SHERLOCK

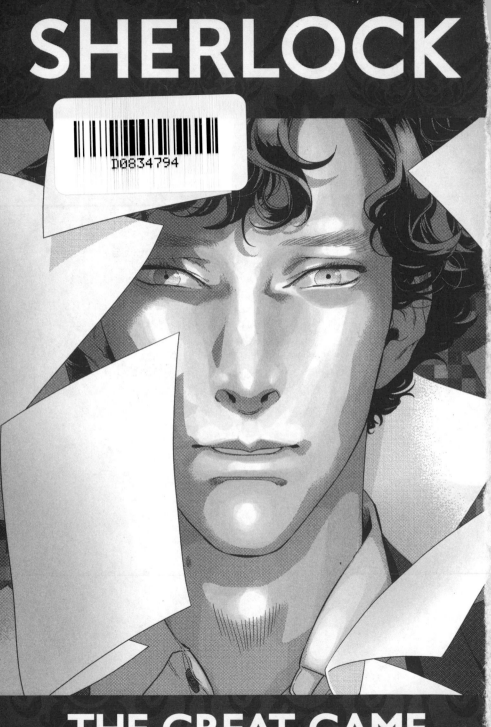

THE GREAT GAME

SHERLOCK

THE GREAT GAME

SCRIPT
MARK GATISS

ADAPTATION/ART
JAY.

LETTERING
AMOONA SAOHIN

Originally published in Japanese by Kadokawa.
This manga is presented in its original right-to-left
reading format.

Based on the TV series **SHERLOCK**
co-created by **STEVEN MOFFAT** & **MARK GATISS**
and adapting Episode Three: The Great Game.

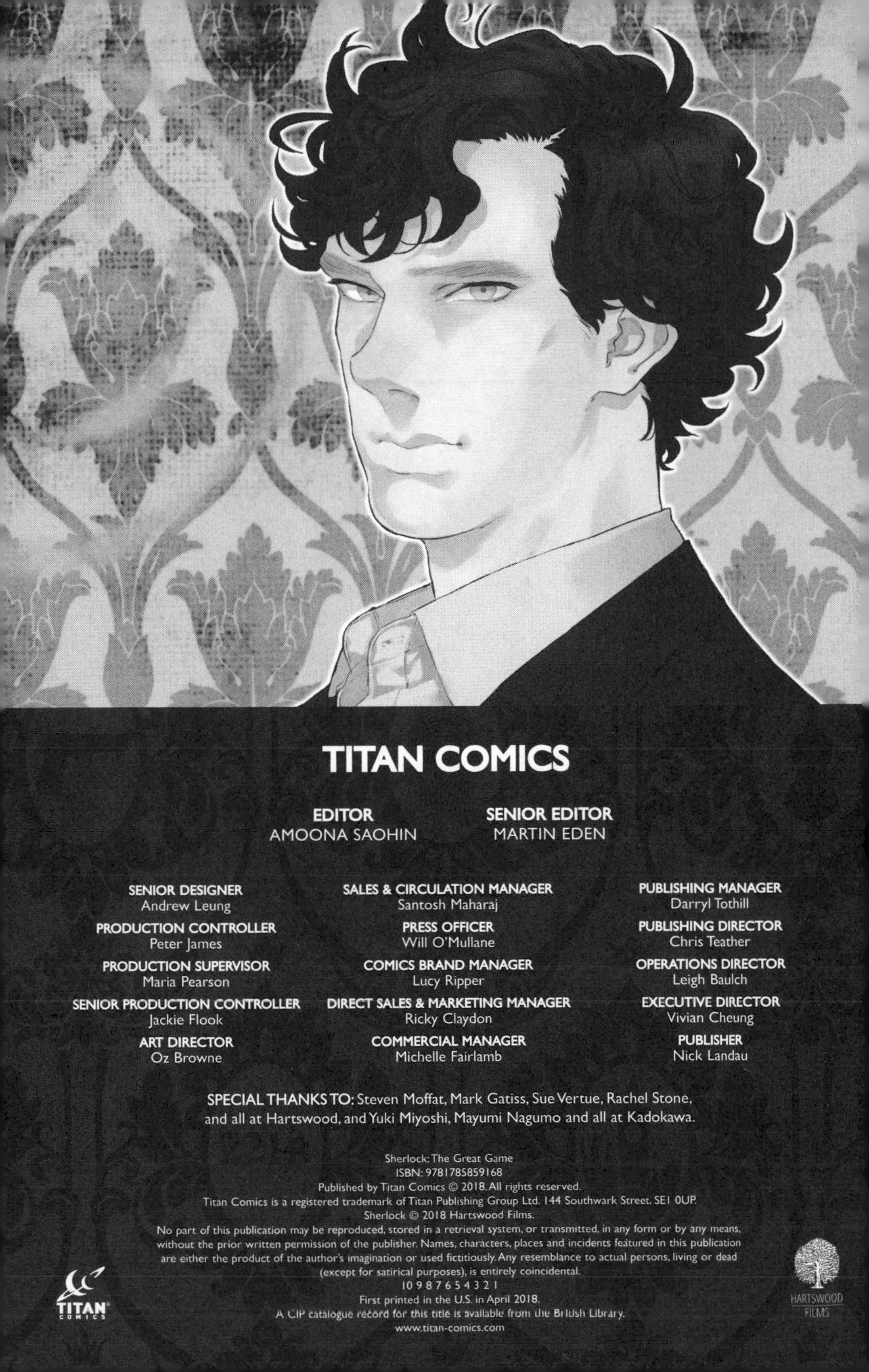

TITAN COMICS

EDITOR
AMOONA SAOHIN

SENIOR EDITOR
MARTIN EDEN

SENIOR DESIGNER
Andrew Leung

PRODUCTION CONTROLLER
Peter James

PRODUCTION SUPERVISOR
Maria Pearson

SENIOR PRODUCTION CONTROLLER
Jackie Flook

ART DIRECTOR
Oz Browne

SALES & CIRCULATION MANAGER
Santosh Maharaj

PRESS OFFICER
Will O'Mullane

COMICS BRAND MANAGER
Lucy Ripper

DIRECT SALES & MARKETING MANAGER
Ricky Claydon

COMMERCIAL MANAGER
Michelle Fairlamb

PUBLISHING MANAGER
Darryl Tothill

PUBLISHING DIRECTOR
Chris Teather

OPERATIONS DIRECTOR
Leigh Baulch

EXECUTIVE DIRECTOR
Vivian Cheung

PUBLISHER
Nick Landau

SPECIAL THANKS TO: Steven Moffat, Mark Gatiss, Sue Vertue, Rachel Stone, and all at Hartswood, and Yuki Miyoshi, Mayumi Nagumo and all at Kadokawa.

Sherlock: The Great Game
ISBN: 9781785859168

10 9 8 7 6 5 4 3 2 1
First printed in the U.S. in April 2018.
A CIP catalogue record for this title is available from the British Library.
www.titan-comics.com

Chapter 1

Illustration by:
Sana Takeda

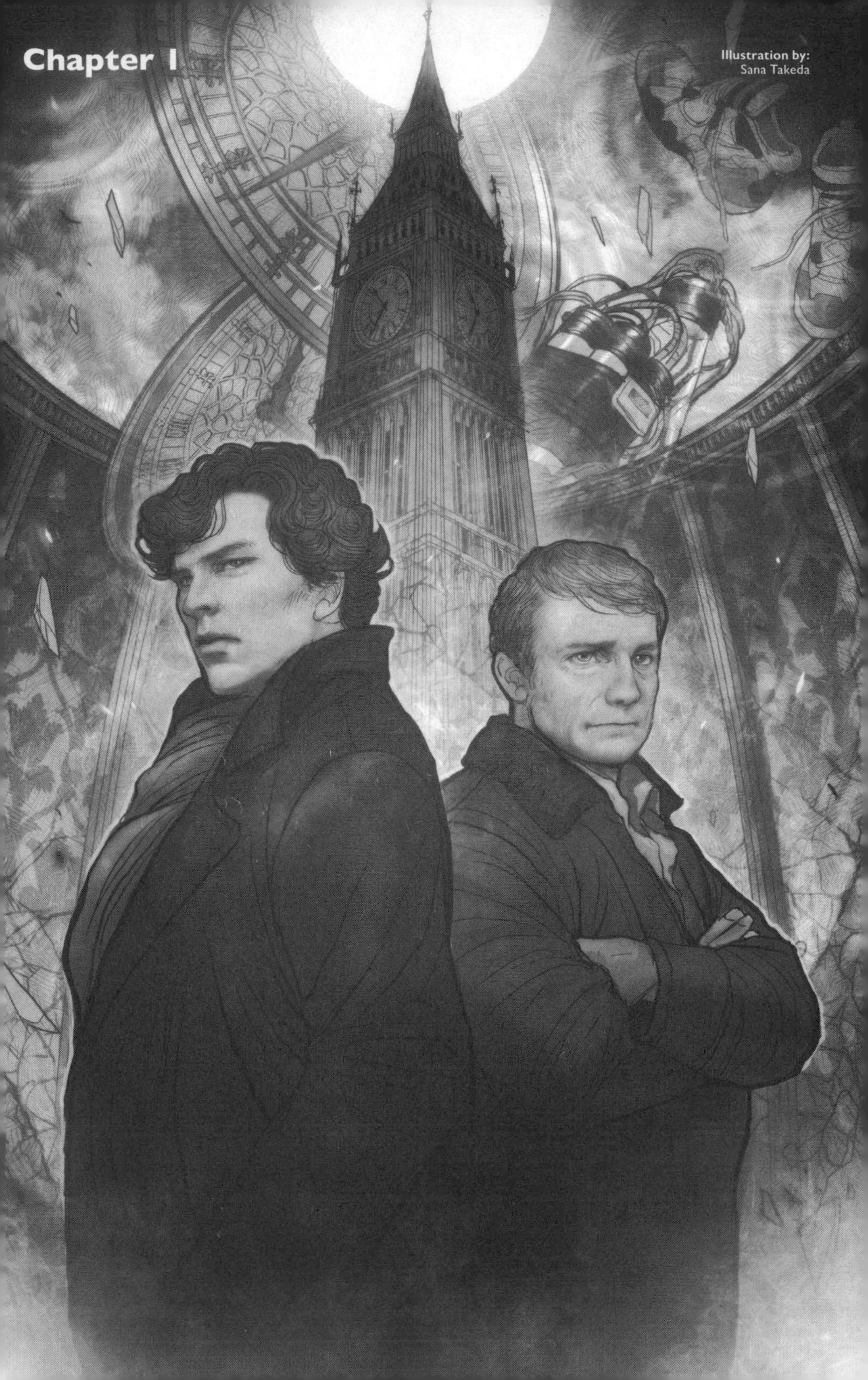

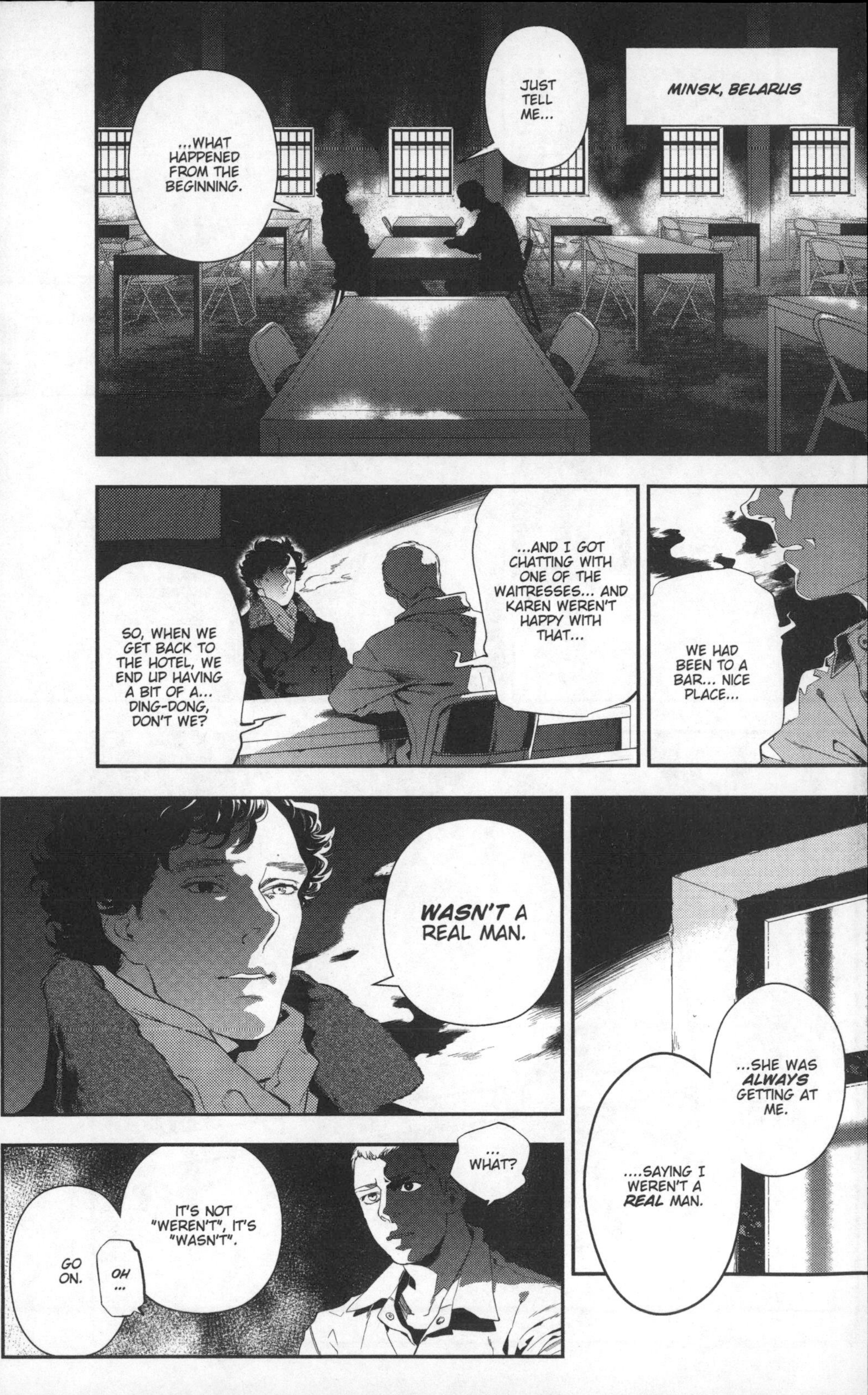
MINSK, BELARUS
JUST TELL ME...
...WHAT HAPPENED FROM THE BEGINNING.
WE HAD BEEN TO A BAR... NICE PLACE...
...AND I GOT CHATTING WITH ONE OF THE WAITRESSES... AND KAREN WEREN'T HAPPY WITH THAT...
SO, WHEN WE GET BACK TO THE HOTEL, WE END UP HAVING A BIT OF A... DING-DONG, DON'T WE?
...SHE WAS ALWAYS GETTING AT ME.
....SAYING I WEREN'T A REAL MAN.
WASN'T A REAL MAN.
... WHAT?
IT'S NOT "WEREN'T", IT'S "WASN'T".
OH ...
GO ON.

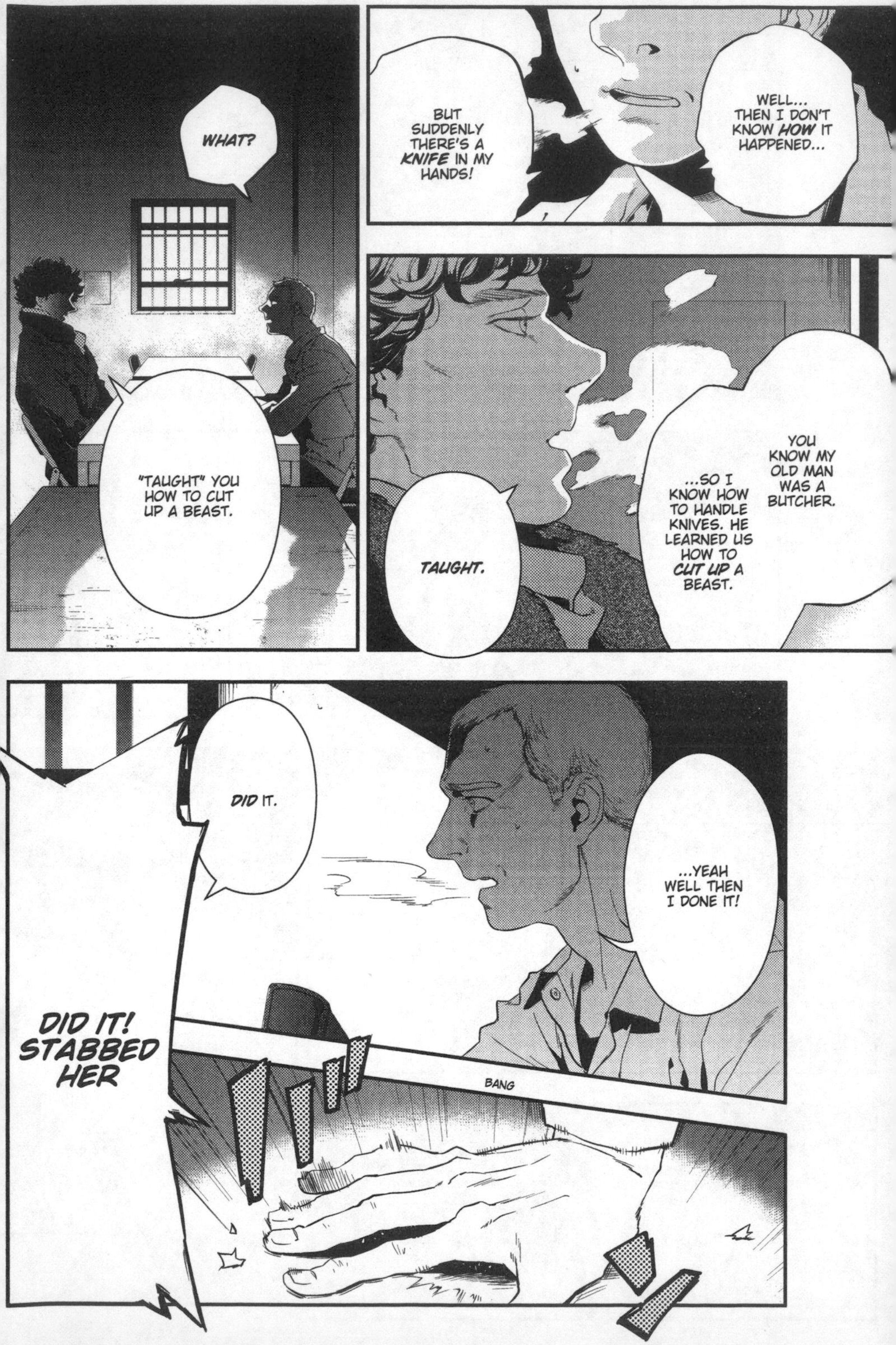
WELL... THEN I DON'T KNOW HOW IT HAPPENED...
BUT SUDDENLY THERE'S A KNIFE IN MY HANDS!
YOU KNOW MY OLD MAN WAS A BUTCHER.
...SO I KNOW HOW TO HANDLE KNIVES. HE LEARNED US HOW TO CUT UP A BEAST.
TAUGHT.
WHAT?
"TAUGHT" YOU HOW TO CUT UP A BEAST.
...YEAH WELL THEN I DONE IT!
DID IT.
BANG
DID IT! STABBED HER

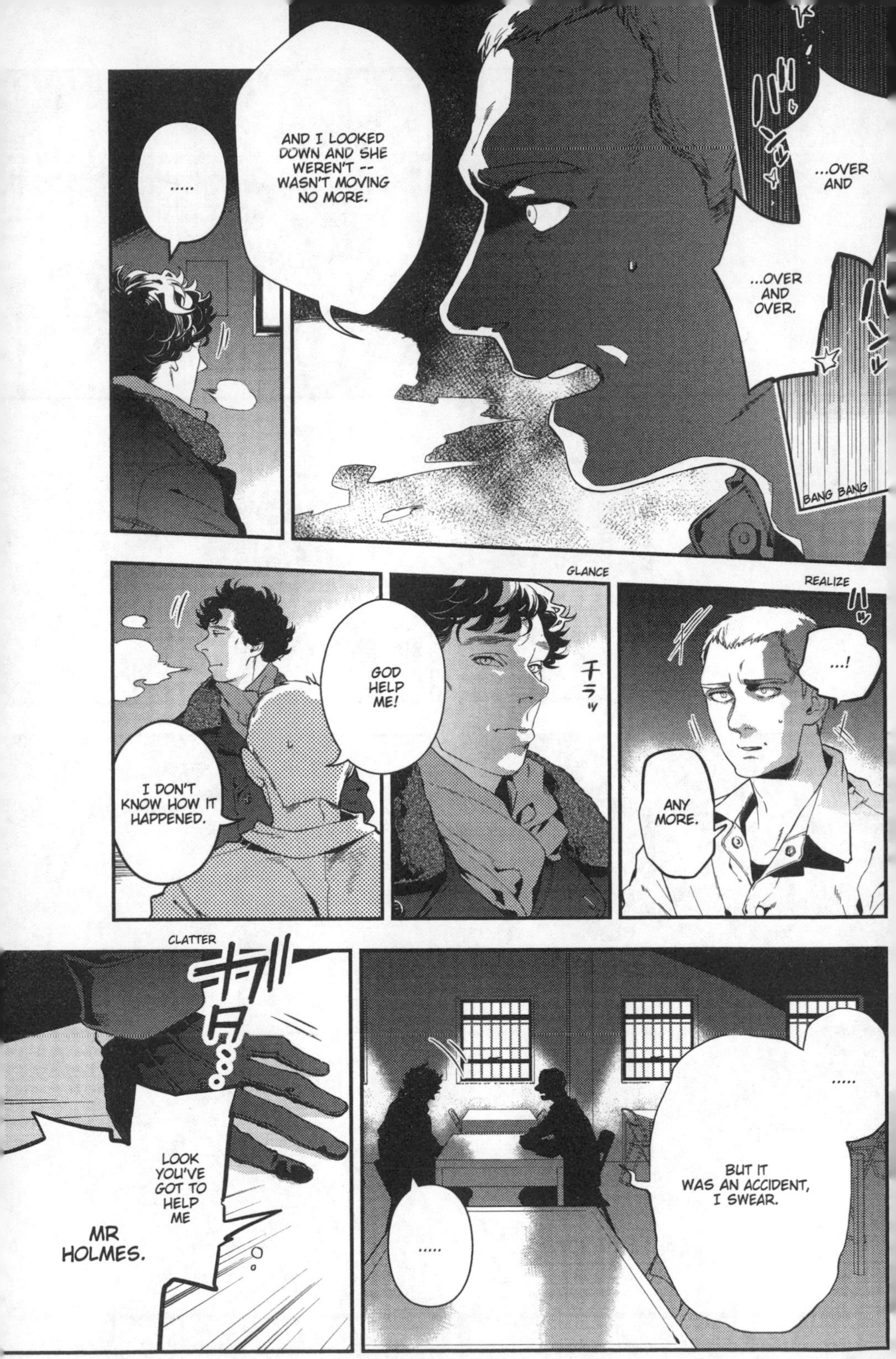
...OVER AND
...OVER AND OVER.
BANG BANG
AND I LOOKED DOWN AND SHE WEREN'T -- WASN'T MOVING NO MORE.
.....
REALIZE
ハッ
...!
ANY MORE.
GLANCE
チラッ
GOD HELP ME!
I DON'T KNOW HOW IT HAPPENED.
.....
BUT IT WAS AN ACCIDENT, I SWEAR.
.....
CLATTER
ガタ
LOOK YOU'VE GOT TO HELP ME
MR HOLMES.

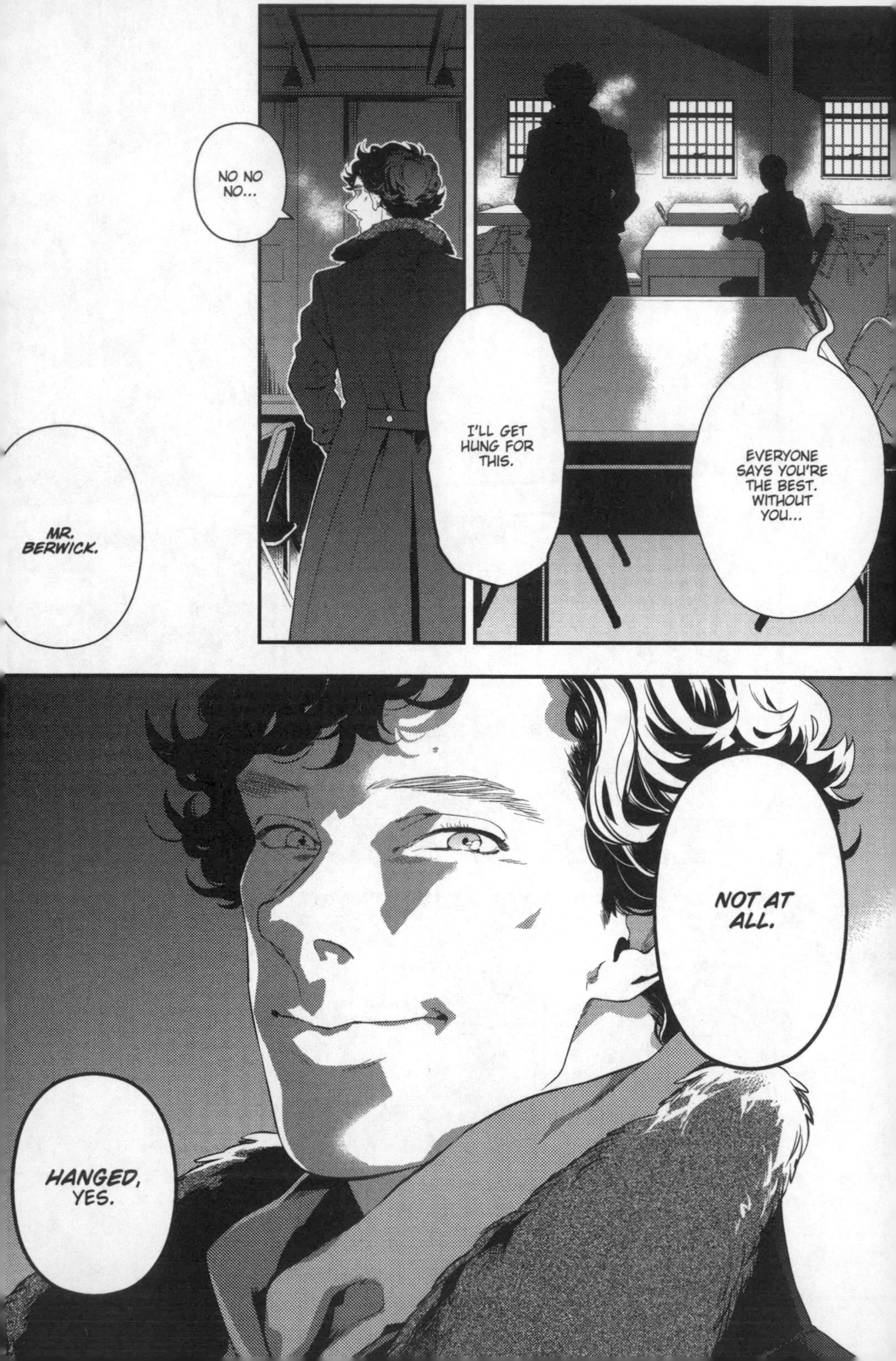
EVERYONE SAYS YOU'RE THE BEST. WITHOUT YOU...
I'LL GET HUNG FOR THIS.
NO NO NO...
MR. BERWICK.
NOT AT ALL.
HANGED, YES.

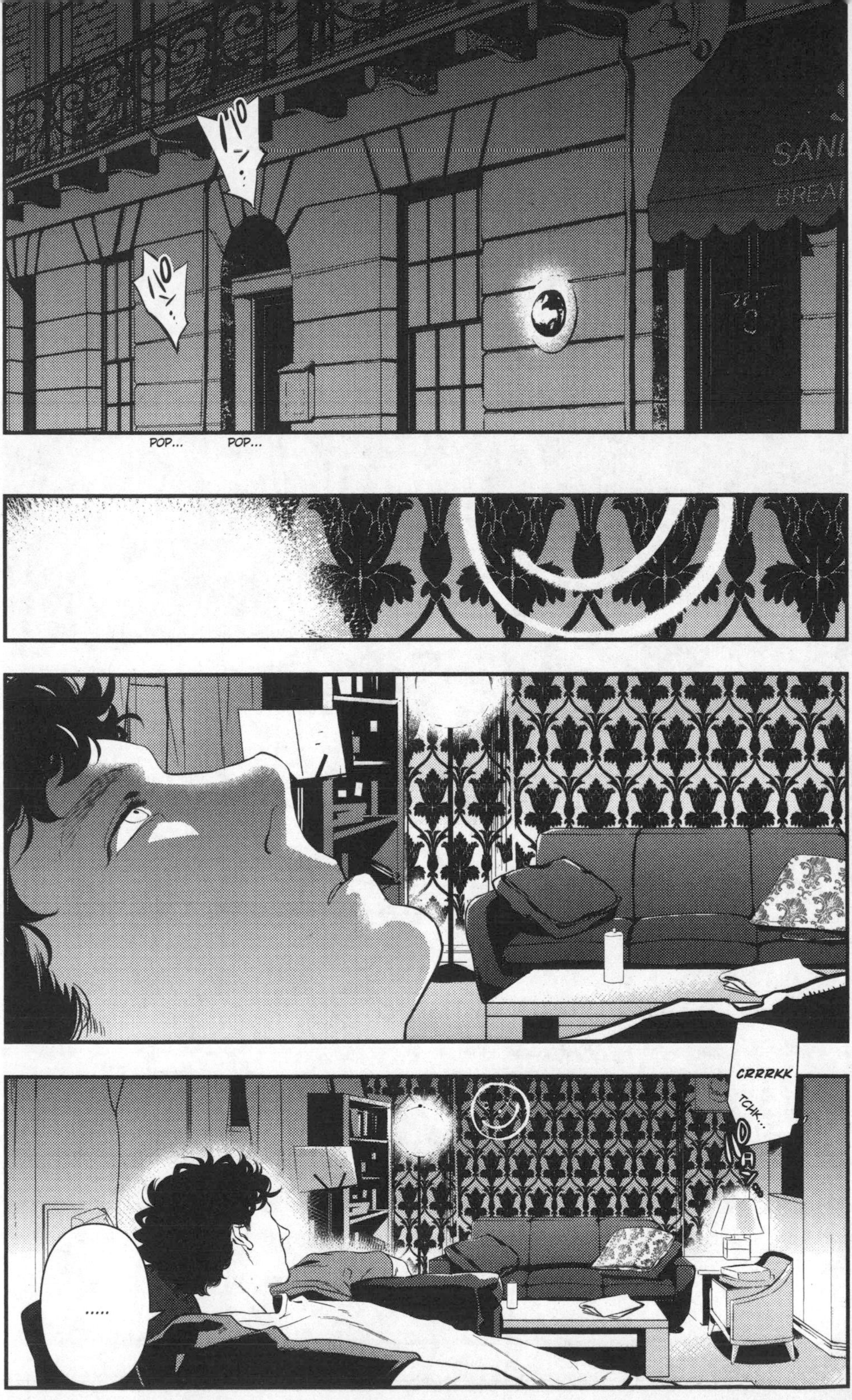

POP...
POP...
CRRRKK
TCHK...
.....

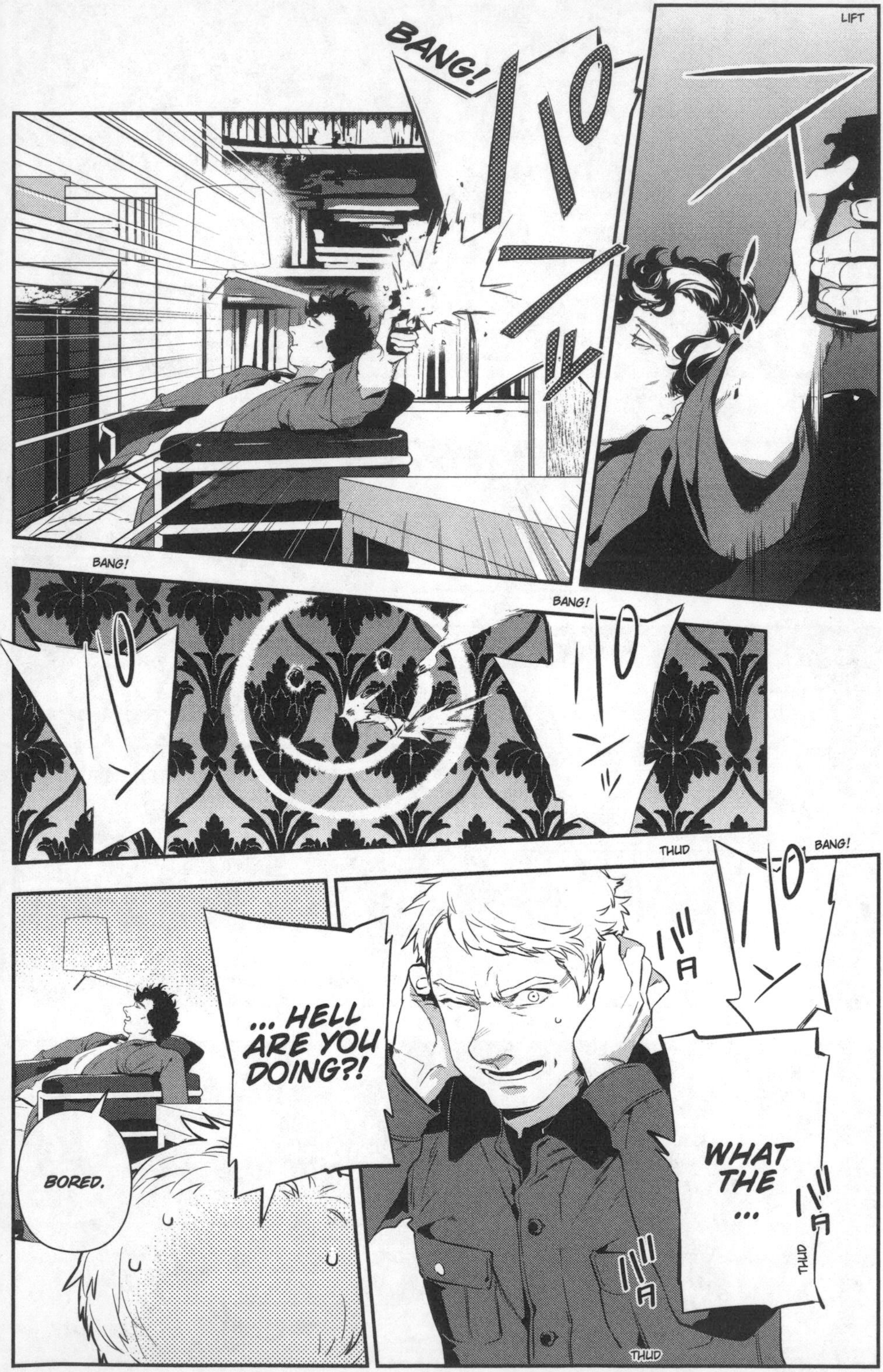
LIFT
BANG!
BANG!
BANG!
THUD
BANG!
WHAT THE ...
THUD
THUD
... HELL ARE YOU DOING?!
BORED.

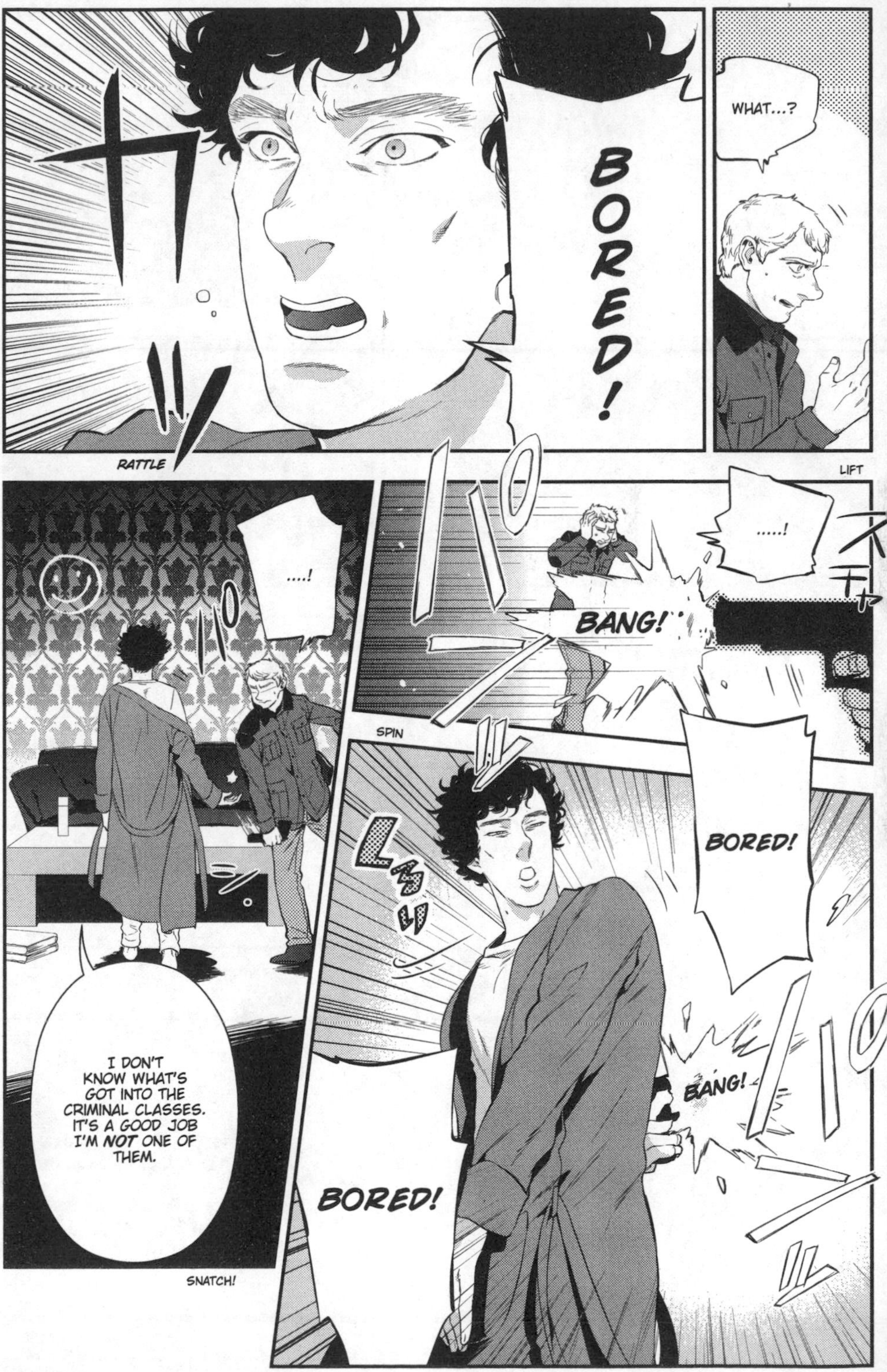

WHAT...?
LIFT
BORED!
RATTLE
....!
BANG!
SPIN
BORED!
BANG!
BORED!
....!
I DON'T KNOW WHAT'S GOT INTO THE CRIMINAL CLASSES. IT'S A GOOD JOB I'M ***NOT*** ONE OF THEM.
SNATCH!

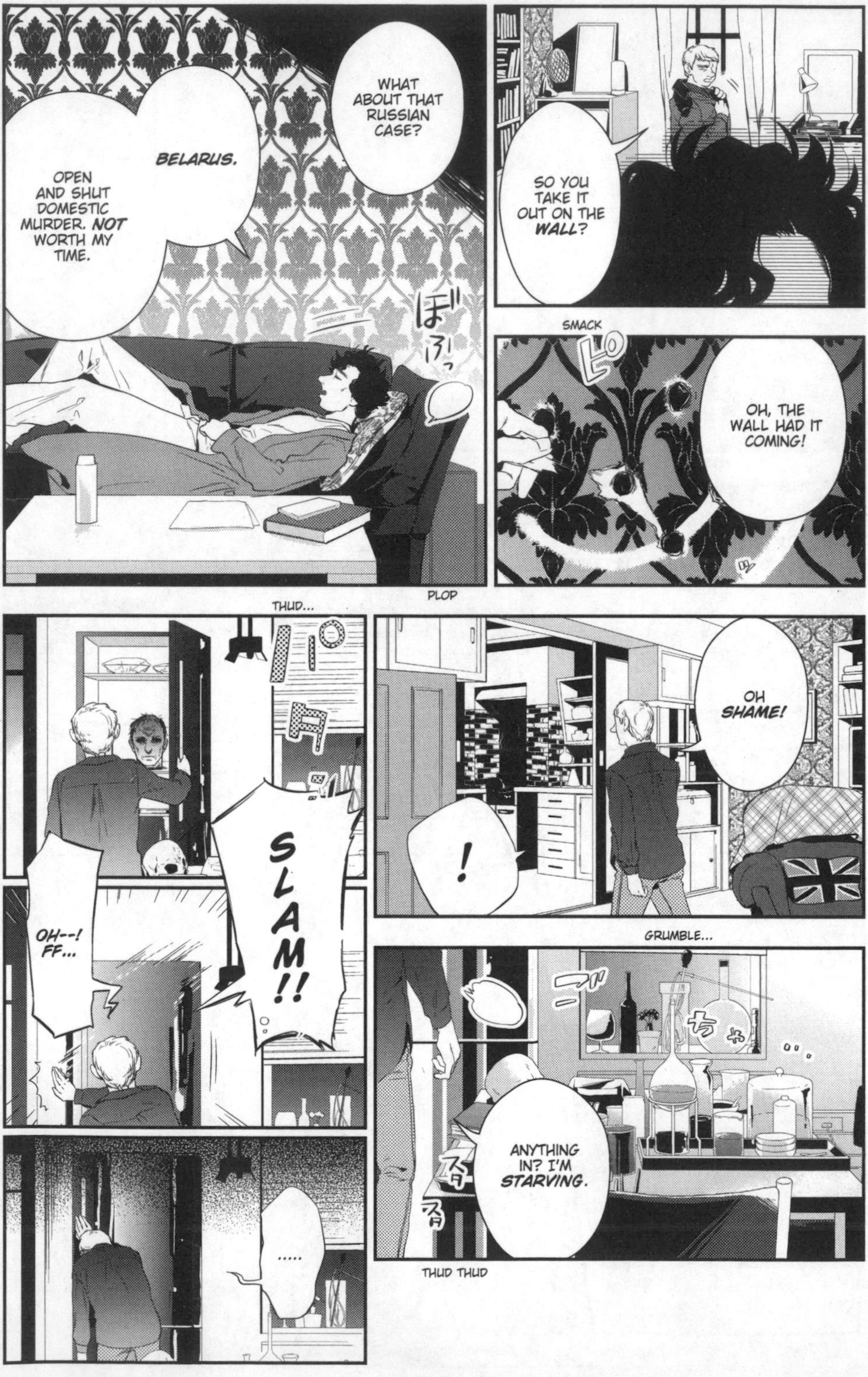
SO YOU TAKE IT OUT ON THE WALL?
SMACK
OH, THE WALL HAD IT COMING!
WHAT ABOUT THAT RUSSIAN CASE?
BELARUS.
OPEN AND SHUT DOMESTIC MURDER. NOT WORTH MY TIME.
PLOP
OH SHAME!
!
GRUMBLE...
ANYTHING IN? I'M STARVING.
THUD THUD
THUD...
SLAM!!
OH--! FF...
.....

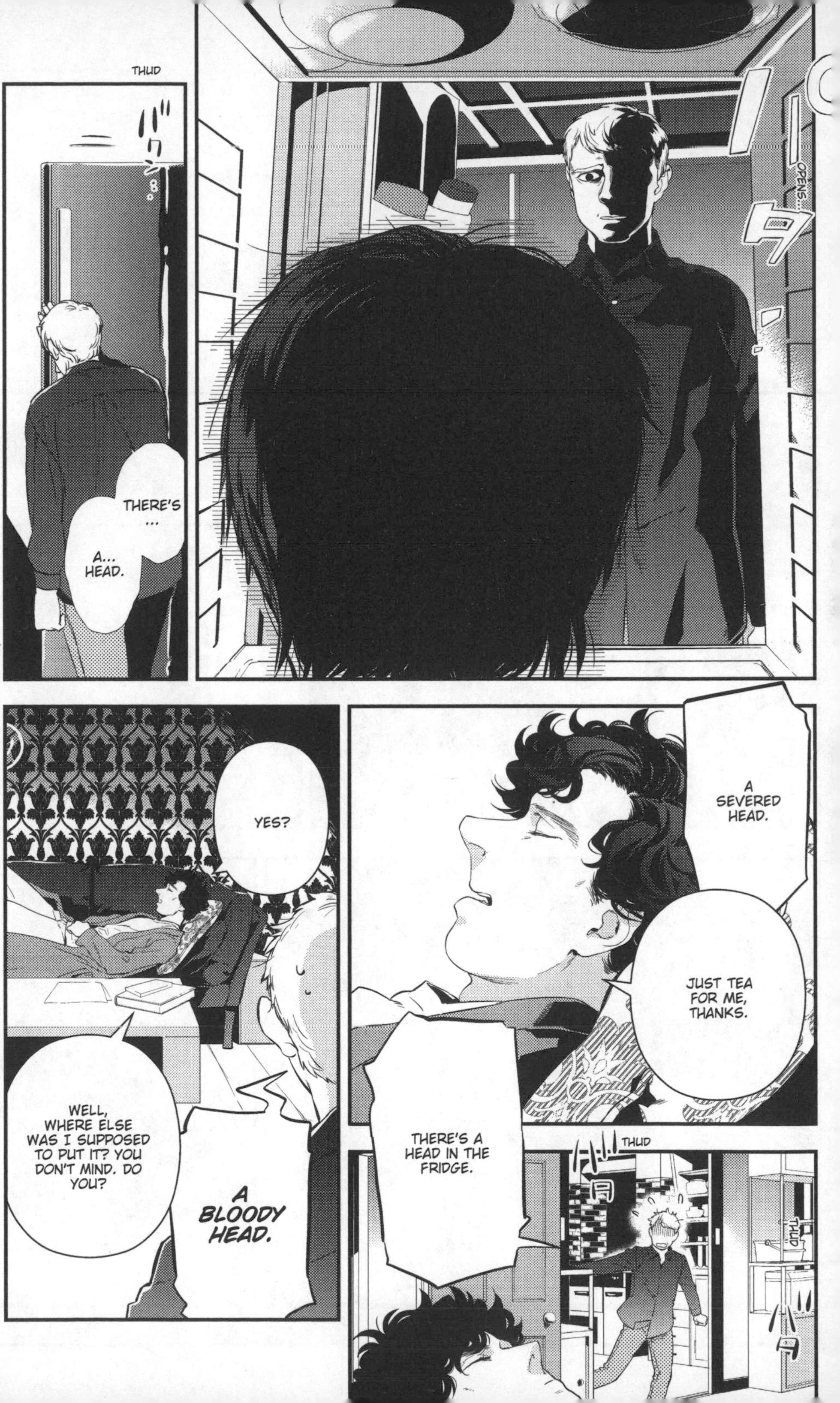
OPENS...
THUD
THERE'S ...
A... HEAD.
A SEVERED HEAD.
JUST TEA FOR ME, THANKS.
THUD
THERE'S A HEAD IN THE FRIDGE.
THUD
YES?
WELL, WHERE ELSE WAS I SUPPOSED TO PUT IT? YOU DON'T MIND. DO YOU?
A BLOODY HEAD.

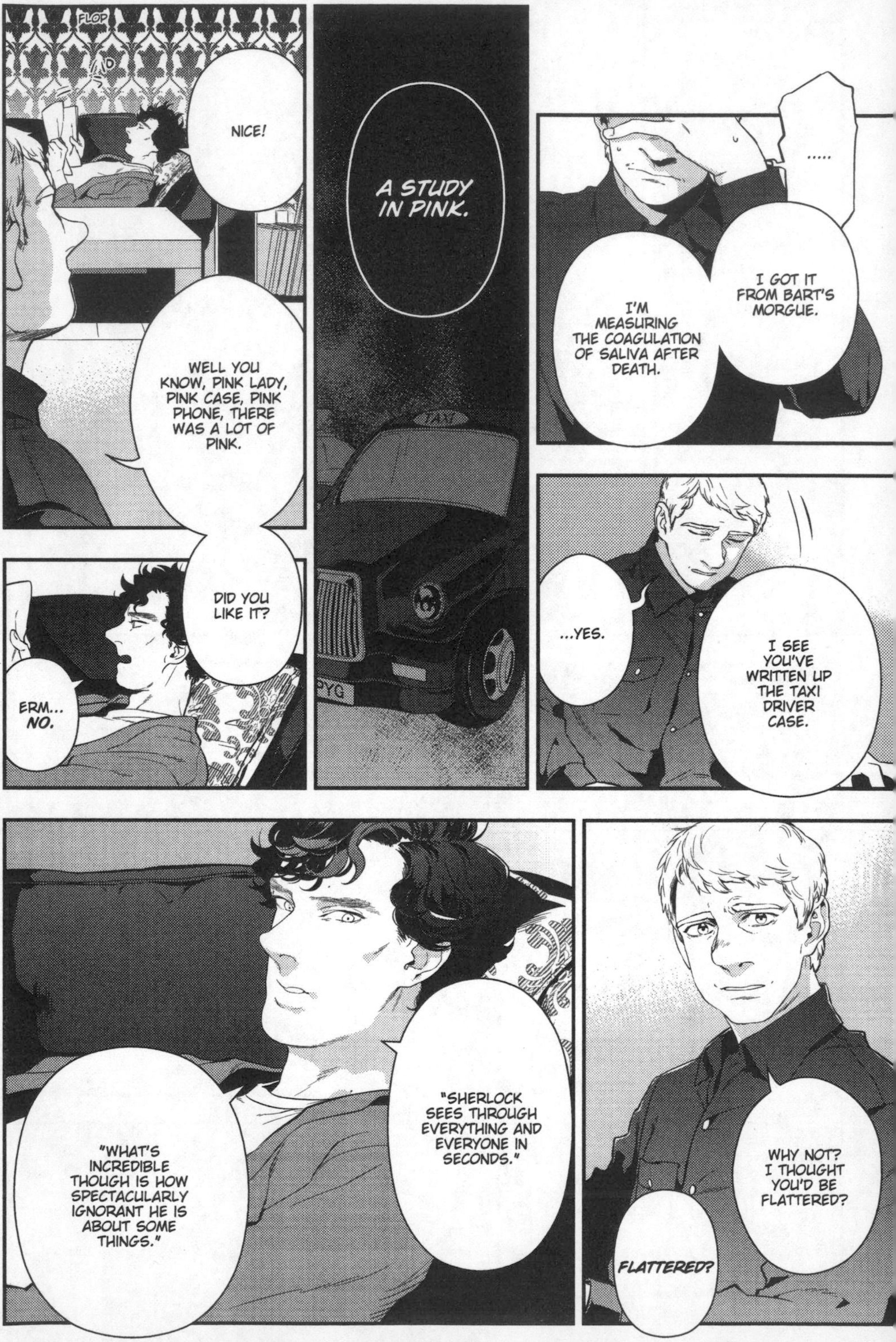
.....
I GOT IT FROM BART'S MORGUE.
I'M MEASURING THE COAGULATION OF SALIVA AFTER DEATH.
I SEE YOU'VE WRITTEN UP THE TAXI DRIVER CASE.
...YES.
A STUDY IN PINK.
TAXI
FLOP
NICE!
WELL YOU KNOW, PINK LADY, PINK CASE, PINK PHONE, THERE WAS A LOT OF PINK.
DID YOU LIKE IT?
ERM... NO.
WHY NOT? I THOUGHT YOU'D BE FLATTERED?
FLATTERED?
"SHERLOCK SEES THROUGH EVERYTHING AND EVERYONE IN SECONDS."
"WHAT'S INCREDIBLE THOUGH IS HOW SPECTACULARLY IGNORANT HE IS ABOUT SOME THINGS."

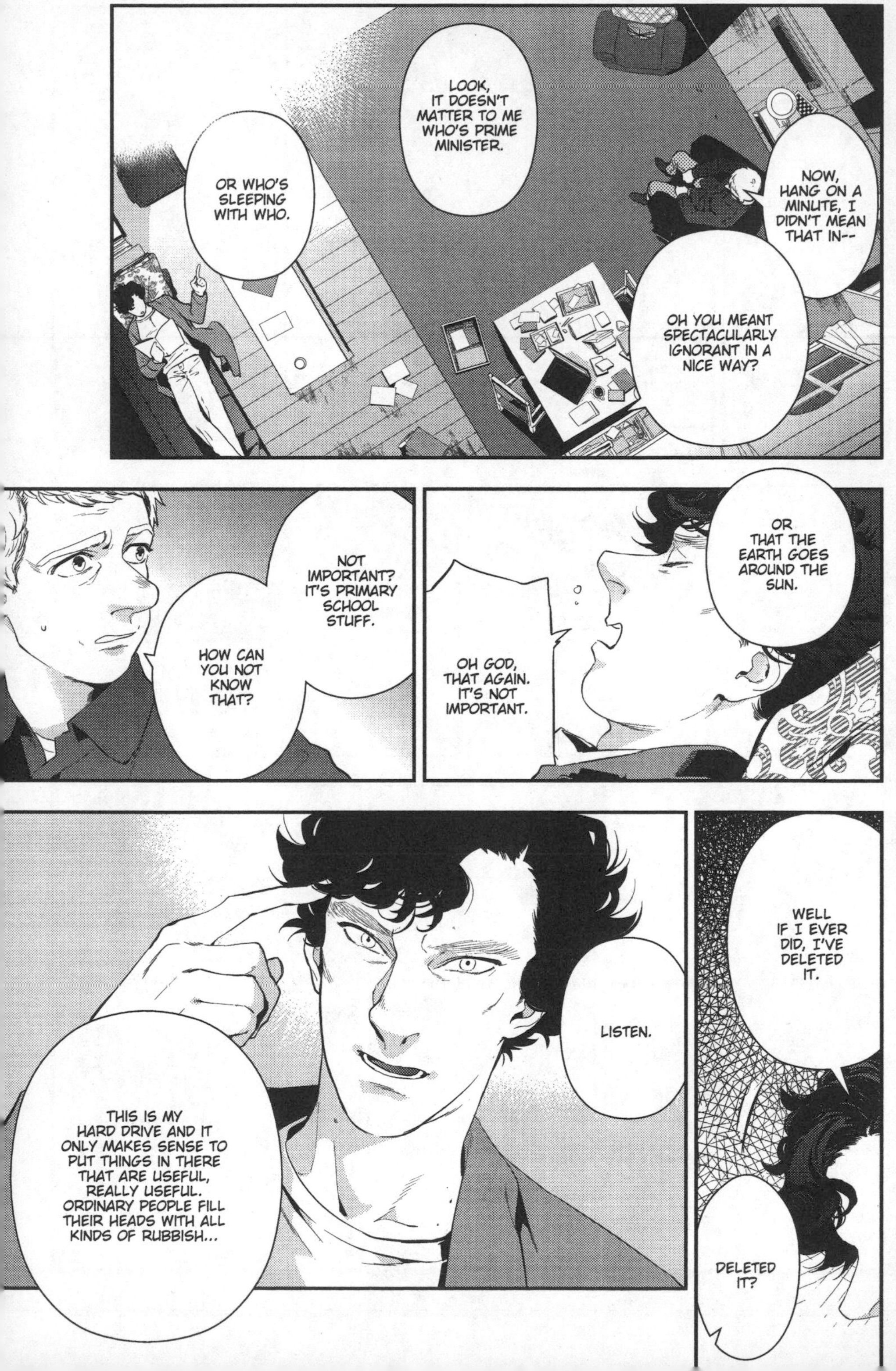
NOW, HANG ON A MINUTE, I DIDN'T MEAN THAT IN--
OH YOU MEANT SPECTACULARLY IGNORANT IN A NICE WAY?
LOOK, IT DOESN'T MATTER TO ME WHO'S PRIME MINISTER.
OR WHO'S SLEEPING WITH WHO.
OR THAT THE EARTH GOES AROUND THE SUN.
OH GOD, THAT AGAIN. IT'S NOT IMPORTANT.
NOT IMPORTANT? IT'S PRIMARY SCHOOL STUFF.
HOW CAN YOU NOT KNOW THAT?
WELL IF I EVER DID, I'VE DELETED IT.
DELETED IT?
LISTEN.
THIS IS MY HARD DRIVE AND IT ONLY MAKES SENSE TO PUT THINGS IN THERE THAT ARE USEFUL, REALLY USEFUL. ORDINARY PEOPLE FILL THEIR HEADS WITH ALL KINDS OF RUBBISH...

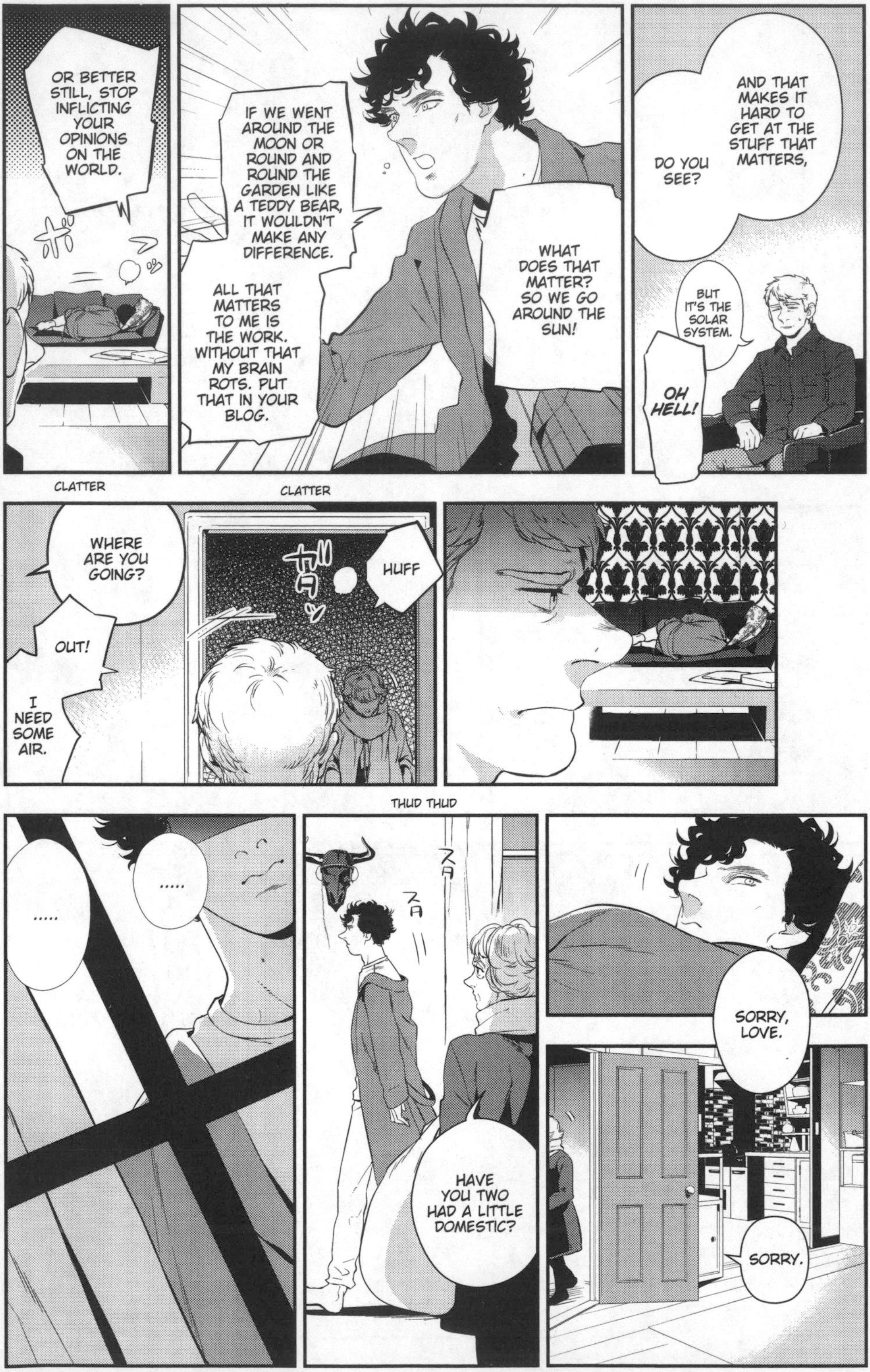
AND THAT MAKES IT HARD TO GET AT THE STUFF THAT MATTERS,
DO YOU SEE?
BUT IT'S THE SOLAR SYSTEM.
OH HELL!
WHAT DOES THAT MATTER? SO WE GO AROUND THE SUN!
IF WE WENT AROUND THE MOON OR ROUND AND ROUND THE GARDEN LIKE A TEDDY BEAR, IT WOULDN'T MAKE ANY DIFFERENCE.
ALL THAT MATTERS TO ME IS THE WORK. WITHOUT THAT MY BRAIN ROTS. PUT THAT IN YOUR BLOG.
OR BETTER STILL, STOP INFLICTING YOUR OPINIONS ON THE WORLD.
CLATTER
CLATTER
HUFF
ガタッ
WHERE ARE YOU GOING?
OUT!
I NEED SOME AIR.
THUD THUD
SORRY, LOVE.
SORRY.
スタ
スタ
HAVE YOU TWO HAD A LITTLE DOMESTIC?
.....
.....

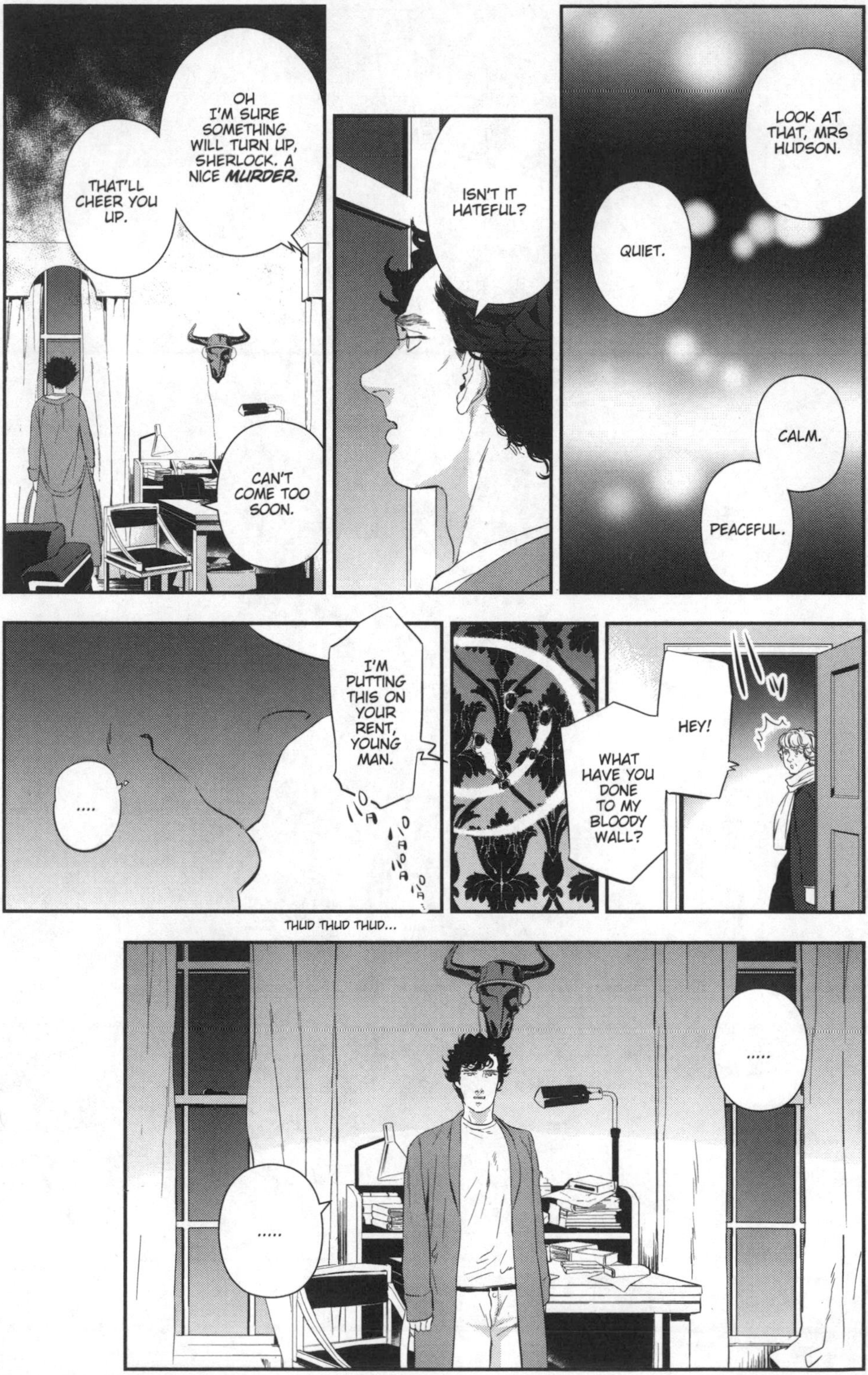
LOOK AT THAT, MRS HUDSON.
QUIET.
CALM.
PEACEFUL.
ISN'T IT HATEFUL?
OH I'M SURE SOMETHING WILL TURN UP, SHERLOCK. A NICE *MURDER.*
THAT'LL CHEER YOU UP.
CAN'T COME TOO SOON.
HEY!
WHAT HAVE YOU DONE TO MY BLOODY WALL?
I'M PUTTING THIS ON YOUR RENT, YOUNG MAN.
....
THUD THUD THUD...
.....
.....

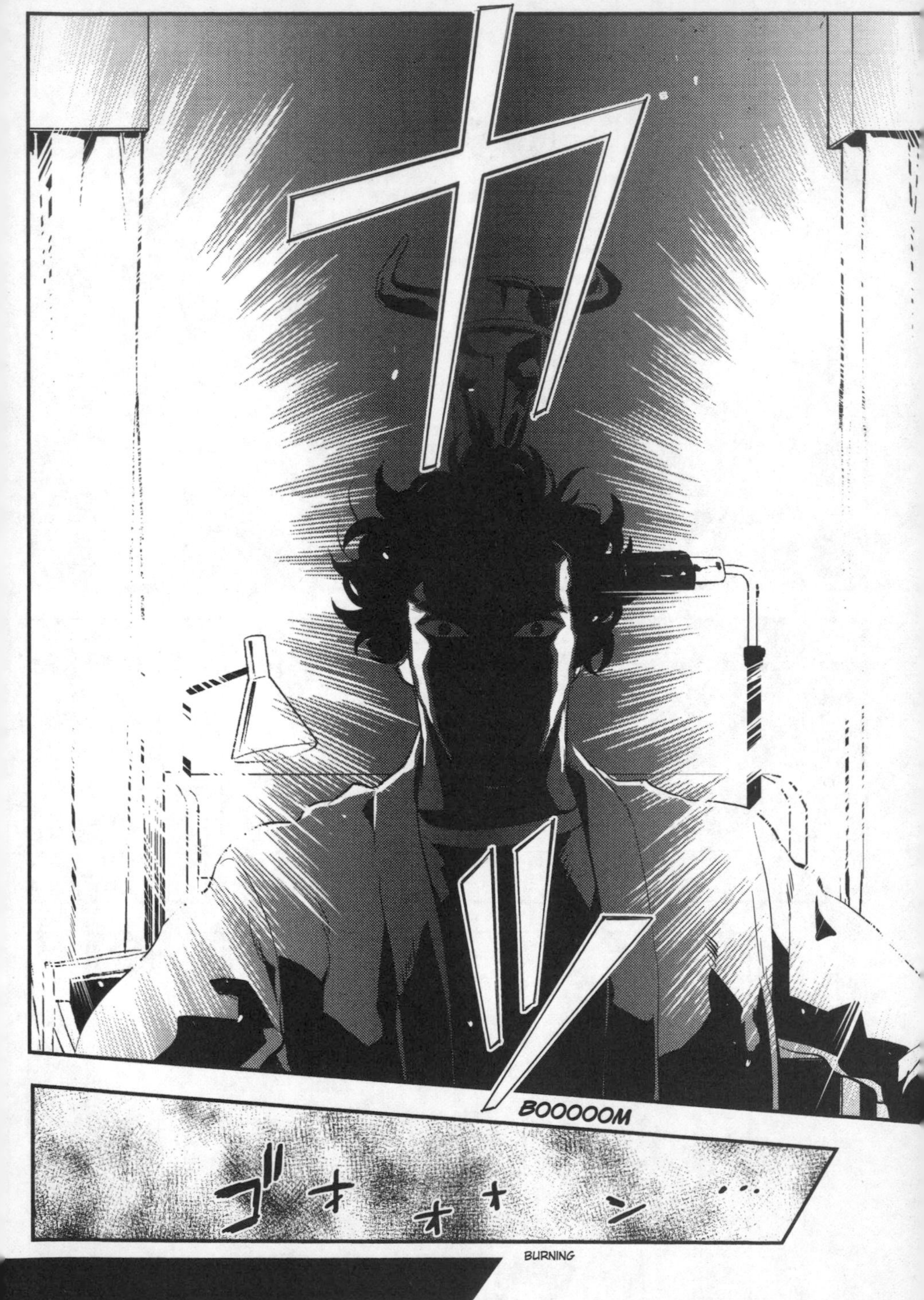
BOOOOOM
ゴオオン…
BURNING

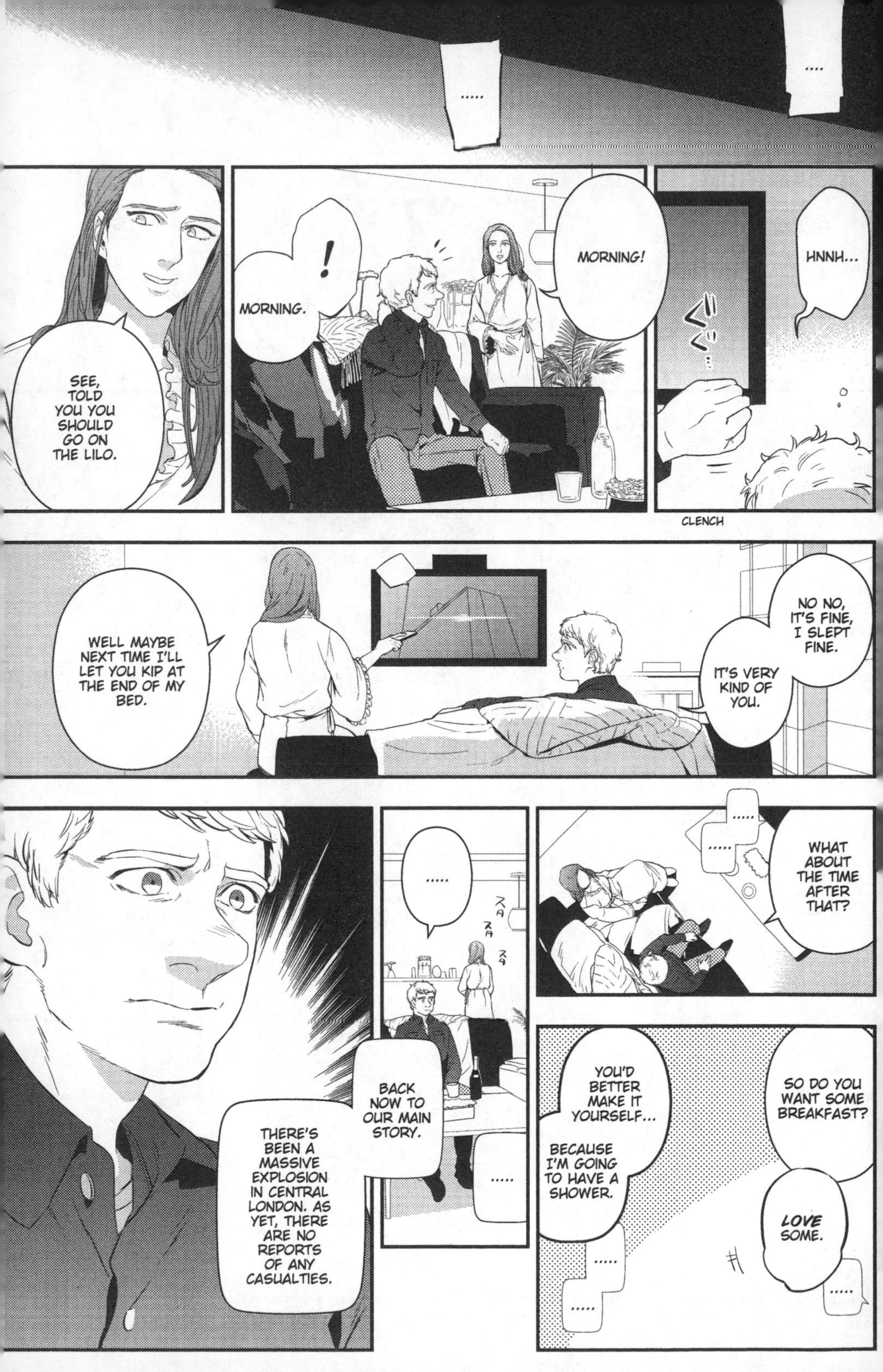
....
.....
HNNH...
CLENCH
MORNING!
!
MORNING.
SEE, TOLD YOU YOU SHOULD GO ON THE LILO.
NO NO, IT'S FINE, I SLEPT FINE.
IT'S VERY KIND OF YOU.
WELL MAYBE NEXT TIME I'LL LET YOU KIP AT THE END OF MY BED.
WHAT ABOUT THE TIME AFTER THAT?
.....
.....
SO DO YOU WANT SOME BREAKFAST?
LOVE SOME.
.....
YOU'D BETTER MAKE IT YOURSELF...
BECAUSE I'M GOING TO HAVE A SHOWER.
.....
.....
.....
BACK NOW TO OUR MAIN STORY.
.....
THERE'S BEEN A MASSIVE EXPLOSION IN CENTRAL LONDON. AS YET, THERE ARE NO REPORTS OF ANY CASUALTIES.

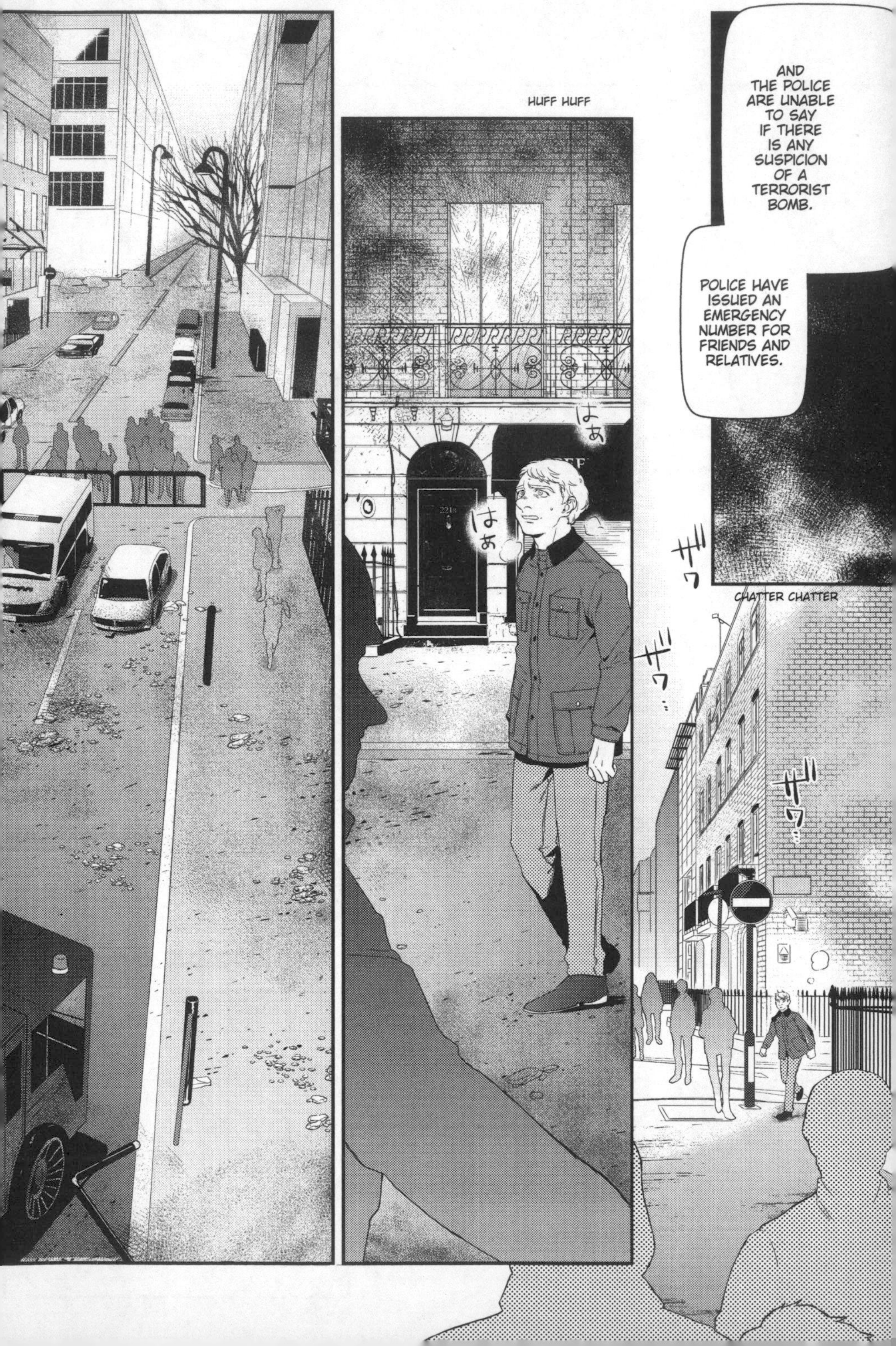
AND THE POLICE ARE UNABLE TO SAY IF THERE IS ANY SUSPICION OF A TERRORIST BOMB.
POLICE HAVE ISSUED AN EMERGENCY NUMBER FOR FRIENDS AND RELATIVES.
ザワ
CHATTER CHATTER
ザワ…
ザワ…
HUFF HUFF
はぁ
はぁ

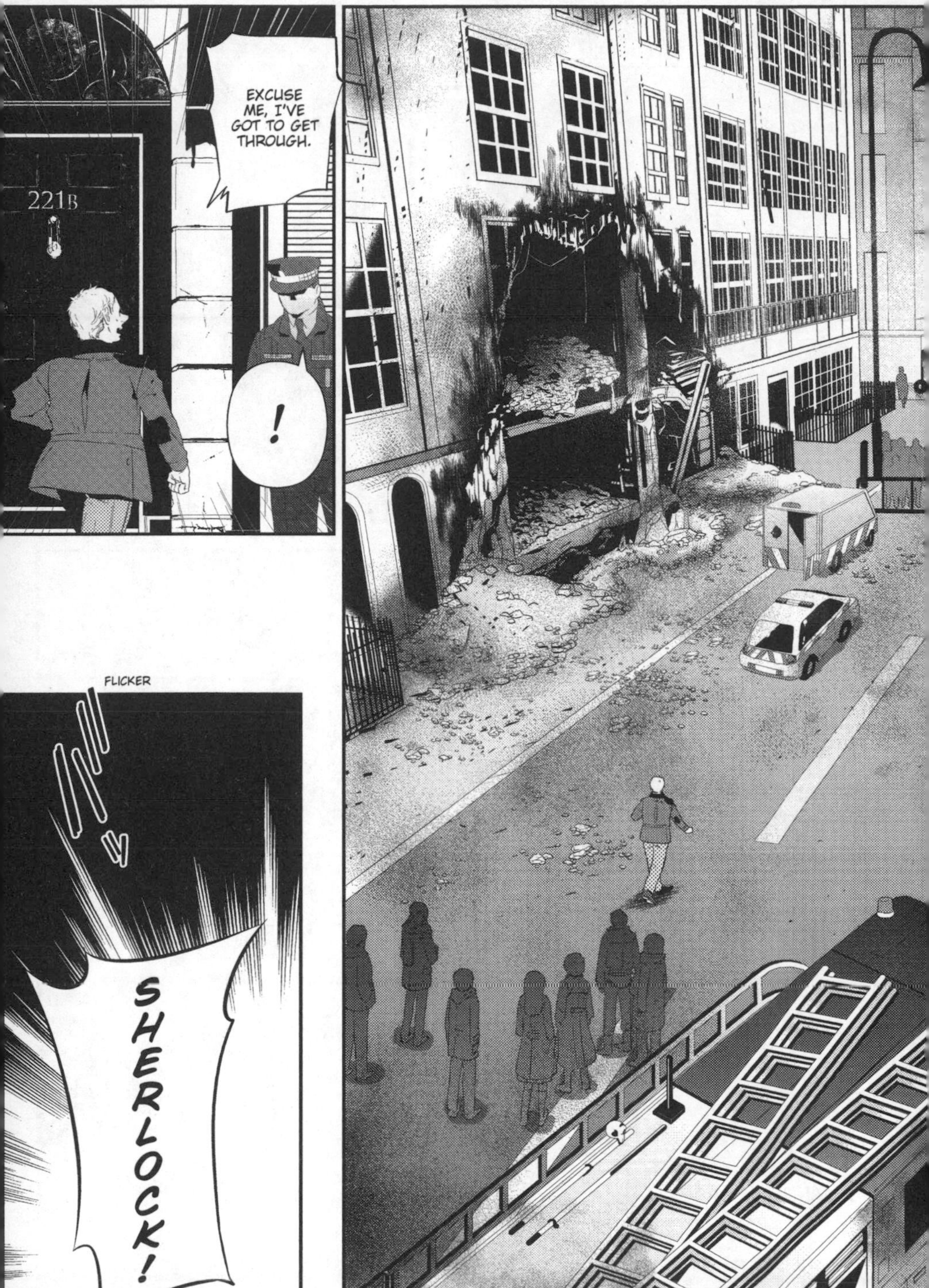
EXCUSE ME, I'VE GOT TO GET THROUGH.
!
FLICKER
SHERLOCK!

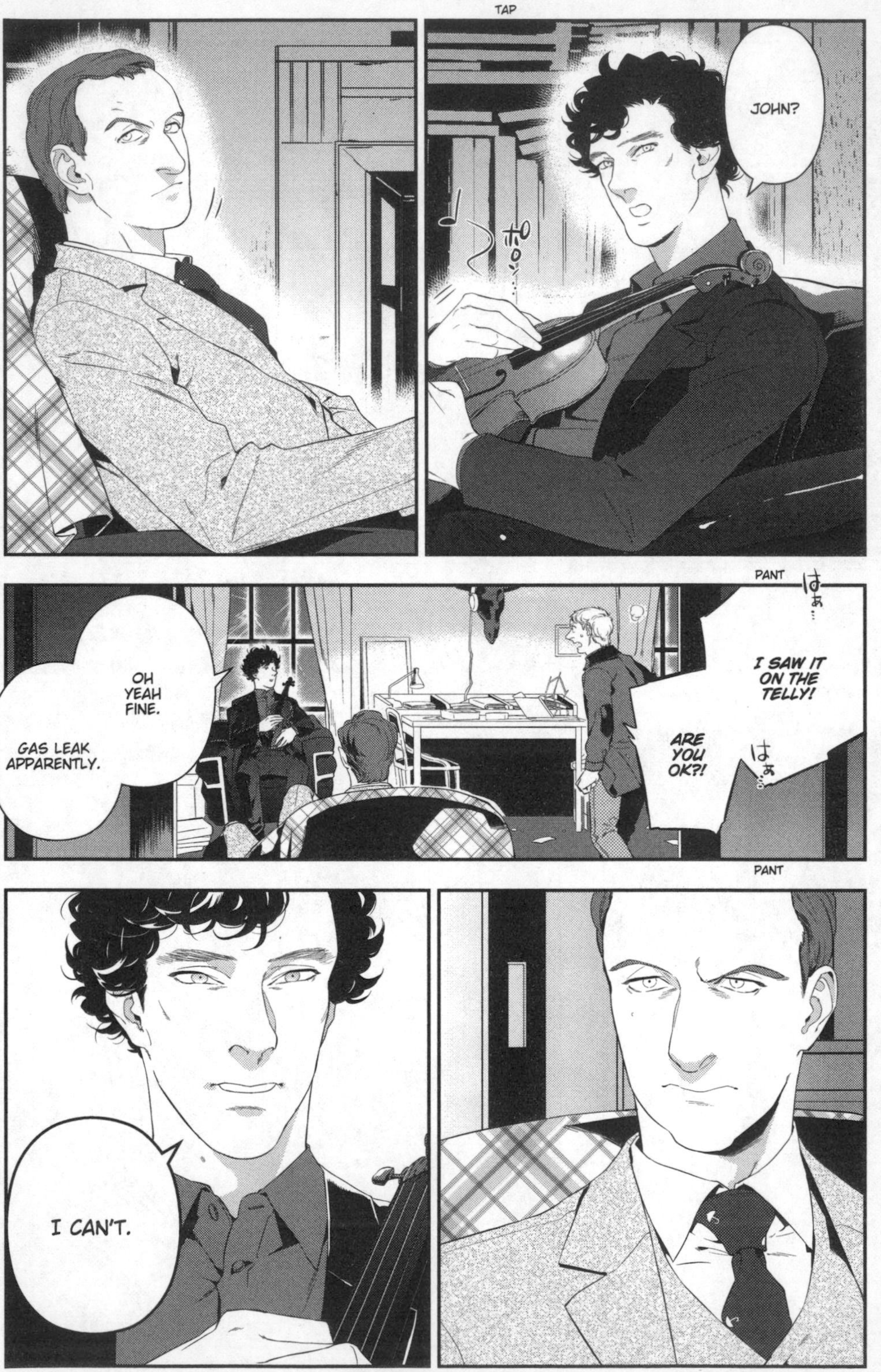
TAP
JOHN?
PANT
はぁ…
I SAW IT ON THE TELLY!
ARE YOU OK?!
はぁ…
OH YEAH FINE.
GAS LEAK APPARENTLY.
PANT
I CAN'T.

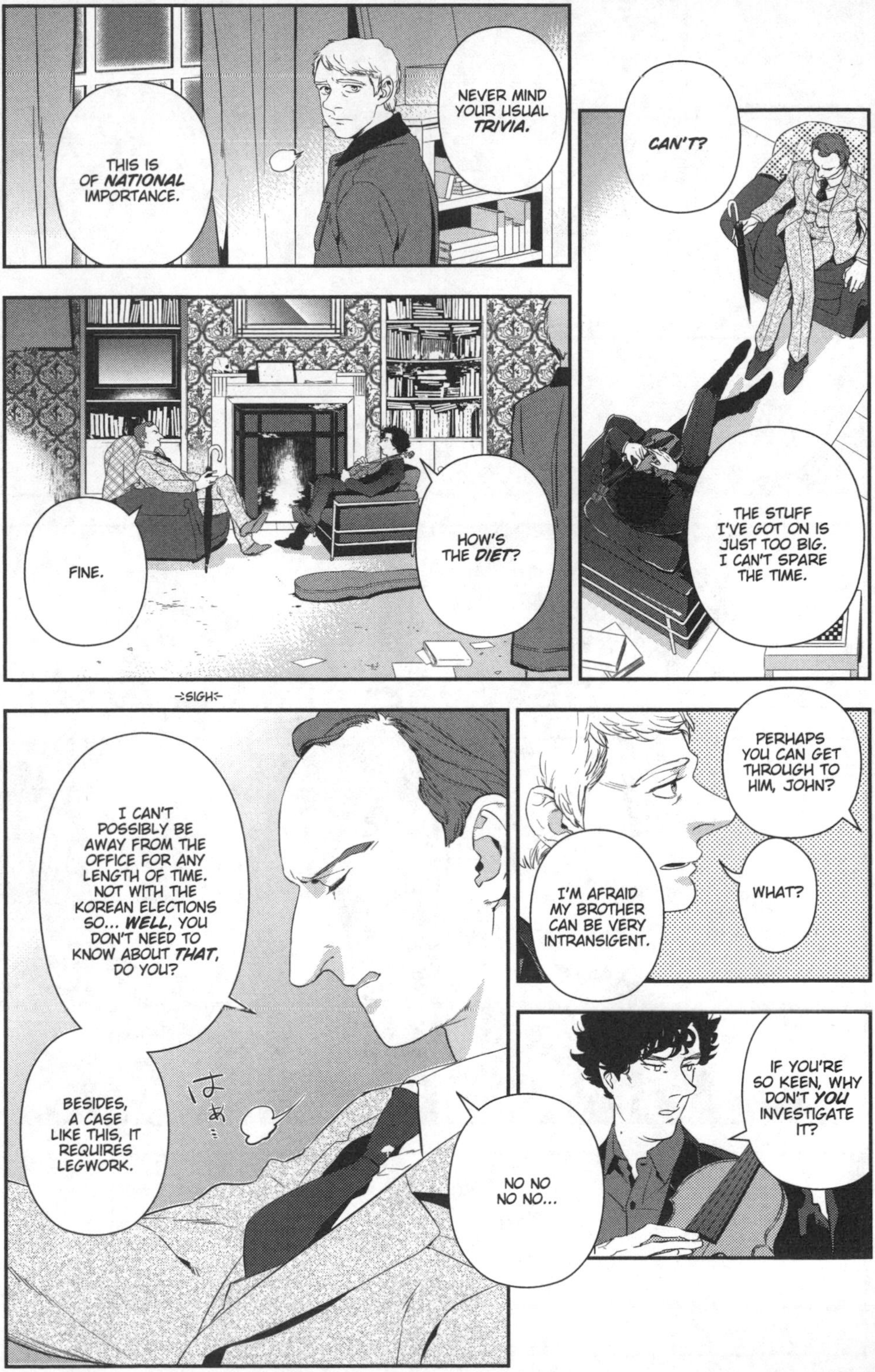
CAN'T?
THE STUFF I'VE GOT ON IS JUST TOO BIG. I CAN'T SPARE THE TIME.
NEVER MIND YOUR USUAL *TRIVIA.*
THIS IS OF *NATIONAL* IMPORTANCE.
HOW'S THE *DIET*?
FINE.
PERHAPS YOU CAN GET THROUGH TO HIM, JOHN?
WHAT?
I'M AFRAID MY BROTHER CAN BE VERY INTRANSIGENT.
IF YOU'RE SO KEEN, WHY DON'T *YOU* INVESTIGATE IT?
-SIGH-
I CAN'T POSSIBLY BE AWAY FROM THE OFFICE FOR ANY LENGTH OF TIME. NOT WITH THE KOREAN ELECTIONS SO... *WELL*, YOU DON'T NEED TO KNOW ABOUT *THAT*, DO YOU?
はぁ…
NO NO NO NO...
BESIDES, A CASE LIKE THIS, IT REQUIRES LEGWORK.

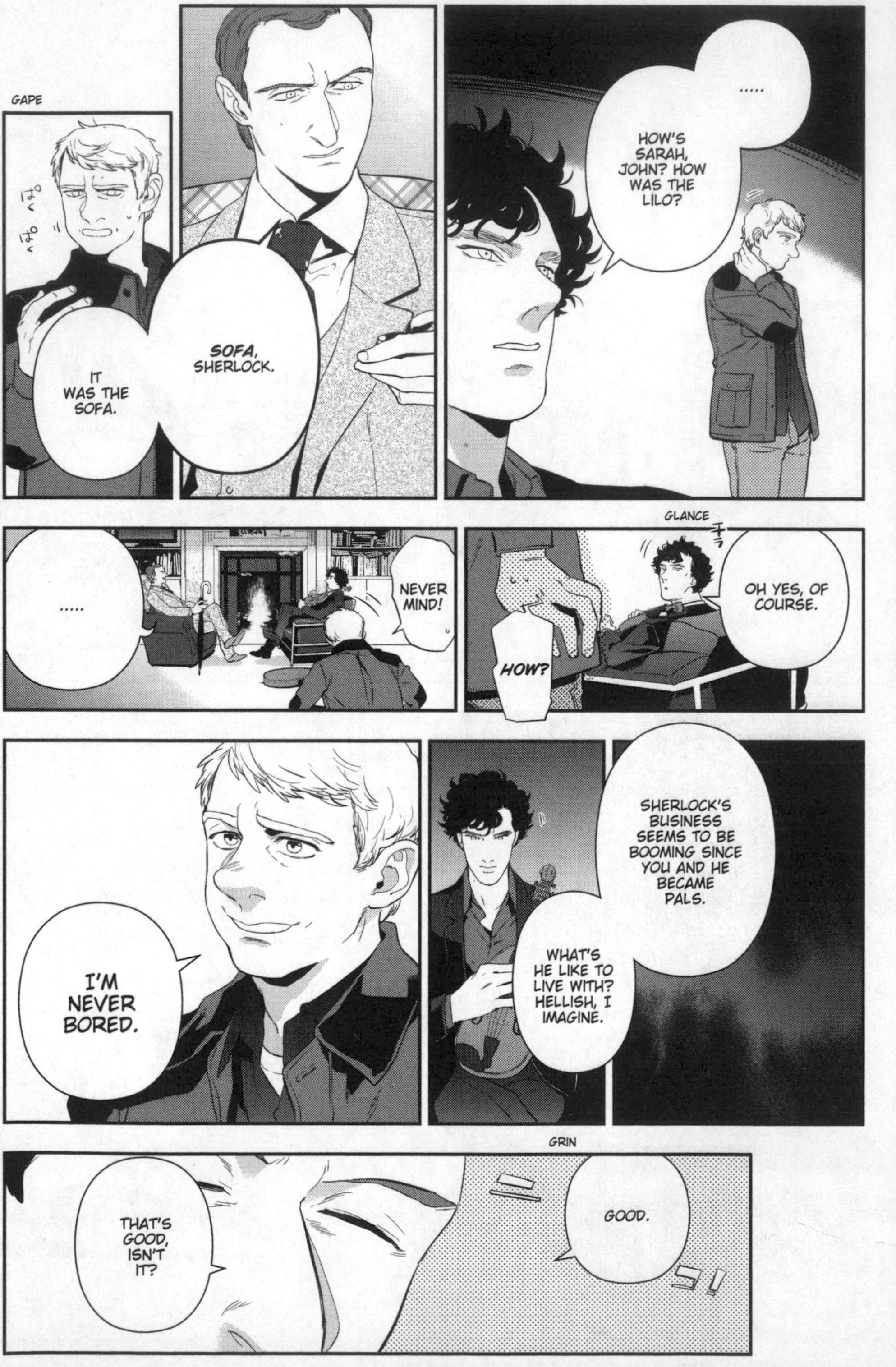
......
HOW'S SARAH, JOHN? HOW WAS THE LILO?
SOFA, SHERLOCK.
GAPE
IT WAS THE SOFA.
GLANCE
OH YES, OF COURSE.
HOW?
NEVER MIND!
......
SHERLOCK'S BUSINESS SEEMS TO BE BOOMING SINCE YOU AND HE BECAME PALS.
WHAT'S HE LIKE TO LIVE WITH? HELLISH, I IMAGINE.
I'M NEVER BORED.
GRIN
GOOD.
THAT'S GOOD, ISN'T IT?

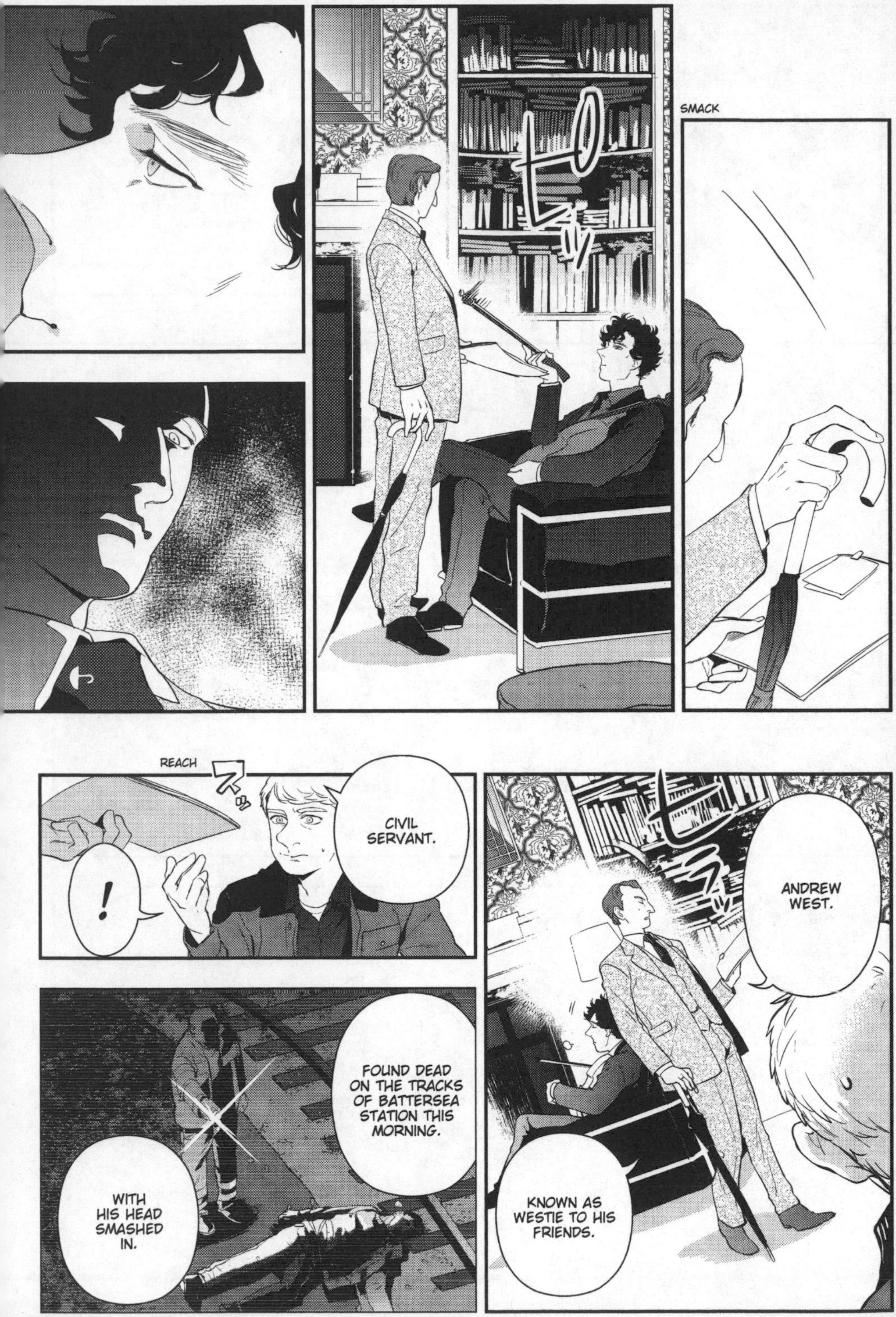
SMACK
ANDREW WEST.
KNOWN AS WESTIE TO HIS FRIENDS.
REACH
CIVIL SERVANT.
!
FOUND DEAD ON THE TRACKS OF BATTERSEA STATION THIS MORNING.
WITH HIS HEAD SMASHED IN.

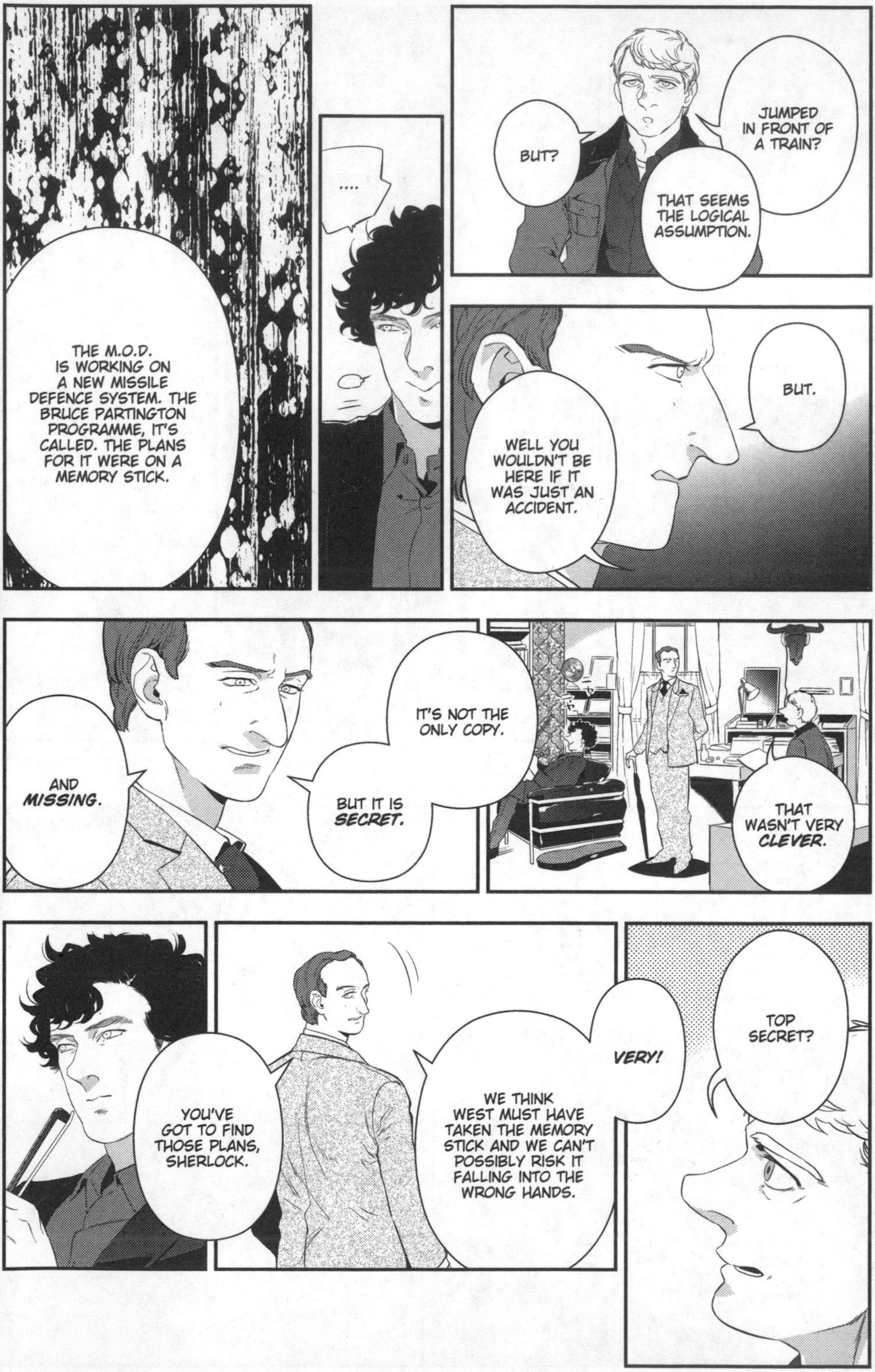
JUMPED IN FRONT OF A TRAIN?
THAT SEEMS THE LOGICAL ASSUMPTION.
BUT?
BUT.
WELL YOU WOULDN'T BE HERE IF IT WAS JUST AN ACCIDENT.
....
THE M.O.D. IS WORKING ON A NEW MISSILE DEFENCE SYSTEM. THE BRUCE PARTINGTON PROGRAMME, IT'S CALLED. THE PLANS FOR IT WERE ON A MEMORY STICK.
THAT WASN'T VERY *CLEVER*.
IT'S NOT THE ONLY COPY.
BUT IT IS *SECRET*.
AND *MISSING*.
TOP SECRET?
VERY!
WE THINK WEST MUST HAVE TAKEN THE MEMORY STICK AND WE CAN'T POSSIBLY RISK IT FALLING INTO THE WRONG HANDS.
YOU'VE GOT TO FIND THOSE PLANS, SHERLOCK.

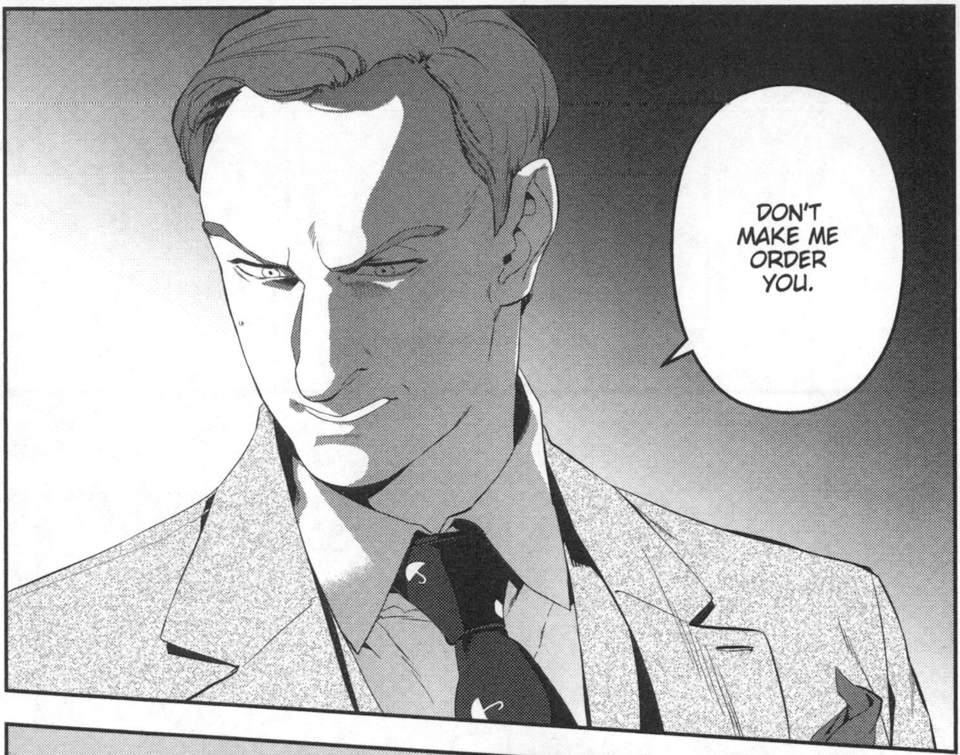
DON'T MAKE ME ORDER YOU.
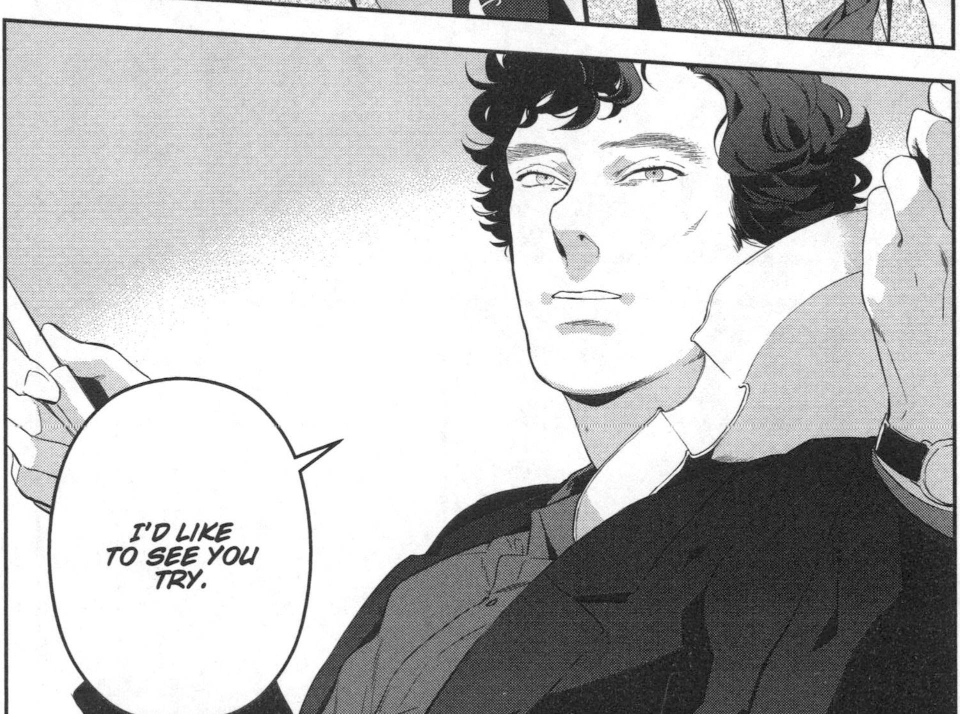
I'D LIKE TO SEE YOU TRY.

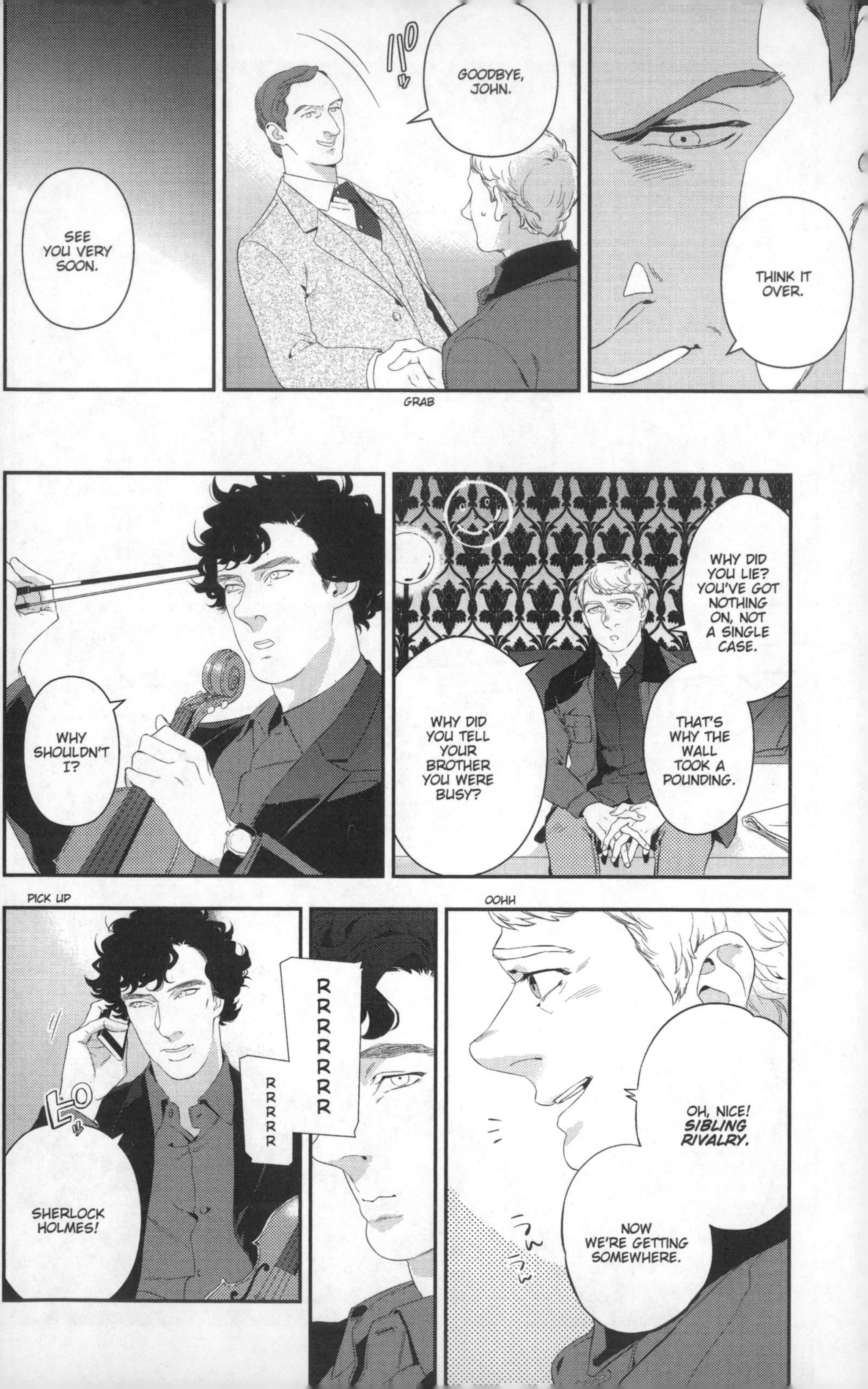
THINK IT OVER.
GOODBYE, JOHN.
GRAB
SEE YOU VERY SOON.
WHY DID YOU LIE? YOU'VE GOT NOTHING ON, NOT A SINGLE CASE.
THAT'S WHY THE WALL TOOK A POUNDING.
WHY DID YOU TELL YOUR BROTHER YOU WERE BUSY?
WHY SHOULDN'T I?
OOHH
OH, NICE! ***SIBLING RIVALRY.***
NOW WE'RE GETTING SOMEWHERE.
RRRRRRR
RRRRR
PICK UP
SHERLOCK HOLMES!

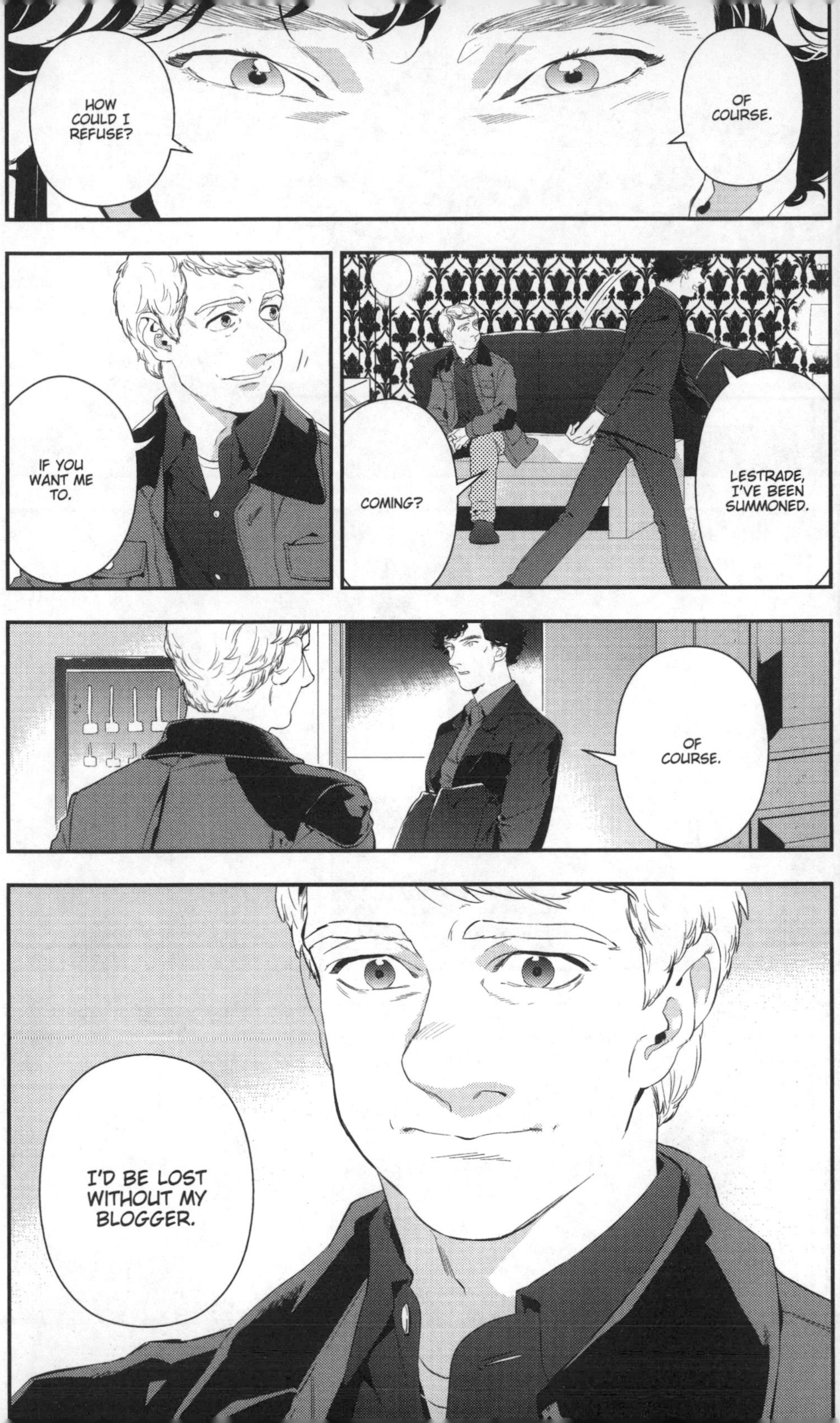
OF COURSE.
HOW COULD I REFUSE?
LESTRADE, I'VE BEEN SUMMONED.
COMING?
IF YOU WANT ME TO.
OF COURSE.
I'D BE LOST WITHOUT MY BLOGGER.

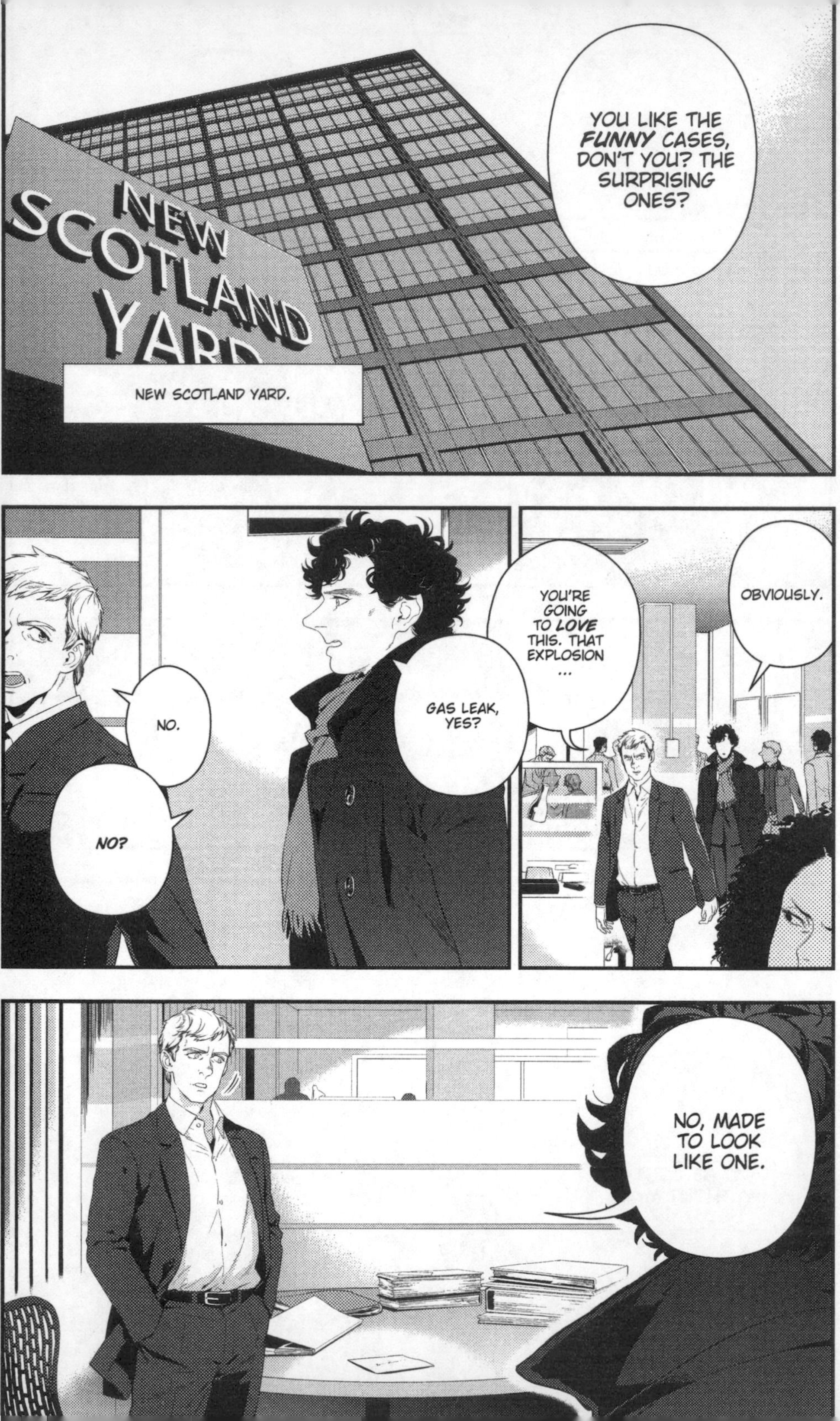
YOU LIKE THE *FUNNY* CASES, DON'T YOU? THE SURPRISING ONES?
NEW SCOTLAND YARD
NEW SCOTLAND YARD.
OBVIOUSLY.
YOU'RE GOING TO *LOVE* THIS. THAT EXPLOSION ...
GAS LEAK, YES?
NO.
NO?
NO, MADE TO LOOK LIKE ONE.

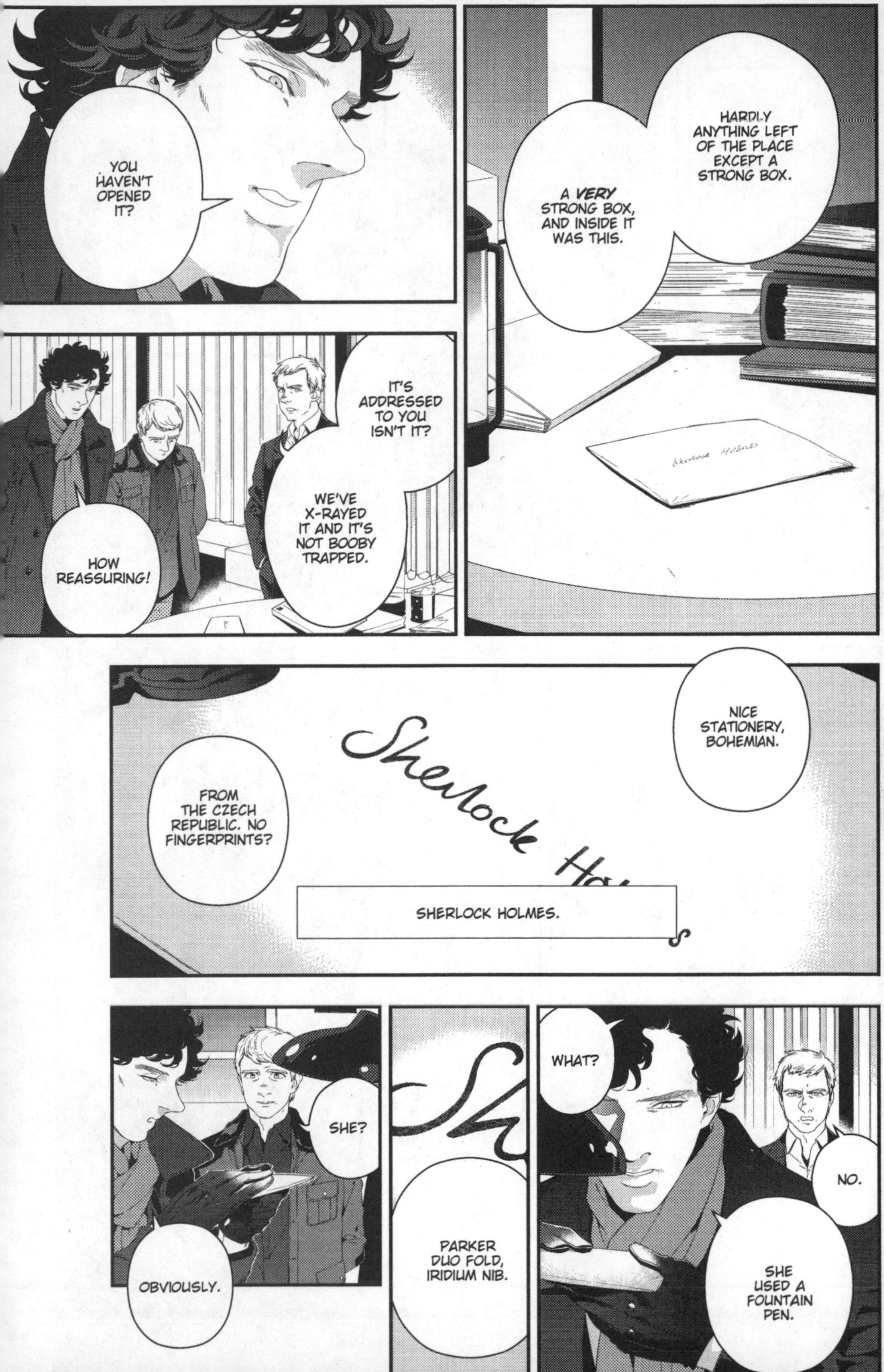
HARDLY ANYTHING LEFT OF THE PLACE EXCEPT A STRONG BOX.
A VERY STRONG BOX, AND INSIDE IT WAS THIS.
YOU HAVEN'T OPENED IT?
IT'S ADDRESSED TO YOU ISN'T IT?
WE'VE X-RAYED IT AND IT'S NOT BOOBY TRAPPED.
HOW REASSURING!
NICE STATIONERY, BOHEMIAN.
FROM THE CZECH REPUBLIC. NO FINGERPRINTS?
SHERLOCK HOLMES.
WHAT?
NO.
SHE USED A FOUNTAIN PEN.
PARKER DUO FOLD, IRIDIUM NIB.
SHE?
OBVIOUSLY.

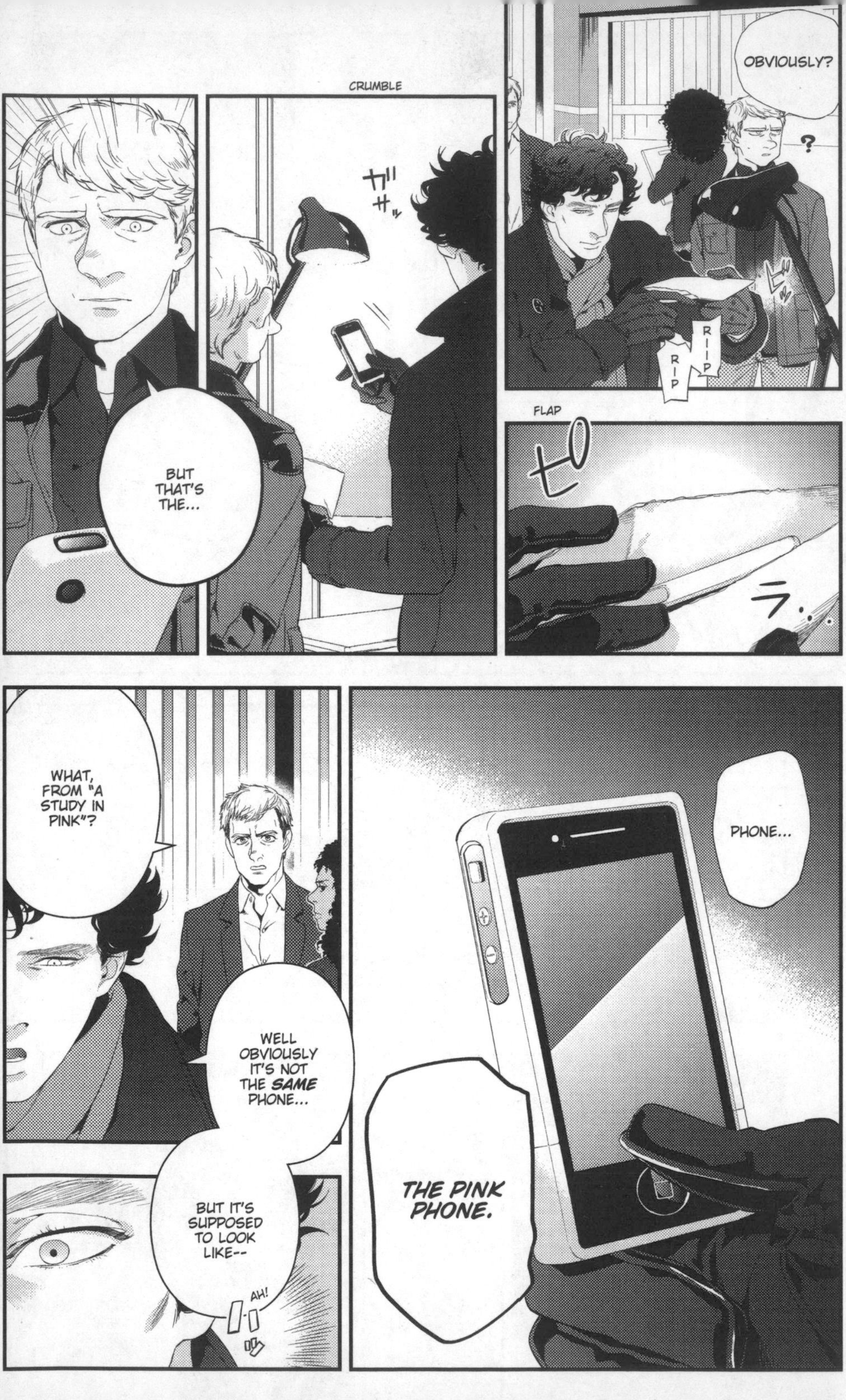
OBVIOUSLY?
RIIP
RIIP
FLAP
CRUMBLE
ガサッ
BUT THAT'S THE...
PHONE...
THE PINK PHONE.
WHAT, FROM "A STUDY IN PINK"?
WELL OBVIOUSLY IT'S NOT THE *SAME* PHONE...
BUT IT'S SUPPOSED TO LOOK LIKE--
AH!

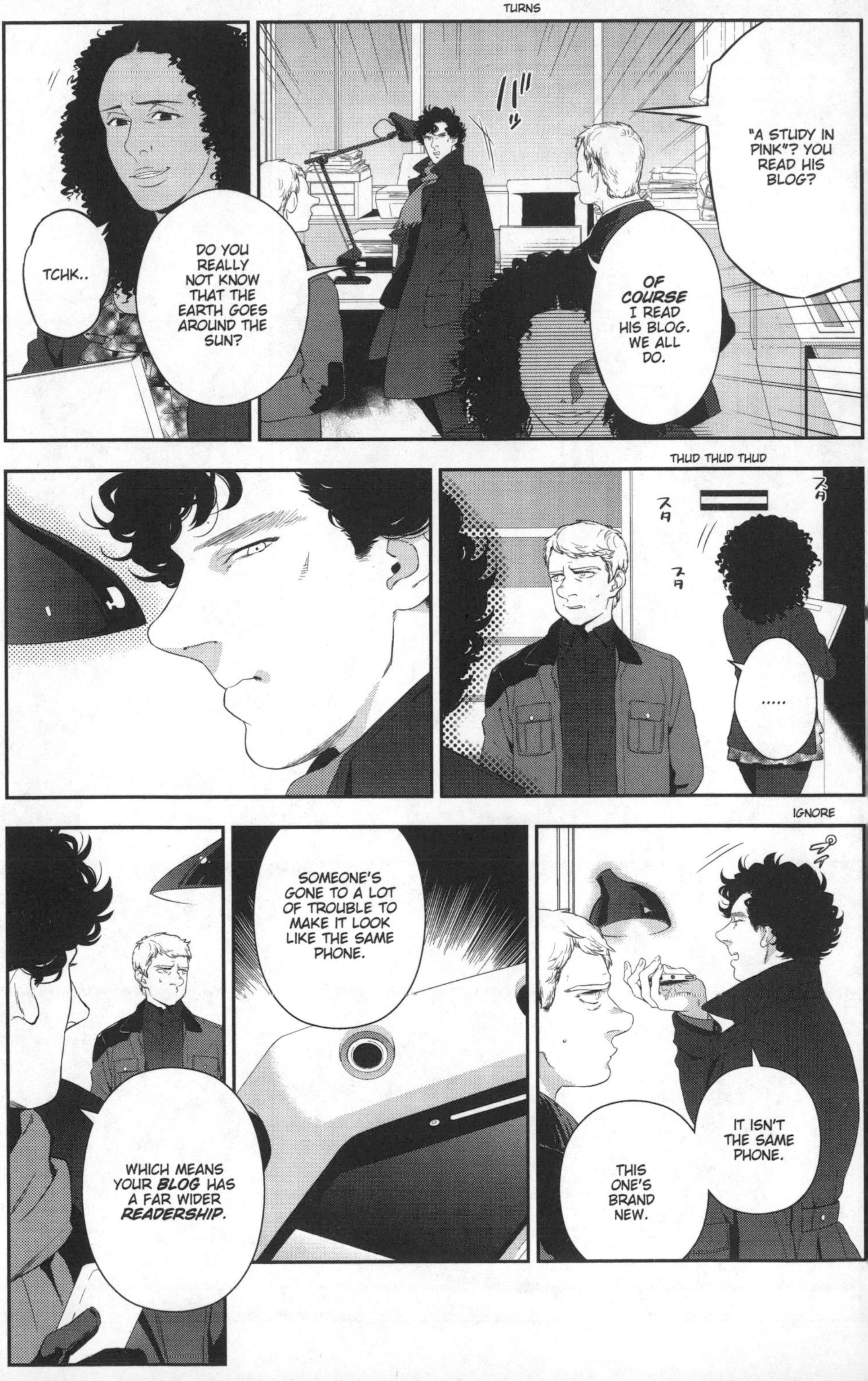
"A STUDY IN PINK"? YOU READ HIS BLOG?
TURNS
OF COURSE I READ HIS BLOG. WE ALL DO.
DO YOU REALLY NOT KNOW THAT THE EARTH GOES AROUND THE SUN?
TCHK..
THUD THUD THUD
.....
IGNORE
IT ISN'T THE SAME PHONE.
THIS ONE'S BRAND NEW.
SOMEONE'S GONE TO A LOT OF TROUBLE TO MAKE IT LOOK LIKE THE SAME PHONE.
WHICH MEANS YOUR BLOG HAS A FAR WIDER READERSHIP.

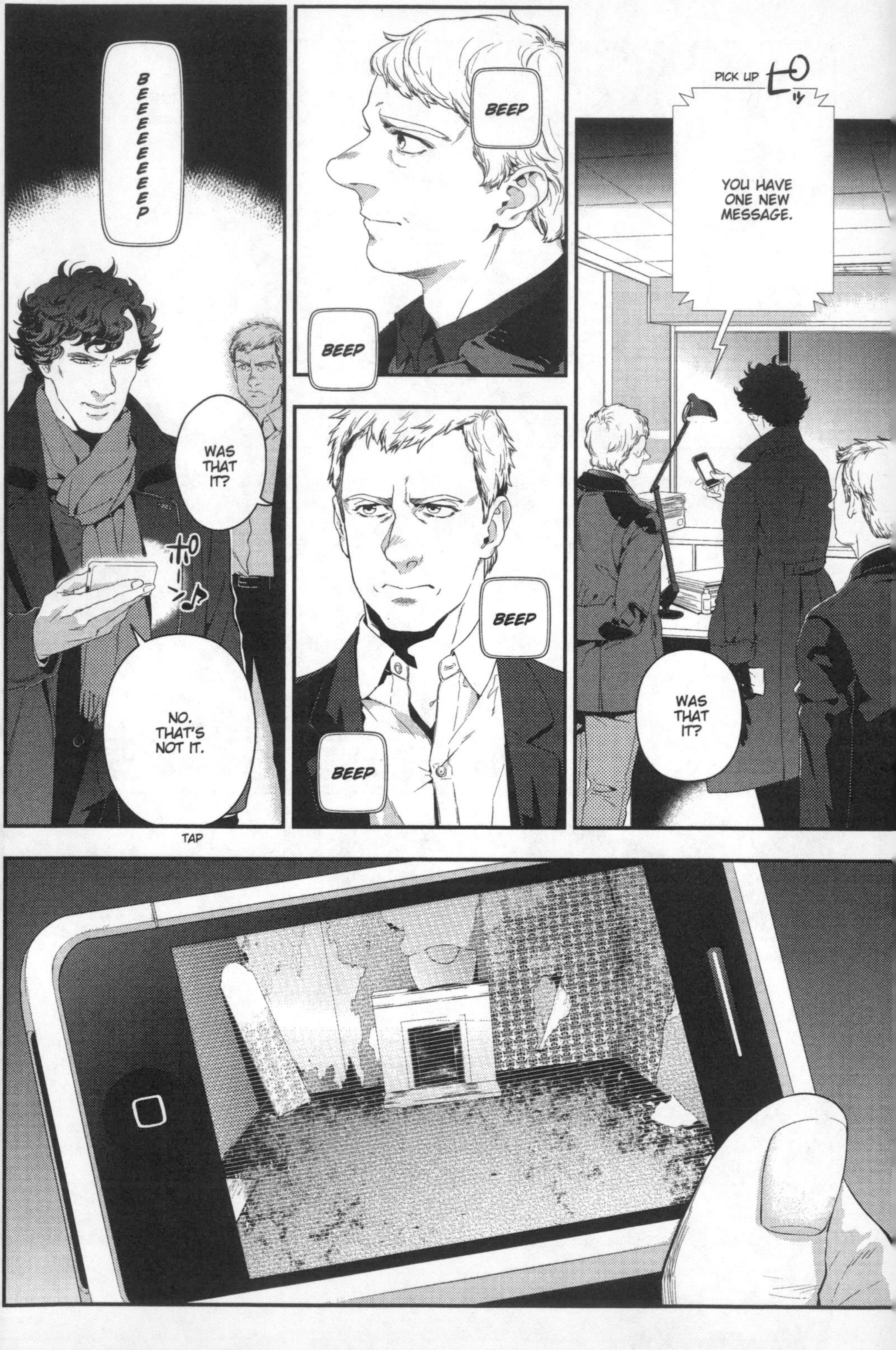
PICK UP
YOU HAVE ONE NEW MESSAGE.
WAS THAT IT?
BEEP
BEEP
BEEP
BEEP
BEEEEEEEEEP
WAS THAT IT?
NO. THAT'S NOT IT.
TAP

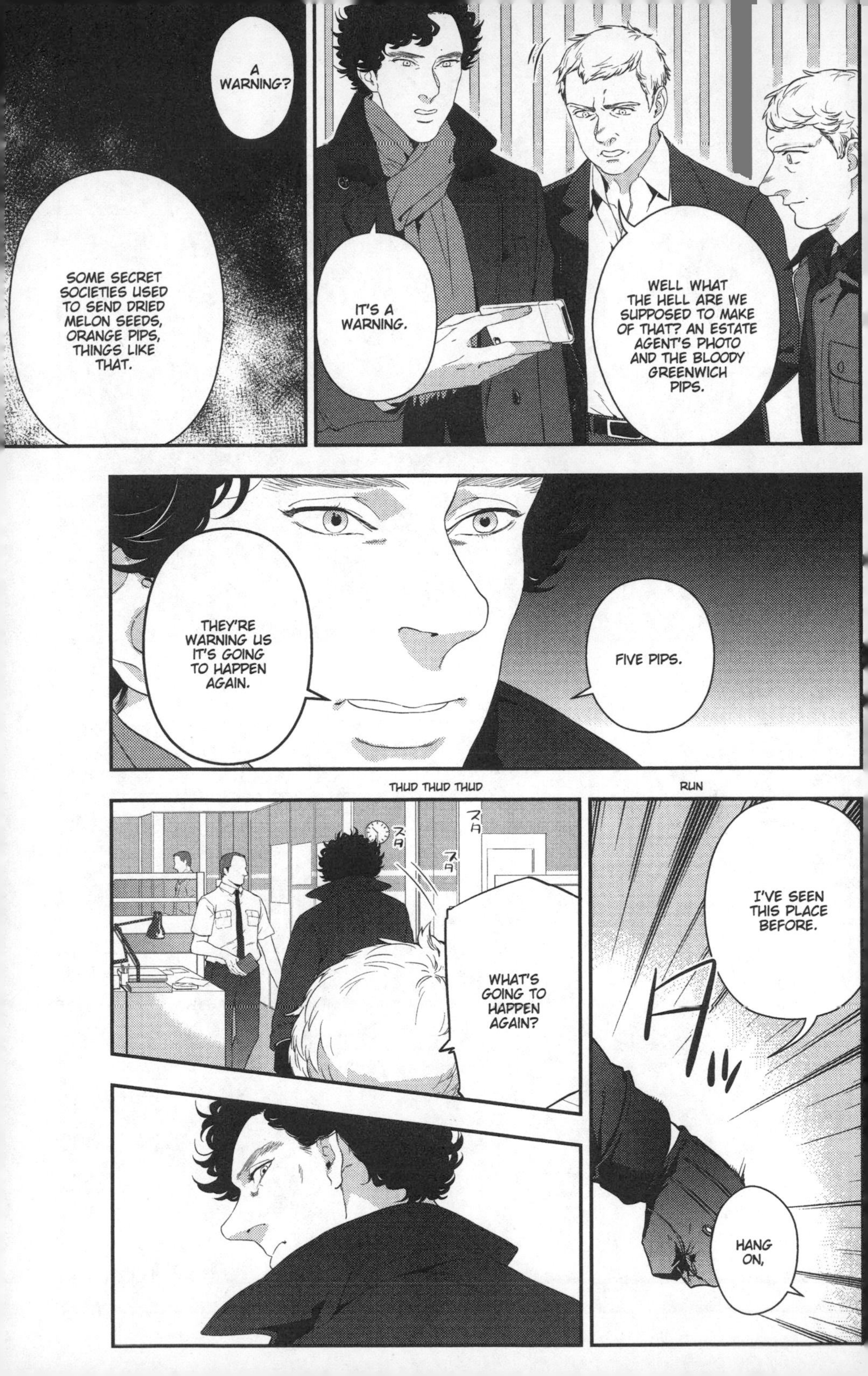
WELL WHAT THE HELL ARE WE SUPPOSED TO MAKE OF THAT? AN ESTATE AGENT'S PHOTO AND THE BLOODY GREENWICH PIPS.
IT'S A WARNING.
A WARNING?
SOME SECRET SOCIETIES USED TO SEND DRIED MELON SEEDS, ORANGE PIPS, THINGS LIKE THAT.
FIVE PIPS.
THEY'RE WARNING US IT'S GOING TO HAPPEN AGAIN.
RUN
I'VE SEEN THIS PLACE BEFORE.
HANG ON,
THUD THUD THUD
スタ
スタ
スタ
WHAT'S GOING TO HAPPEN AGAIN?

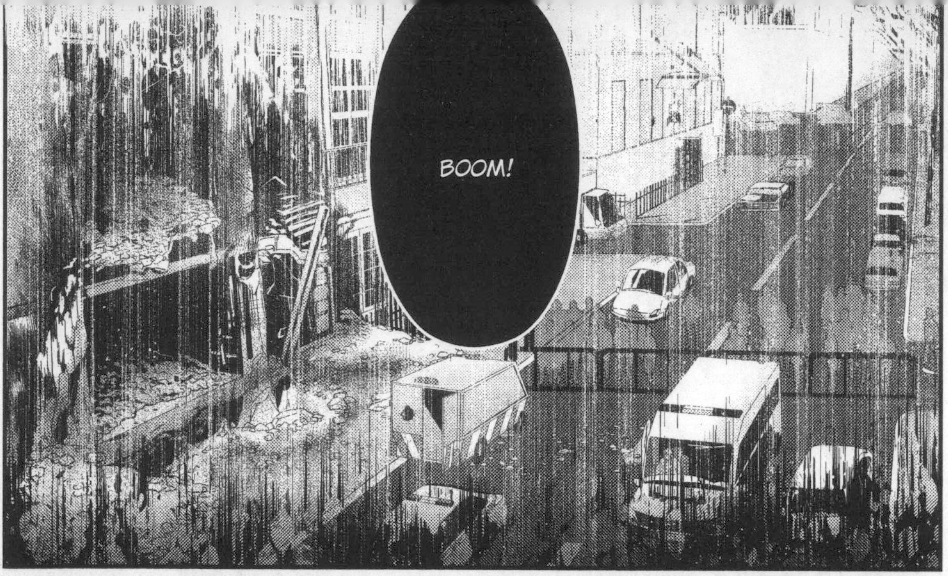
BOOM!

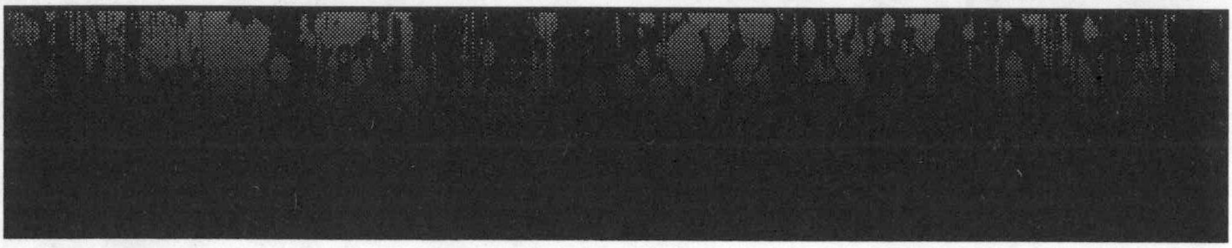

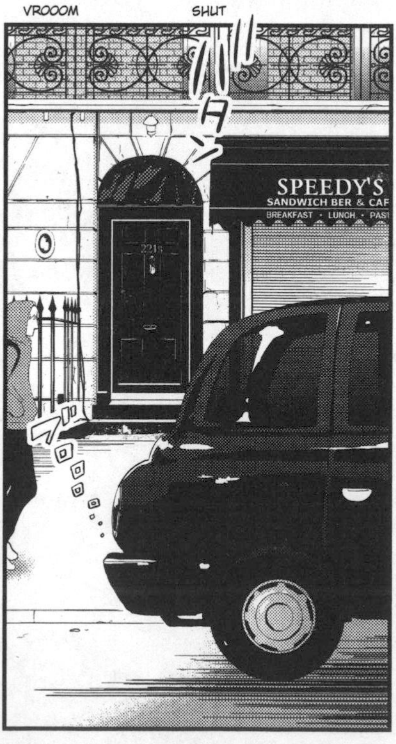
SHUT
VROOOM
SPEEDY'S
SANDWICH BER & CAF
BREAKFAST • LUNCH • PAST

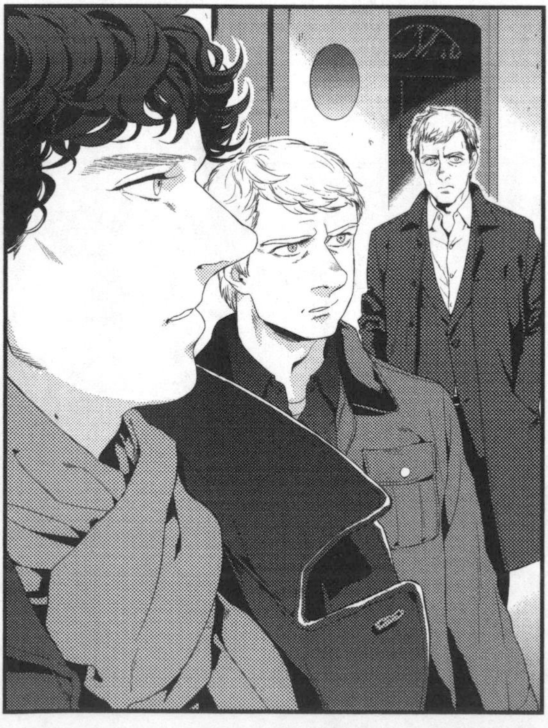

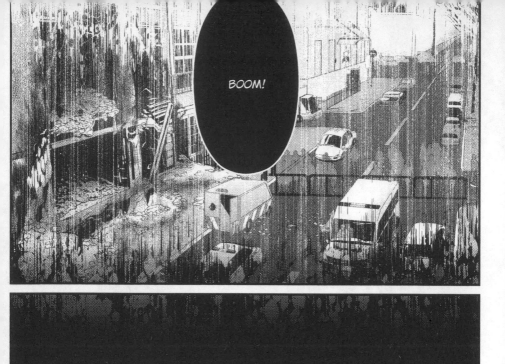

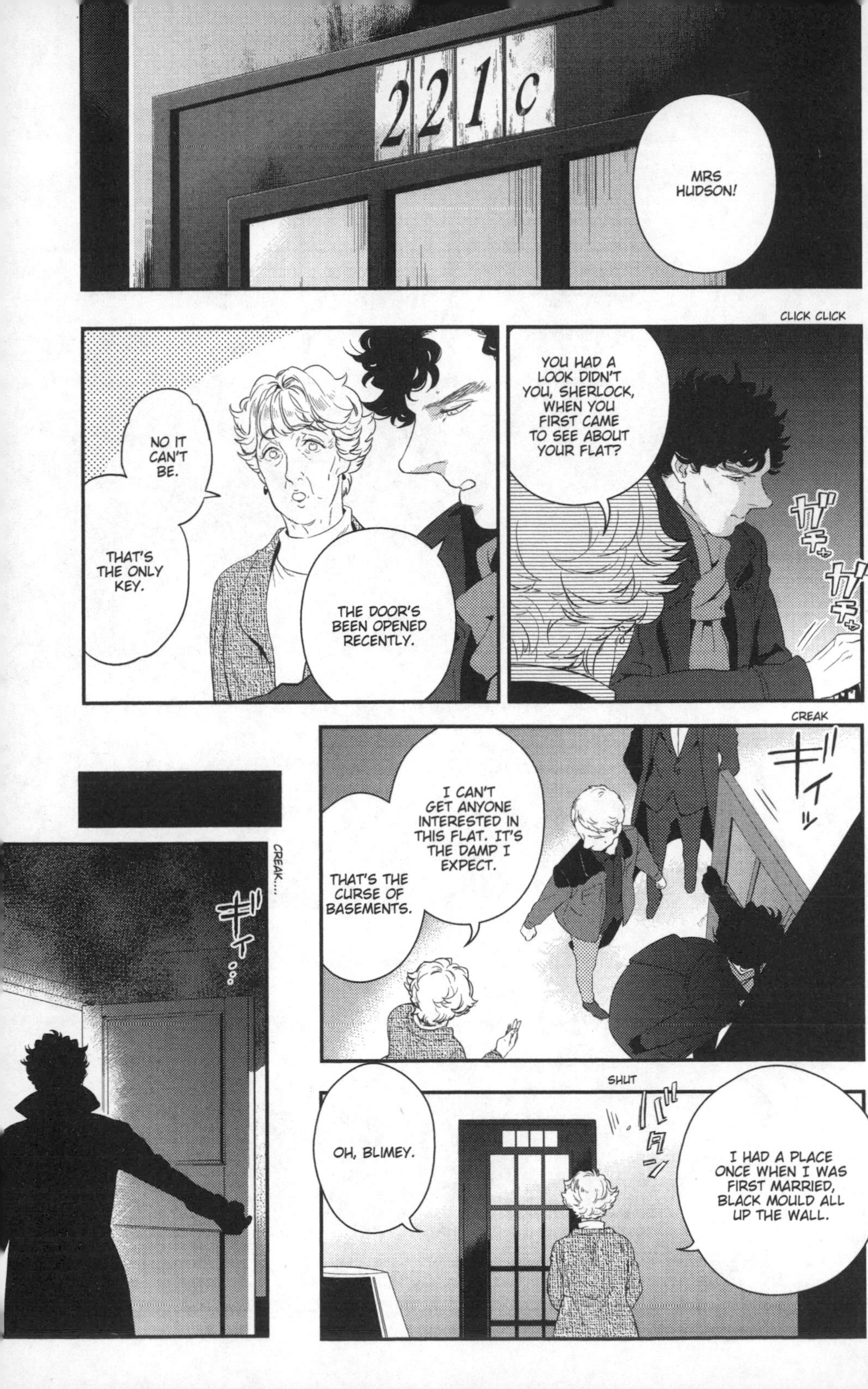
221c
MRS HUDSON!
CLICK CLICK
ガチャ ガチャ
YOU HAD A LOOK DIDN'T YOU, SHERLOCK, WHEN YOU FIRST CAME TO SEE ABOUT YOUR FLAT?
THE DOOR'S BEEN OPENED RECENTLY.
NO IT CAN'T BE.
THAT'S THE ONLY KEY.
CREAK
ギィッ
I CAN'T GET ANYONE INTERESTED IN THIS FLAT. IT'S THE DAMP I EXPECT.
THAT'S THE CURSE OF BASEMENTS.
SHUT
バタン
I HAD A PLACE ONCE WHEN I WAS FIRST MARRIED, BLACK MOULD ALL UP THE WALL.
OH, BLIMEY.
CREAK...
ギィ…

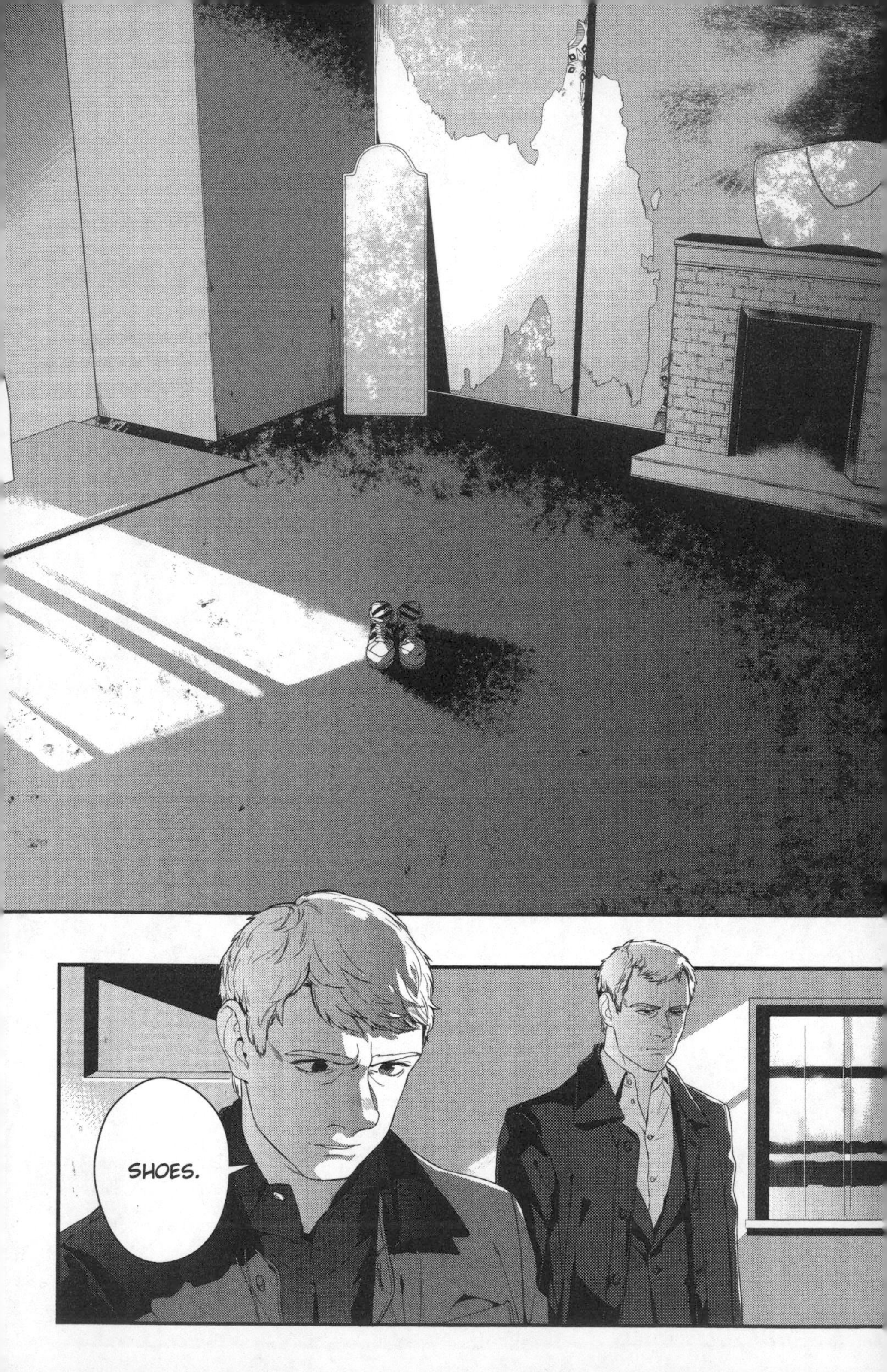
SHOES.

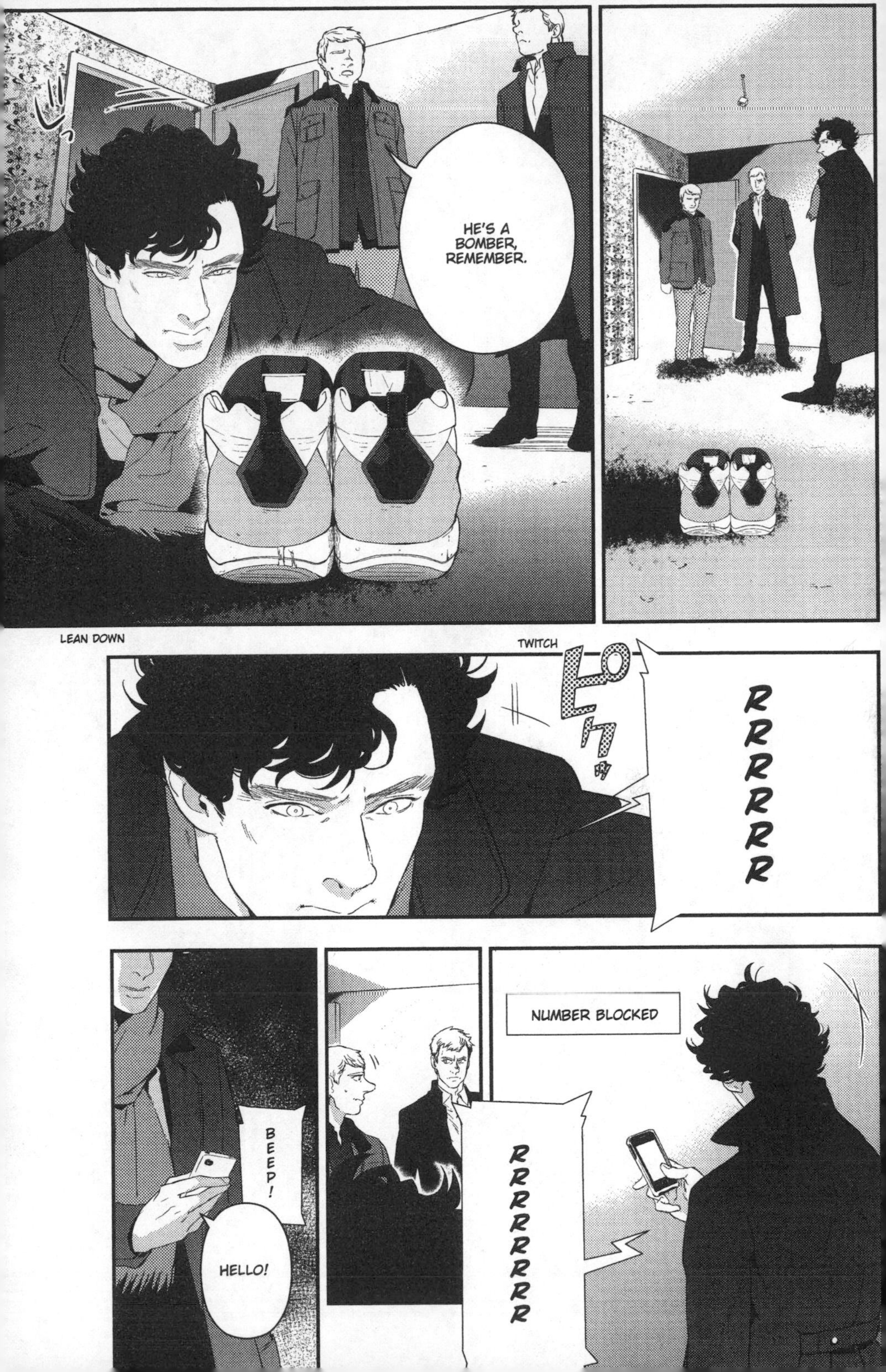
HE'S A BOMBER, REMEMBER.
LEAN DOWN
TWITCH
RRRRRR
NUMBER BLOCKED
RRRRRRRR
BEEP!
HELLO!

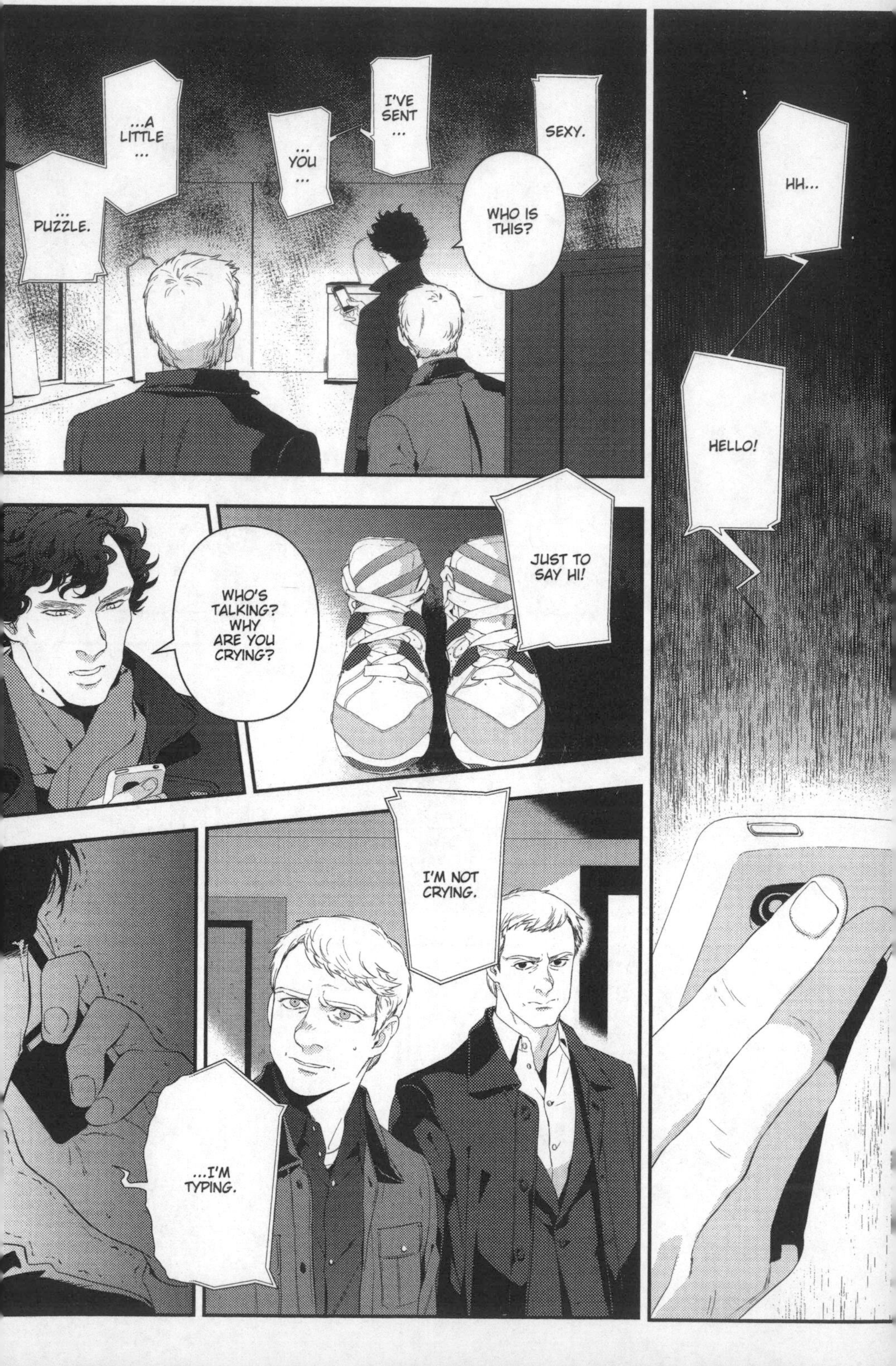
HH...
HELLO!
SEXY.
WHO IS THIS?
I'VE SENT ...
... YOU ...
...A LITTLE ...
... PUZZLE.
JUST TO SAY HI!
WHO'S TALKING? WHY ARE YOU CRYING?
I'M NOT CRYING.
...I'M TYPING.

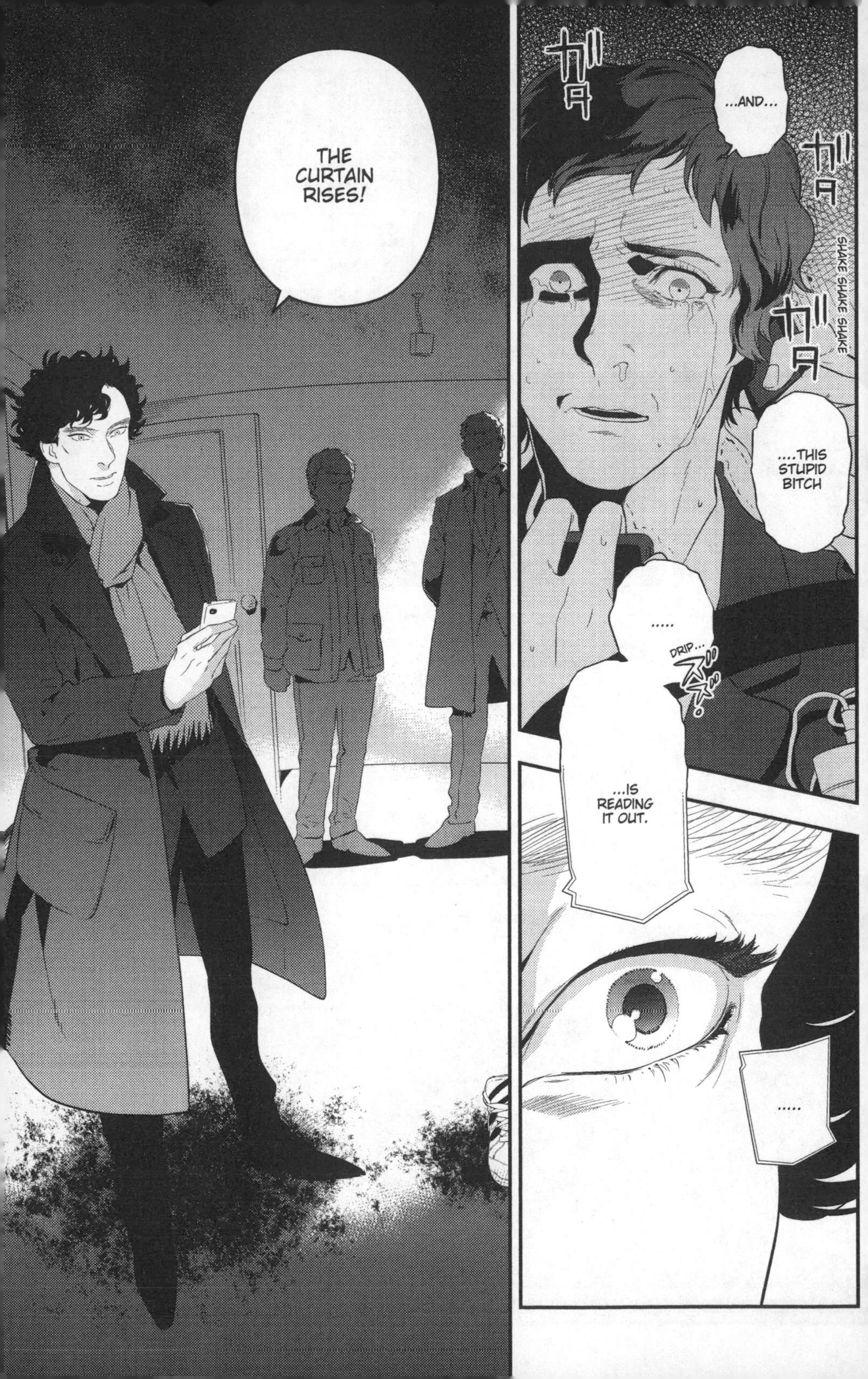
...AND...
SHAKE SHAKE SHAKE
....THIS STUPID BITCH
.....
DRIP...
...IS READING IT OUT.
.....
THE CURTAIN RISES!

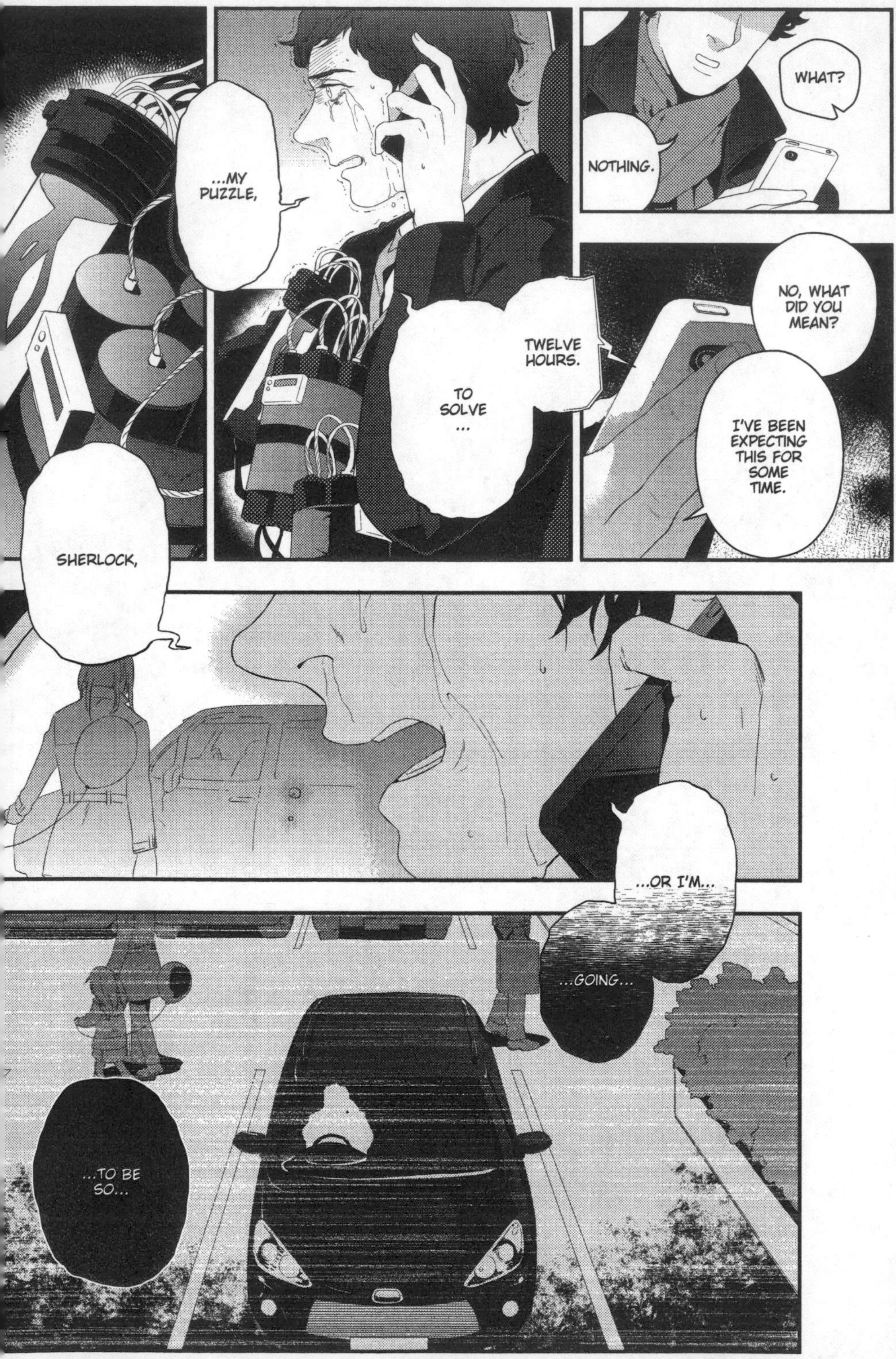
WHAT?
NOTHING.
NO, WHAT DID YOU MEAN?
I'VE BEEN EXPECTING THIS FOR SOME TIME.
TWELVE HOURS.
TO SOLVE ...
...MY PUZZLE,
SHERLOCK,
...OR I'M...
...GOING...
...TO BE SO...

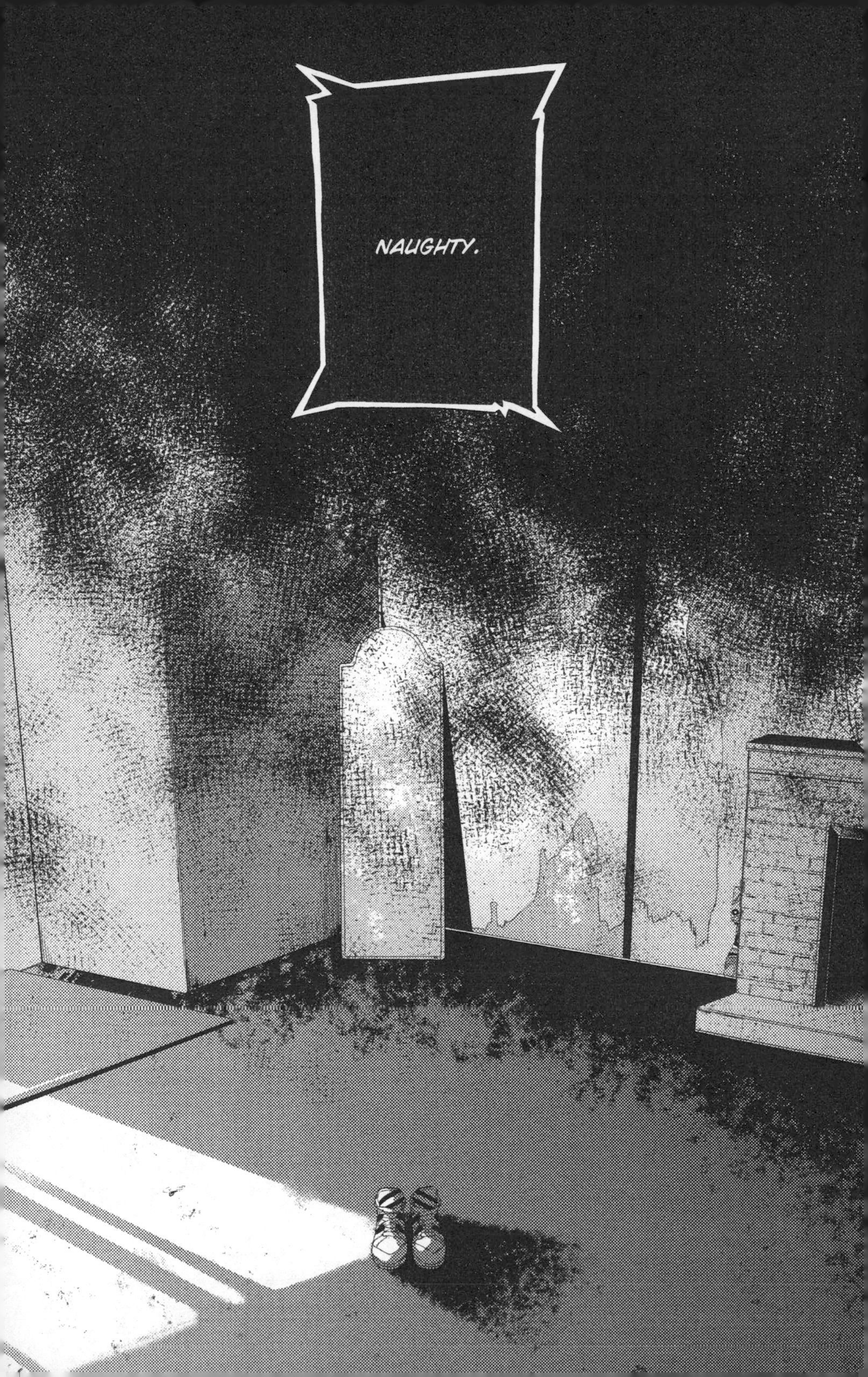
NAUGHTY.

Illustration by:
Will Brooks

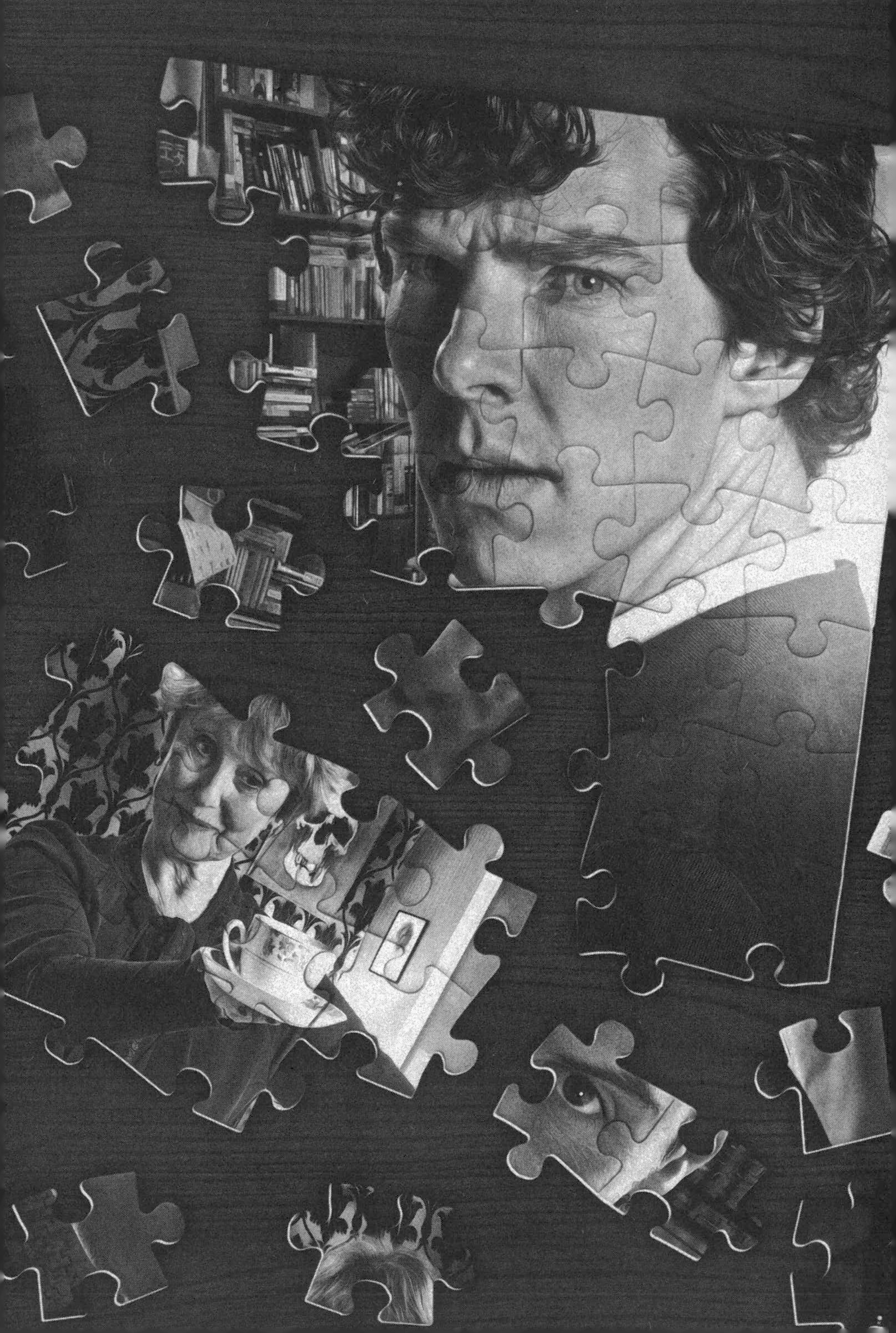

Chapter 2

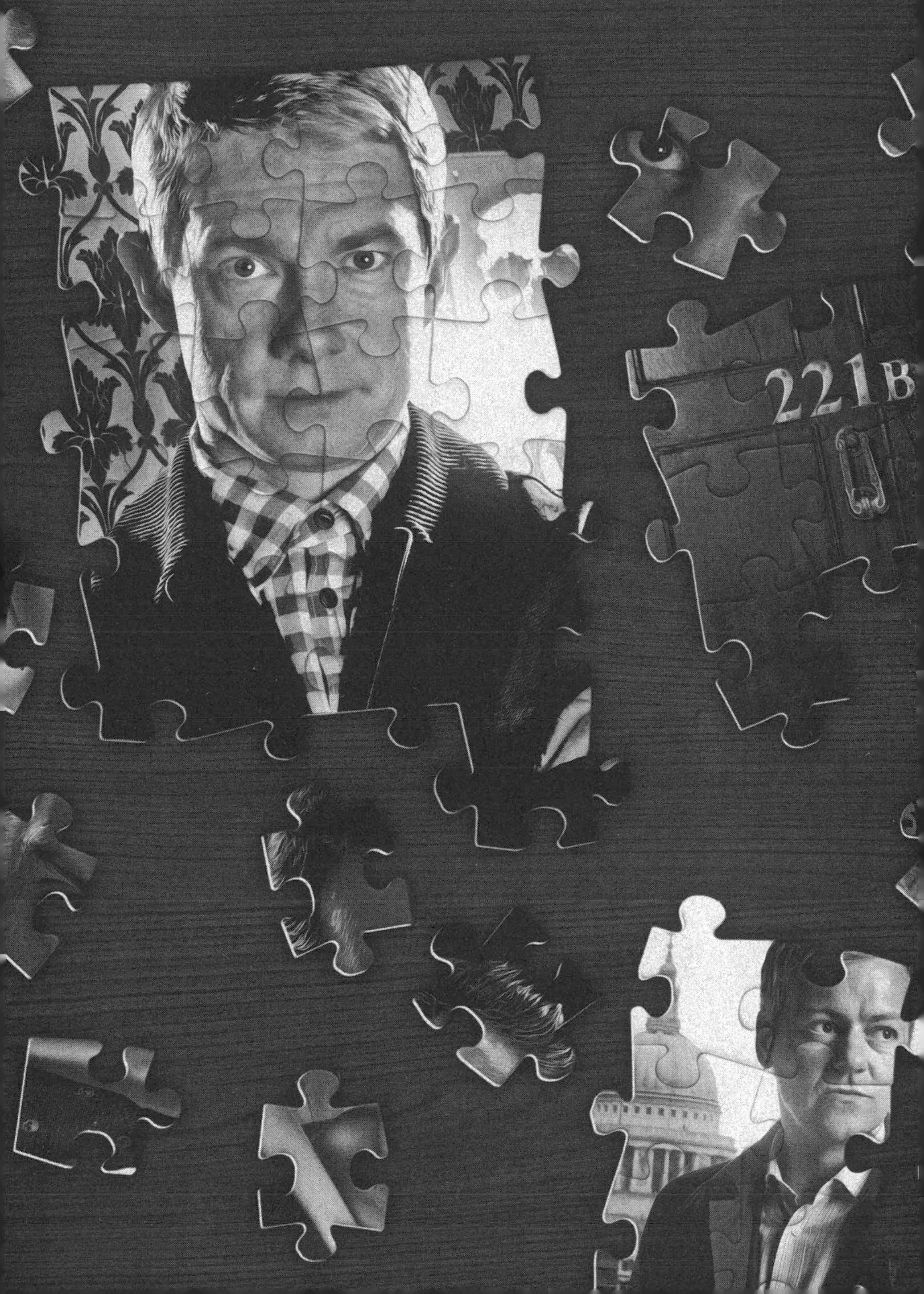

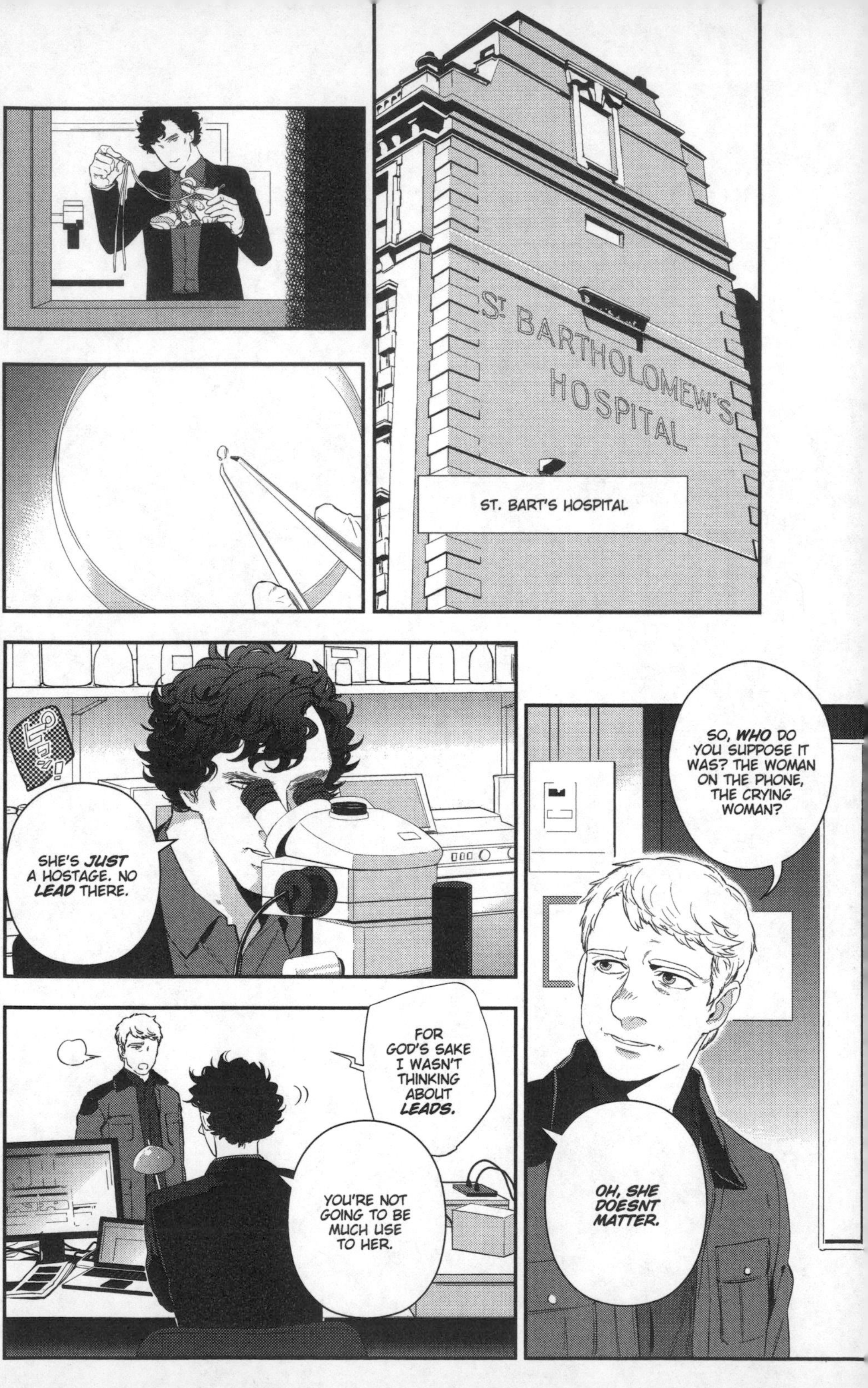

ST BARTHOLOMEW'S HOSPITAL
ST. BART'S HOSPITAL
SO, WHO DO YOU SUPPOSE IT WAS? THE WOMAN ON THE PHONE, THE CRYING WOMAN?
OH, SHE DOESNT MATTER.
SHE'S JUST A HOSTAGE. NO LEAD THERE.
FOR GOD'S SAKE I WASN'T THINKING ABOUT LEADS.
YOU'RE NOT GOING TO BE MUCH USE TO HER.

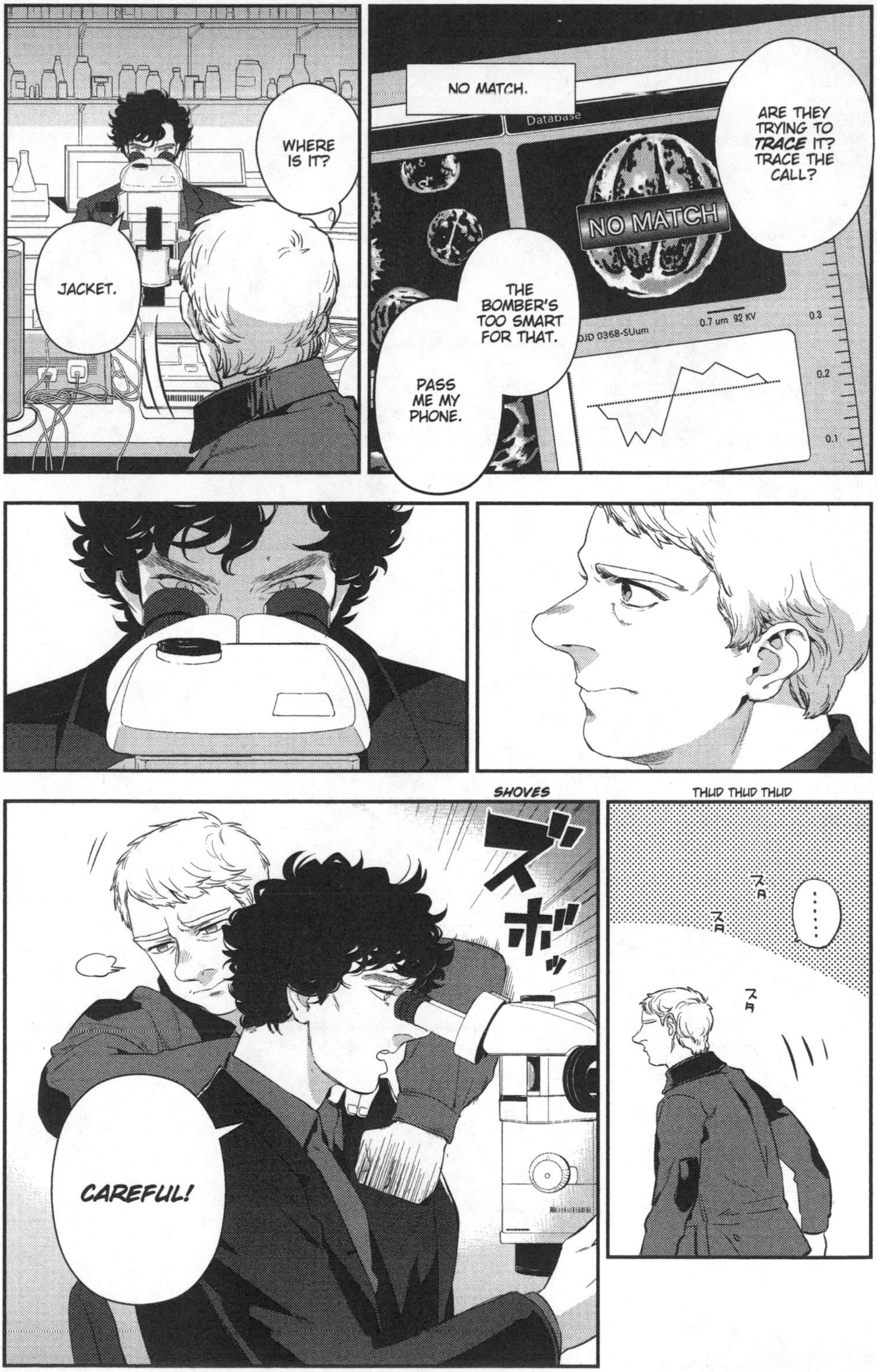
NO MATCH.
Database
NO MATCH
ARE THEY TRYING TO *TRACE* IT? TRACE THE CALL?
THE BOMBER'S TOO SMART FOR THAT.
PASS ME MY PHONE.
0.7 um 92 KV
WHERE IS IT?
JACKET.
THUD THUD THUD
スタ
スタ
……
スタ
SHOVES
ズボッ
CAREFUL!

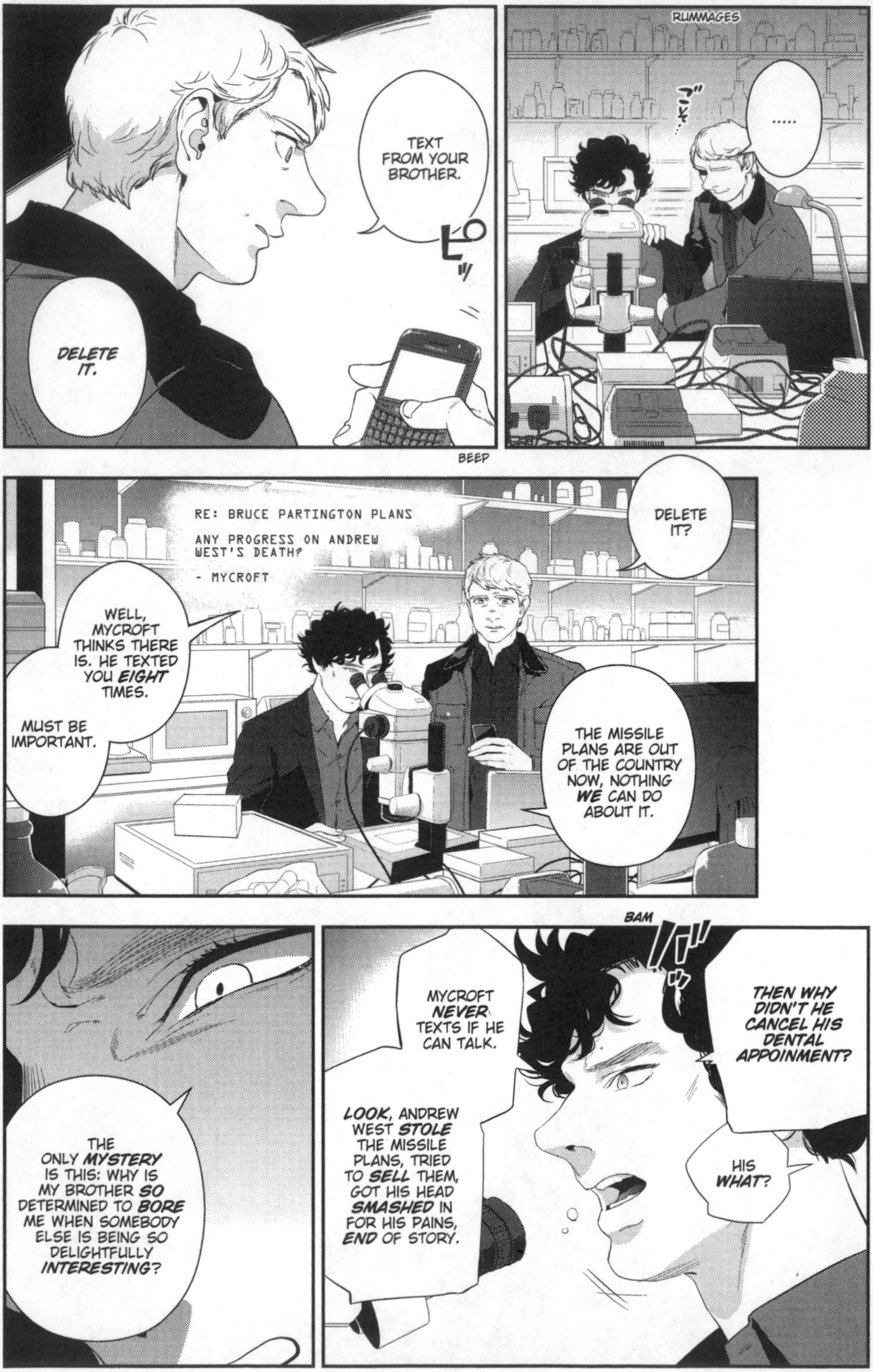
RUMMAGES
......
TEXT FROM YOUR BROTHER.
ピッ
DELETE IT.
BEEP
DELETE IT?
RE: BRUCE PARTINGTON PLANS
ANY PROGRESS ON ANDREW WEST'S DEATH?
- MYCROFT
THE MISSILE PLANS ARE OUT OF THE COUNTRY NOW, NOTHING WE CAN DO ABOUT IT.
WELL, MYCROFT THINKS THERE IS. HE TEXTED YOU EIGHT TIMES.
MUST BE IMPORTANT.
BAM
MYCROFT NEVER TEXTS IF HE CAN TALK.
LOOK, ANDREW WEST STOLE THE MISSILE PLANS, TRIED TO SELL THEM, GOT HIS HEAD SMASHED IN FOR HIS PAINS, END OF STORY.
THEN WHY DIDN'T HE CANCEL HIS DENTAL APPOINMENT?
HIS WHAT?
THE ONLY MYSTERY IS THIS: WHY IS MY BROTHER SO DETERMINED TO BORE ME WHEN SOMEBODY ELSE IS BEING SO DELIGHTFULLY INTERESTING?

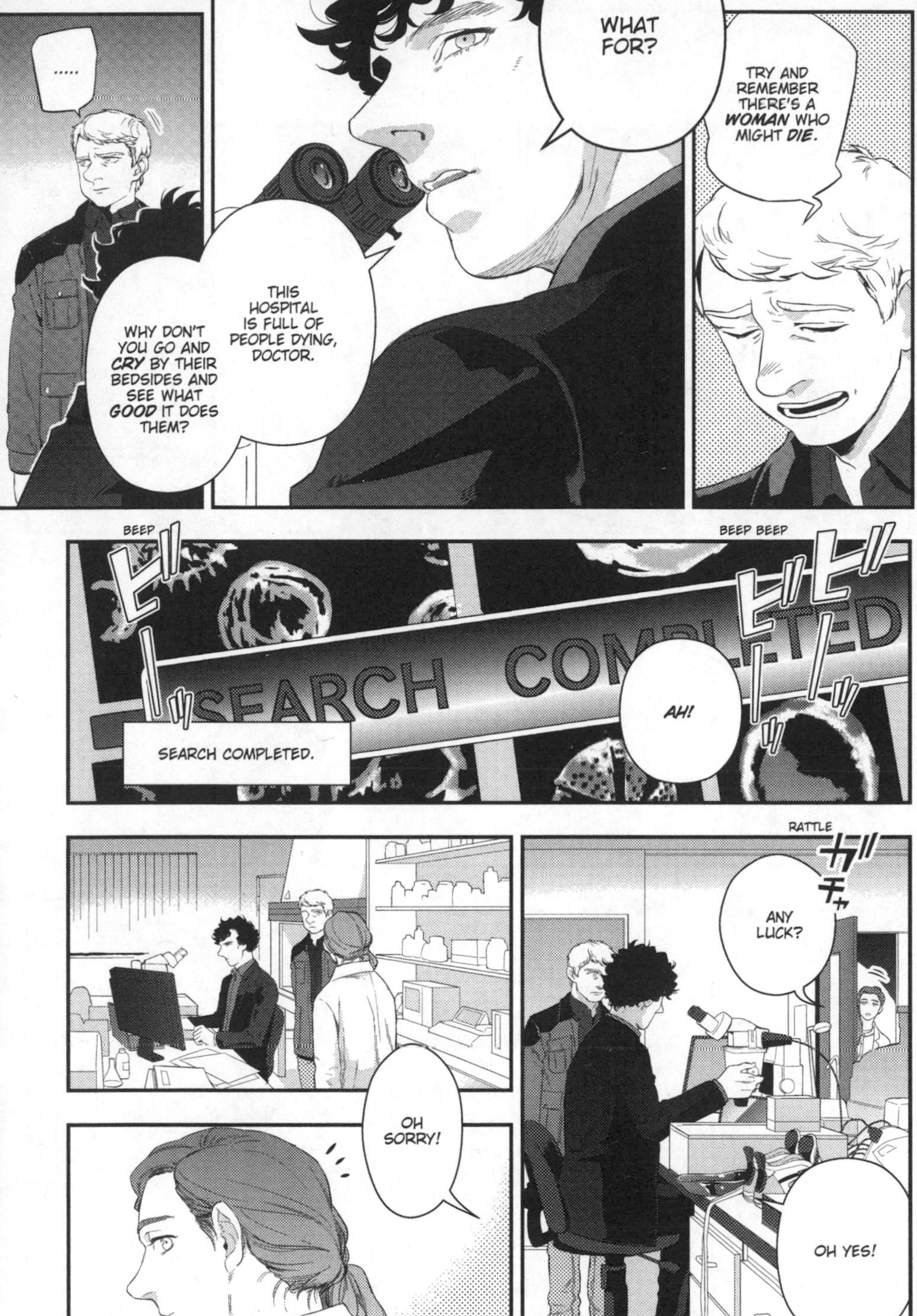
TRY AND REMEMBER THERE'S A ***WOMAN*** WHO MIGHT ***DIE.***
WHAT FOR?
THIS HOSPITAL IS FULL OF PEOPLE DYING, DOCTOR.
WHY DON'T YOU GO AND ***CRY*** BY THEIR BEDSIDES AND SEE WHAT ***GOOD*** IT DOES THEM?
.....
BEEP BEEP
ビビ
SEARCH COMPLETED
AH!
BEEP
ビ
SEARCH COMPLETED.
RATTLE
ガチャ
ANY LUCK?
OH YES!
OH SORRY!

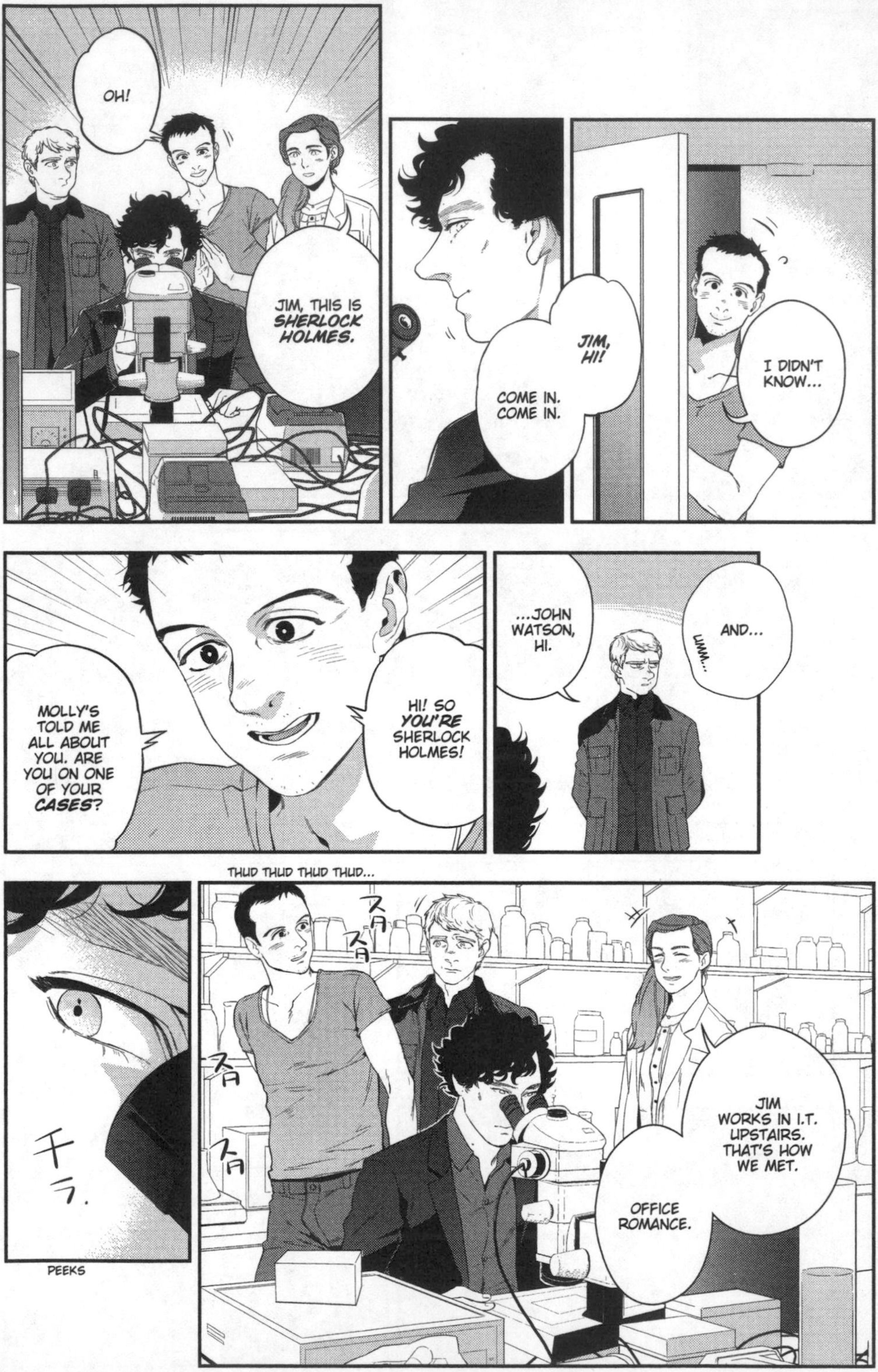
I DIDN'T KNOW...
JIM, HI!
COME IN. COME IN.
OH!
JIM, THIS IS *SHERLOCK HOLMES.*
AND...
UMM...
...JOHN WATSON, HI.
HI! SO *YOU'RE* SHERLOCK HOLMES!
MOLLY'S TOLD ME ALL ABOUT YOU. ARE YOU ON ONE OF YOUR *CASES*?
THUD THUD THUD THUD...
スタ
スタ
スタ
スタ
JIM WORKS IN I.T. UPSTAIRS. THAT'S HOW WE MET.
OFFICE ROMANCE.
チラ.
PEEKS

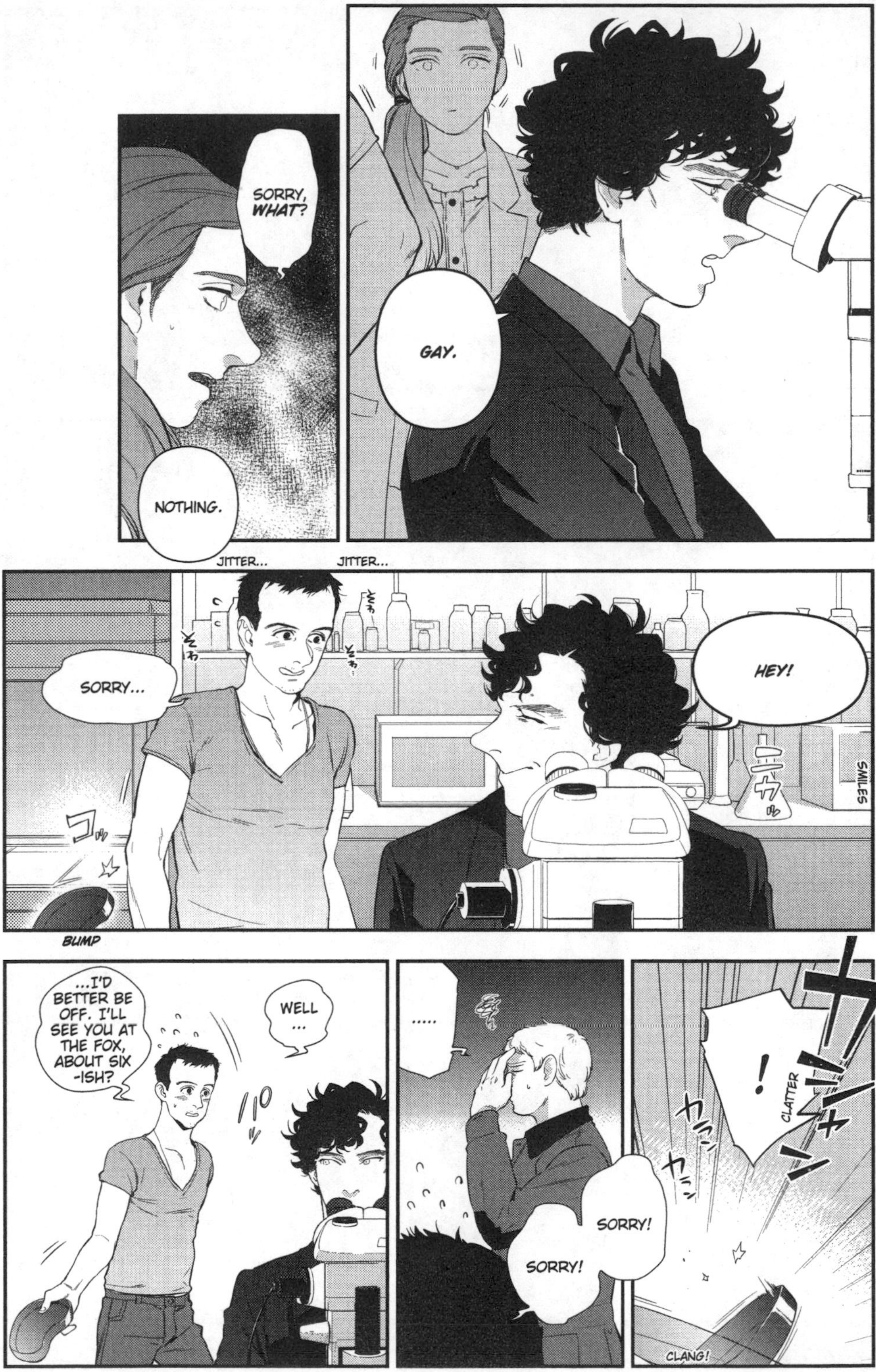
GAY.
SORRY, WHAT?
NOTHING.
JITTER...
JITTER...
HEY!
SMILES
SORRY...
BUMP
!
CLATTER
CLANG!
.....
SORRY!
SORRY!
WELL ...
...I'D BETTER BE OFF. I'LL SEE YOU AT THE FOX, ABOUT SIX -ISH?

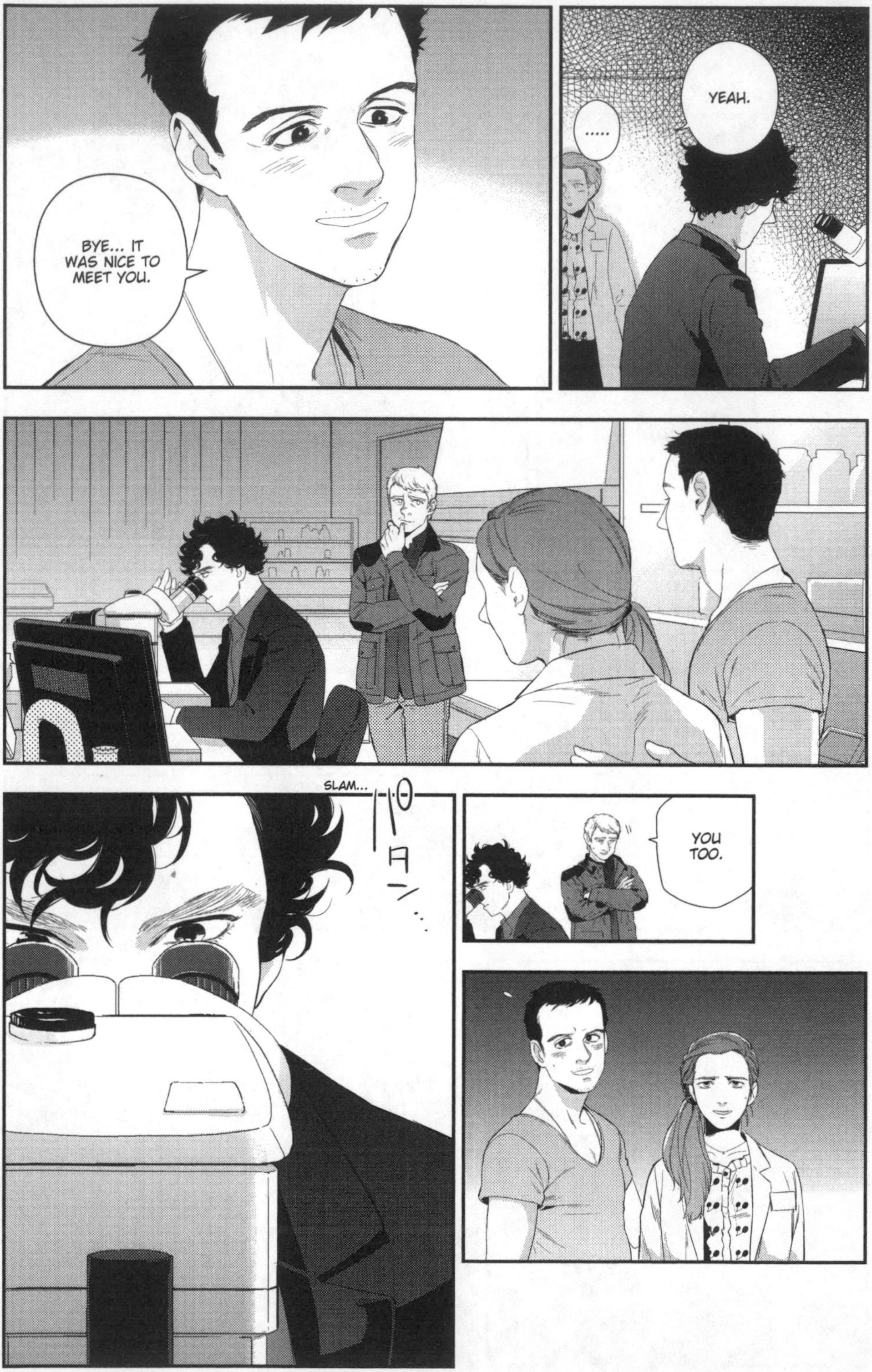
YEAH.
.....
BYE... IT WAS NICE TO MEET YOU.
YOU TOO.
SLAM...
バタン…

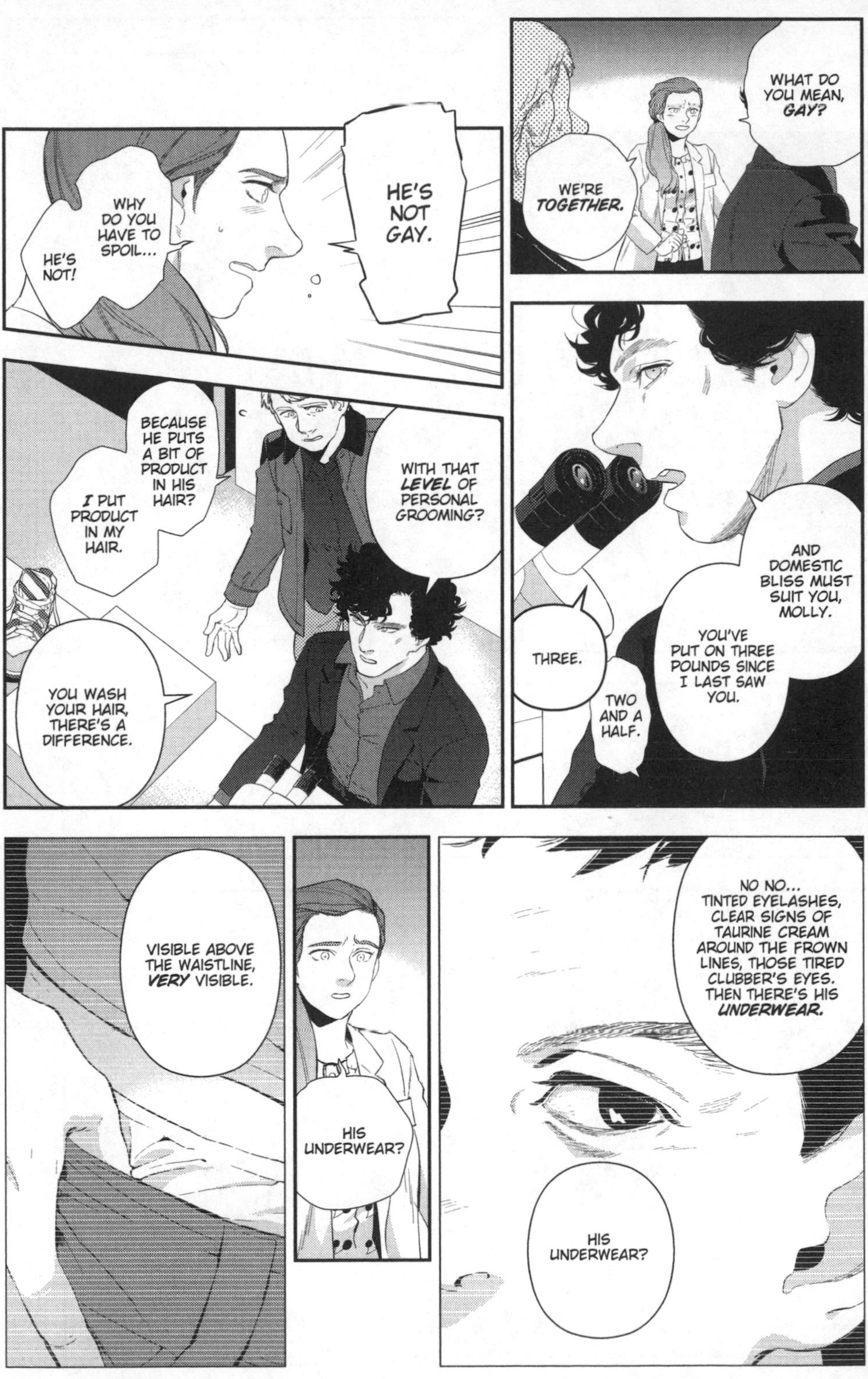
WHAT DO YOU MEAN, GAY?
WE'RE TOGETHER.
HE'S NOT GAY.
WHY DO YOU HAVE TO SPOIL...
HE'S NOT!
AND DOMESTIC BLISS MUST SUIT YOU, MOLLY.
YOU'VE PUT ON THREE POUNDS SINCE I LAST SAW YOU.
TWO AND A HALF.
THREE.
WITH THAT LEVEL OF PERSONAL GROOMING?
BECAUSE HE PUTS A BIT OF PRODUCT IN HIS HAIR?
I PUT PRODUCT IN MY HAIR.
YOU WASH YOUR HAIR, THERE'S A DIFFERENCE.
NO NO... TINTED EYELASHES, CLEAR SIGNS OF TAURINE CREAM AROUND THE FROWN LINES, THOSE TIRED CLUBBER'S EYES. THEN THERE'S HIS UNDERWEAR.
HIS UNDERWEAR?
HIS UNDERWEAR?
VISIBLE ABOVE THE WAISTLINE, VERY VISIBLE.

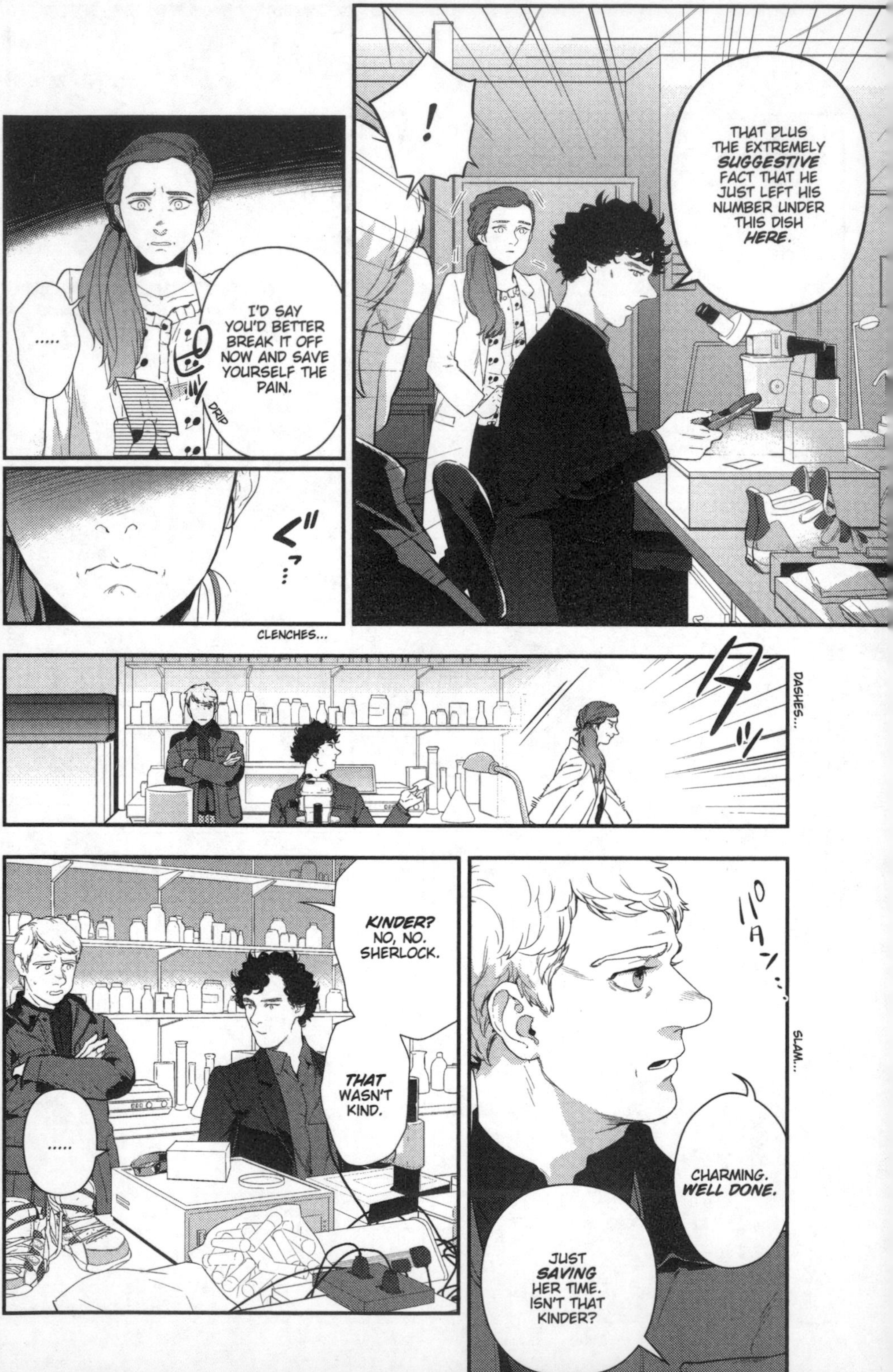
THAT PLUS THE EXTREMELY **SUGGESTIVE** FACT THAT HE JUST LEFT HIS NUMBER UNDER THIS DISH **HERE**.
!
I'D SAY YOU'D BETTER BREAK IT OFF NOW AND SAVE YOURSELF THE PAIN.
......
DRIP
CLENCHES...
DASHES...
SLAM...
CHARMING. **WELL DONE.**
JUST **SAVING** HER TIME. ISN'T THAT KINDER?
KINDER? NO, NO. SHERLOCK.
THAT WASN'T KIND.
......

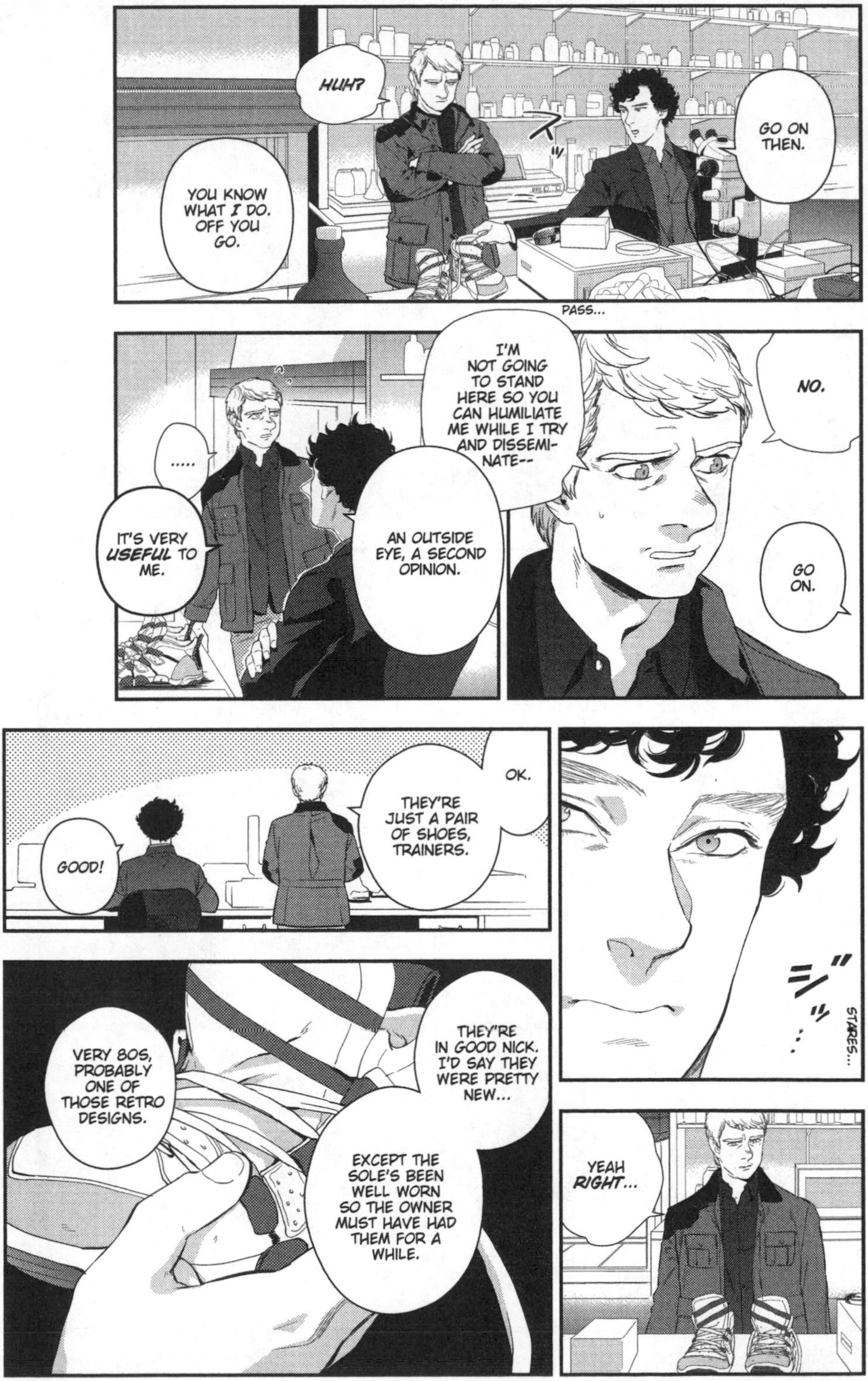
GO ON THEN.
HUH?
YOU KNOW WHAT I DO. OFF YOU GO.
PASS...
I'M NOT GOING TO STAND HERE SO YOU CAN HUMILIATE ME WHILE I TRY AND DISSEMI-NATE--
NO.
GO ON.
AN OUTSIDE EYE, A SECOND OPINION.
......
IT'S VERY USEFUL TO ME.
STARES...
YEAH RIGHT...
OK.
THEY'RE JUST A PAIR OF SHOES, TRAINERS.
GOOD!
THEY'RE IN GOOD NICK. I'D SAY THEY WERE PRETTY NEW...
VERY 80S, PROBABLY ONE OF THOSE RETRO DESIGNS.
EXCEPT THE SOLE'S BEEN WELL WORN SO THE OWNER MUST HAVE HAD THEM FOR A WHILE.

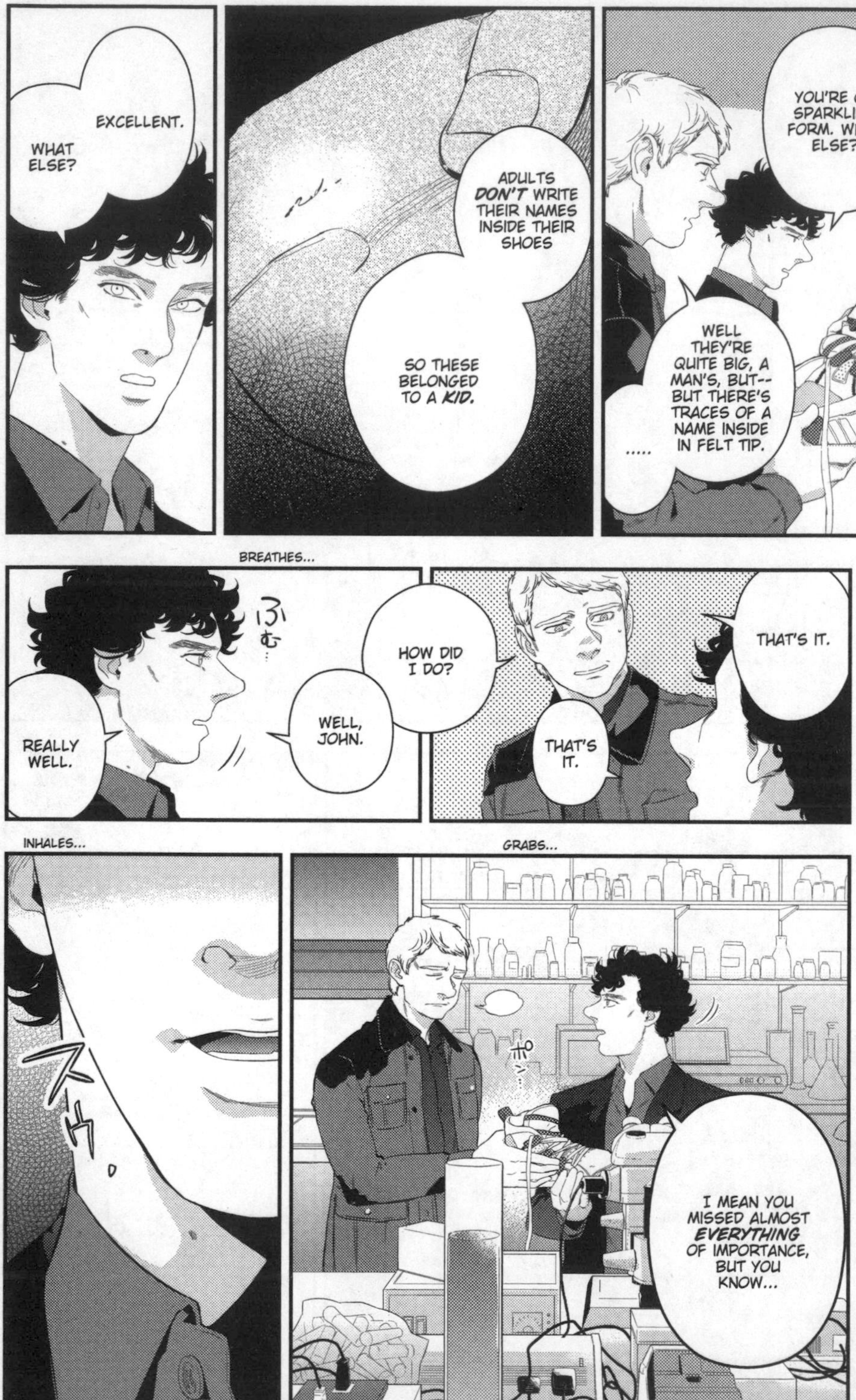
YOU'RE ON SPARKLING FORM. WHAT ELSE?
WELL THEY'RE QUITE BIG, A MAN'S, BUT-- BUT THERE'S TRACES OF A NAME INSIDE IN FELT TIP.
.....
ADULTS **DON'T** WRITE THEIR NAMES INSIDE THEIR SHOES
SO THESE BELONGED TO A **KID.**
EXCELLENT.
WHAT ELSE?
THAT'S IT.
HOW DID I DO?
THAT'S IT.
BREATHES...
ふむ…
WELL, JOHN.
REALLY WELL.
GRABS...
ポン…
I MEAN YOU MISSED ALMOST **EVERYTHING** OF IMPORTANCE, BUT YOU KNOW...
INHALES...
スゥ

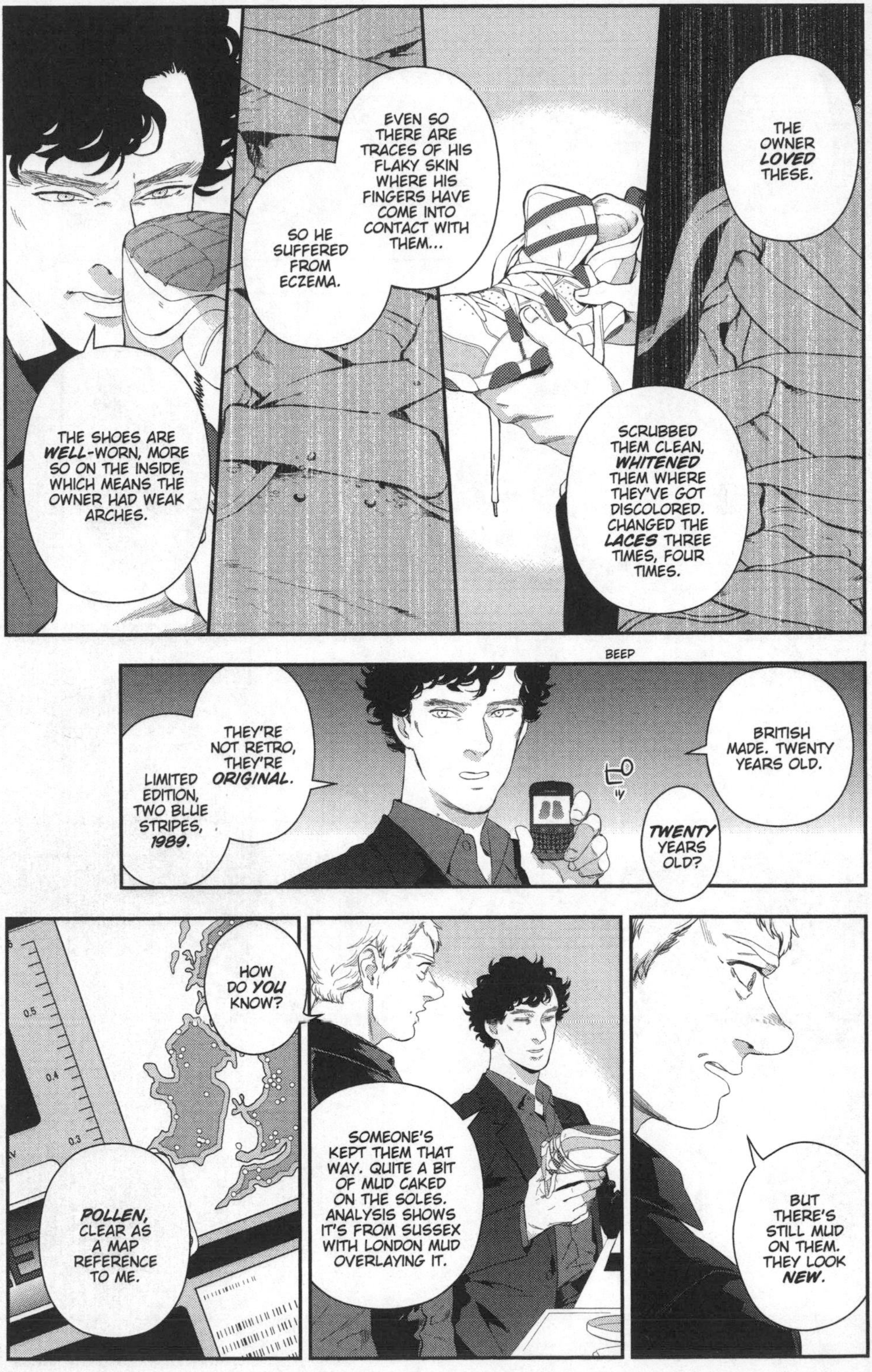
THE OWNER LOVED THESE.
SCRUBBED THEM CLEAN, WHITENED THEM WHERE THEY'VE GOT DISCOLORED. CHANGED THE LACES THREE TIMES, FOUR TIMES.
EVEN SO THERE ARE TRACES OF HIS FLAKY SKIN WHERE HIS FINGERS HAVE COME INTO CONTACT WITH THEM...
SO HE SUFFERED FROM ECZEMA.
THE SHOES ARE WELL-WORN, MORE SO ON THE INSIDE, WHICH MEANS THE OWNER HAD WEAK ARCHES.
BEEP
BRITISH MADE. TWENTY YEARS OLD.
TWENTY YEARS OLD?
THEY'RE NOT RETRO, THEY'RE ORIGINAL.
LIMITED EDITION, TWO BLUE STRIPES, 1989.
BUT THERE'S STILL MUD ON THEM. THEY LOOK NEW.
SOMEONE'S KEPT THEM THAT WAY. QUITE A BIT OF MUD CAKED ON THE SOLES. ANALYSIS SHOWS IT'S FROM SUSSEX WITH LONDON MUD OVERLAYING IT.
HOW DO YOU KNOW?
POLLEN, CLEAR AS A MAP REFERENCE TO ME.

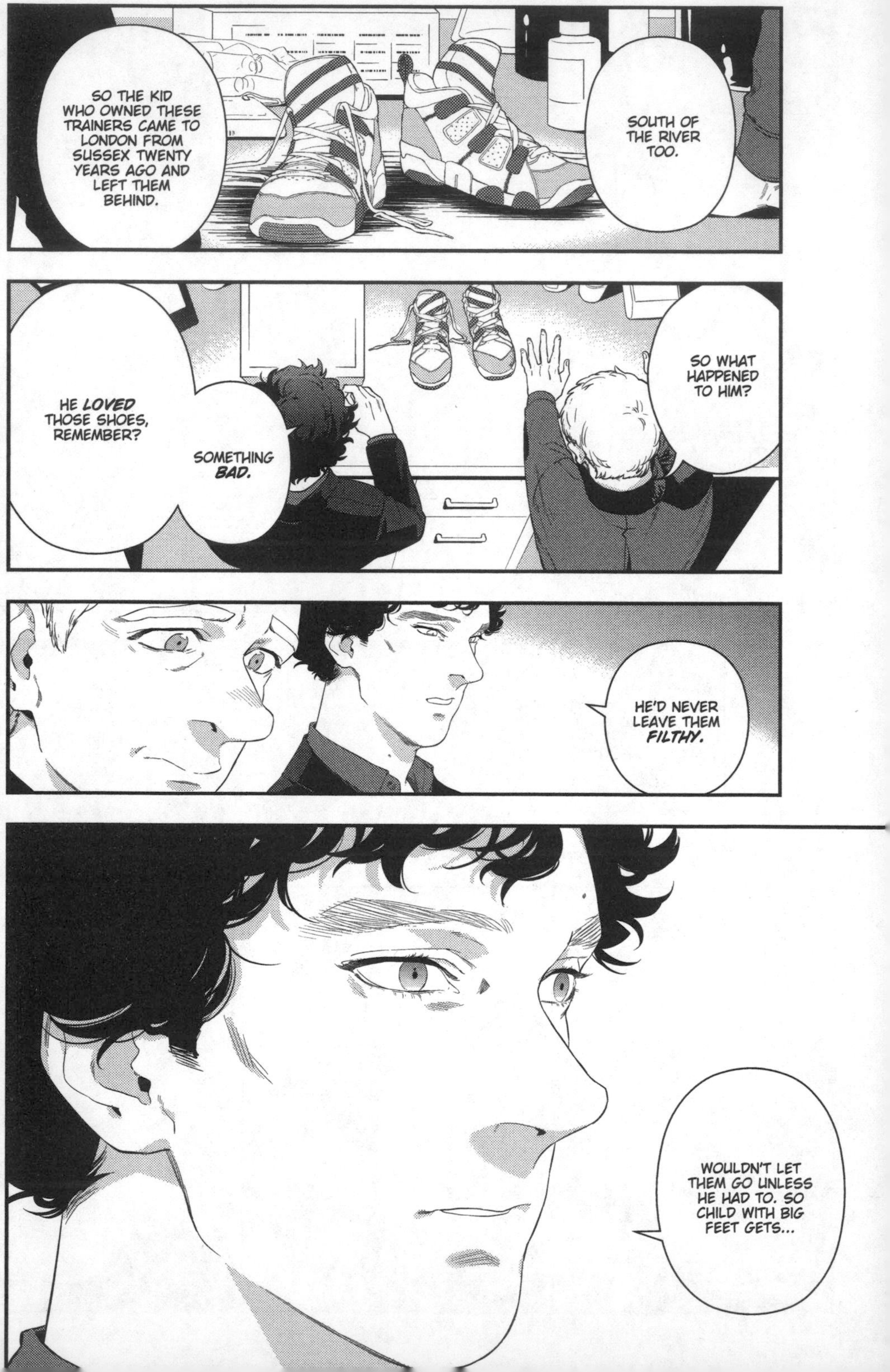
SO THE KID WHO OWNED THESE TRAINERS CAME TO LONDON FROM SUSSEX TWENTY YEARS AGO AND LEFT THEM BEHIND.
SOUTH OF THE RIVER TOO.
SO WHAT HAPPENED TO HIM?
SOMETHING *BAD.*
HE *LOVED* THOSE SHOES, REMEMBER?
HE'D NEVER LEAVE THEM *FILTHY.*
WOULDN'T LET THEM GO UNLESS HE HAD TO. SO CHILD WITH BIG FEET GETS...

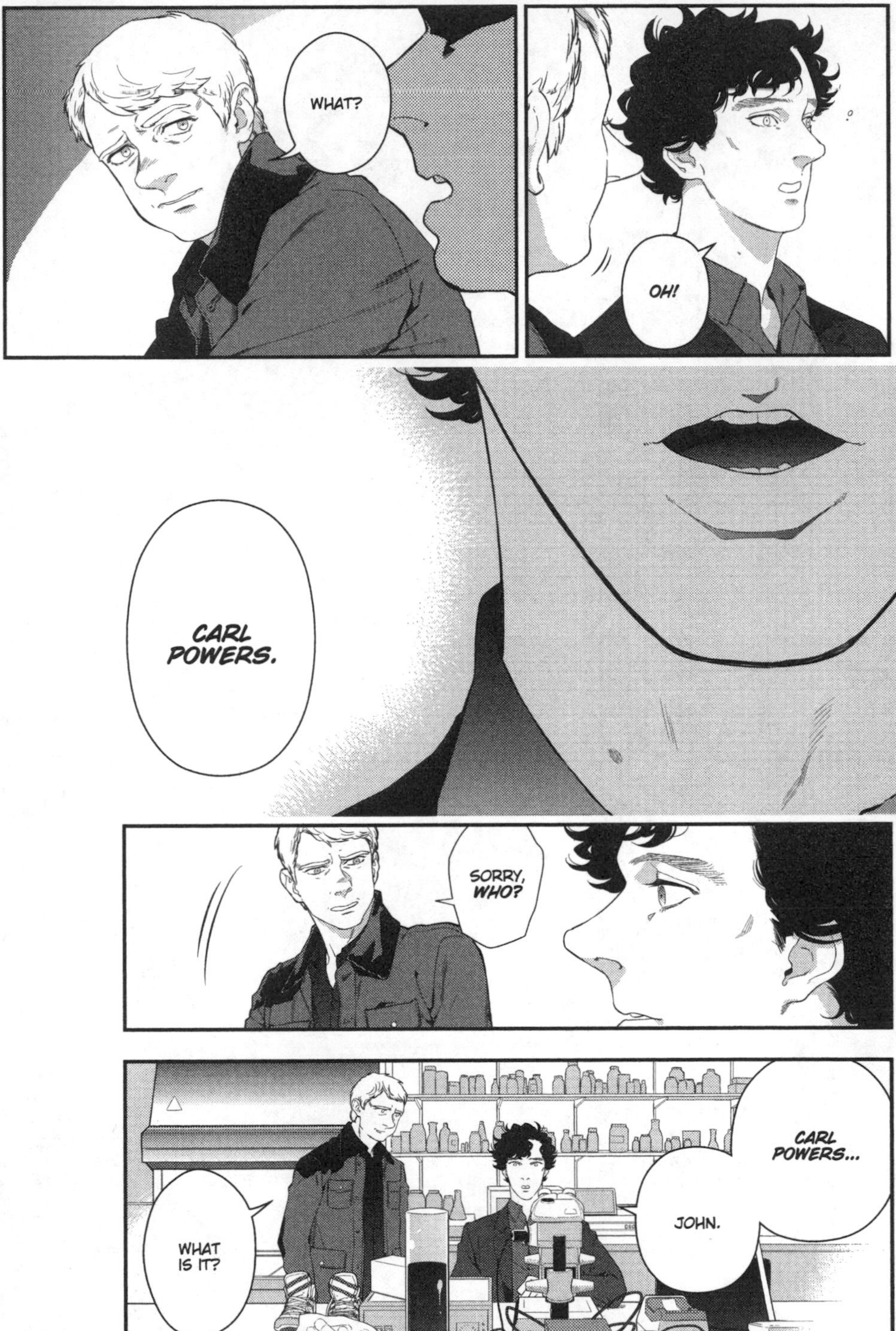
OH!
WHAT?
CARL POWERS.
SORRY, WHO?
CARL POWERS...
JOHN.
WHAT IS IT?

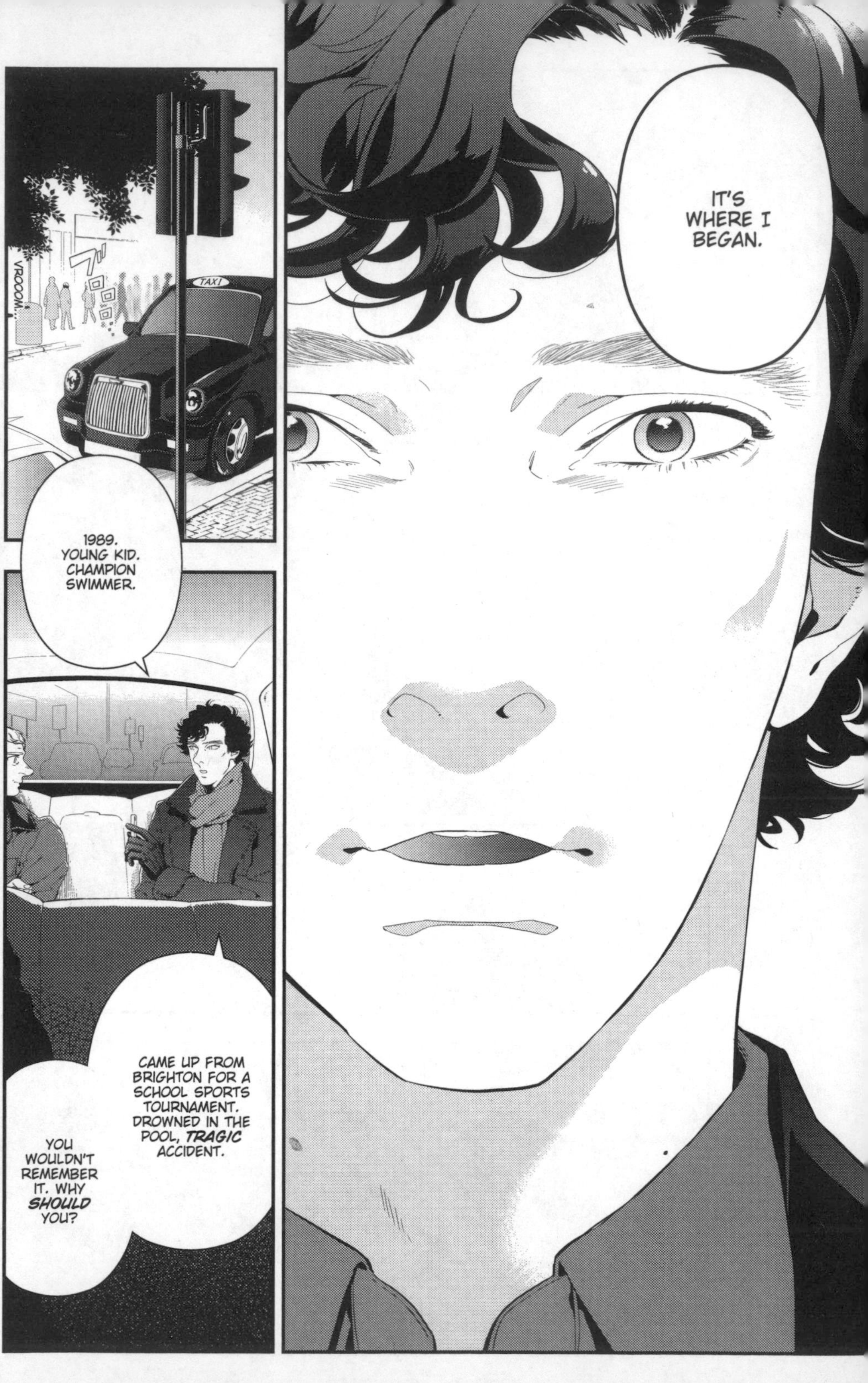
IT'S WHERE I BEGAN.
VROOOM...
1989. YOUNG KID. CHAMPION SWIMMER.
CAME UP FROM BRIGHTON FOR A SCHOOL SPORTS TOURNAMENT. DROWNED IN THE POOL, ***TRAGIC*** ACCIDENT.
YOU WOULDN'T REMEMBER IT. WHY ***SHOULD*** YOU?

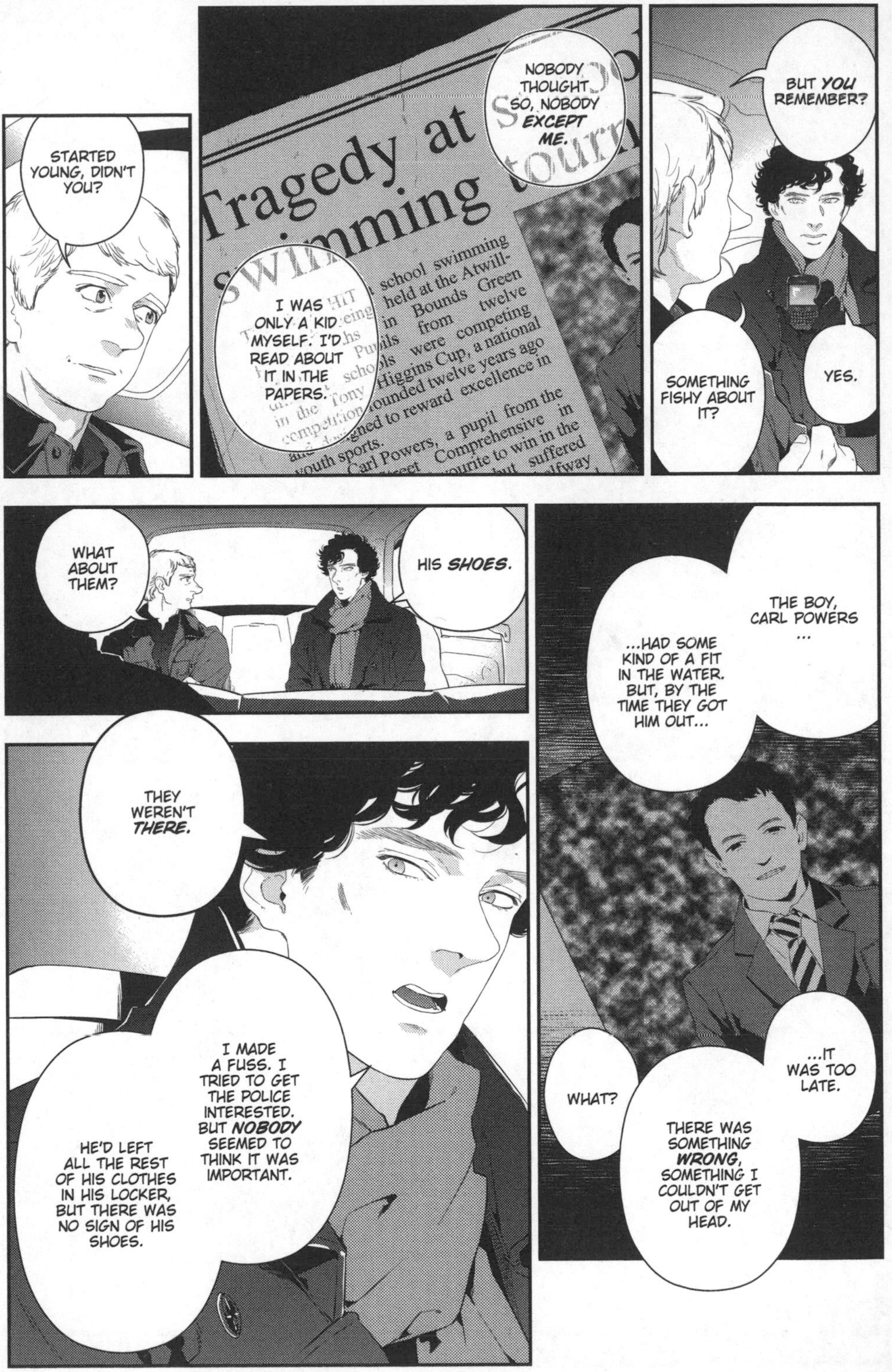
BUT *YOU* REMEMBER?
YES.
SOMETHING FISHY ABOUT IT?
NOBODY THOUGHT SO, NOBODY *EXCEPT ME.*
Tragedy at
I WAS ONLY A KID MYSELF. I'D READ ABOUT IT IN THE PAPERS.
STARTED YOUNG, DIDN'T YOU?
THE BOY, CARL POWERS ...
...HAD SOME KIND OF A FIT IN THE WATER. BUT, BY THE TIME THEY GOT HIM OUT...
...IT WAS TOO LATE.
WHAT?
THERE WAS SOMETHING *WRONG*, SOMETHING I COULDN'T GET OUT OF MY HEAD.
HIS *SHOES*.
WHAT ABOUT THEM?
THEY WEREN'T *THERE.*
I MADE A FUSS. I TRIED TO GET THE POLICE INTERESTED. BUT *NOBODY* SEEMED TO THINK IT WAS IMPORTANT.
HE'D LEFT ALL THE REST OF HIS CLOTHES IN HIS LOCKER, BUT THERE WAS NO SIGN OF HIS SHOES.

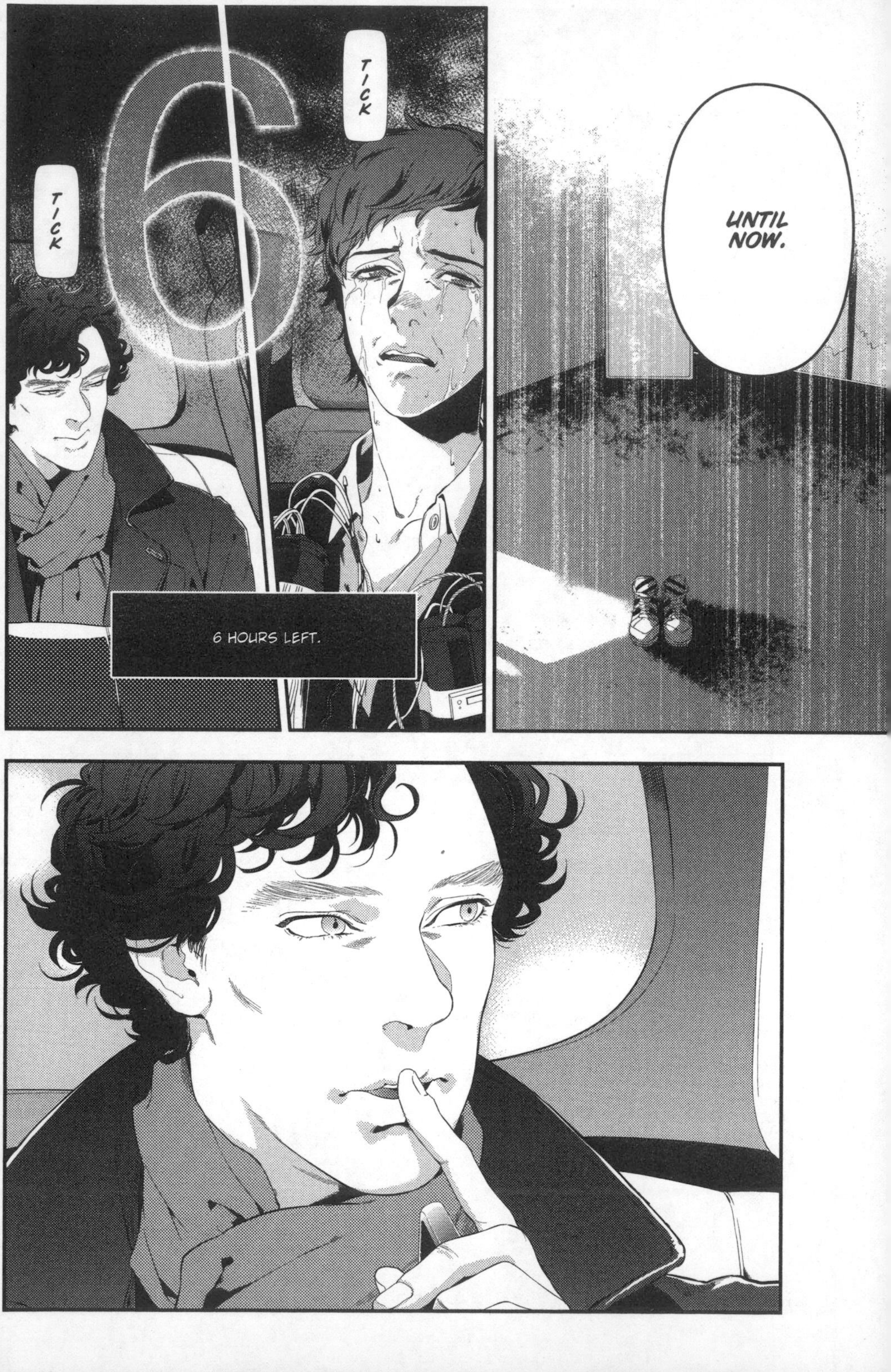
UNTIL NOW.
TICK
TICK
6 HOURS LEFT.

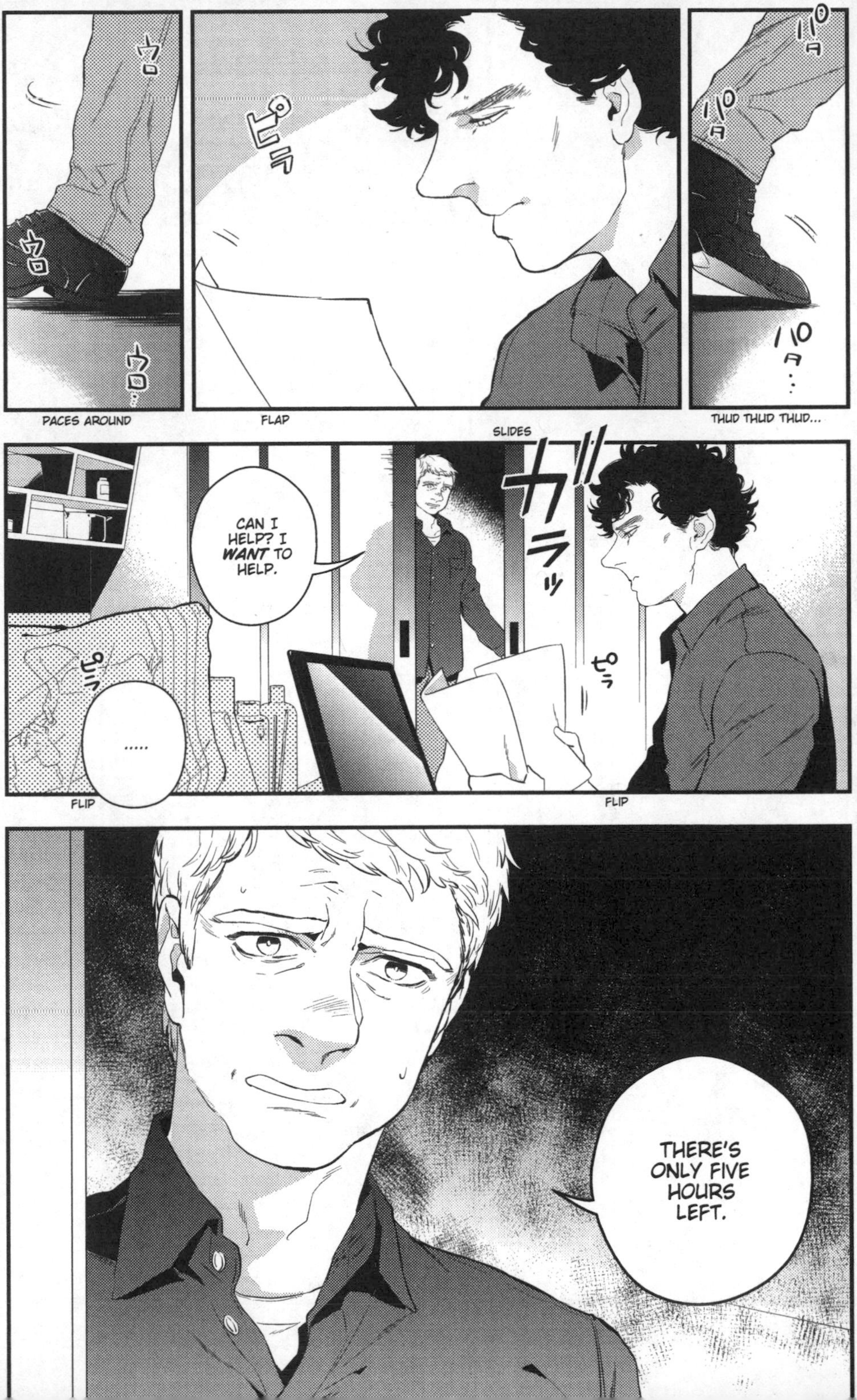
パタ パタ パタ…
THUD THUD THUD...
ピラ
FLAP
ウロ ウロ ウロ…
PACES AROUND
ガラッ
SLIDES
CAN I HELP? I *WANT* TO HELP.
ピラ
FLIP
......
ピラ
FLIP
THERE'S ONLY FIVE HOURS LEFT.

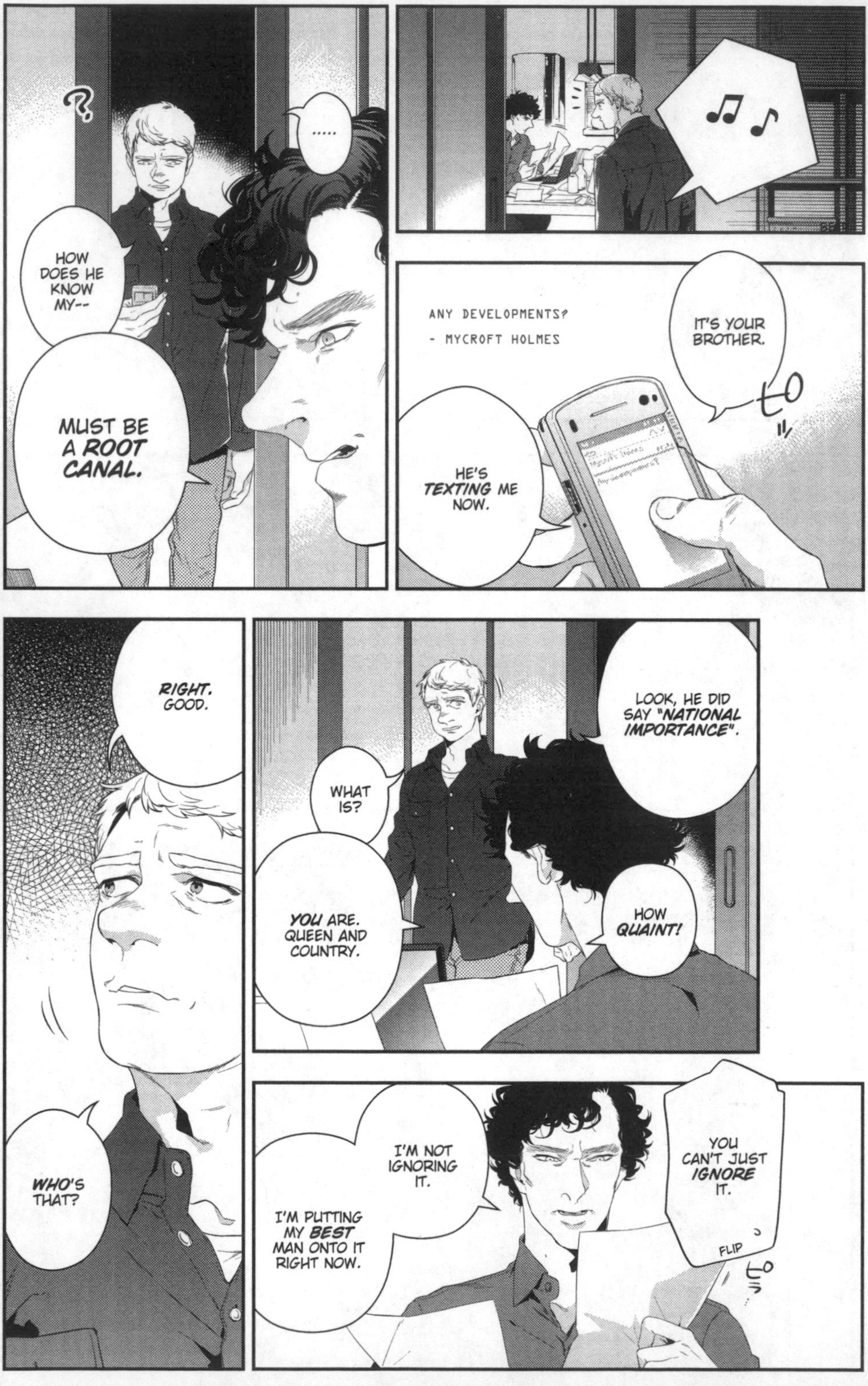
?
......
HOW DOES HE KNOW MY--
MUST BE A ROOT CANAL.
♫ ♪
ANY DEVELOPMENTS?
- MYCROFT HOLMES
IT'S YOUR BROTHER.
HE'S TEXTING ME NOW.
RIGHT. GOOD.
WHO'S THAT?
LOOK, HE DID SAY "NATIONAL IMPORTANCE".
WHAT IS?
YOU ARE. QUEEN AND COUNTRY.
HOW QUAINT!
YOU CAN'T JUST IGNORE IT.
I'M NOT IGNORING IT.
I'M PUTTING MY BEST MAN ONTO IT RIGHT NOW.
FLIP

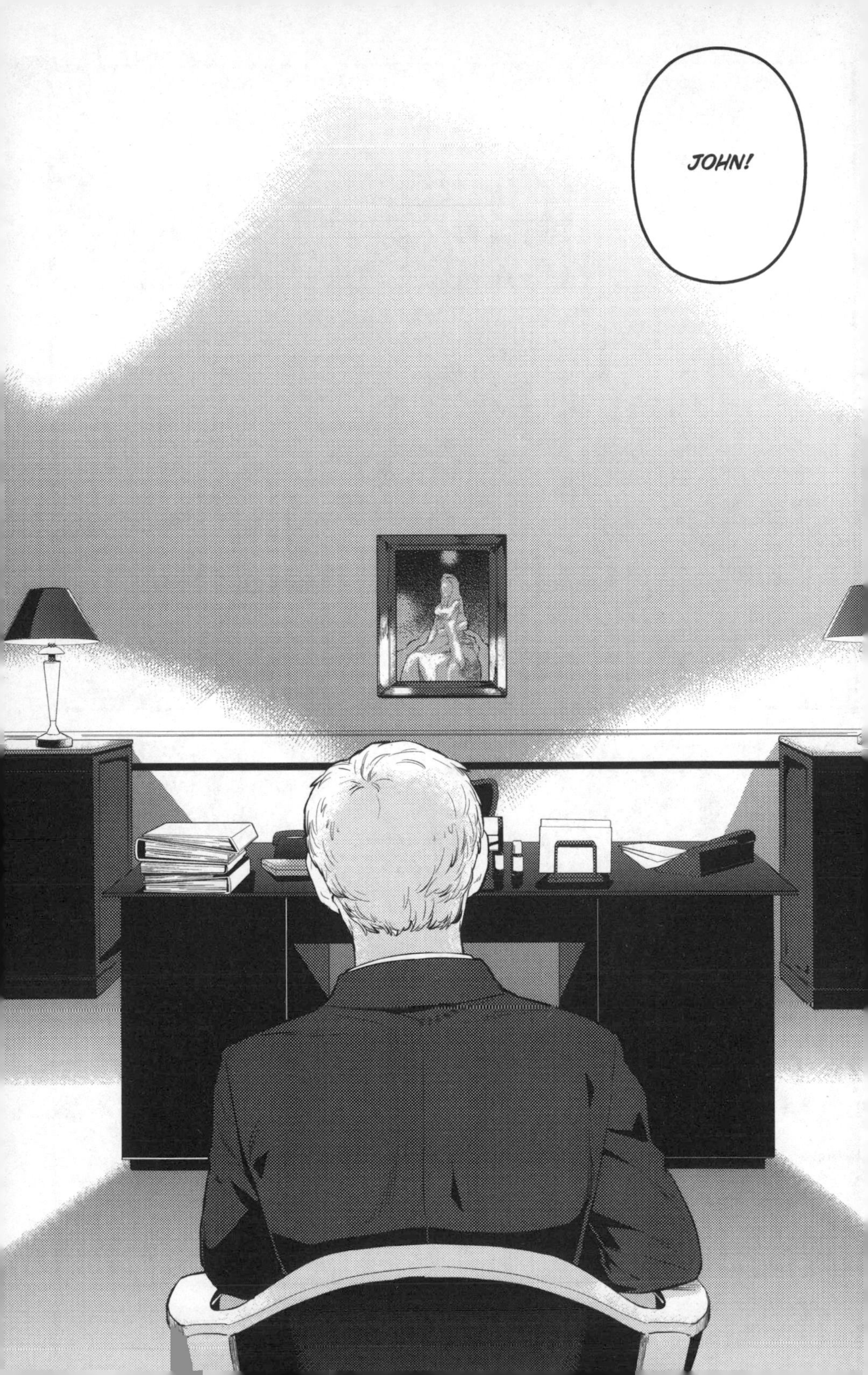
JOHN!

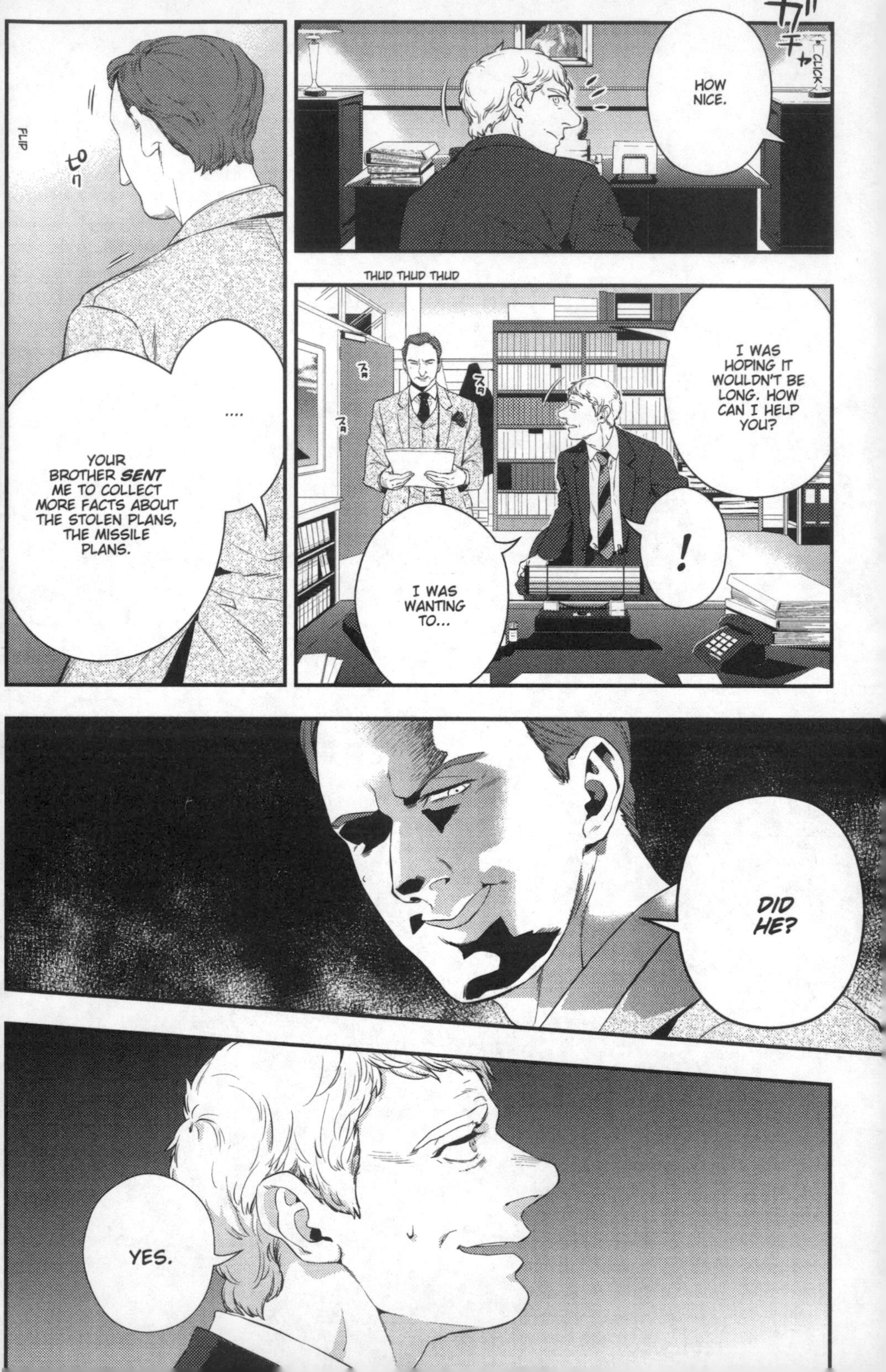
ガチャ
CLICK
HOW NICE.
THUD THUD THUD
I WAS HOPING IT WOULDN'T BE LONG. HOW CAN I HELP YOU?
!
I WAS WANTING TO...
FLIP
....
YOUR BROTHER **SENT** ME TO COLLECT MORE FACTS ABOUT THE STOLEN PLANS, THE MISSILE PLANS.
DID HE?
YES.

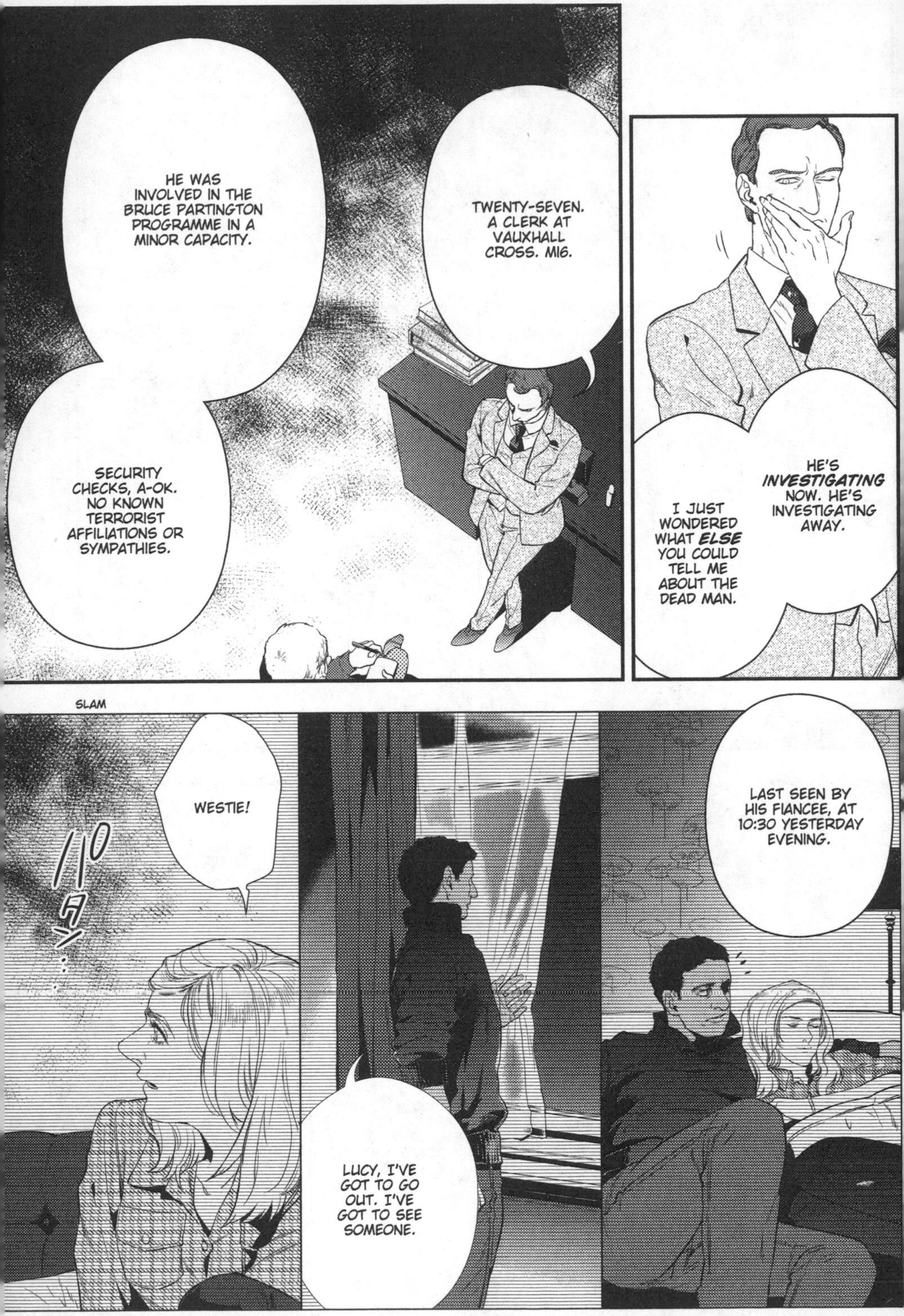
HE'S INVESTIGATING NOW. HE'S INVESTIGATING AWAY.
I JUST WONDERED WHAT ELSE YOU COULD TELL ME ABOUT THE DEAD MAN.
TWENTY-SEVEN. A CLERK AT VAUXHALL CROSS. MI6.
HE WAS INVOLVED IN THE BRUCE PARTINGTON PROGRAMME IN A MINOR CAPACITY.
SECURITY CHECKS, A-OK. NO KNOWN TERRORIST AFFILIATIONS OR SYMPATHIES.
LAST SEEN BY HIS FIANCEE, AT 10:30 YESTERDAY EVENING.
LUCY, I'VE GOT TO GO OUT. I'VE GOT TO SEE SOMEONE.
SLAM
パタン…
WESTIE!

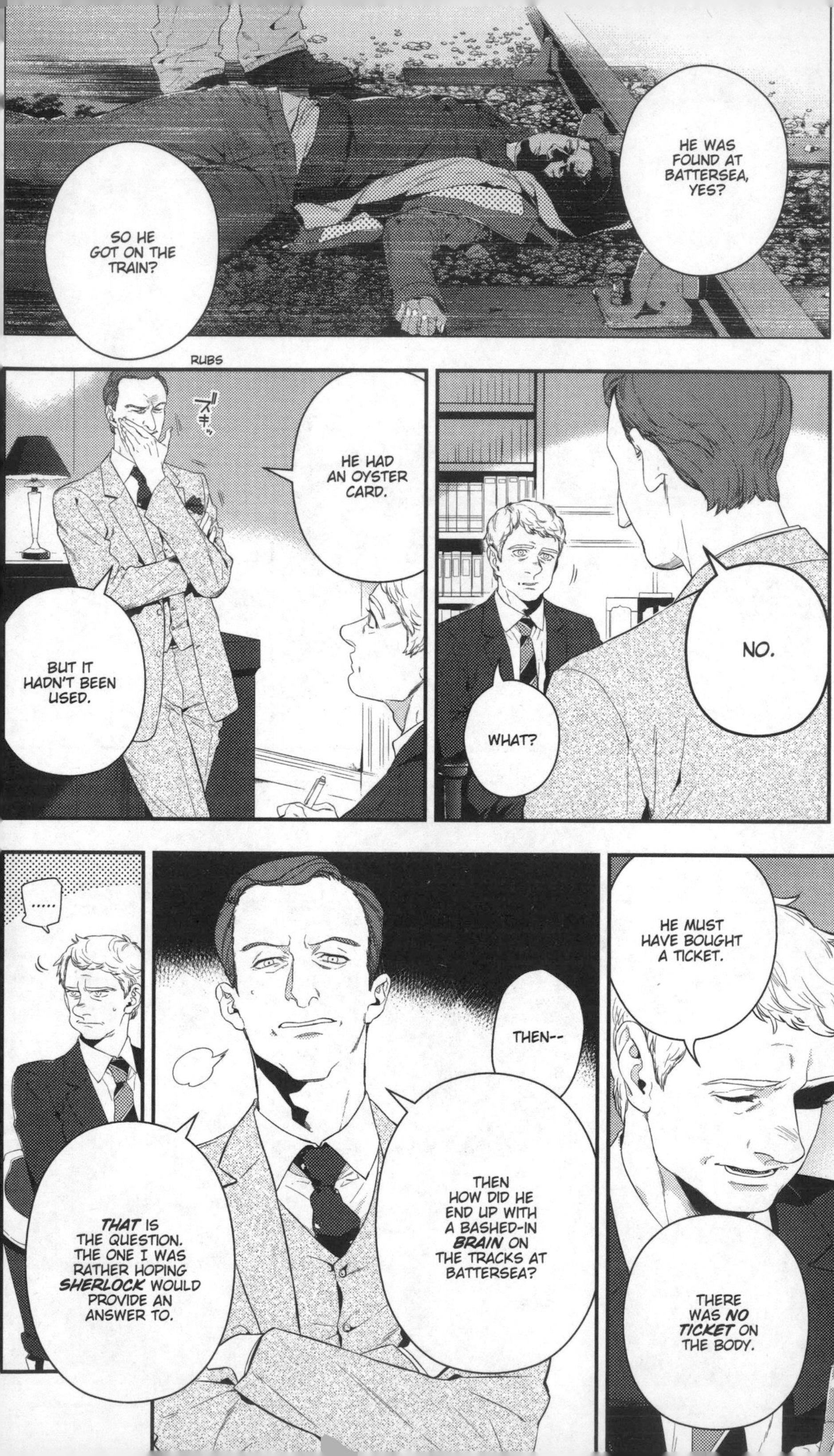
HE WAS FOUND AT BATTERSEA, YES?
SO HE GOT ON THE TRAIN?
RUBS
NO.
WHAT?
ズキッ
HE HAD AN OYSTER CARD.
BUT IT HADN'T BEEN USED.
HE MUST HAVE BOUGHT A TICKET.
THERE WAS *NO TICKET* ON THE BODY.
THEN--
THEN HOW DID HE END UP WITH A BASHED-IN *BRAIN* ON THE TRACKS AT BATTERSEA?
THAT IS THE QUESTION. THE ONE I WAS RATHER HOPING *SHERLOCK* WOULD PROVIDE AN ANSWER TO.
......

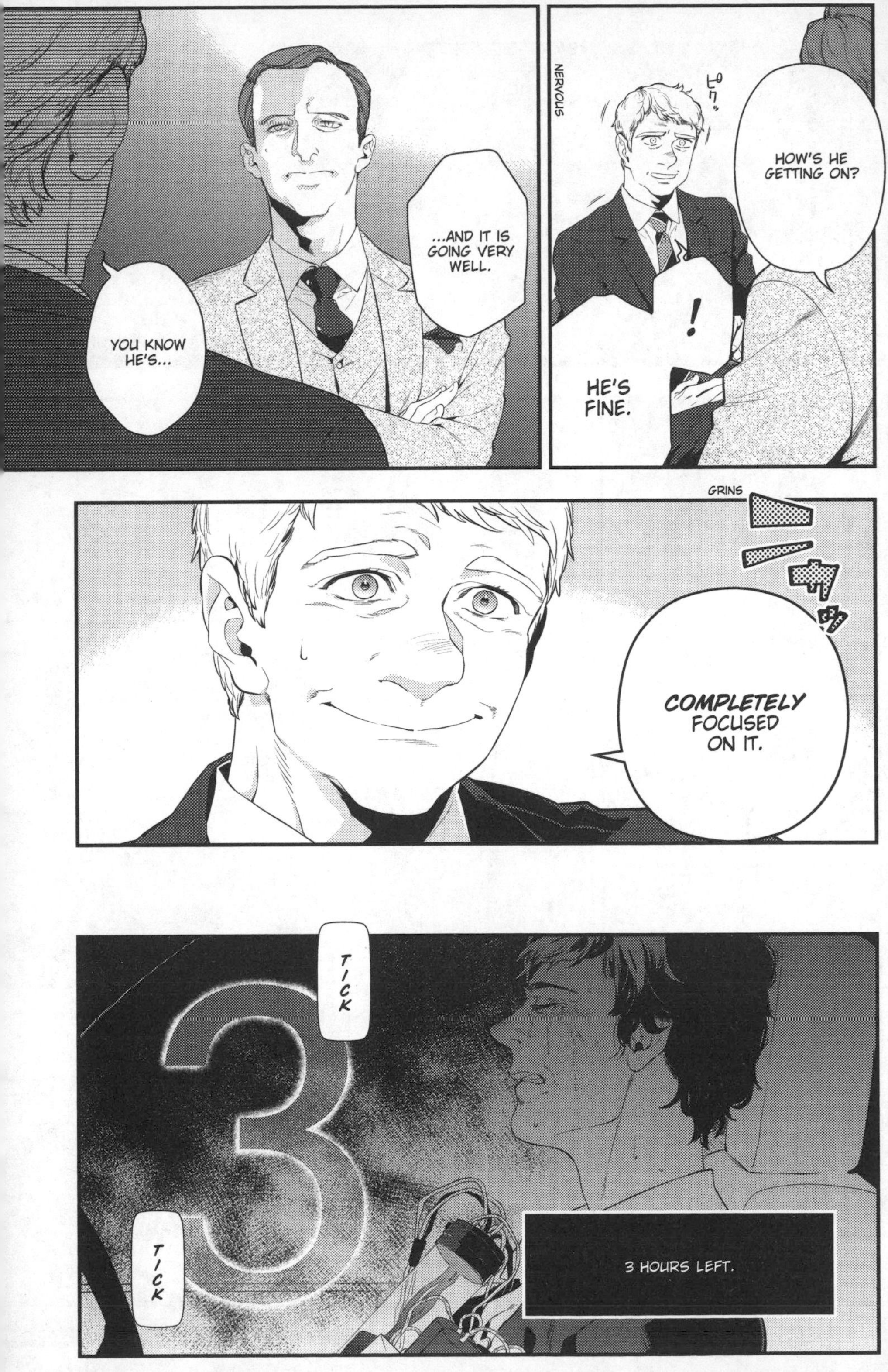
NERVOUS
ピクッ
HOW'S HE GETTING ON?
!
HE'S FINE.
...AND IT IS GOING VERY WELL.
YOU KNOW HE'S...
GRINS
COMPLETELY FOCUSED ON IT.
TICK
3
TICK
3 HOURS LEFT.

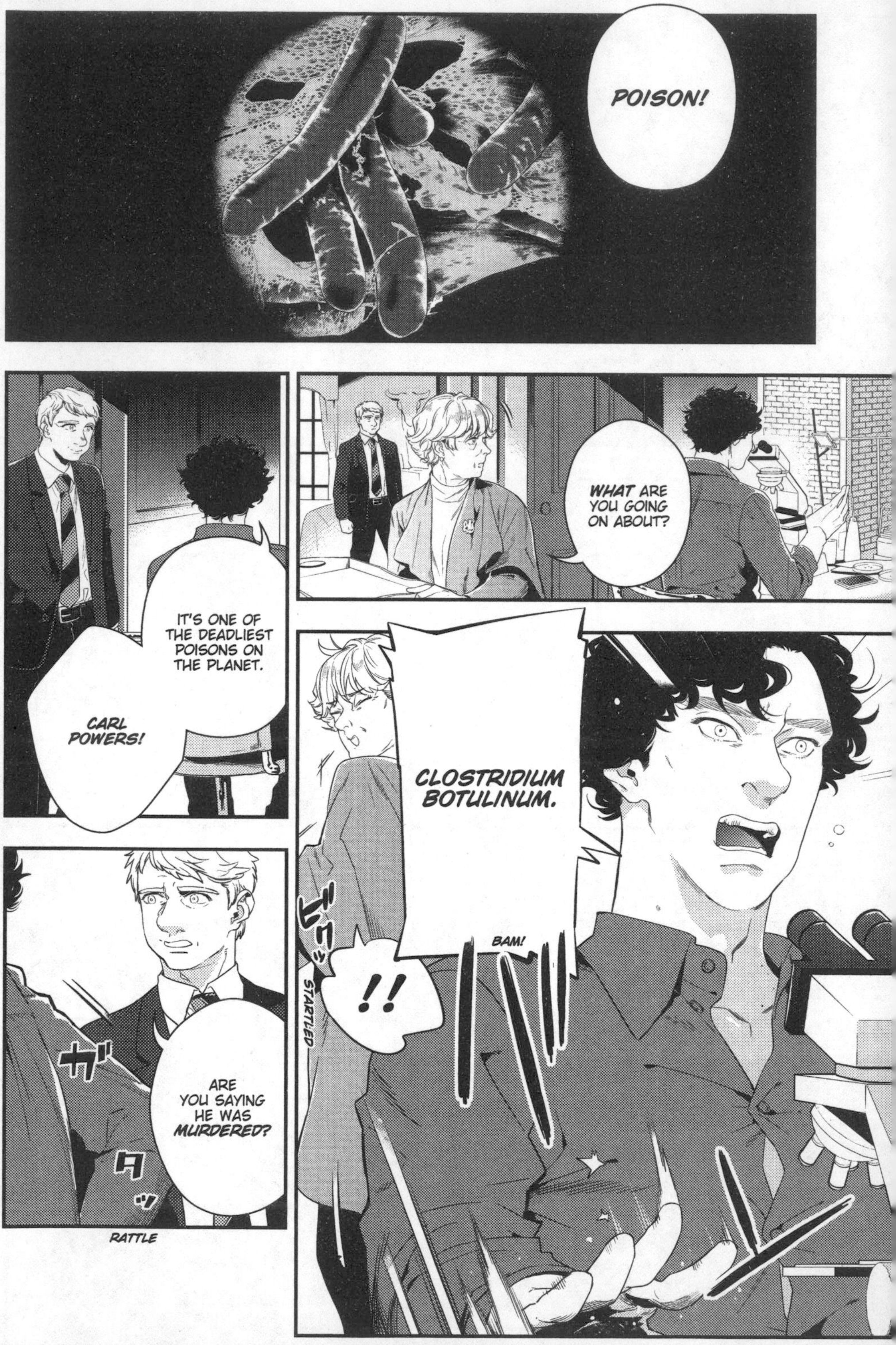
POISON!
WHAT ARE YOU GOING ON ABOUT?
CLOSTRIDIUM BOTULINUM.
BAM!
!!
STARTLED
IT'S ONE OF THE DEADLIEST POISONS ON THE PLANET.
CARL POWERS!
ARE YOU SAYING HE WAS MURDERED?
RATTLE

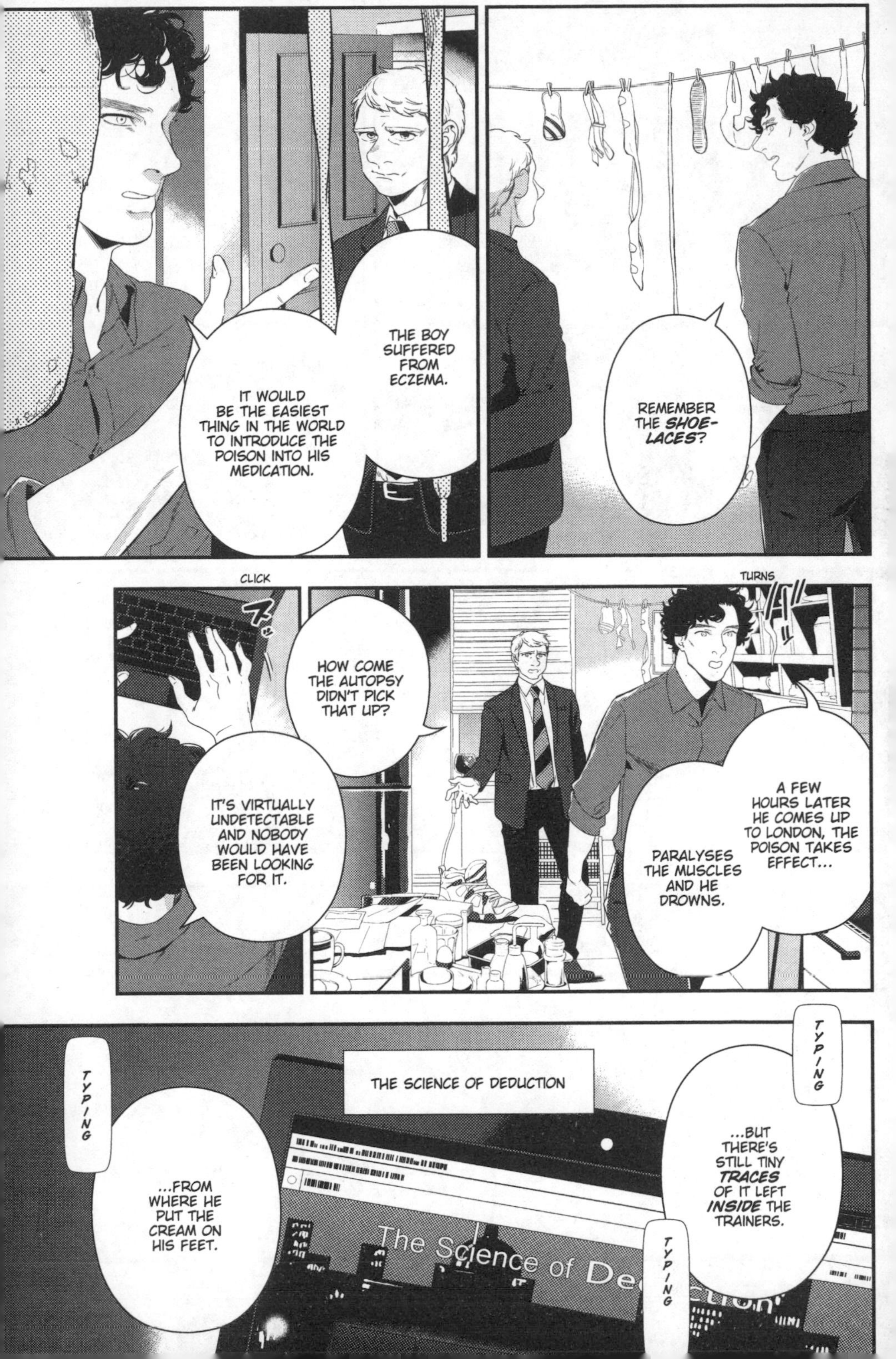
REMEMBER THE *SHOE-LACES*?
THE BOY SUFFERED FROM ECZEMA.
IT WOULD BE THE EASIEST THING IN THE WORLD TO INTRODUCE THE POISON INTO HIS MEDICATION.
TURNS
A FEW HOURS LATER HE COMES UP TO LONDON, THE POISON TAKES EFFECT...
PARALYSES THE MUSCLES AND HE DROWNS.
HOW COME THE AUTOPSY DIDN'T PICK THAT UP?
CLICK
IT'S VIRTUALLY UNDETECTABLE AND NOBODY WOULD HAVE BEEN LOOKING FOR IT.
TYPING
...BUT THERE'S STILL TINY *TRACES* OF IT LEFT *INSIDE* THE TRAINERS.
TYPING
THE SCIENCE OF DEDUCTION
TYPING
...FROM WHERE HE PUT THE CREAM ON HIS FEET.

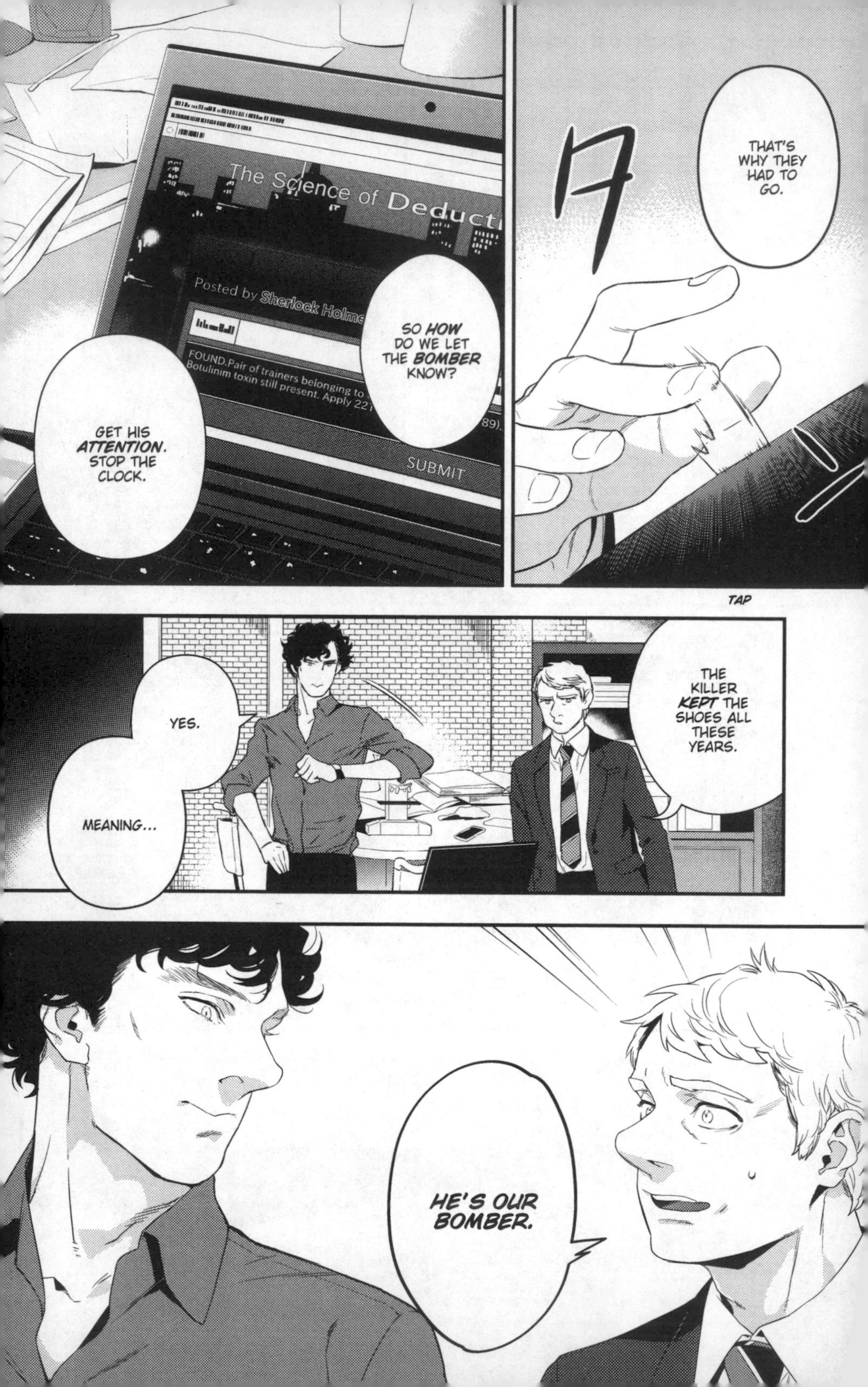
THAT'S WHY THEY HAD TO GO.
The Science of Deducti
Posted by Sherlock Holme
FOUND.Pair of trainers belonging to
Botulinim toxin still present. Apply 221
SUBMIT
SO *HOW* DO WE LET THE *BOMBER* KNOW?
GET HIS *ATTENTION*. STOP THE CLOCK.
TAP
THE KILLER *KEPT* THE SHOES ALL THESE YEARS.
YES.
MEANING...
HE'S OUR BOMBER.

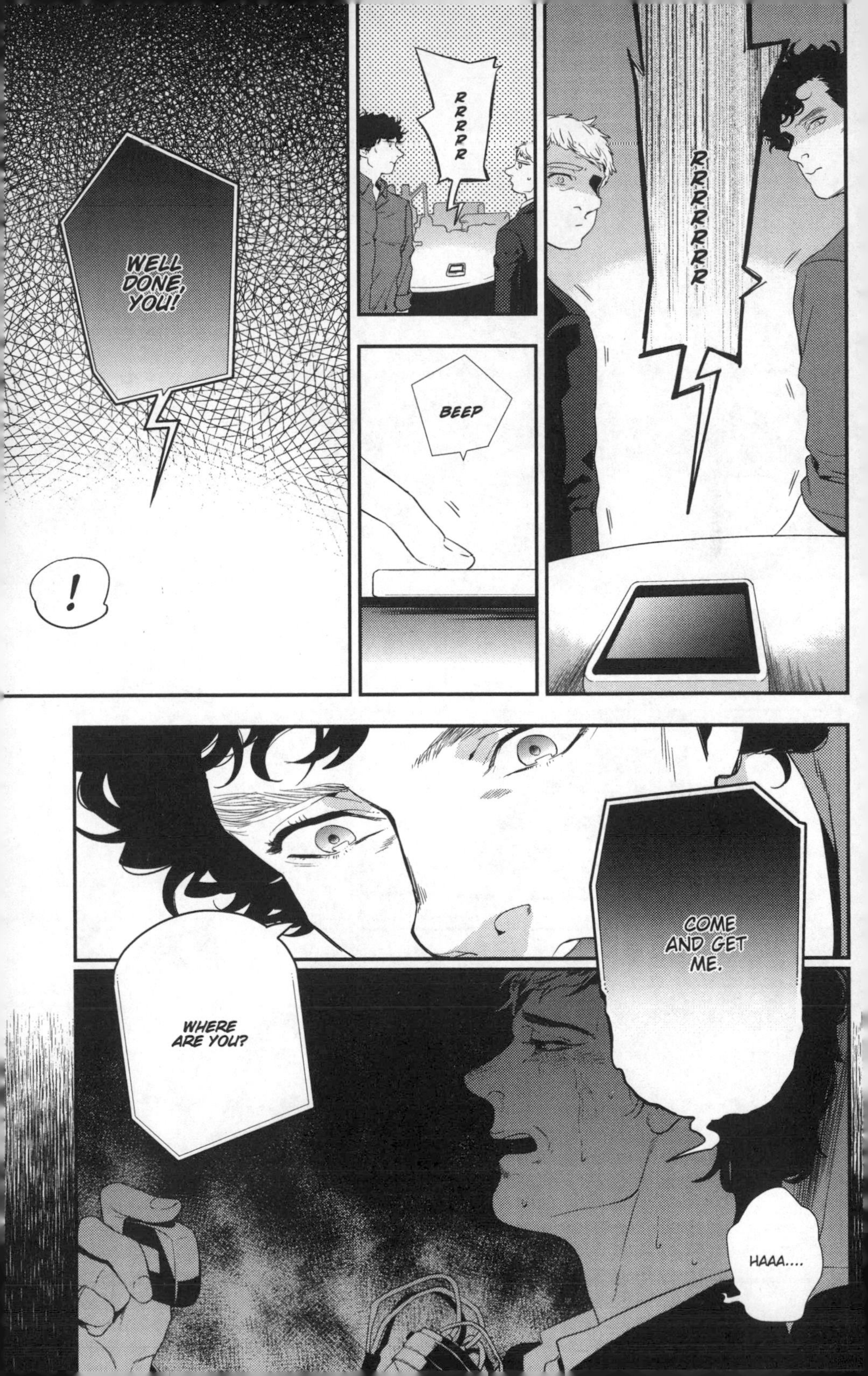
RRRRRRRR
RRRRR
BEEP
WELL DONE, YOU!
!
COME AND GET ME.
WHERE ARE YOU?
HAAA....

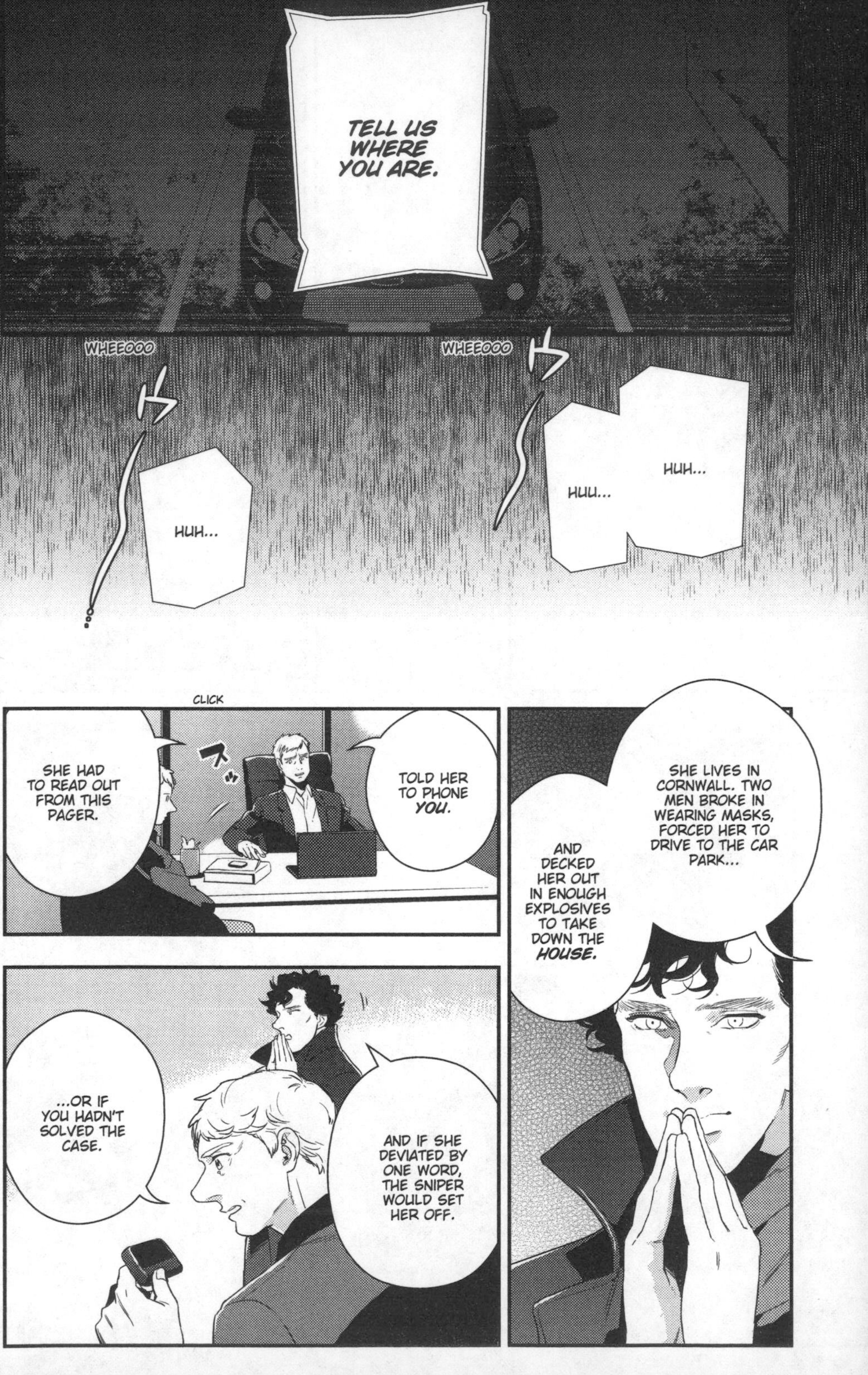
TELL US WHERE YOU ARE.
WHEEOOO
HUH...
HUU...
WHEEOOO
HUH...
SHE LIVES IN CORNWALL. TWO MEN BROKE IN WEARING MASKS, FORCED HER TO DRIVE TO THE CAR PARK...
AND DECKED HER OUT IN ENOUGH EXPLOSIVES TO TAKE DOWN THE *HOUSE.*
CLICK
TOLD HER TO PHONE *YOU.*
SHE HAD TO READ OUT FROM THIS PAGER.
AND IF SHE DEVIATED BY ONE WORD, THE SNIPER WOULD SET HER OFF.
...OR IF YOU HADN'T SOLVED THE CASE.

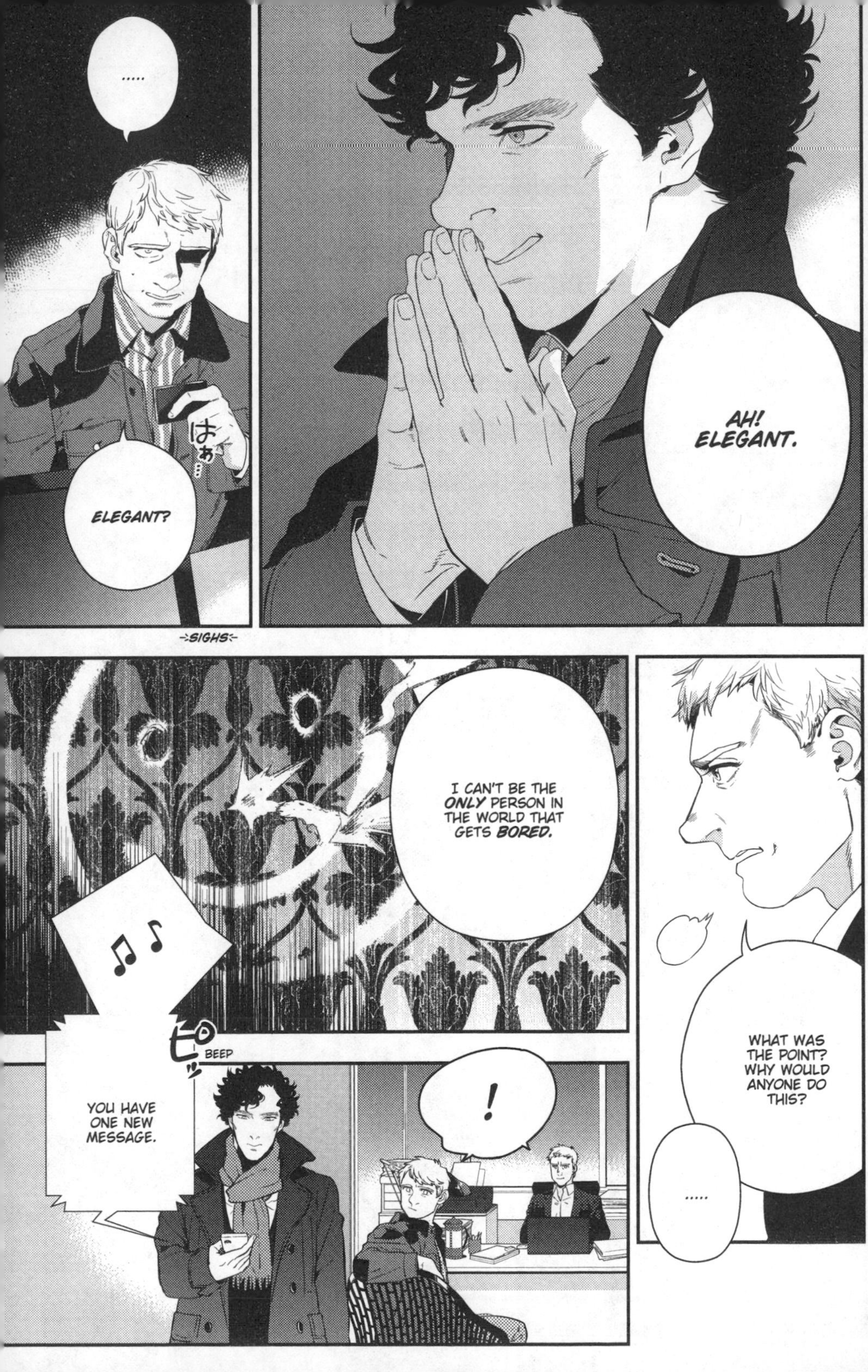
AH! ELEGANT.
.....
はぁ…
ELEGANT?
SIGHS
WHAT WAS THE POINT? WHY WOULD ANYONE DO THIS?
.....
I CAN'T BE THE ONLY PERSON IN THE WORLD THAT GETS BORED.
♫ ♪
ピ
BEEP
YOU HAVE ONE NEW MESSAGE.
!

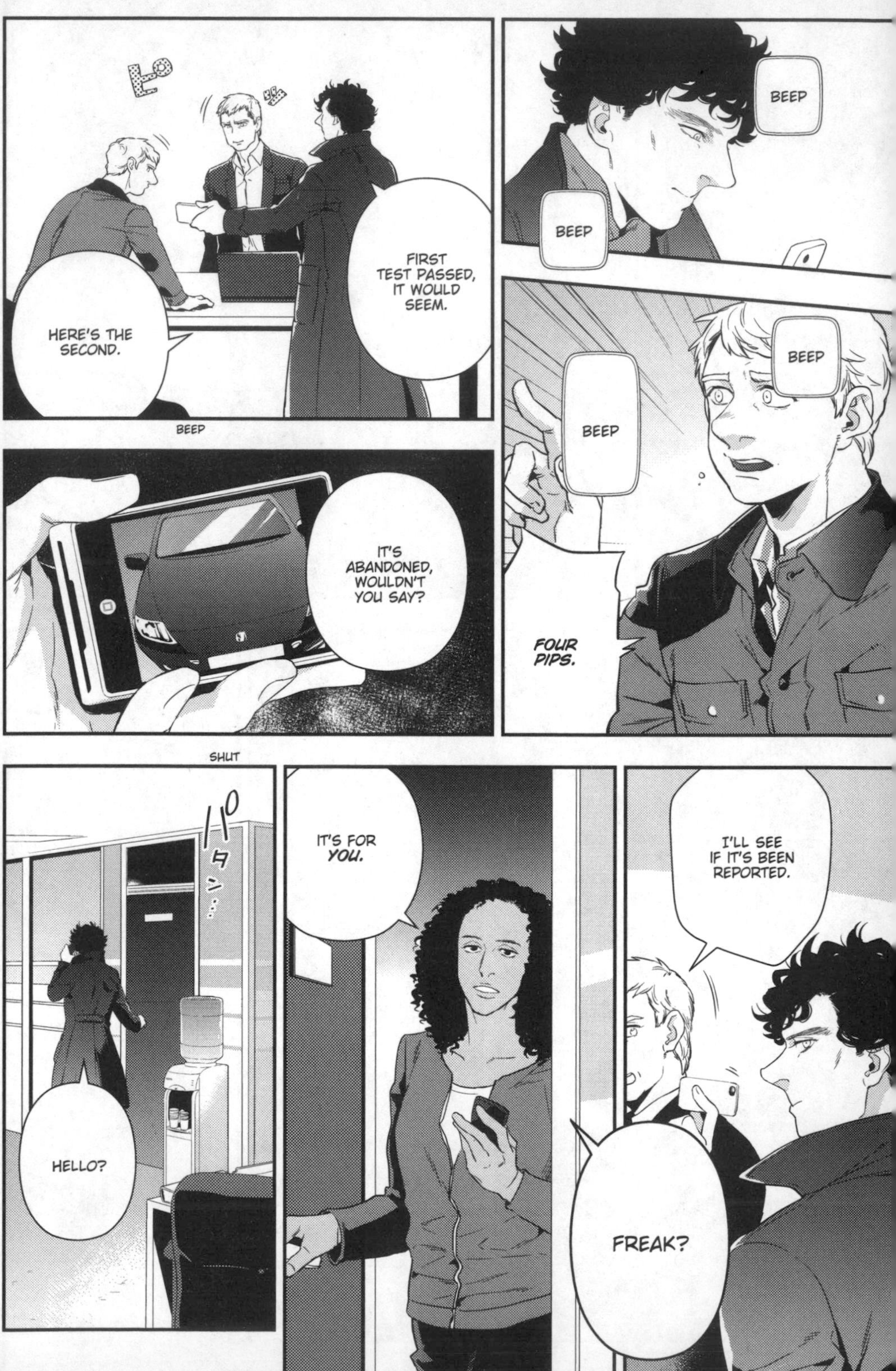
BEEP
BEEP
FIRST TEST PASSED, IT WOULD SEEM.
HERE'S THE SECOND.
BEEP
BEEP
BEEP
FOUR PIPS.
IT'S ABANDONED, WOULDN'T YOU SAY?
I'LL SEE IF IT'S BEEN REPORTED.
FREAK?
IT'S FOR *YOU.*
SHUT
HELLO?

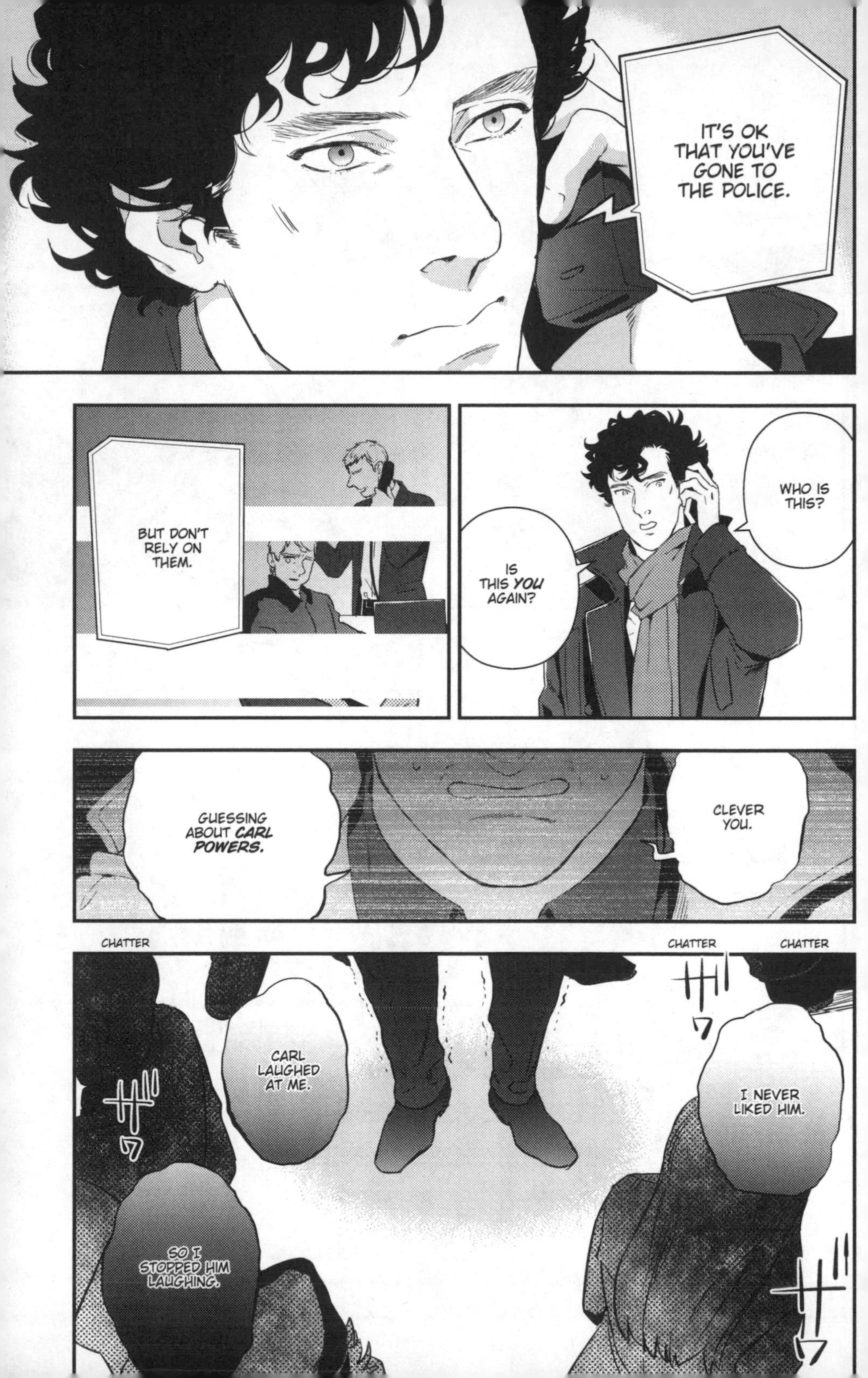
IT'S OK THAT YOU'VE GONE TO THE POLICE.
WHO IS THIS?
IS THIS *YOU* AGAIN?
BUT DON'T RELY ON THEM.
CLEVER YOU.
GUESSING ABOUT ***CARL POWERS.***
CHATTER
CHATTER
CHATTER
I NEVER LIKED HIM.
CARL LAUGHED AT ME.
SO I STOPPED HIM LAUGHING.

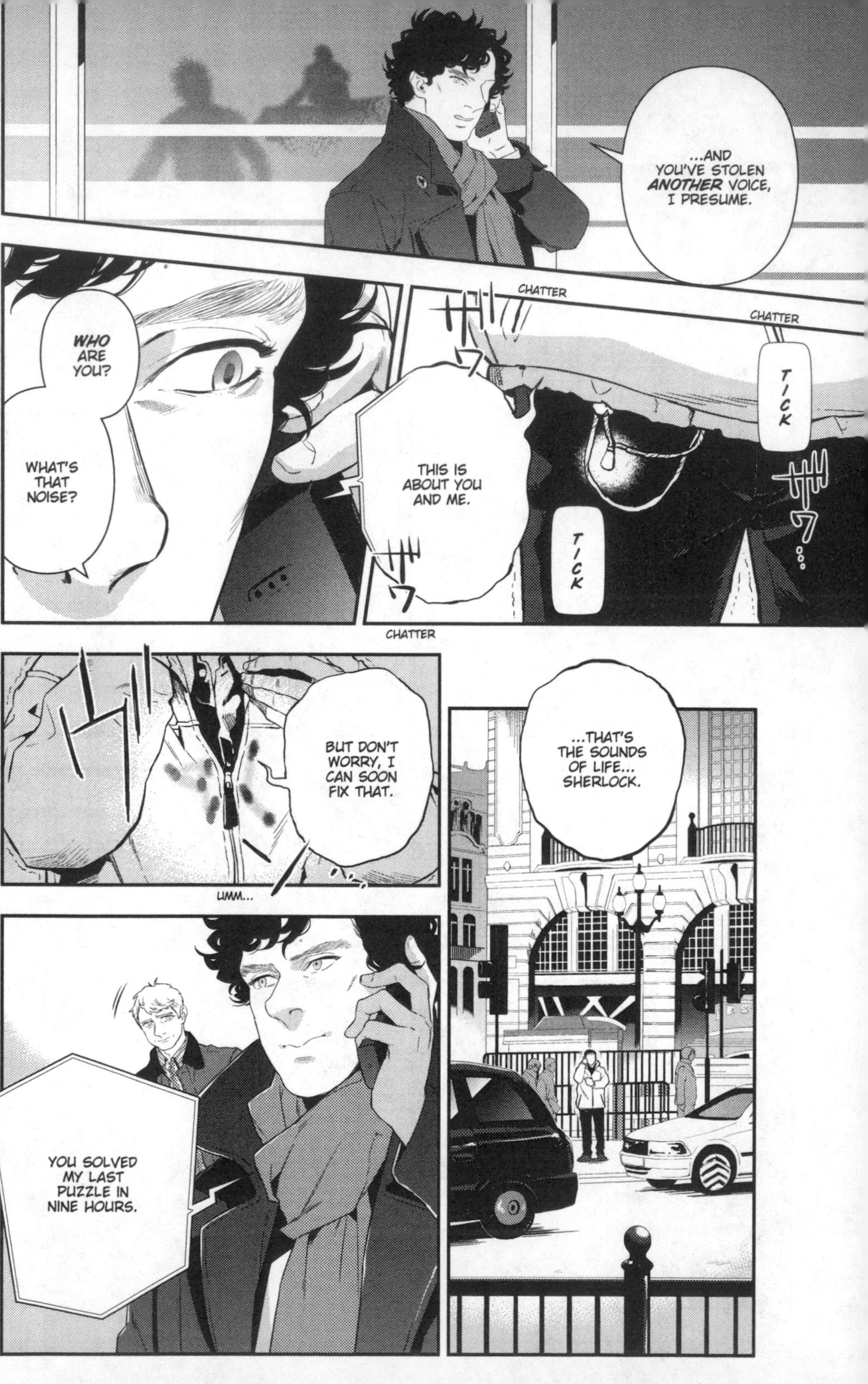
...AND YOU'VE STOLEN **ANOTHER** VOICE, I PRESUME.
CHATTER
CHATTER
TICK
THIS IS ABOUT YOU AND ME.
TICK
WHO ARE YOU?
WHAT'S THAT NOISE?
CHATTER
...THAT'S THE SOUNDS OF LIFE... SHERLOCK.
BUT DON'T WORRY, I CAN SOON FIX THAT.
UMM...
YOU SOLVED MY LAST PUZZLE IN NINE HOURS.

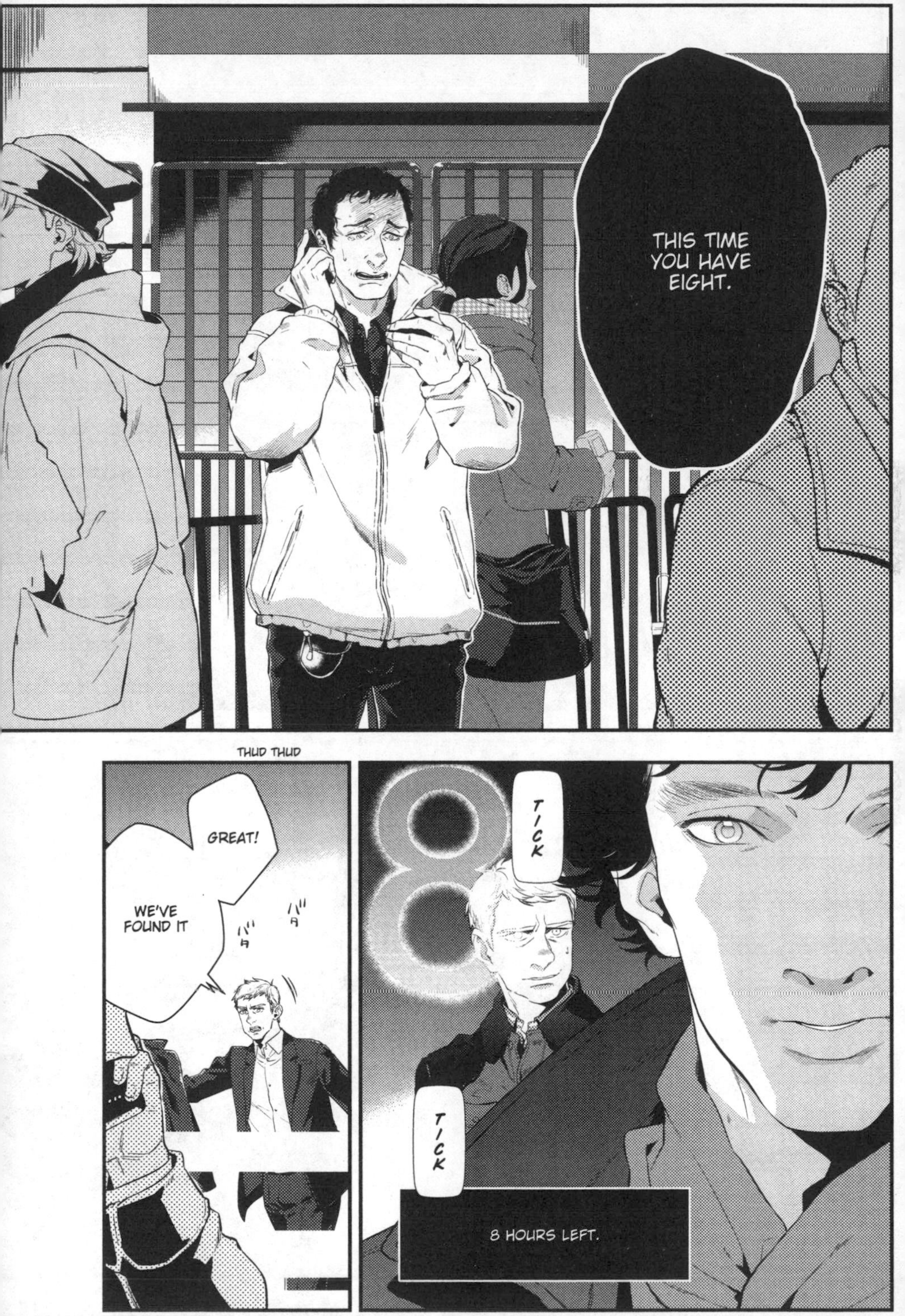
THIS TIME YOU HAVE EIGHT.
8
TICK
TICK
8 HOURS LEFT.
THUD THUD
GREAT!
WE'VE FOUND IT
バタ
バタ

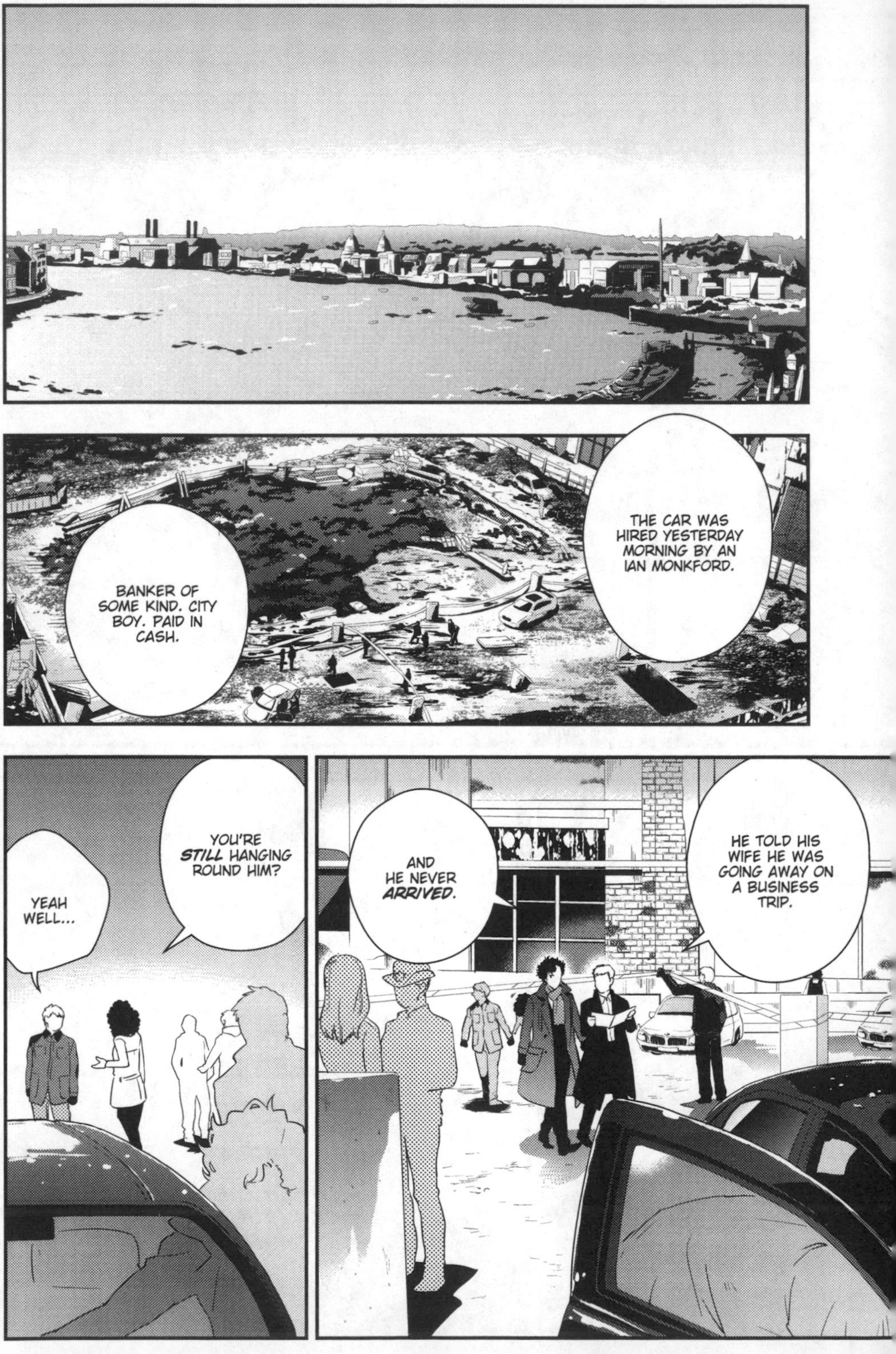
THE CAR WAS HIRED YESTERDAY MORNING BY AN IAN MONKFORD.
BANKER OF SOME KIND. CITY BOY. PAID IN CASH.
HE TOLD HIS WIFE HE WAS GOING AWAY ON A BUSINESS TRIP.
AND HE NEVER *ARRIVED*.
YOU'RE *STILL* HANGING ROUND HIM?
YEAH WELL...

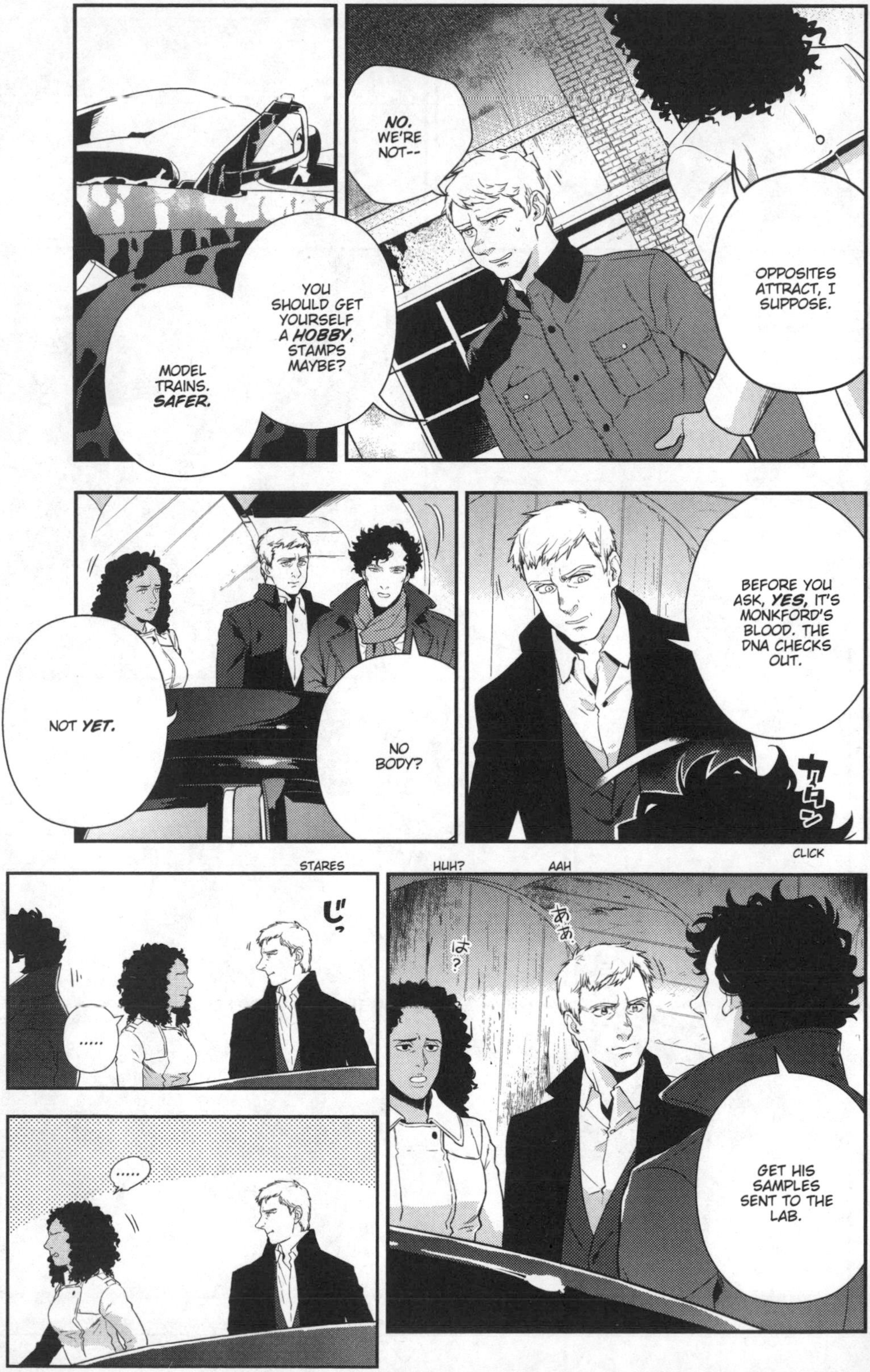
OPPOSITES ATTRACT, I SUPPOSE.
NO. WE'RE NOT--
YOU SHOULD GET YOURSELF A HOBBY, STAMPS MAYBE?
MODEL TRAINS. SAFER.
BEFORE YOU ASK, YES, IT'S MONKFORD'S BLOOD. THE DNA CHECKS OUT.
カタン
CLICK
NO BODY?
NOT YET.
ああ
AAH
は？
HUH?
GET HIS SAMPLES SENT TO THE LAB.
じっ
STARES
......
......

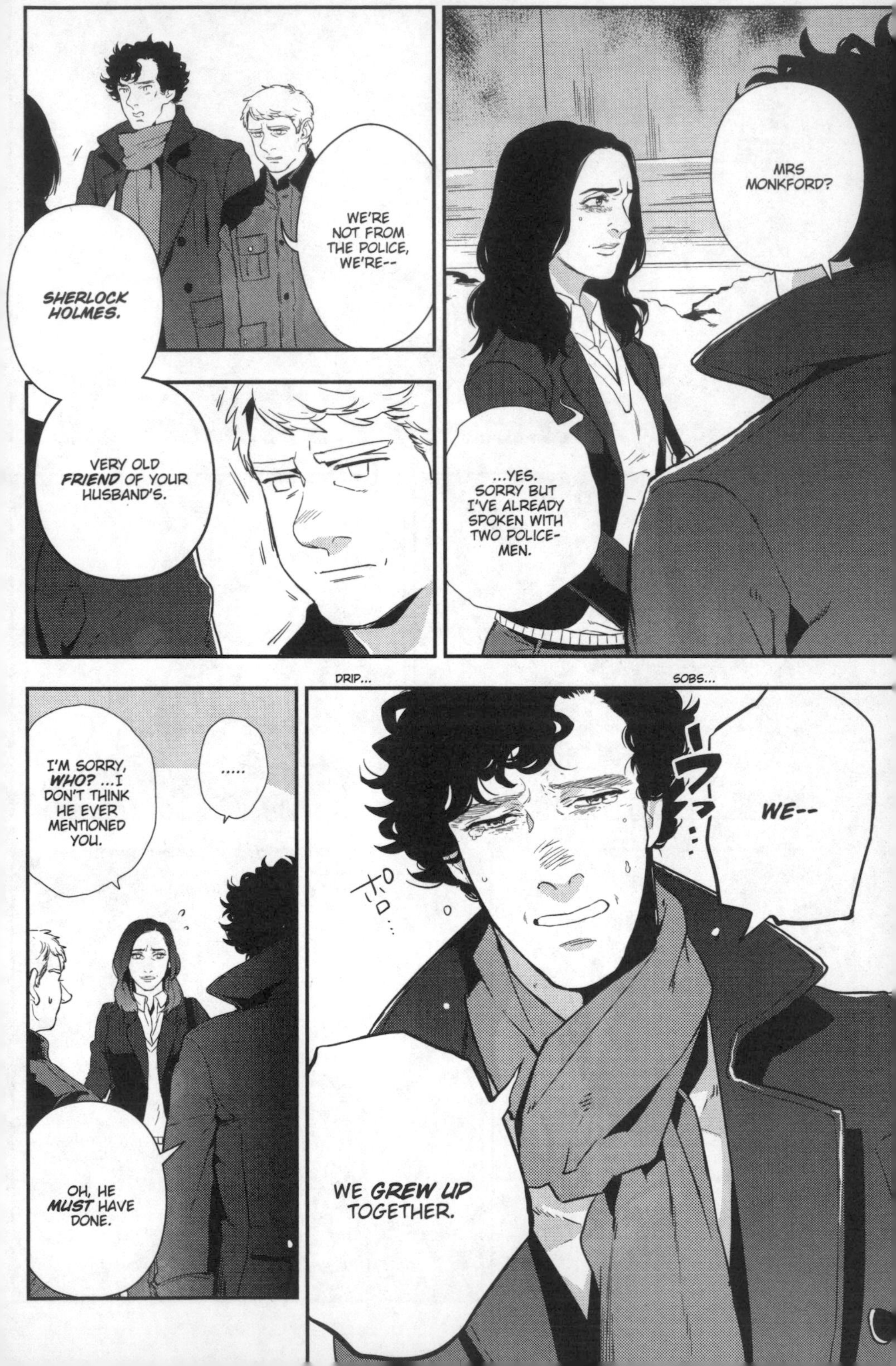
MRS MONKFORD?
...YES. SORRY BUT I'VE ALREADY SPOKEN WITH TWO POLICEMEN.
WE'RE NOT FROM THE POLICE, WE'RE--
SHERLOCK HOLMES.
VERY OLD FRIEND OF YOUR HUSBAND'S.
SOBS...
DRIP...
WE--
WE GREW UP TOGETHER.
I'M SORRY, WHO? ...I DON'T THINK HE EVER MENTIONED YOU.
.....
OH, HE MUST HAVE DONE.

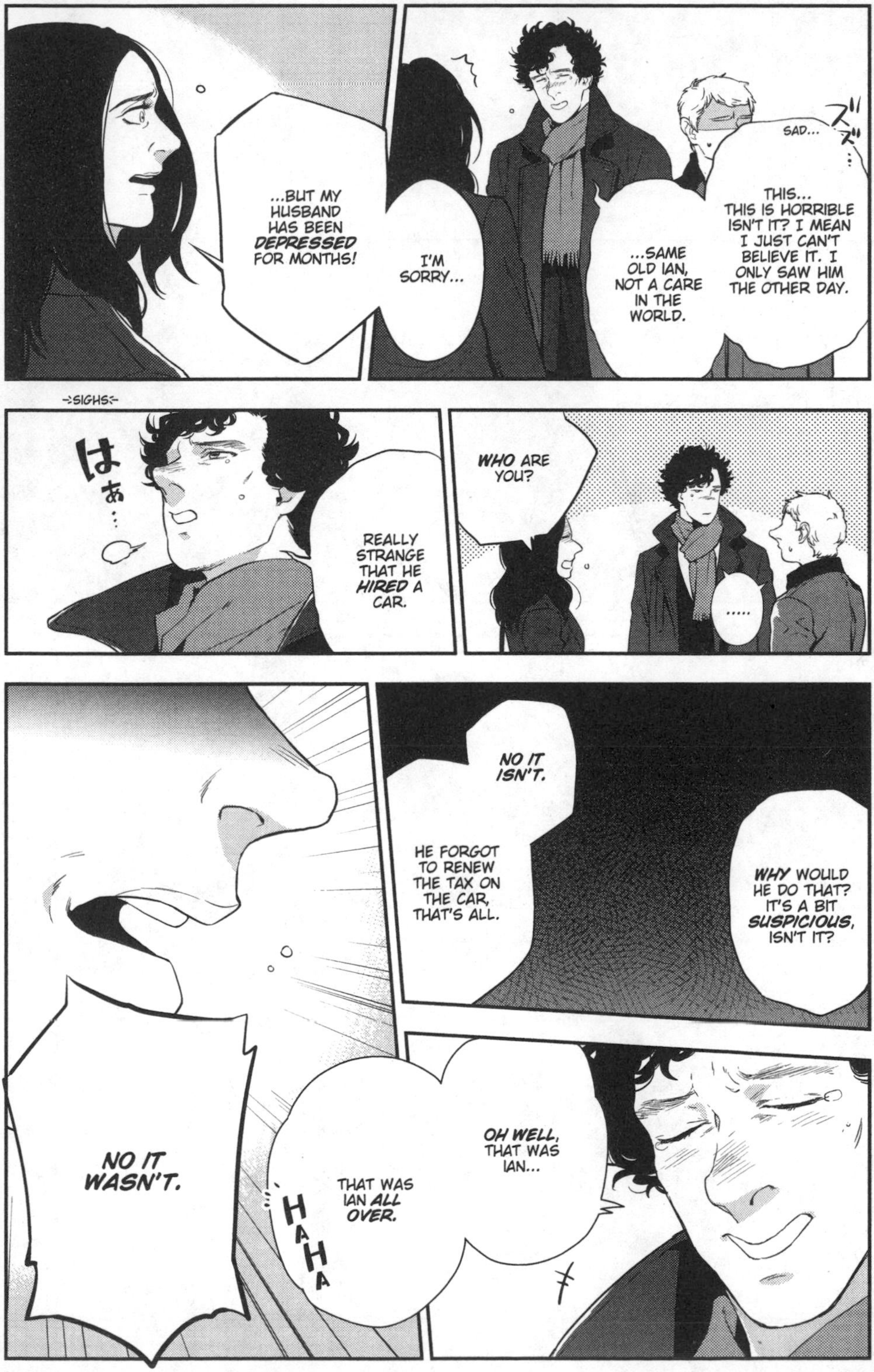
SAD...
THIS... THIS IS HORRIBLE ISN'T IT? I MEAN I JUST CAN'T BELIEVE IT. I ONLY SAW HIM THE OTHER DAY.
...SAME OLD IAN, NOT A CARE IN THE WORLD.
I'M SORRY...
...BUT MY HUSBAND HAS BEEN DEPRESSED FOR MONTHS!
WHO ARE YOU?
.....
-SIGHS-
はぁ…
REALLY STRANGE THAT HE HIRED A CAR.
WHY WOULD HE DO THAT? IT'S A BIT SUSPICIOUS, ISN'T IT?
NO IT ISN'T.
HE FORGOT TO RENEW THE TAX ON THE CAR, THAT'S ALL.
OH WELL, THAT WAS IAN...
THAT WAS IAN ALL OVER.
HAHA
NO IT WASN'T.

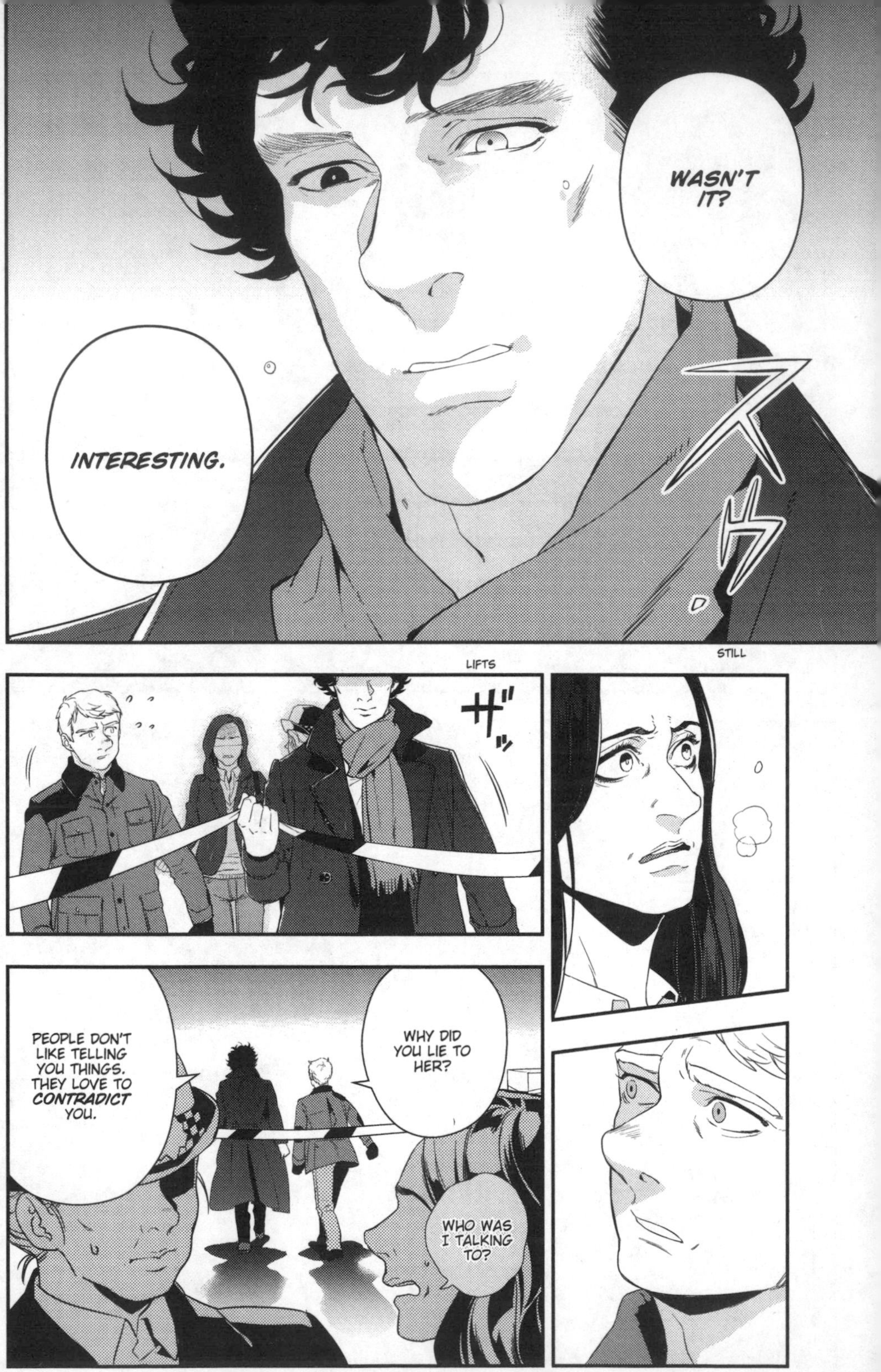
WASN'T IT?
INTERESTING.
スッ
STILL
ザッ
LIFTS
WHY DID YOU LIE TO HER?
PEOPLE DON'T LIKE TELLING YOU THINGS. THEY LOVE TO CONTRADICT YOU.
WHO WAS I TALKING TO?

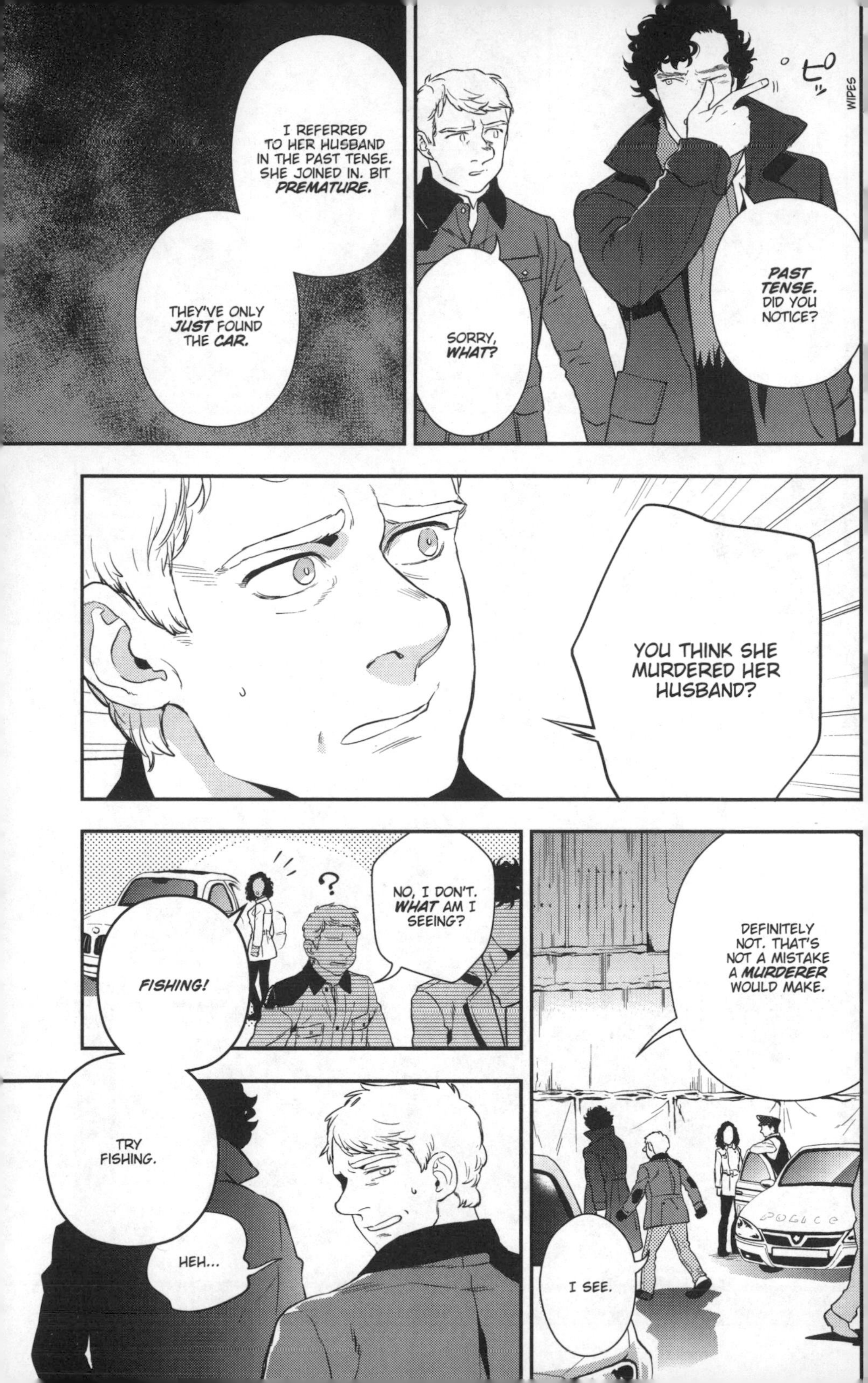
ピッ
WIPES
PAST TENSE. DID YOU NOTICE?
SORRY, WHAT?
I REFERRED TO HER HUSBAND IN THE PAST TENSE. SHE JOINED IN. BIT PREMATURE.
THEY'VE ONLY JUST FOUND THE CAR.
YOU THINK SHE MURDERED HER HUSBAND?
DEFINITELY NOT. THAT'S NOT A MISTAKE A MURDERER WOULD MAKE.
I SEE.
NO, I DON'T. WHAT AM I SEEING?
FISHING!
TRY FISHING.
HEH...

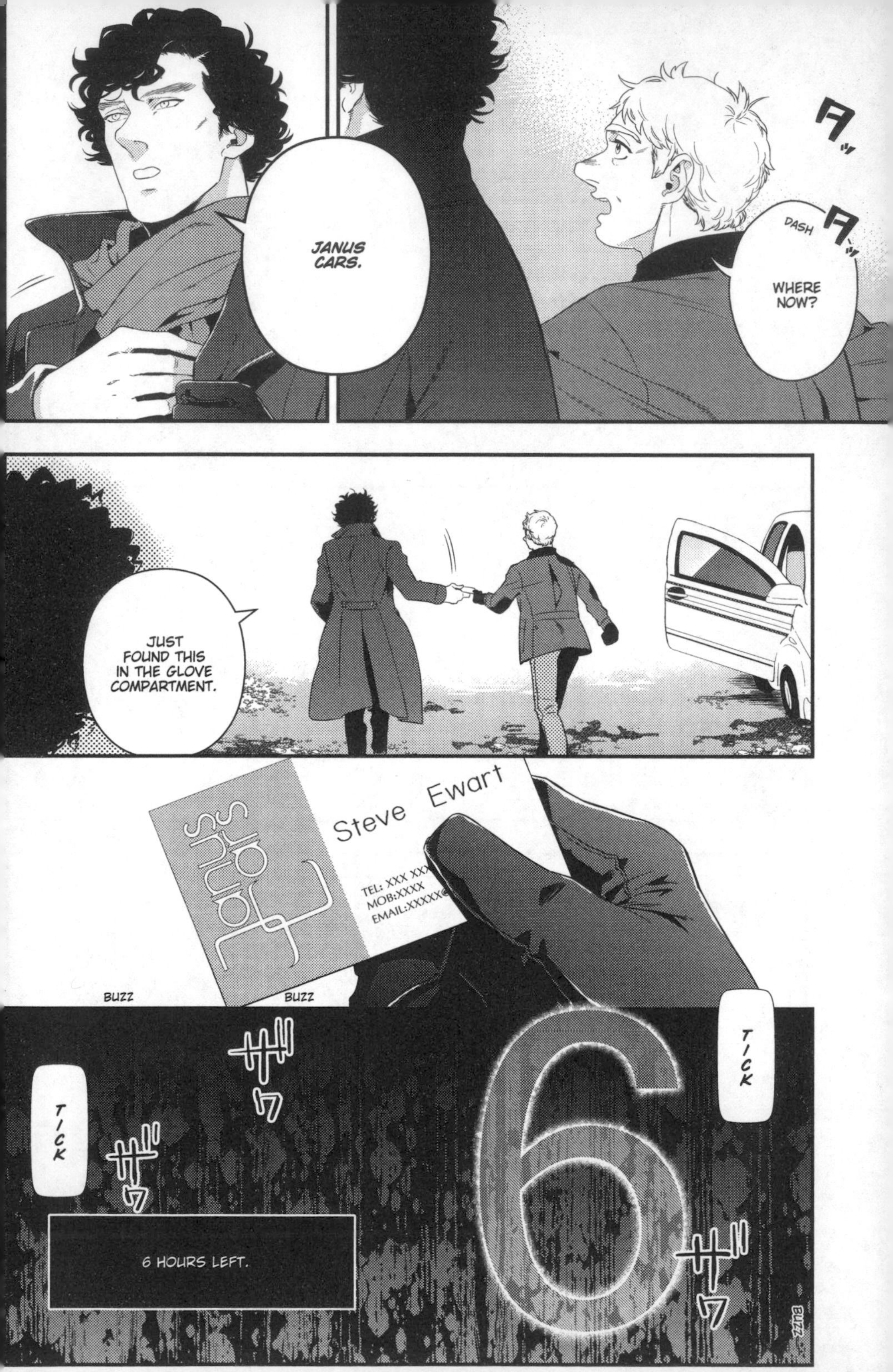
DASH
WHERE NOW?
JANUS CARS.
JUST FOUND THIS IN THE GLOVE COMPARTMENT.
Steve Ewart
TEL: XXX XXX
MOB:XXXX
BUZZ
BUZZ
TICK
TICK
6
6 HOURS LEFT.
BUZZ

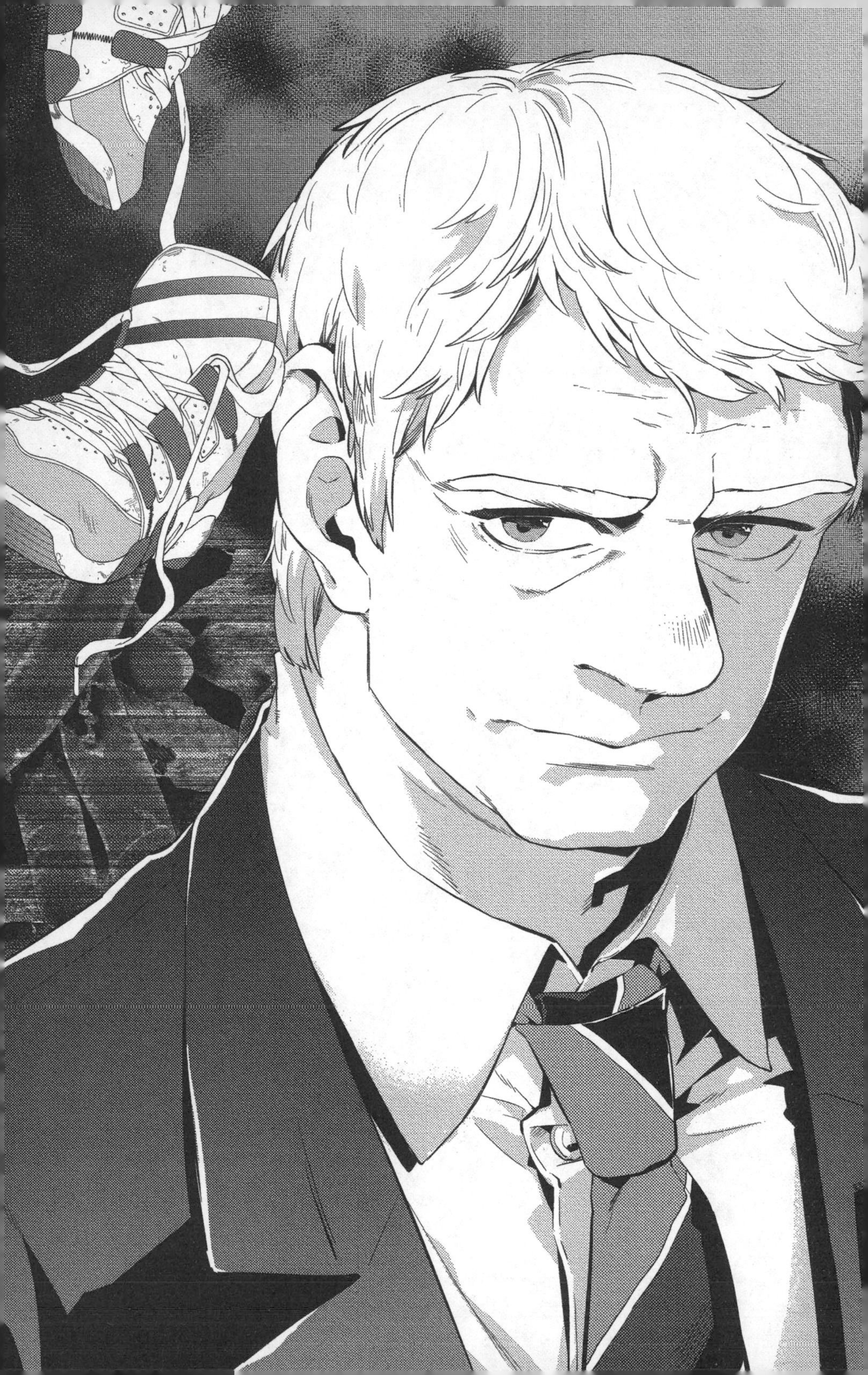

Chapter 3

Illustration by:
Mike Dowling

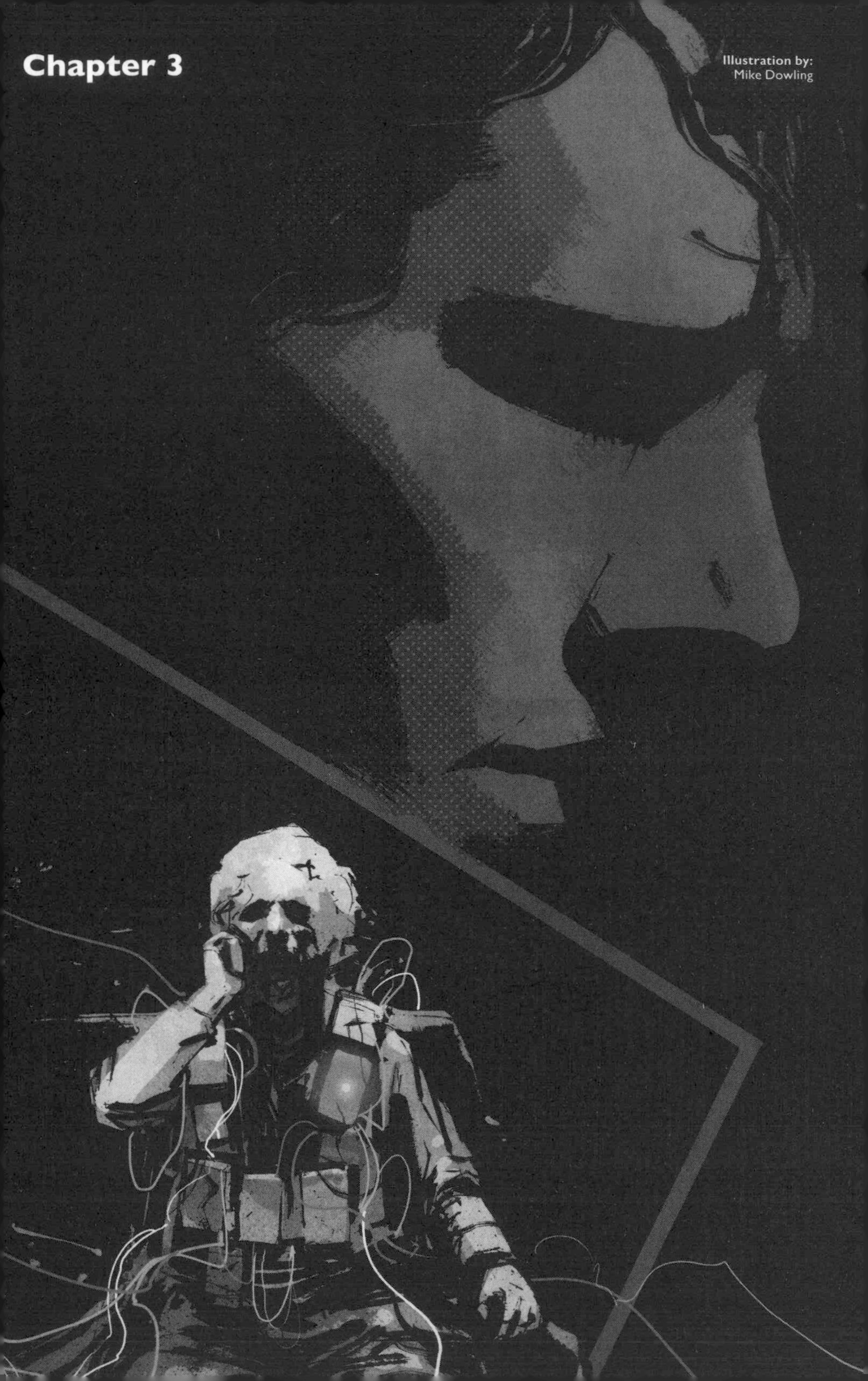

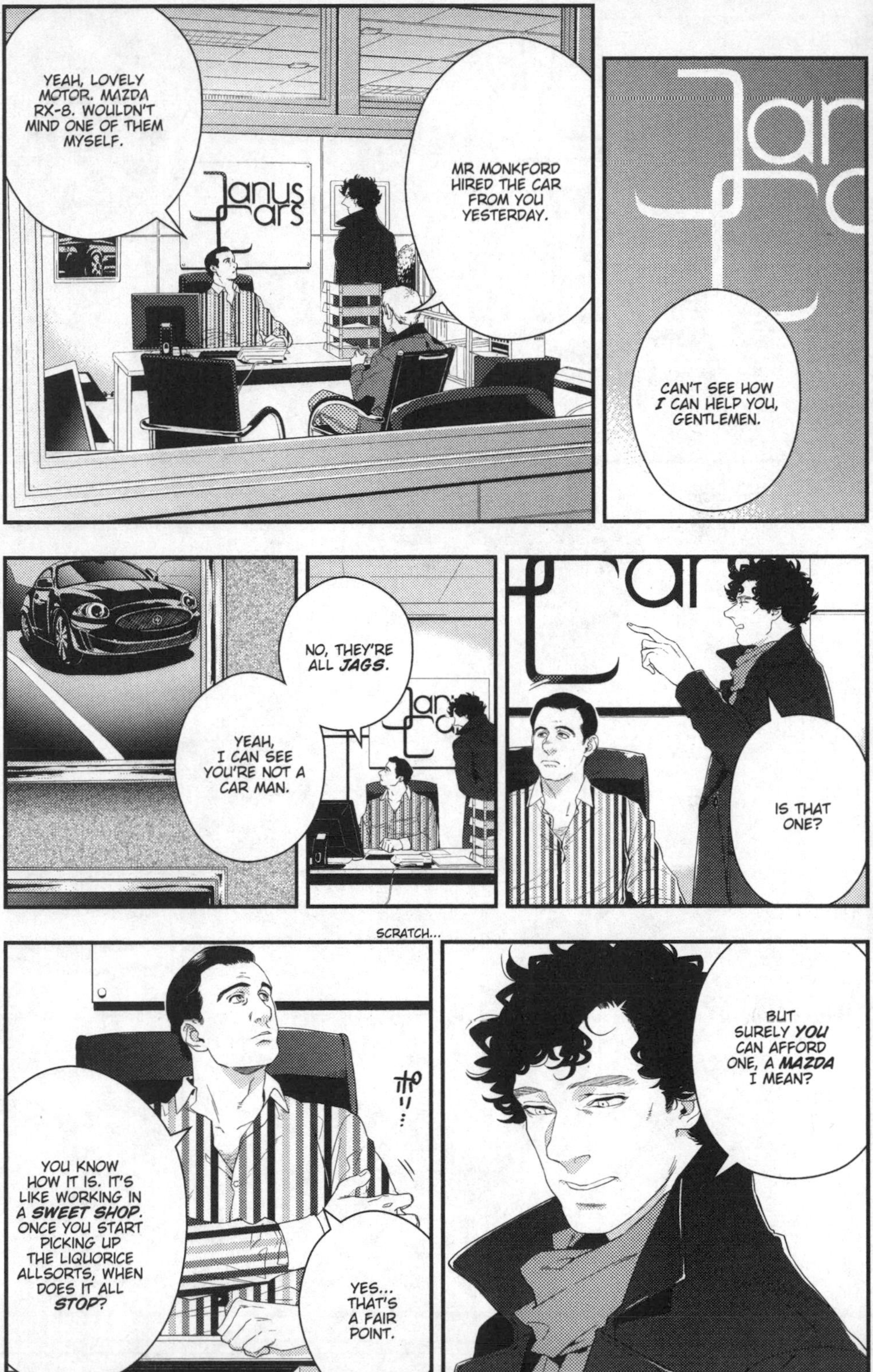
CAN'T SEE HOW *I* CAN HELP YOU, GENTLEMEN.
MR MONKFORD HIRED THE CAR FROM YOU YESTERDAY.
YEAH, LOVELY MOTOR. MAZDA RX-8. WOULDN'T MIND ONE OF THEM MYSELF.
IS THAT ONE?
NO, THEY'RE ALL ***JAGS***.
YEAH, I CAN SEE YOU'RE NOT A CAR MAN.
SCRATCH...
BUT SURELY ***YOU*** CAN AFFORD ONE, A ***MAZDA*** I MEAN?
ポリ…
YOU KNOW HOW IT IS. IT'S LIKE WORKING IN A ***SWEET SHOP***. ONCE YOU START PICKING UP THE LIQUORICE ALLSORTS, WHEN DOES IT ALL ***STOP***?
YES... THAT'S A FAIR POINT.

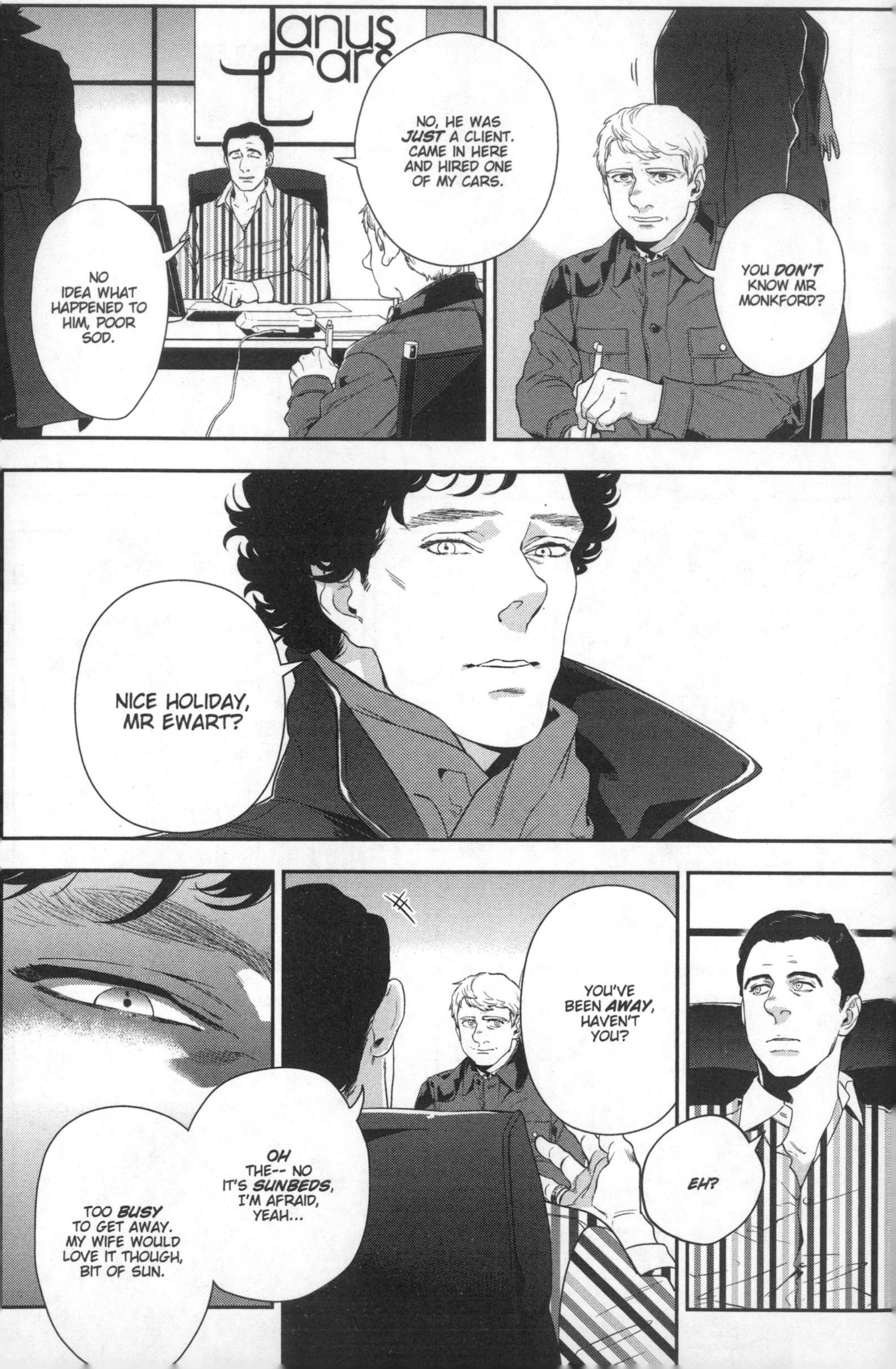
YOU DON'T KNOW MR MONKFORD?
NO, HE WAS JUST A CLIENT. CAME IN HERE AND HIRED ONE OF MY CARS.
NO IDEA WHAT HAPPENED TO HIM, POOR SOD.
NICE HOLIDAY, MR EWART?
EH?
YOU'VE BEEN AWAY, HAVEN'T YOU?
OH THE-- NO IT'S SUNBEDS, I'M AFRAID, YEAH...
TOO BUSY TO GET AWAY. MY WIFE WOULD LOVE IT THOUGH, BIT OF SUN.

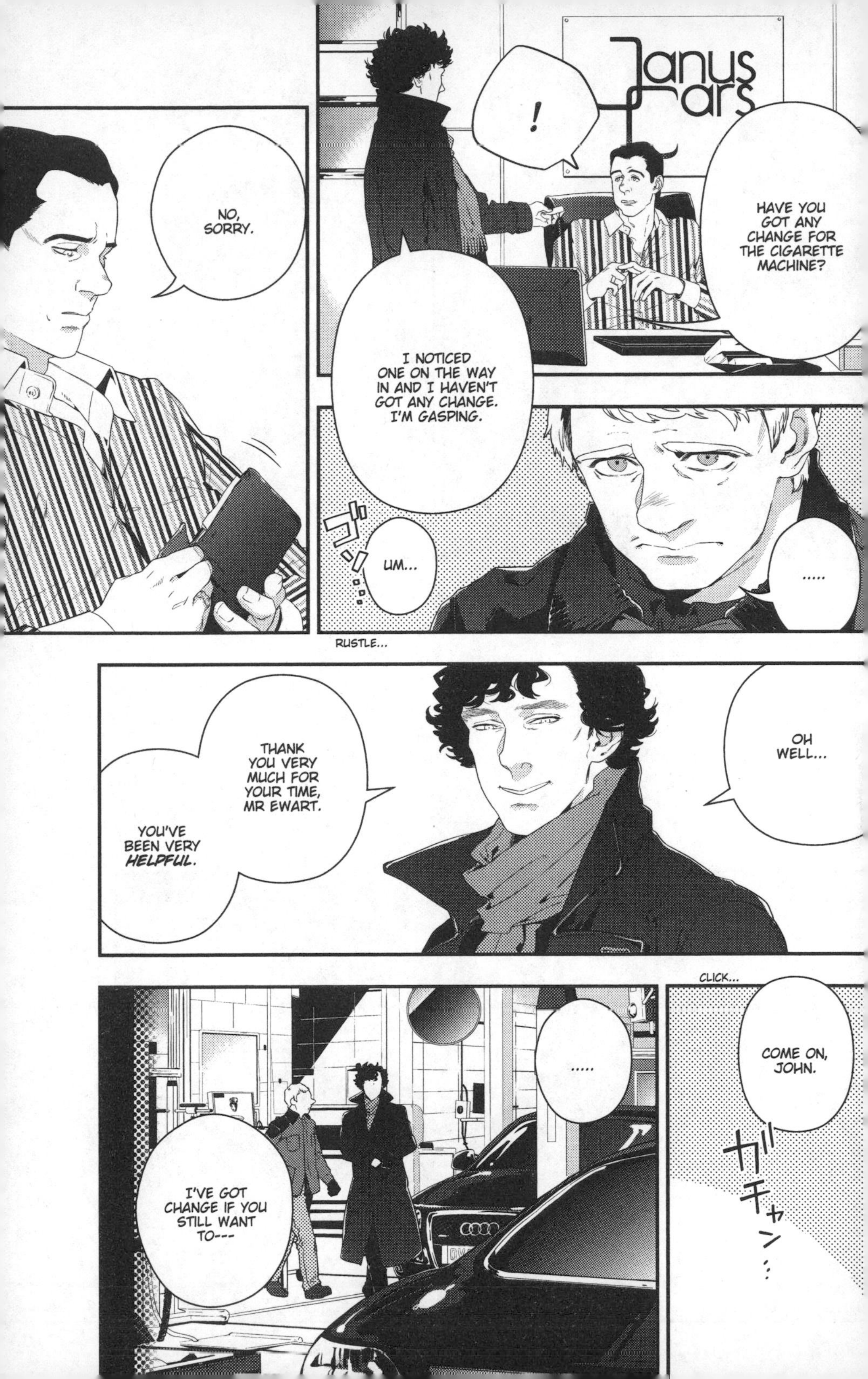
Janus Cars
!
HAVE YOU GOT ANY CHANGE FOR THE CIGARETTE MACHINE?
I NOTICED ONE ON THE WAY IN AND I HAVEN'T GOT ANY CHANGE. I'M GASPING.
.....
UM...
NO, SORRY.
RUSTLE...
OH WELL...
THANK YOU VERY MUCH FOR YOUR TIME, MR EWART.
YOU'VE BEEN VERY ***HELPFUL***.
CLICK...
COME ON, JOHN.
ガチャン...
.....
I'VE GOT CHANGE IF YOU STILL WANT TO---

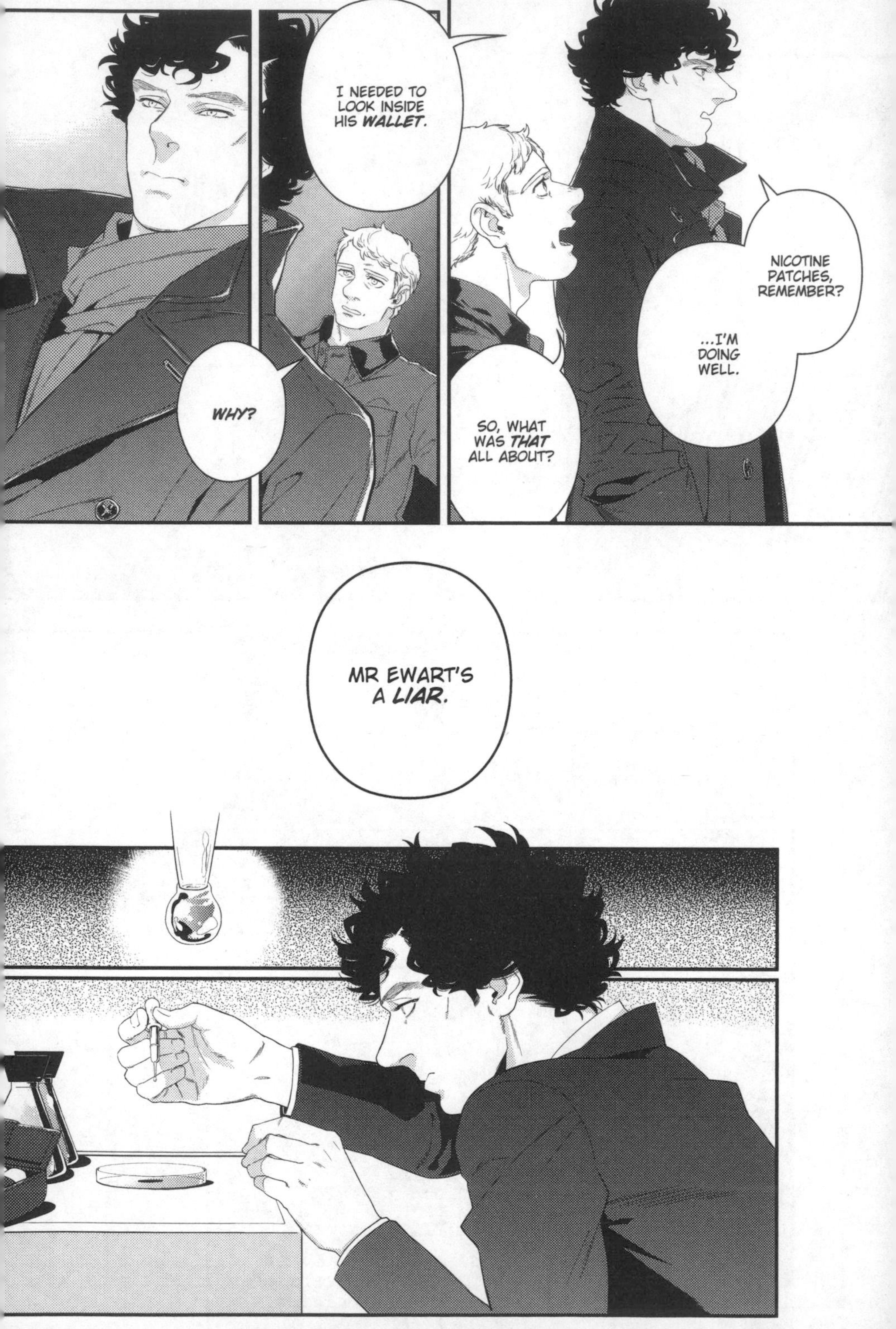
NICOTINE PATCHES, REMEMBER?
...I'M DOING WELL.
SO, WHAT WAS *THAT* ALL ABOUT?
I NEEDED TO LOOK INSIDE HIS *WALLET*.
WHY?
MR EWART'S A *LIAR*.

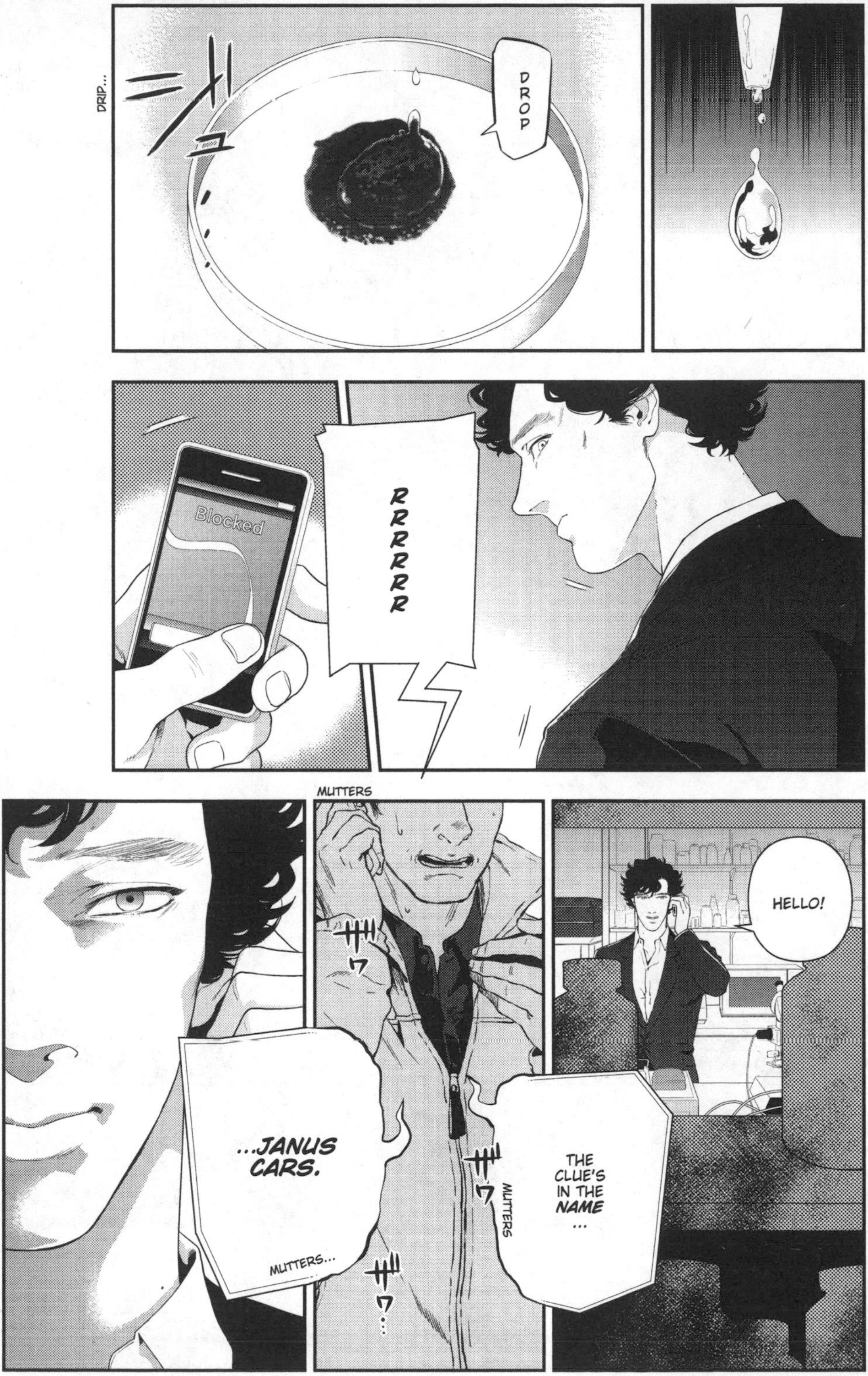
DROP
DRIP...
RRRRRR
Blocked
HELLO!
MUTTERS
THE CLUE'S IN THE NAME...
MUTTERS
...JANUS CARS.
MUTTERS...

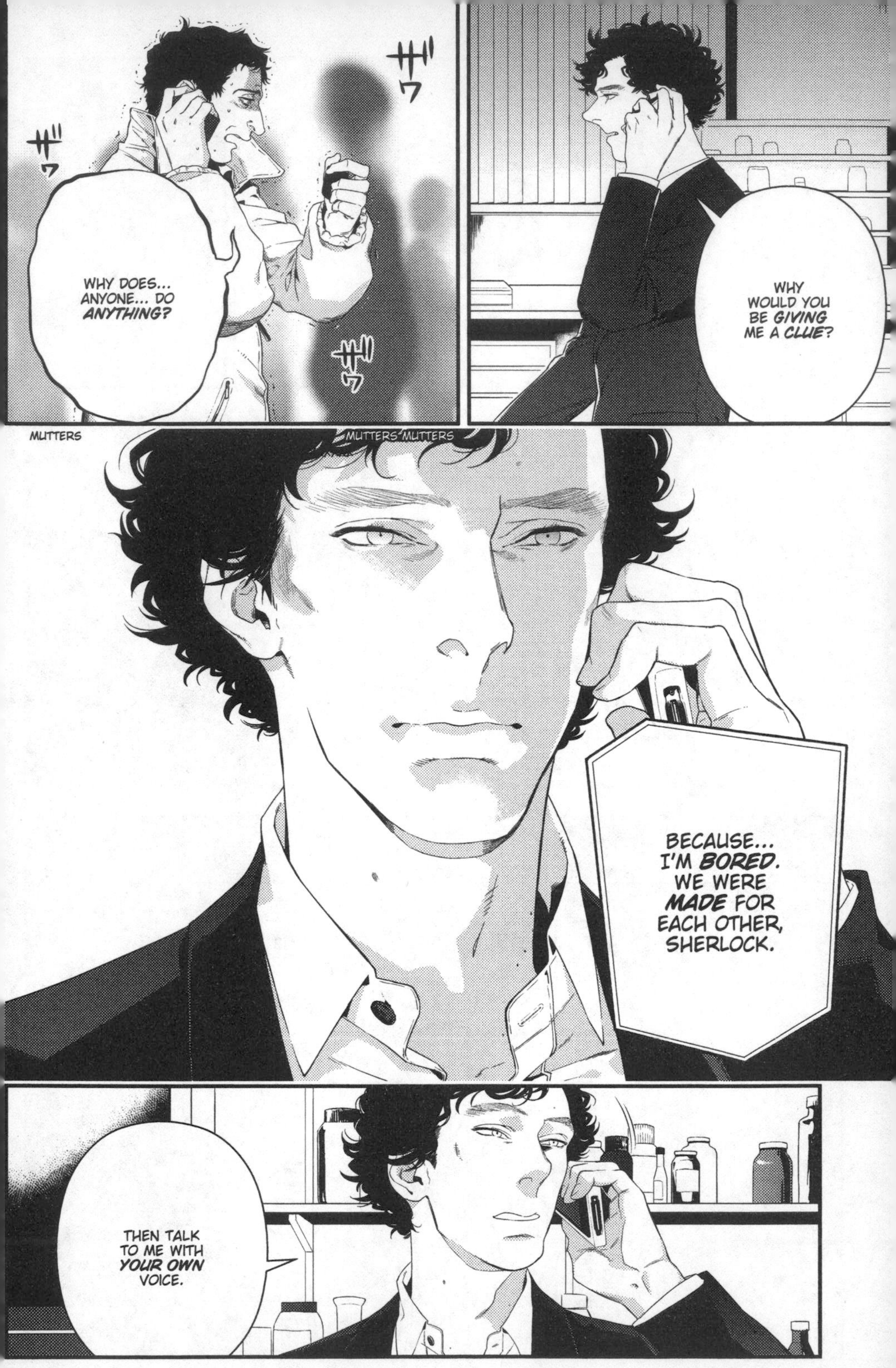
WHY WOULD YOU BE *GIVING* ME A *CLUE*?
ザワ
ザワ
WHY DOES... ANYONE... DO *ANYTHING*?
ザワ
MUTTERS MUTTERS
MUTTERS
BECAUSE... I'M *BORED*. WE WERE *MADE* FOR EACH OTHER, SHERLOCK.
THEN TALK TO ME WITH *YOUR OWN* VOICE.

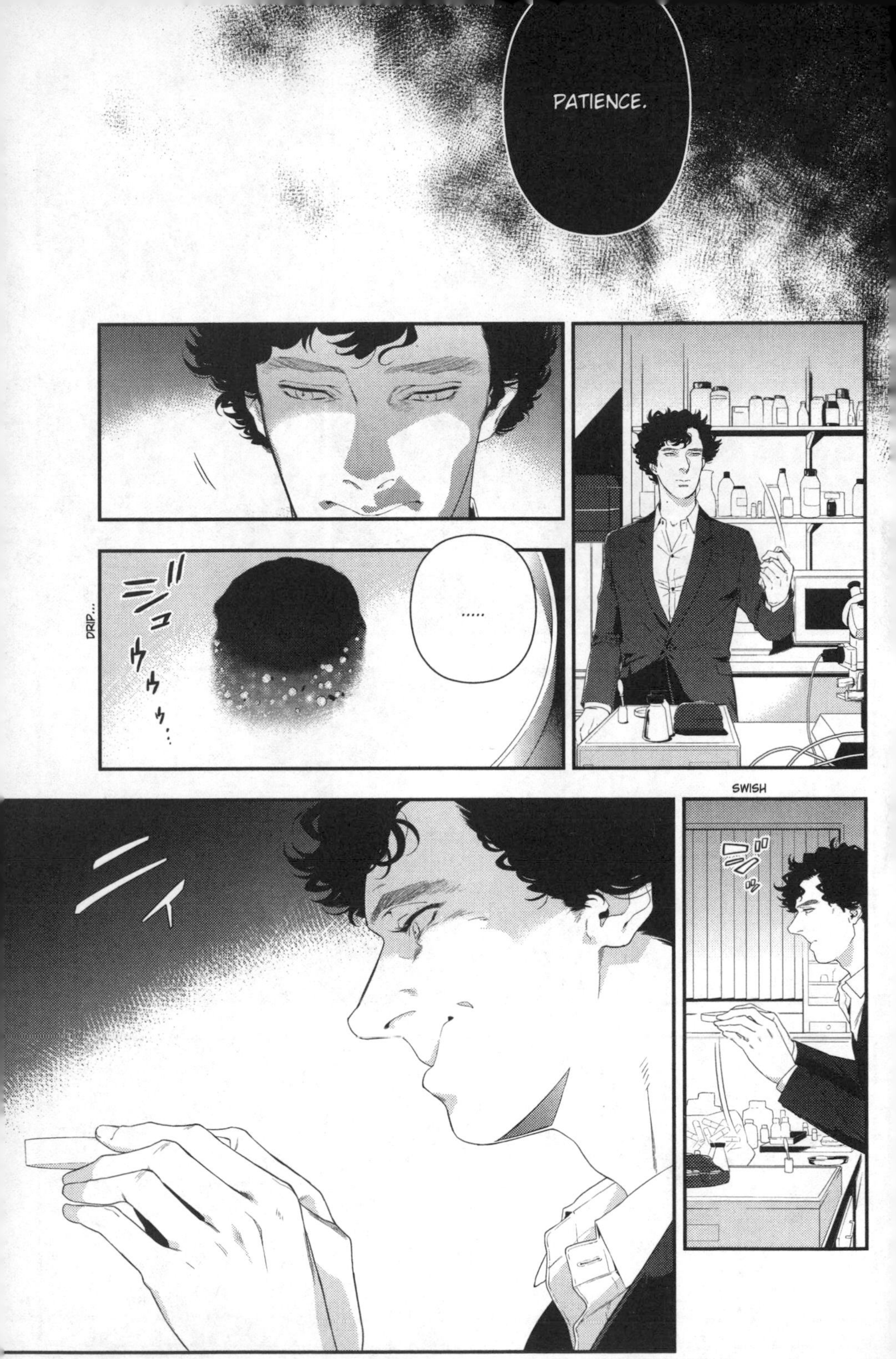
PATIENCE.
.....
DRIP...
ジュゥゥゥ...
SWISH
ニィ

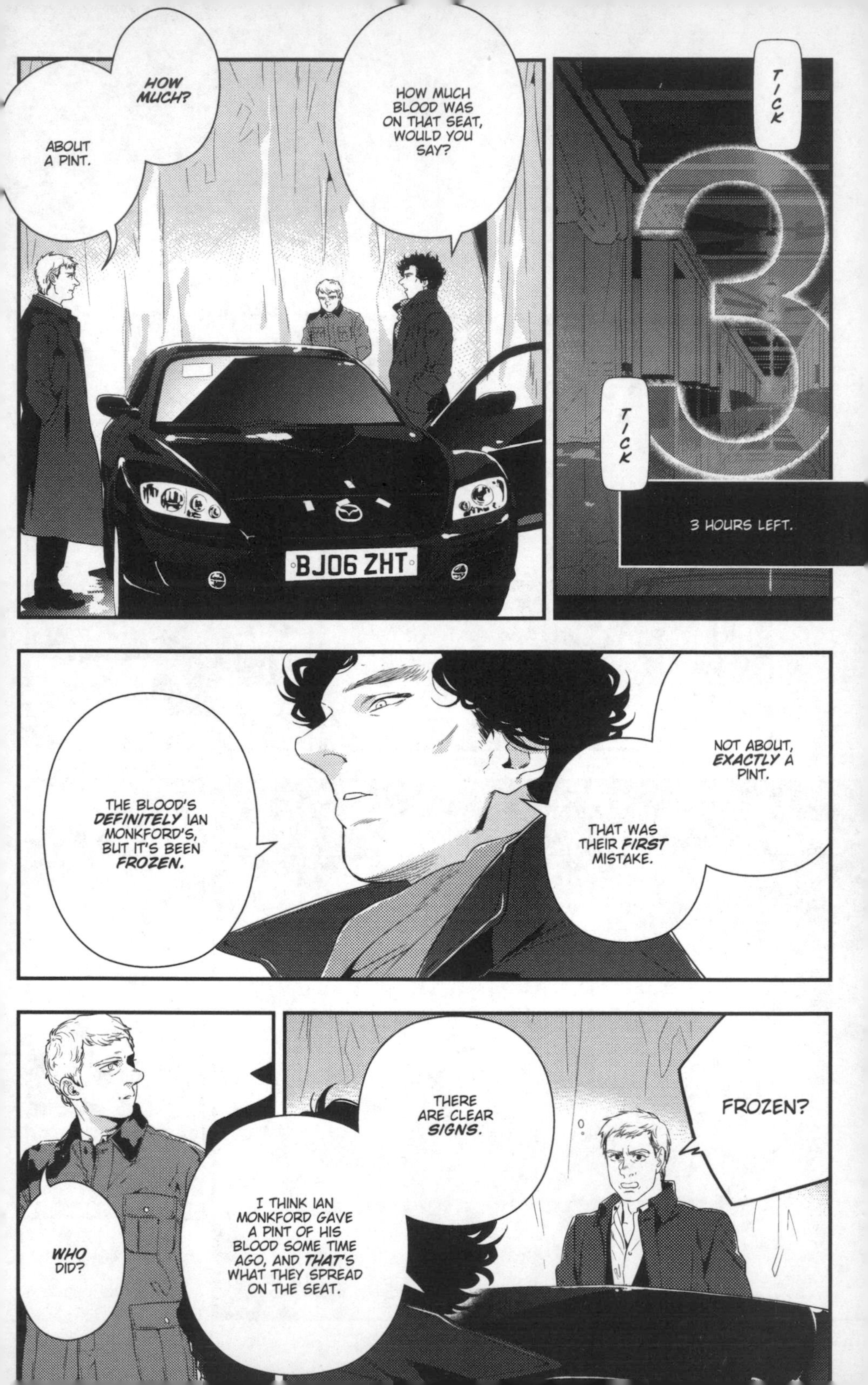
TICK
TICK
3 HOURS LEFT.
HOW MUCH BLOOD WAS ON THAT SEAT, WOULD YOU SAY?
HOW MUCH?
ABOUT A PINT.
BJ06 ZHT
NOT ABOUT, EXACTLY A PINT.
THAT WAS THEIR FIRST MISTAKE.
THE BLOOD'S DEFINITELY IAN MONKFORD'S, BUT IT'S BEEN FROZEN.
FROZEN?
THERE ARE CLEAR SIGNS.
I THINK IAN MONKFORD GAVE A PINT OF HIS BLOOD SOME TIME AGO, AND THAT'S WHAT THEY SPREAD ON THE SEAT.
WHO DID?

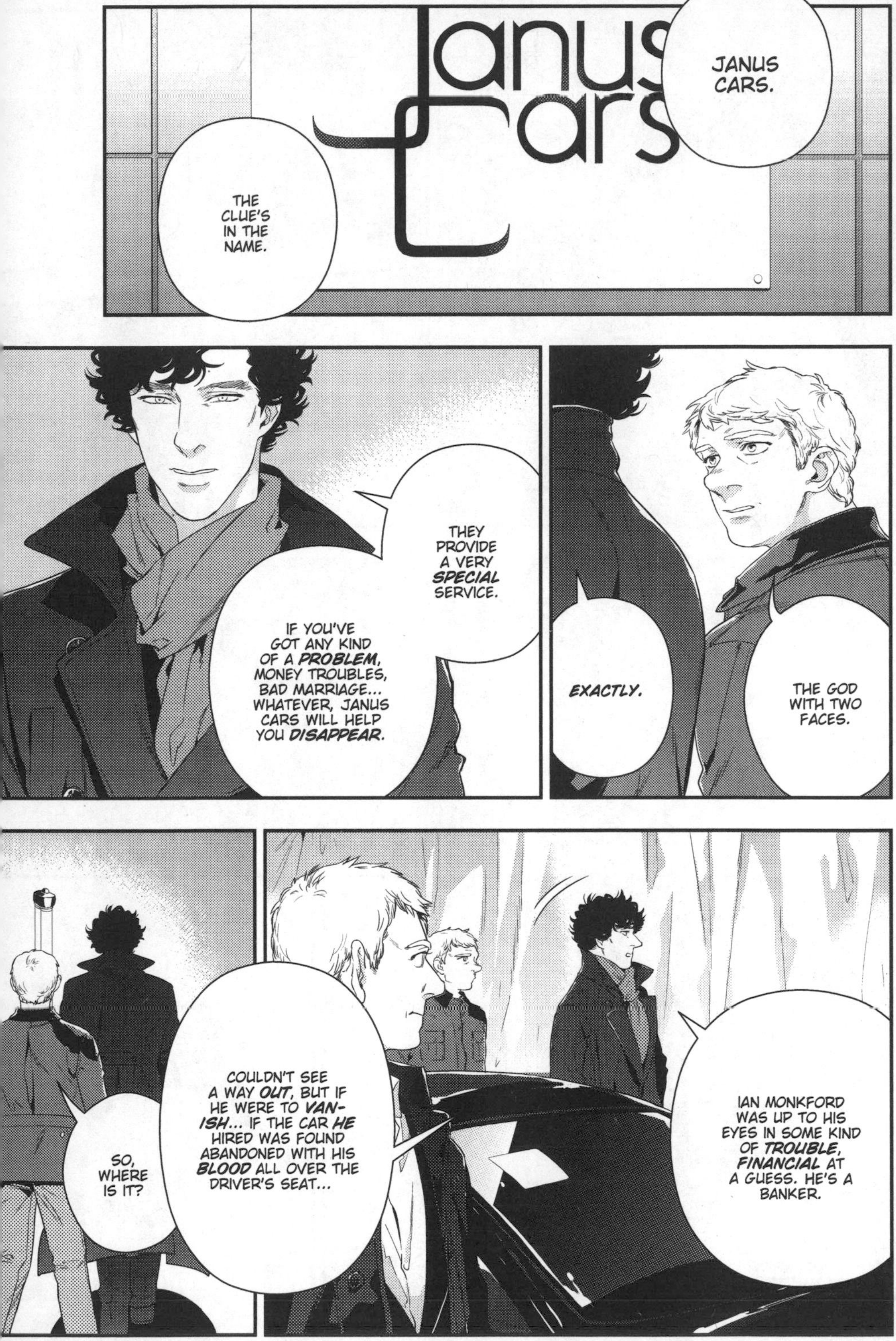
Janus Cars
JANUS CARS.
THE CLUE'S IN THE NAME.
THE GOD WITH TWO FACES.
EXACTLY.
THEY PROVIDE A VERY SPECIAL SERVICE.
IF YOU'VE GOT ANY KIND OF A PROBLEM, MONEY TROUBLES, BAD MARRIAGE... WHATEVER, JANUS CARS WILL HELP YOU DISAPPEAR.
IAN MONKFORD WAS UP TO HIS EYES IN SOME KIND OF TROUBLE, FINANCIAL AT A GUESS. HE'S A BANKER.
COULDN'T SEE A WAY OUT, BUT IF HE WERE TO VAN-ISH... IF THE CAR HE HIRED WAS FOUND ABANDONED WITH HIS BLOOD ALL OVER THE DRIVER'S SEAT...
SO, WHERE IS IT?

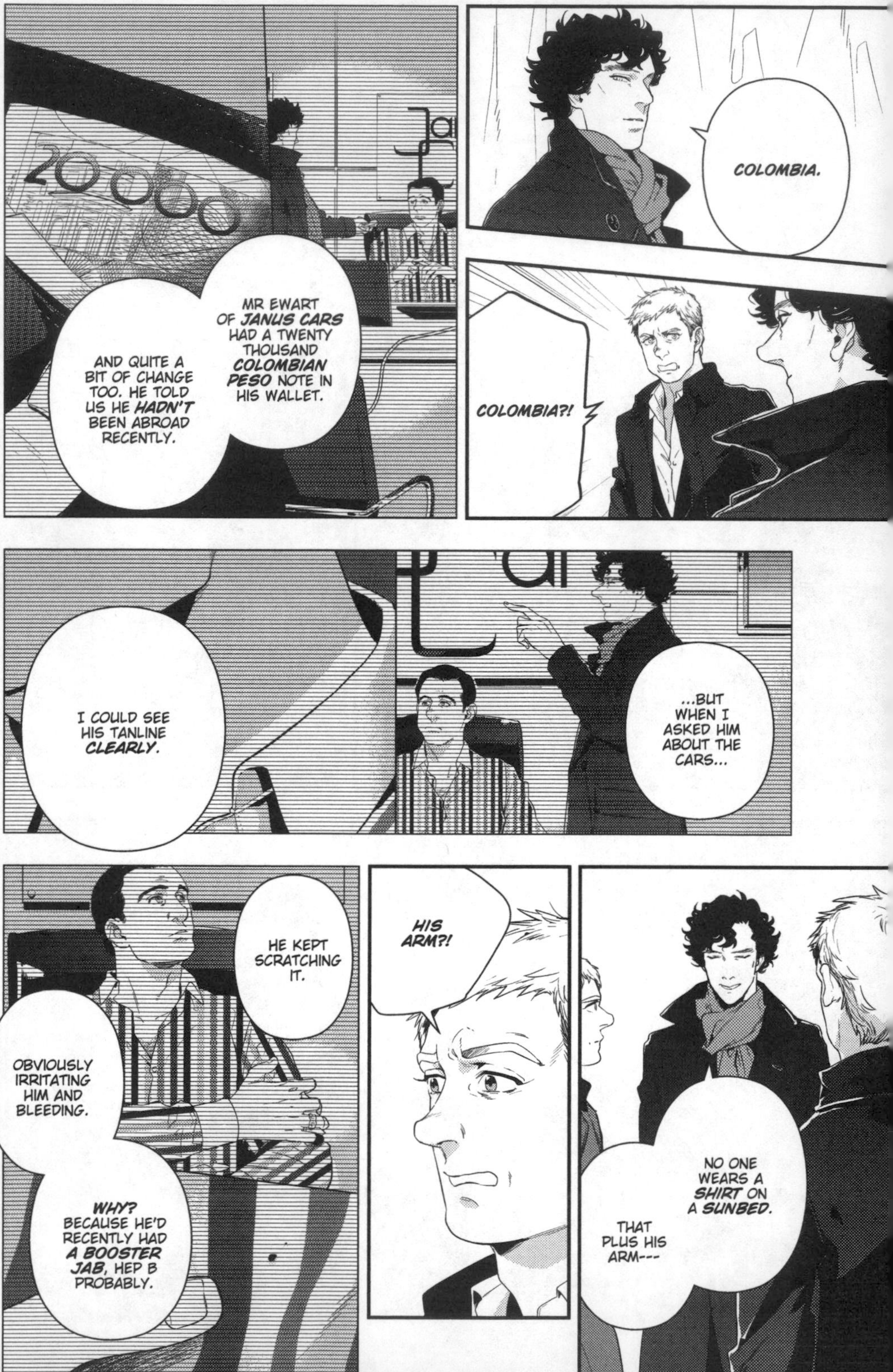
COLOMBIA.
COLOMBIA?!
MR EWART OF ***JANUS CARS*** HAD A TWENTY THOUSAND ***COLOMBIAN PESO*** NOTE IN HIS WALLET.
AND QUITE A BIT OF CHANGE TOO. HE TOLD US HE ***HADN'T*** BEEN ABROAD RECENTLY.
...BUT WHEN I ASKED HIM ABOUT THE CARS...
I COULD SEE HIS TANLINE ***CLEARLY.***
NO ONE WEARS A ***SHIRT*** ON A ***SUNBED.***
THAT PLUS HIS ARM---
HIS ARM?!
HE KEPT SCRATCHING IT.
OBVIOUSLY IRRITATING HIM AND BLEEDING.
WHY? BECAUSE HE'D RECENTLY HAD ***A BOOSTER JAB***, HEP B PROBABLY.

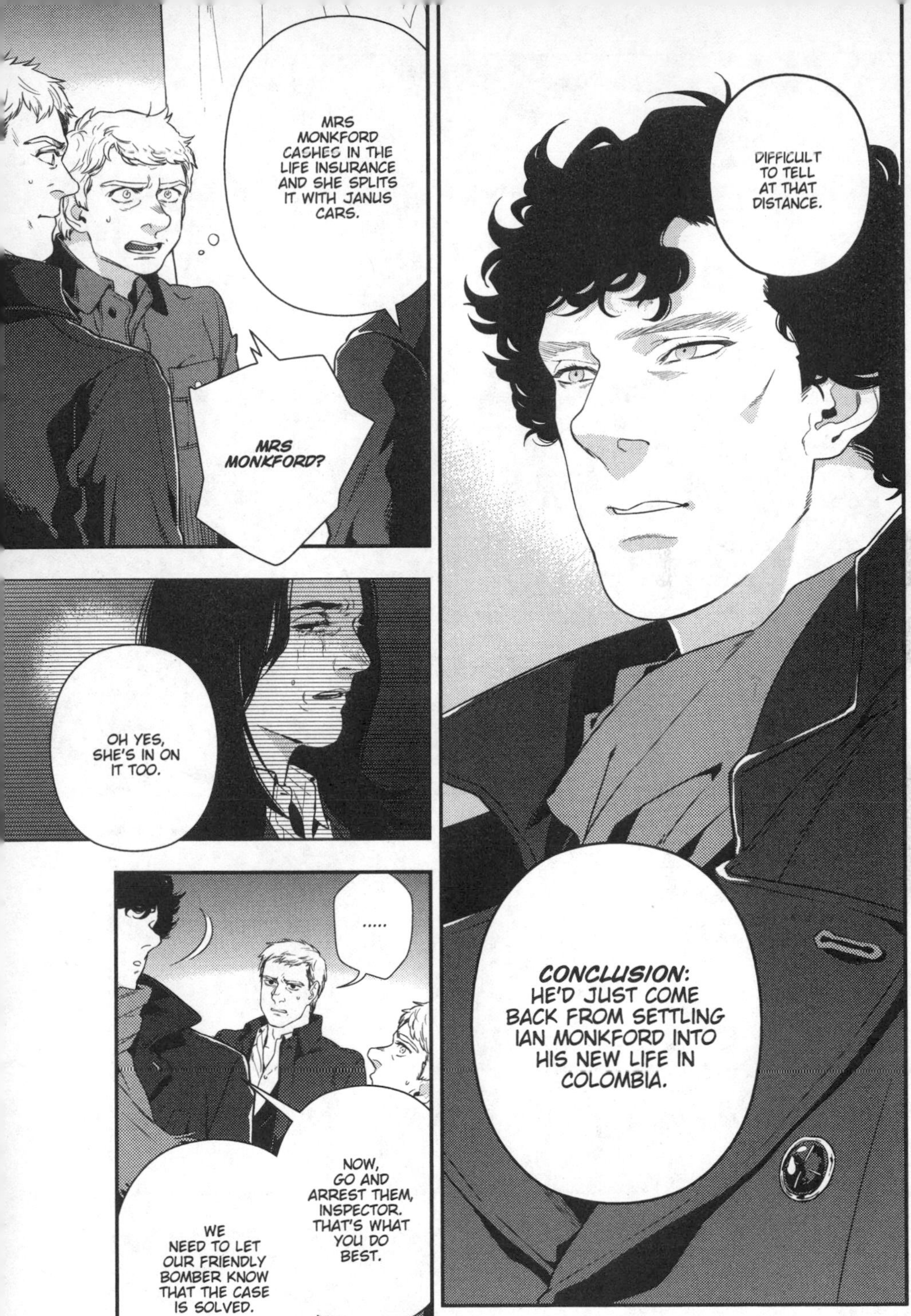
DIFFICULT TO TELL AT THAT DISTANCE.
CONCLUSION: HE'D JUST COME BACK FROM SETTLING IAN MONKFORD INTO HIS NEW LIFE IN COLOMBIA.
MRS MONKFORD CASHES IN THE LIFE INSURANCE AND SHE SPLITS IT WITH JANUS CARS.
MRS MONKFORD?
OH YES, SHE'S IN ON IT TOO.
.....
NOW, GO AND ARREST THEM, INSPECTOR. THAT'S WHAT YOU DO BEST.
WE NEED TO LET OUR FRIENDLY BOMBER KNOW THAT THE CASE IS SOLVED.

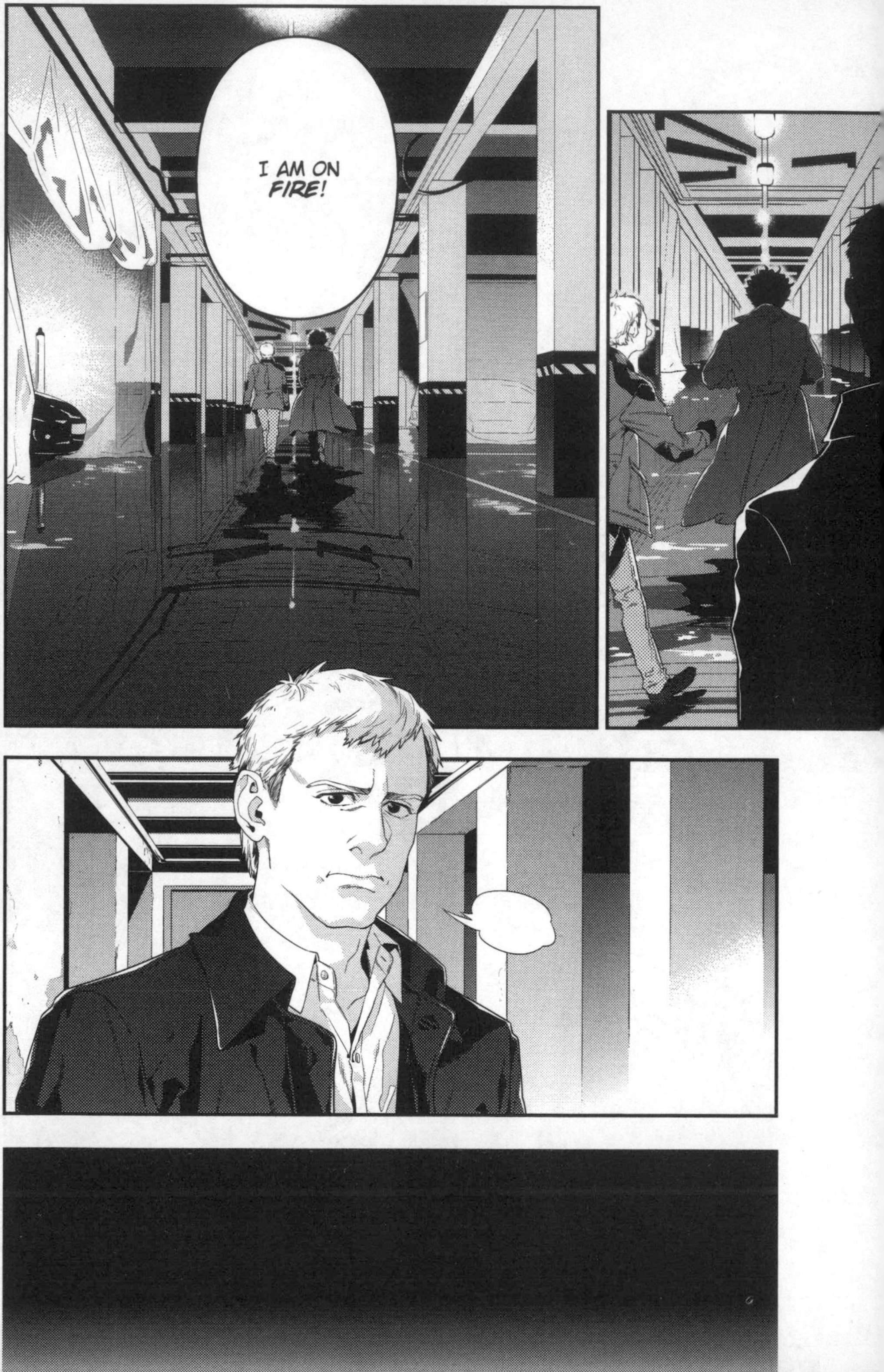
I AM ON *FIRE!*

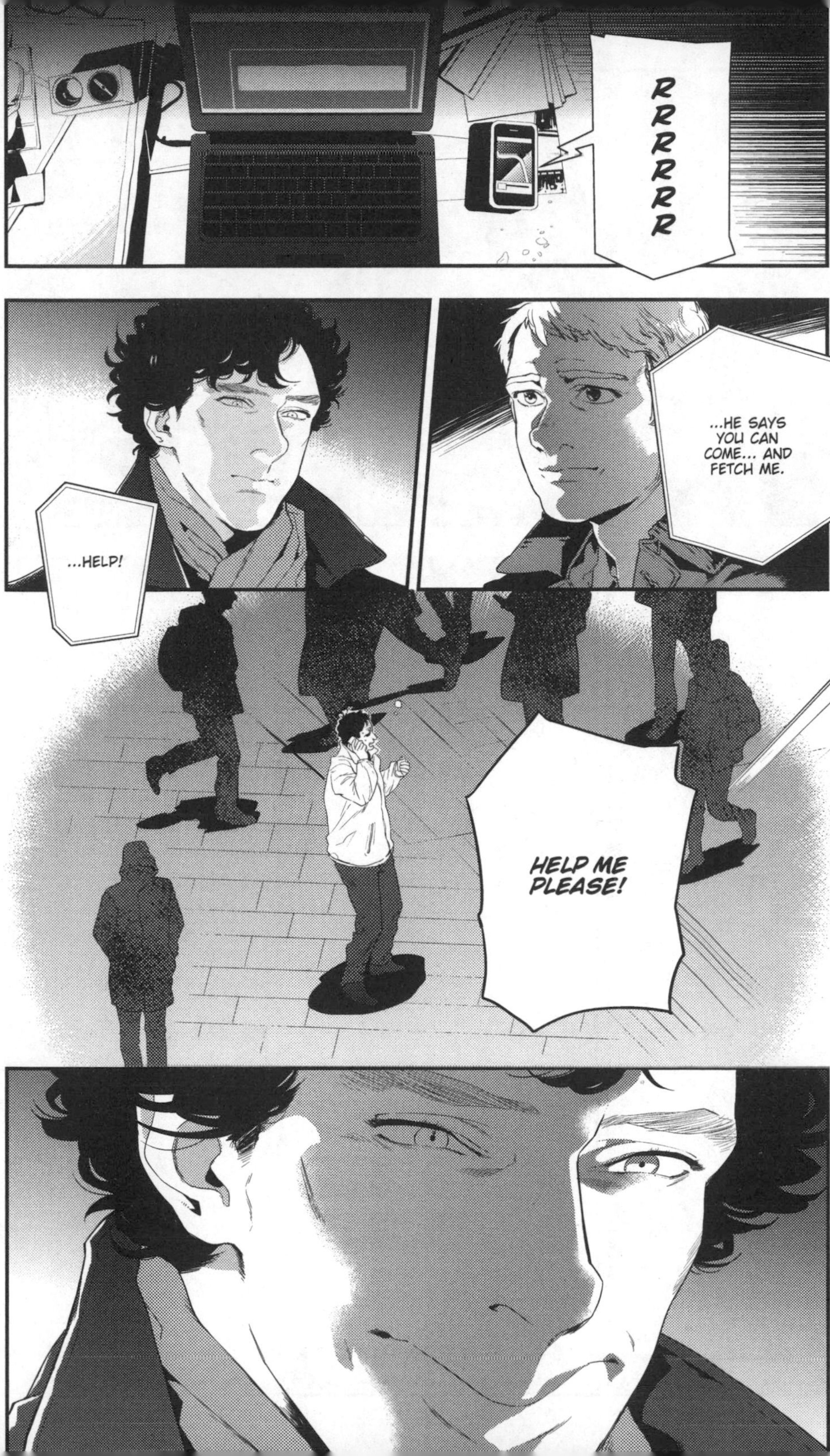
RRRRRR
...HE SAYS YOU CAN COME... AND FETCH ME.
...HELP!
HELP ME PLEASE!

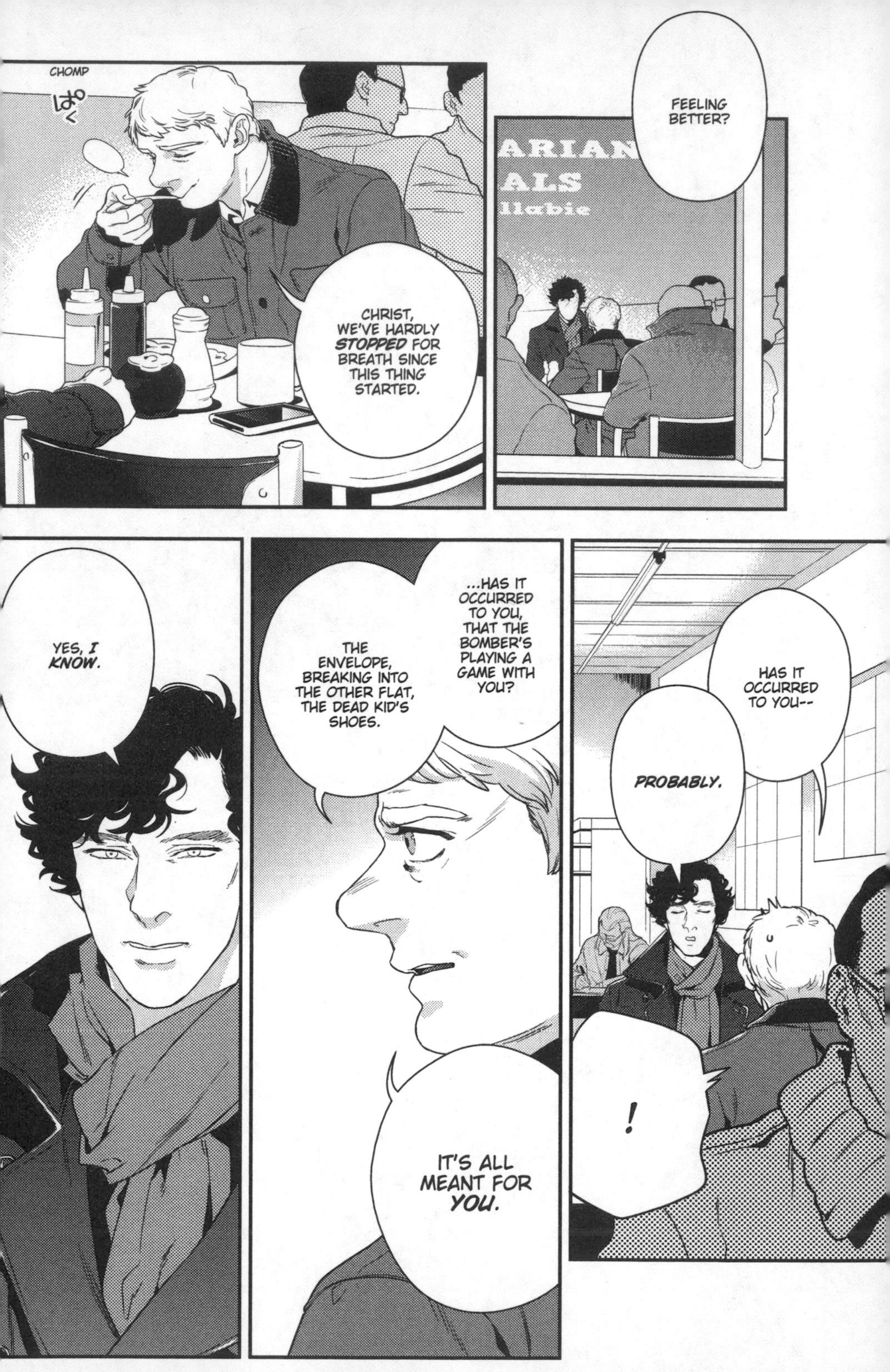
FEELING BETTER?
ARIAN
ALS
llabie
CHOMP
ぱく
CHRIST, WE'VE HARDLY *STOPPED* FOR BREATH SINCE THIS THING STARTED.
HAS IT OCCURRED TO YOU--
PROBABLY.
!
...HAS IT OCCURRED TO YOU, THAT THE BOMBER'S PLAYING A GAME WITH YOU?
THE ENVELOPE, BREAKING INTO THE OTHER FLAT, THE DEAD KID'S SHOES.
IT'S ALL MEANT FOR *YOU*.
YES, *I KNOW*.

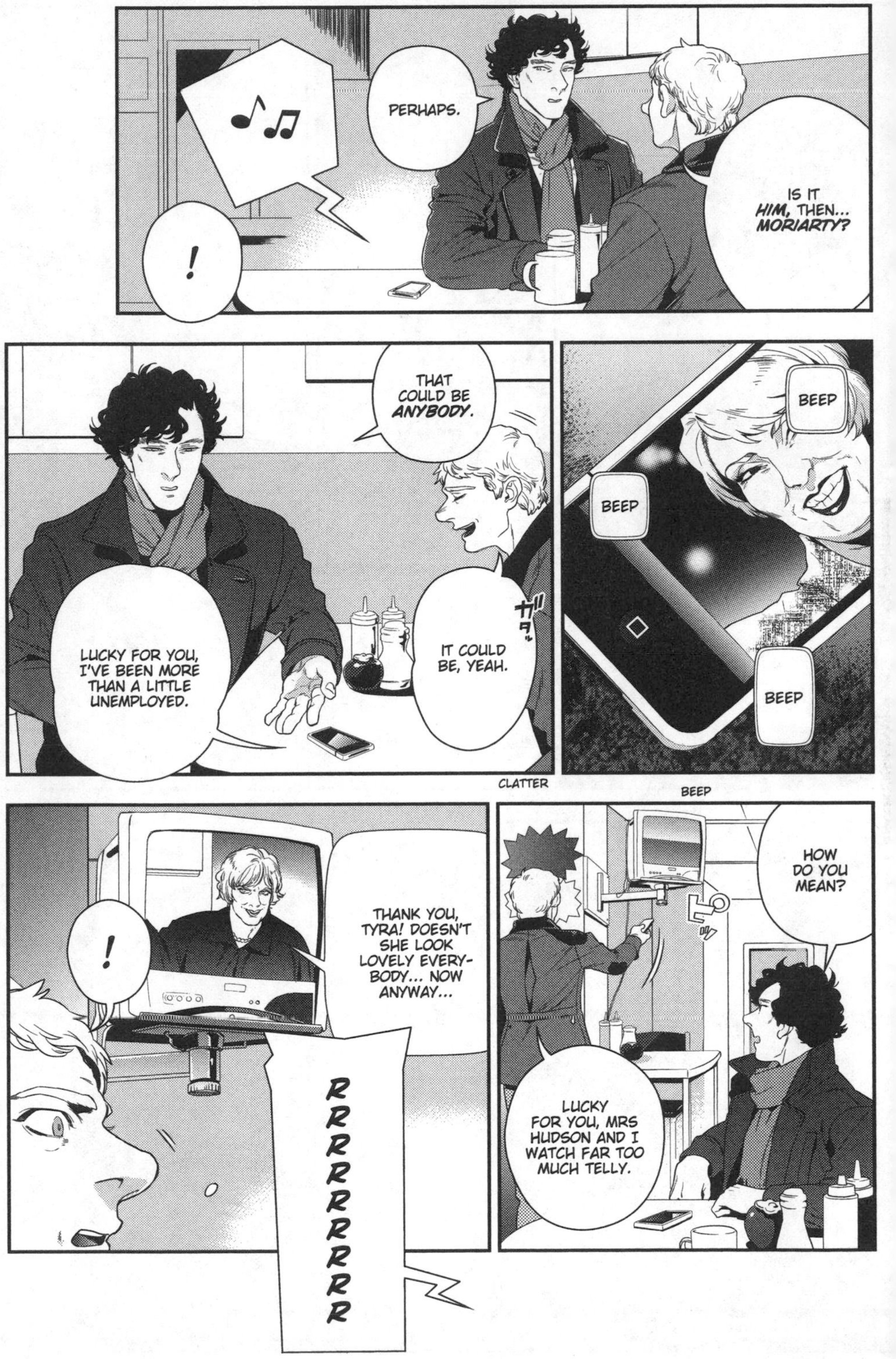
IS IT *HIM*, THEN... *MORIARTY?*
PERHAPS.
♪♫
!
BEEP
BEEP
BEEP
BEEP
THAT COULD BE *ANYBODY*.
IT COULD BE, YEAH.
ガタ
LUCKY FOR YOU, I'VE BEEN MORE THAN A LITTLE UNEMPLOYED.
CLATTER
HOW DO YOU MEAN?
ピッ
LUCKY FOR YOU, MRS HUDSON AND I WATCH FAR TOO MUCH TELLY.
THANK YOU, TYRA! DOESN'T SHE LOOK LOVELY EVERY-BODY... NOW ANYWAY...
!
RRRRRRRRR

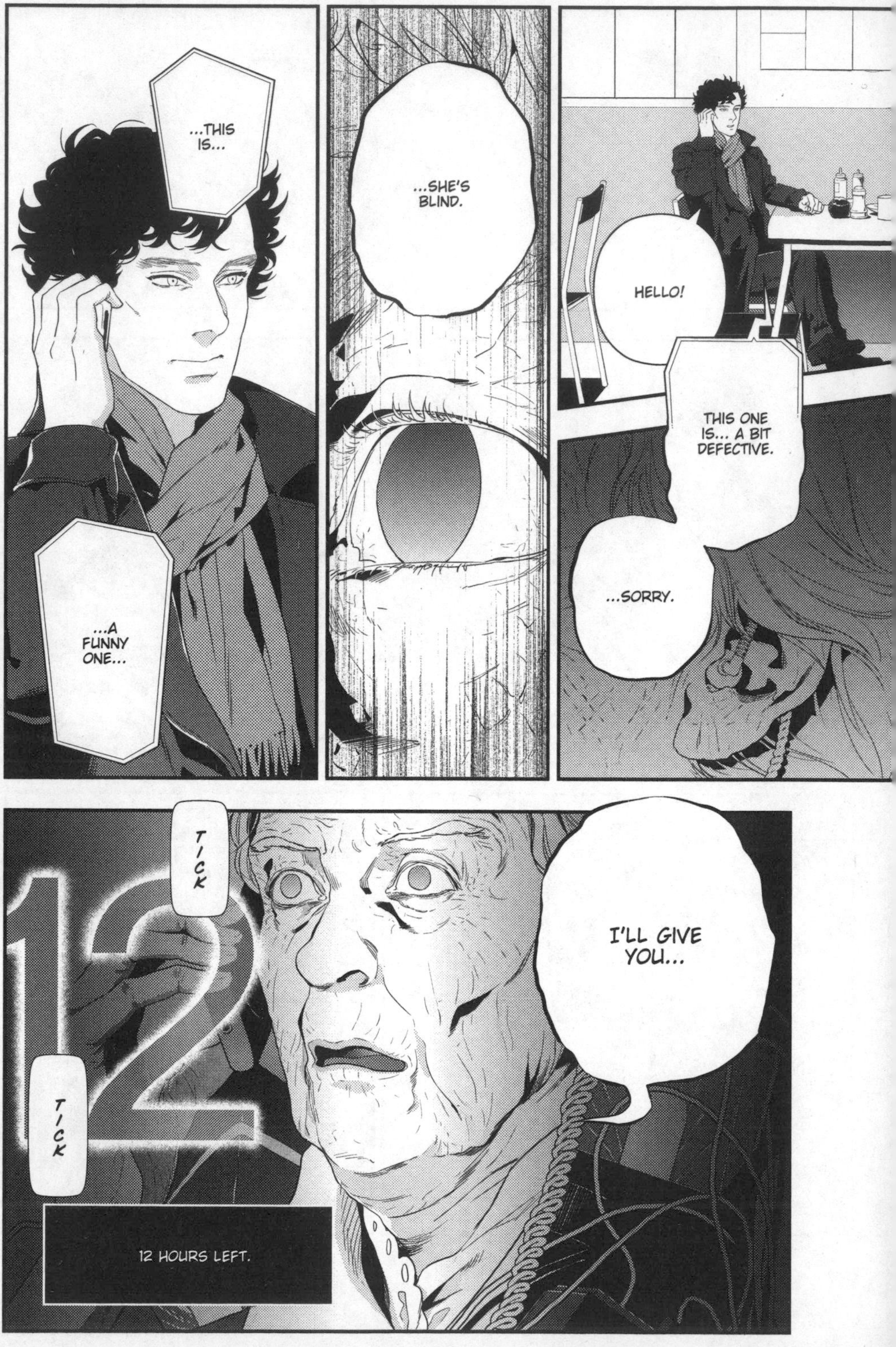
HELLO!
THIS ONE IS... A BIT DEFECTIVE.
...SORRY.
...SHE'S BLIND.
...THIS IS...
...A FUNNY ONE...
I'LL GIVE YOU...
TICK
12
TICK
12 HOURS LEFT.

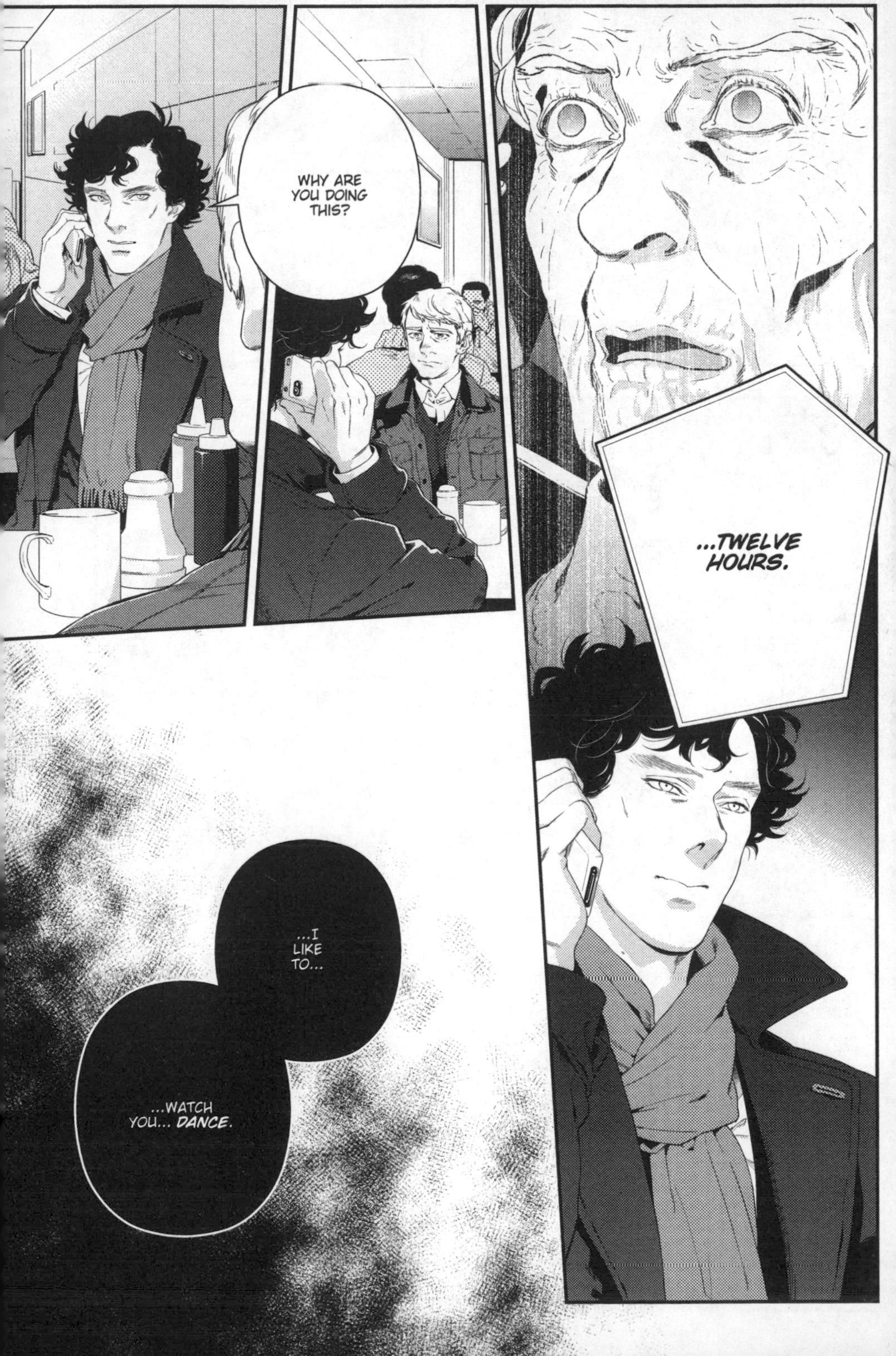
...TWELVE HOURS.
WHY ARE YOU DOING THIS?
...I LIKE TO...
...WATCH YOU... *DANCE*.

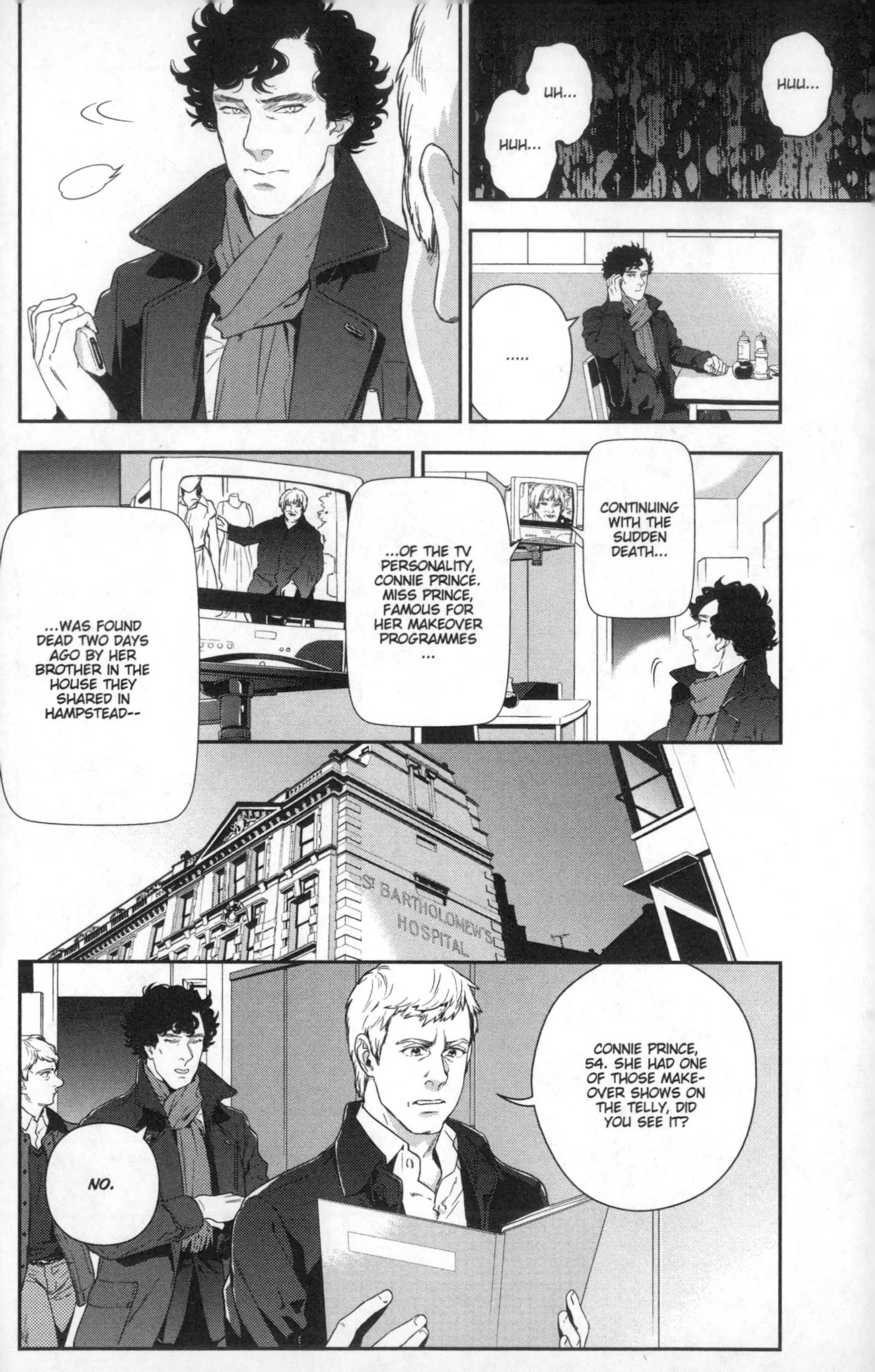
HUU...
UH...
HUH...
.....
CONTINUING WITH THE SUDDEN DEATH...
...OF THE TV PERSONALITY, CONNIE PRINCE. MISS PRINCE, FAMOUS FOR HER MAKEOVER PROGRAMMES ...
...WAS FOUND DEAD TWO DAYS AGO BY HER BROTHER IN THE HOUSE THEY SHARED IN HAMPSTEAD--
ST BARTHOLOMEW'S HOSPITAL
CONNIE PRINCE, 54. SHE HAD ONE OF THOSE MAKE-OVER SHOWS ON THE TELLY, DID YOU SEE IT?
NO.

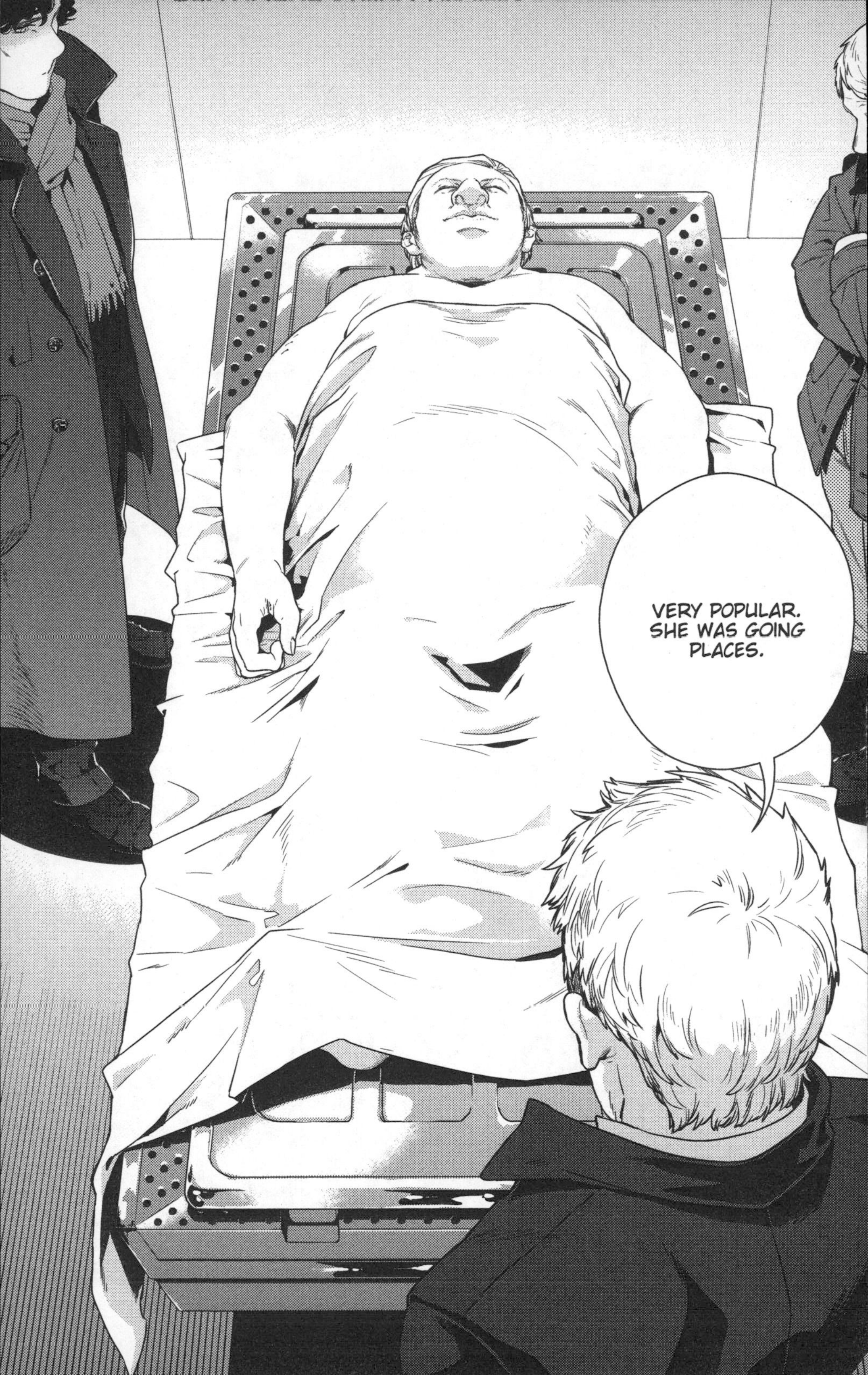
VERY POPULAR. SHE WAS GOING PLACES.

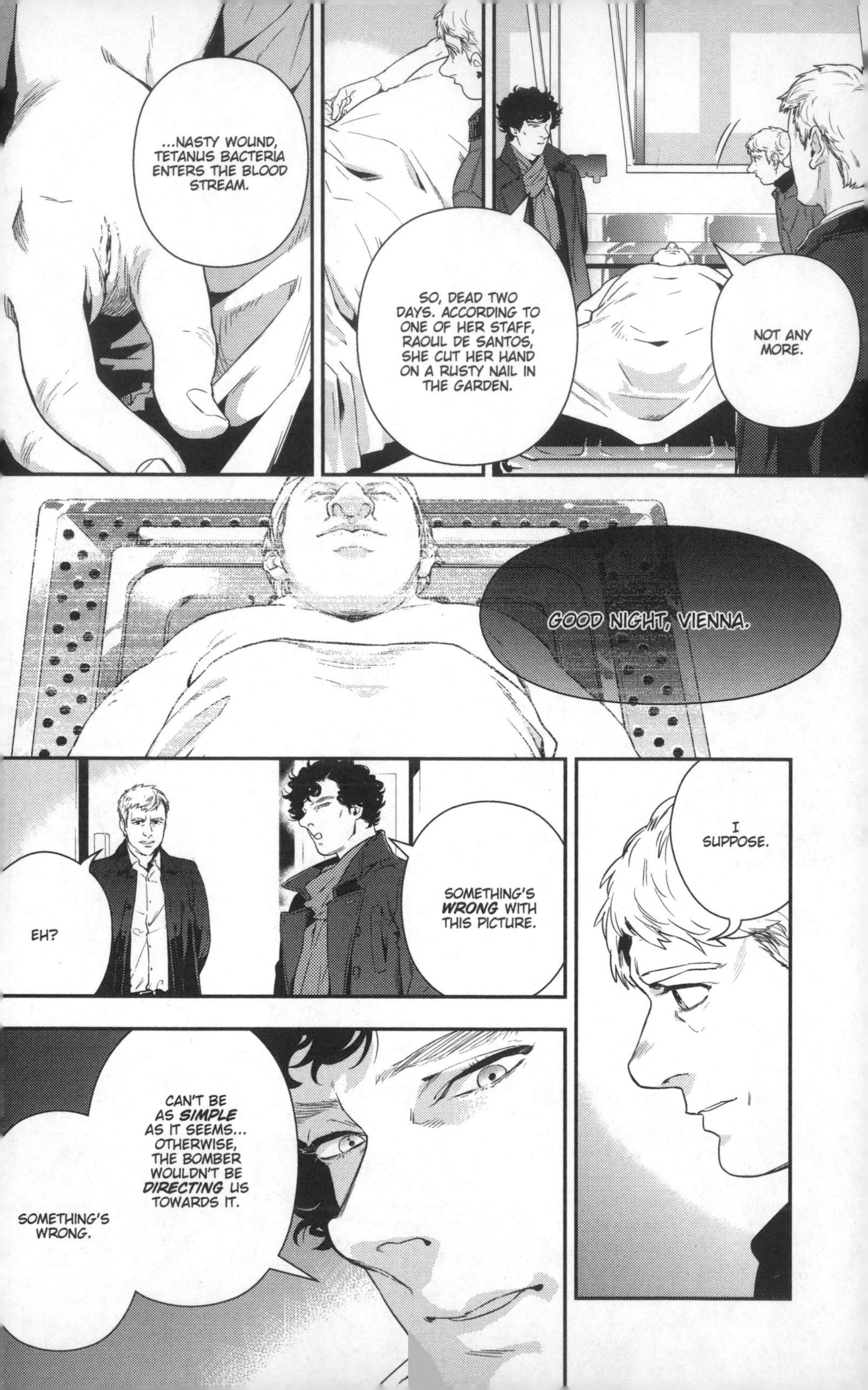
NOT ANY MORE.
SO, DEAD TWO DAYS. ACCORDING TO ONE OF HER STAFF, RAOUL DE SANTOS, SHE CUT HER HAND ON A RUSTY NAIL IN THE GARDEN.
...NASTY WOUND, TETANUS BACTERIA ENTERS THE BLOOD STREAM.
GOOD NIGHT, VIENNA.
I SUPPOSE.
SOMETHING'S **WRONG** WITH THIS PICTURE.
EH?
CAN'T BE AS **SIMPLE** AS IT SEEMS... OTHERWISE, THE BOMBER WOULDN'T BE **DIRECTING** US TOWARDS IT.
SOMETHING'S WRONG.

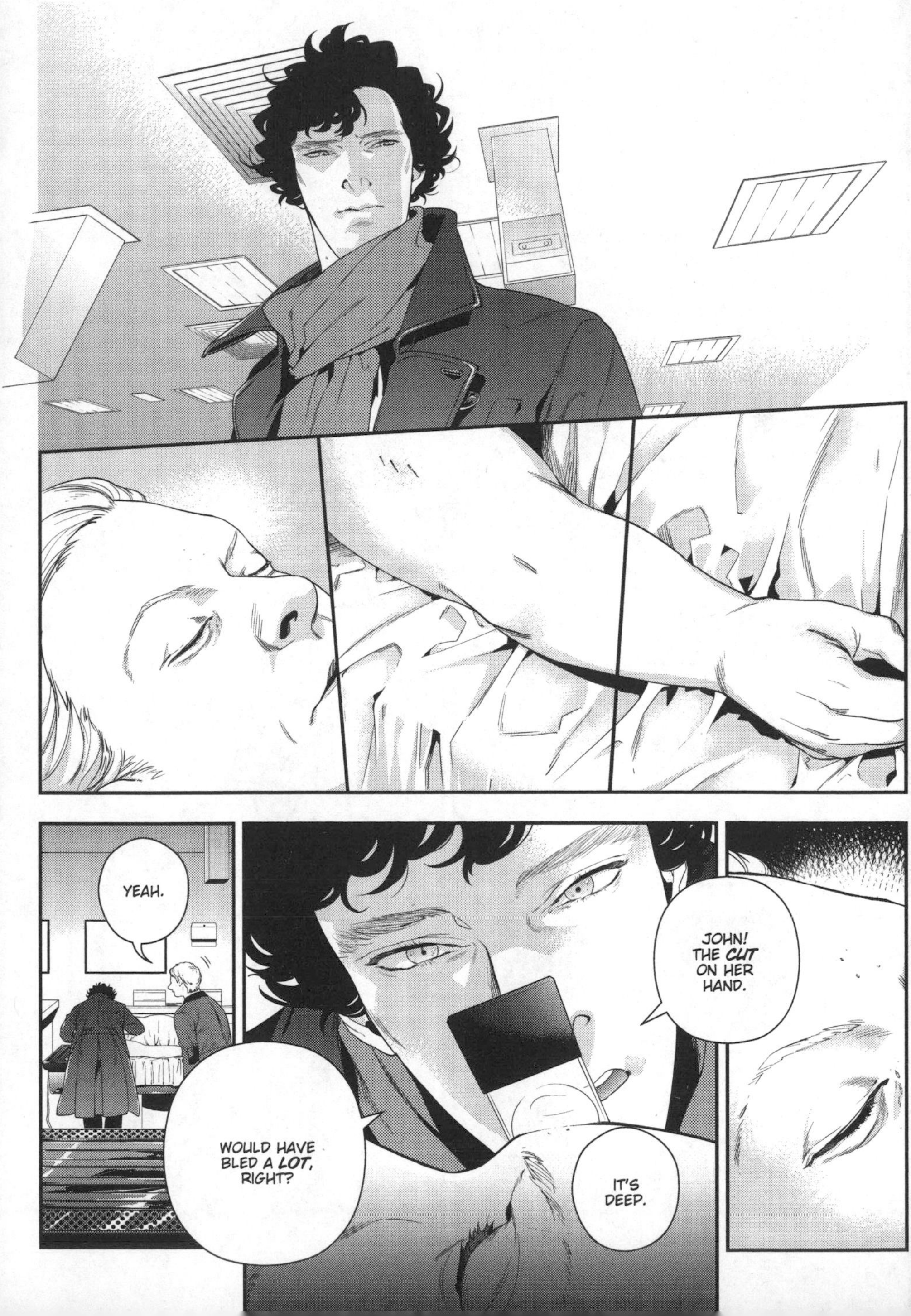
JOHN! THE *CUT* ON HER HAND.
IT'S DEEP.
WOULD HAVE BLED A *LOT*, RIGHT?
YEAH.

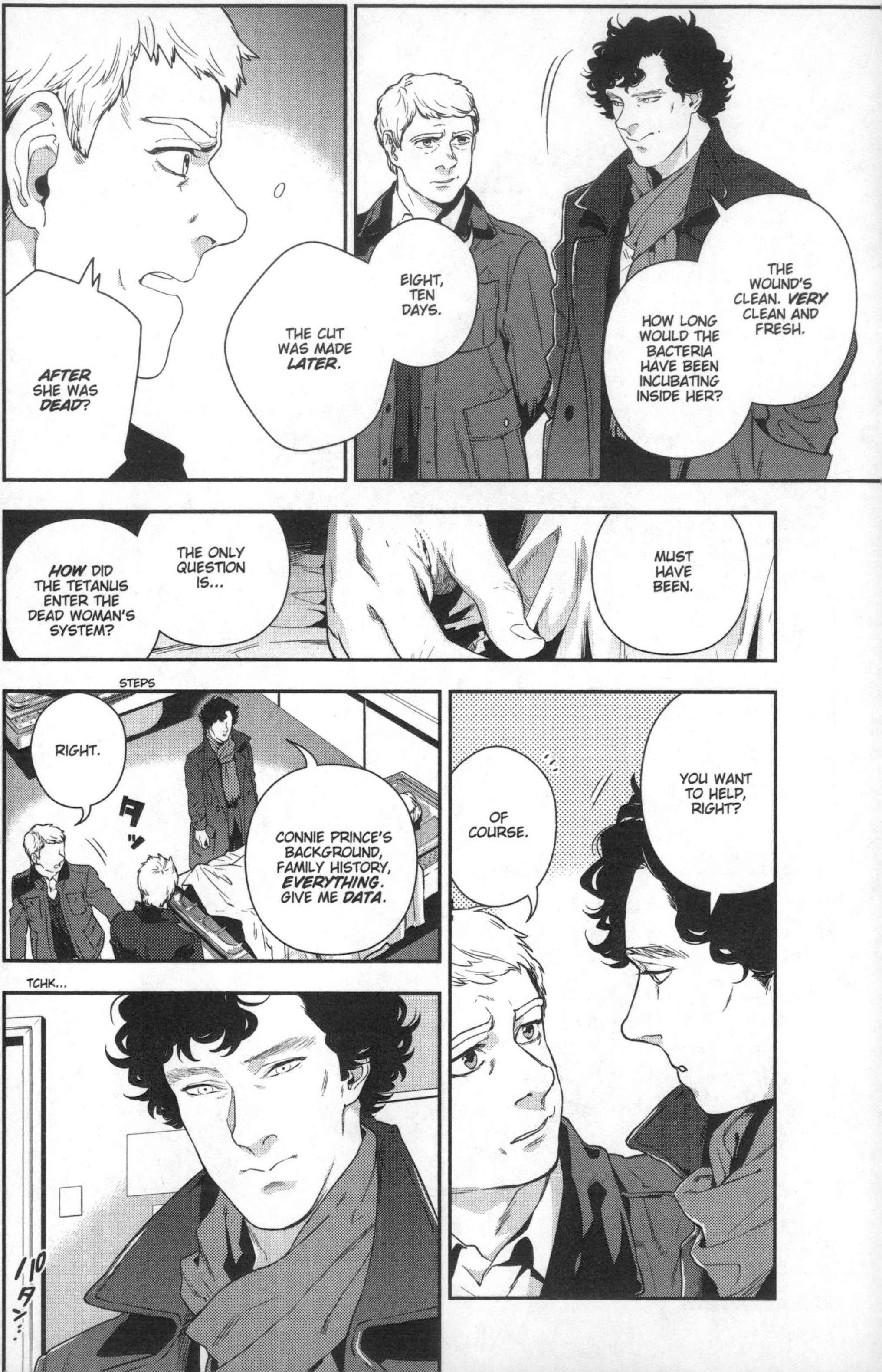
THE WOUND'S CLEAN. VERY CLEAN AND FRESH.
HOW LONG WOULD THE BACTERIA HAVE BEEN INCUBATING INSIDE HER?
EIGHT, TEN DAYS.
THE CUT WAS MADE LATER.
AFTER SHE WAS DEAD?
MUST HAVE BEEN.
THE ONLY QUESTION IS...
HOW DID THE TETANUS ENTER THE DEAD WOMAN'S SYSTEM?
YOU WANT TO HELP, RIGHT?
OF COURSE.
STEPS
タッ
CONNIE PRINCE'S BACKGROUND, FAMILY HISTORY, EVERYTHING. GIVE ME DATA.
RIGHT.
TCHK...

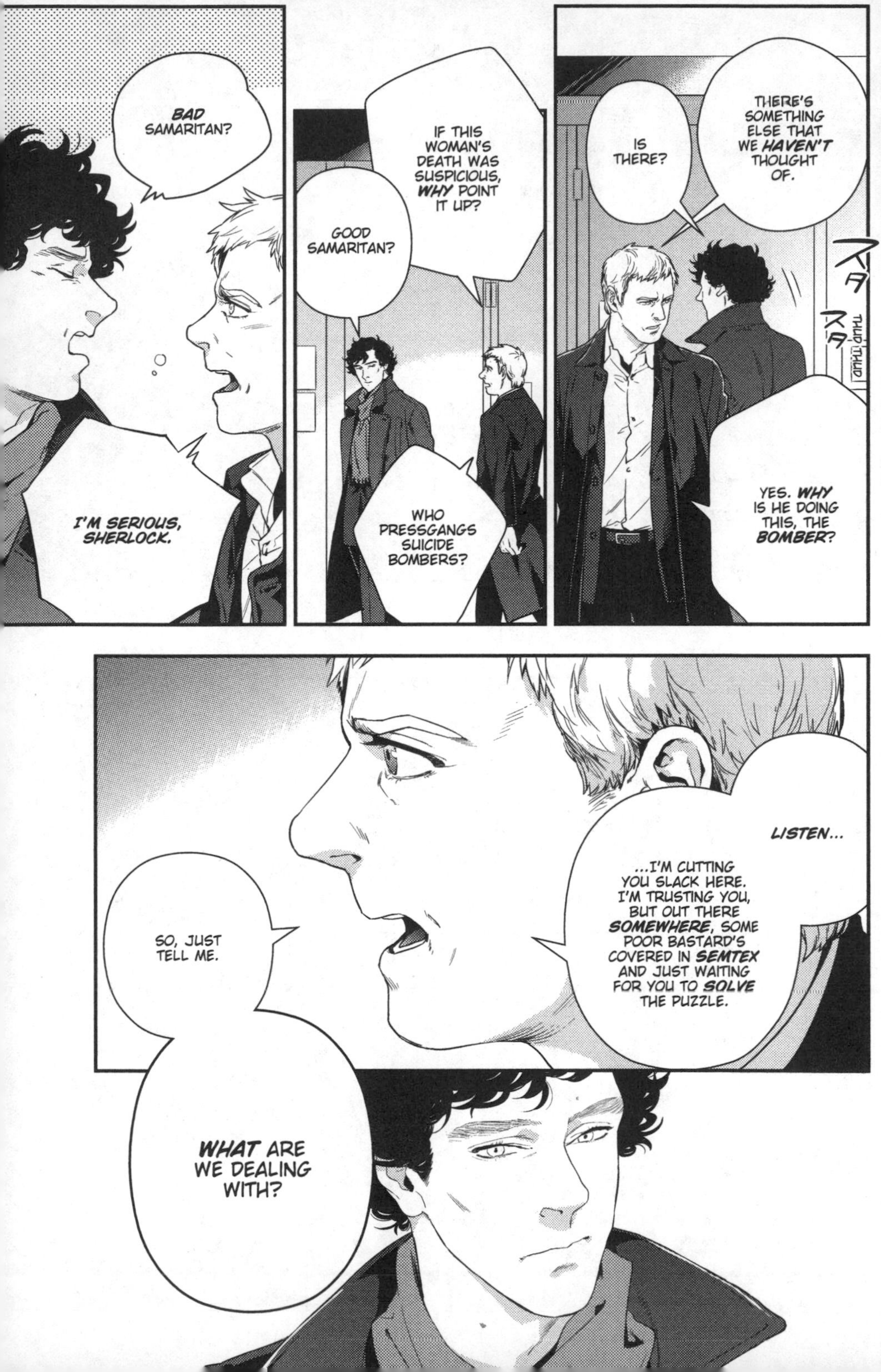
THERE'S SOMETHING ELSE THAT WE *HAVEN'T* THOUGHT OF.
IS THERE?
スタ スタ
THUD THUD
YES. *WHY* IS HE DOING THIS, THE *BOMBER*?
IF THIS WOMAN'S DEATH WAS SUSPICIOUS, *WHY* POINT IT UP?
GOOD SAMARITAN?
WHO PRESSGANGS SUICIDE BOMBERS?
BAD SAMARITAN?
I'M SERIOUS, SHERLOCK.
LISTEN...
...I'M CUTTING YOU SLACK HERE. I'M TRUSTING YOU, BUT OUT THERE *SOMEWHERE*, SOME POOR BASTARD'S COVERED IN *SEMTEX* AND JUST WAITING FOR YOU TO *SOLVE* THE PUZZLE.
SO, JUST TELL ME.
WHAT ARE WE DEALING WITH?

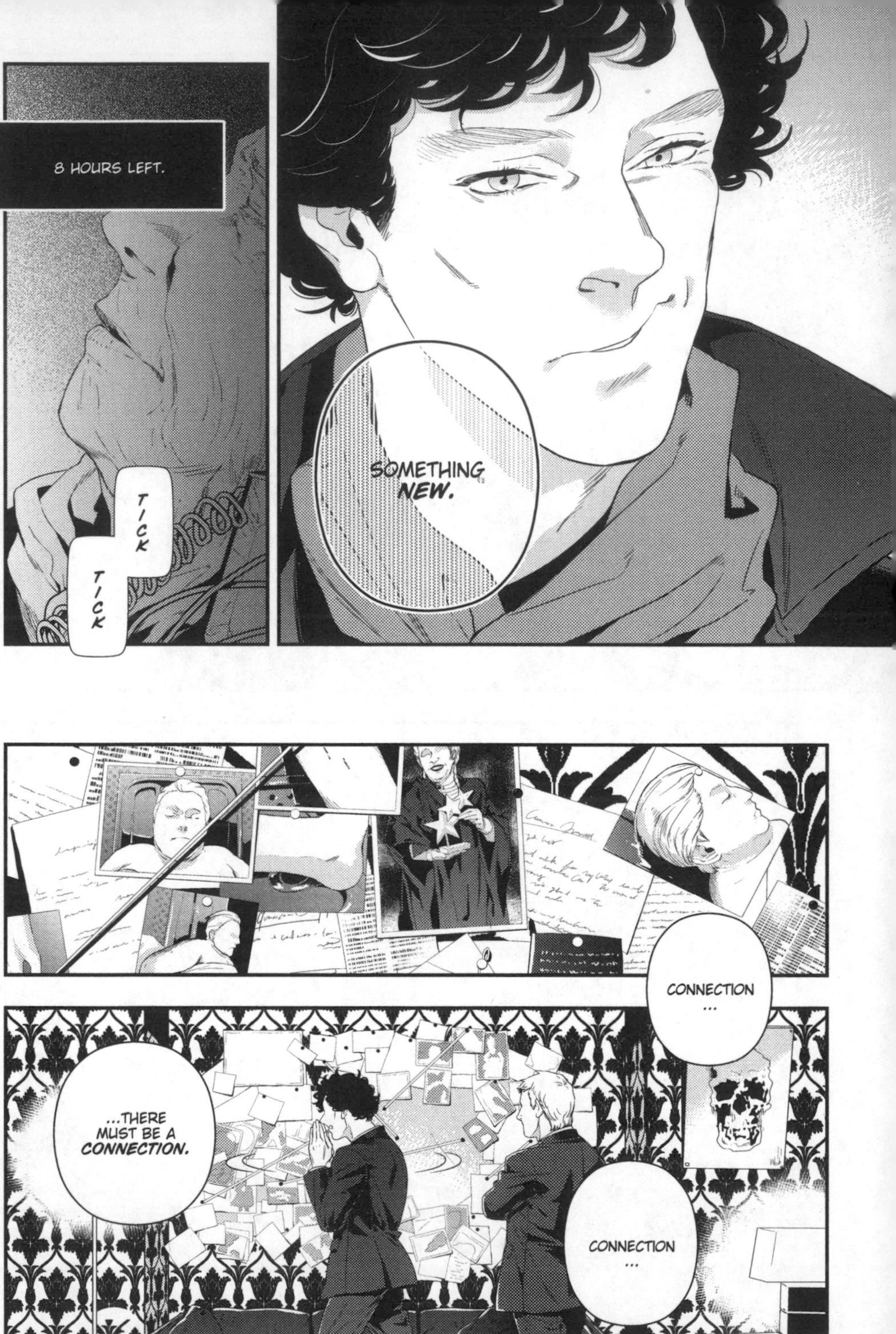
SOMETHING NEW.
8 HOURS LEFT.
TICK
TICK
CONNECTION ...
CONNECTION ...
...THERE MUST BE A CONNECTION.

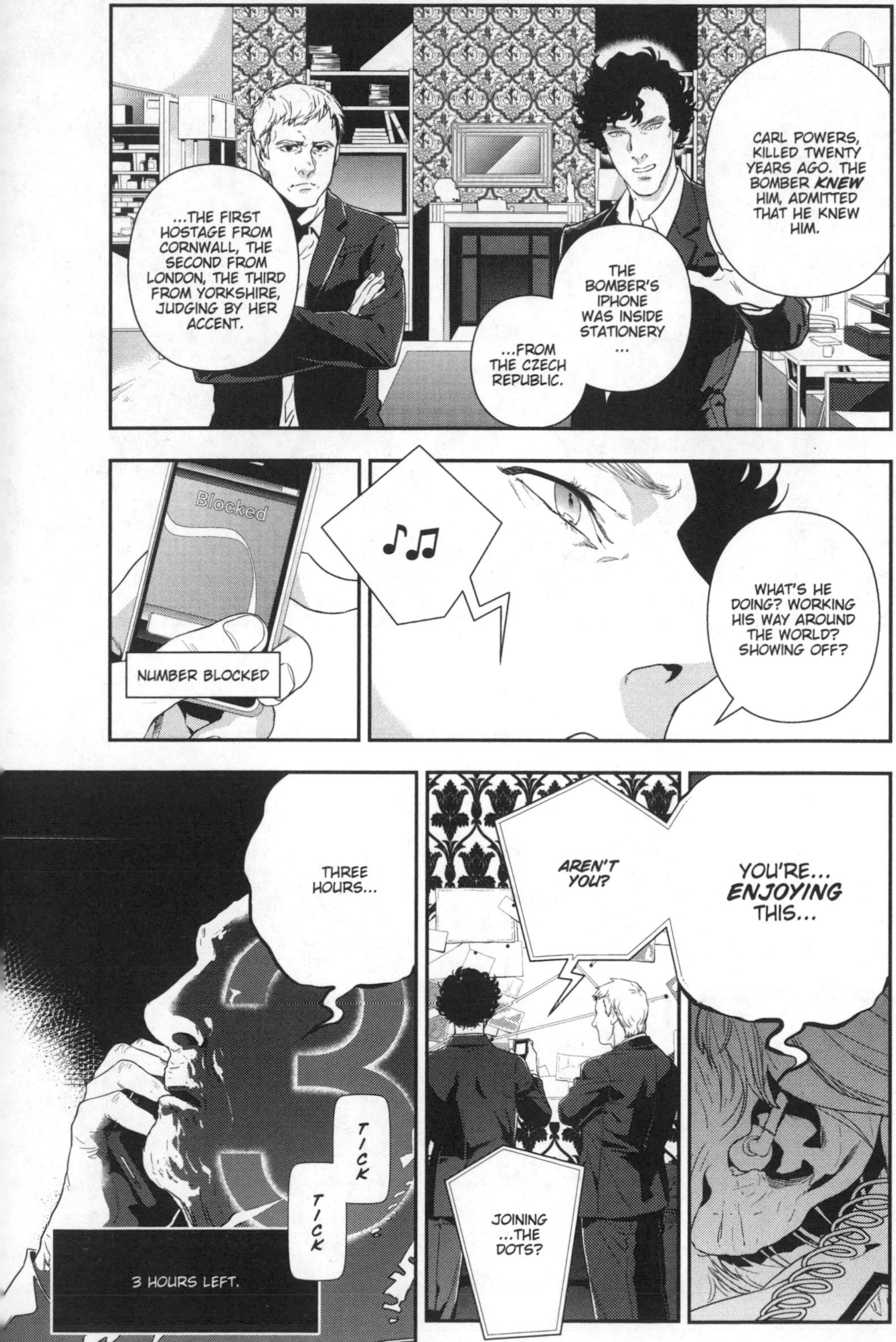
CARL POWERS, KILLED TWENTY YEARS AGO. THE BOMBER *KNEW* HIM, ADMITTED THAT HE KNEW HIM.
THE BOMBER'S IPHONE WAS INSIDE STATIONERY ...
...FROM THE CZECH REPUBLIC.
...THE FIRST HOSTAGE FROM CORNWALL, THE SECOND FROM LONDON, THE THIRD FROM YORKSHIRE, JUDGING BY HER ACCENT.
♪♫
WHAT'S HE DOING? WORKING HIS WAY AROUND THE WORLD? SHOWING OFF?
Blocked
NUMBER BLOCKED
YOU'RE... *ENJOYING* THIS...
AREN'T YOU?
JOINING ...THE DOTS?
THREE HOURS...
TICK
TICK
3 HOURS LEFT.

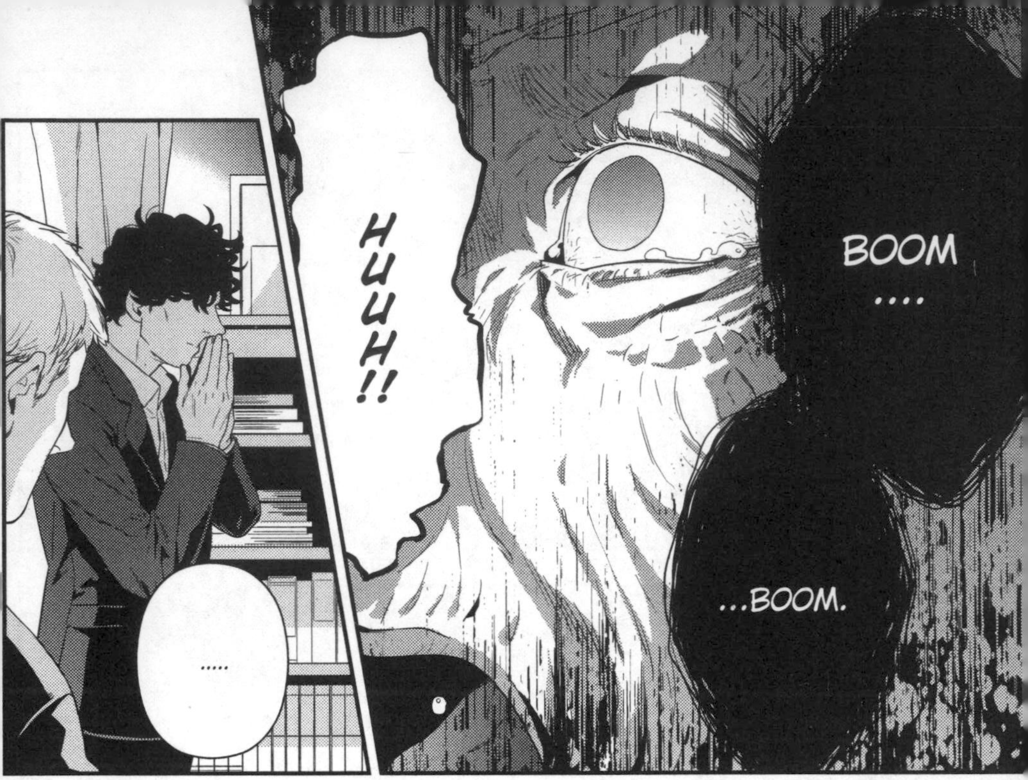
BOOM ....
HUUH!!
...BOOM.
.....

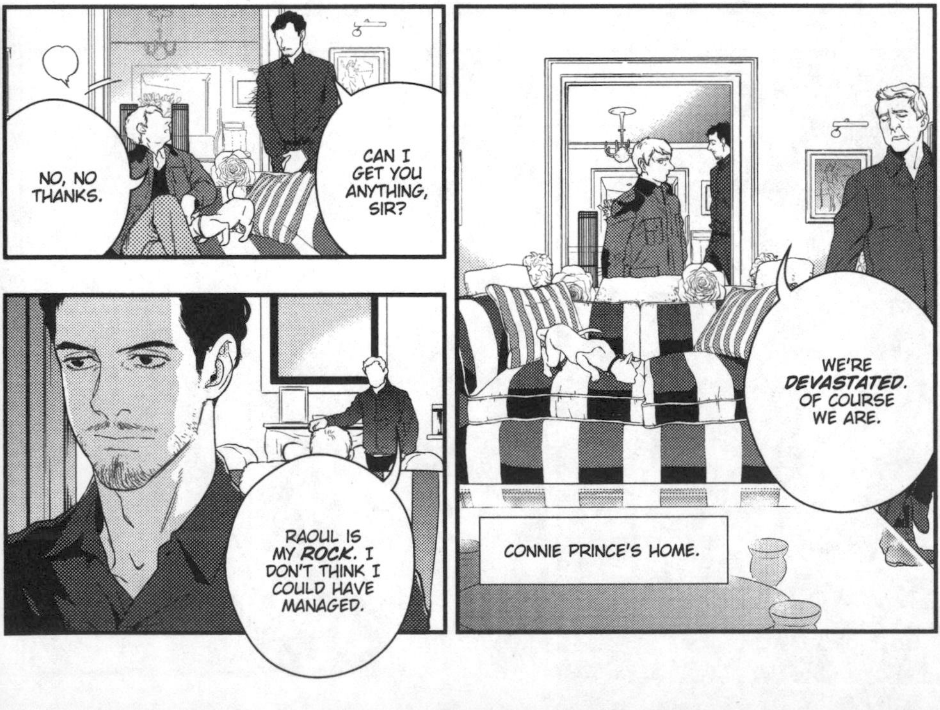
WE'RE *DEVASTATED*. OF COURSE WE ARE.
CONNIE PRINCE'S HOME.
CAN I GET YOU ANYTHING, SIR?
NO, NO THANKS.
RAOUL IS MY *ROCK*. I DON'T THINK I COULD HAVE MANAGED.

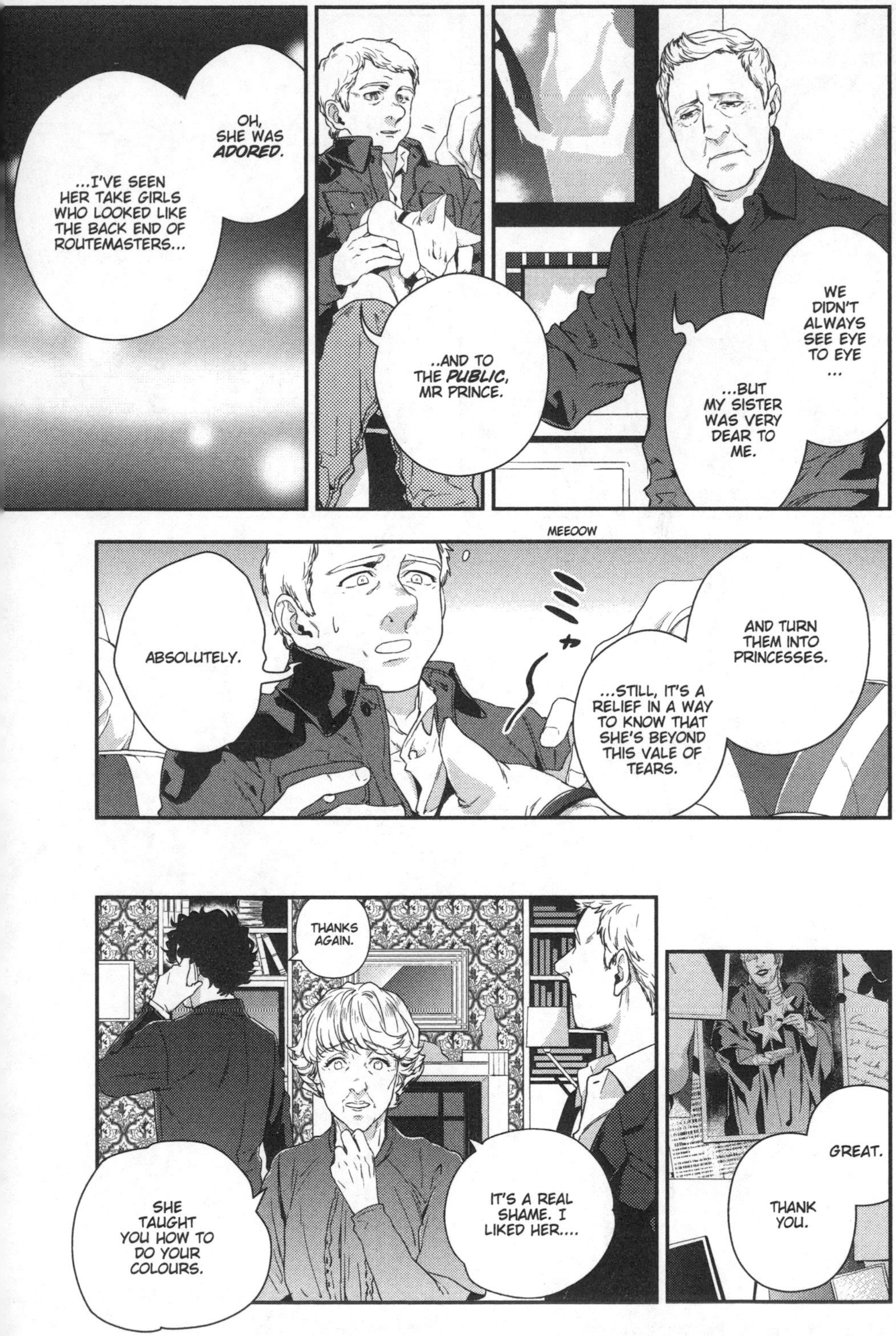
WE DIDN'T ALWAYS SEE EYE TO EYE ...
...BUT MY SISTER WAS VERY DEAR TO ME.
..AND TO THE *PUBLIC*, MR PRINCE.
OH, SHE WAS *ADORED*.
...I'VE SEEN HER TAKE GIRLS WHO LOOKED LIKE THE BACK END OF ROUTEMASTERS...
MEEOOW
AND TURN THEM INTO PRINCESSES.
...STILL, IT'S A RELIEF IN A WAY TO KNOW THAT SHE'S BEYOND THIS VALE OF TEARS.
ABSOLUTELY.
GREAT.
THANK YOU.
THANKS AGAIN.
IT'S A REAL SHAME. I LIKED HER....
SHE TAUGHT YOU HOW TO DO YOUR COLOURS.

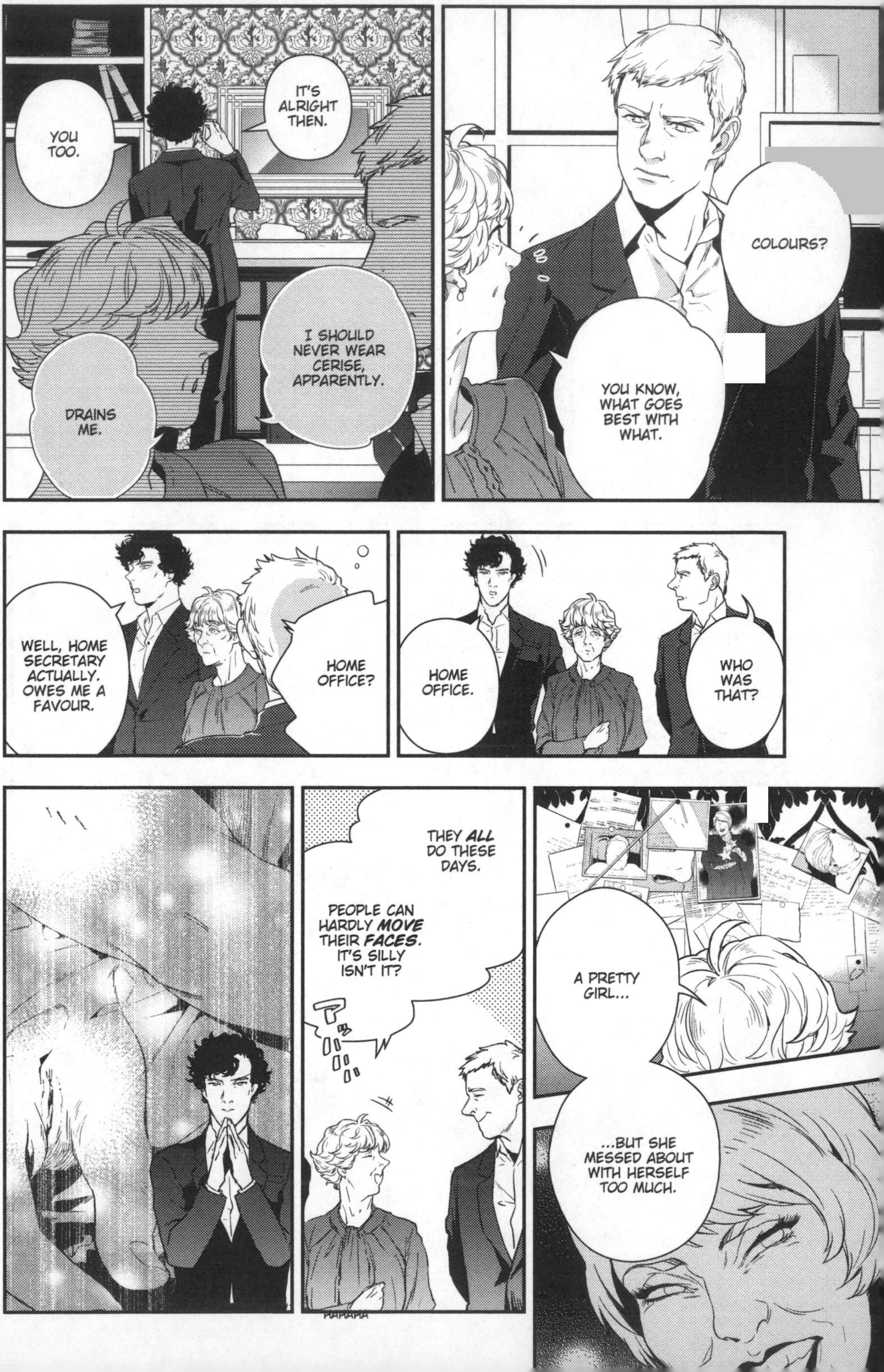
COLOURS?
YOU KNOW, WHAT GOES BEST WITH WHAT.
IT'S ALRIGHT THEN.
YOU TOO.
I SHOULD NEVER WEAR CERISE, APPARENTLY.
DRAINS ME.
WHO WAS THAT?
HOME OFFICE.
HOME OFFICE?
WELL, HOME SECRETARY ACTUALLY. OWES ME A FAVOUR.
A PRETTY GIRL...
...BUT SHE MESSED ABOUT WITH HERSELF TOO MUCH.
THEY **ALL** DO THESE DAYS.
PEOPLE CAN HARDLY **MOVE** THEIR **FACES**. IT'S SILLY ISN'T IT?
HAHAHA

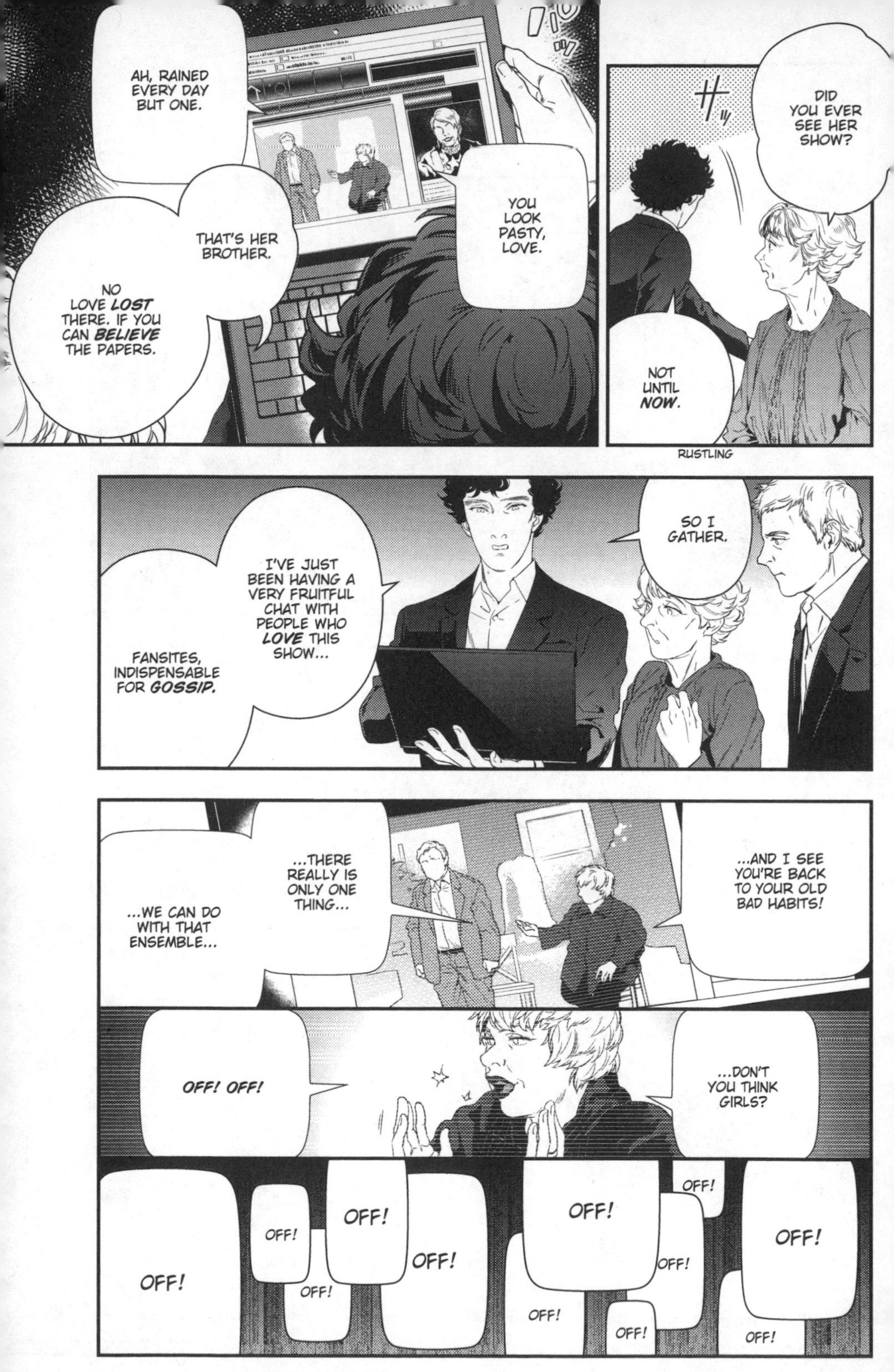
DID YOU EVER SEE HER SHOW?
NOT UNTIL NOW.
RUSTLING
AH, RAINED EVERY DAY BUT ONE.
YOU LOOK PASTY, LOVE.
THAT'S HER BROTHER.
NO LOVE LOST THERE. IF YOU CAN BELIEVE THE PAPERS.
SO I GATHER.
I'VE JUST BEEN HAVING A VERY FRUITFUL CHAT WITH PEOPLE WHO LOVE THIS SHOW...
FANSITES, INDISPENSABLE FOR GOSSIP.
...AND I SEE YOU'RE BACK TO YOUR OLD BAD HABITS!
...THERE REALLY IS ONLY ONE THING...
...WE CAN DO WITH THAT ENSEMBLE...
...DON'T YOU THINK GIRLS?
OFF! OFF!
OFF!
OFF!
OFF!
OFF!
OFF!
OFF!
OFF!
OFF!
OFF!
OFF!
OFF!
OFF!
OFF!
OFF!

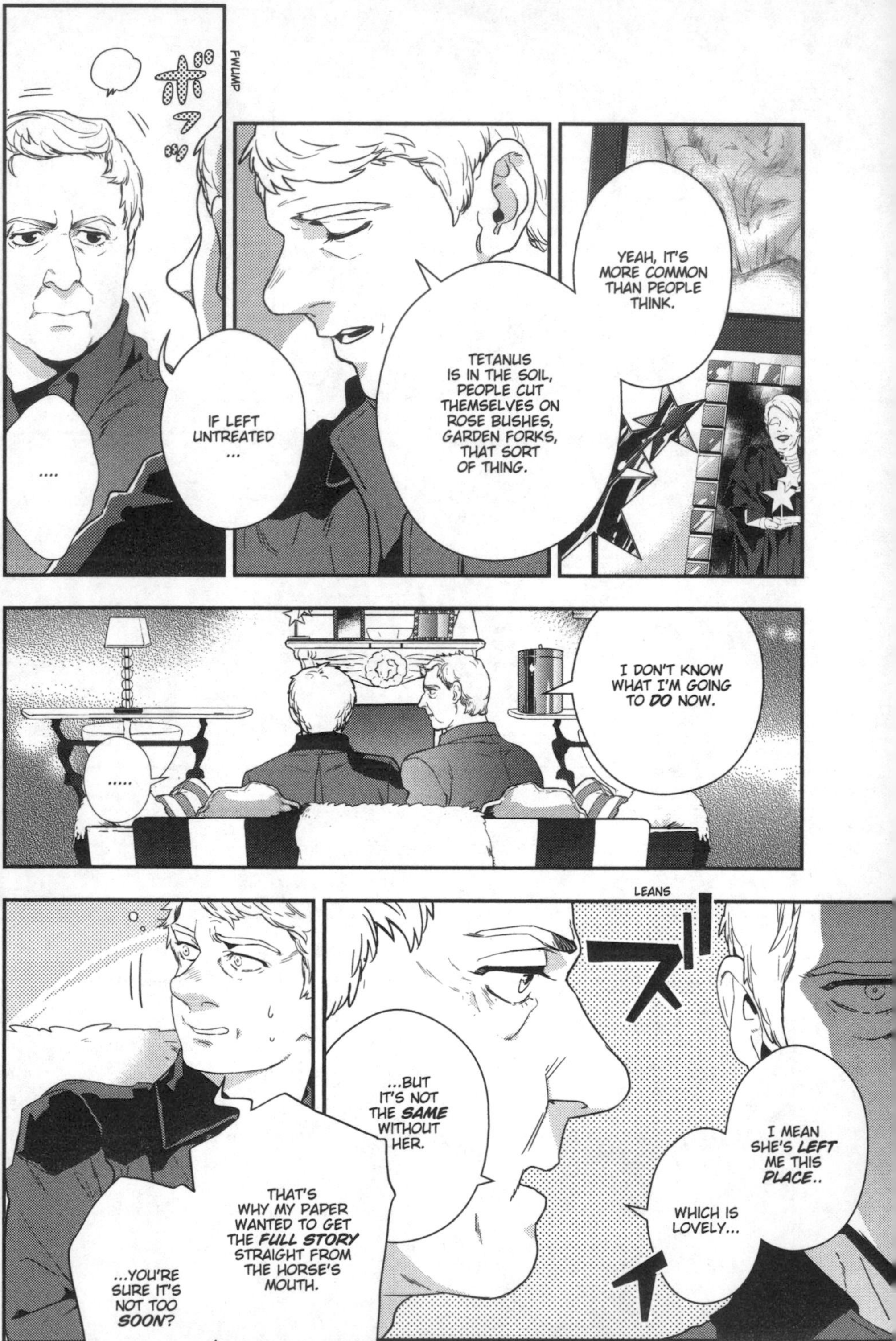
YEAH, IT'S MORE COMMON THAN PEOPLE THINK.
TETANUS IS IN THE SOIL, PEOPLE CUT THEMSELVES ON ROSE BUSHES, GARDEN FORKS, THAT SORT OF THING.
FWUMP
IF LEFT UNTREATED ...
....
I DON'T KNOW WHAT I'M GOING TO **DO** NOW.
.....
LEANS
I MEAN SHE'S **LEFT** ME THIS **PLACE**..
WHICH IS LOVELY...
...BUT IT'S NOT THE **SAME** WITHOUT HER.
THAT'S WHY MY PAPER WANTED TO GET THE **FULL STORY** STRAIGHT FROM THE HORSE'S MOUTH.
...YOU'RE SURE IT'S NOT TOO **SOON**?

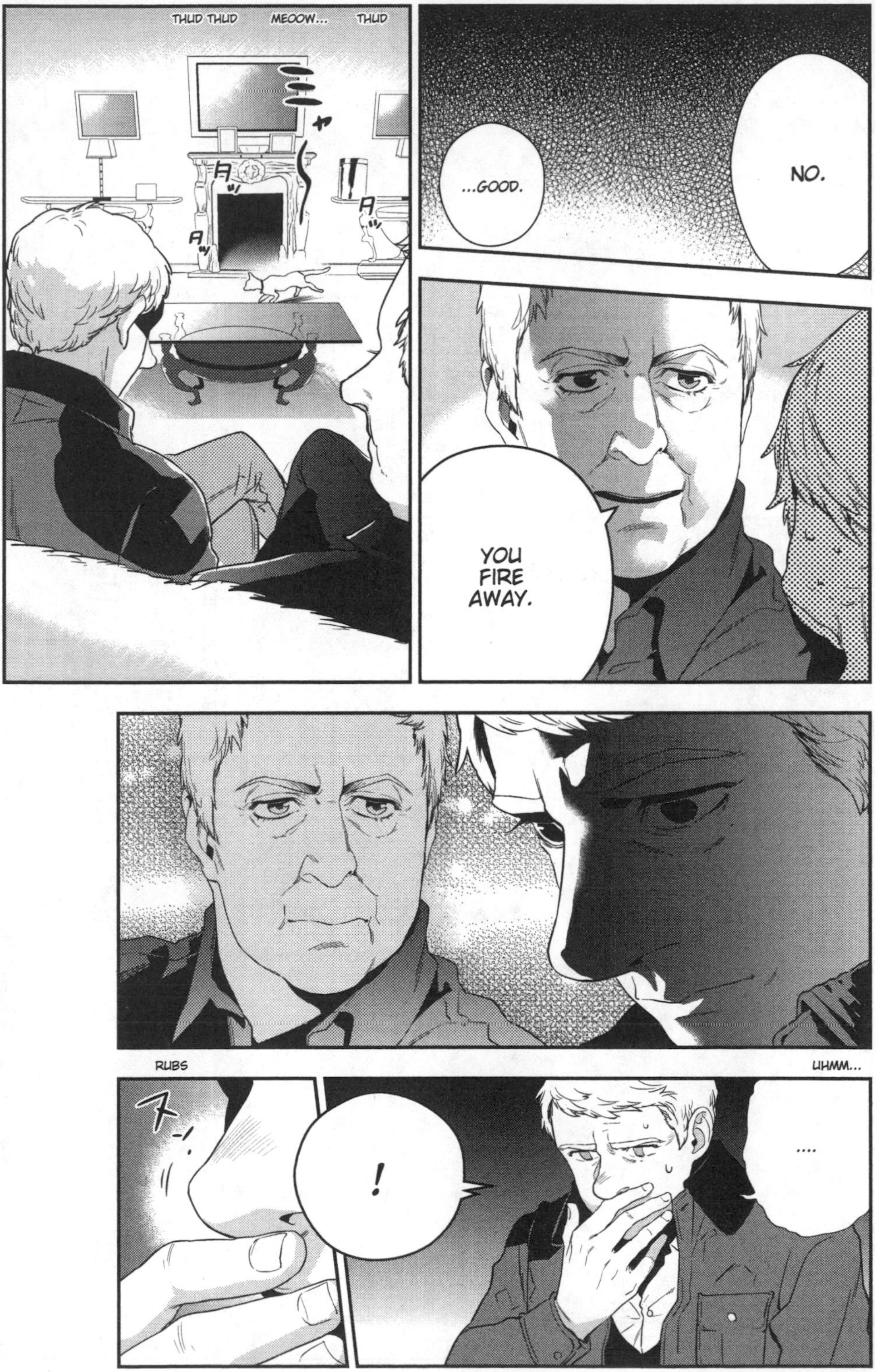
NO.
...GOOD.
YOU FIRE AWAY.
THUD THUD
MEOOW...
THUD
UHMM...
....
!
RUBS

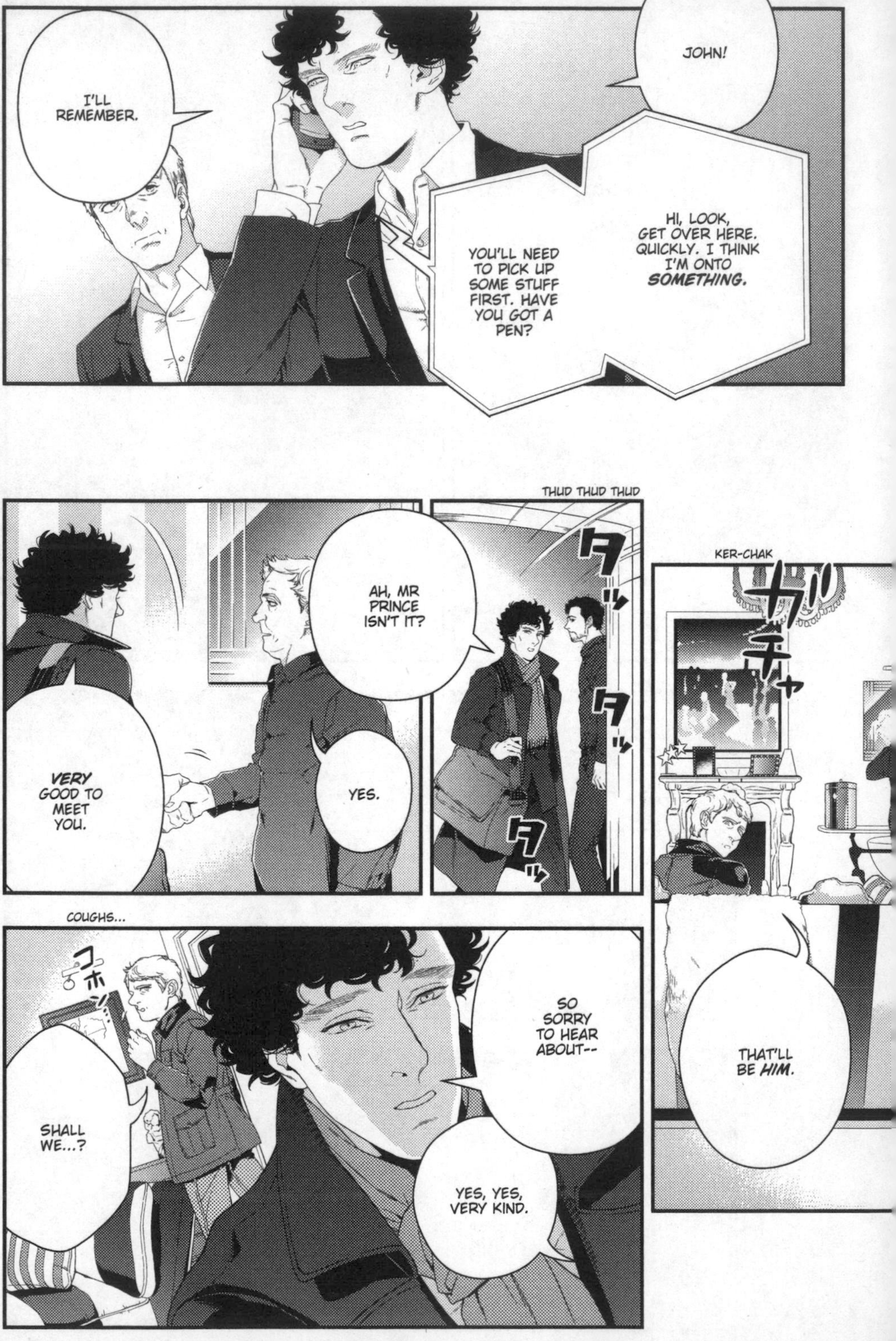
JOHN!
HI, LOOK, GET OVER HERE. QUICKLY. I THINK I'M ONTO *SOMETHING.*
YOU'LL NEED TO PICK UP SOME STUFF FIRST. HAVE YOU GOT A PEN?
I'LL REMEMBER.
KER-CHAK
THAT'LL BE *HIM*.
THUD THUD THUD
AH, MR PRINCE ISN'T IT?
YES.
VERY GOOD TO MEET YOU.
COUGHS...
SO SORRY TO HEAR ABOUT--
YES, YES, VERY KIND.
SHALL WE...?

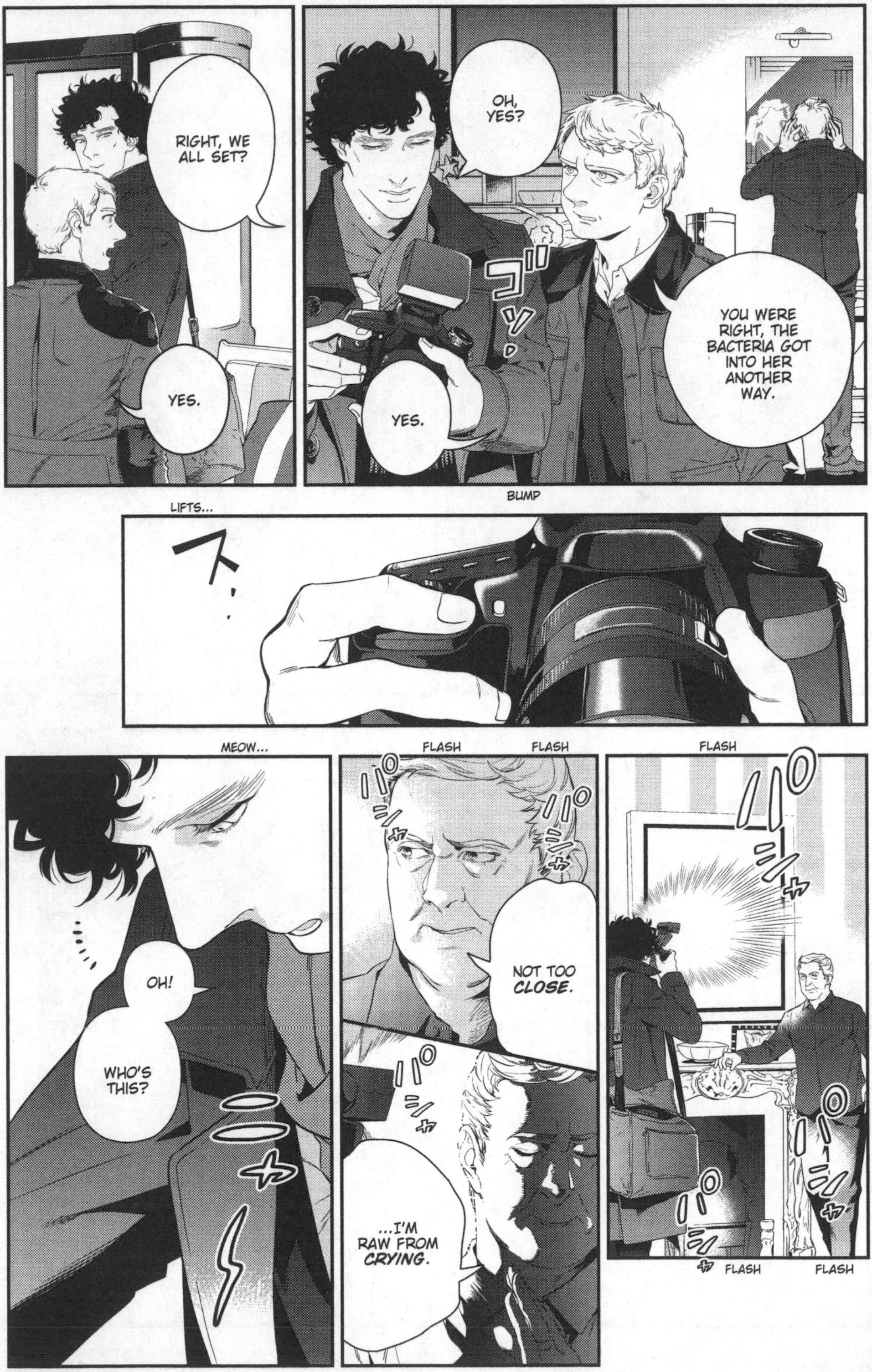
YOU WERE RIGHT, THE BACTERIA GOT INTO HER ANOTHER WAY.
OH, YES?
YES.
BUMP
RIGHT, WE ALL SET?
YES.
LIFTS...
FLASH
FLASH
FLASH
FLASH
FLASH
NOT TOO CLOSE.
...I'M RAW FROM CRYING.
MEOW...
OH!
WHO'S THIS?

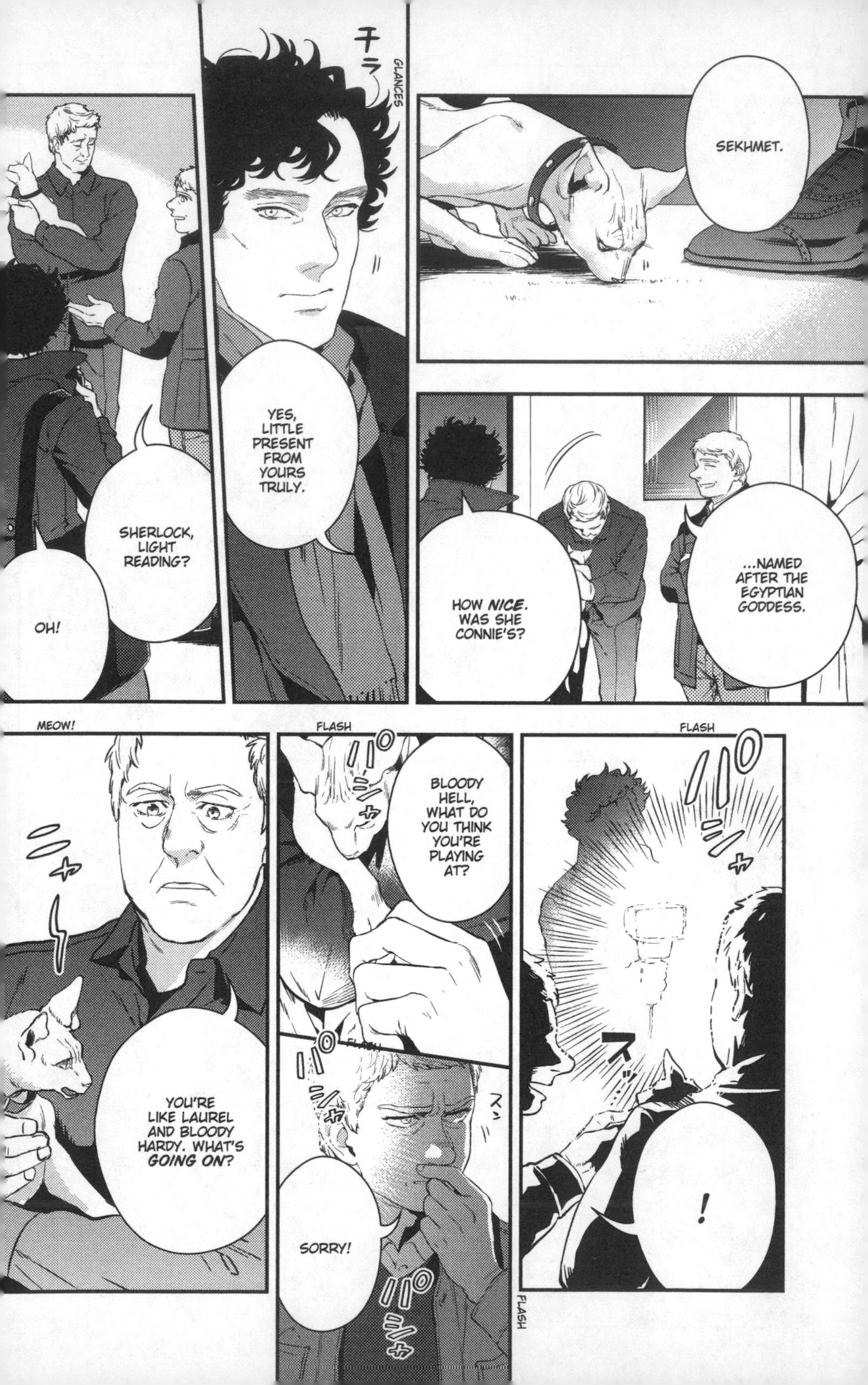
SEKHMET.
...NAMED AFTER THE EGYPTIAN GODDESS.
HOW NICE. WAS SHE CONNIE'S?
GLANCES
YES, LITTLE PRESENT FROM YOURS TRULY.
SHERLOCK, LIGHT READING?
OH!
FLASH
!
FLASH
BLOODY HELL, WHAT DO YOU THINK YOU'RE PLAYING AT?
SORRY!
FLASH
MEOW!
YOU'RE LIKE LAUREL AND BLOODY HARDY. WHAT'S *GOING ON*?

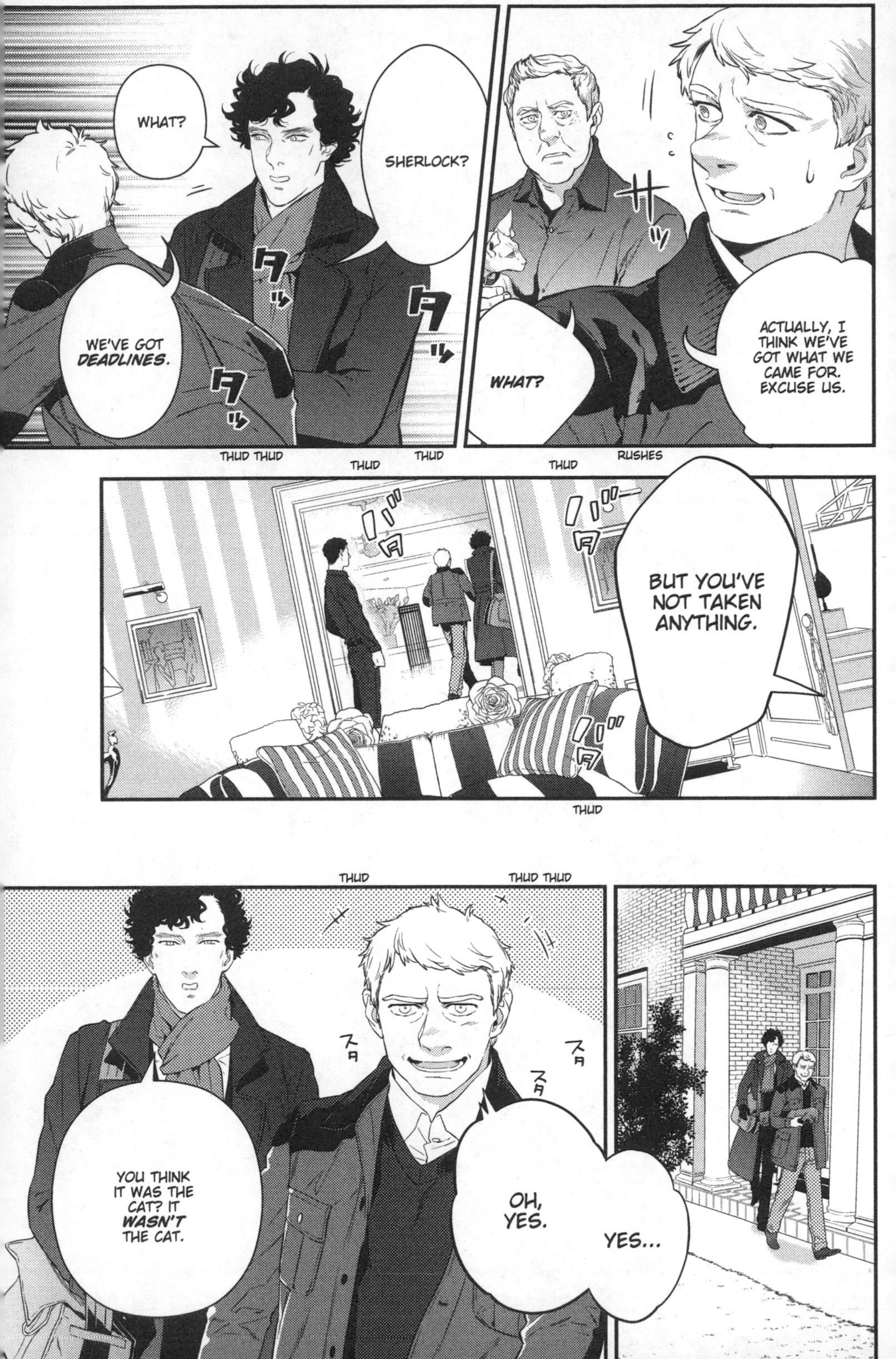
ACTUALLY, I THINK WE'VE GOT WHAT WE CAME FOR. EXCUSE US.
WHAT?
SHERLOCK?
WHAT?
WE'VE GOT DEADLINES.
RUSHES
THUD
THUD
THUD
THUD THUD
BUT YOU'VE NOT TAKEN ANYTHING.
THUD
THUD THUD
THUD
OH, YES.
YES...
YOU THINK IT WAS THE CAT? IT WASN'T THE CAT.

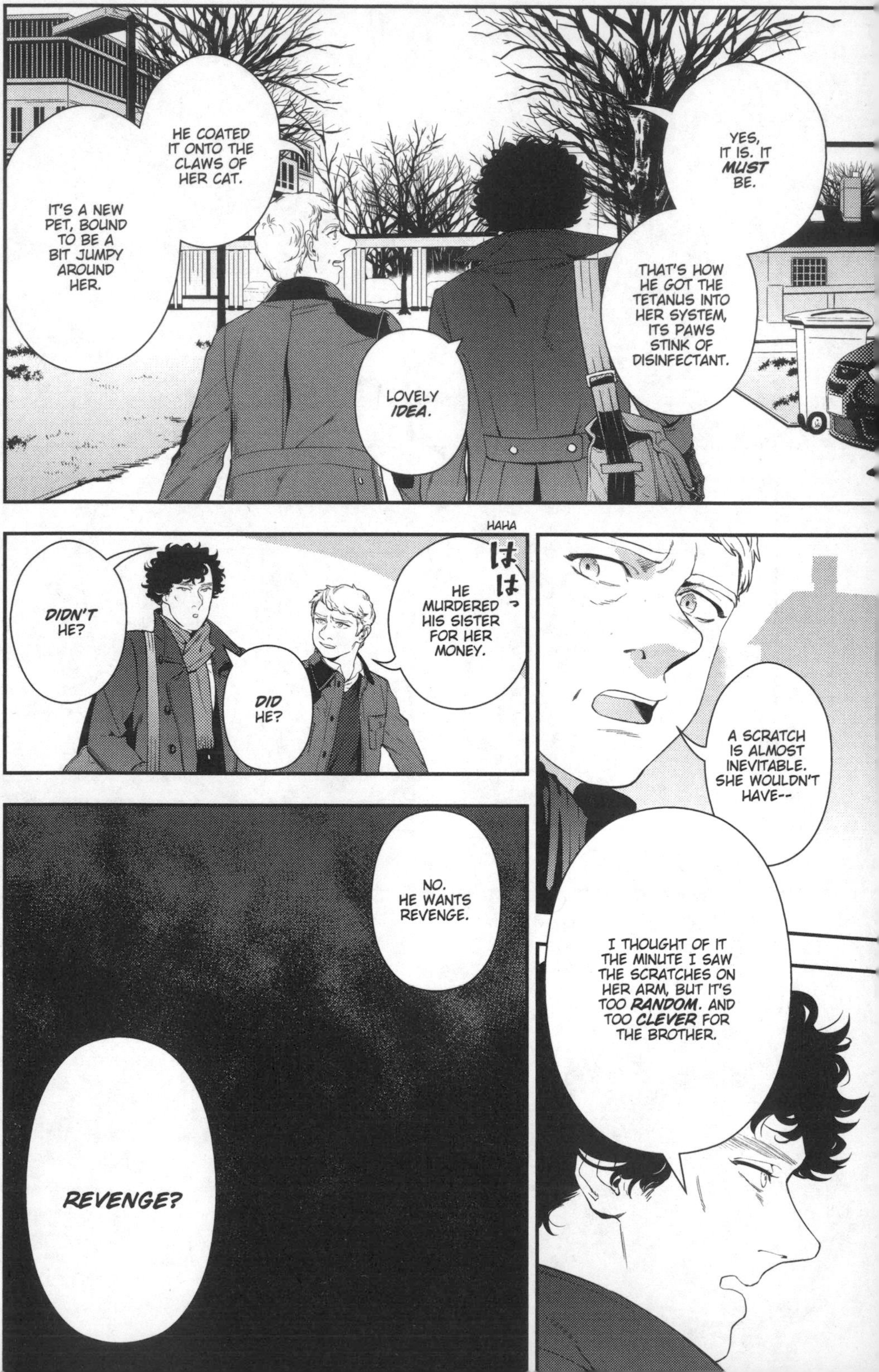
YES, IT IS. IT *MUST* BE.
THAT'S HOW HE GOT THE TETANUS INTO HER SYSTEM, ITS PAWS STINK OF DISINFECTANT.
HE COATED IT ONTO THE CLAWS OF HER CAT.
LOVELY *IDEA*.
IT'S A NEW PET, BOUND TO BE A BIT JUMPY AROUND HER.
A SCRATCH IS ALMOST INEVITABLE. SHE WOULDN'T HAVE--
HAHA
はは
HE MURDERED HIS SISTER FOR HER MONEY.
DID HE?
DIDN'T HE?
I THOUGHT OF IT THE MINUTE I SAW THE SCRATCHES ON HER ARM, BUT IT'S TOO ***RANDOM***. AND TOO ***CLEVER*** FOR THE BROTHER.
NO. HE WANTS REVENGE.
REVENGE?

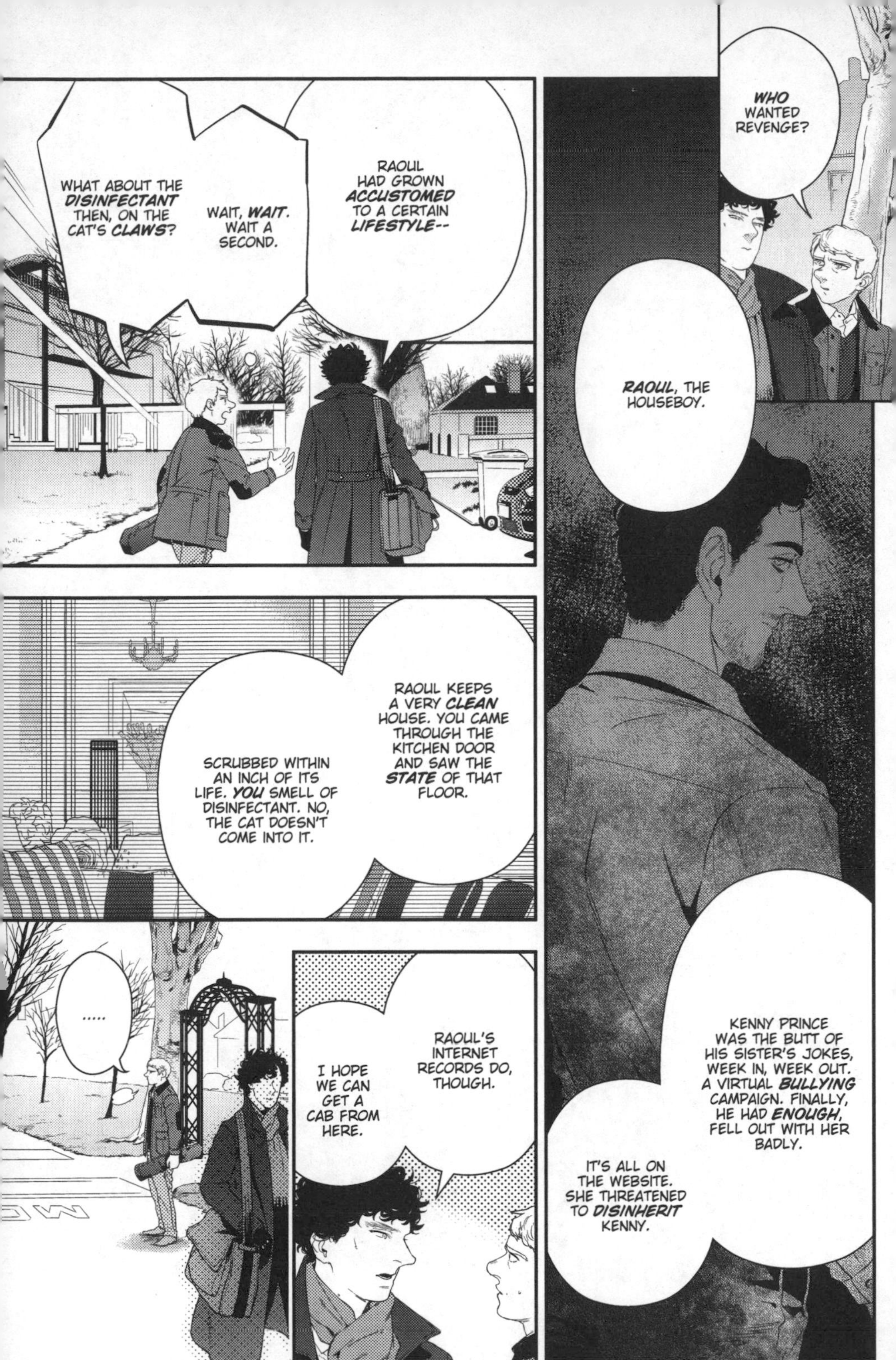
WHO WANTED REVENGE?
RAOUL, THE HOUSEBOY.
KENNY PRINCE WAS THE BUTT OF HIS SISTER'S JOKES, WEEK IN, WEEK OUT. A VIRTUAL BULLYING CAMPAIGN. FINALLY, HE HAD ENOUGH, FELL OUT WITH HER BADLY.
IT'S ALL ON THE WEBSITE. SHE THREATENED TO DISINHERIT KENNY.
RAOUL HAD GROWN ACCUSTOMED TO A CERTAIN LIFESTYLE--
WAIT, WAIT. WAIT A SECOND.
WHAT ABOUT THE DISINFECTANT THEN, ON THE CAT'S CLAWS?
RAOUL KEEPS A VERY CLEAN HOUSE. YOU CAME THROUGH THE KITCHEN DOOR AND SAW THE STATE OF THAT FLOOR.
SCRUBBED WITHIN AN INCH OF ITS LIFE. YOU SMELL OF DISINFECTANT. NO, THE CAT DOESN'T COME INTO IT.
RAOUL'S INTERNET RECORDS DO, THOUGH.
I HOPE WE CAN GET A CAB FROM HERE.
.....

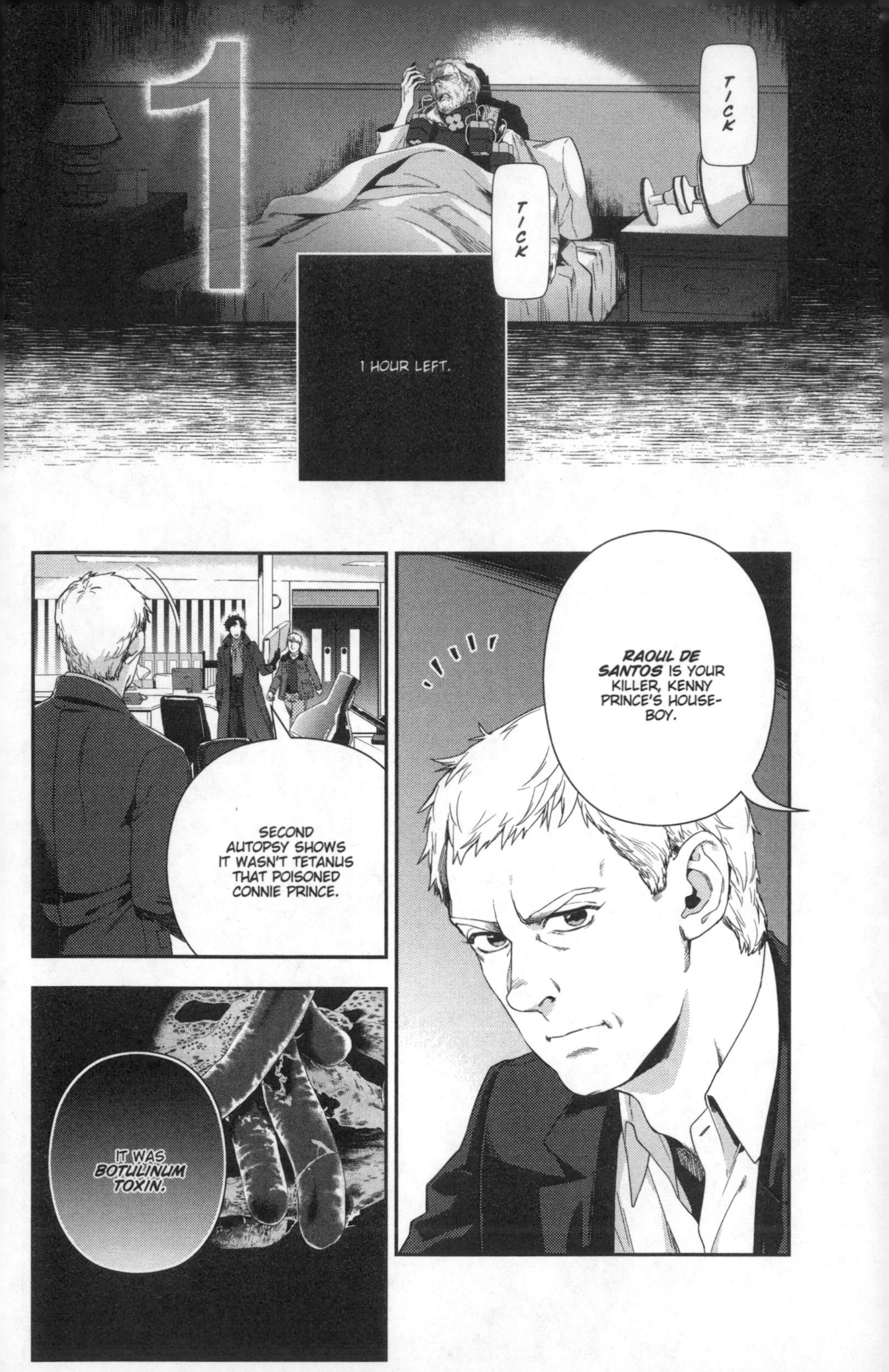
TICK
TICK
1 HOUR LEFT.
RAOUL DE SANTOS IS YOUR KILLER, KENNY PRINCE'S HOUSE-BOY.
SECOND AUTOPSY SHOWS IT WASN'T TETANUS THAT POISONED CONNIE PRINCE.
IT WAS BOTULINUM TOXIN.

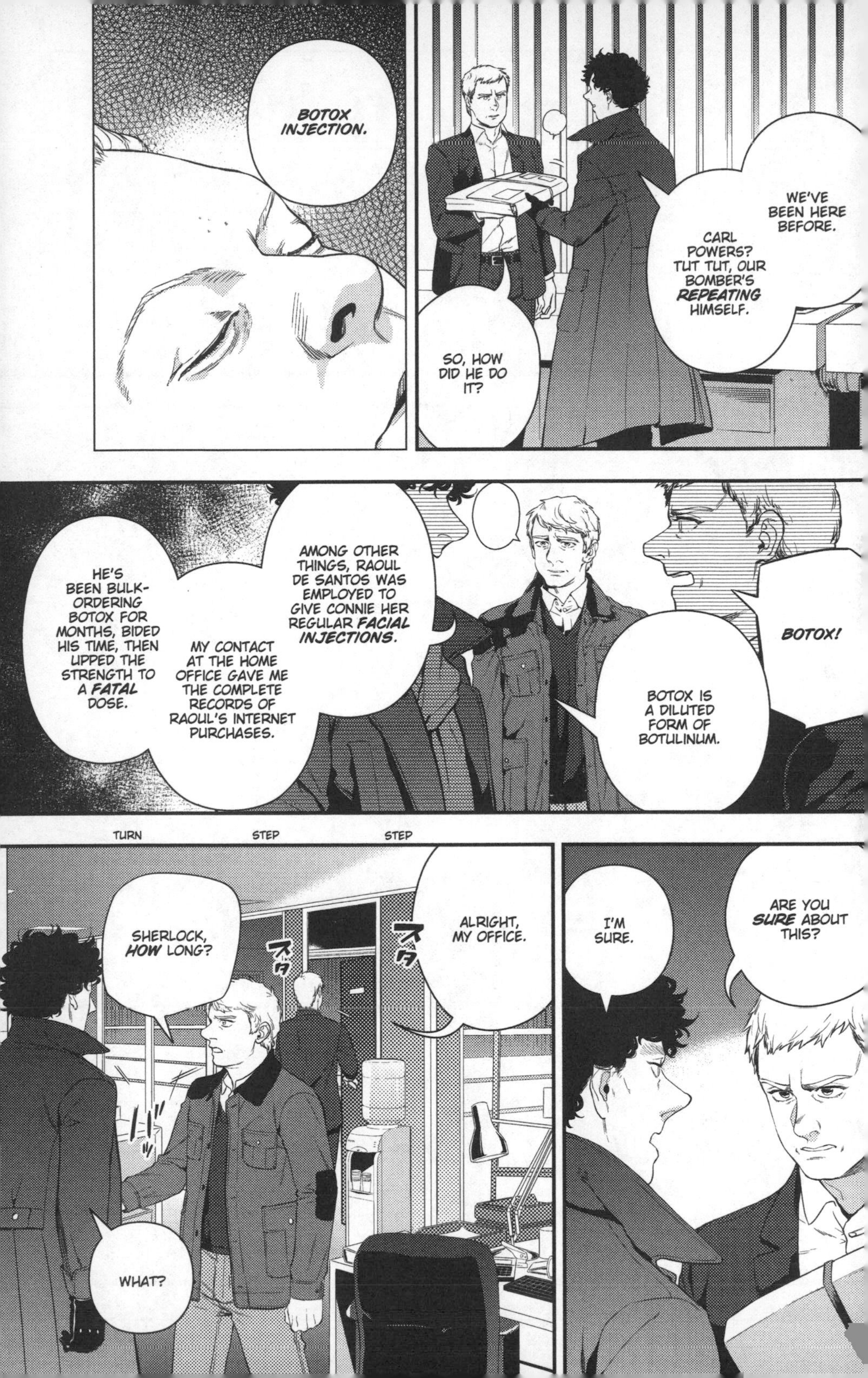
WE'VE BEEN HERE BEFORE.
CARL POWERS? TUT TUT, OUR BOMBER'S *REPEATING* HIMSELF.
SO, HOW DID HE DO IT?
BOTOX INJECTION.
BOTOX!
BOTOX IS A DILUTED FORM OF BOTULINUM.
AMONG OTHER THINGS, RAOUL DE SANTOS WAS EMPLOYED TO GIVE CONNIE HER REGULAR *FACIAL INJECTIONS*.
MY CONTACT AT THE HOME OFFICE GAVE ME THE COMPLETE RECORDS OF RAOUL'S INTERNET PURCHASES.
HE'S BEEN BULK-ORDERING BOTOX FOR MONTHS, BIDED HIS TIME, THEN UPPED THE STRENGTH TO A *FATAL* DOSE.
ARE YOU *SURE* ABOUT THIS?
I'M SURE.
STEP
ALRIGHT, MY OFFICE.
STEP
TURN
SHERLOCK, *HOW* LONG?
WHAT?

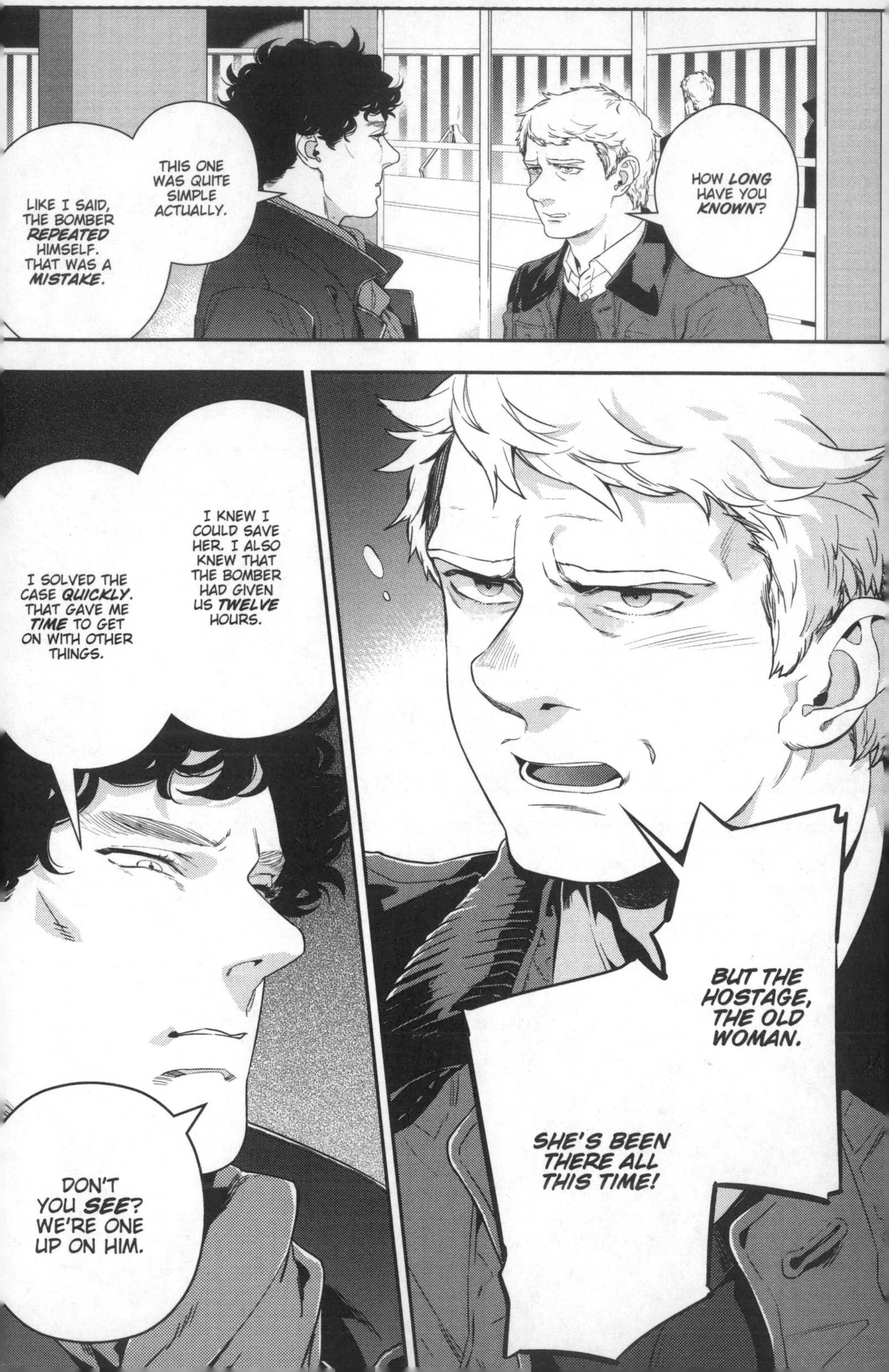
HOW *LONG* HAVE YOU *KNOWN*?
LIKE I SAID, THE BOMBER *REPEATED* HIMSELF. THAT WAS A *MISTAKE*. THIS ONE WAS QUITE SIMPLE ACTUALLY.
BUT THE HOSTAGE, THE OLD WOMAN.
SHE'S BEEN THERE ALL THIS TIME!
I SOLVED THE CASE *QUICKLY*. THAT GAVE ME *TIME* TO GET ON WITH OTHER THINGS. I KNEW I COULD SAVE HER. I ALSO KNEW THAT THE BOMBER HAD GIVEN US *TWELVE* HOURS.
DON'T YOU *SEE*? WE'RE ONE UP ON HIM.

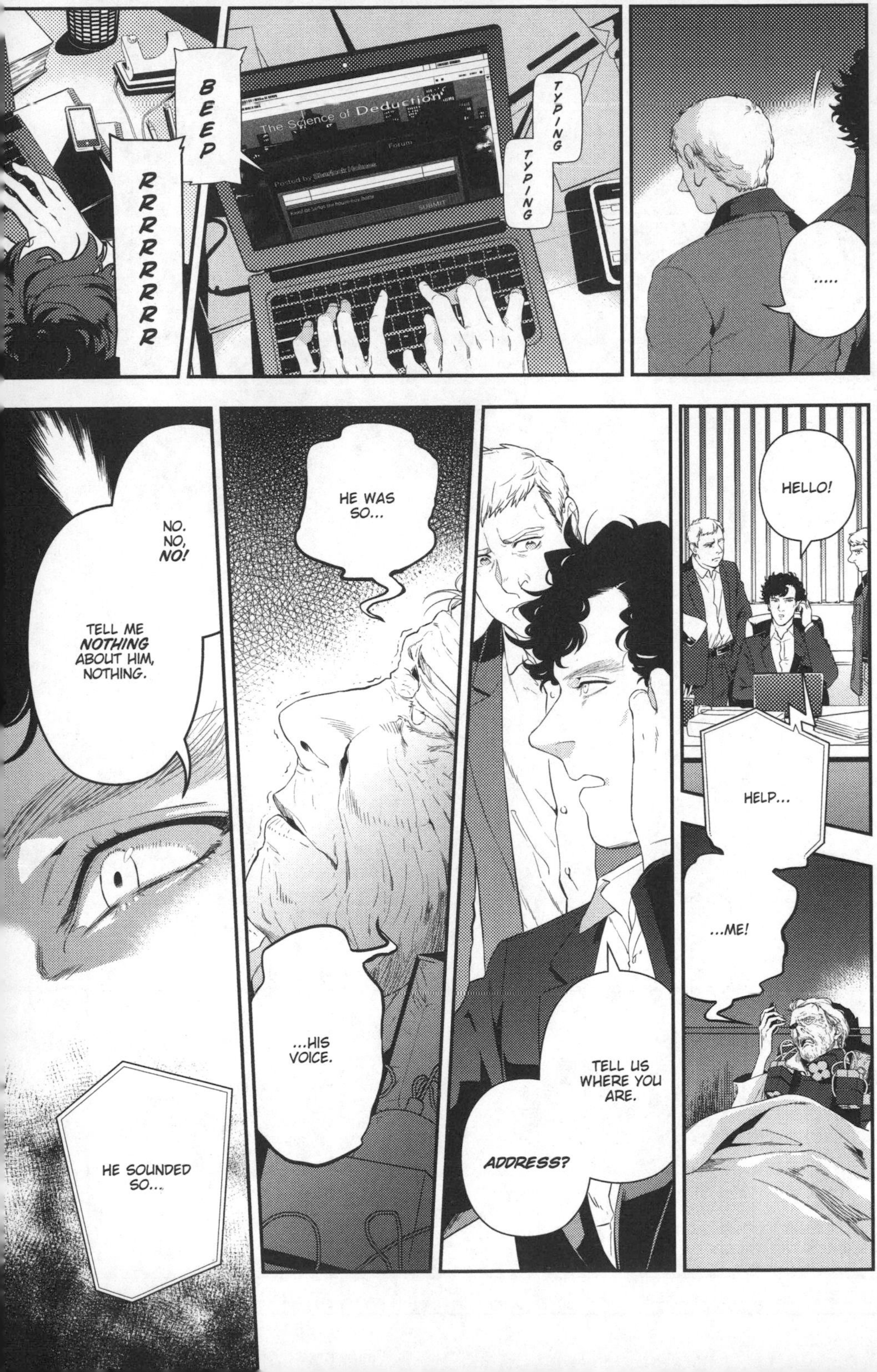
.....
TYPING
TYPING
The Science of Deduction
Forum
Posted by Sherlock Holmes
SUBMIT
BEEP
RRRRRRRR
HELLO!
HELP...
...ME!
TELL US WHERE YOU ARE.
ADDRESS?
HE WAS SO...
...HIS VOICE.
NO. NO, NO!
TELL ME NOTHING ABOUT HIM, NOTHING.
HE SOUNDED SO...

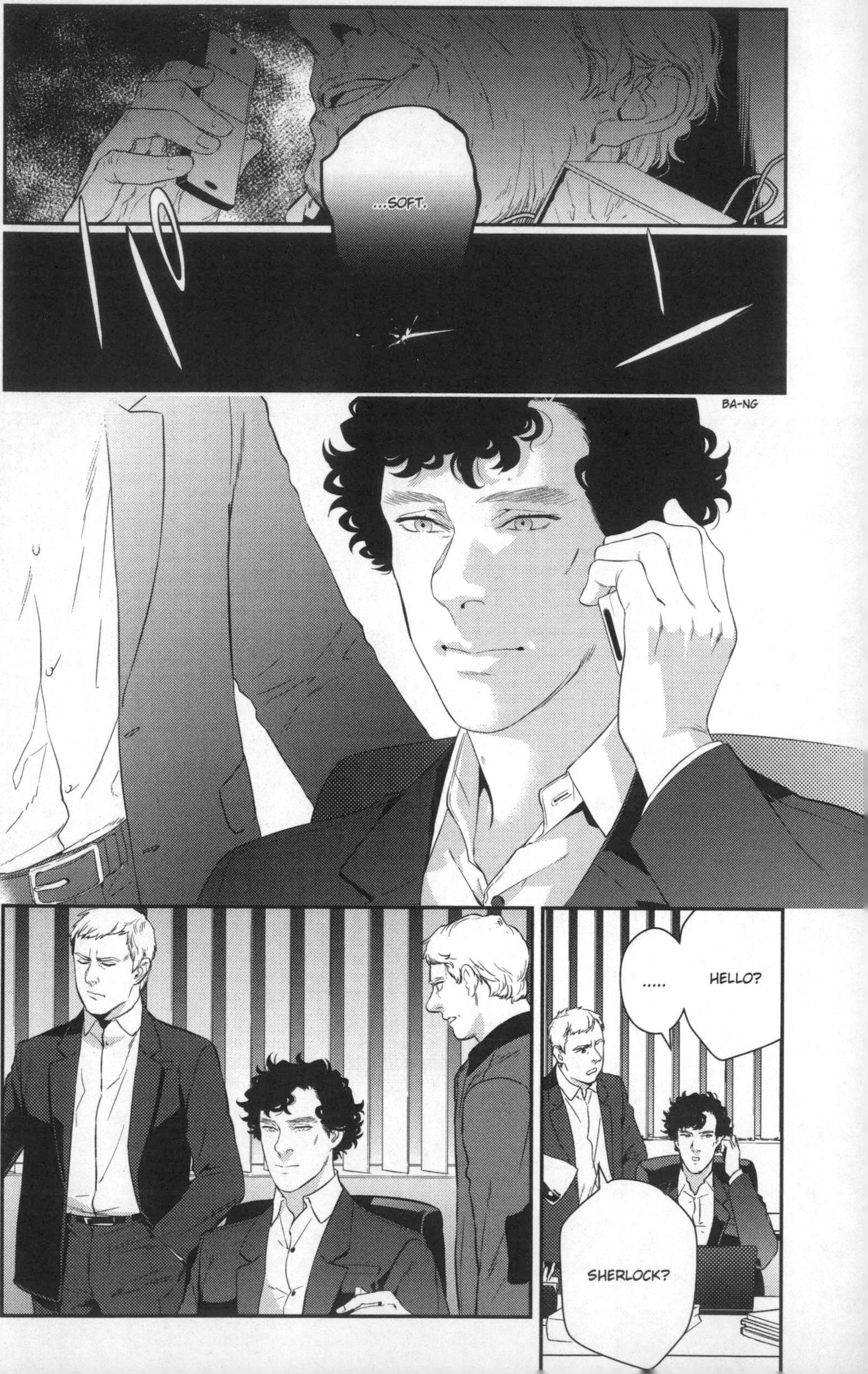
...SOFT.
BA-NG
HELLO?
.....
SHERLOCK?

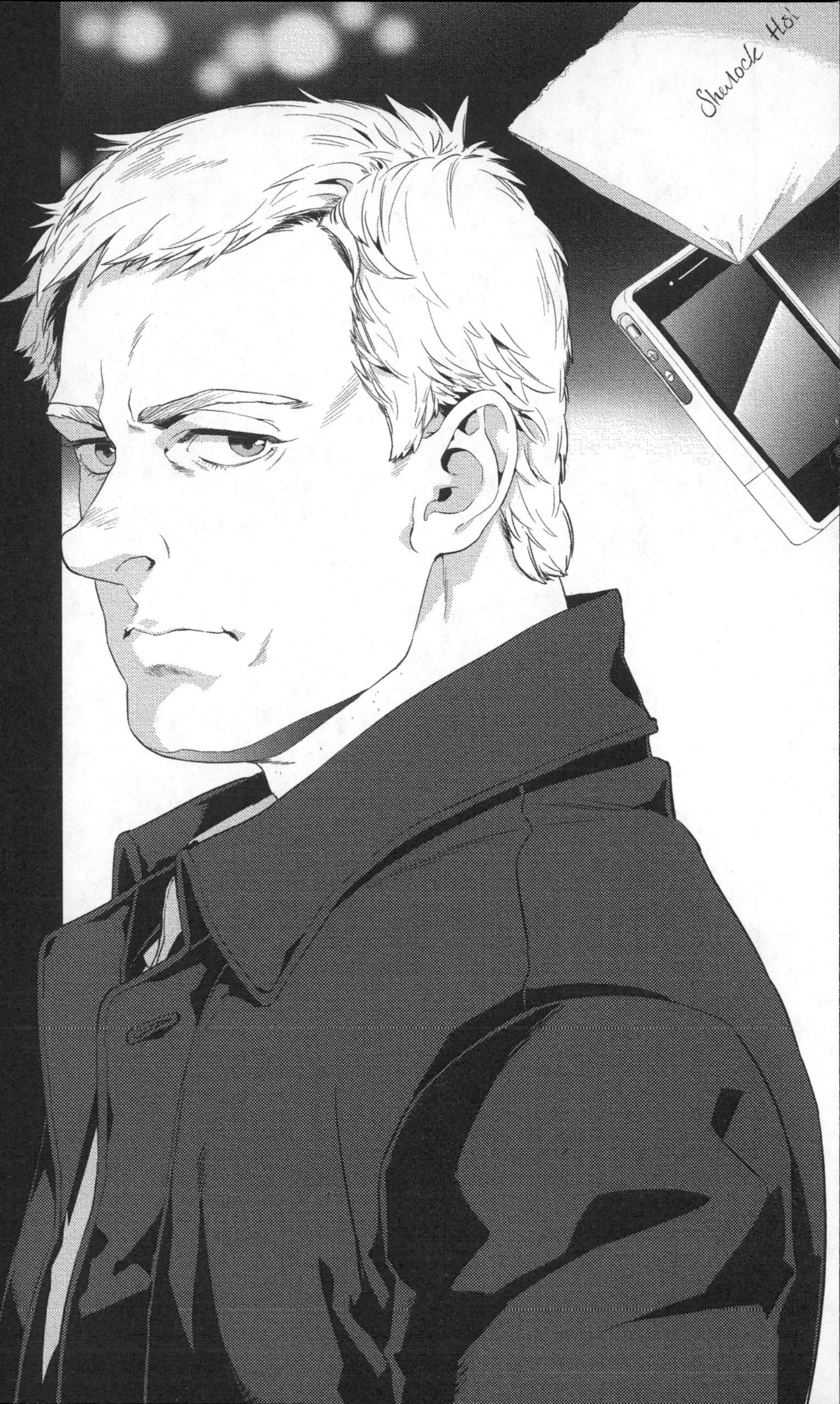

Sherlock

Chapter 4

Illustration by:
Mark Buckingham

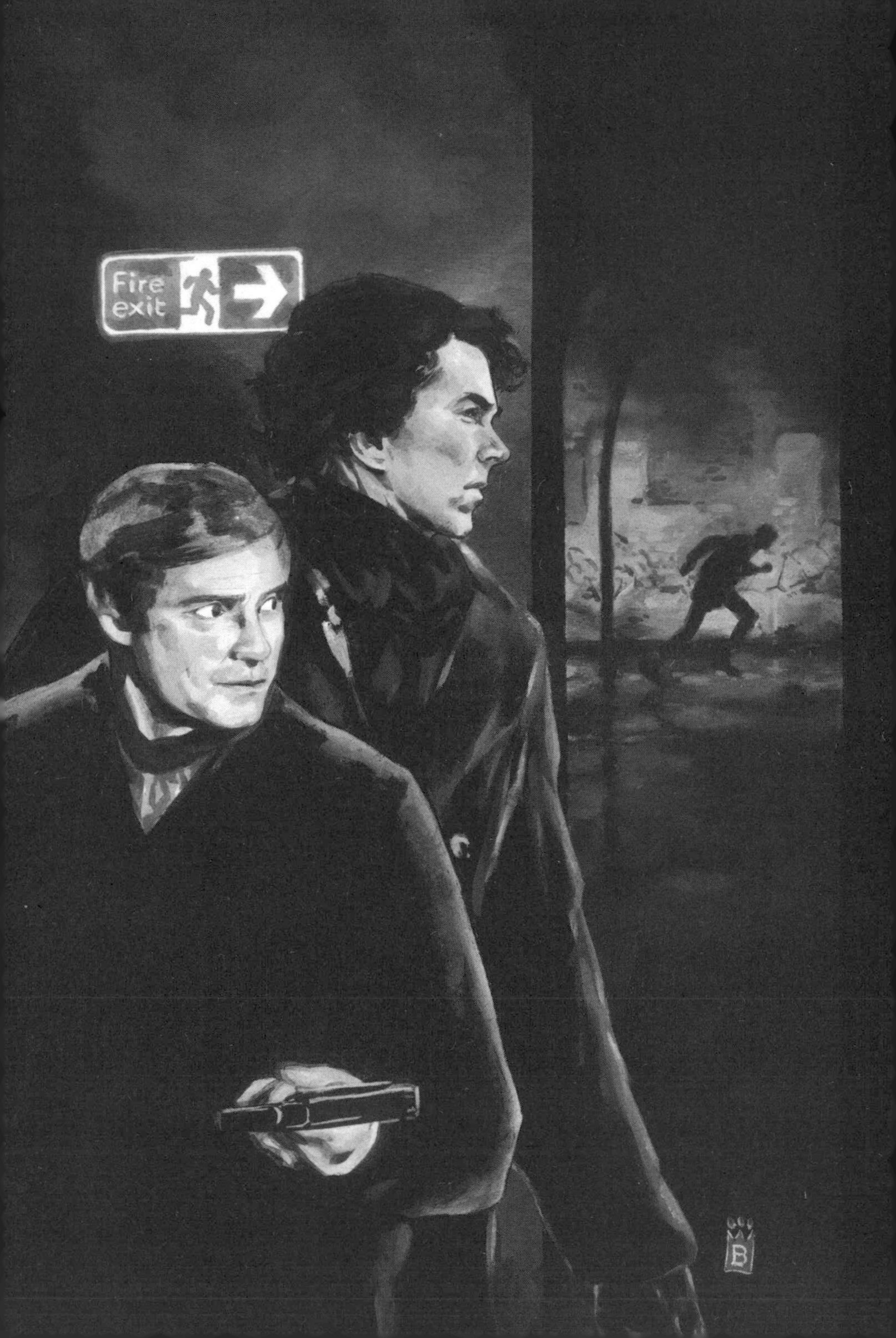
Fire
exit

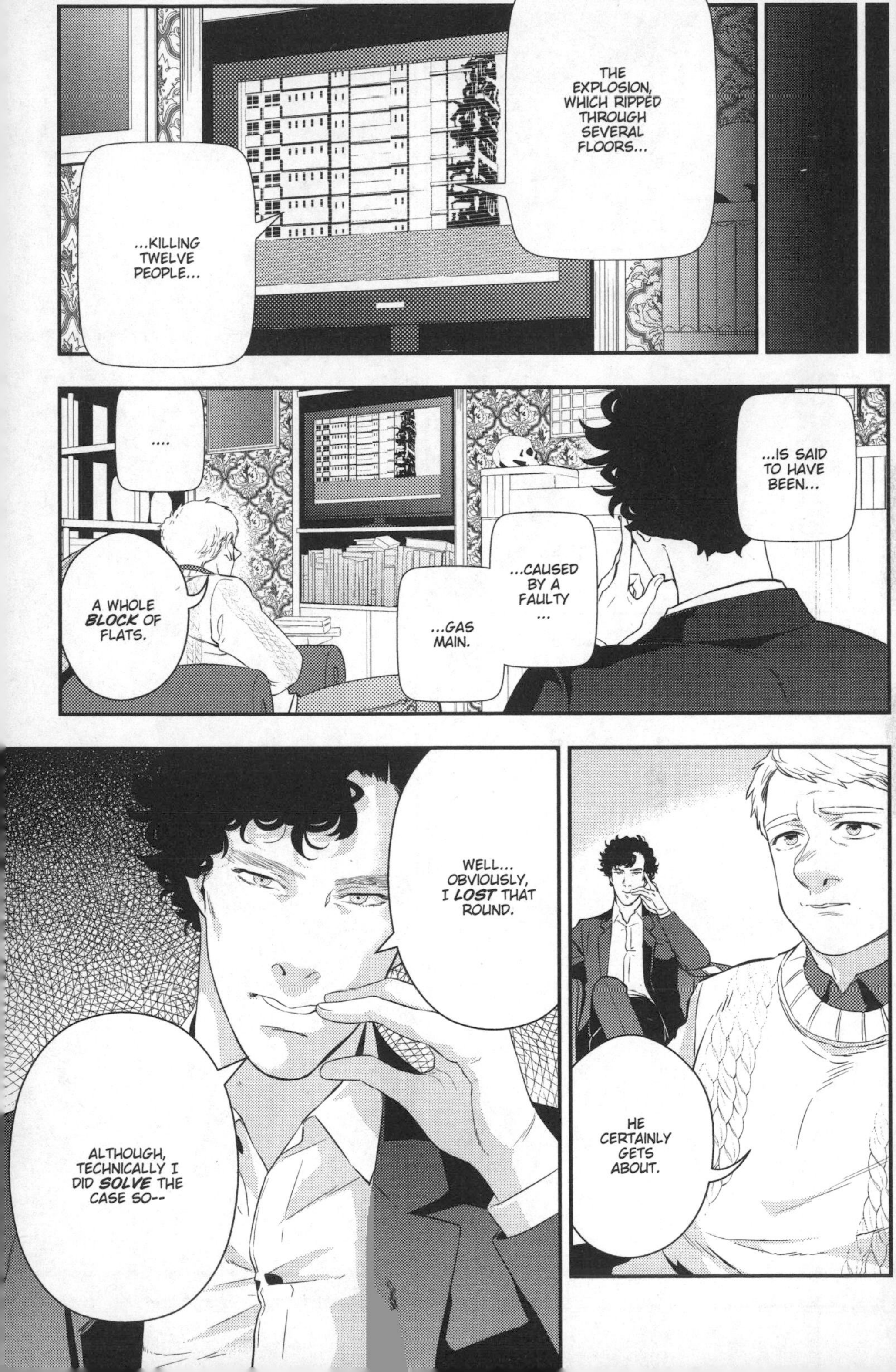
THE EXPLOSION, WHICH RIPPED THROUGH SEVERAL FLOORS...
...KILLING TWELVE PEOPLE...
...IS SAID TO HAVE BEEN...
...CAUSED BY A FAULTY ...
...GAS MAIN.
....
A WHOLE BLOCK OF FLATS.
HE CERTAINLY GETS ABOUT.
WELL... OBVIOUSLY, I LOST THAT ROUND.
ALTHOUGH, TECHNICALLY I DID SOLVE THE CASE SO--

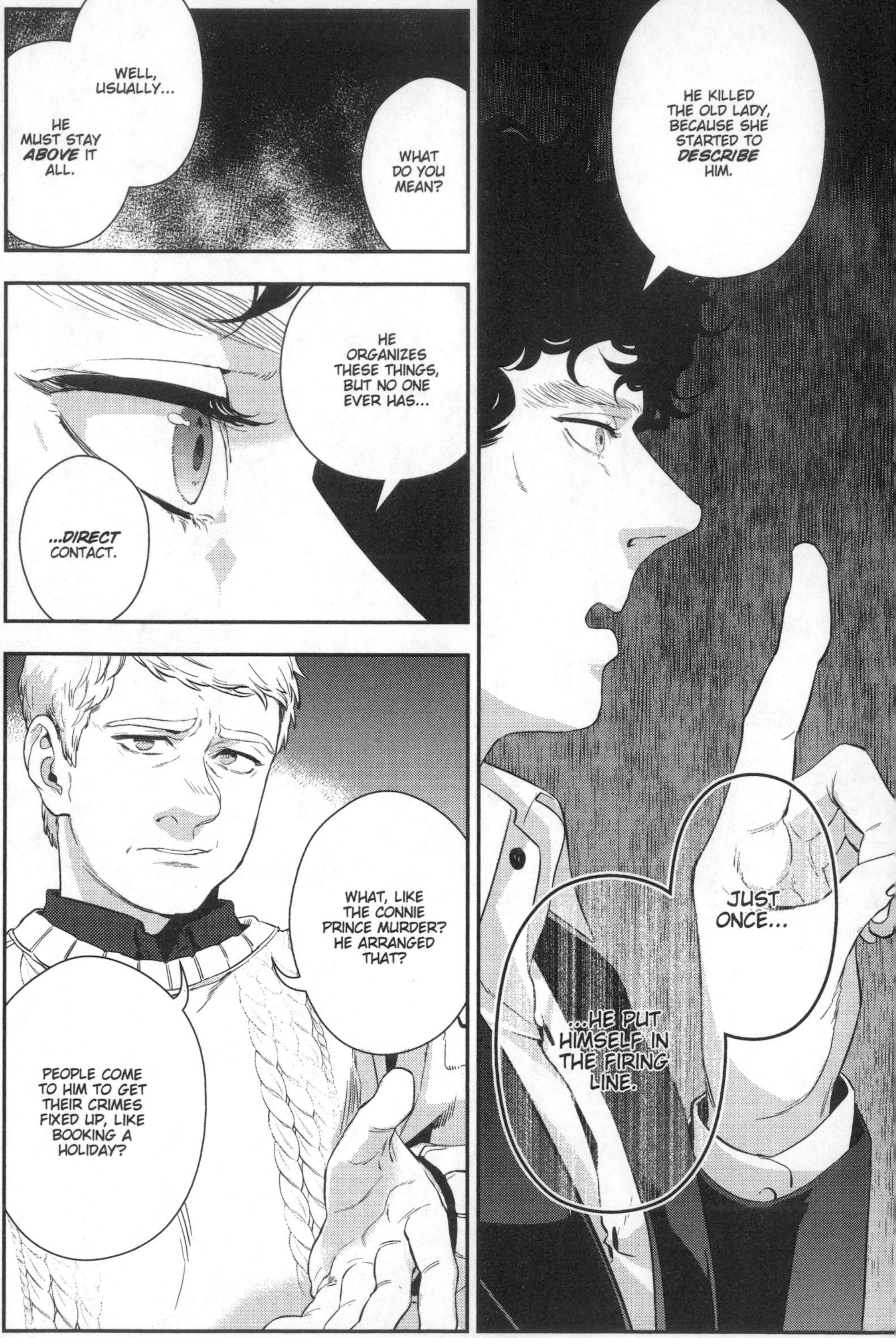
HE KILLED THE OLD LADY, BECAUSE SHE STARTED TO *DESCRIBE* HIM.
JUST ONCE...
...HE PUT HIMSELF IN THE FIRING LINE.
WHAT DO YOU MEAN?
WELL, USUALLY...
HE MUST STAY *ABOVE* IT ALL.
HE ORGANIZES THESE THINGS, BUT NO ONE EVER HAS...
...*DIRECT* CONTACT.
WHAT, LIKE THE CONNIE PRINCE MURDER? HE ARRANGED THAT?
PEOPLE COME TO HIM TO GET THEIR CRIMES FIXED UP, LIKE BOOKING A HOLIDAY?

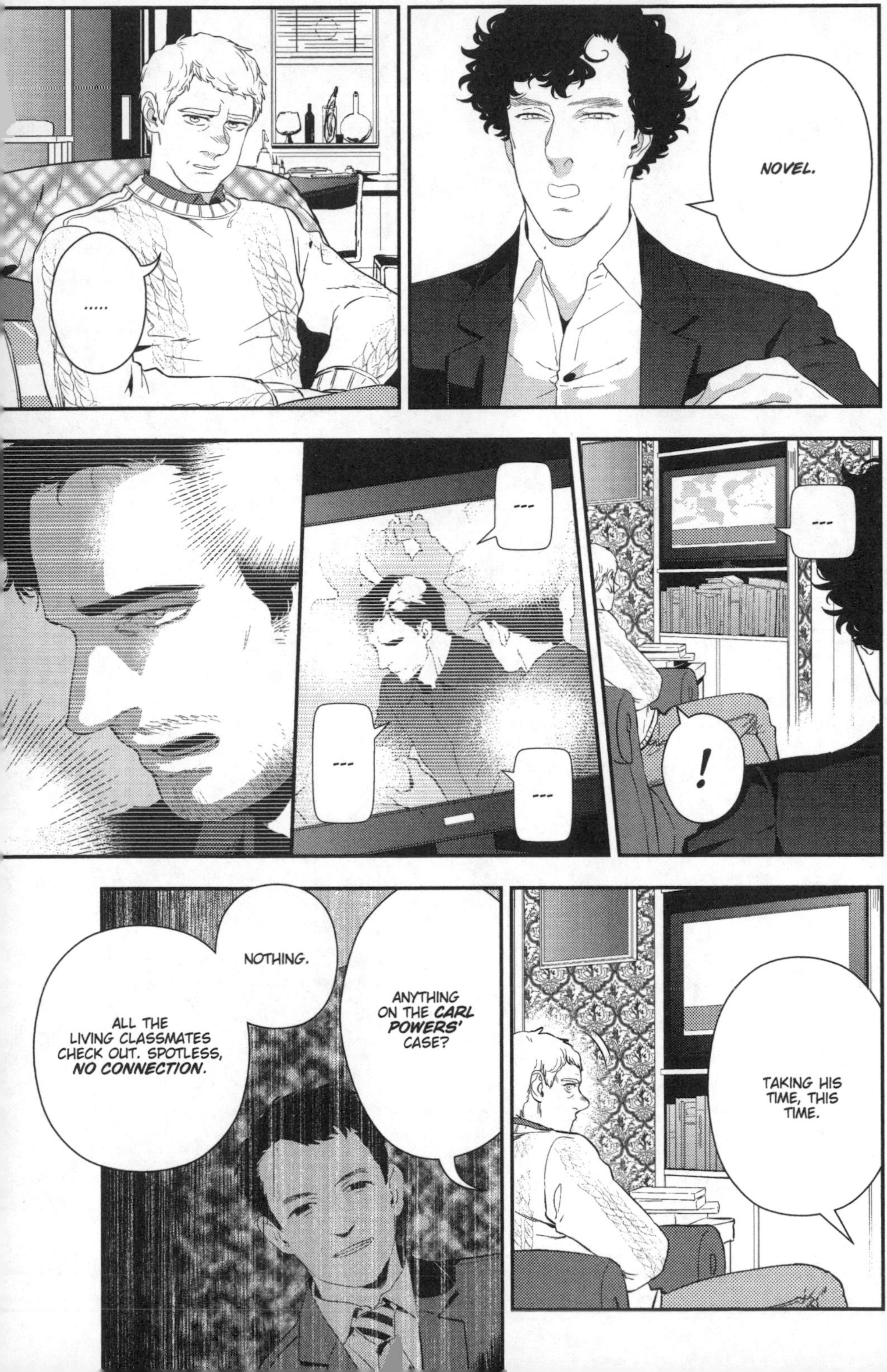
NOVEL.
.....

!

TAKING HIS TIME, THIS TIME.
ANYTHING ON THE **CARL POWERS'** CASE?
NOTHING.
ALL THE LIVING CLASSMATES CHECK OUT. SPOTLESS, **NO CONNECTION**.

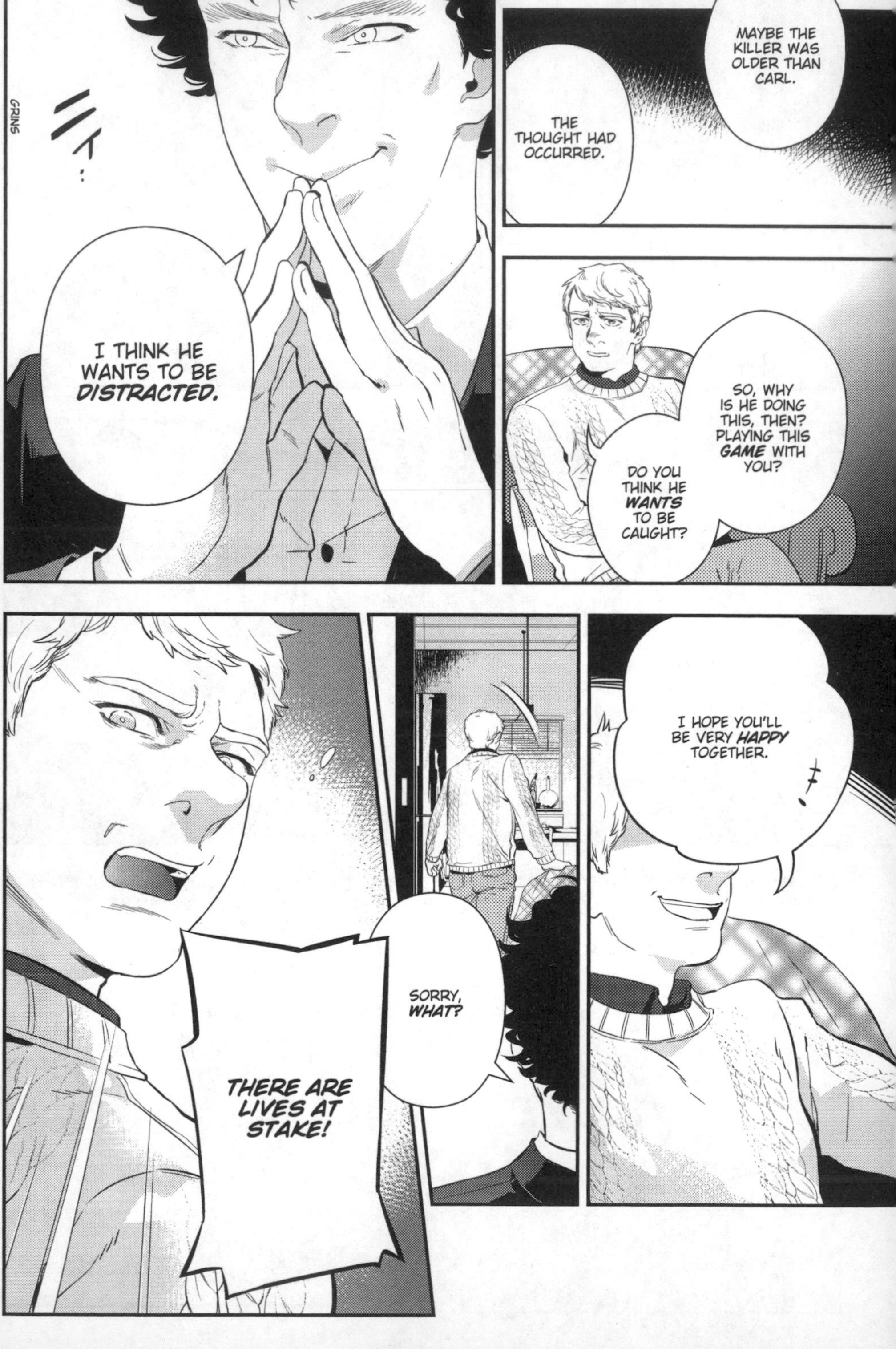
MAYBE THE KILLER WAS OLDER THAN CARL.
THE THOUGHT HAD OCCURRED.
SO, WHY IS HE DOING THIS, THEN? PLAYING THIS GAME WITH YOU?
DO YOU THINK HE WANTS TO BE CAUGHT?
GRINS
I THINK HE WANTS TO BE DISTRACTED.
I HOPE YOU'LL BE VERY HAPPY TOGETHER.
SORRY, WHAT?
THERE ARE LIVES AT STAKE!

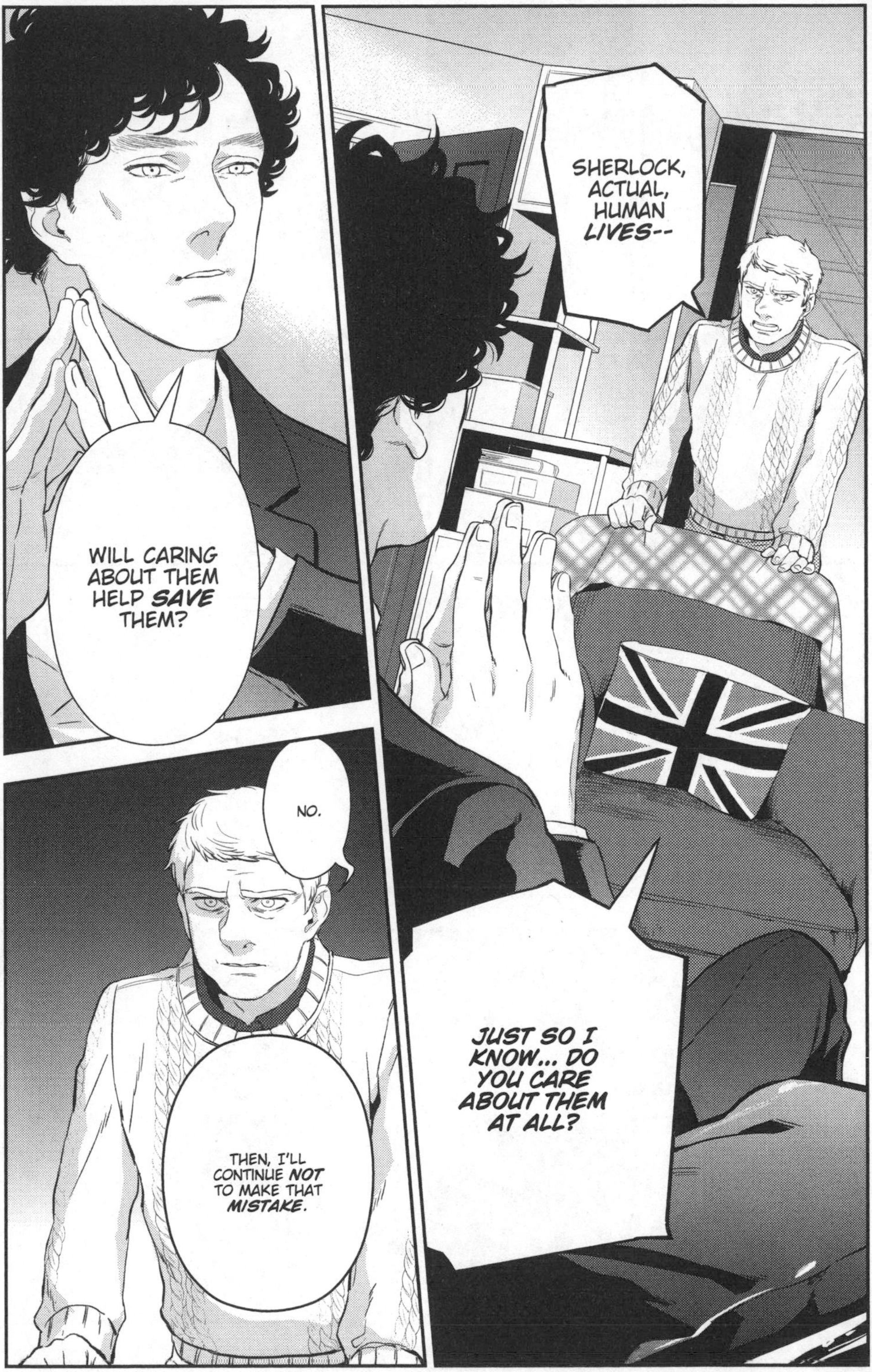
SHERLOCK, ACTUAL, HUMAN *LIVES*--
JUST SO I KNOW... DO YOU CARE ABOUT THEM AT ALL?
WILL CARING ABOUT THEM HELP *SAVE* THEM?
NO.
THEN, I'LL CONTINUE *NOT* TO MAKE THAT *MISTAKE*.

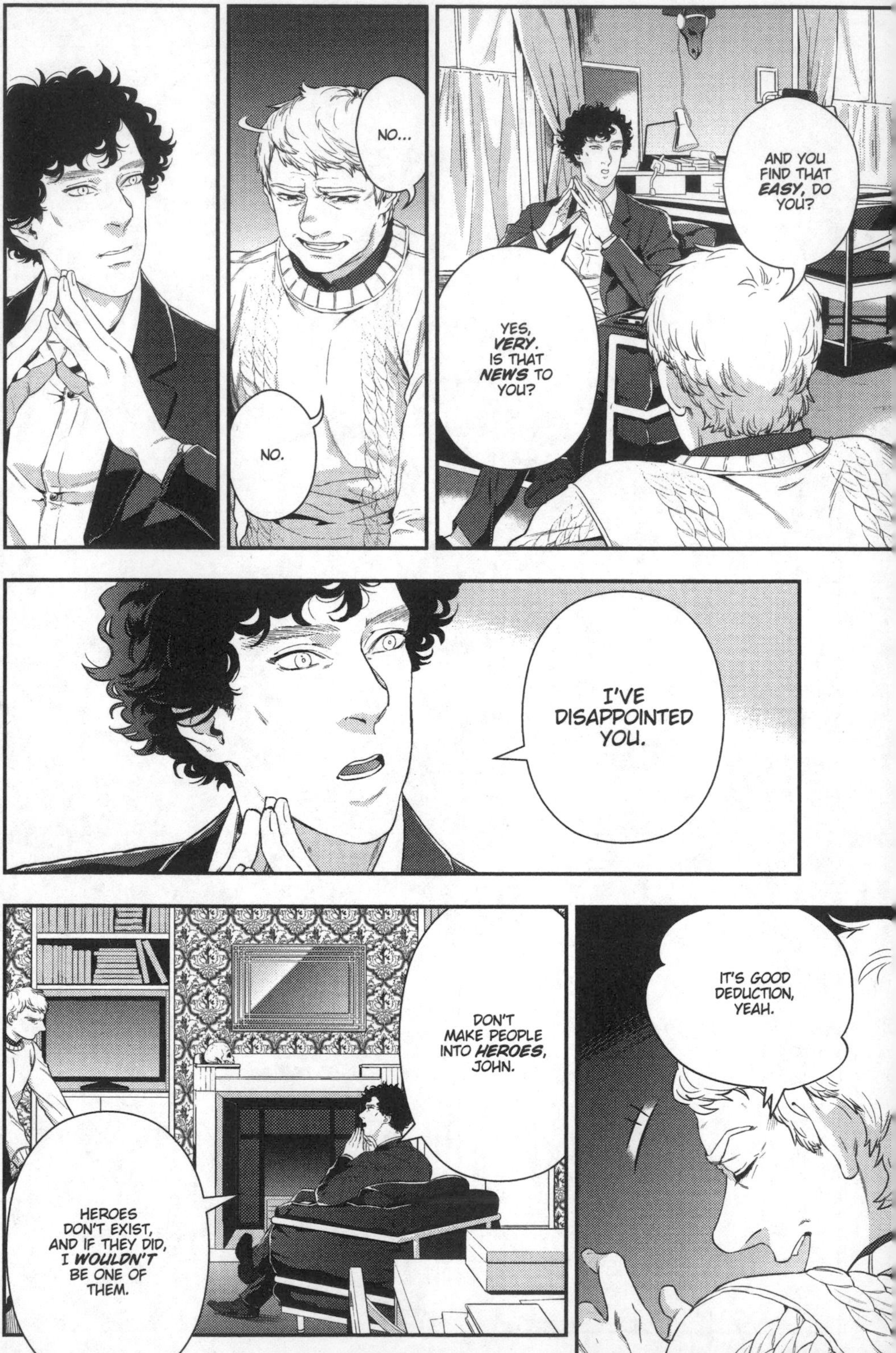
AND YOU FIND THAT **EASY**, DO YOU?
YES, **VERY**. IS THAT **NEWS** TO YOU?
NO...
NO.
I'VE DISAPPOINTED YOU.
IT'S GOOD DEDUCTION, YEAH.
DON'T MAKE PEOPLE INTO **HEROES**, JOHN.
HEROES DON'T EXIST, AND IF THEY DID, I **WOULDN'T** BE ONE OF THEM.

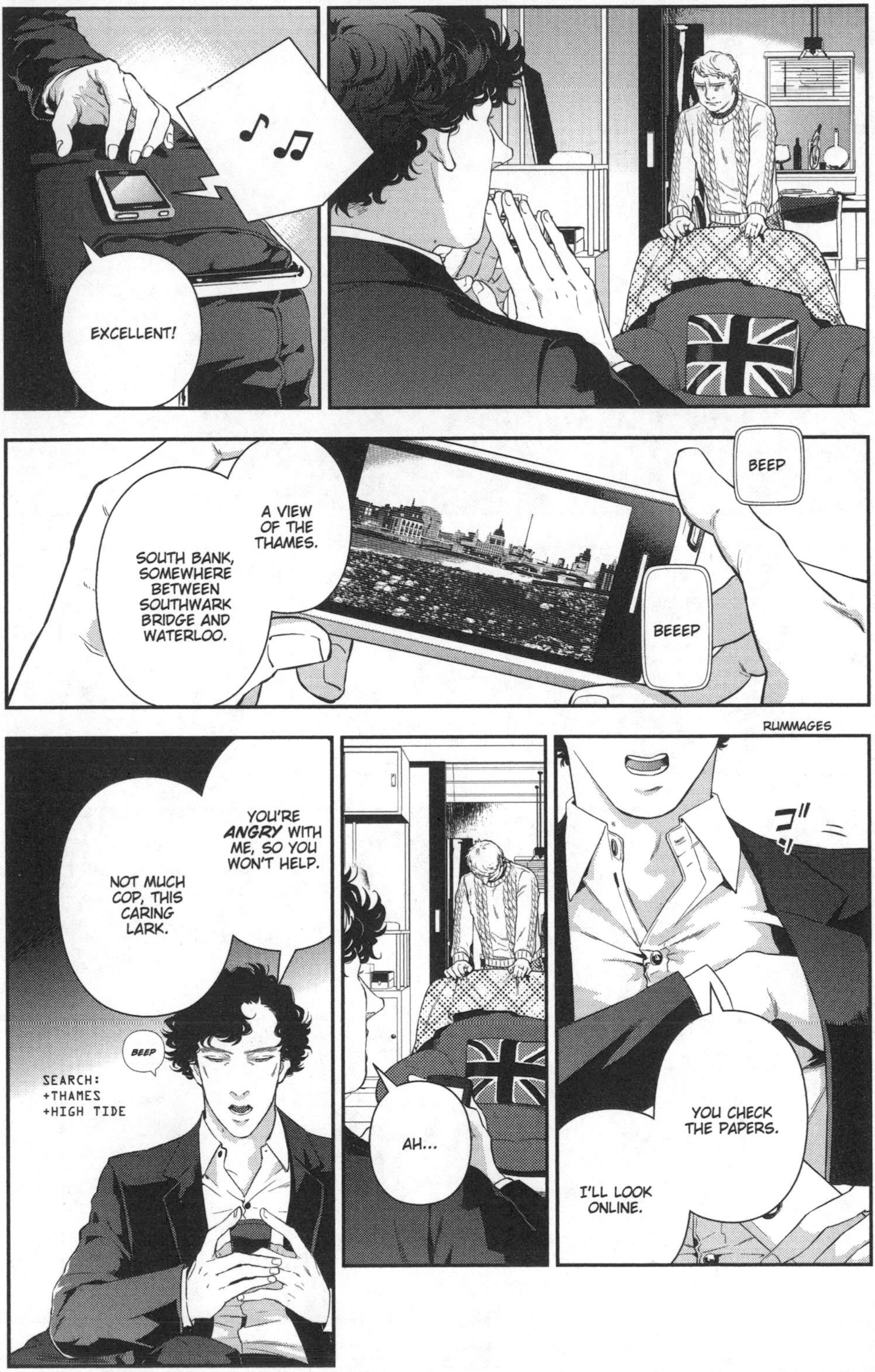
♪ ♫
EXCELLENT!
BEEP
A VIEW OF THE THAMES.
SOUTH BANK, SOMEWHERE BETWEEN SOUTHWARK BRIDGE AND WATERLOO.
BEEEP
RUMMAGES
ゴ
YOU CHECK THE PAPERS.
I'LL LOOK ONLINE.
AH...
YOU'RE *ANGRY* WITH ME, SO YOU WON'T HELP.
NOT MUCH COP, THIS CARING LARK.
BEEP
SEARCH:
+THAMES
+HIGH TIDE

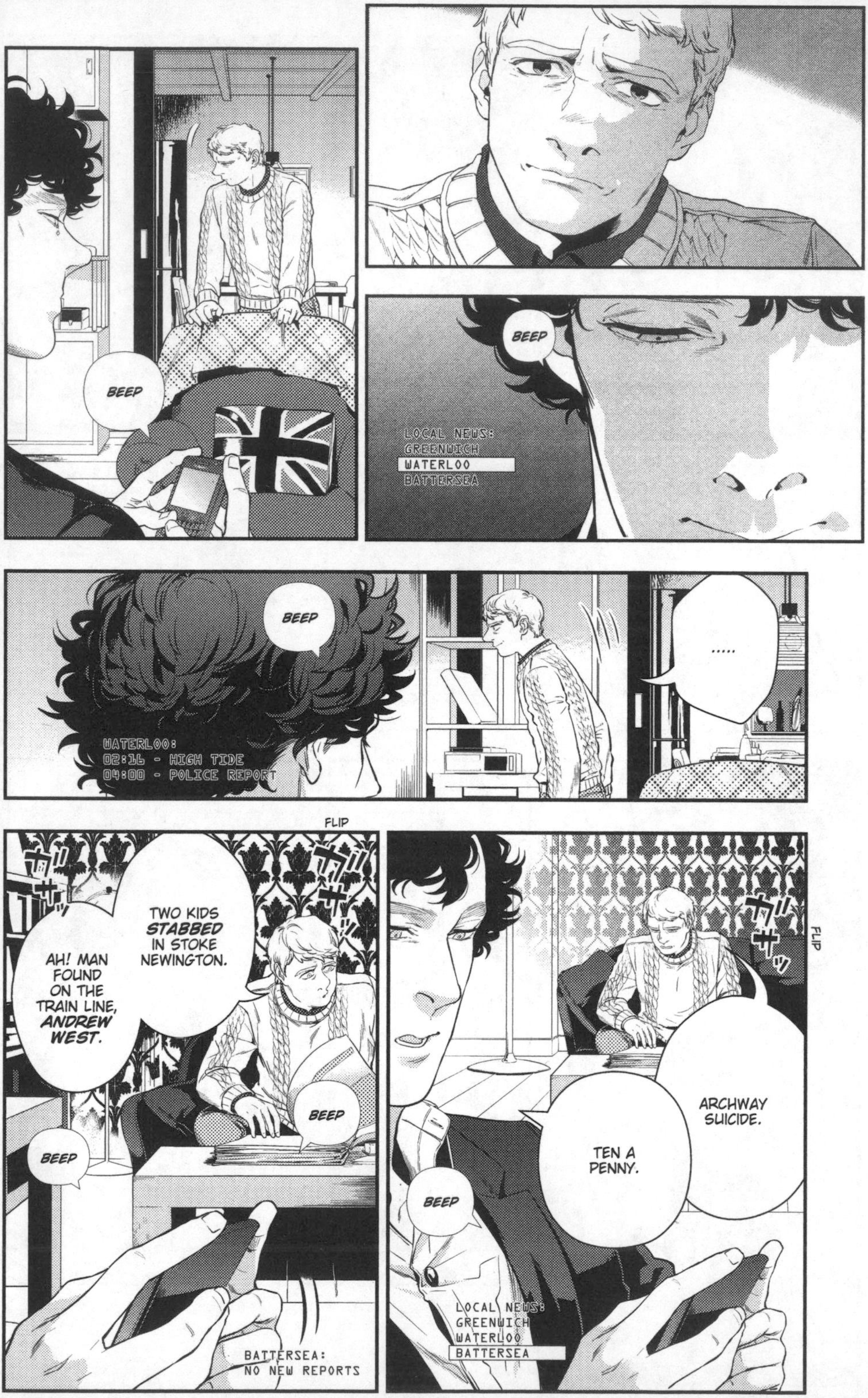
BEEP
LOCAL NEWS:
GREENWICH
WATERLOO
BATTERSEA
BEEP
.....
BEEP
WATERLOO:
02:16 - HIGH TIDE
04:00 - POLICE REPORT
FLIP
FLIP
ガサッ
ARCHWAY SUICIDE.
TEN A PENNY.
BEEP
LOCAL NEWS:
GREENWICH
WATERLOO
BATTERSEA
ガサッ
TWO KIDS *STABBED* IN STOKE NEWINGTON.
AH! MAN FOUND ON THE TRAIN LINE, *ANDREW WEST*.
BEEP
BEEP
BATTERSEA:
NO NEW REPORTS

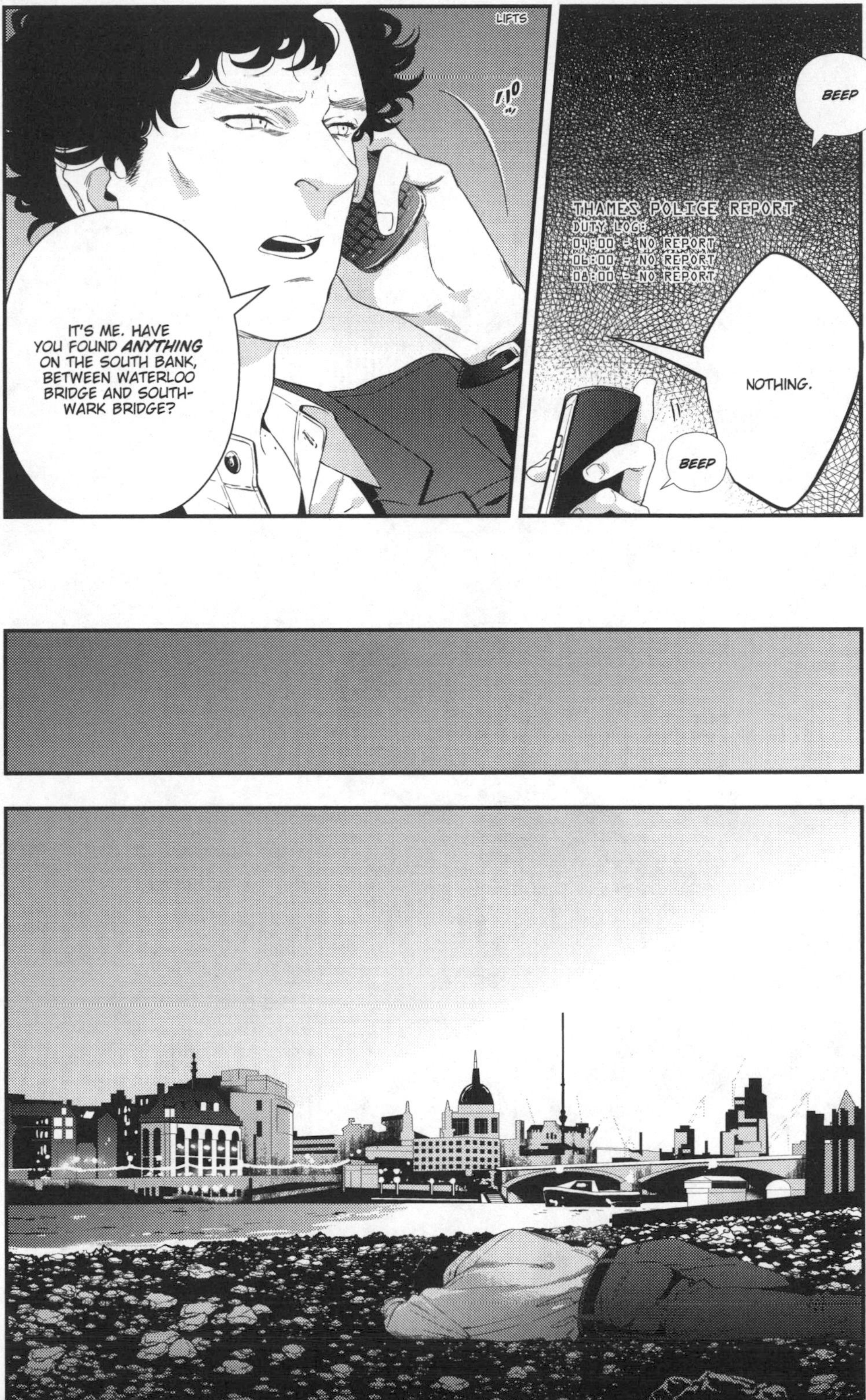
BEEP
THAMES POLICE REPORT
DUTY LOG:
04:00 - NO REPORT
06:00 - NO REPORT
08:00 - NO REPORT
NOTHING.
BEEP
LIFTS
IT'S ME. HAVE YOU FOUND ANYTHING ON THE SOUTH BANK, BETWEEN WATERLOO BRIDGE AND SOUTH-WARK BRIDGE?

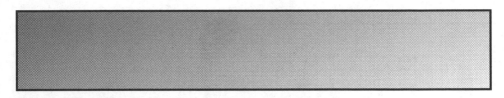

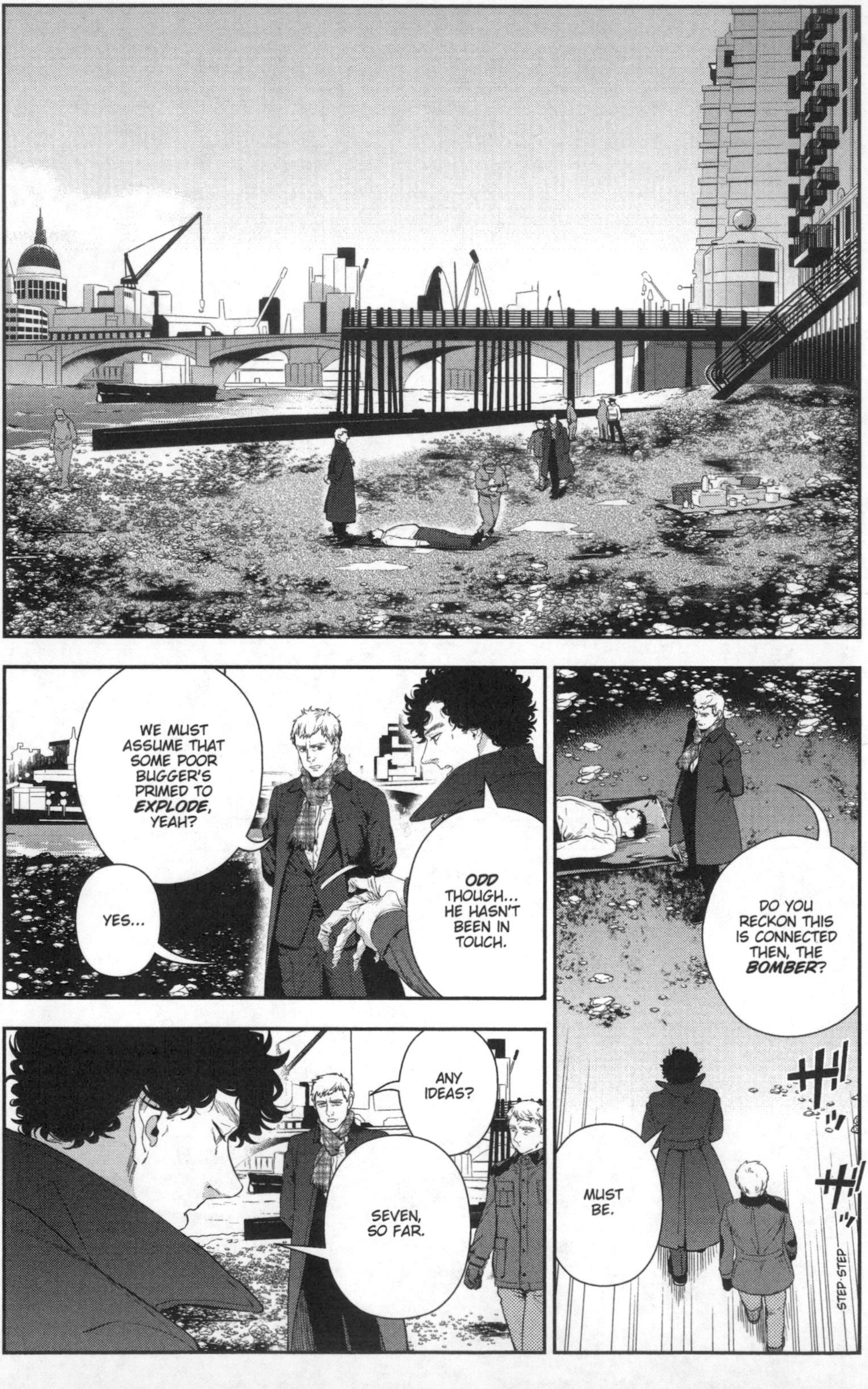
DO YOU RECKON THIS IS CONNECTED THEN, THE ***BOMBER?***
MUST BE.
ザッ
ザッ
STEP-STEP
ODD THOUGH... HE HASN'T BEEN IN TOUCH.
WE MUST ASSUME THAT SOME POOR BUGGER'S PRIMED TO ***EXPLODE***, YEAH?
YES...
ANY IDEAS?
SEVEN, SO FAR.

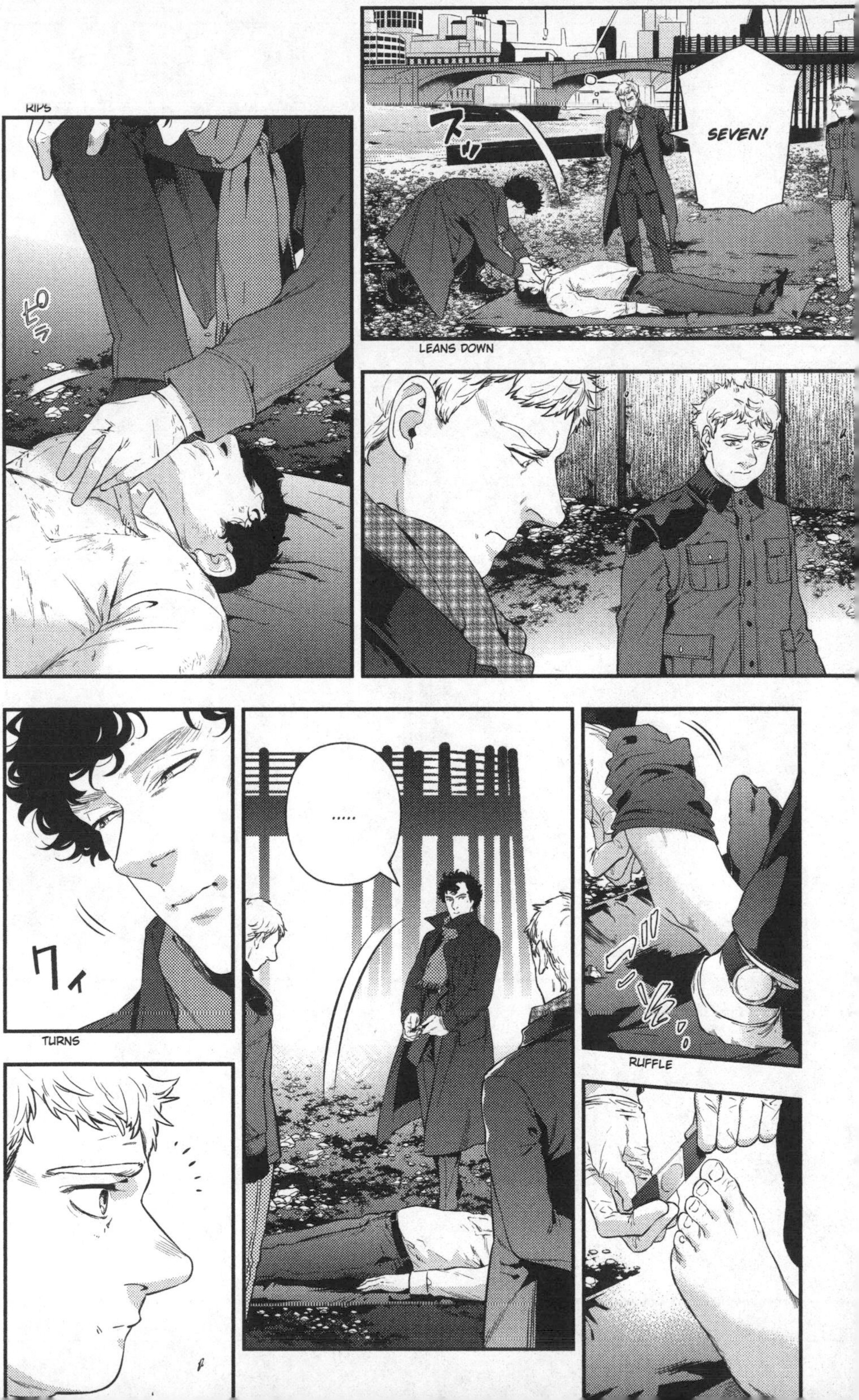
SEVEN!
ズッ
LEANS DOWN
RIPS
ピラ
RUFFLE
.....
TURNS

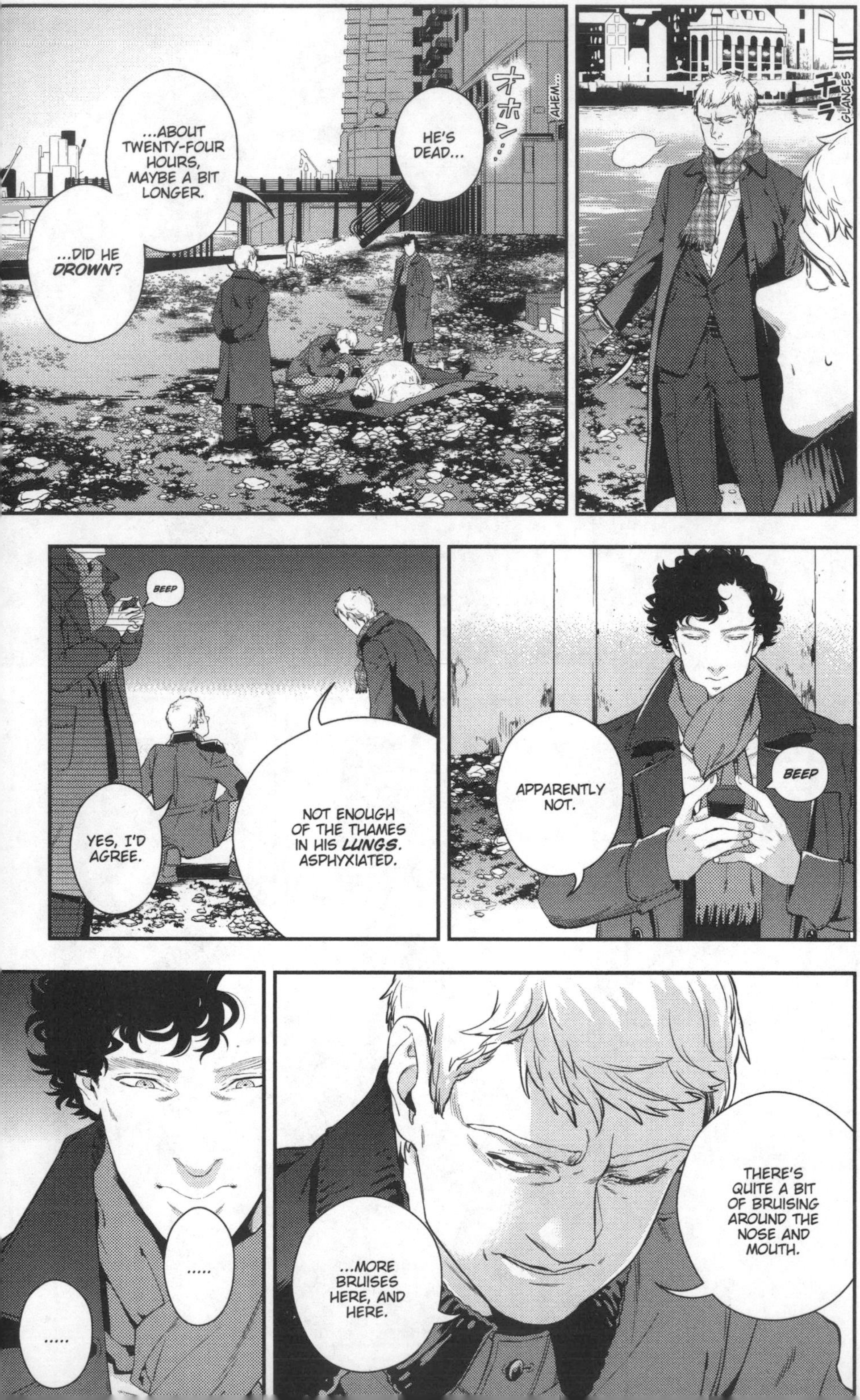
チラ
GLANCES
オホン…
AHEM...
HE'S DEAD...
...ABOUT TWENTY-FOUR HOURS, MAYBE A BIT LONGER.
...DID HE *DROWN*?
BEEP
APPARENTLY NOT.
BEEP
NOT ENOUGH OF THE THAMES IN HIS *LUNGS*. ASPHYXIATED.
YES, I'D AGREE.
THERE'S QUITE A BIT OF BRUISING AROUND THE NOSE AND MOUTH.
...MORE BRUISES HERE, AND HERE.
.....
.....

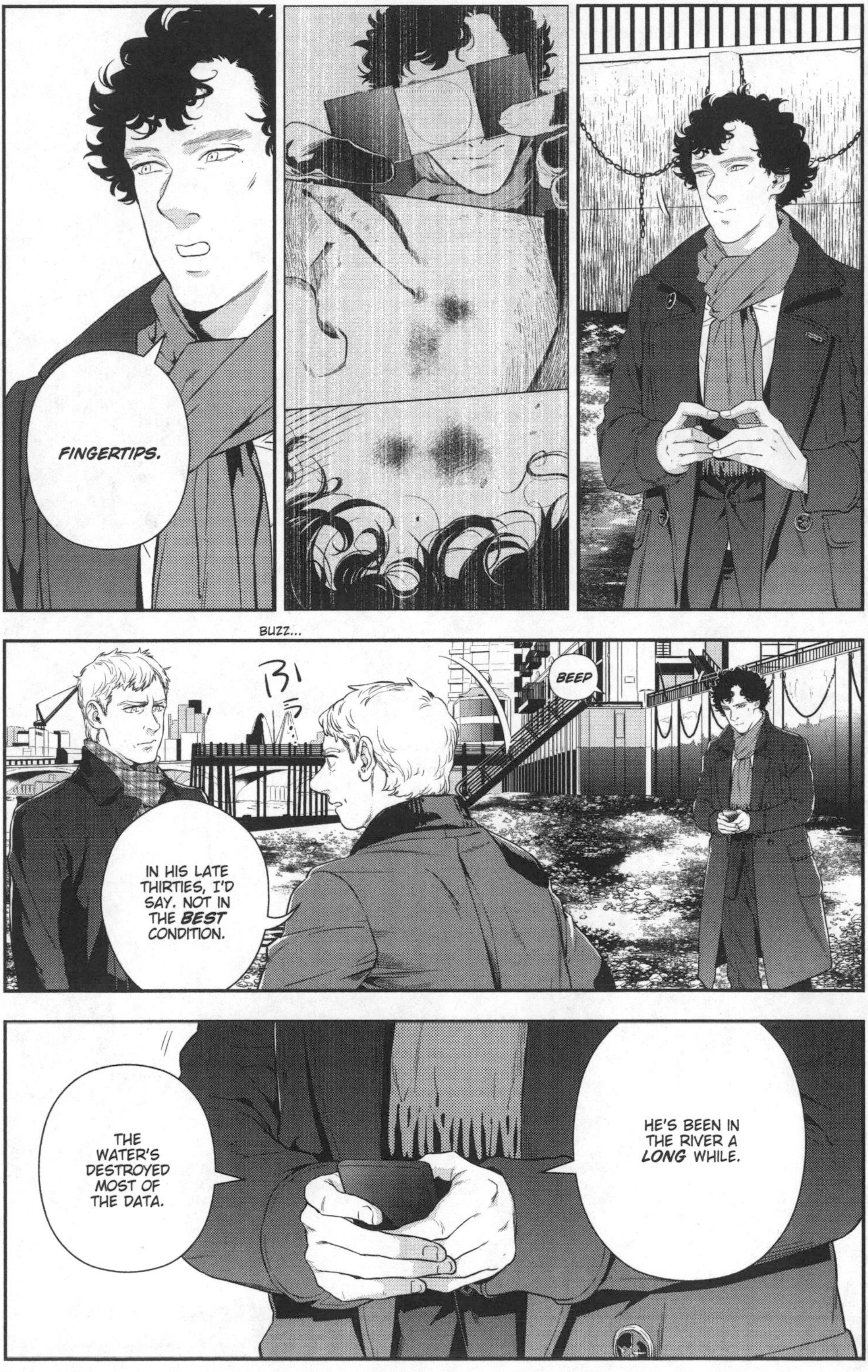
FINGERTIPS.
BUZZ...
BEEP
IN HIS LATE THIRTIES, I'D SAY. NOT IN THE BEST CONDITION.
HE'S BEEN IN THE RIVER A LONG WHILE.
THE WATER'S DESTROYED MOST OF THE DATA.

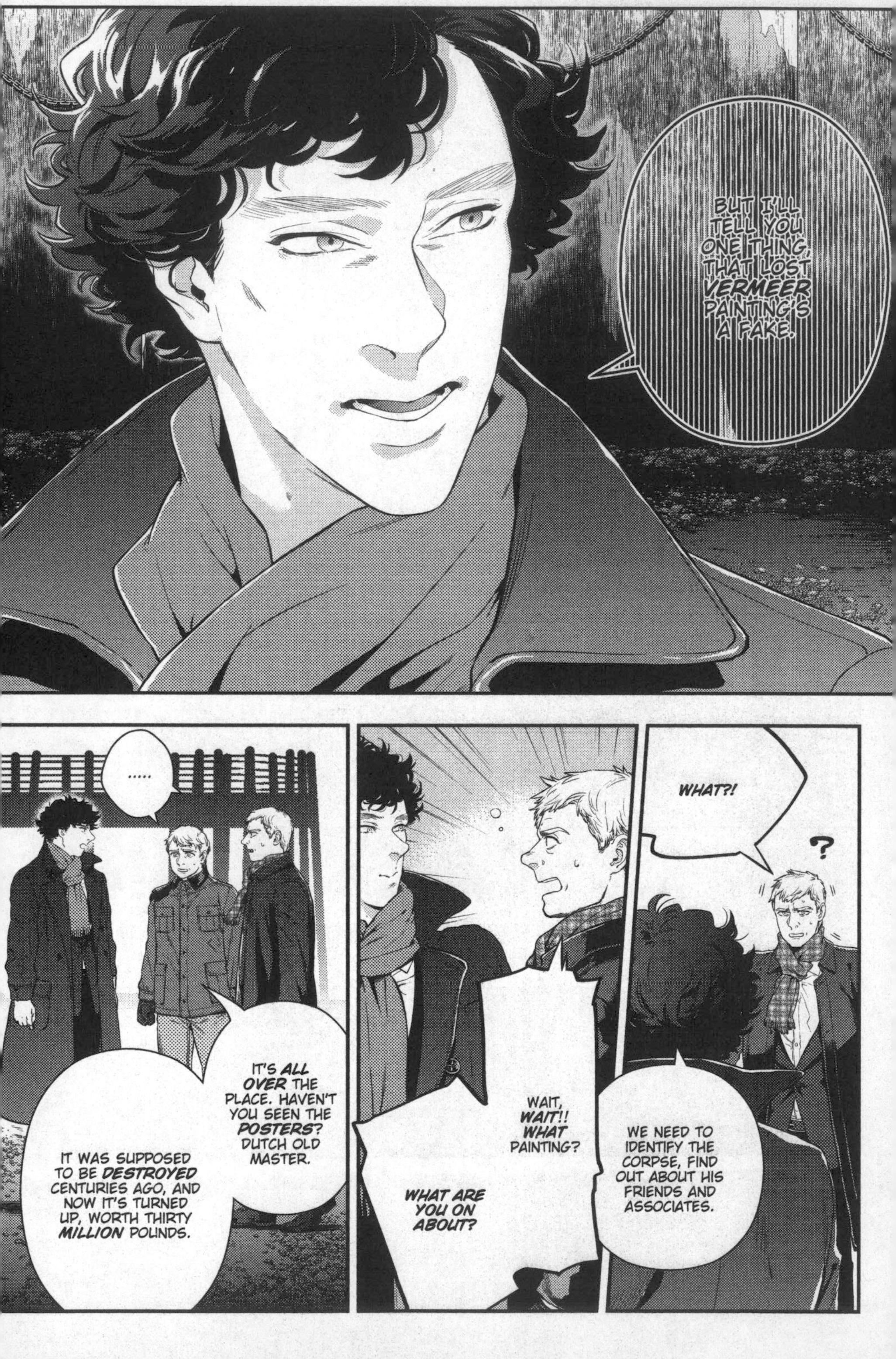
BUT I'LL TELL YOU ONE THING, THAT LOST VERMEER PAINTING'S A FAKE.
WHAT?!
WE NEED TO IDENTIFY THE CORPSE, FIND OUT ABOUT HIS FRIENDS AND ASSOCIATES.
WAIT, WAIT!! WHAT PAINTING?
WHAT ARE YOU ON ABOUT?
.....
IT'S ALL OVER THE PLACE. HAVEN'T YOU SEEN THE POSTERS? DUTCH OLD MASTER.
IT WAS SUPPOSED TO BE DESTROYED CENTURIES AGO, AND NOW IT'S TURNED UP, WORTH THIRTY MILLION POUNDS.

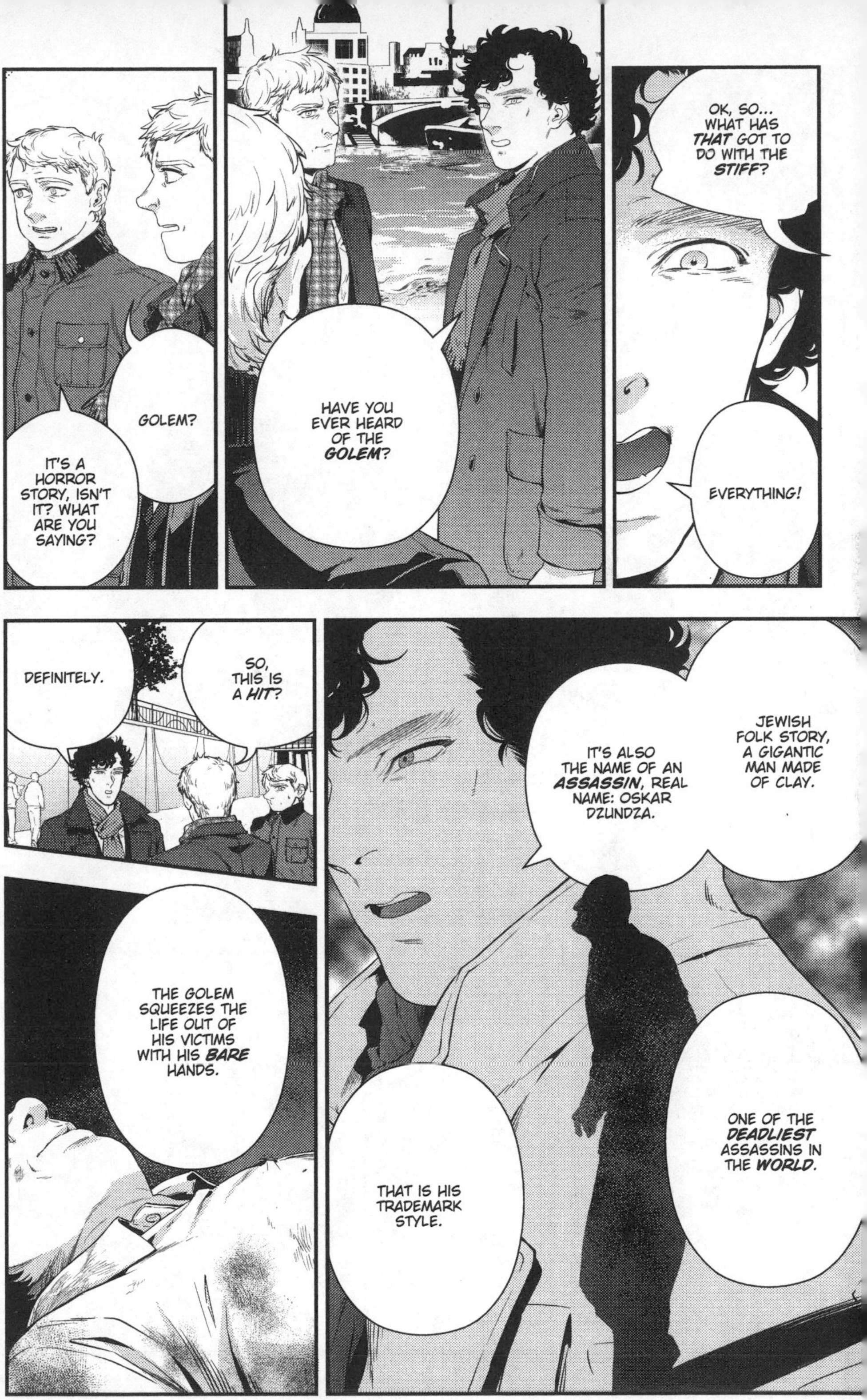
OK, SO... WHAT HAS *THAT* GOT TO DO WITH THE *STIFF*?
EVERYTHING!
HAVE YOU EVER HEARD OF THE *GOLEM*?
GOLEM?
IT'S A HORROR STORY, ISN'T IT? WHAT ARE YOU SAYING?
JEWISH FOLK STORY, A GIGANTIC MAN MADE OF CLAY.
IT'S ALSO THE NAME OF AN *ASSASSIN*, REAL NAME: OSKAR DZUNDZA.
ONE OF THE *DEADLIEST* ASSASSINS IN THE *WORLD*.
THAT IS HIS TRADEMARK STYLE.
SO, THIS IS A *HIT*?
DEFINITELY.
THE GOLEM SQUEEZES THE LIFE OUT OF HIS VICTIMS WITH HIS *BARE* HANDS.

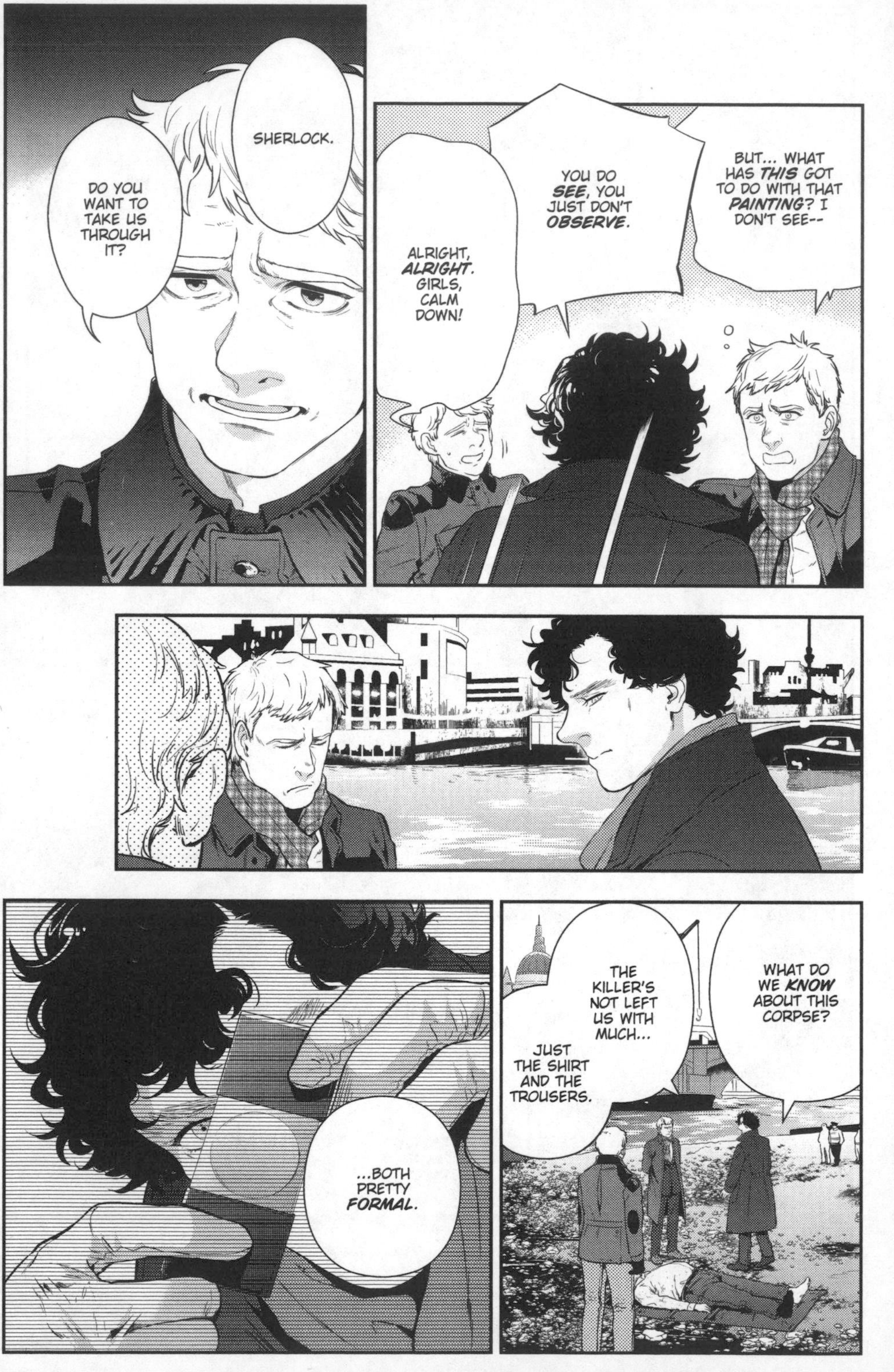
BUT... WHAT HAS **THIS** GOT TO DO WITH THAT **PAINTING**? I DON'T SEE--
YOU DO **SEE**, YOU JUST DON'T **OBSERVE**.
ALRIGHT, **ALRIGHT**. GIRLS, CALM DOWN!
SHERLOCK.
DO YOU WANT TO TAKE US THROUGH IT?
WHAT DO WE **KNOW** ABOUT THIS CORPSE?
THE KILLER'S NOT LEFT US WITH MUCH...
JUST THE SHIRT AND THE TROUSERS.
...BOTH PRETTY **FORMAL**.

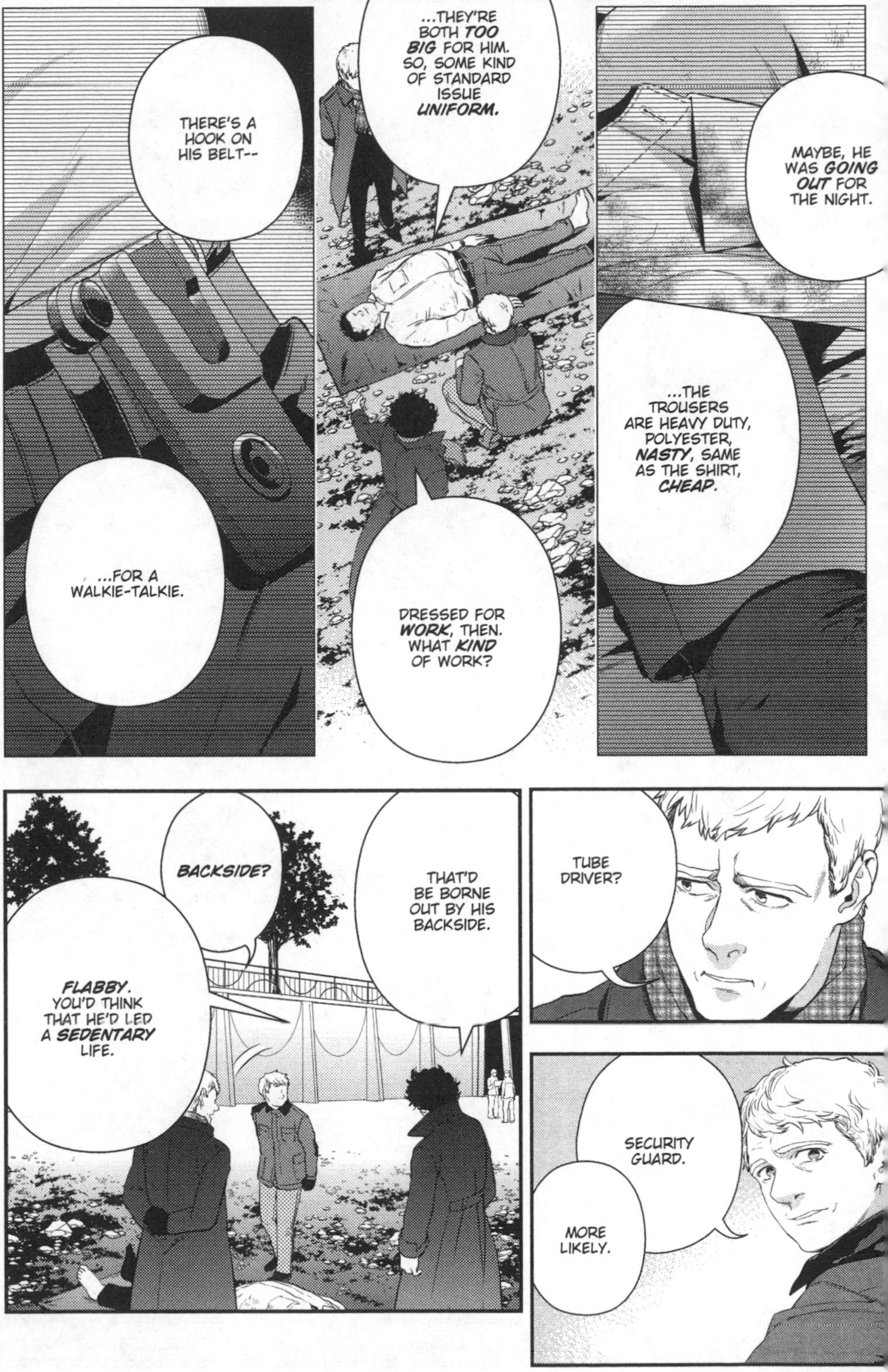
MAYBE, HE WAS **GOING OUT** FOR THE NIGHT.
...THE TROUSERS ARE HEAVY DUTY, POLYESTER, **NASTY**, SAME AS THE SHIRT, **CHEAP**.
...THEY'RE BOTH **TOO BIG** FOR HIM. SO, SOME KIND OF STANDARD ISSUE **UNIFORM.**
DRESSED FOR **WORK**, THEN. WHAT **KIND** OF WORK?
THERE'S A HOOK ON HIS BELT--
...FOR A WALKIE-TALKIE.
TUBE DRIVER?
SECURITY GUARD.
MORE LIKELY.
THAT'D BE BORNE OUT BY HIS BACKSIDE.
BACKSIDE?
FLABBY. YOU'D THINK THAT HE'D LED A **SEDENTARY** LIFE.

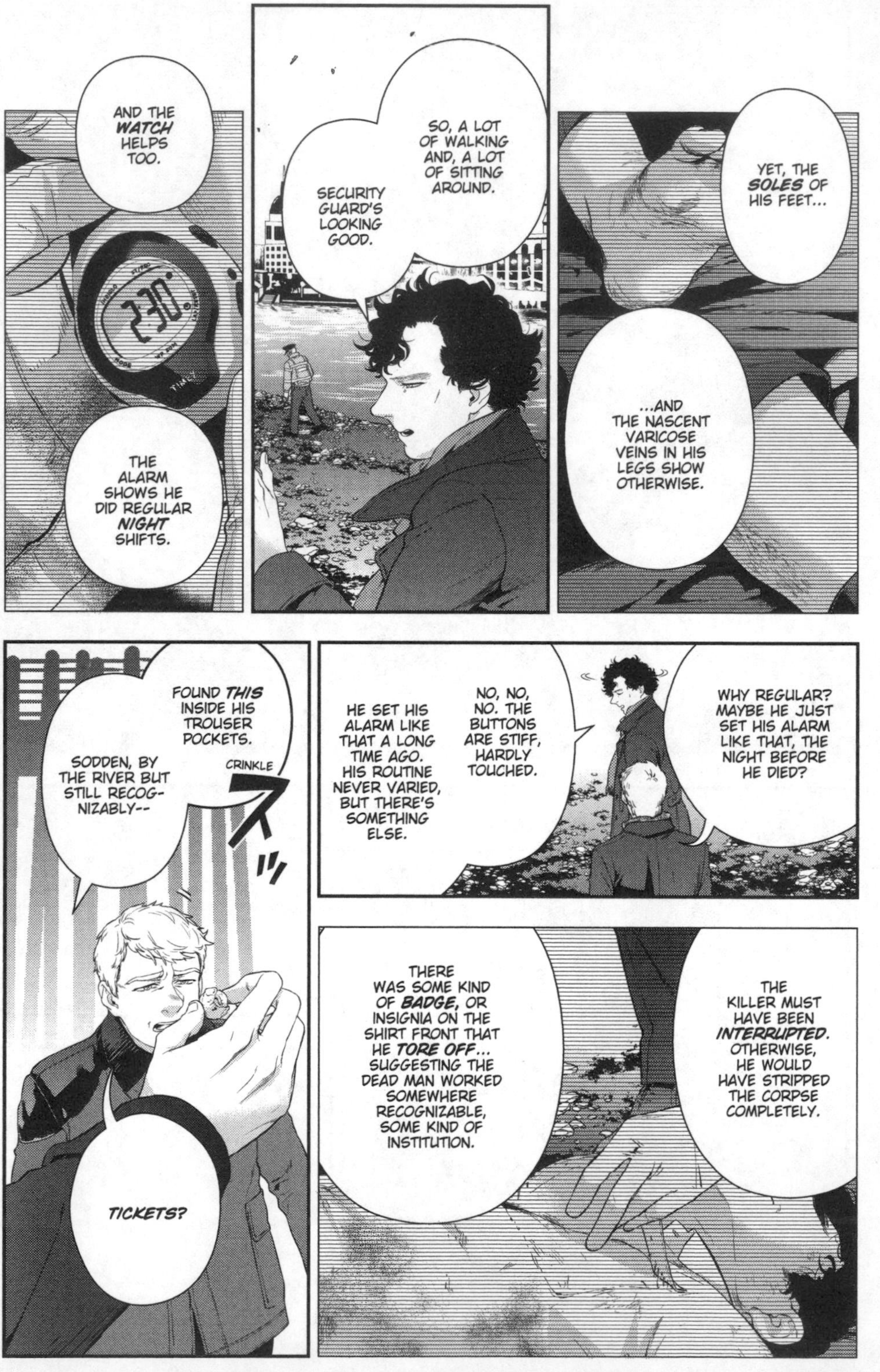
YET, THE *SOLES* OF HIS FEET...
...AND THE NASCENT VARICOSE VEINS IN HIS LEGS SHOW OTHERWISE.
SO, A LOT OF WALKING AND, A LOT OF SITTING AROUND.
SECURITY GUARD'S LOOKING GOOD.
AND THE *WATCH* HELPS TOO.
THE ALARM SHOWS HE DID REGULAR *NIGHT* SHIFTS.
WHY REGULAR? MAYBE HE JUST SET HIS ALARM LIKE THAT, THE NIGHT BEFORE HE DIED?
NO, NO, NO. THE BUTTONS ARE STIFF, HARDLY TOUCHED.
HE SET HIS ALARM LIKE THAT A LONG TIME AGO. HIS ROUTINE NEVER VARIED, BUT THERE'S SOMETHING ELSE.
THE KILLER MUST HAVE BEEN *INTERRUPTED*. OTHERWISE, HE WOULD HAVE STRIPPED THE CORPSE COMPLETELY.
THERE WAS SOME KIND OF *BADGE*, OR INSIGNIA ON THE SHIRT FRONT THAT HE *TORE OFF*... SUGGESTING THE DEAD MAN WORKED SOMEWHERE RECOGNIZABLE, SOME KIND OF INSTITUTION.
FOUND *THIS* INSIDE HIS TROUSER POCKETS.
SODDEN, BY THE RIVER BUT STILL RECOG-NIZABLY--
CRINKLE
TICKETS?

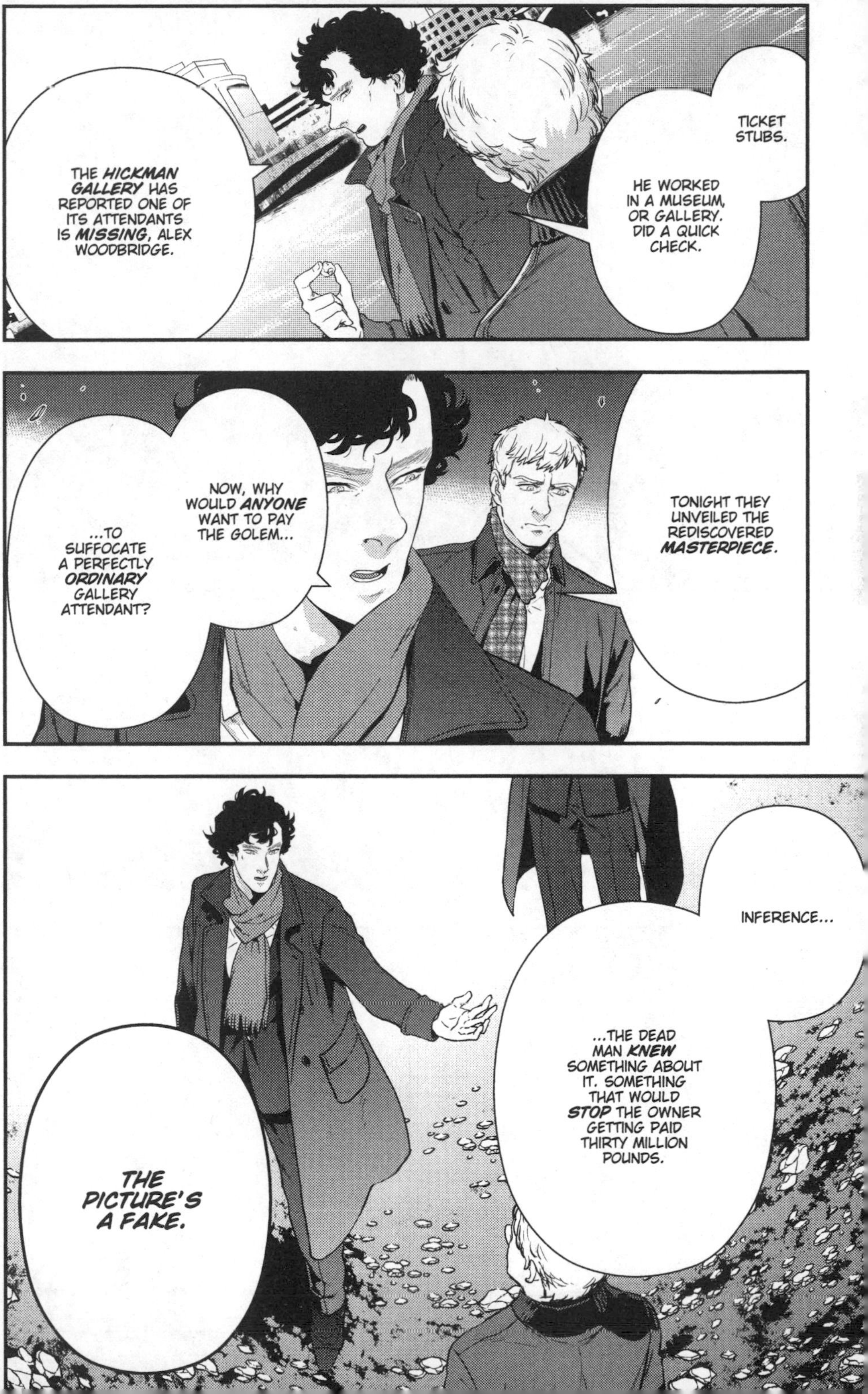
TICKET STUBS.
HE WORKED IN A MUSEUM, OR GALLERY. DID A QUICK CHECK.
THE *HICKMAN GALLERY* HAS REPORTED ONE OF ITS ATTENDANTS IS *MISSING*, ALEX WOODBRIDGE.
TONIGHT THEY UNVEILED THE REDISCOVERED *MASTERPIECE*.
NOW, WHY WOULD *ANYONE* WANT TO PAY THE GOLEM...
...TO SUFFOCATE A PERFECTLY *ORDINARY* GALLERY ATTENDANT?
INFERENCE...
...THE DEAD MAN *KNEW* SOMETHING ABOUT IT. SOMETHING THAT WOULD *STOP* THE OWNER GETTING PAID THIRTY MILLION POUNDS.
THE PICTURE'S A FAKE.

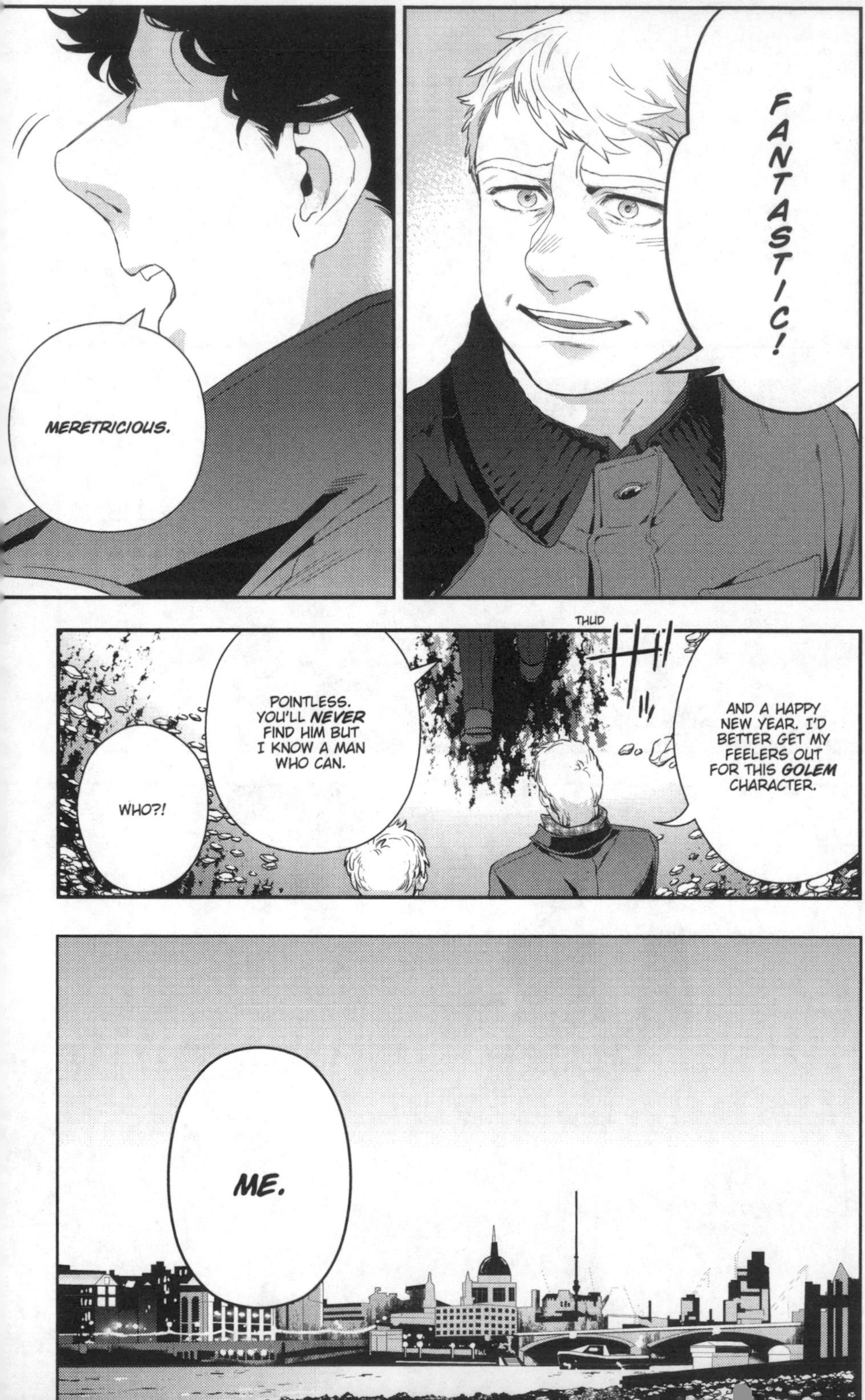
FANTASTIC!
MERETRICIOUS.
THUD
AND A HAPPY NEW YEAR. I'D BETTER GET MY FEELERS OUT FOR THIS GOLEM CHARACTER.
POINTLESS. YOU'LL NEVER FIND HIM BUT I KNOW A MAN WHO CAN.
WHO?!
ME.

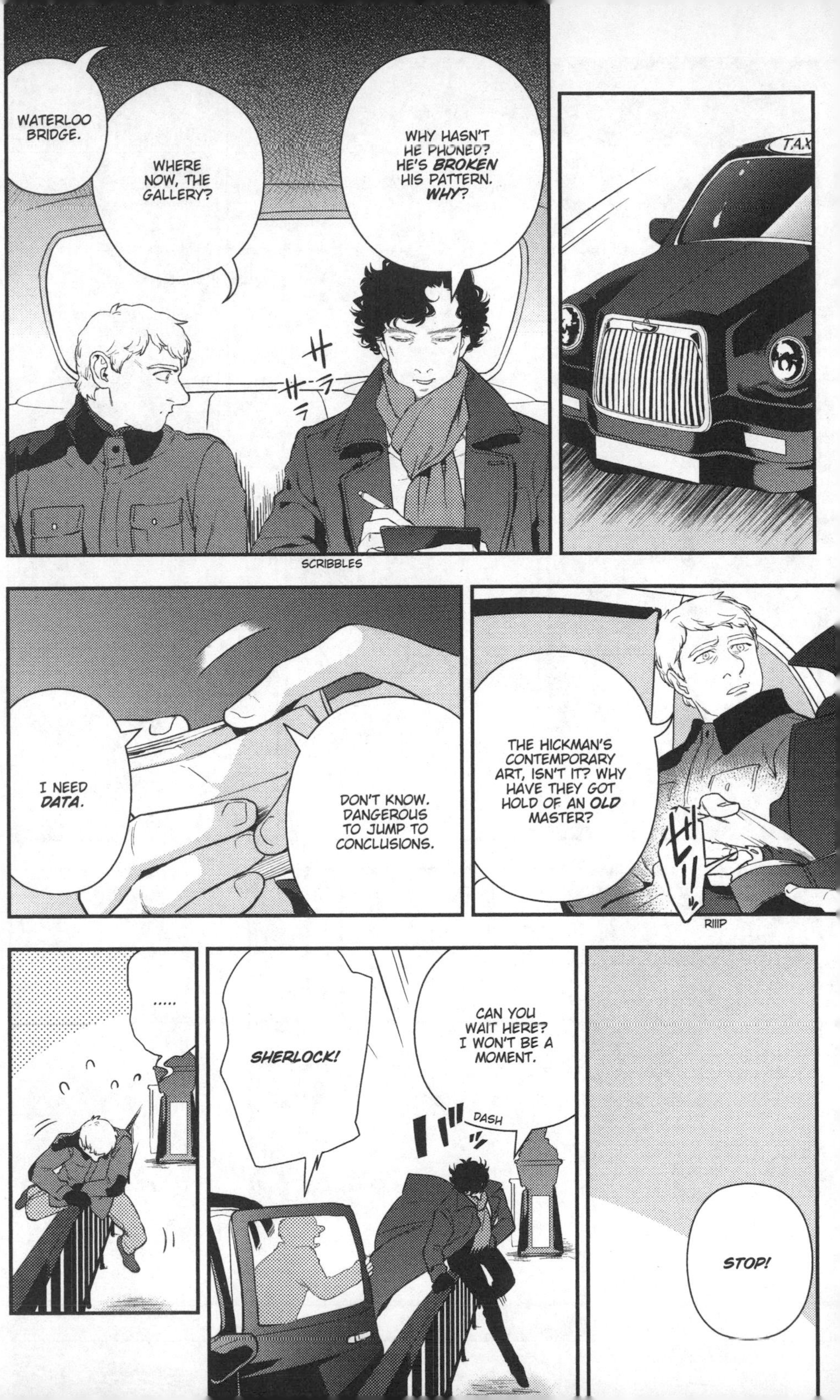
WHY HASN'T HE PHONED? HE'S **BROKEN** HIS PATTERN. **WHY**?
WHERE NOW, THE GALLERY?
WATERLOO BRIDGE.
SCRIBBLES
THE HICKMAN'S CONTEMPORARY ART, ISN'T IT? WHY HAVE THEY GOT HOLD OF AN **OLD** MASTER?
RIIIP
DON'T KNOW. DANGEROUS TO JUMP TO CONCLUSIONS.
I NEED **DATA**.
STOP!
CAN YOU WAIT HERE? I WON'T BE A MOMENT.
DASH
SHERLOCK!
.....

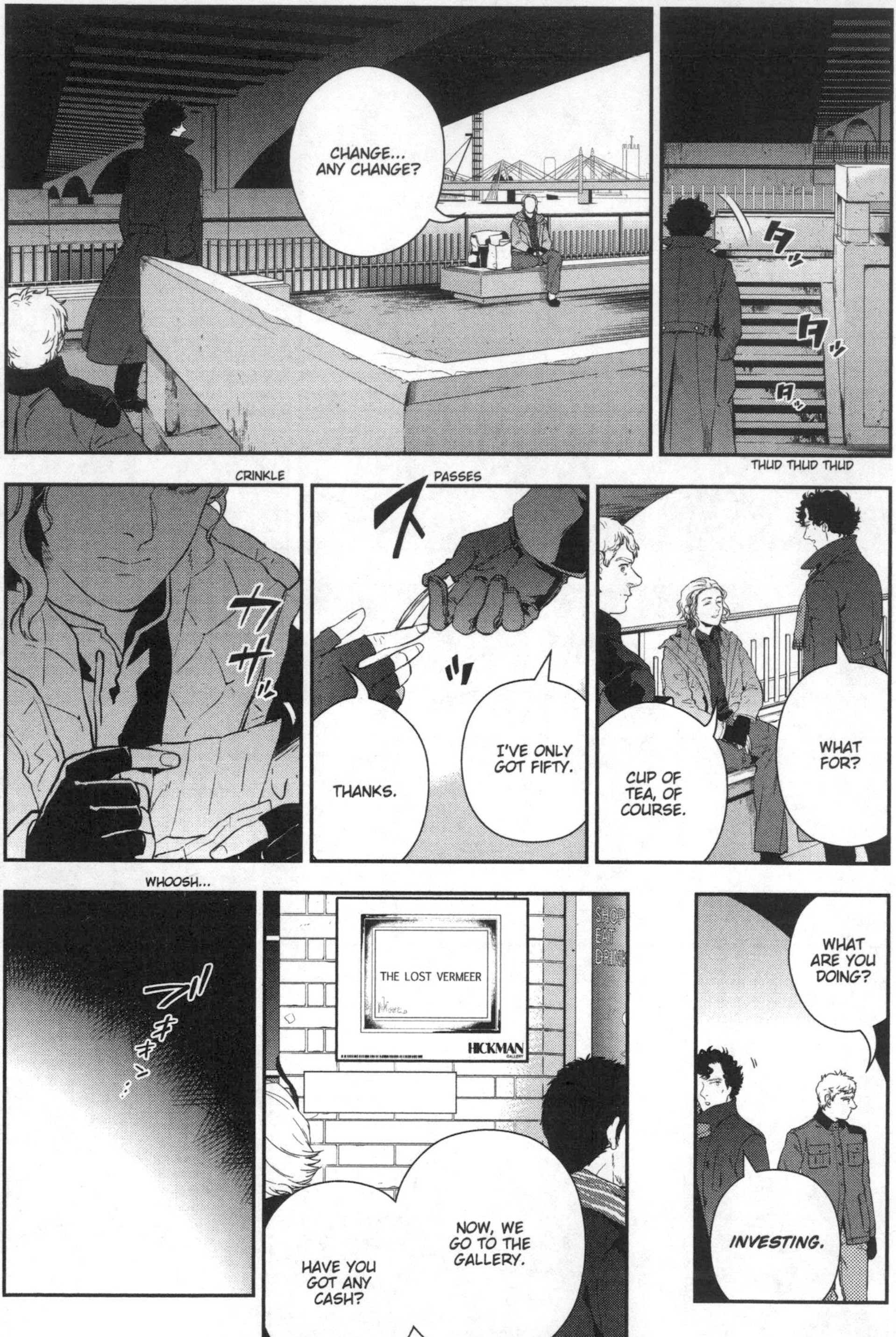

THUD THUD THUD
CHANGE... ANY CHANGE?
WHAT FOR?
CUP OF TEA, OF COURSE.
PASSES
I'VE ONLY GOT FIFTY.
THANKS.
CRINKLE
WHAT ARE YOU DOING?
INVESTING.
THE LOST VERMEER
HICKMAN GALLERY
SHOP EAT DRINK
NOW, WE GO TO THE GALLERY.
HAVE YOU GOT ANY CASH?
WHOOSH...

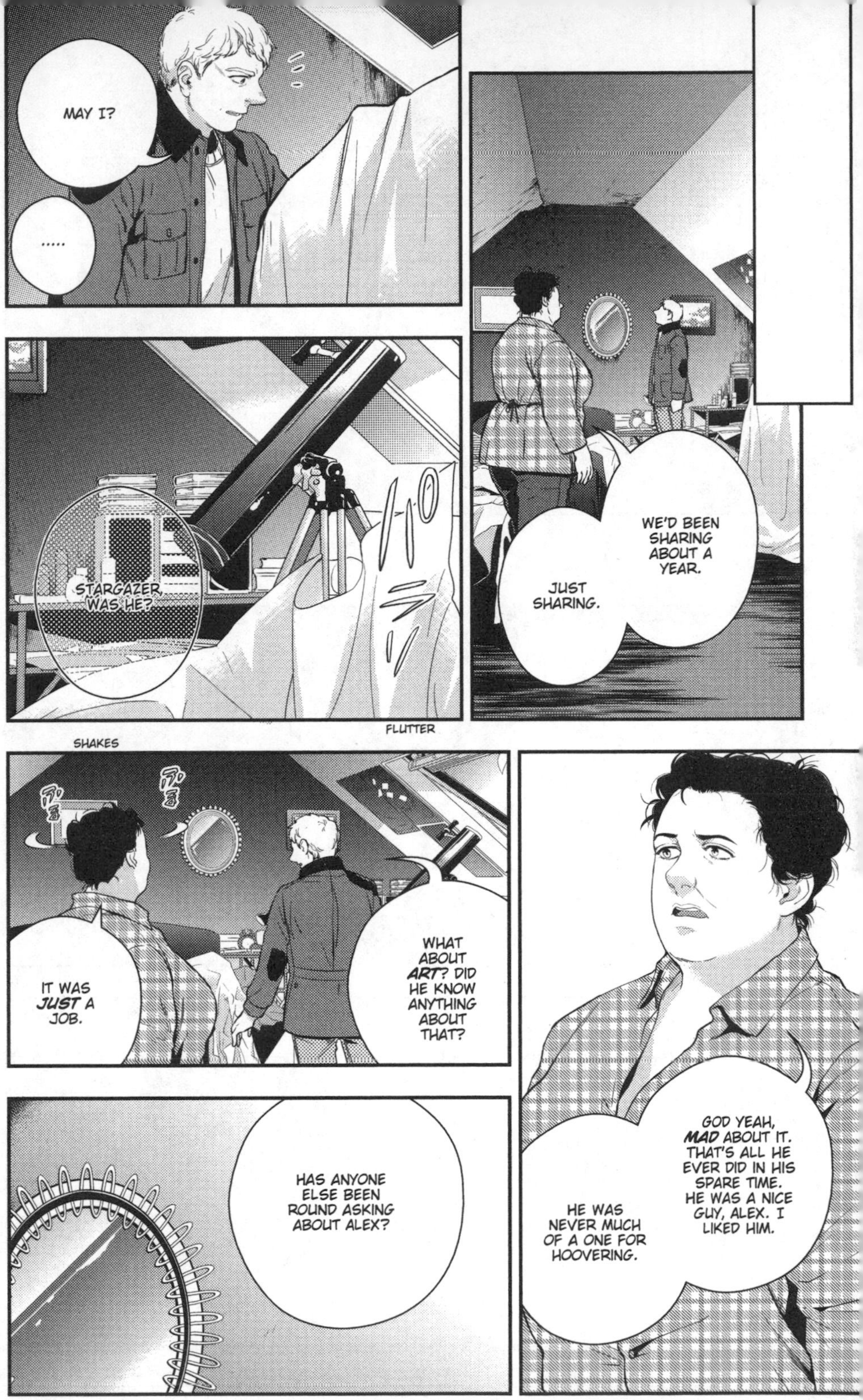
WE'D BEEN SHARING ABOUT A YEAR.
JUST SHARING.
MAY I?
.....
STARGAZER, WAS HE?
FLUTTER
SHAKES
GOD YEAH, MAD ABOUT IT. THAT'S ALL HE EVER DID IN HIS SPARE TIME. HE WAS A NICE GUY, ALEX. I LIKED HIM.
HE WAS NEVER MUCH OF A ONE FOR HOOVERING.
WHAT ABOUT ART? DID HE KNOW ANYTHING ABOUT THAT?
IT WAS JUST A JOB.
HAS ANYONE ELSE BEEN ROUND ASKING ABOUT ALEX?

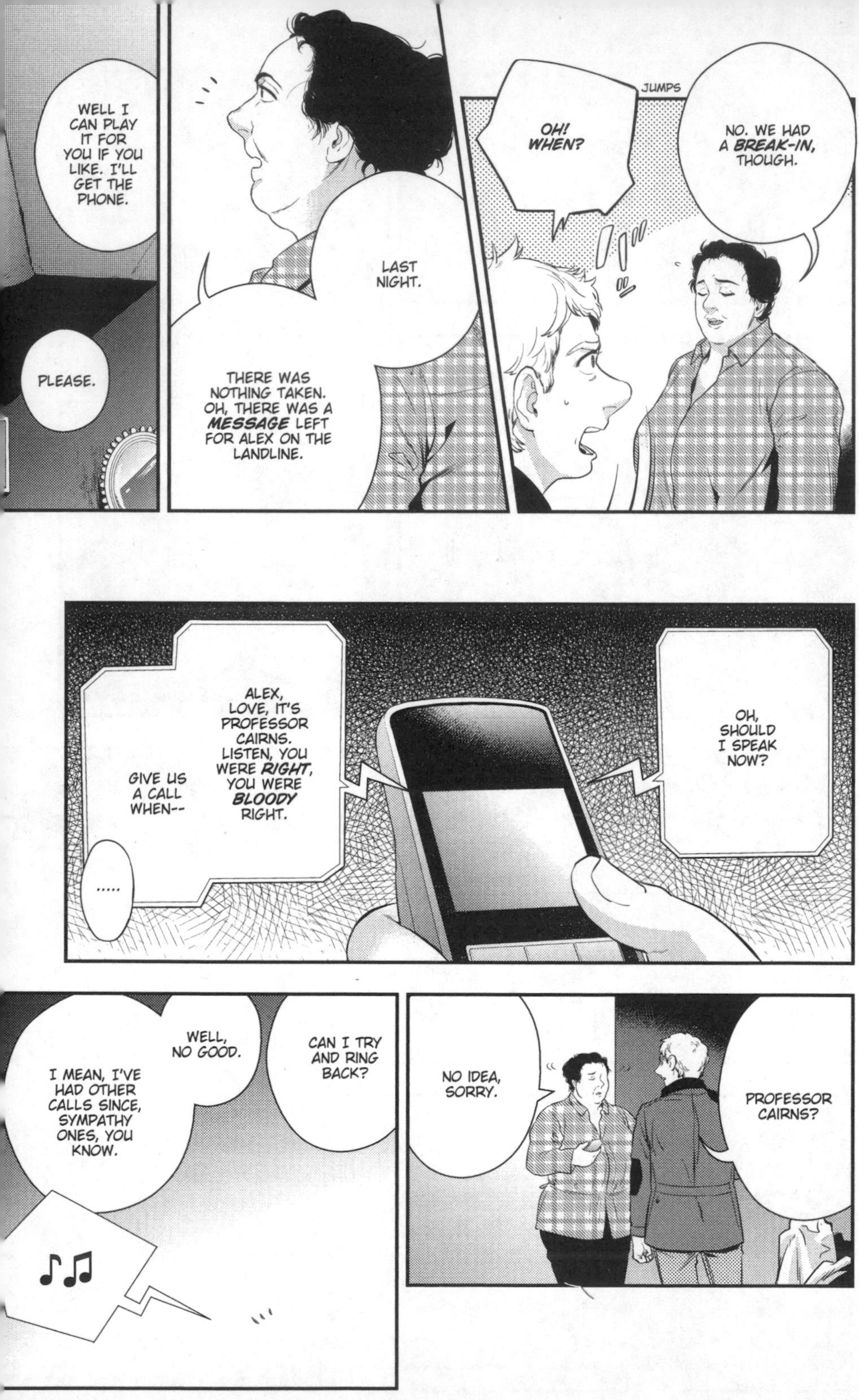
NO. WE HAD A BREAK-IN, THOUGH.
JUMPS
OH! WHEN?
LAST NIGHT.
THERE WAS NOTHING TAKEN. OH, THERE WAS A MESSAGE LEFT FOR ALEX ON THE LANDLINE.
WELL I CAN PLAY IT FOR YOU IF YOU LIKE. I'LL GET THE PHONE.
PLEASE.
OH, SHOULD I SPEAK NOW?
ALEX, LOVE, IT'S PROFESSOR CAIRNS. LISTEN, YOU WERE RIGHT, YOU WERE BLOODY RIGHT.
GIVE US A CALL WHEN--
.....
PROFESSOR CAIRNS?
NO IDEA, SORRY.
CAN I TRY AND RING BACK?
WELL, NO GOOD.
I MEAN, I'VE HAD OTHER CALLS SINCE, SYMPATHY ONES, YOU KNOW.
♪♫

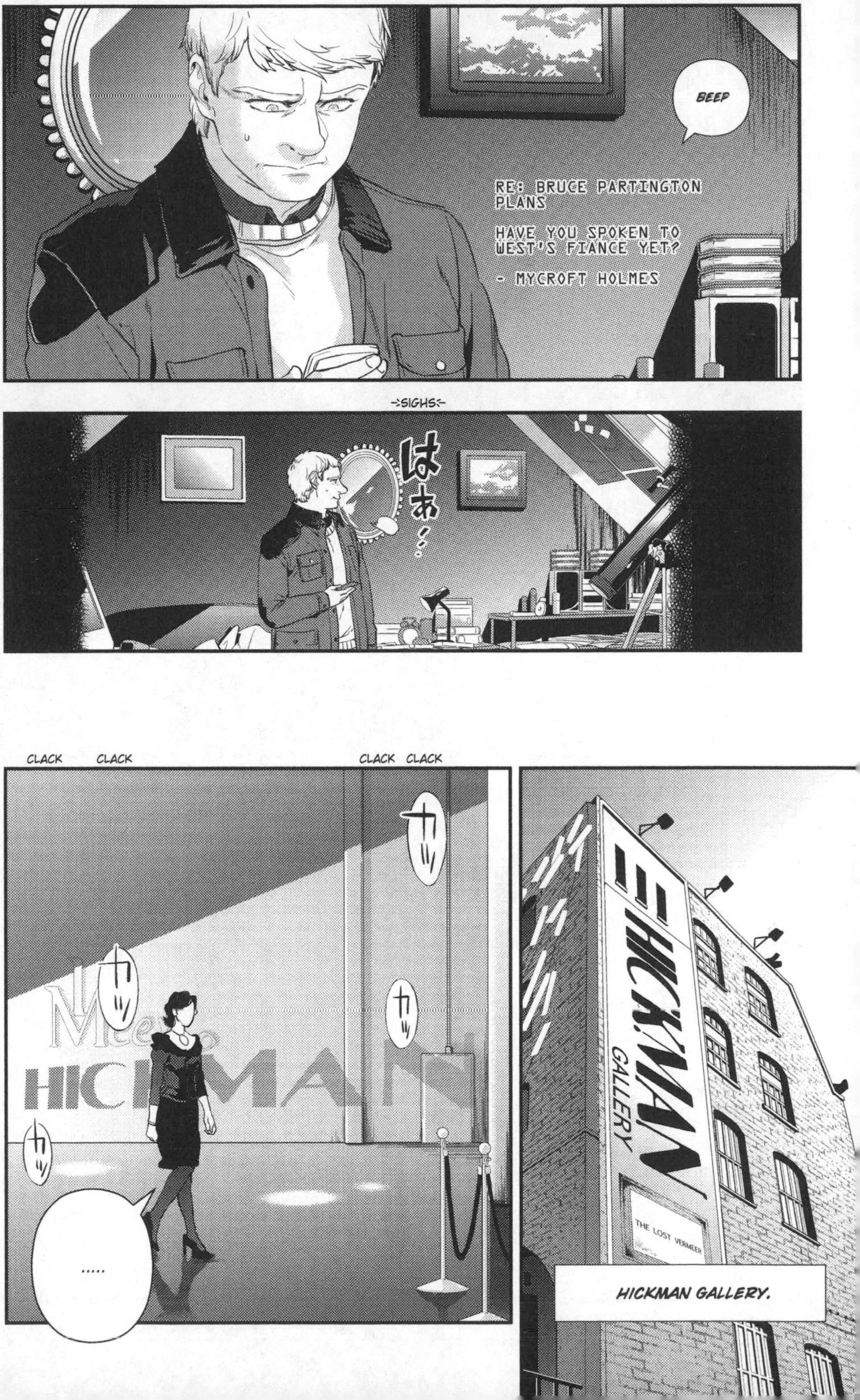
BEEP
RE: BRUCE PARTINGTON PLANS
HAVE YOU SPOKEN TO WEST'S FIANCE YET?
- MYCROFT HOLMES
-SIGHS-
はぁ!
HICKMAN GALLERY
THE LOST VERMEER
HICKMAN GALLERY.
CLACK CLACK CLACK CLACK
カッ
カッ
カッ
カッ
......

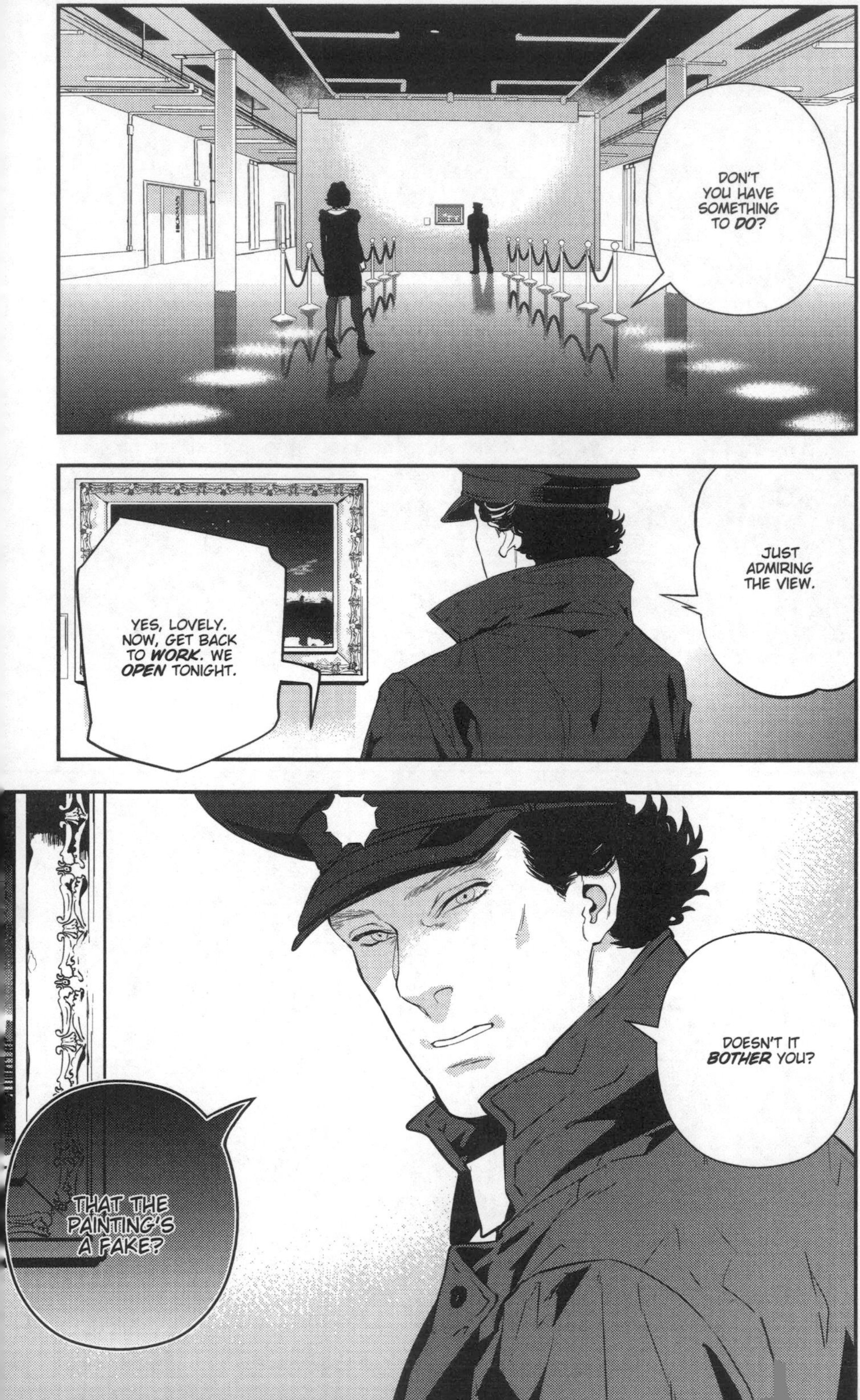
DON'T YOU HAVE SOMETHING TO *DO*?
JUST ADMIRING THE VIEW.
YES, LOVELY. NOW, GET BACK TO *WORK*. WE *OPEN* TONIGHT.
DOESN'T IT *BOTHER* YOU?
THAT THE PAINTING'S A FAKE?

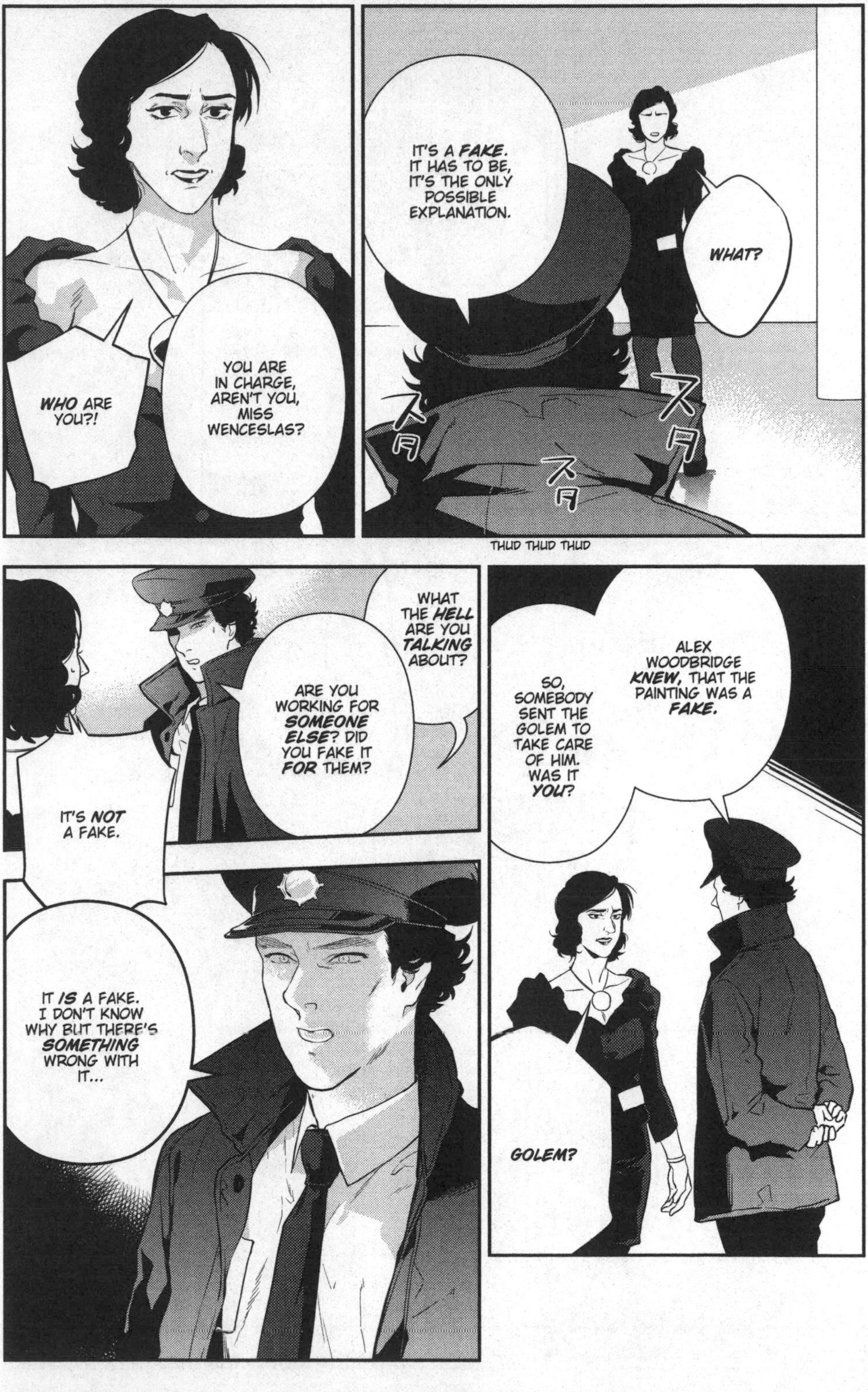
IT'S A **FAKE**. IT HAS TO BE, IT'S THE ONLY POSSIBLE EXPLANATION.
WHAT?
スタ
スタ
スタ
THUD THUD THUD
YOU ARE IN CHARGE, AREN'T YOU, MISS WENCESLAS?
WHO ARE YOU?!
ALEX WOODBRIDGE **KNEW**, THAT THE PAINTING WAS A **FAKE.**
SO, SOMEBODY SENT THE GOLEM TO TAKE CARE OF HIM. WAS IT **YOU**?
GOLEM?
WHAT THE **HELL** ARE YOU **TALKING** ABOUT?
ARE YOU WORKING FOR **SOMEONE ELSE**? DID YOU FAKE IT **FOR** THEM?
IT'S **NOT** A FAKE.
IT **IS** A FAKE. I DON'T KNOW WHY BUT THERE'S **SOMETHING** WRONG WITH IT...

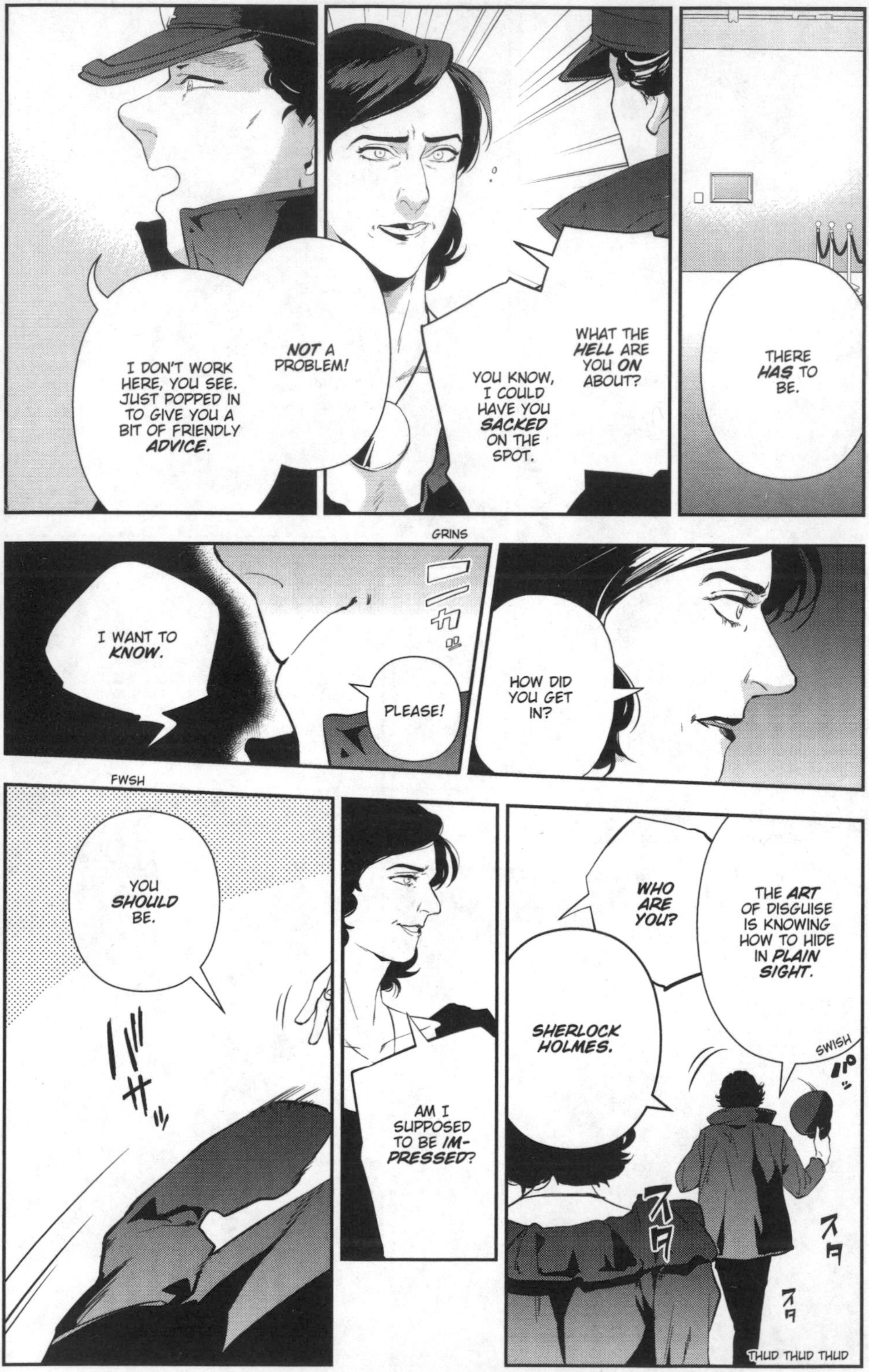
THERE HAS TO BE.
WHAT THE HELL ARE YOU ON ABOUT?
YOU KNOW, I COULD HAVE YOU SACKED ON THE SPOT.
NOT A PROBLEM!
I DON'T WORK HERE, YOU SEE. JUST POPPED IN TO GIVE YOU A BIT OF FRIENDLY ADVICE.
GRINS
HOW DID YOU GET IN?
PLEASE!
I WANT TO KNOW.
THE ART OF DISGUISE IS KNOWING HOW TO HIDE IN PLAIN SIGHT.
WHO ARE YOU?
SHERLOCK HOLMES.
SWISH
THUD THUD THUD
AM I SUPPOSED TO BE IM-PRESSED?
FWSH
YOU SHOULD BE.

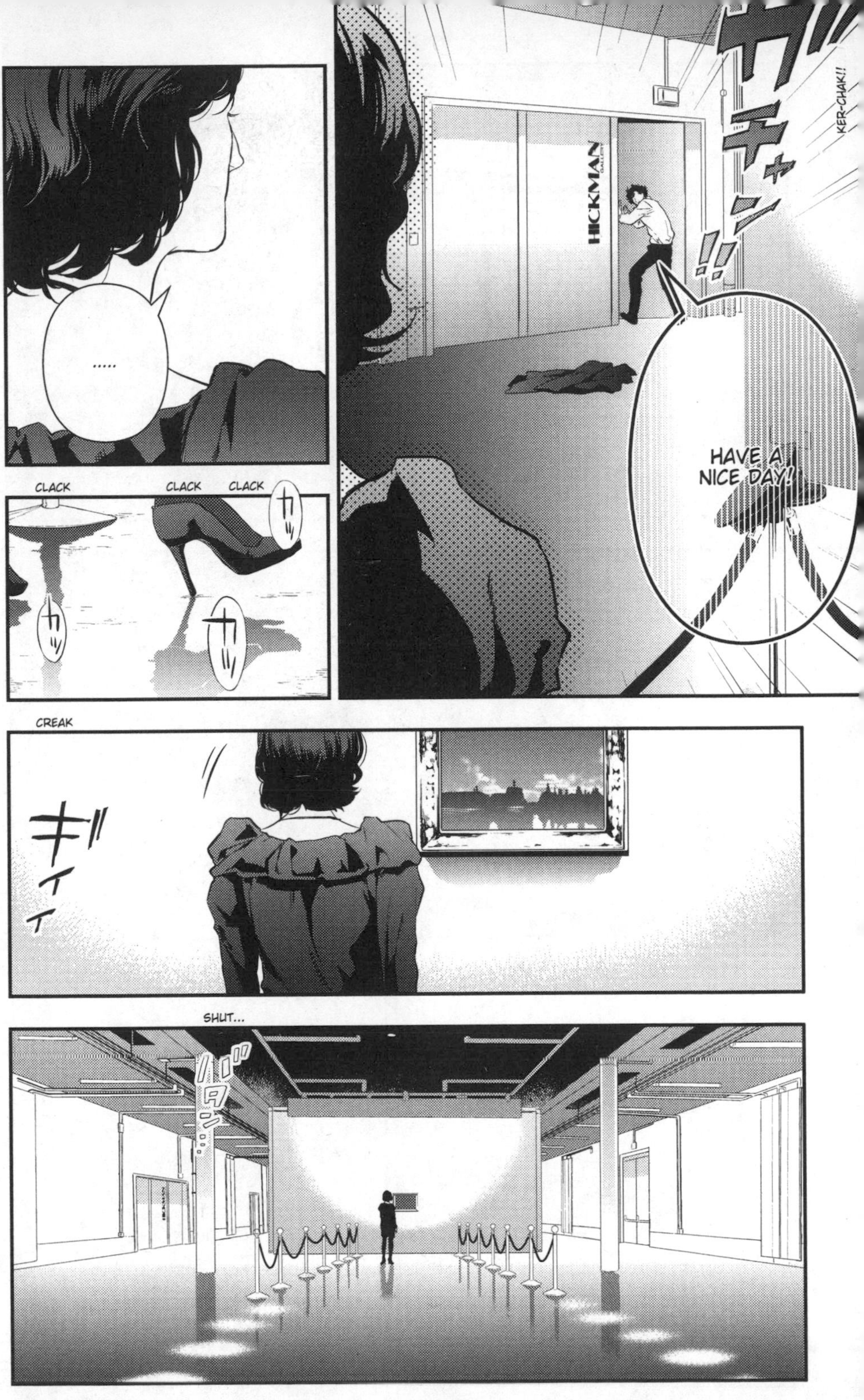
KER-CHAK!!
ガチャン!!
HICKMAN
HAVE A NICE DAY!
.....
CLACK CLACK CLACK
カッ
カッ
カッ
CREAK
ギイイ
SHUT...
バタン…。

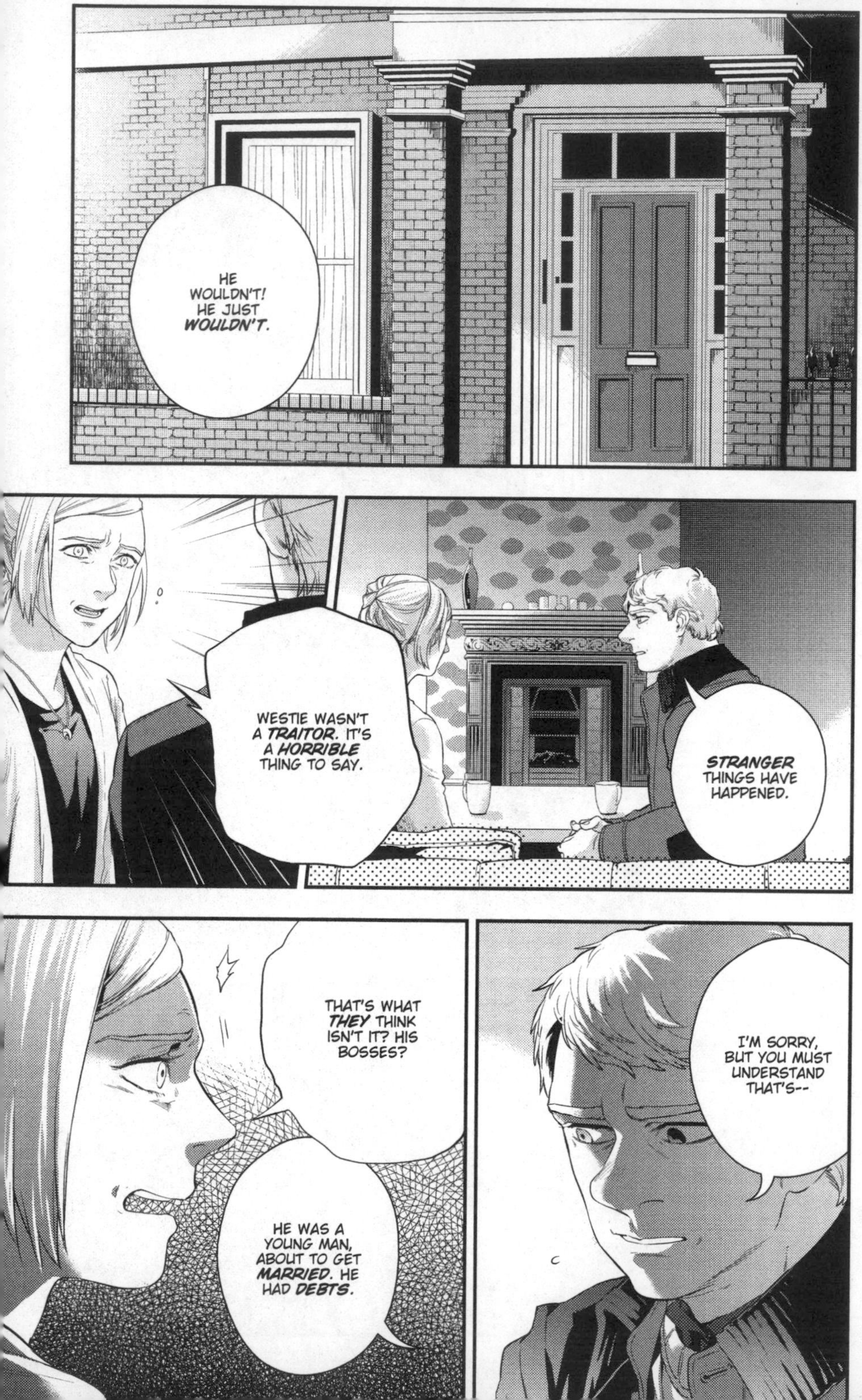
HE WOULDN'T! HE JUST ***WOULDN'T***.
WESTIE WASN'T A ***TRAITOR***. IT'S A ***HORRIBLE*** THING TO SAY.
STRANGER THINGS HAVE HAPPENED.
THAT'S WHAT ***THEY*** THINK ISN'T IT? HIS BOSSES?
HE WAS A YOUNG MAN, ABOUT TO GET ***MARRIED***. HE HAD ***DEBTS***.
I'M SORRY, BUT YOU MUST UNDERSTAND THAT'S--

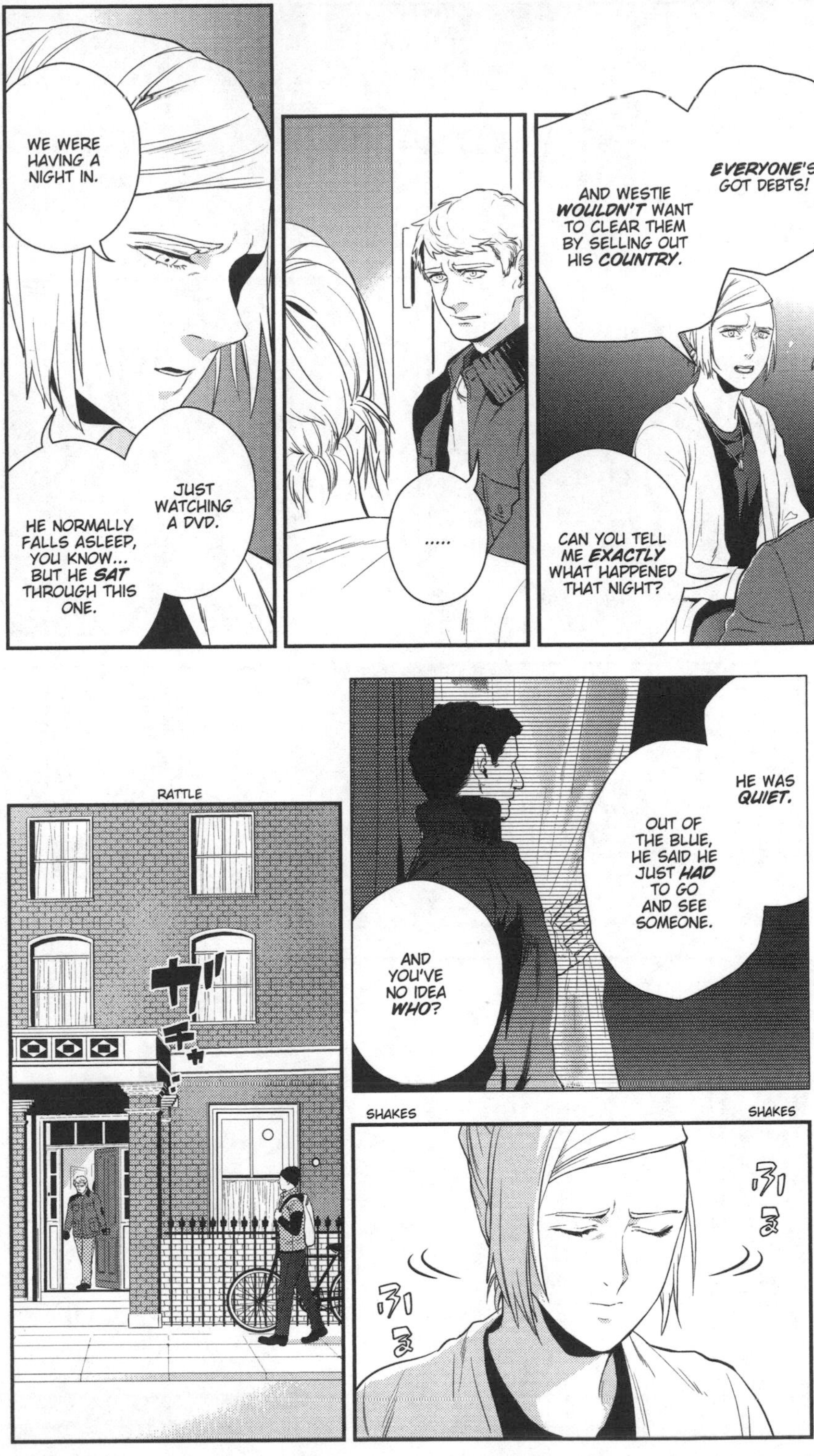
EVERYONE'S GOT DEBTS!
AND WESTIE WOULDN'T WANT TO CLEAR THEM BY SELLING OUT HIS COUNTRY.
CAN YOU TELL ME EXACTLY WHAT HAPPENED THAT NIGHT?
.....
WE WERE HAVING A NIGHT IN.
JUST WATCHING A DVD.
HE NORMALLY FALLS ASLEEP, YOU KNOW... BUT HE SAT THROUGH THIS ONE.
HE WAS QUIET.
OUT OF THE BLUE, HE SAID HE JUST HAD TO GO AND SEE SOMEONE.
AND YOU'VE NO IDEA WHO?
SHAKES
SHAKES
ふるふる
RATTLE
ガチャ

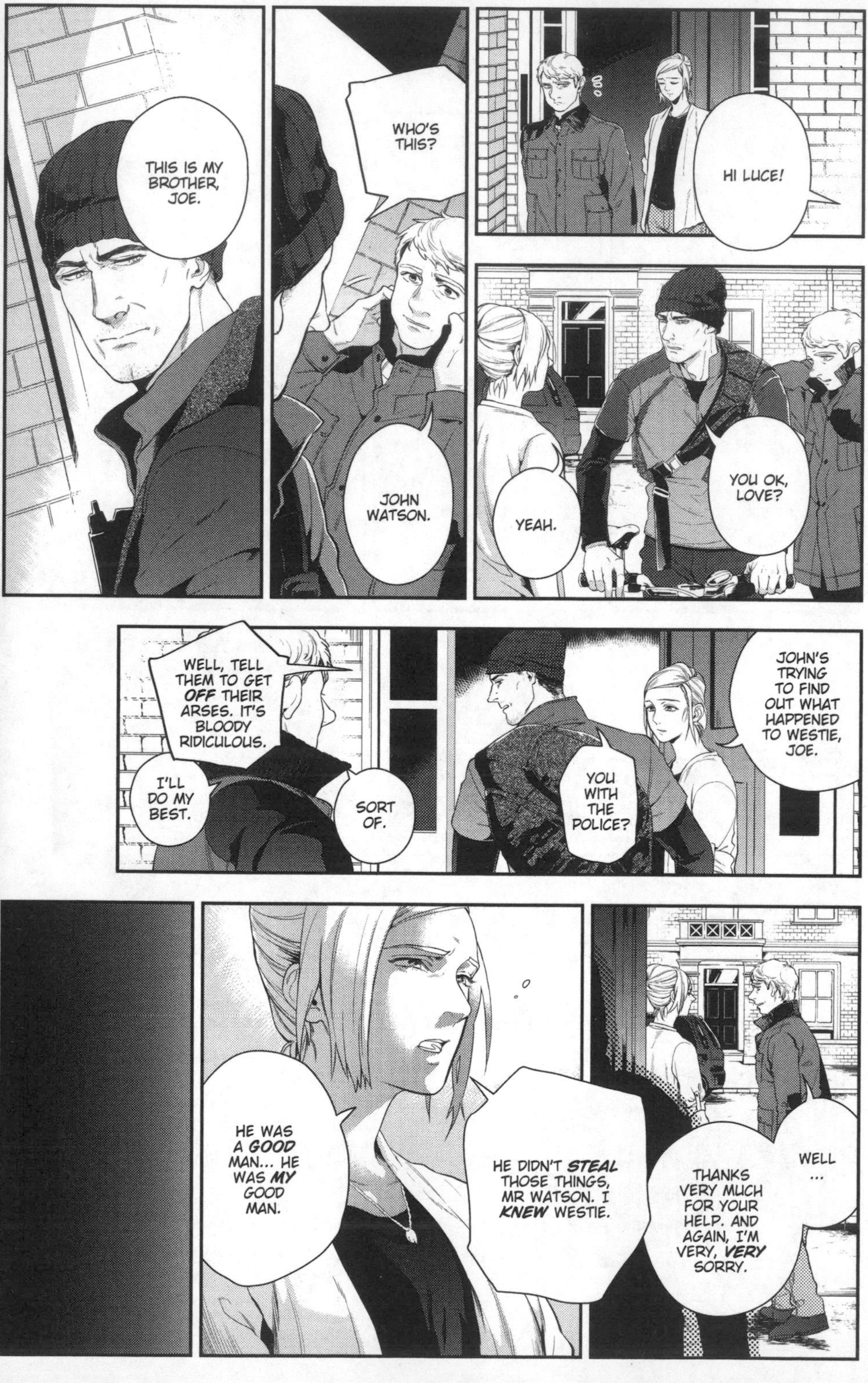
HI LUCE!
YOU OK, LOVE?
YEAH.
WHO'S THIS?
JOHN WATSON.
THIS IS MY BROTHER, JOE.
JOHN'S TRYING TO FIND OUT WHAT HAPPENED TO WESTIE, JOE.
YOU WITH THE POLICE?
SORT OF.
WELL, TELL THEM TO GET *OFF* THEIR ARSES. IT'S BLOODY RIDICULOUS.
I'LL DO MY BEST.
WELL ...
THANKS VERY MUCH FOR YOUR HELP. AND AGAIN, I'M VERY, *VERY* SORRY.
HE DIDN'T *STEAL* THOSE THINGS, MR WATSON. I *KNEW* WESTIE.
HE WAS A *GOOD* MAN... HE WAS *MY* GOOD MAN.

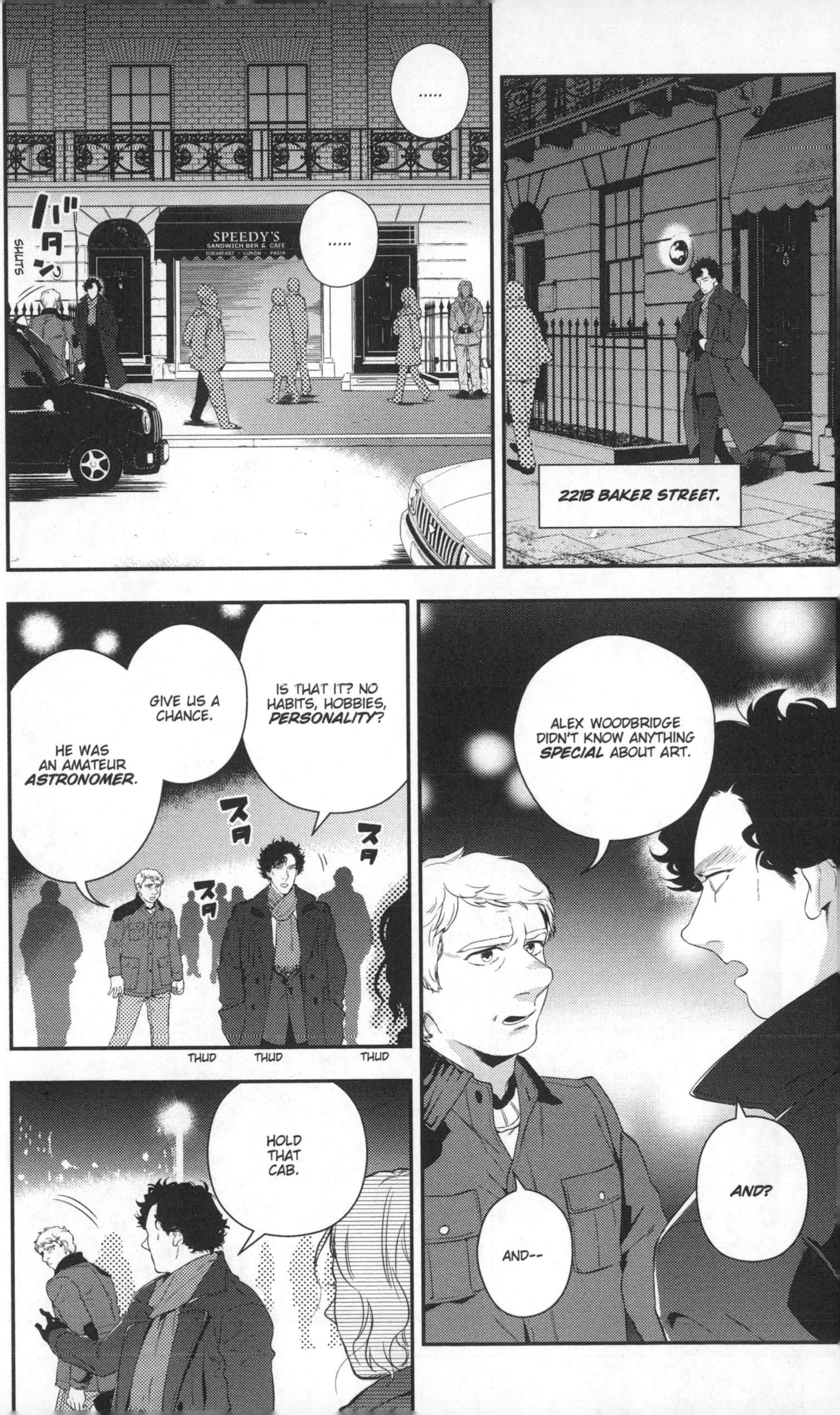
221B BAKER STREET.
......
......
SPEEDY'S
SANDWICH BER & CAFE
BREAKFAST · LUNCH · PASTA
バタン
SHUTS
ALEX WOODBRIDGE DIDN'T KNOW ANYTHING SPECIAL ABOUT ART.
AND?
AND--
IS THAT IT? NO HABITS, HOBBIES, PERSONALITY?
GIVE US A CHANCE.
HE WAS AN AMATEUR ASTRONOMER.
スタ
スタ
スタ
THUD
THUD
THUD
HOLD THAT CAB.

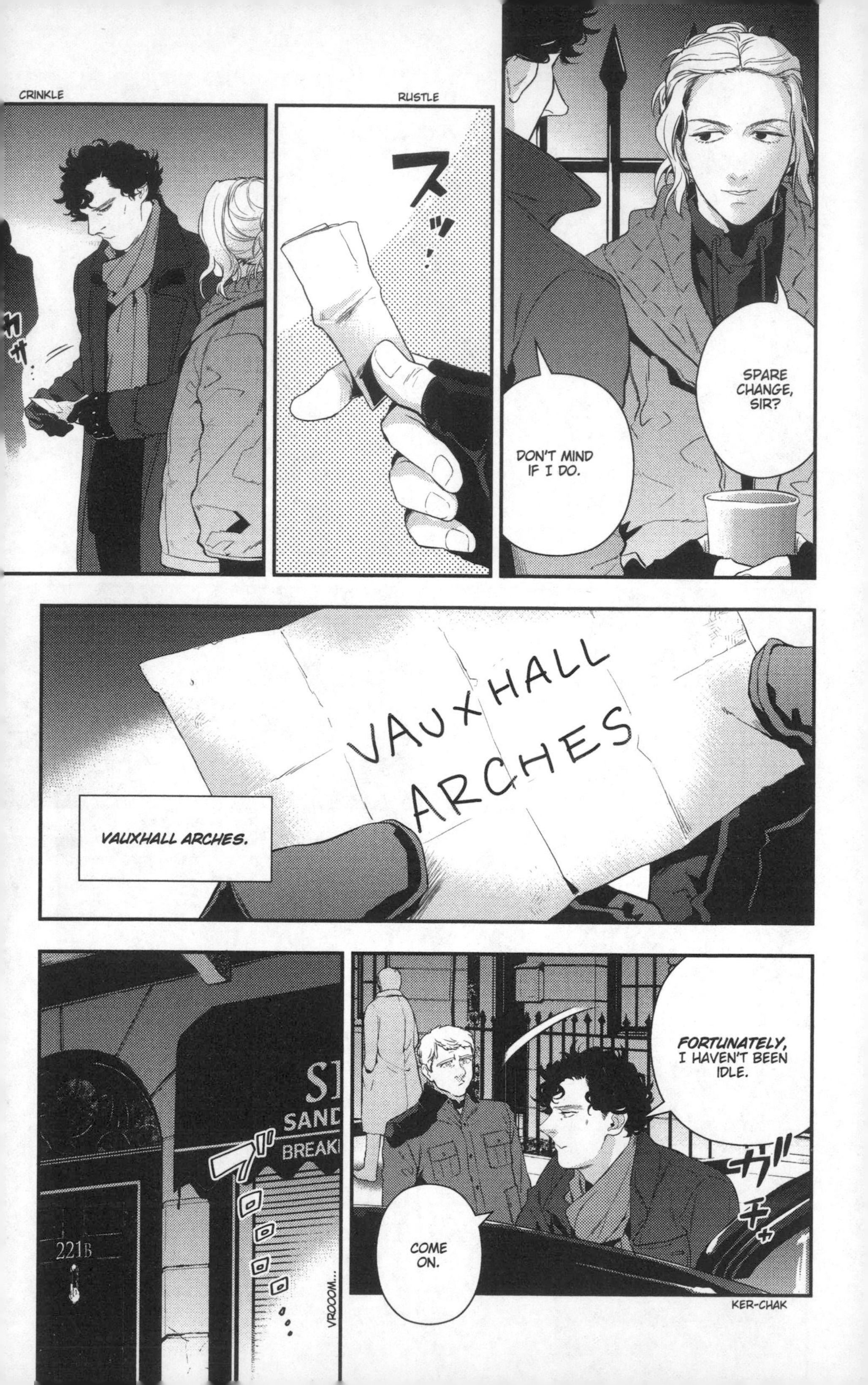
SPARE CHANGE, SIR?
DON'T MIND IF I DO.
RUSTLE
スッ
CRINKLE
VAUXHALL ARCHES
VAUXHALL ARCHES.
FORTUNATELY, I HAVEN'T BEEN IDLE.
COME ON.
KER-CHAK
VROOOM...
221B

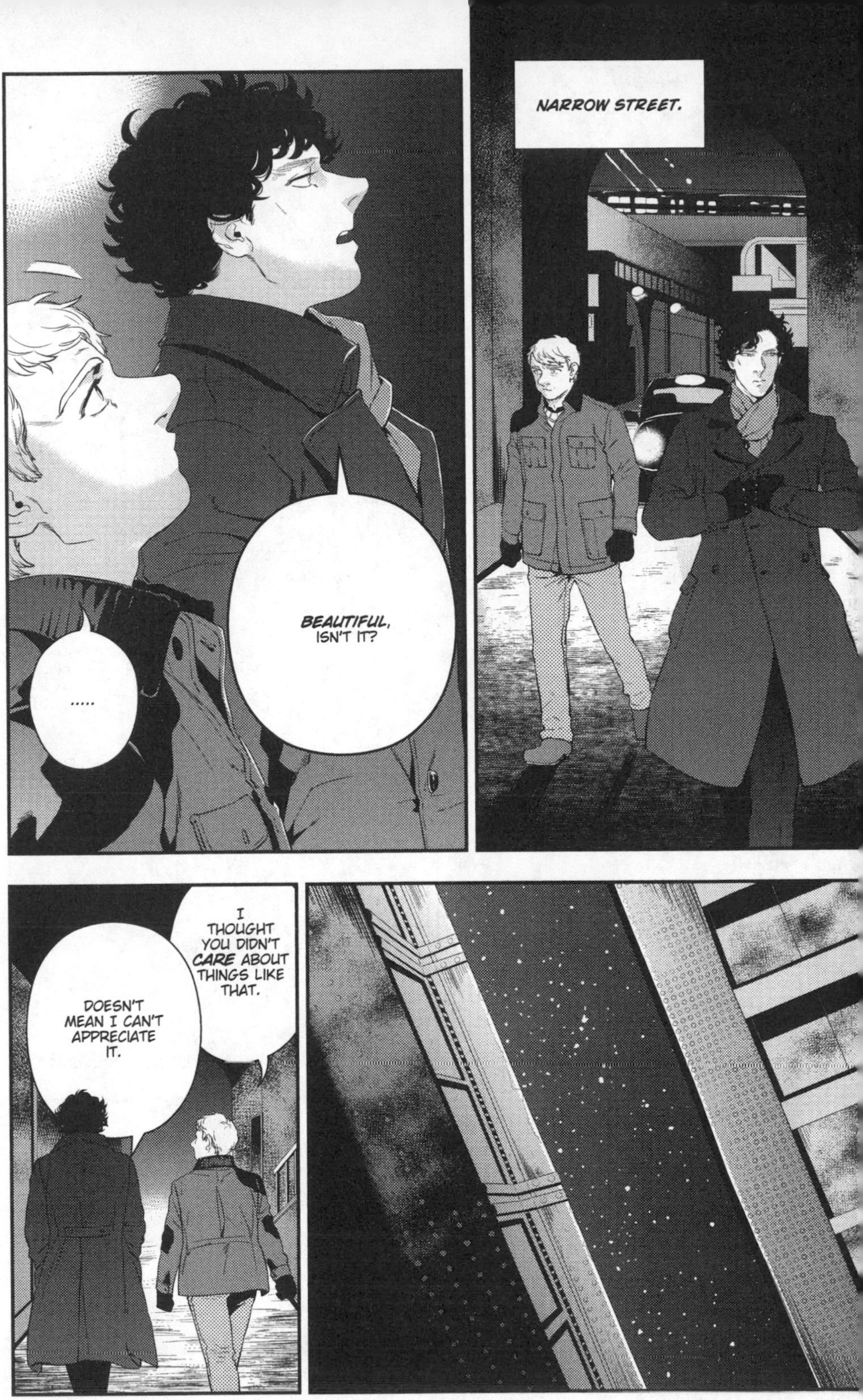
NARROW STREET.
BEAUTIFUL, ISN'T IT?
.....
I THOUGHT YOU DIDN'T CARE ABOUT THINGS LIKE THAT.
DOESN'T MEAN I CAN'T APPRECIATE IT.

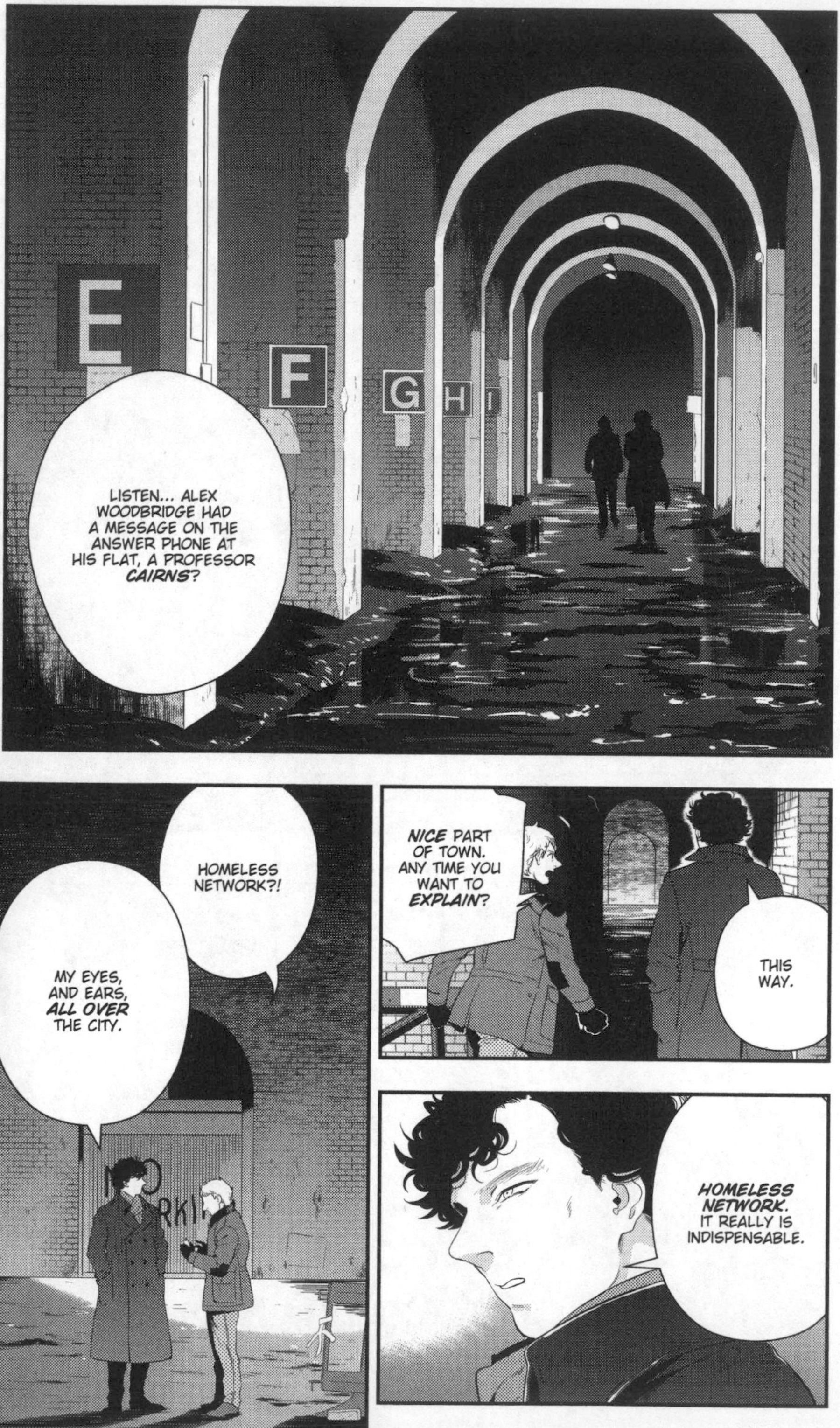
LISTEN... ALEX WOODBRIDGE HAD A MESSAGE ON THE ANSWER PHONE AT HIS FLAT, A PROFESSOR *CAIRNS*?
NICE PART OF TOWN. ANY TIME YOU WANT TO *EXPLAIN*?
THIS WAY.
HOMELESS NETWORK. IT REALLY IS INDISPENSABLE.
HOMELESS NETWORK?!
MY EYES, AND EARS, *ALL OVER* THE CITY.

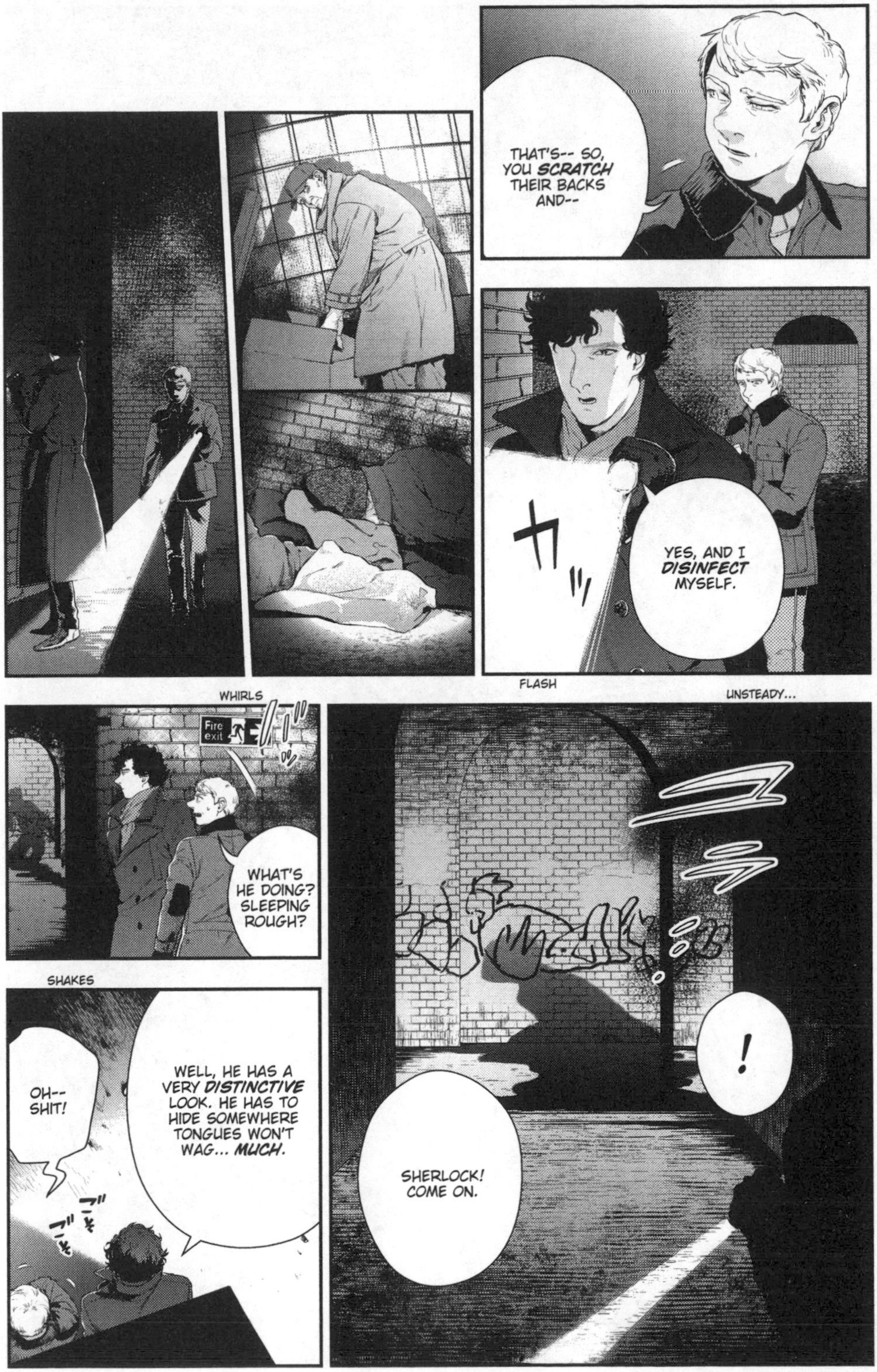
THAT'S-- SO, YOU SCRATCH THEIR BACKS AND--
YES, AND I DISINFECT MYSELF.
FLASH
UNSTEADY...
!
SHERLOCK! COME ON.
WHIRLS
WHAT'S HE DOING? SLEEPING ROUGH?
Fire exit
SHAKES
WELL, HE HAS A VERY DISTINCTIVE LOOK. HE HAS TO HIDE SOMEWHERE TONGUES WON'T WAG... MUCH.
OH-- SHIT!

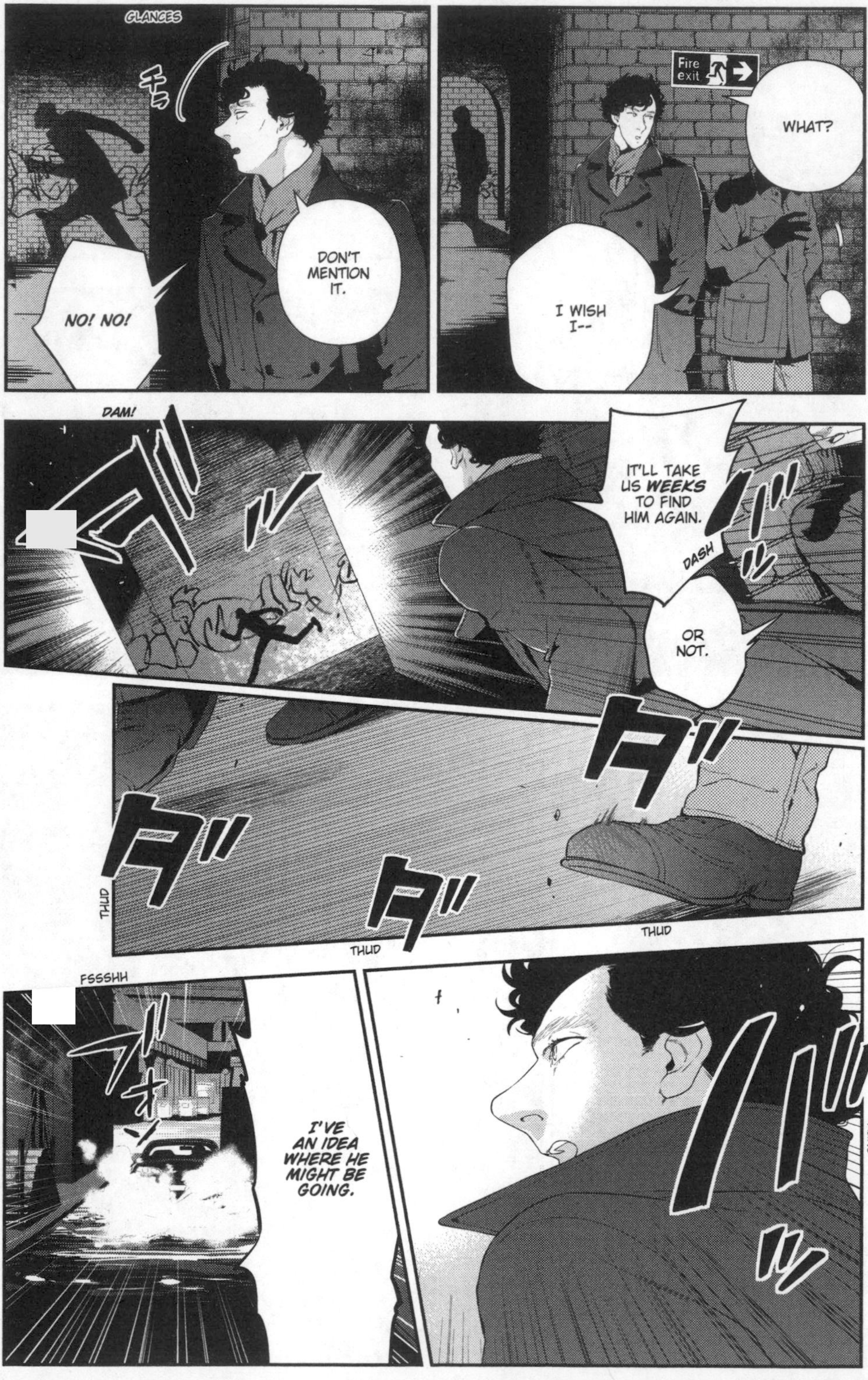
WHAT?
I WISH I--
GLANCES
DON'T MENTION IT.
NO! NO!
IT'LL TAKE US **WEEKS** TO FIND HIM AGAIN.
DASH
OR NOT.
DAM!
THUD
THUD
THUD
RUNS
FSSSHH
I'VE AN IDEA WHERE HE MIGHT BE GOING.
Fire exit

SOMEONE LEFT ALEX WOODBRIDGE A MESSAGE.

.....

I *TOLD* YOU.

WHAT?

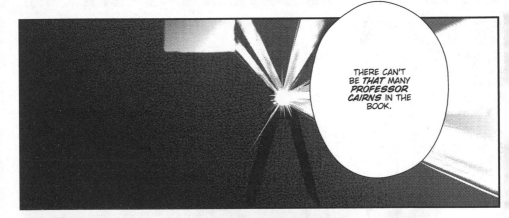

THERE CAN'T BE *THAT* MANY *PROFESSOR CAIRNS* IN THE BOOK.

JUPITER, THE FIFTH PLANET IN OUR SOLAR SYSTEM AND THE LARGEST.

JUPITER IS A GAS GIANT.

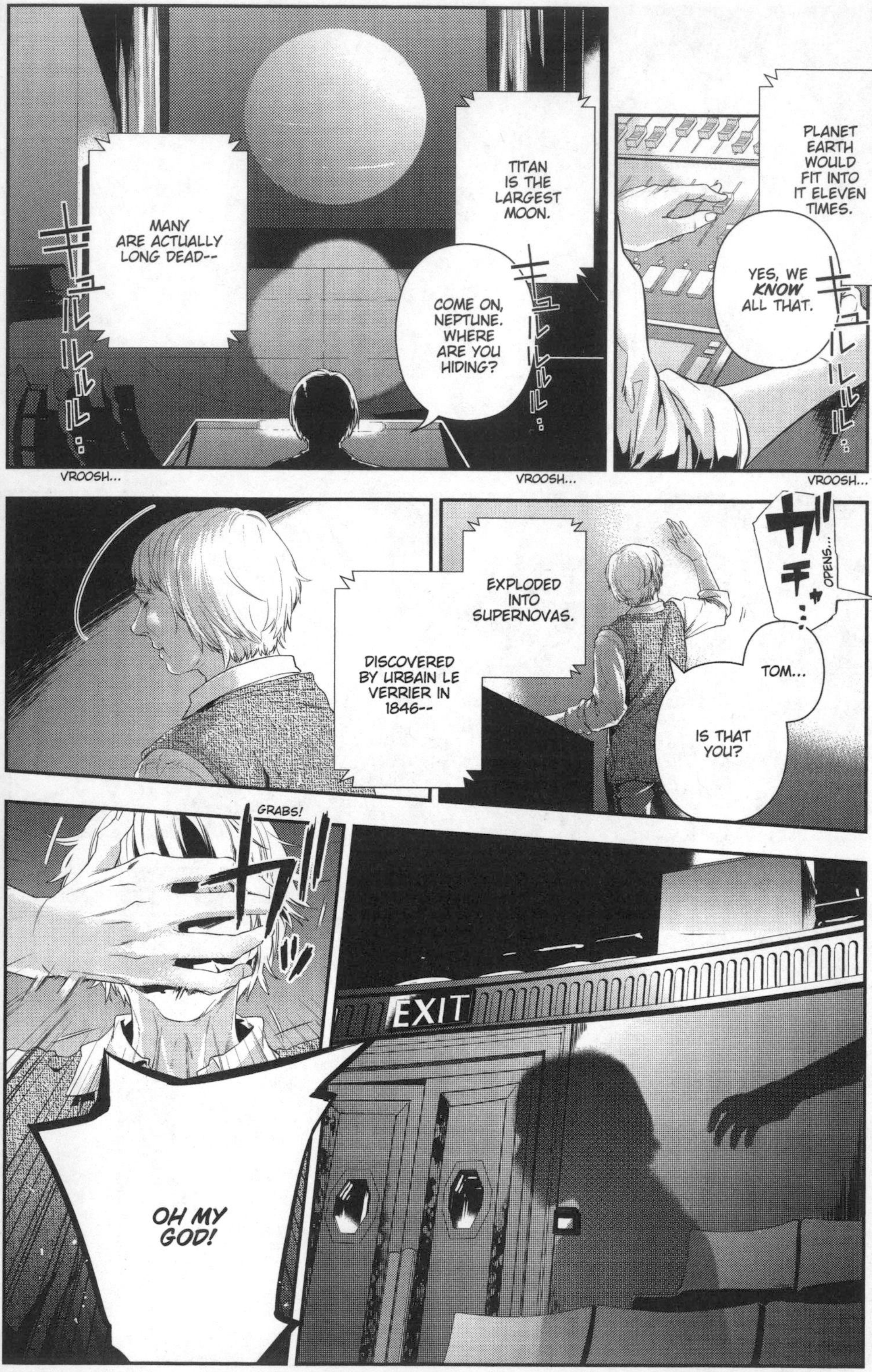

PLANET EARTH WOULD FIT INTO IT ELEVEN TIMES.
YES, WE **KNOW** ALL THAT.
キュルルル。
VROOSH...
TITAN IS THE LARGEST MOON.
COME ON, NEPTUNE. WHERE ARE YOU HIDING?
キュルルル。
VROOSH...
MANY ARE ACTUALLY LONG DEAD--
キュルルル。
VROOSH...
ガチャ
OPENS...
EXPLODED INTO SUPERNOVAS.
TOM...
IS THAT YOU?
DISCOVERED BY URBAIN LE VERRIER IN 1846--
EXIT
GRABS!
ガッ
OH MY GOD!

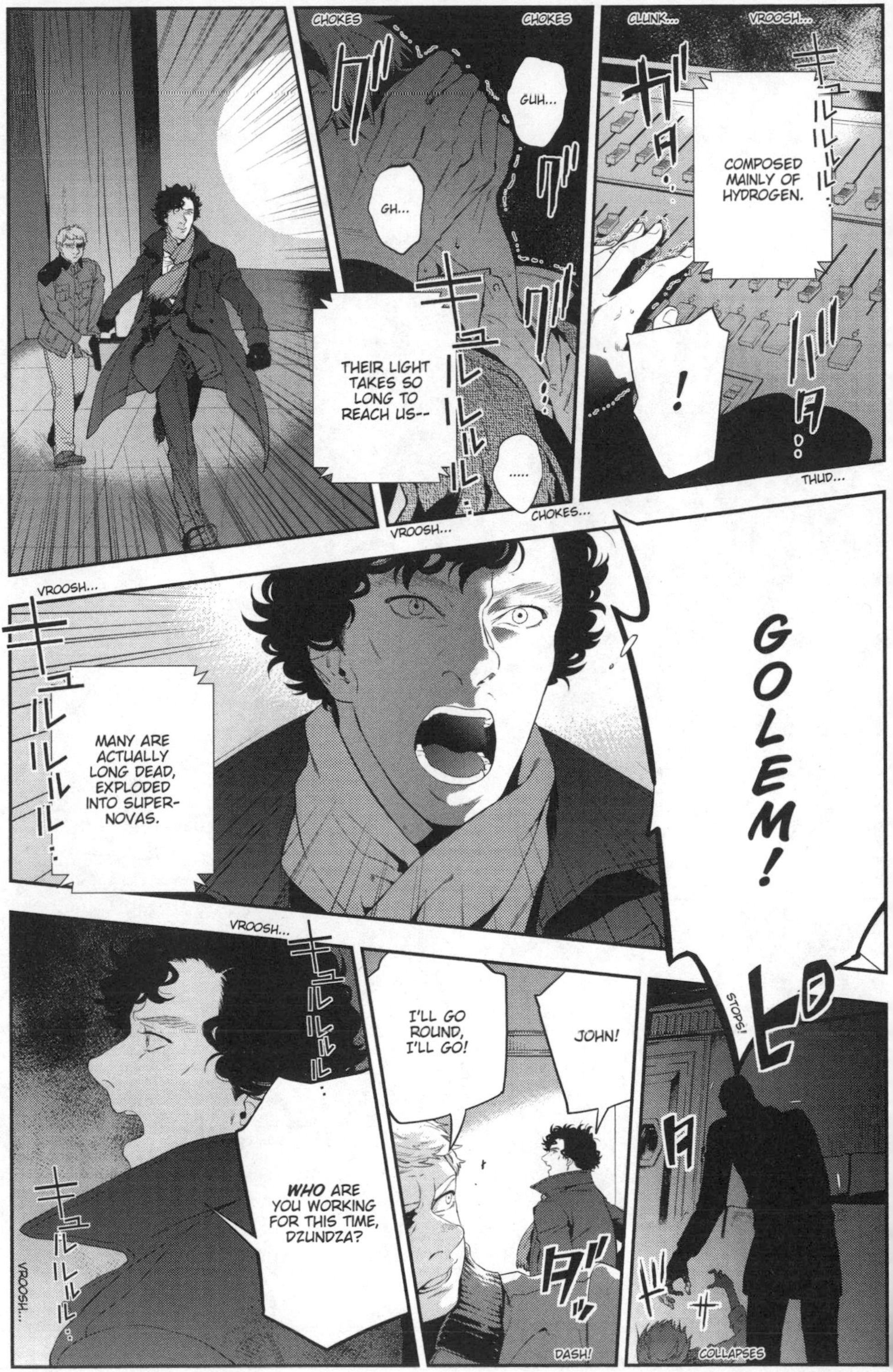
CLUNK...
VROOSH...
COMPOSED MAINLY OF HYDROGEN.
!
THUD...
CHOKES
CHOKES
GUH...
GH...
THEIR LIGHT TAKES SO LONG TO REACH US--
.....
CHOKES...
VROOSH...
GOLEM!
VROOSH...
MANY ARE ACTUALLY LONG DEAD, EXPLODED INTO SUPER-NOVAS.
STOPS!
COLLAPSES
JOHN!
I'LL GO ROUND, I'LL GO!
DASH!
VROOSH...
WHO ARE YOU WORKING FOR THIS TIME, DZUNDZA?
VROOSH...

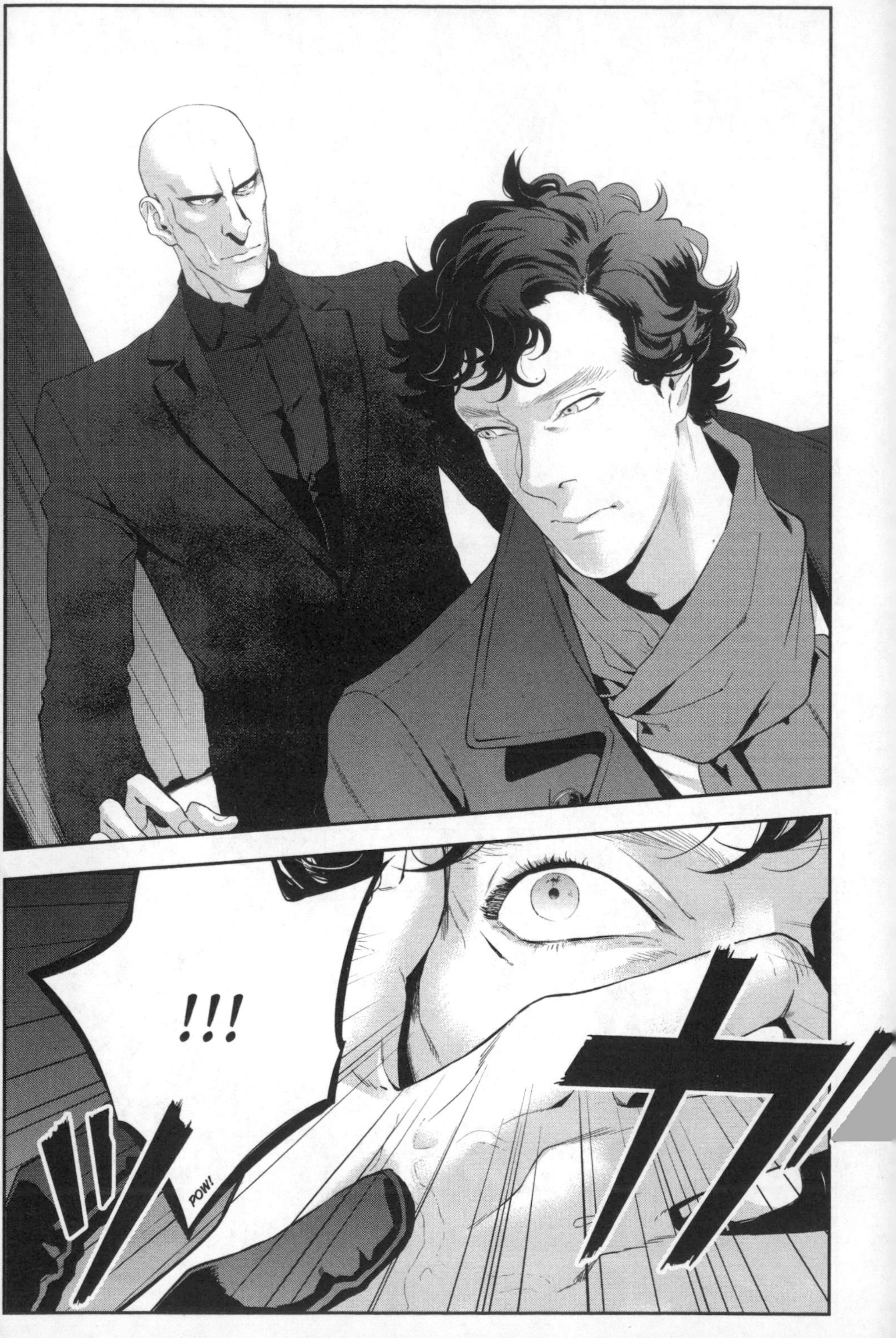
!!!
POW!

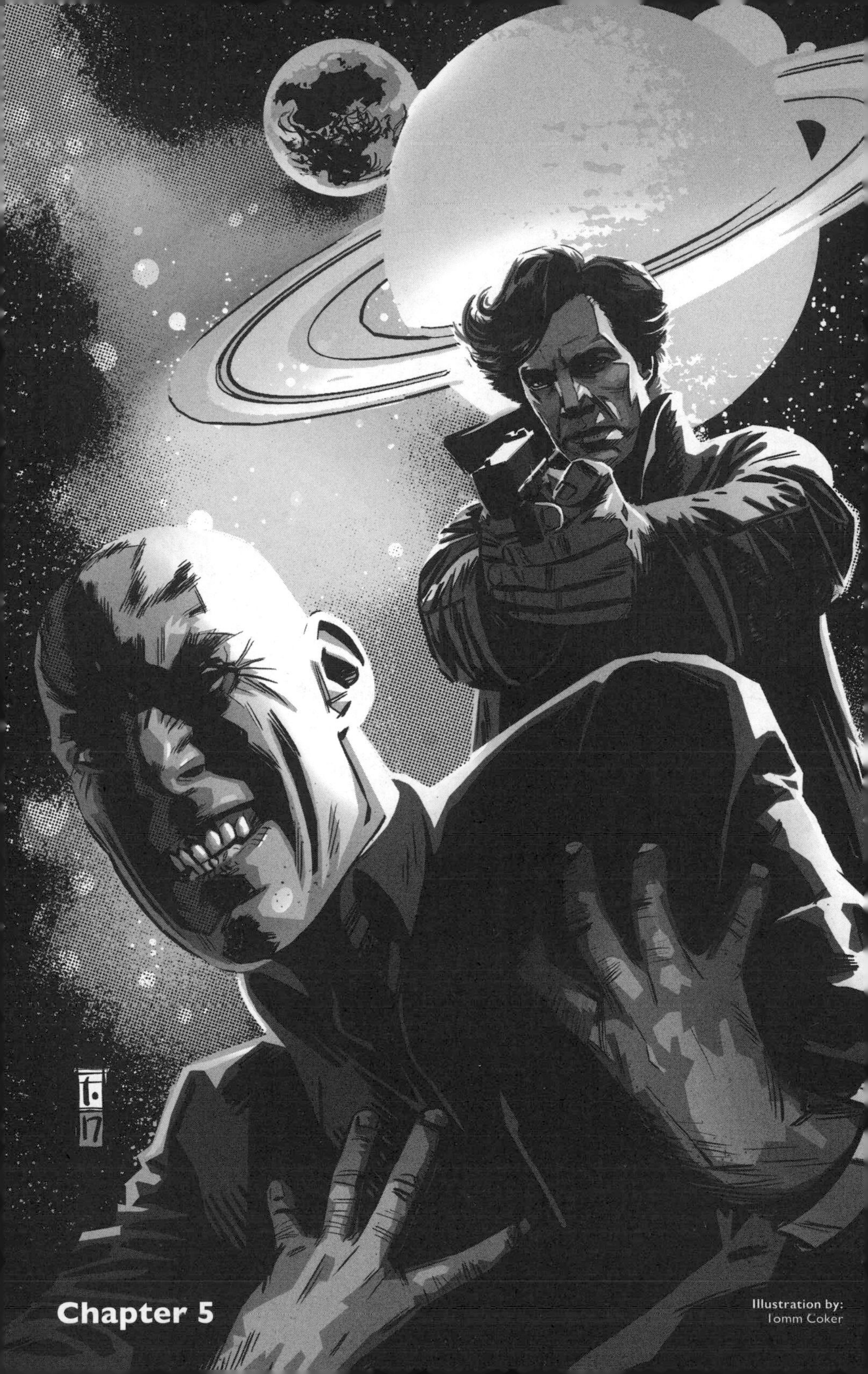

Chapter 5

Illustration by:
Tomm Coker

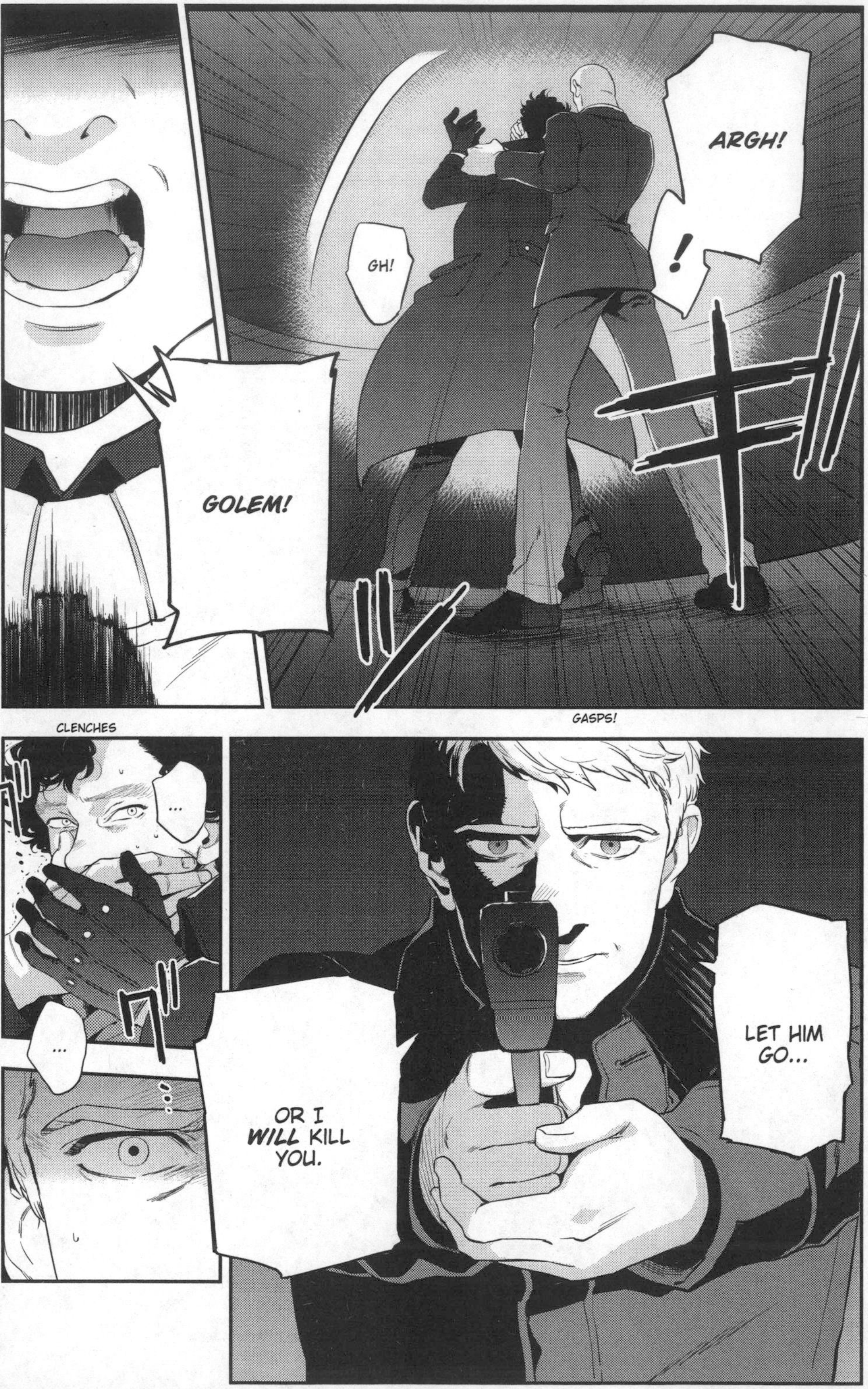
ARGH!
!
GH!
GOLEM!
GASPS!
LET HIM GO...
OR I WILL KILL YOU.
CLENCHES
...
...

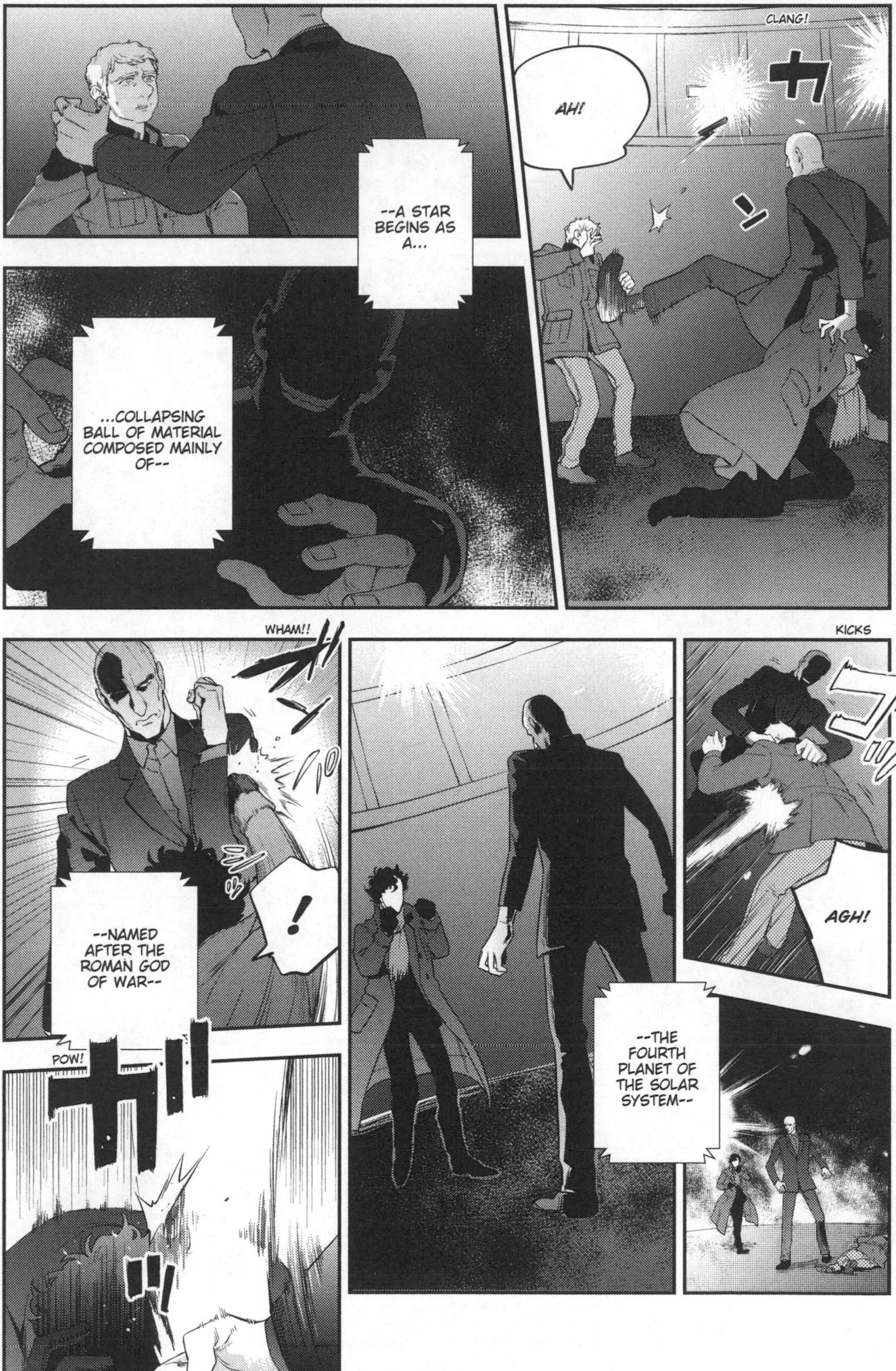
CLANG!
AH!
--A STAR BEGINS AS A...
...COLLAPSING BALL OF MATERIAL COMPOSED MAINLY OF--
KICKS
AGH!
--THE FOURTH PLANET OF THE SOLAR SYSTEM--
WHAM!!
!
--NAMED AFTER THE ROMAN GOD OF WAR--
POW!

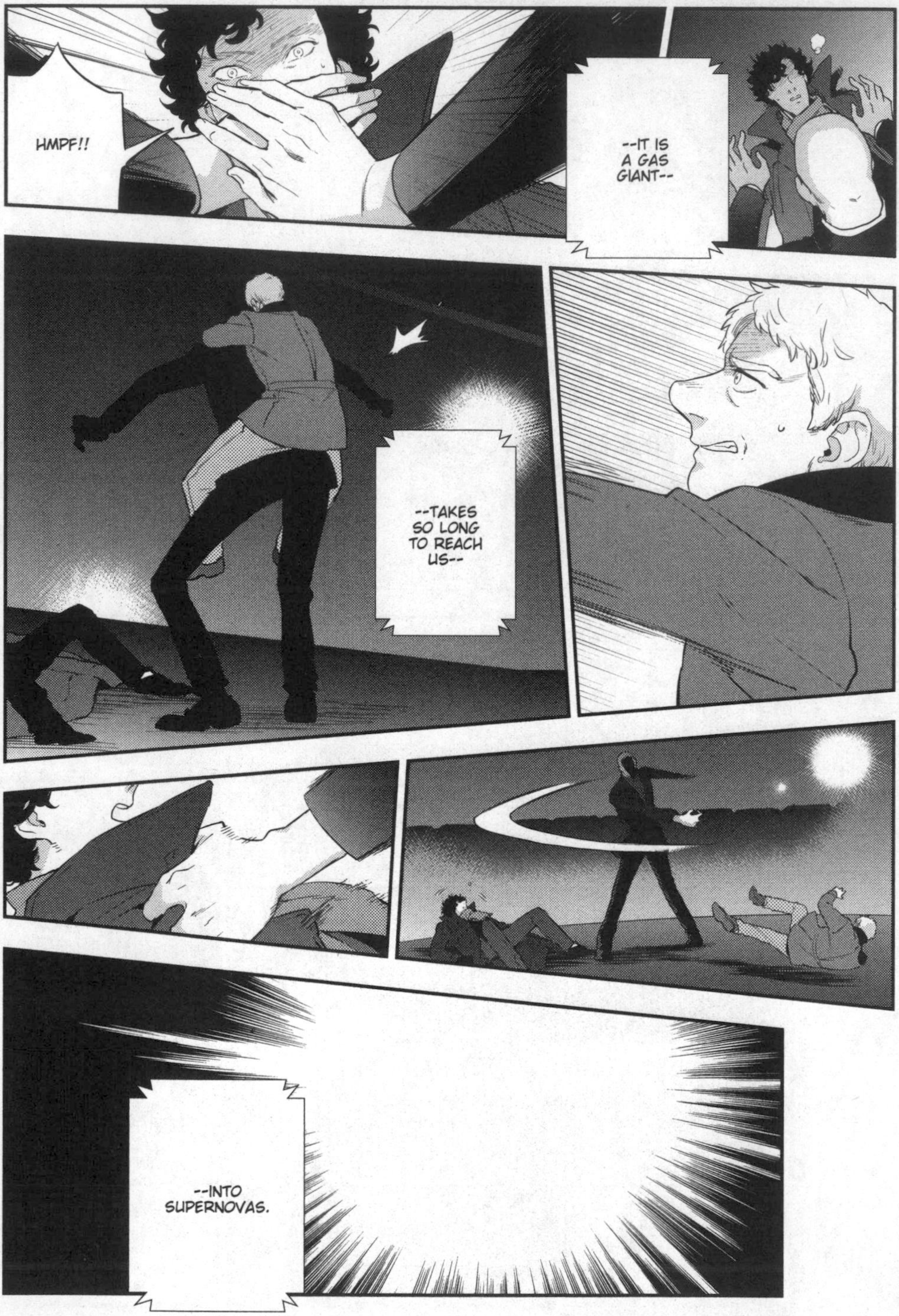
--IT IS A GAS GIANT--
HMPF!!
--TAKES SO LONG TO REACH US--
--INTO SUPERNOVAS.

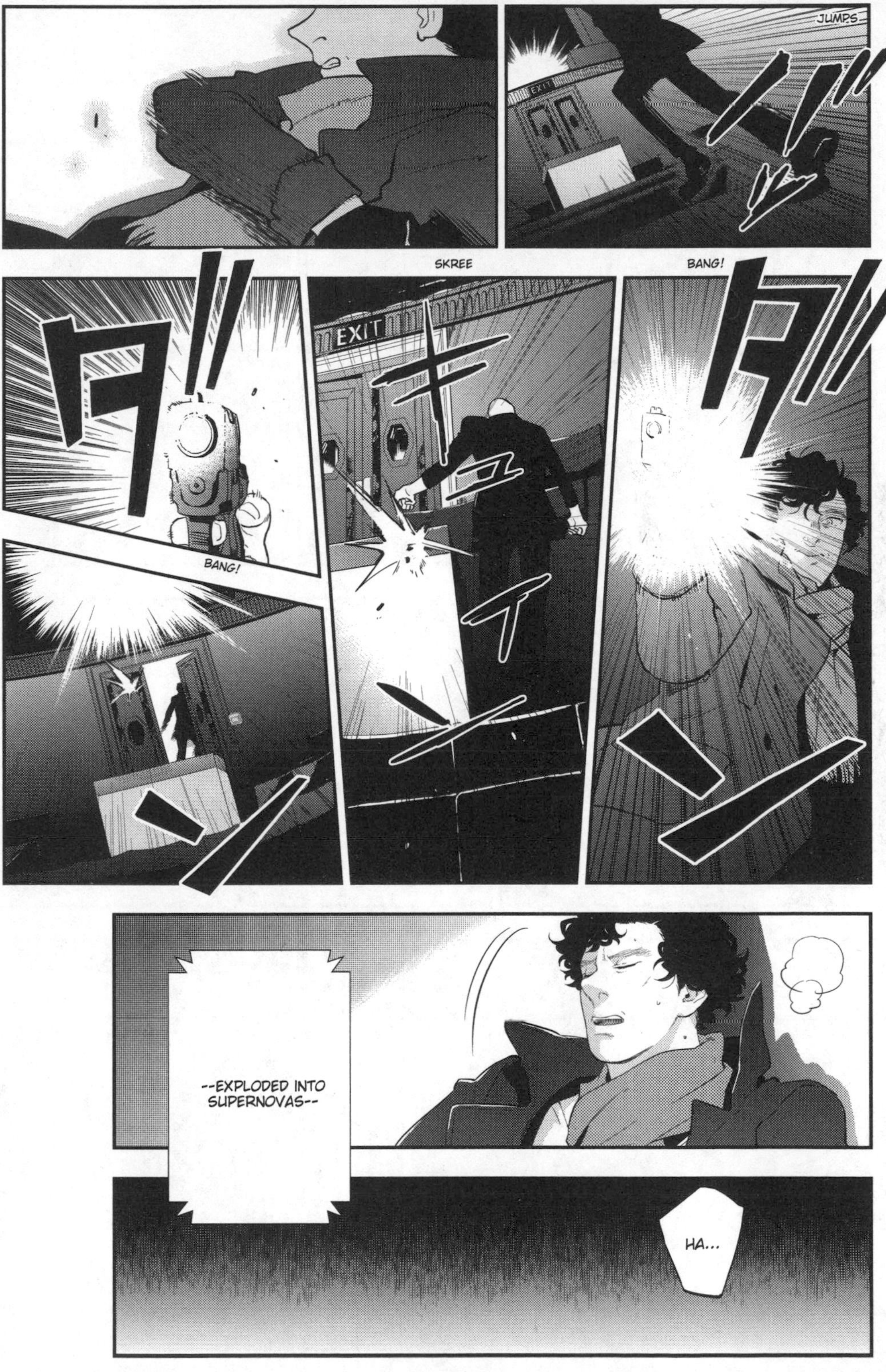
JUMPS
BANG!
SKREE
BANG!
--EXPLODED INTO SUPERNOVAS--
HA...

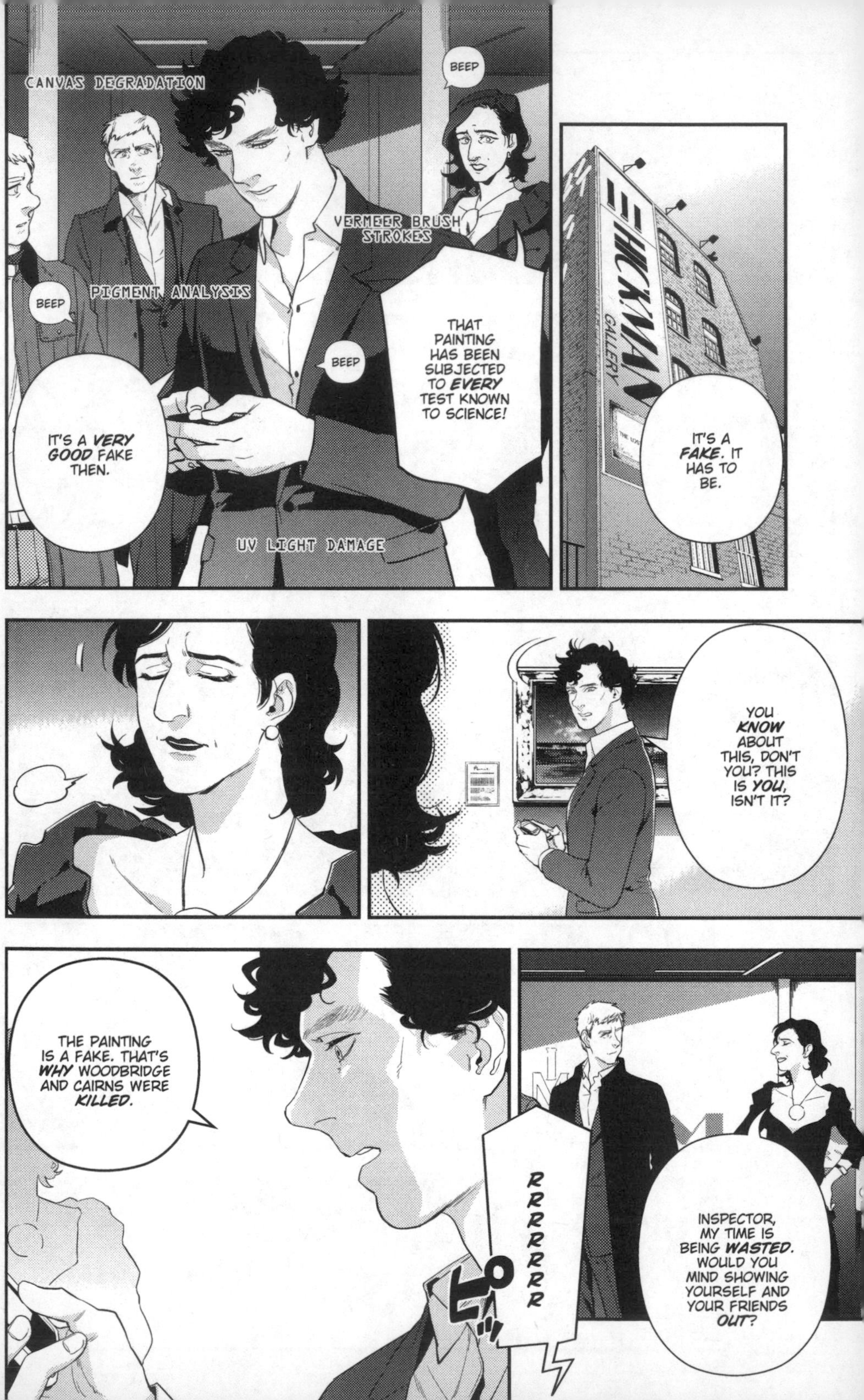
IT'S A FAKE. IT HAS TO BE.
BEEP
CANVAS DEGRADATION
VERMEER BRUSH STROKES
THAT PAINTING HAS BEEN SUBJECTED TO EVERY TEST KNOWN TO SCIENCE!
BEEP
PIGMENT ANALYSIS
BEEP
IT'S A VERY GOOD FAKE THEN.
UV LIGHT DAMAGE
YOU KNOW ABOUT THIS, DON'T YOU? THIS IS YOU, ISN'T IT?
INSPECTOR, MY TIME IS BEING WASTED. WOULD YOU MIND SHOWING YOURSELF AND YOUR FRIENDS OUT?
THE PAINTING IS A FAKE. THAT'S WHY WOODBRIDGE AND CAIRNS WERE KILLED.
RRRRRR
ピッ

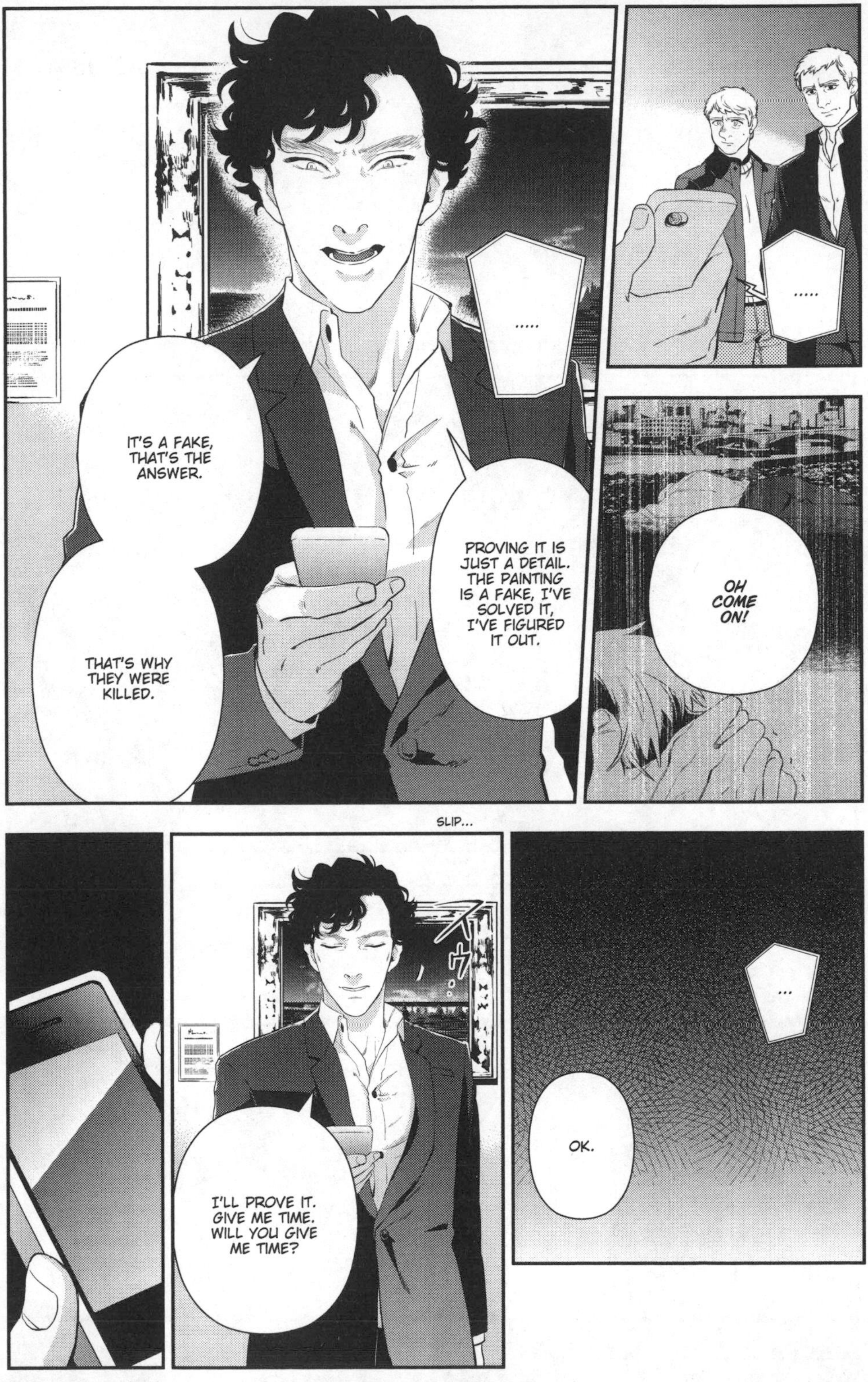
.....
OH COME ON!
.....
IT'S A FAKE, THAT'S THE ANSWER.
THAT'S WHY THEY WERE KILLED.
PROVING IT IS JUST A DETAIL. THE PAINTING IS A FAKE, I'VE SOLVED IT, I'VE FIGURED IT OUT.
SLIP...
...
OK.
スゥ…
I'LL PROVE IT. GIVE ME TIME. WILL YOU GIVE ME TIME?

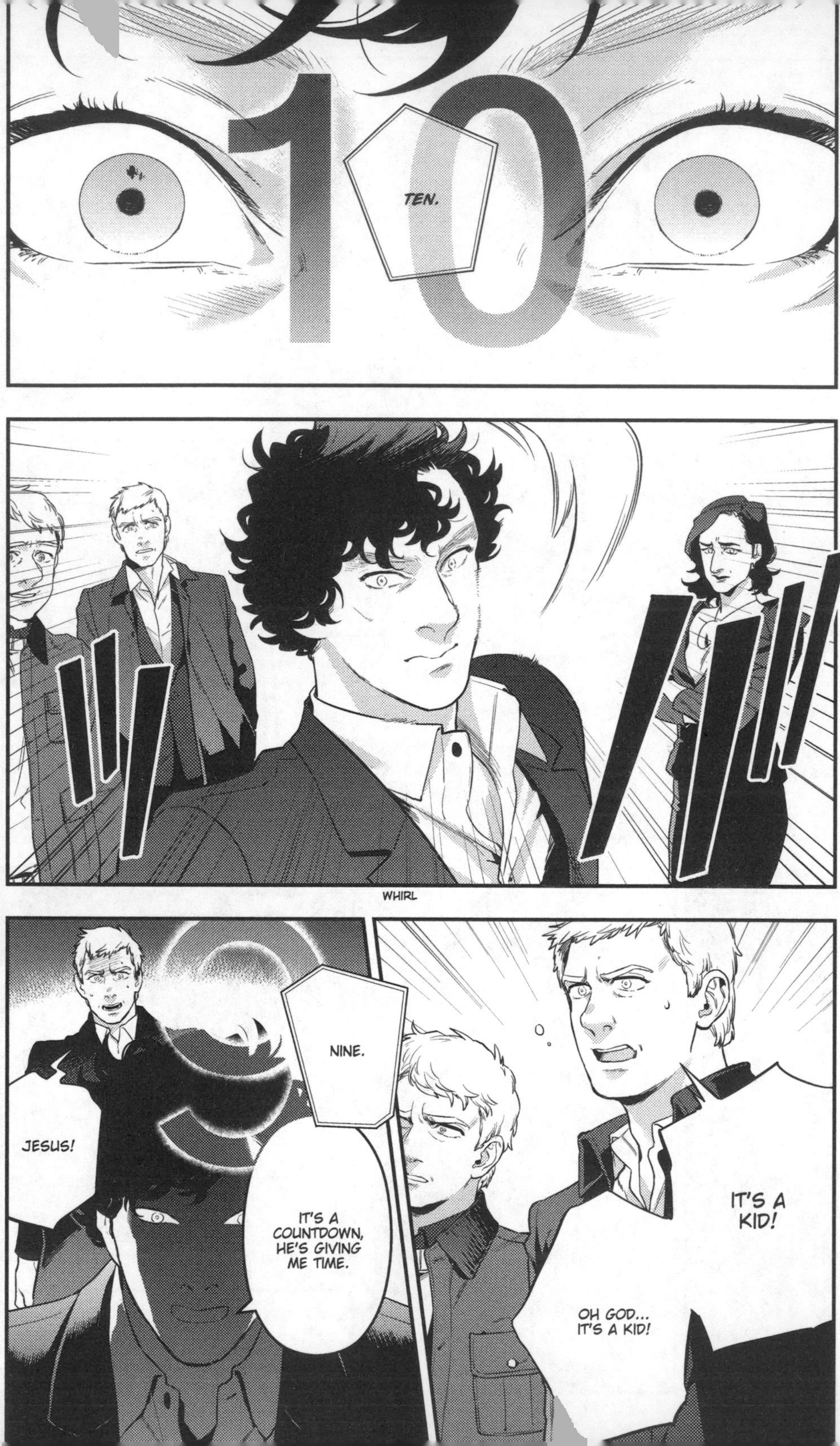
TEN.
WHIRL
IT'S A KID!
OH GOD... IT'S A KID!
NINE.
IT'S A COUNTDOWN, HE'S GIVING ME TIME.
JESUS!

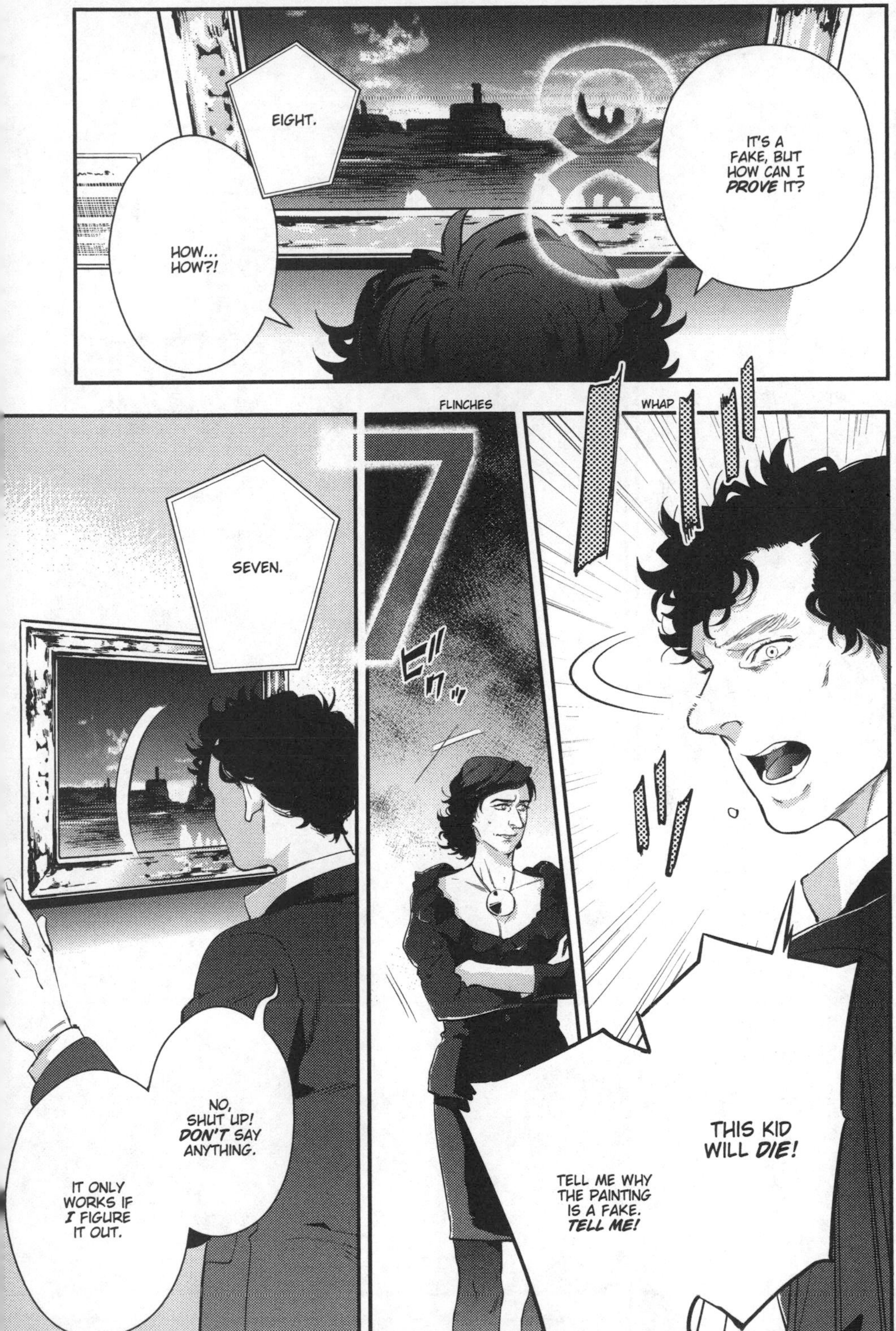
IT'S A FAKE, BUT HOW CAN I *PROVE* IT?
EIGHT.
HOW... HOW?!
WHAP
THIS KID WILL *DIE!*
TELL ME WHY THE PAINTING IS A FAKE. *TELL ME!*
FLINCHES
ビクッ
SEVEN.
NO, SHUT UP! *DON'T* SAY ANYTHING.
IT ONLY WORKS IF *I* FIGURE IT OUT.

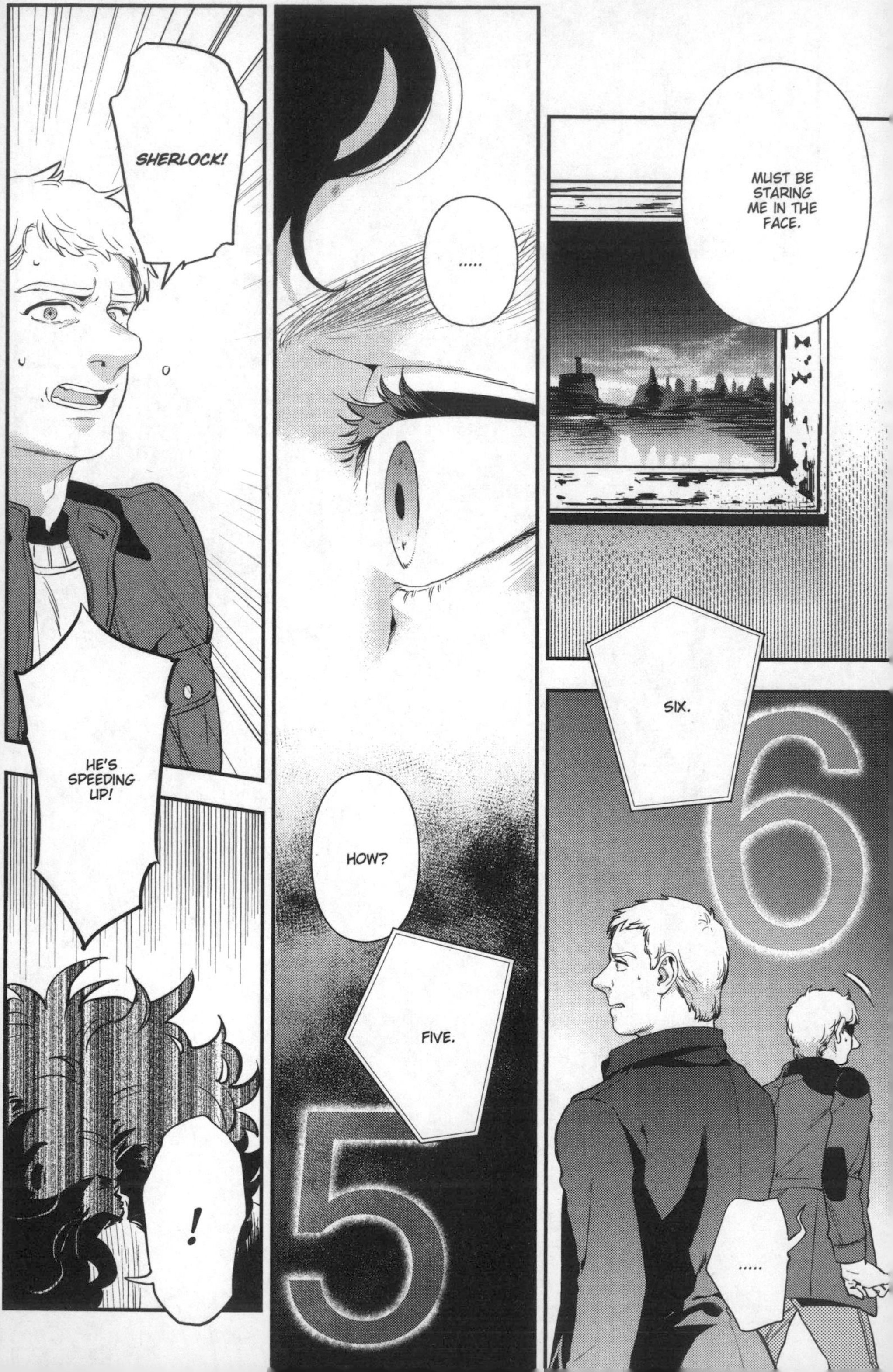
MUST BE STARING ME IN THE FACE.
SIX.
.....
.....
HOW?
FIVE.
SHERLOCK!
HE'S SPEEDING UP!
!

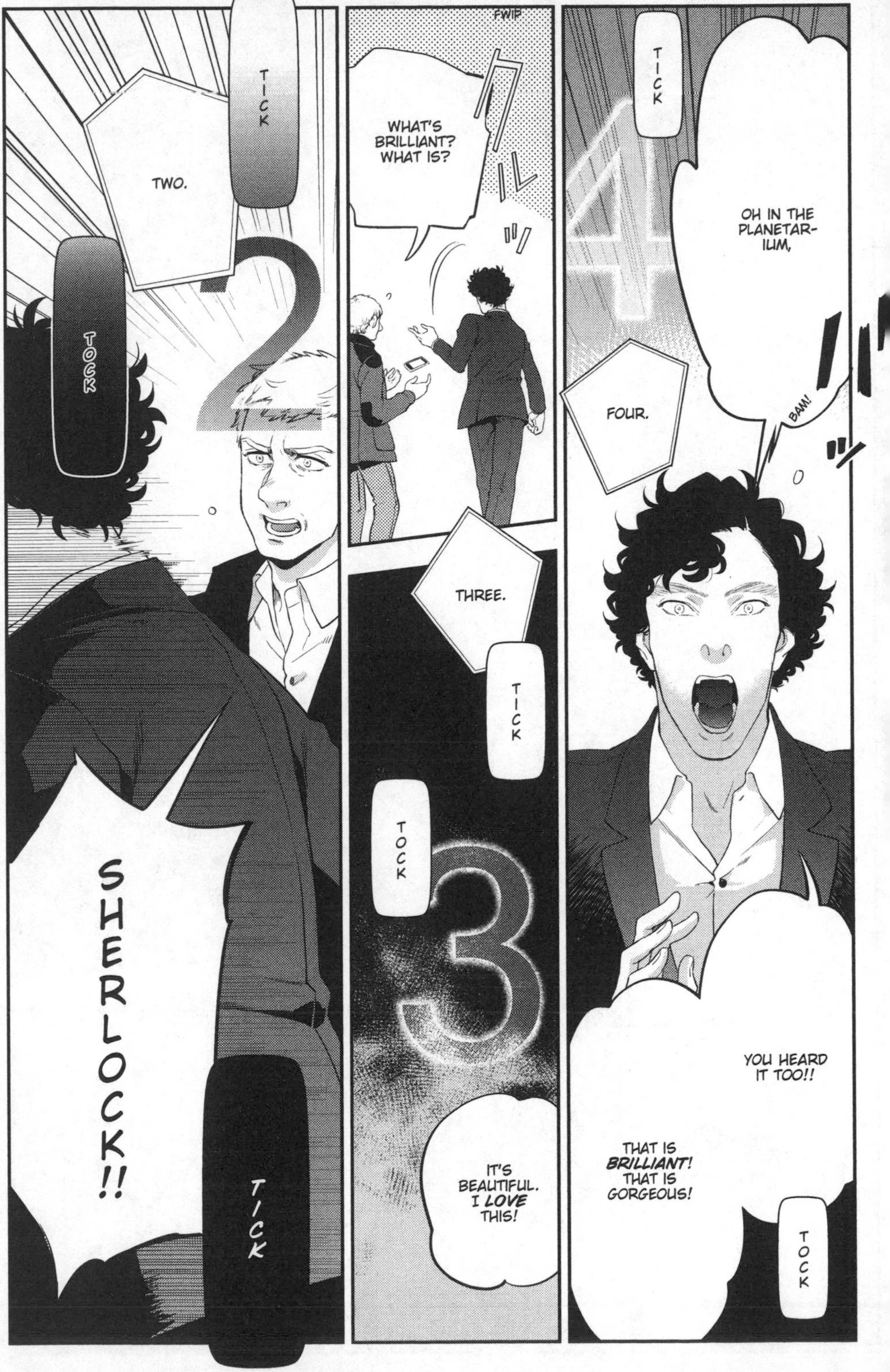
TICK
OH IN THE PLANETARIUM,
FOUR.
BAM!
YOU HEARD IT TOO!!
THAT IS *BRILLIANT*! THAT IS GORGEOUS!
TOCK
FWIP
WHAT'S BRILLIANT? WHAT IS?
THREE.
TICK
TOCK
IT'S BEAUTIFUL. I *LOVE* THIS!
TICK
TWO.
TOCK
SHERLOCK!!
TICK

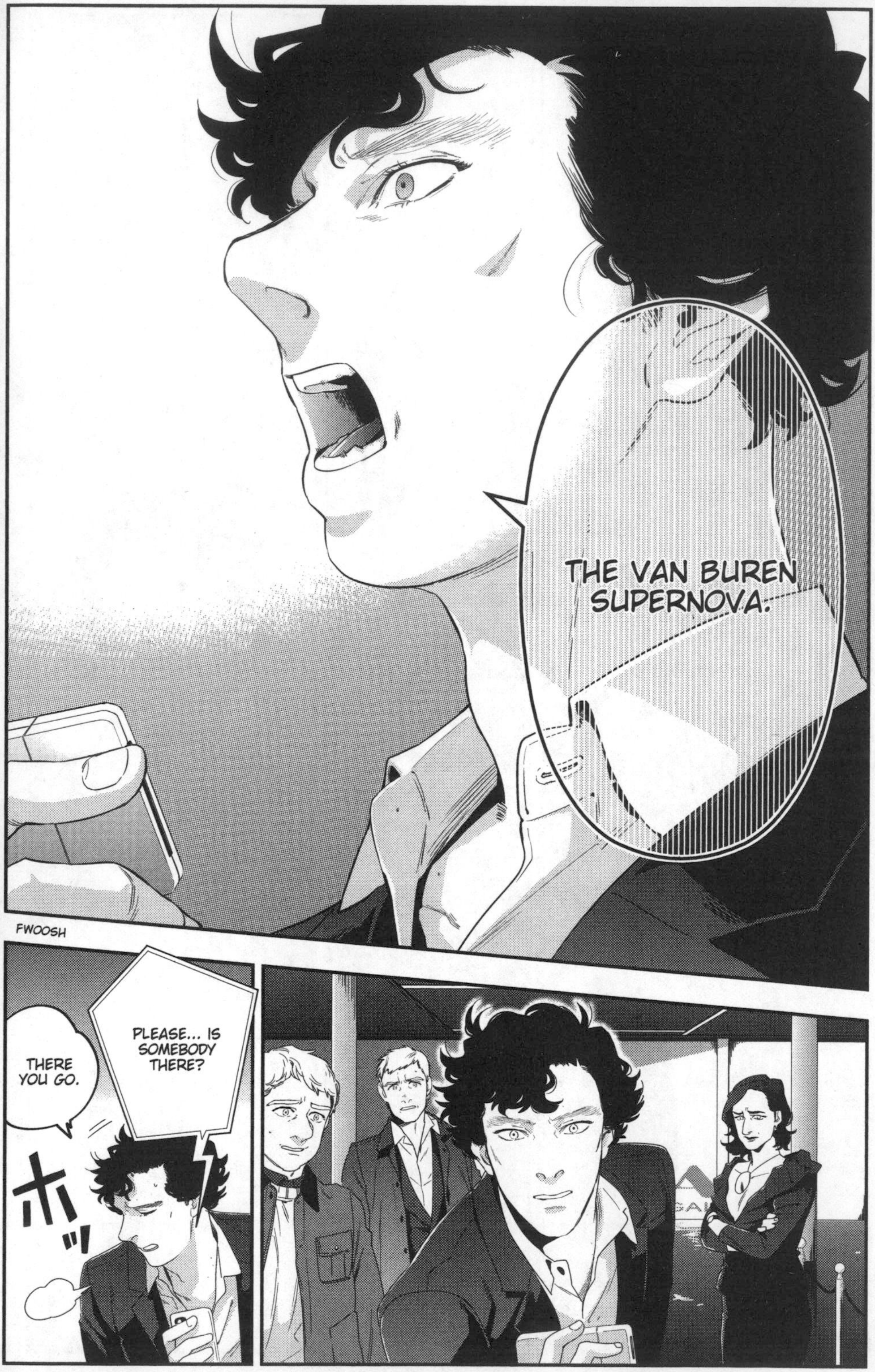
THE VAN BUREN SUPERNOVA.
FWOOSH
PLEASE... IS SOMEBODY THERE?
THERE YOU GO.
ホッ

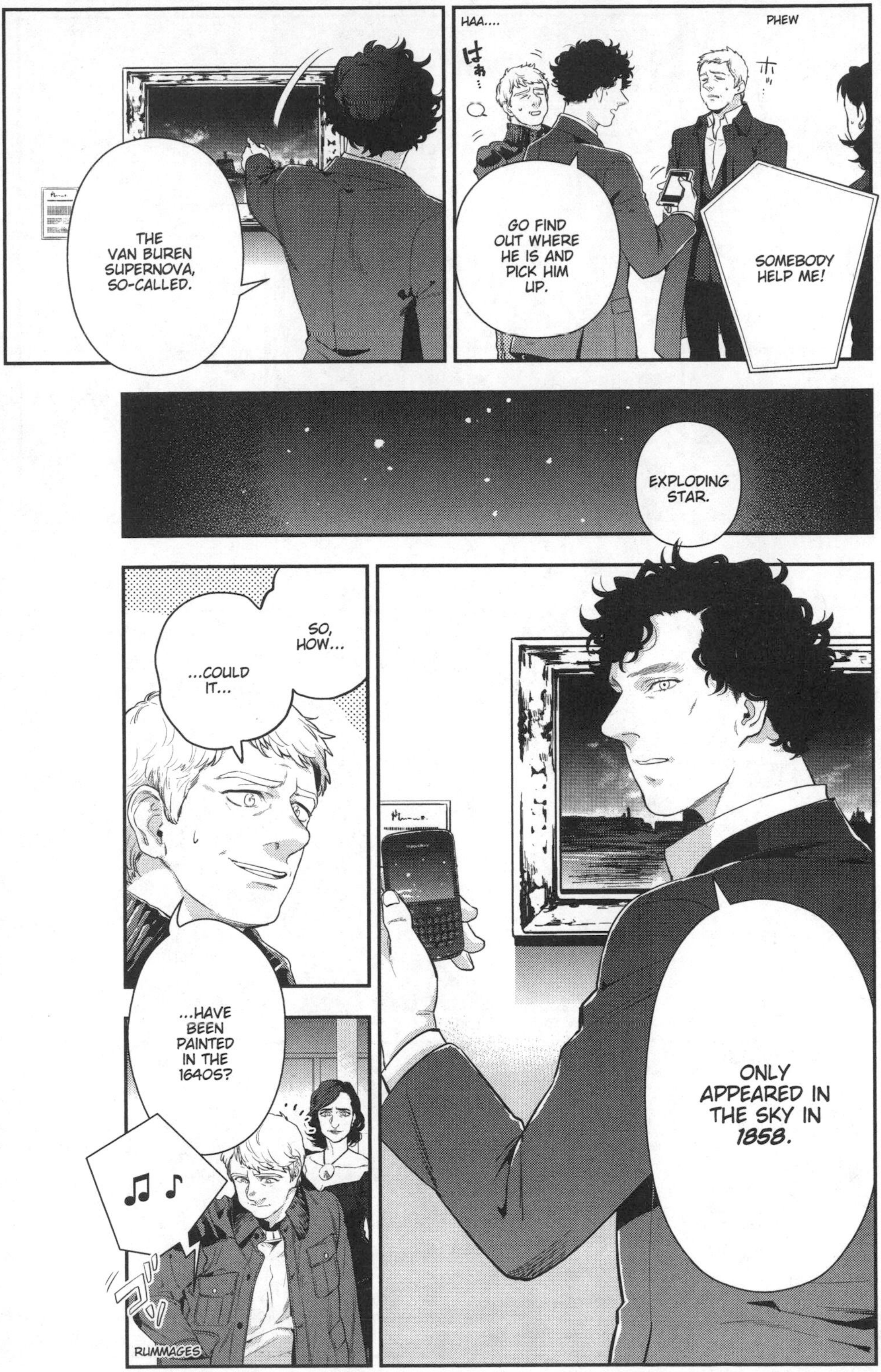
PHEW
HAA....
GO FIND OUT WHERE HE IS AND PICK HIM UP.
SOMEBODY HELP ME!
THE VAN BUREN SUPERNOVA, SO-CALLED.
EXPLODING STAR.
ONLY APPEARED IN THE SKY IN 1858.
SO, HOW...
...COULD IT...
...HAVE BEEN PAINTED IN THE 1640S?
♫ ♪
RUMMAGES

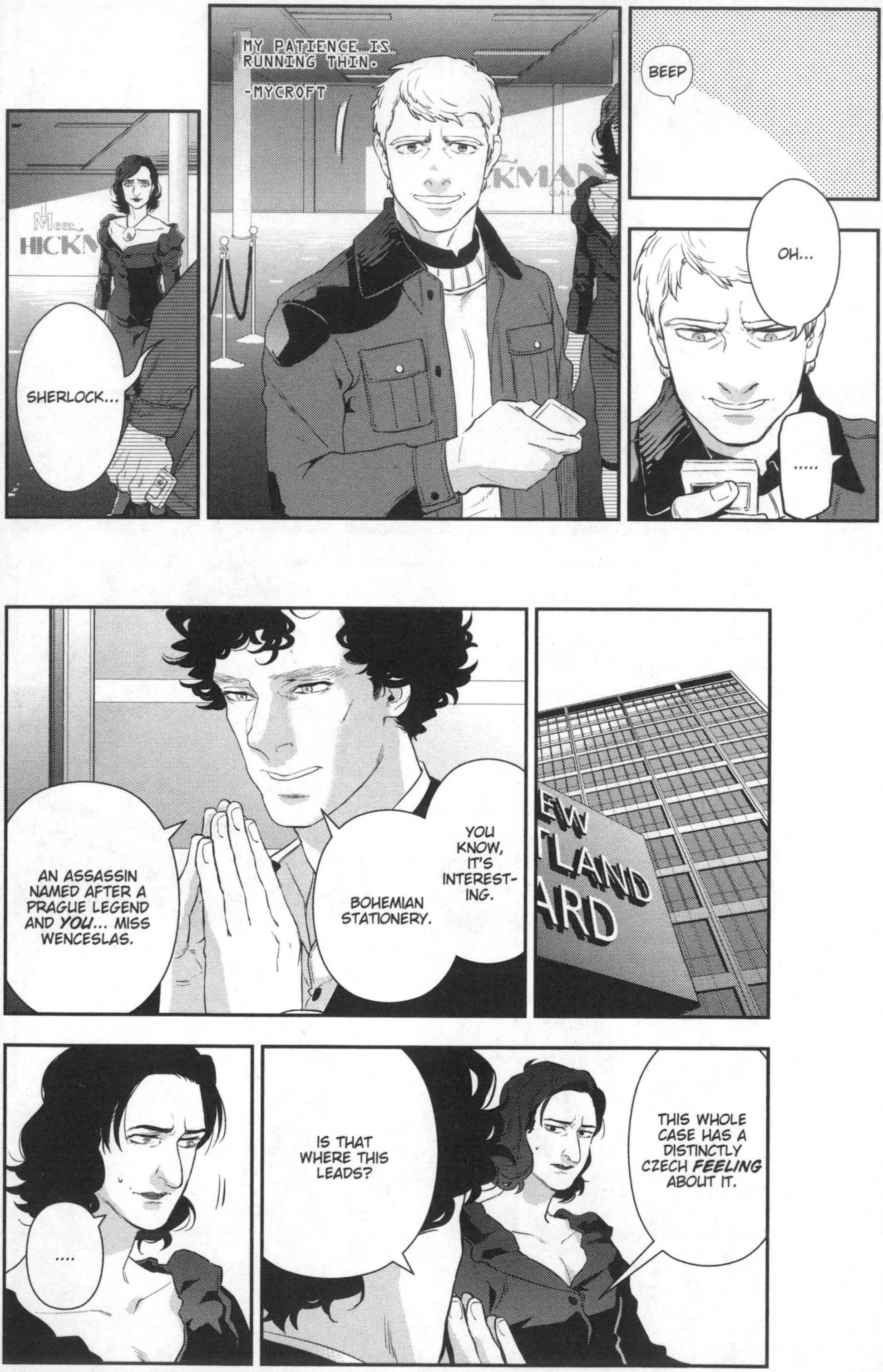
BEEP
OH...
.....
MY PATIENCE IS RUNNING THIN.
-MYCROFT
SHERLOCK...
YOU KNOW, IT'S INTEREST-ING.
BOHEMIAN STATIONERY.
AN ASSASSIN NAMED AFTER A PRAGUE LEGEND AND *YOU*... MISS WENCESLAS.
THIS WHOLE CASE HAS A DISTINCTLY CZECH *FEELING* ABOUT IT.
IS THAT WHERE THIS LEADS?
....

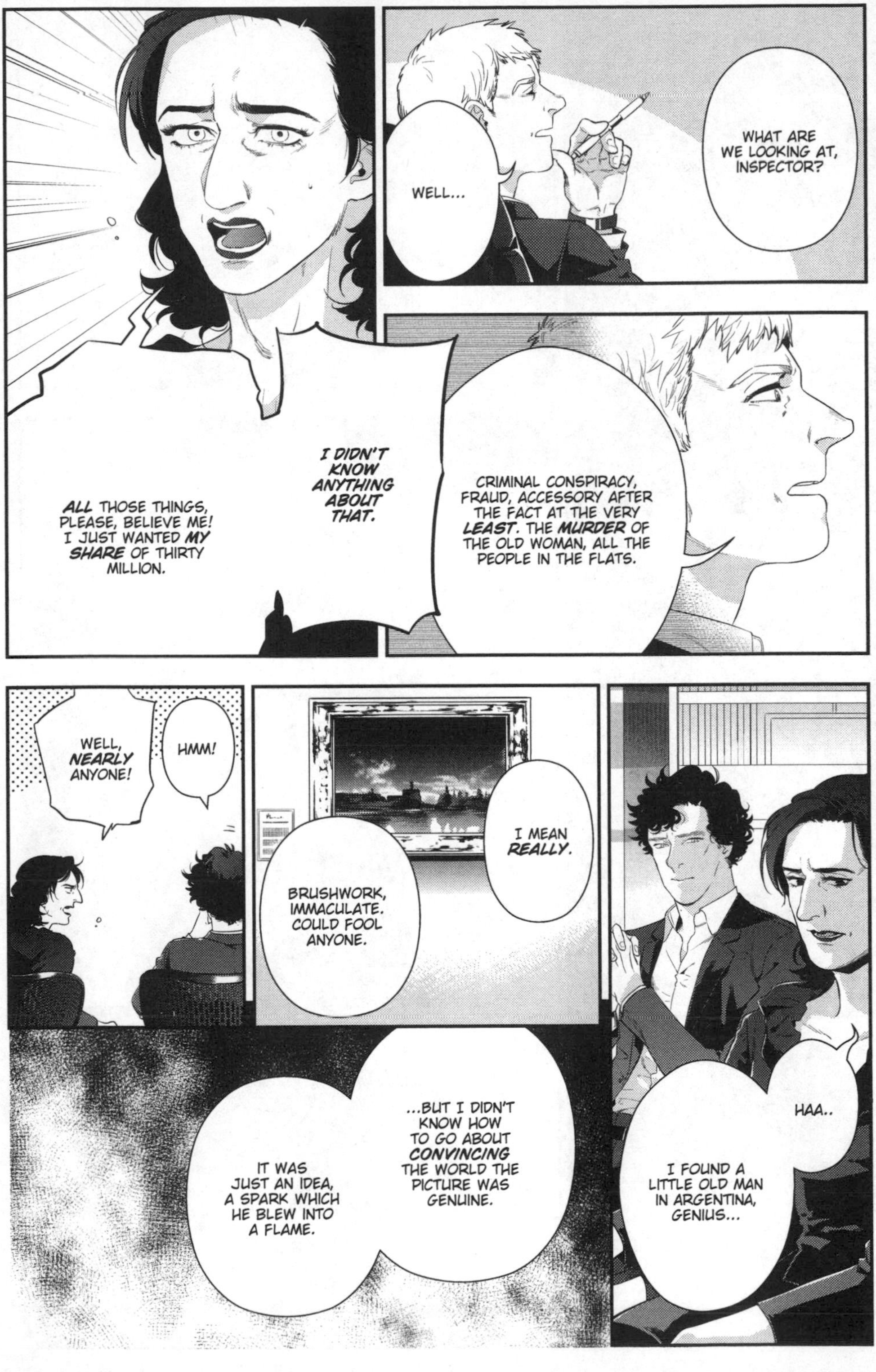
WHAT ARE WE LOOKING AT, INSPECTOR?
WELL...
CRIMINAL CONSPIRACY, FRAUD, ACCESSORY AFTER THE FACT AT THE VERY *LEAST*. THE *MURDER* OF THE OLD WOMAN, ALL THE PEOPLE IN THE FLATS.
I DIDN'T KNOW ANYTHING ABOUT THAT.
ALL THOSE THINGS, PLEASE, BELIEVE ME! I JUST WANTED *MY SHARE* OF THIRTY MILLION.
HAA..
I FOUND A LITTLE OLD MAN IN ARGENTINA, GENIUS...
I MEAN *REALLY*.
BRUSHWORK, IMMACULATE. COULD FOOL ANYONE.
HMM!
WELL, *NEARLY* ANYONE!
...BUT I DIDN'T KNOW HOW TO GO ABOUT *CONVINCING* THE WORLD THE PICTURE WAS GENUINE.
IT WAS JUST AN IDEA, A SPARK WHICH HE BLEW INTO A FLAME.

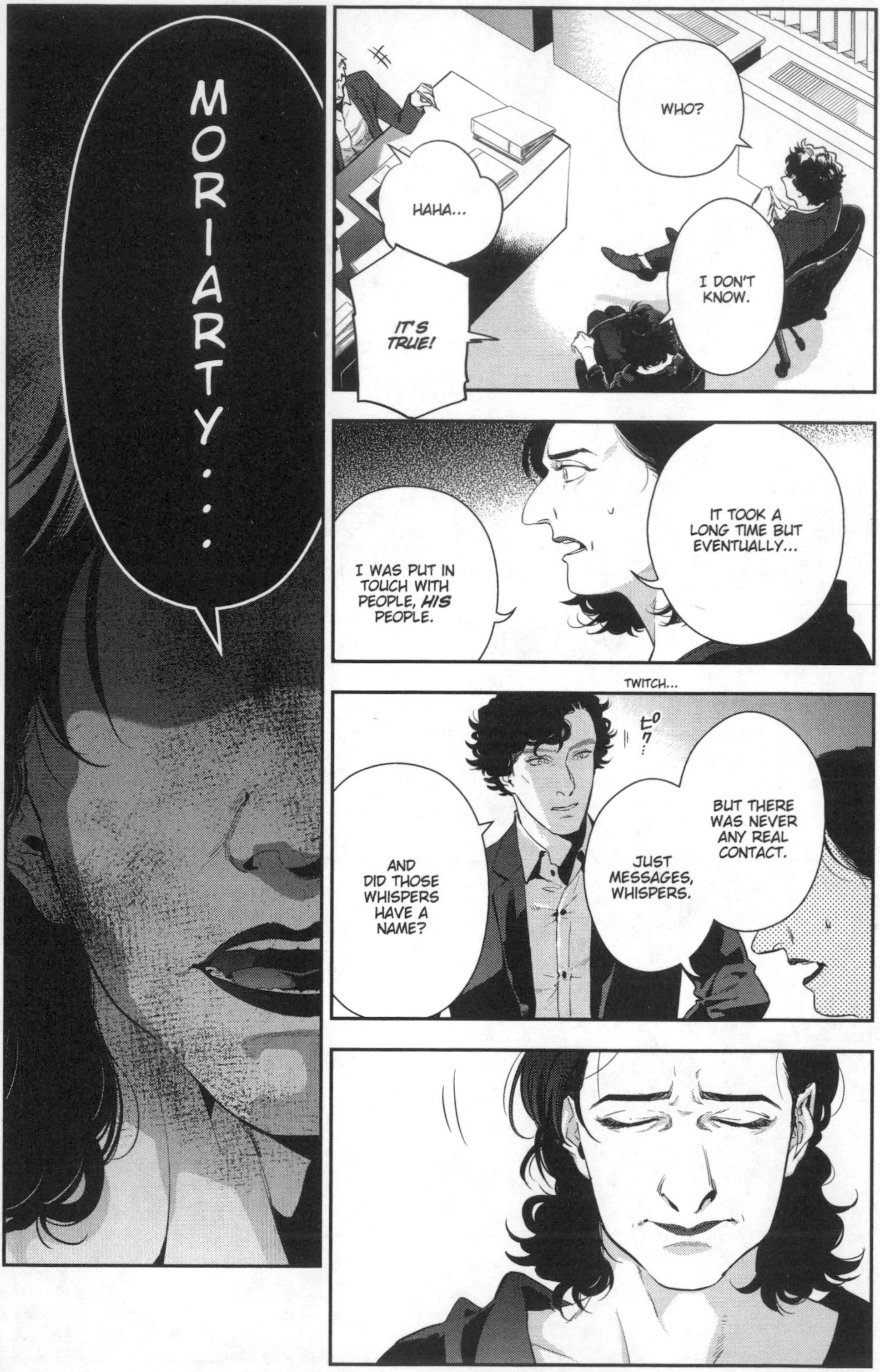
WHO?
I DON'T KNOW.
HAHA...
IT'S TRUE!
IT TOOK A LONG TIME BUT EVENTUALLY...
I WAS PUT IN TOUCH WITH PEOPLE, *HIS* PEOPLE.
TWITCH...
BUT THERE WAS NEVER ANY REAL CONTACT.
JUST MESSAGES, WHISPERS.
AND DID THOSE WHISPERS HAVE A NAME?
MORIARTY...

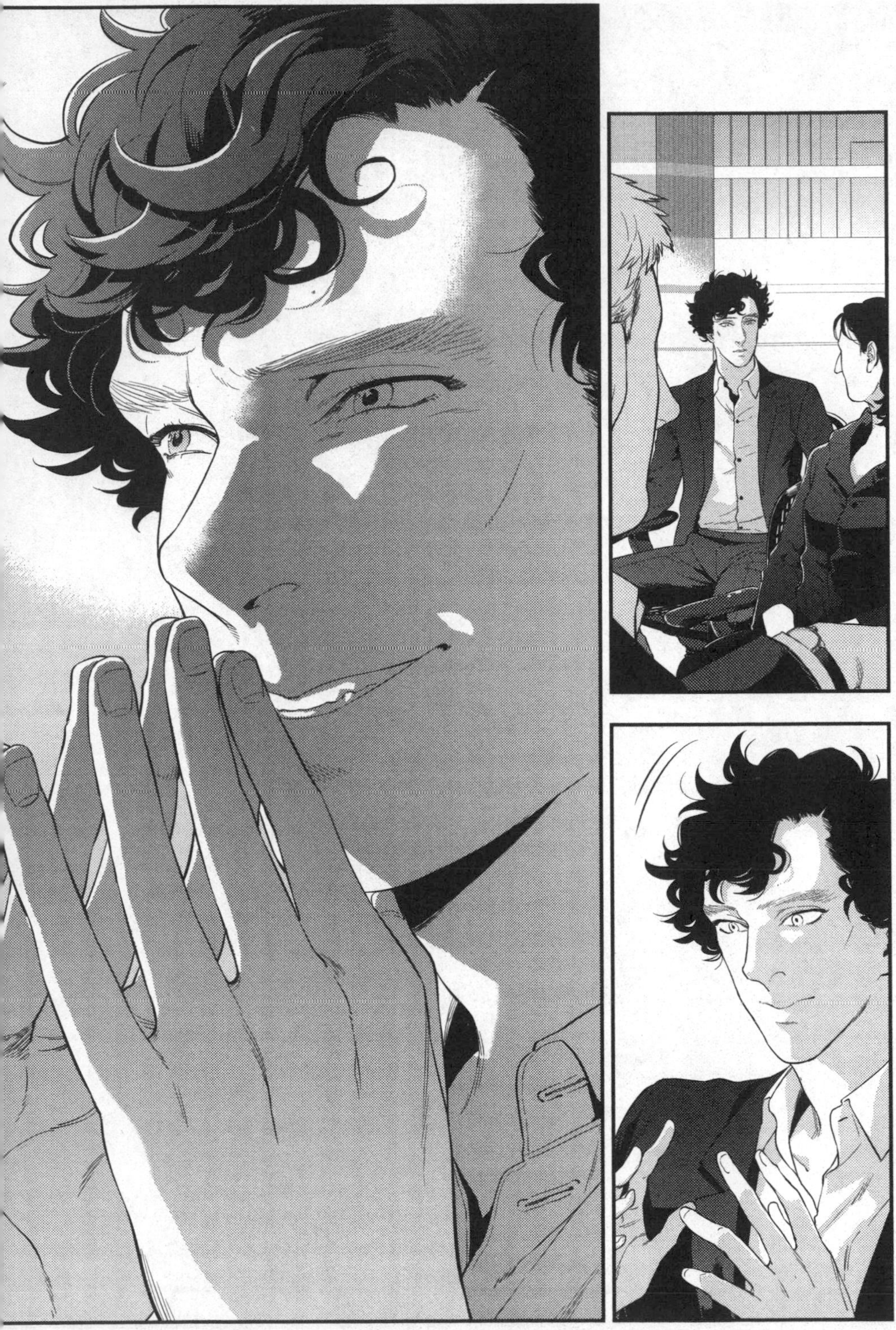

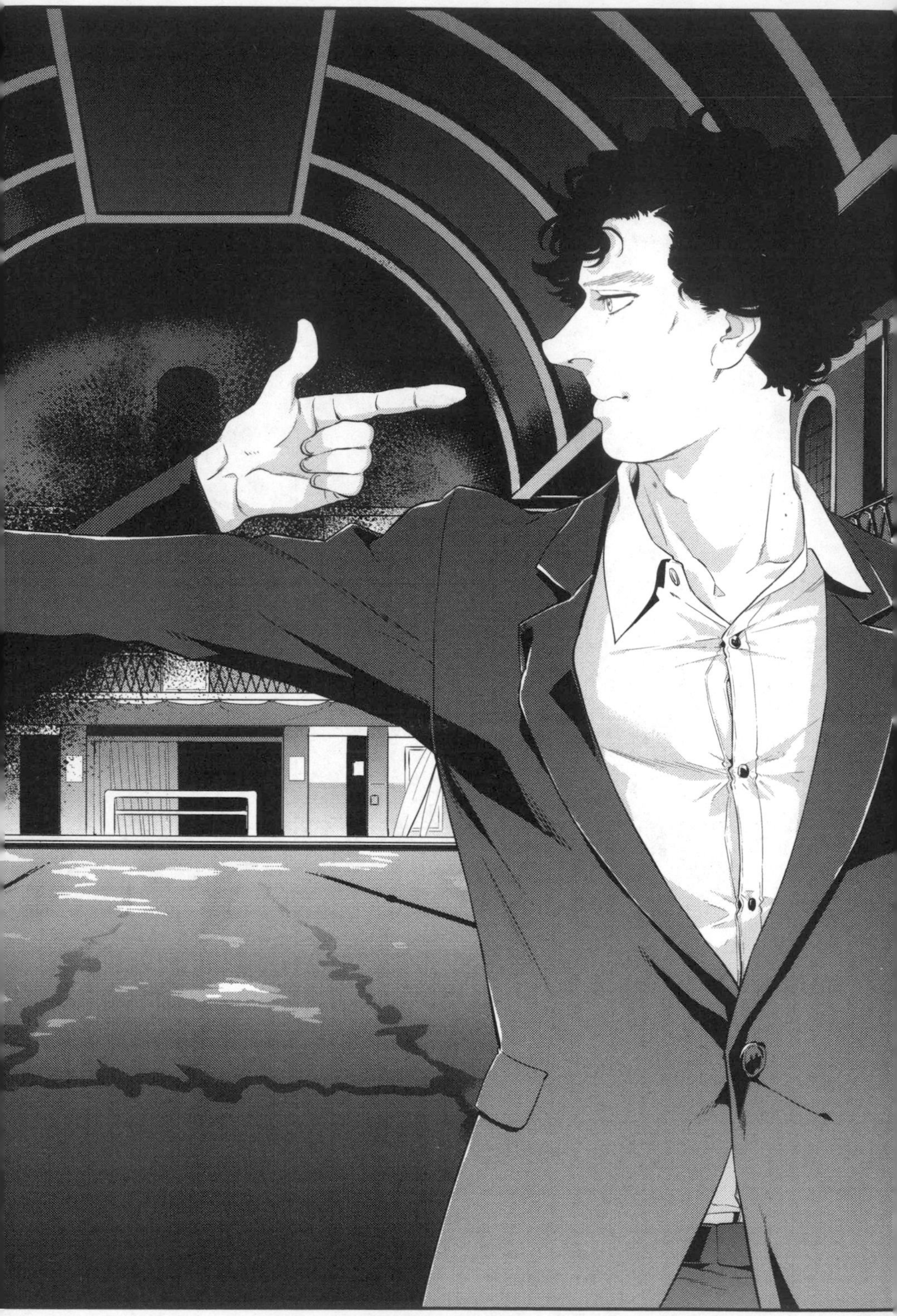

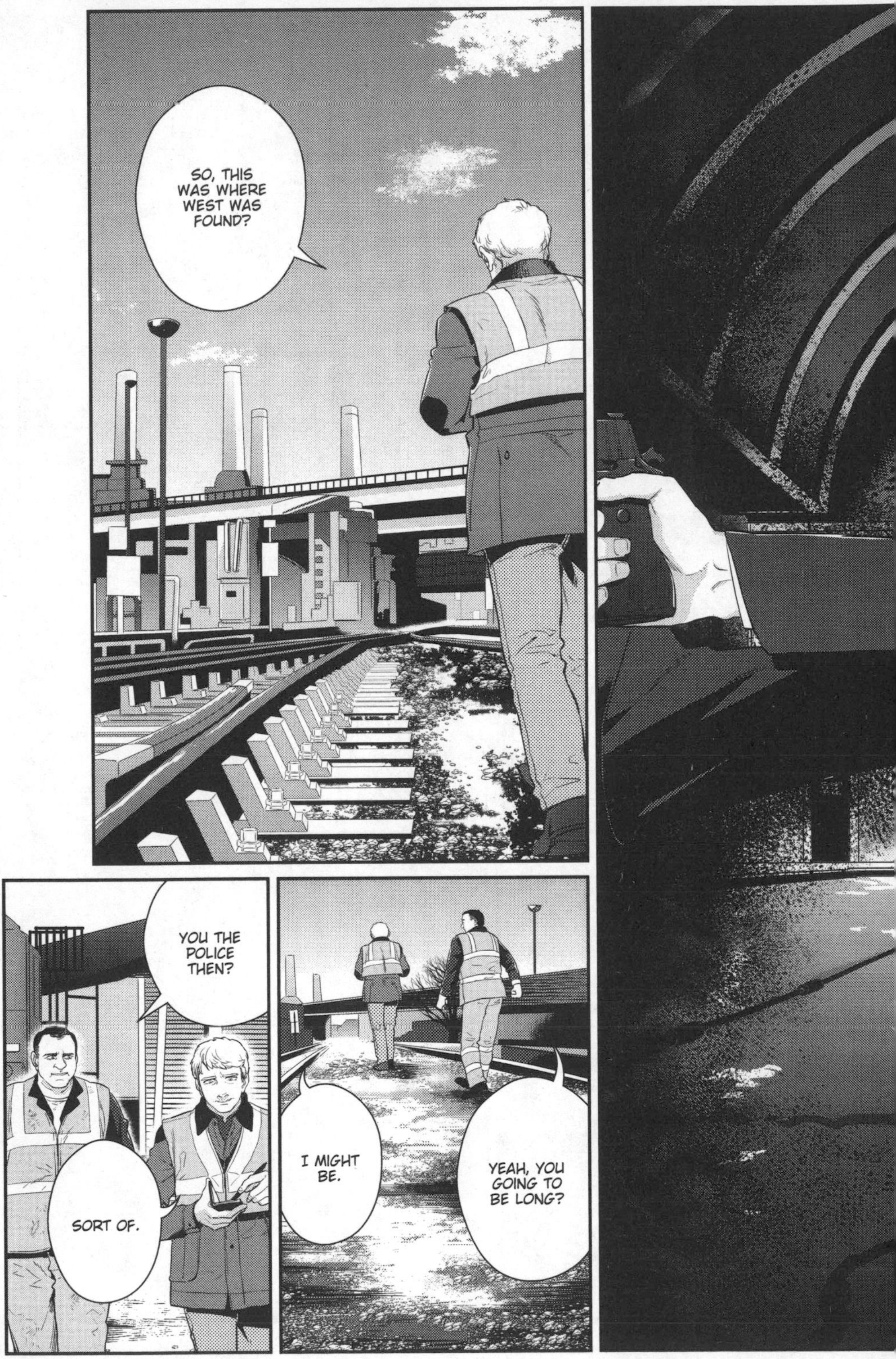
SO, THIS WAS WHERE WEST WAS FOUND?
YEAH, YOU GOING TO BE LONG?
I MIGHT BE.
YOU THE POLICE THEN?
SORT OF.

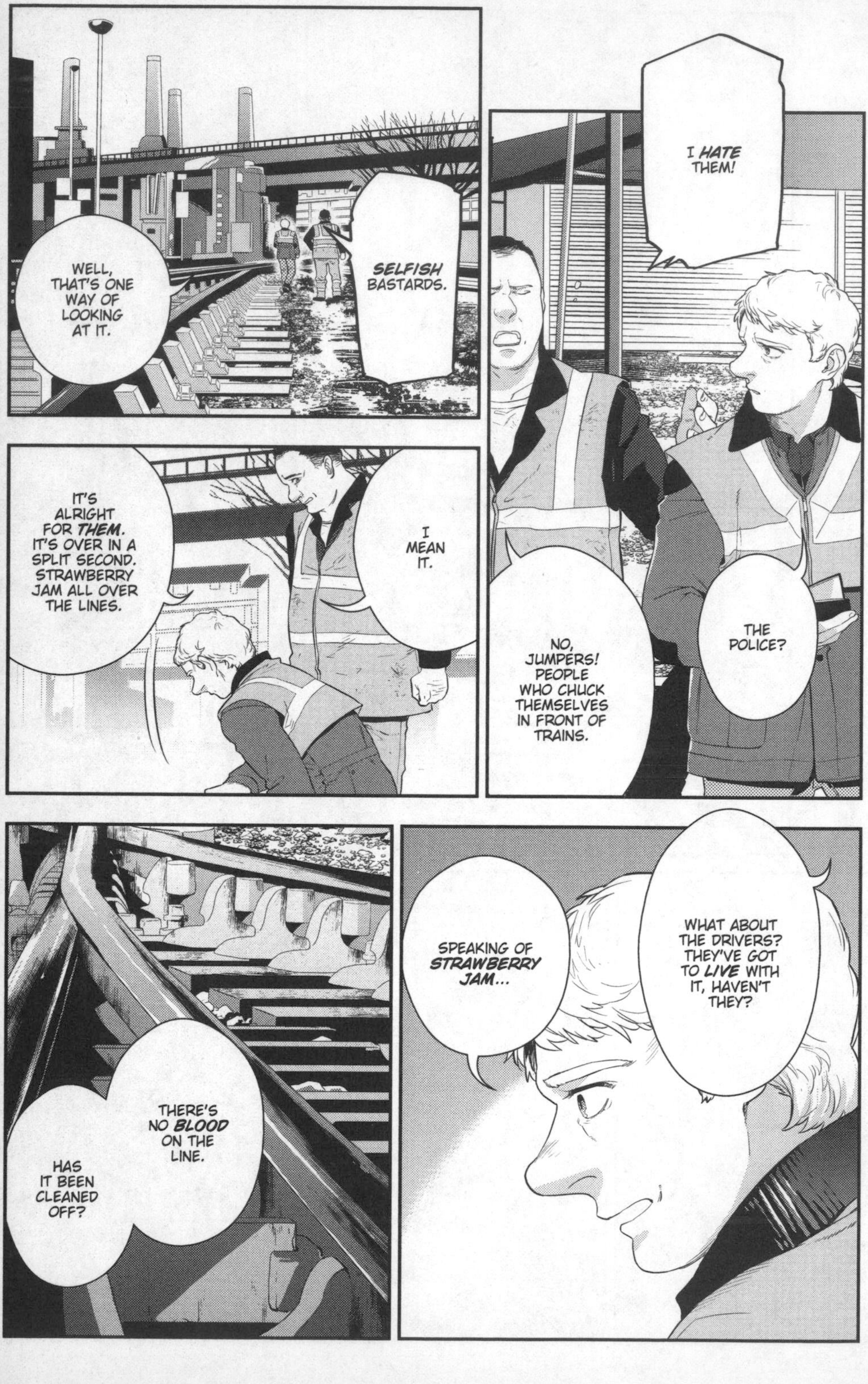
I *HATE* THEM!
THE POLICE?
NO, JUMPERS! PEOPLE WHO CHUCK THEMSELVES IN FRONT OF TRAINS.
SELFISH BASTARDS.
WELL, THAT'S ONE WAY OF LOOKING AT IT.
I MEAN IT.
IT'S ALRIGHT FOR *THEM*. IT'S OVER IN A SPLIT SECOND. STRAWBERRY JAM ALL OVER THE LINES.
WHAT ABOUT THE DRIVERS? THEY'VE GOT TO *LIVE* WITH IT, HAVEN'T THEY?
SPEAKING OF *STRAWBERRY JAM*...
THERE'S NO *BLOOD* ON THE LINE.
HAS IT BEEN CLEANED OFF?

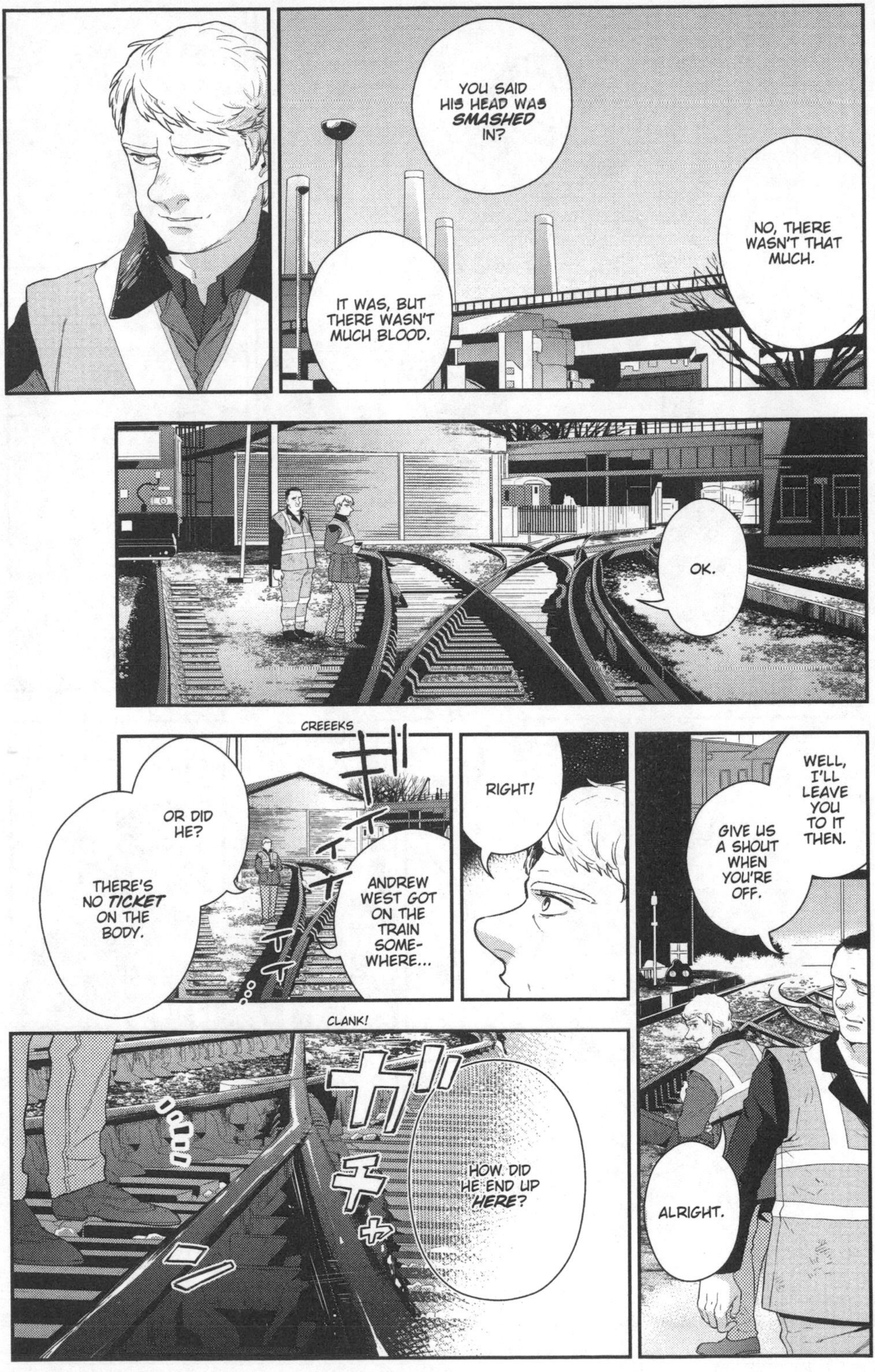
YOU SAID HIS HEAD WAS **SMASHED** IN?
IT WAS, BUT THERE WASN'T MUCH BLOOD.
NO, THERE WASN'T THAT MUCH.
OK.
WELL, I'LL LEAVE YOU TO IT THEN.
GIVE US A SHOUT WHEN YOU'RE OFF.
ALRIGHT.
RIGHT!
CREEEKS
ANDREW WEST GOT ON THE TRAIN SOME-WHERE...
OR DID HE?
THERE'S NO ***TICKET*** ON THE BODY.
CLANK!
HOW DID HE END UP ***HERE***?

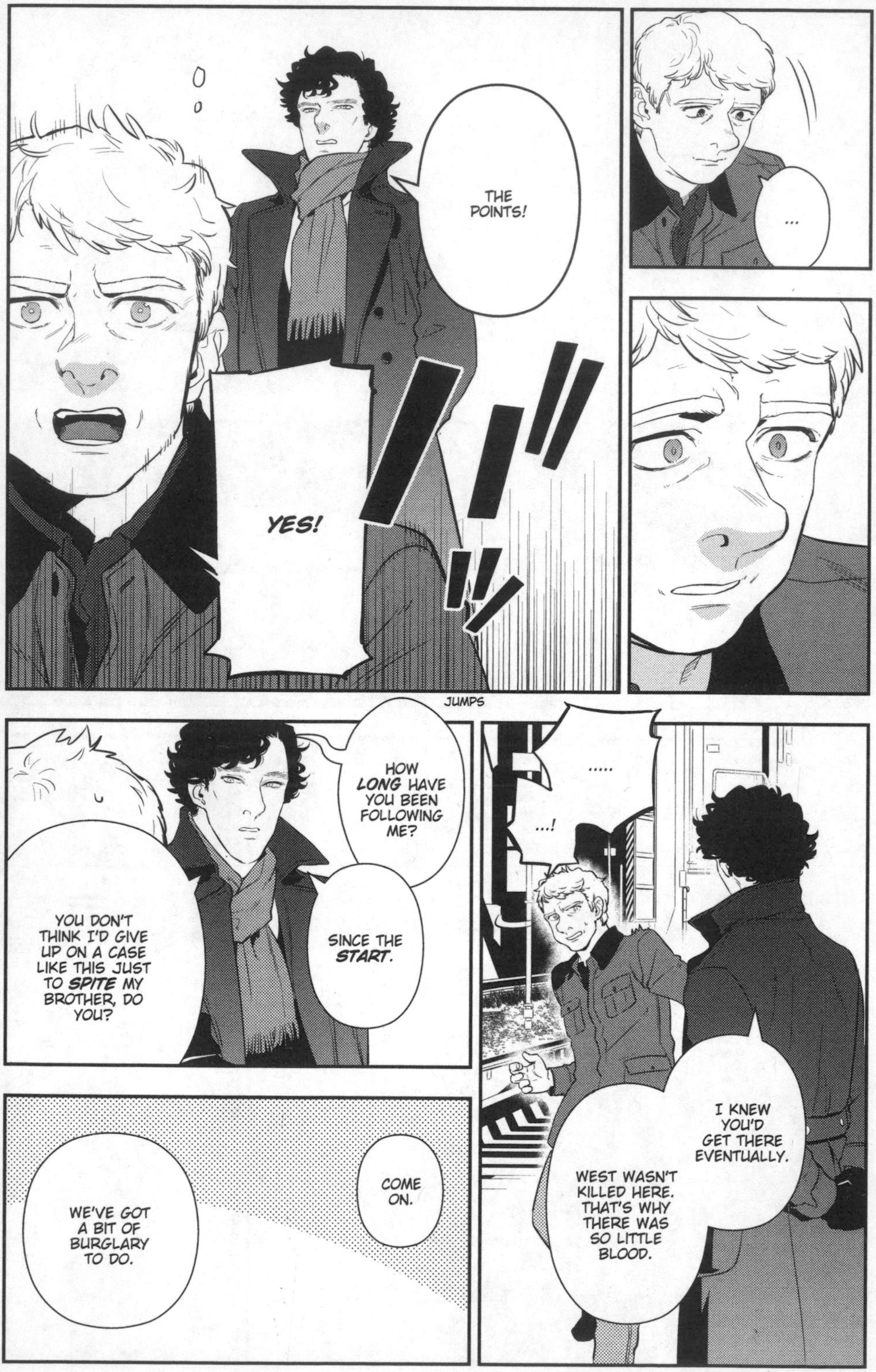
...
THE POINTS!
YES!
JUMPS
.....
...!
I KNEW YOU'D GET THERE EVENTUALLY.
WEST WASN'T KILLED HERE. THAT'S WHY THERE WAS SO LITTLE BLOOD.
HOW LONG HAVE YOU BEEN FOLLOWING ME?
SINCE THE START.
YOU DON'T THINK I'D GIVE UP ON A CASE LIKE THIS JUST TO SPITE MY BROTHER, DO YOU?
COME ON.
WE'VE GOT A BIT OF BURGLARY TO DO.

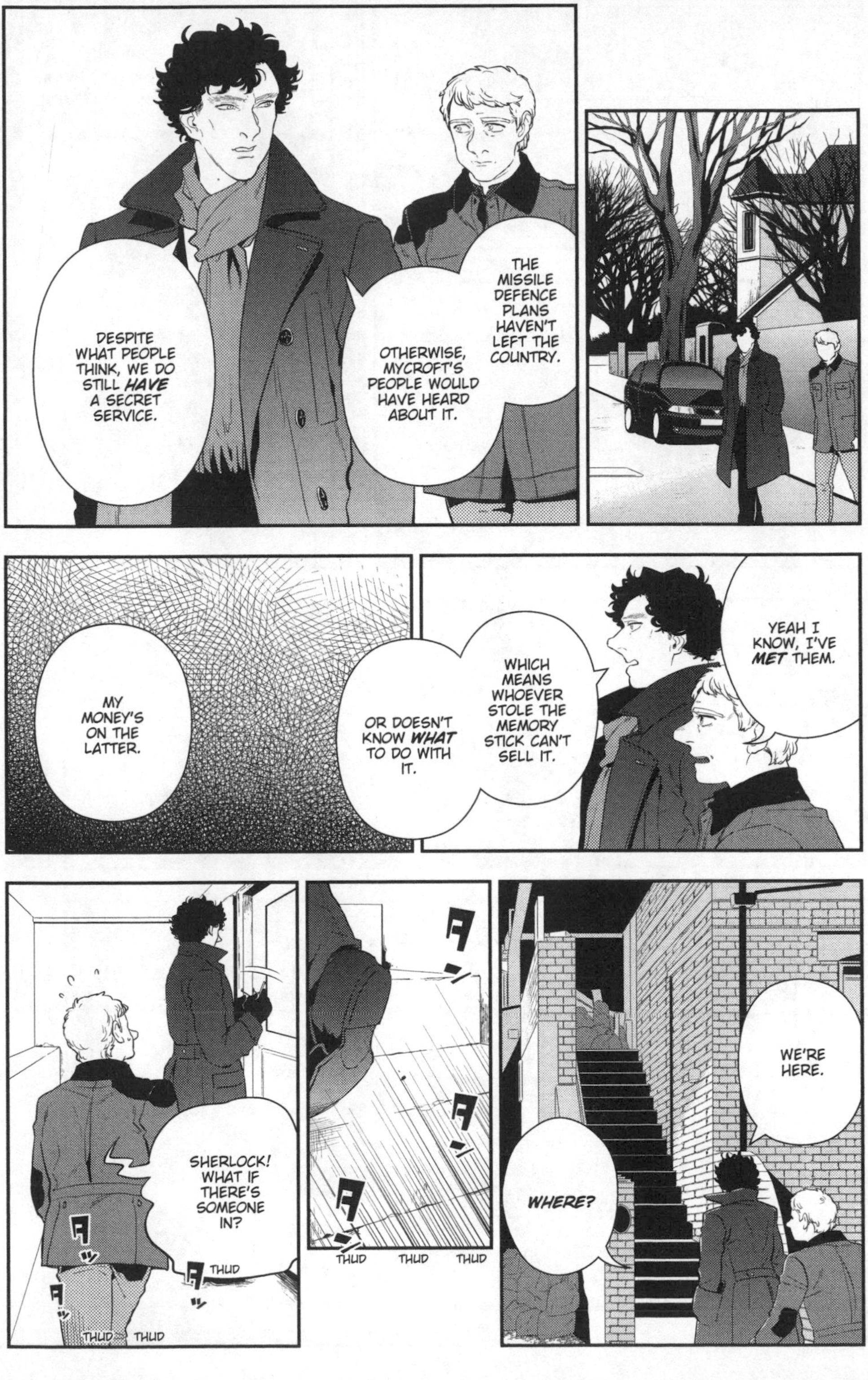
THE MISSILE DEFENCE PLANS HAVEN'T LEFT THE COUNTRY.
OTHERWISE, MYCROFT'S PEOPLE WOULD HAVE HEARD ABOUT IT.
DESPITE WHAT PEOPLE THINK, WE DO STILL ***HAVE*** A SECRET SERVICE.
YEAH I KNOW, I'VE ***MET*** THEM.
WHICH MEANS WHOEVER STOLE THE MEMORY STICK CAN'T SELL IT.
OR DOESN'T KNOW ***WHAT*** TO DO WITH IT.
MY MONEY'S ON THE LATTER.
WE'RE HERE.
WHERE?
THUD THUD THUD
SHERLOCK! WHAT IF THERE'S SOMEONE IN?
THUD
THUD THUD

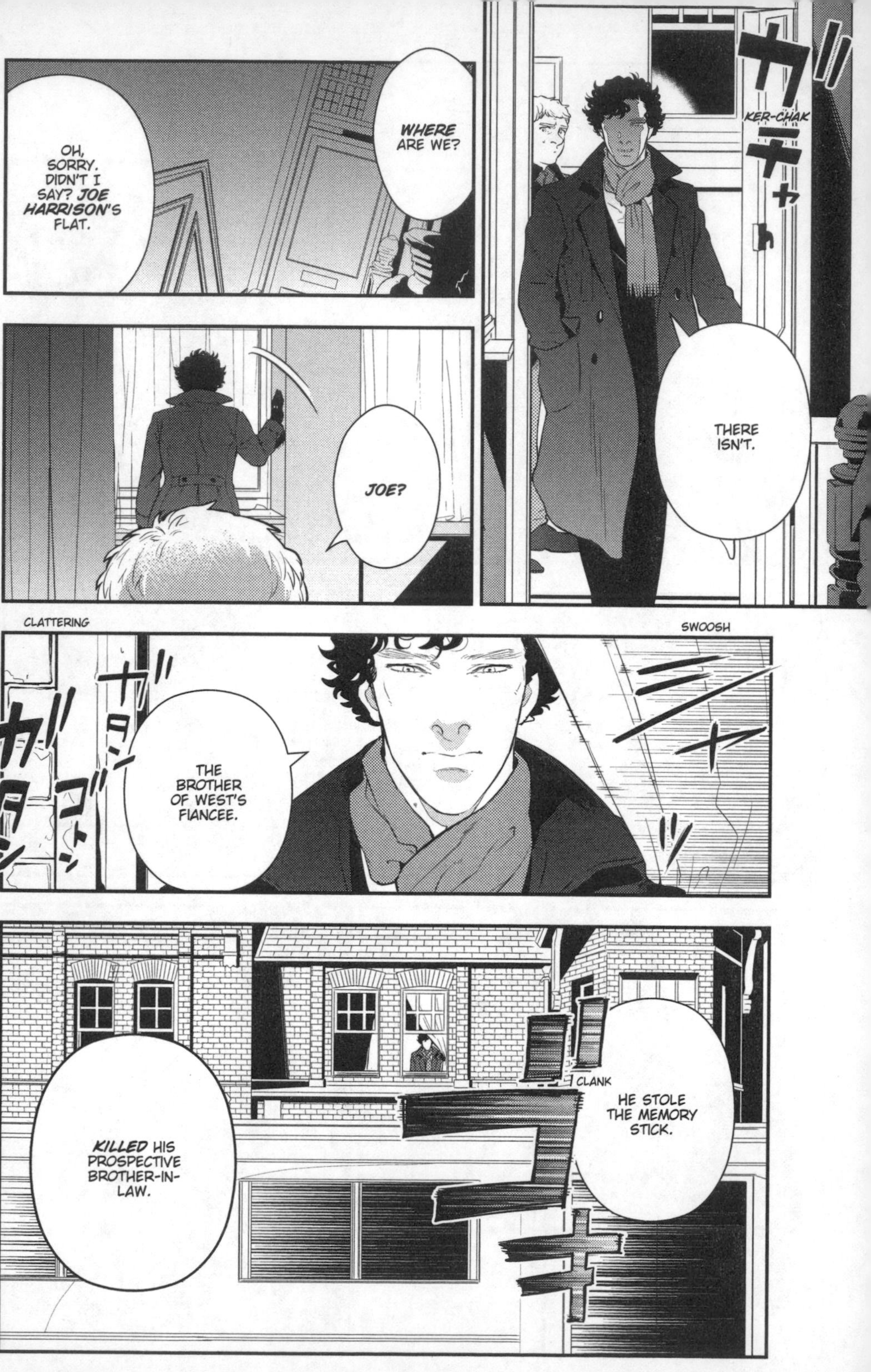
KER-CHAK
THERE ISN'T.
WHERE ARE WE?
OH, SORRY. DIDN'T I SAY? JOE HARRISON'S FLAT.
JOE?
SWOOSH
THE BROTHER OF WEST'S FIANCEE.
CLATTERING
CLANK
HE STOLE THE MEMORY STICK.
KILLED HIS PROSPECTIVE BROTHER-IN-LAW.

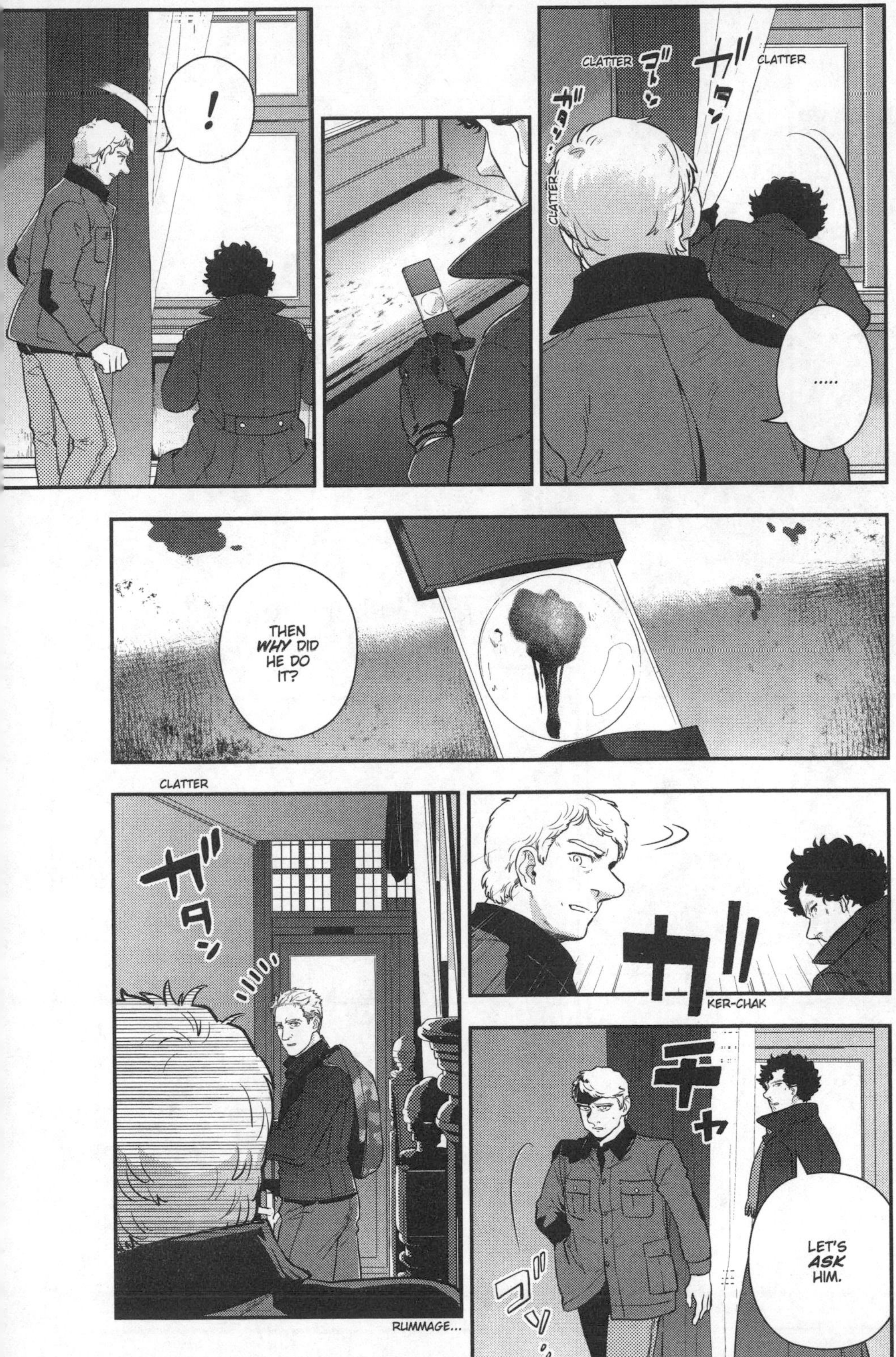
CLATTER
CLATTER
CLATTER
.....
!
THEN *WHY* DID HE DO IT?
KER-CHAK
LET'S *ASK* HIM.
CLATTER
RUMMAGE...

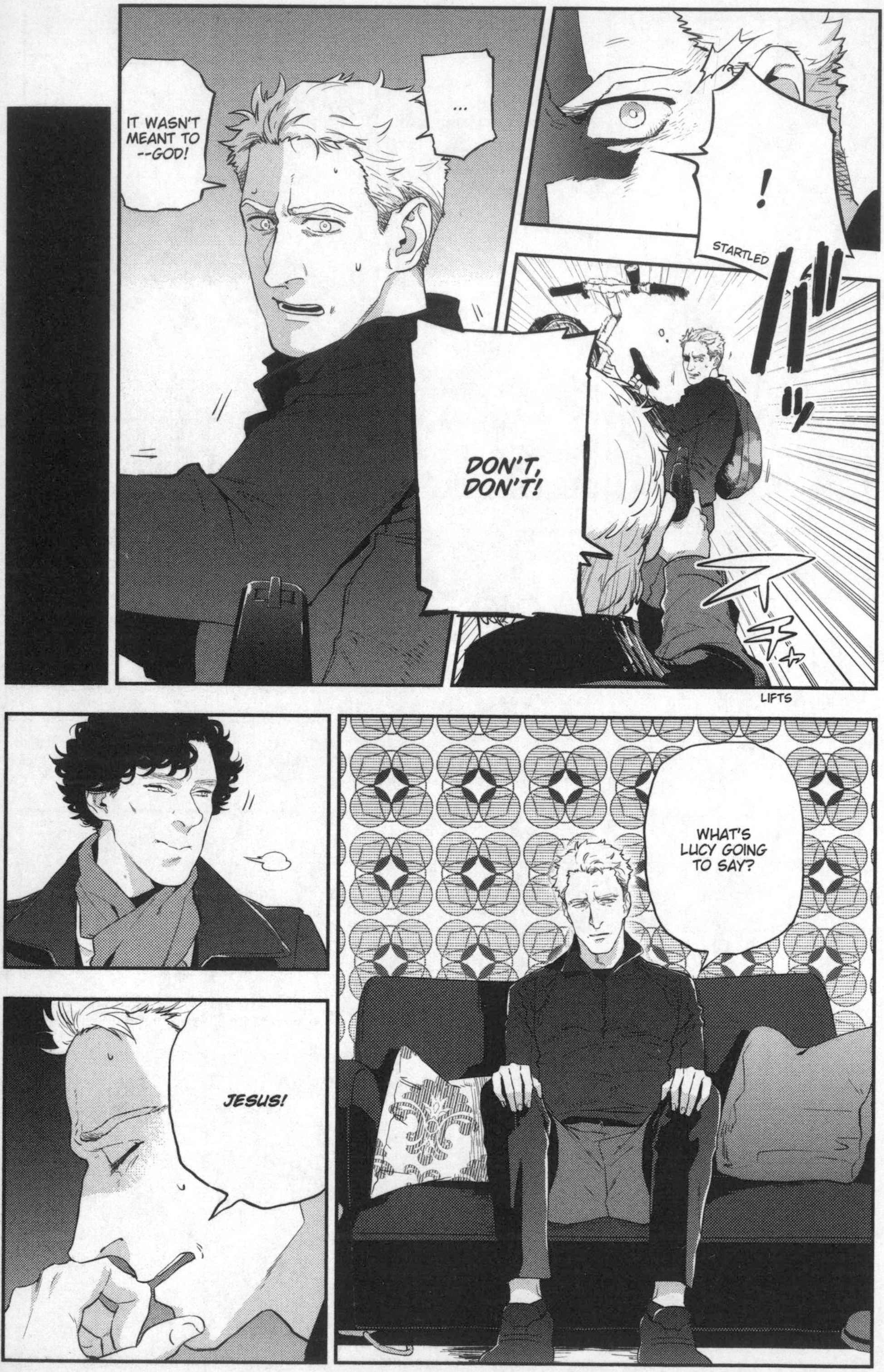
!
STARTLED
DON'T, DON'T!
...
IT WASN'T MEANT TO --GOD!
LIFTS
WHAT'S LUCY GOING TO SAY?
JESUS!

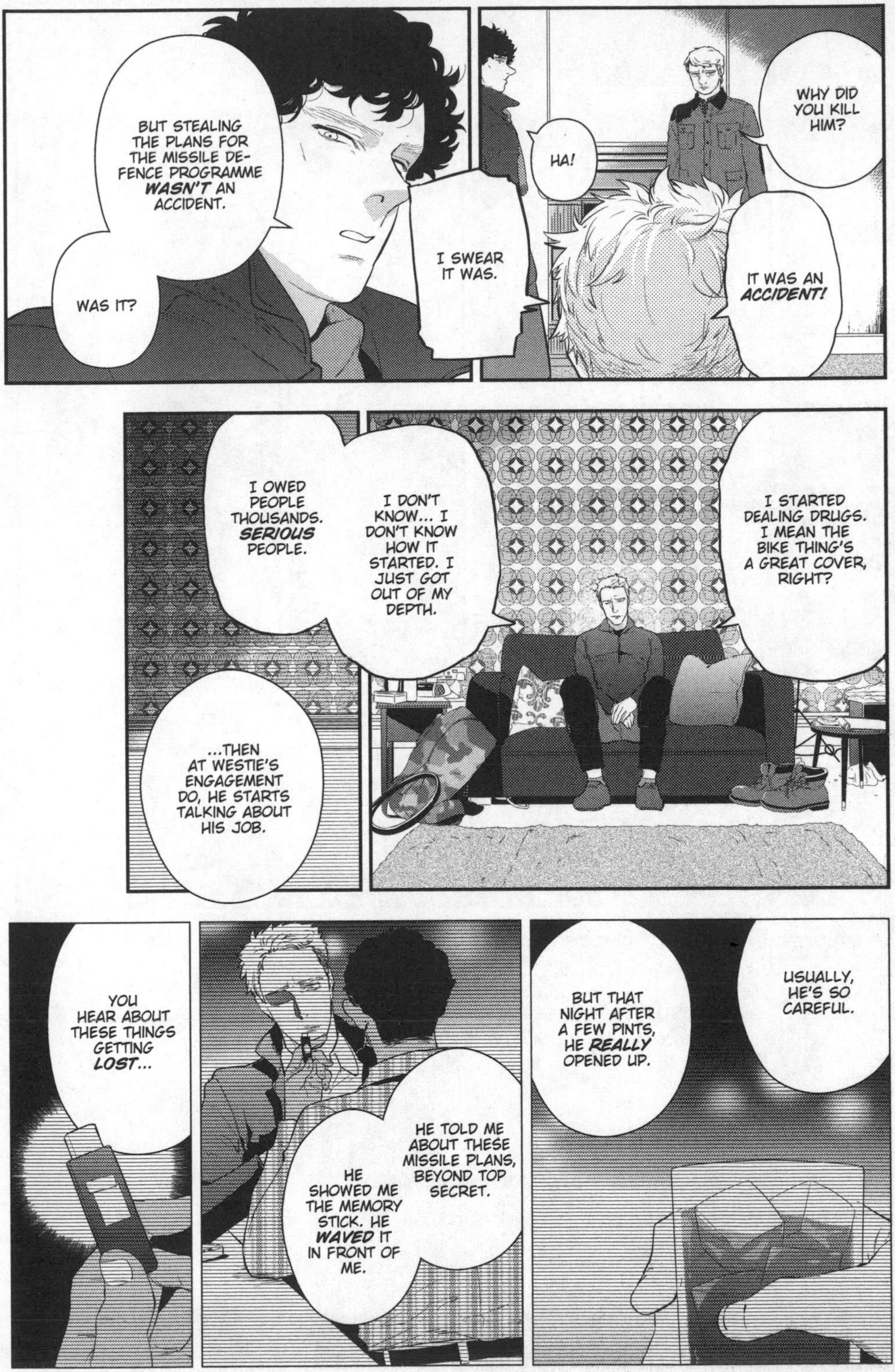
WHY DID YOU KILL HIM?
HA!
IT WAS AN ACCIDENT!
I SWEAR IT WAS.
BUT STEALING THE PLANS FOR THE MISSILE DE-FENCE PROGRAMME WASN'T AN ACCIDENT.
WAS IT?
I STARTED DEALING DRUGS. I MEAN THE BIKE THING'S A GREAT COVER, RIGHT?
I DON'T KNOW... I DON'T KNOW HOW IT STARTED. I JUST GOT OUT OF MY DEPTH.
I OWED PEOPLE THOUSANDS. SERIOUS PEOPLE.
...THEN AT WESTIE'S ENGAGEMENT DO, HE STARTS TALKING ABOUT HIS JOB.
USUALLY, HE'S SO CAREFUL.
BUT THAT NIGHT AFTER A FEW PINTS, HE REALLY OPENED UP.
HE TOLD ME ABOUT THESE MISSILE PLANS, BEYOND TOP SECRET.
HE SHOWED ME THE MEMORY STICK. HE WAVED IT IN FRONT OF ME.
YOU HEAR ABOUT THESE THINGS GETTING LOST...

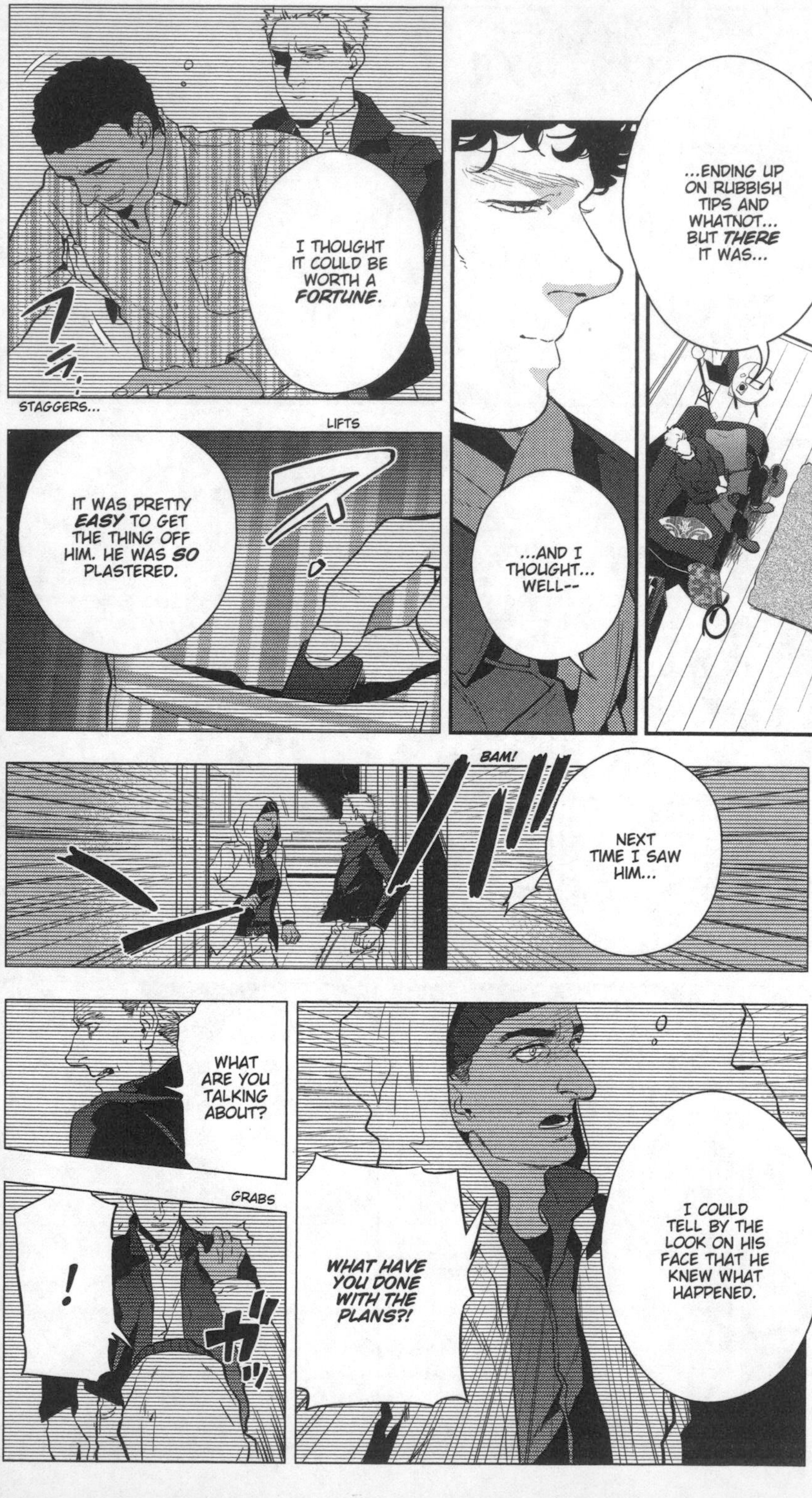
...ENDING UP ON RUBBISH TIPS AND WHATNOT... BUT THERE IT WAS...
...AND I THOUGHT... WELL--
I THOUGHT IT COULD BE WORTH A FORTUNE.
STAGGERS...
LIFTS
IT WAS PRETTY EASY TO GET THE THING OFF HIM. HE WAS SO PLASTERED.
BAM!
NEXT TIME I SAW HIM...
I COULD TELL BY THE LOOK ON HIS FACE THAT HE KNEW WHAT HAPPENED.
WHAT HAVE YOU DONE WITH THE PLANS?!
WHAT ARE YOU TALKING ABOUT?
GRABS
!

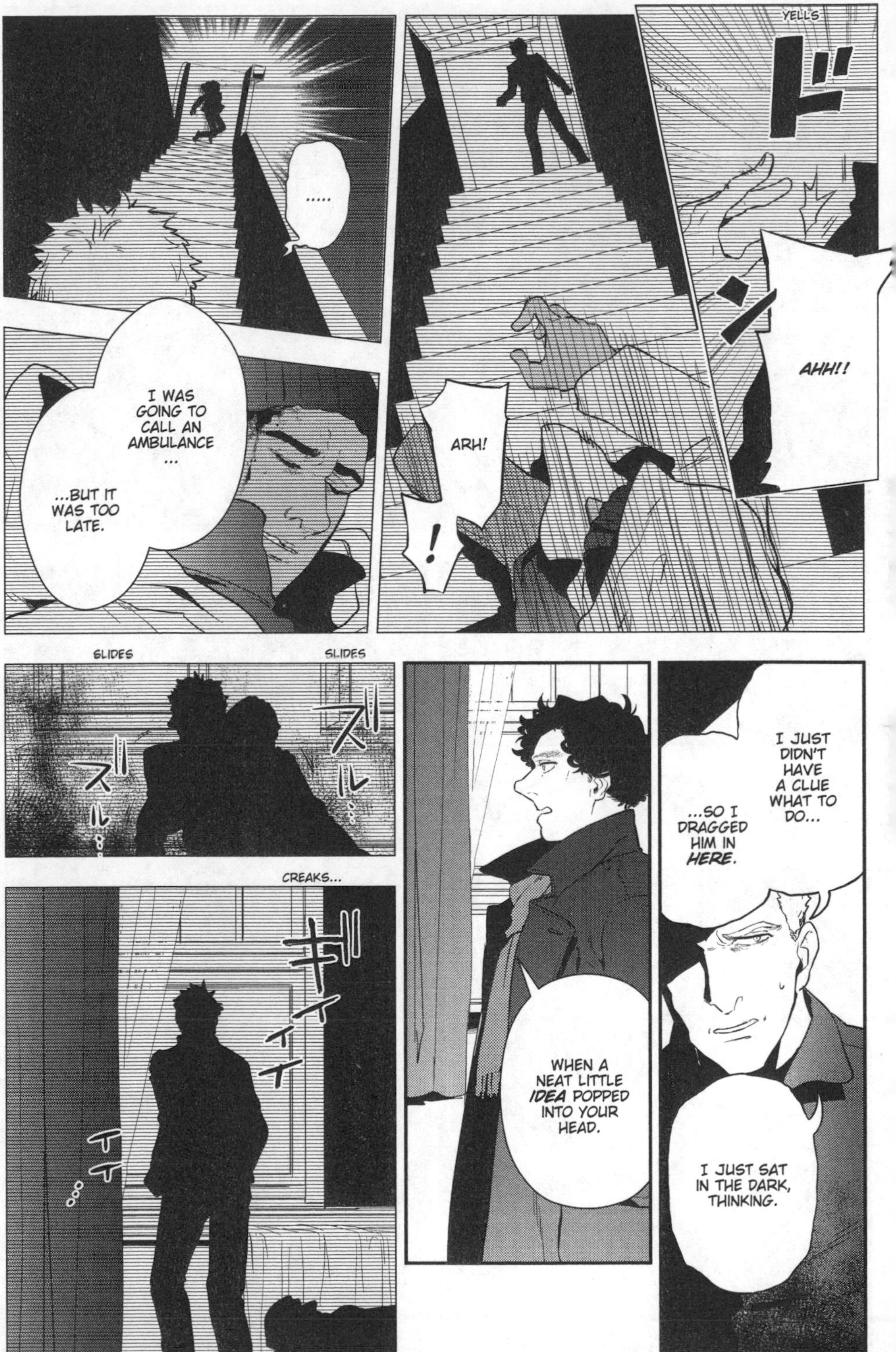
YELL'S
ド
AHH!!
ARH!
!
.....
I WAS GOING TO CALL AN AMBULANCE ...
...BUT IT WAS TOO LATE.
I JUST DIDN'T HAVE A CLUE WHAT TO DO...
...SO I DRAGGED HIM IN *HERE*.
I JUST SAT IN THE DARK, THINKING.
WHEN A NEAT LITTLE *IDEA* POPPED INTO YOUR HEAD.
SLIDES
SLIDES
ズル
ズル
CREAKS...
ギイイイ
イイ

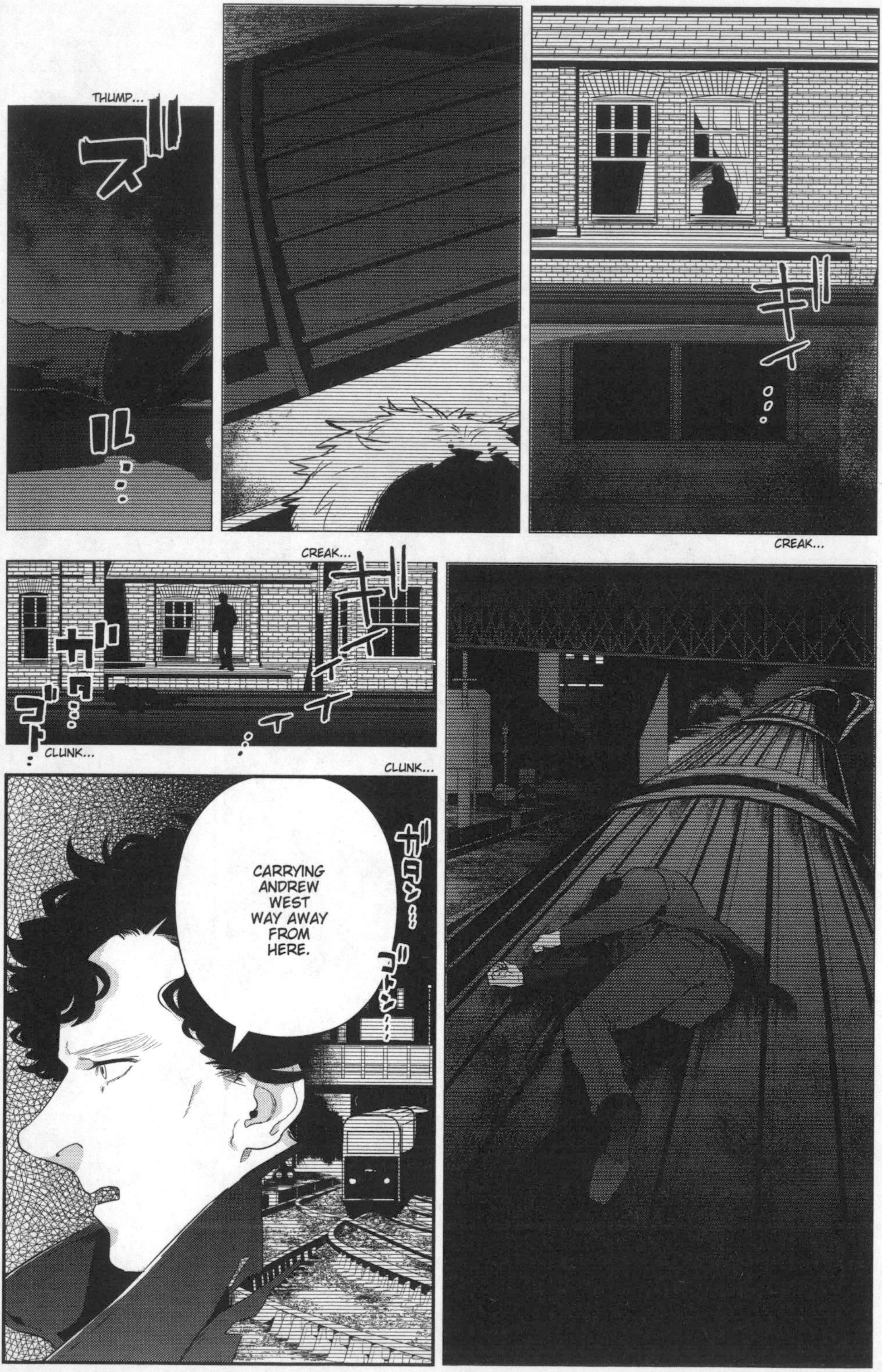
CREAK...
THUMP...
CREAK...
CLUNK...
CLUNK...
CARRYING ANDREW WEST WAY AWAY FROM HERE.

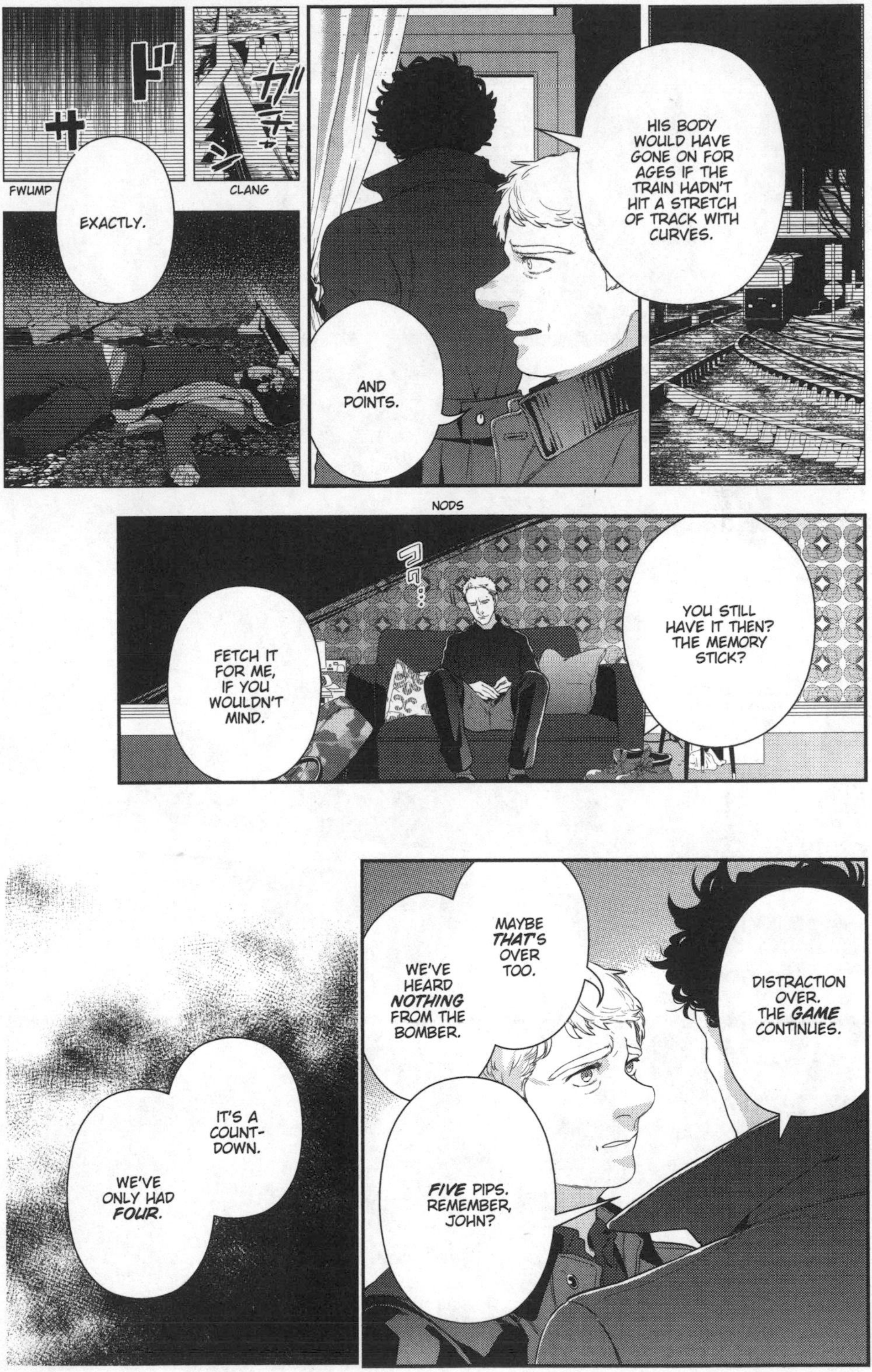
HIS BODY WOULD HAVE GONE ON FOR AGES IF THE TRAIN HADN'T HIT A STRETCH OF TRACK WITH CURVES.
AND POINTS.
CLANG
FWUMP
EXACTLY.
NODS
YOU STILL HAVE IT THEN? THE MEMORY STICK?
FETCH IT FOR ME, IF YOU WOULDN'T MIND.
DISTRACTION OVER. THE *GAME* CONTINUES.
WE'VE HEARD *NOTHING* FROM THE BOMBER.
MAYBE *THAT*'S OVER TOO.
FIVE PIPS. REMEMBER, JOHN?
IT'S A COUNT-DOWN.
WE'VE ONLY HAD *FOUR*.

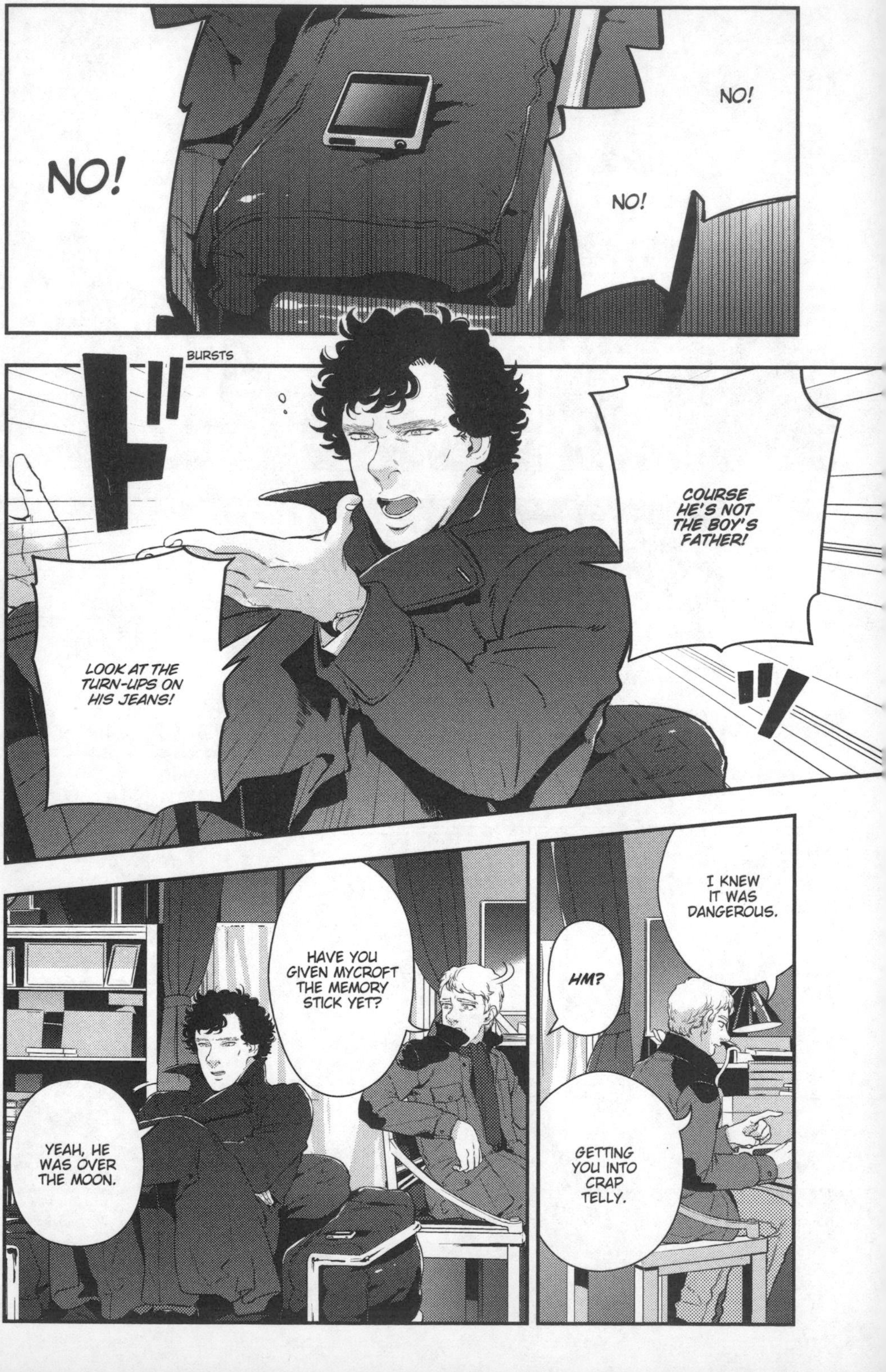
NO!
NO!
NO!
COURSE HE'S NOT THE BOY'S FATHER!
BURSTS
LOOK AT THE TURN-UPS ON HIS JEANS!
I KNEW IT WAS DANGEROUS.
HM?
GETTING YOU INTO CRAP TELLY.
HAVE YOU GIVEN MYCROFT THE MEMORY STICK YET?
YEAH, HE WAS OVER THE MOON.

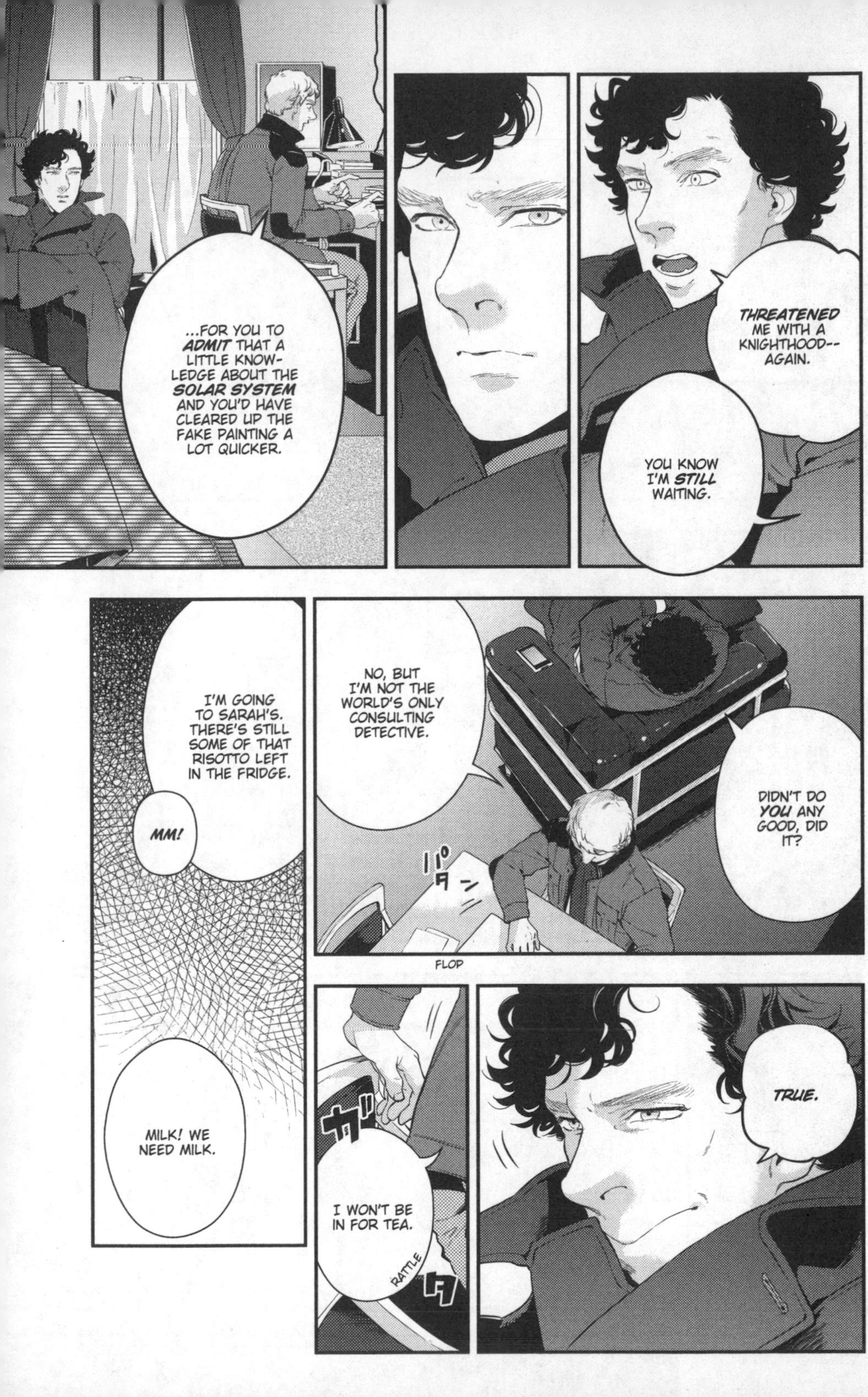
THREATENED ME WITH A KNIGHTHOOD-- AGAIN.
YOU KNOW I'M STILL WAITING.
...FOR YOU TO ADMIT THAT A LITTLE KNOW-LEDGE ABOUT THE SOLAR SYSTEM AND YOU'D HAVE CLEARED UP THE FAKE PAINTING A LOT QUICKER.
DIDN'T DO YOU ANY GOOD, DID IT?
NO, BUT I'M NOT THE WORLD'S ONLY CONSULTING DETECTIVE.
FLOP
TRUE.
I WON'T BE IN FOR TEA.
RATTLE
I'M GOING TO SARAH'S. THERE'S STILL SOME OF THAT RISOTTO LEFT IN THE FRIDGE.
MM!
MILK! WE NEED MILK.

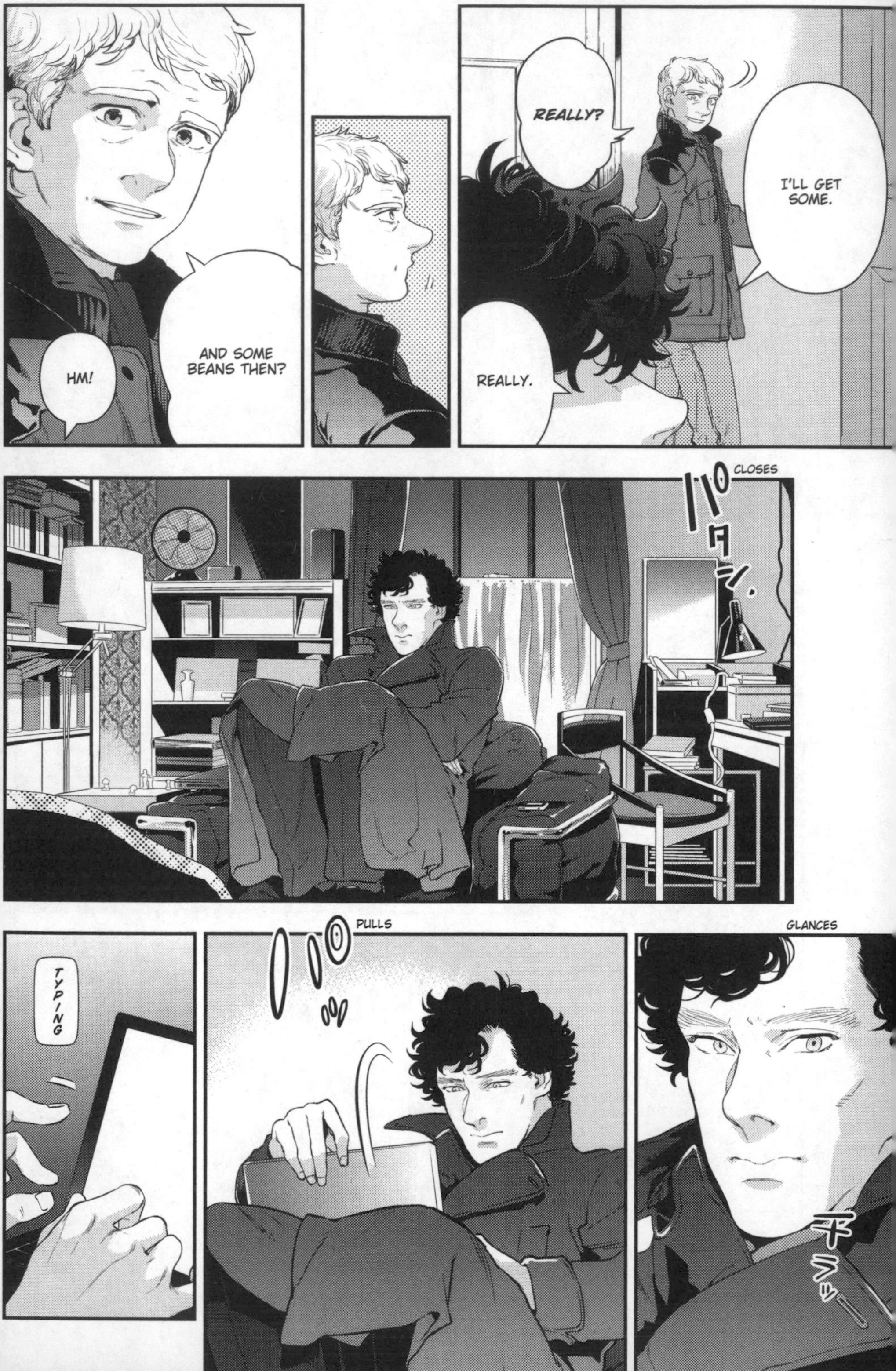
REALLY?
I'LL GET SOME.
REALLY.
AND SOME BEANS THEN?
HM!
CLOSES
バタン
GLANCES
チラッ
PULLS
TYPING

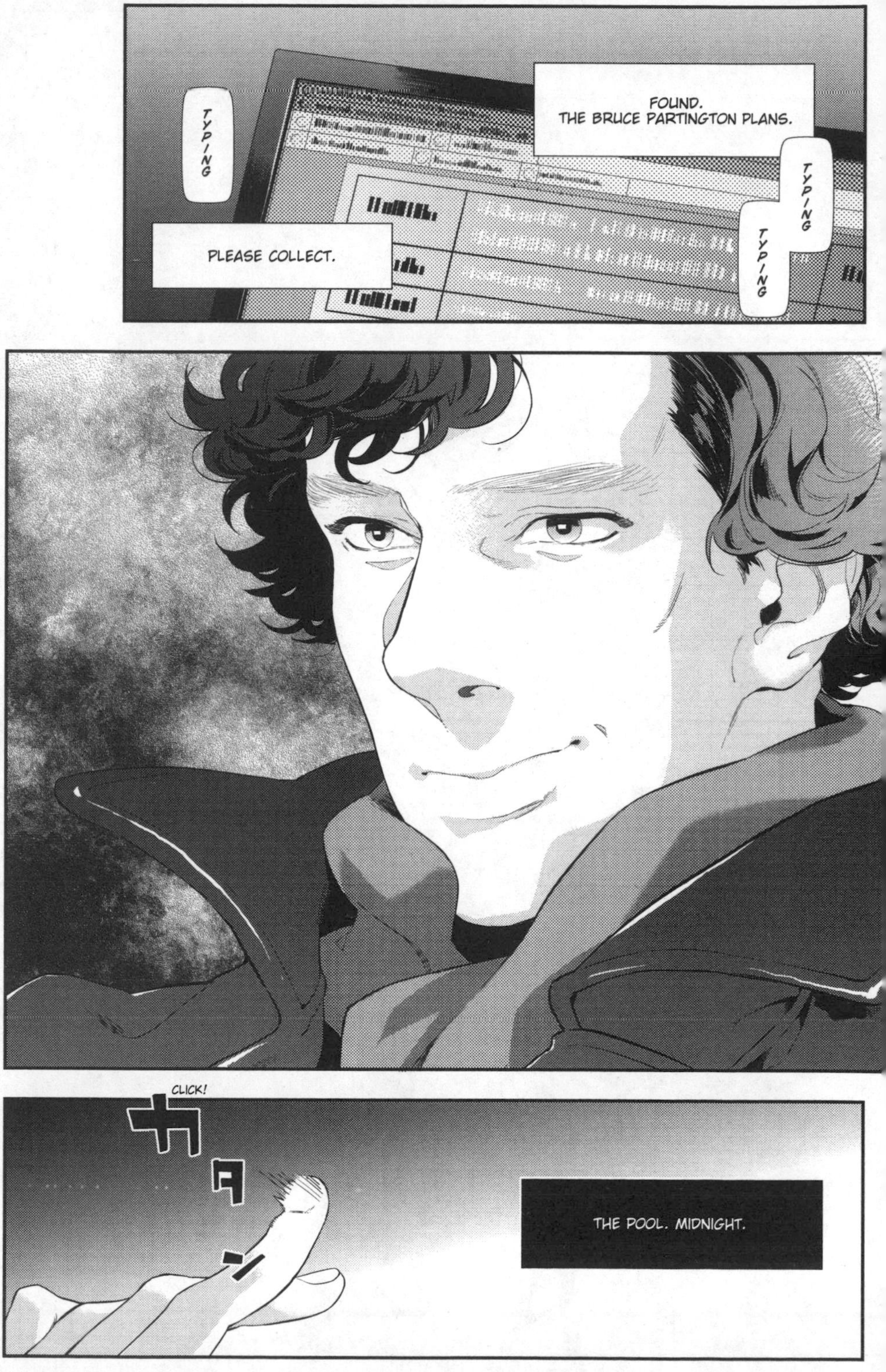
FOUND.
THE BRUCE PARTINGTON PLANS.
TYPING
TYPING
TYPING
PLEASE COLLECT.
CLICK!
THE POOL. MIDNIGHT.

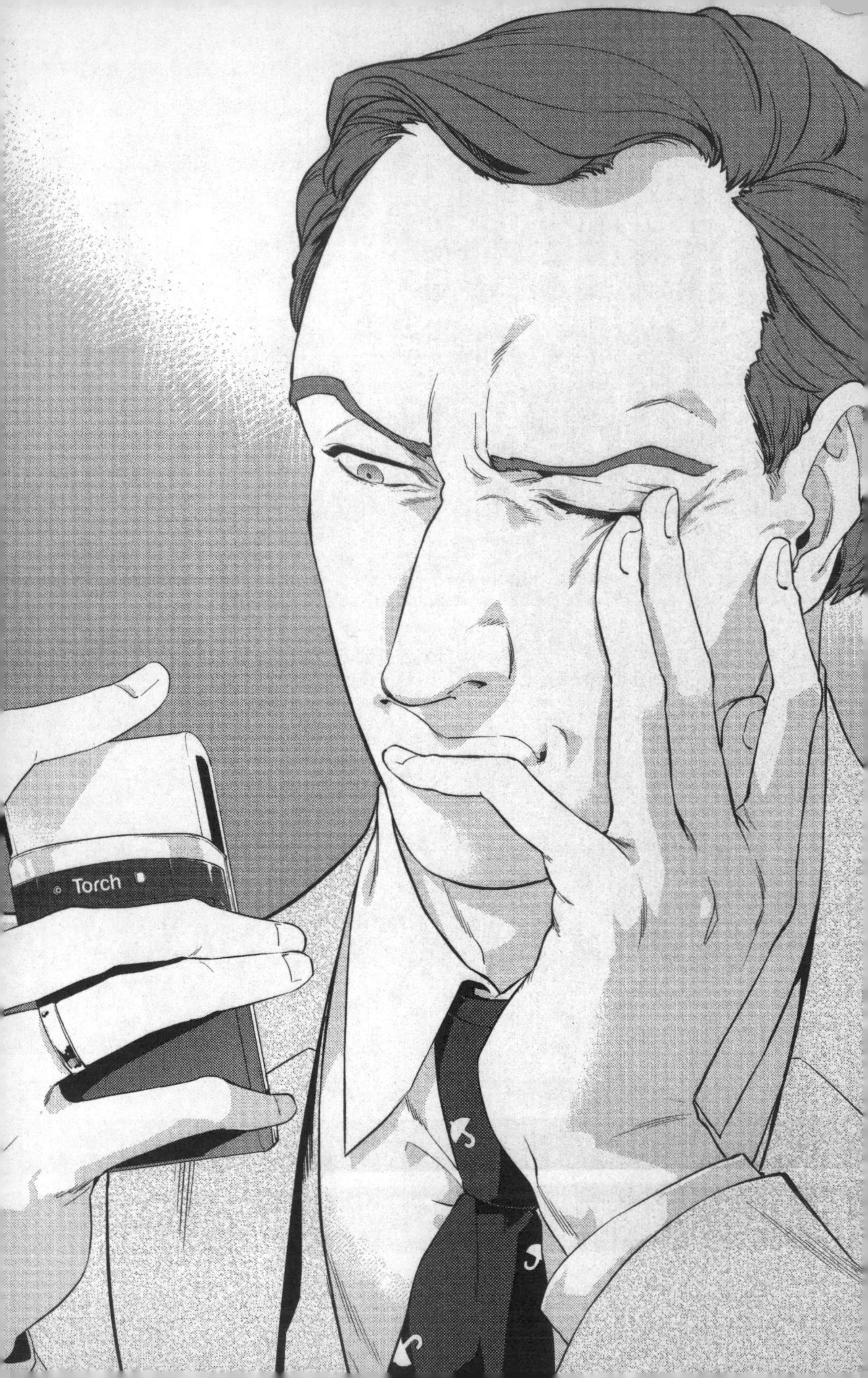
Torch

Chapter 6

Illustration by:
Simon Myers

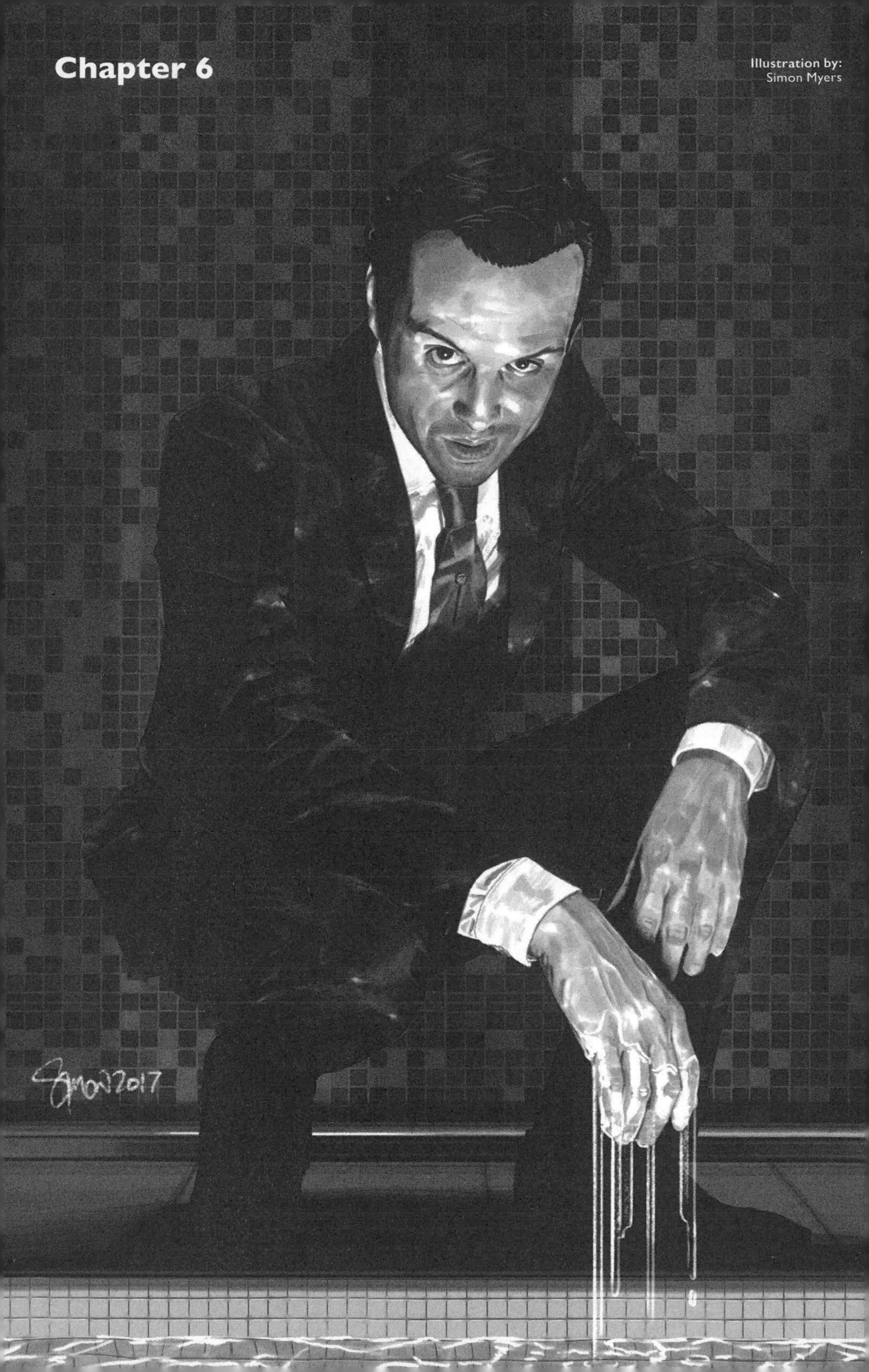
Simon 2017

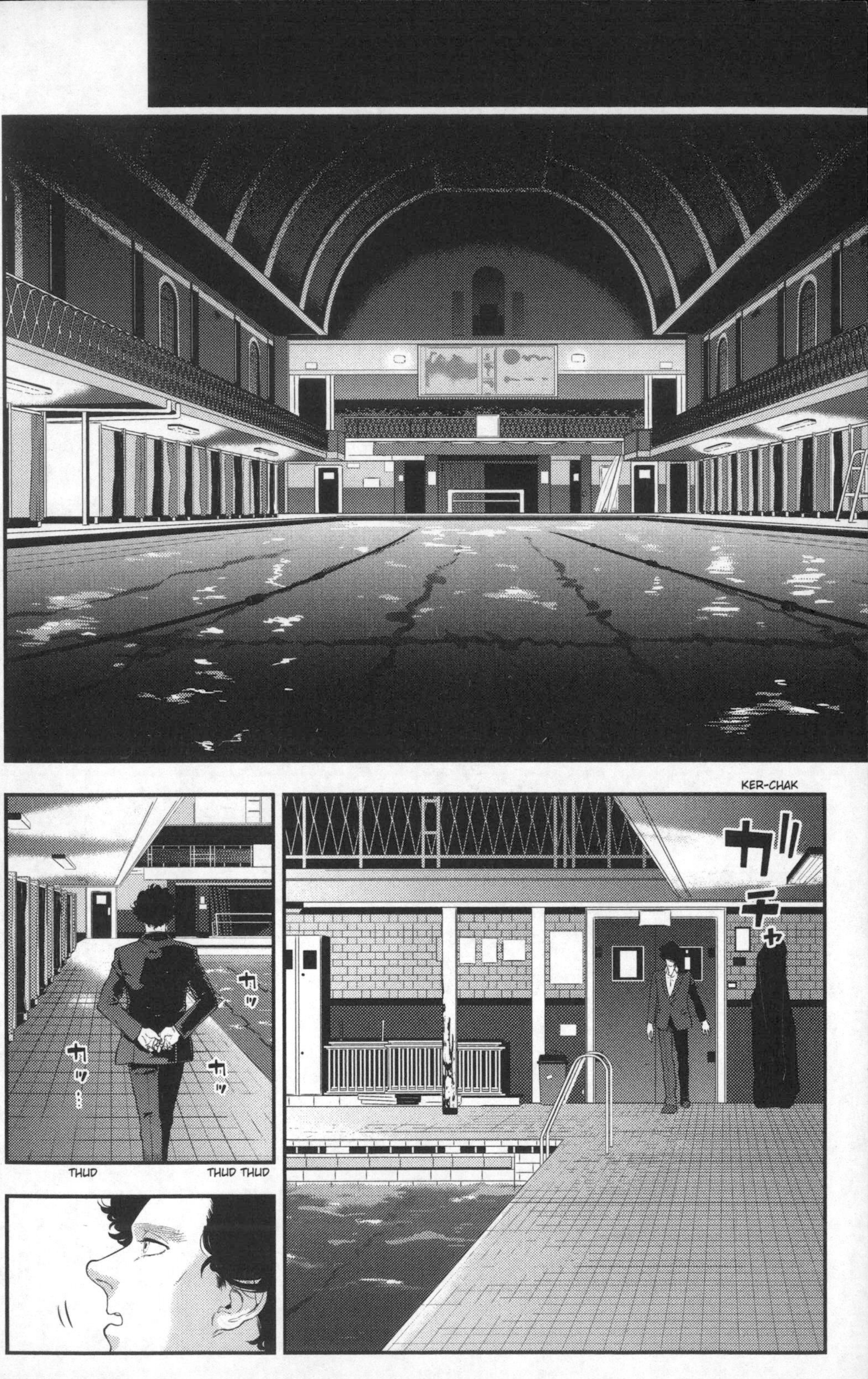
KER-CHAK
ガチャ
カッ
カッ
カッ…
THUD THUD
THUD

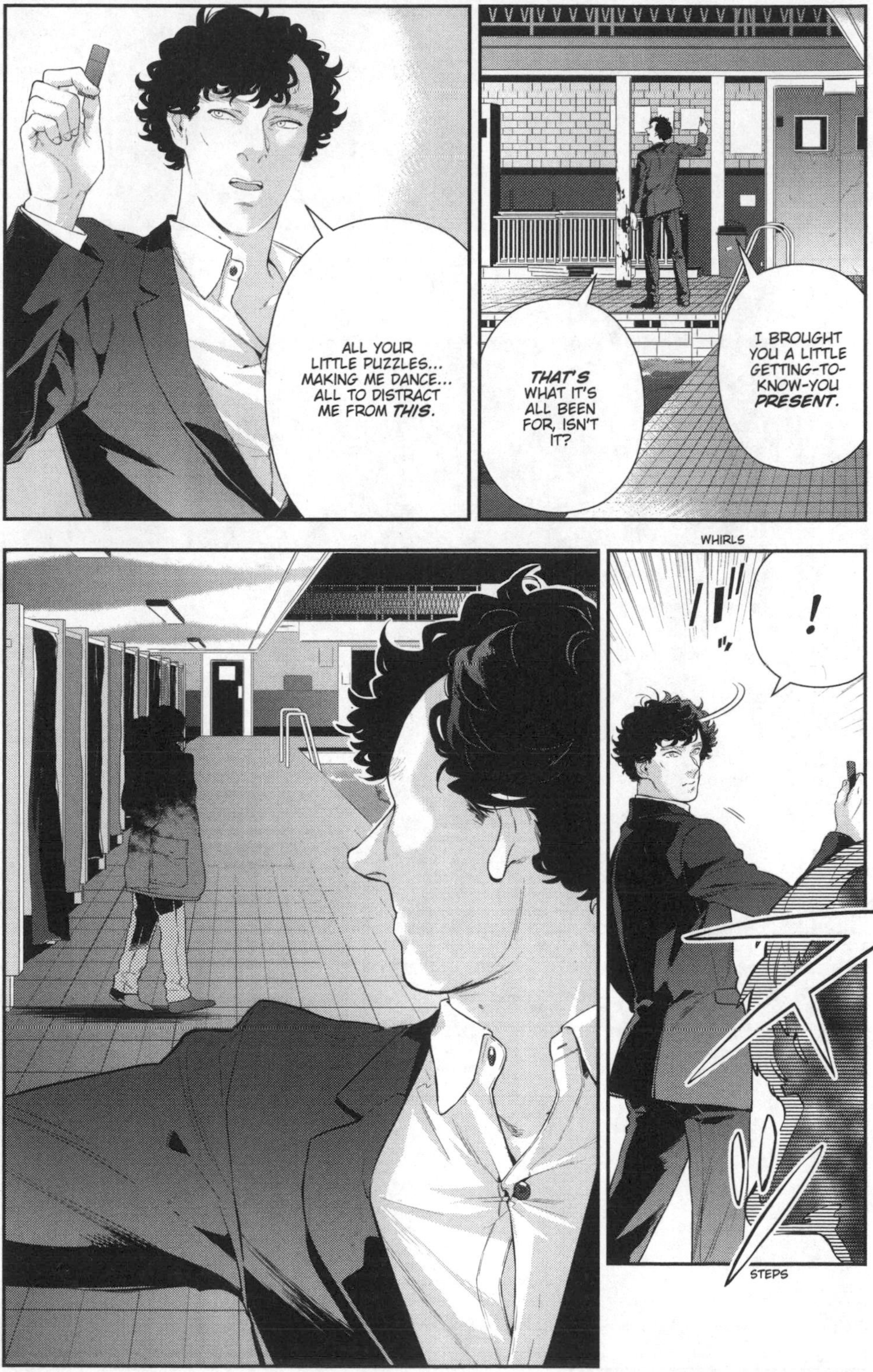
I BROUGHT YOU A LITTLE GETTING-TO-KNOW-YOU *PRESENT*.
THAT'S WHAT IT'S ALL BEEN FOR, ISN'T IT?
ALL YOUR LITTLE PUZZLES... MAKING ME DANCE... ALL TO DISTRACT ME FROM *THIS*.
WHIRLS
!
STEPS

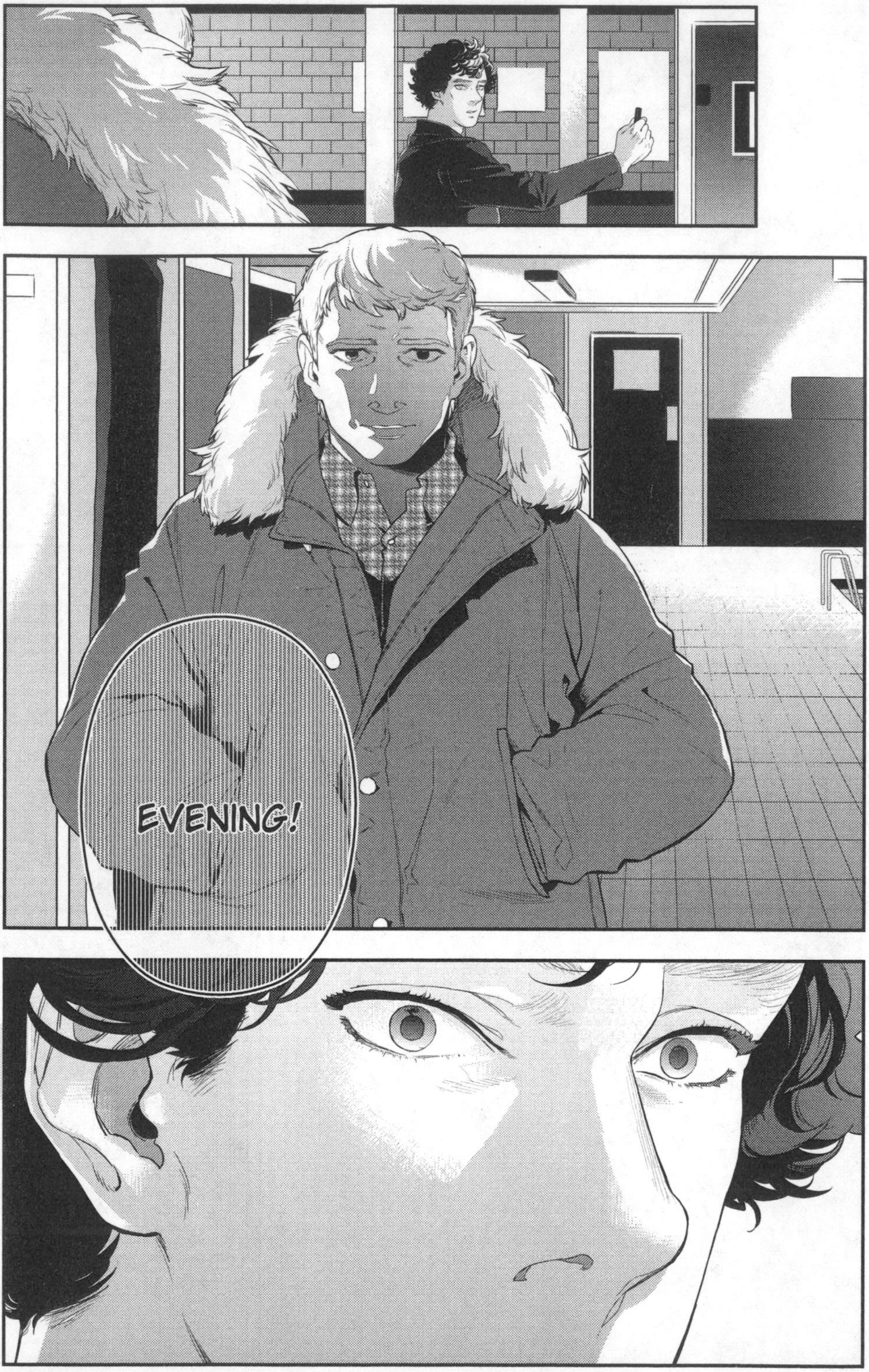
EVENING!

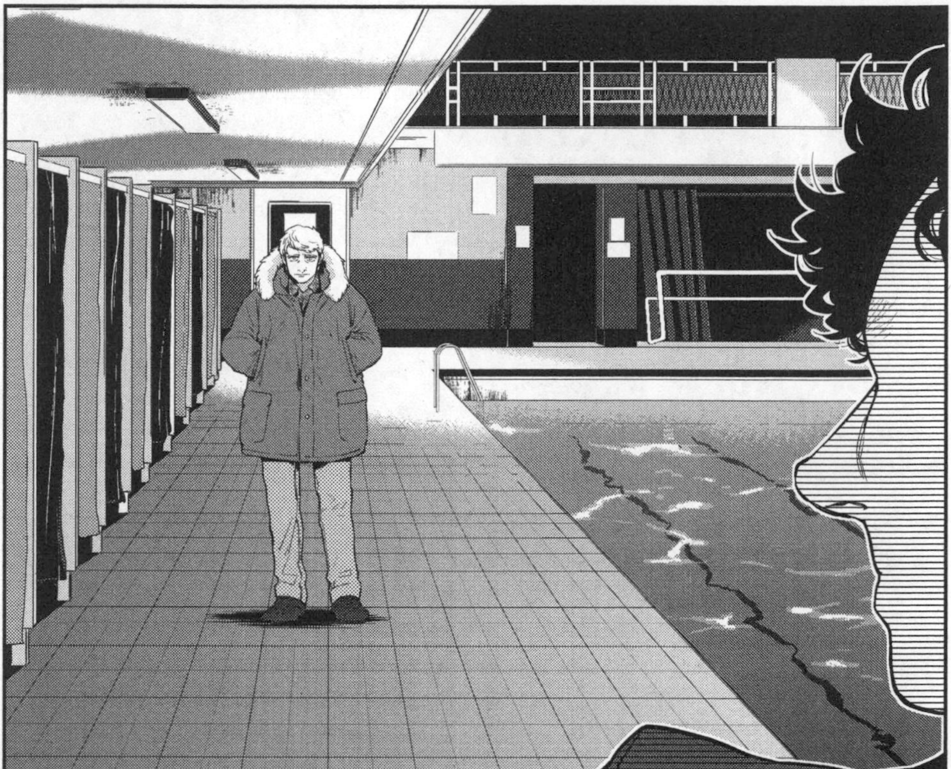

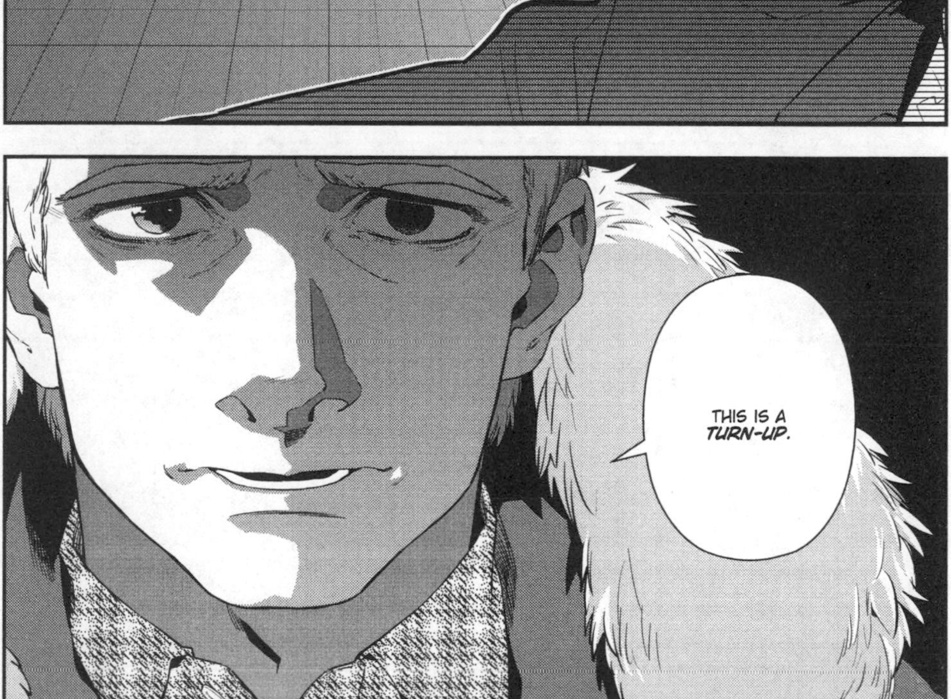
THIS IS A *TURN-UP*.

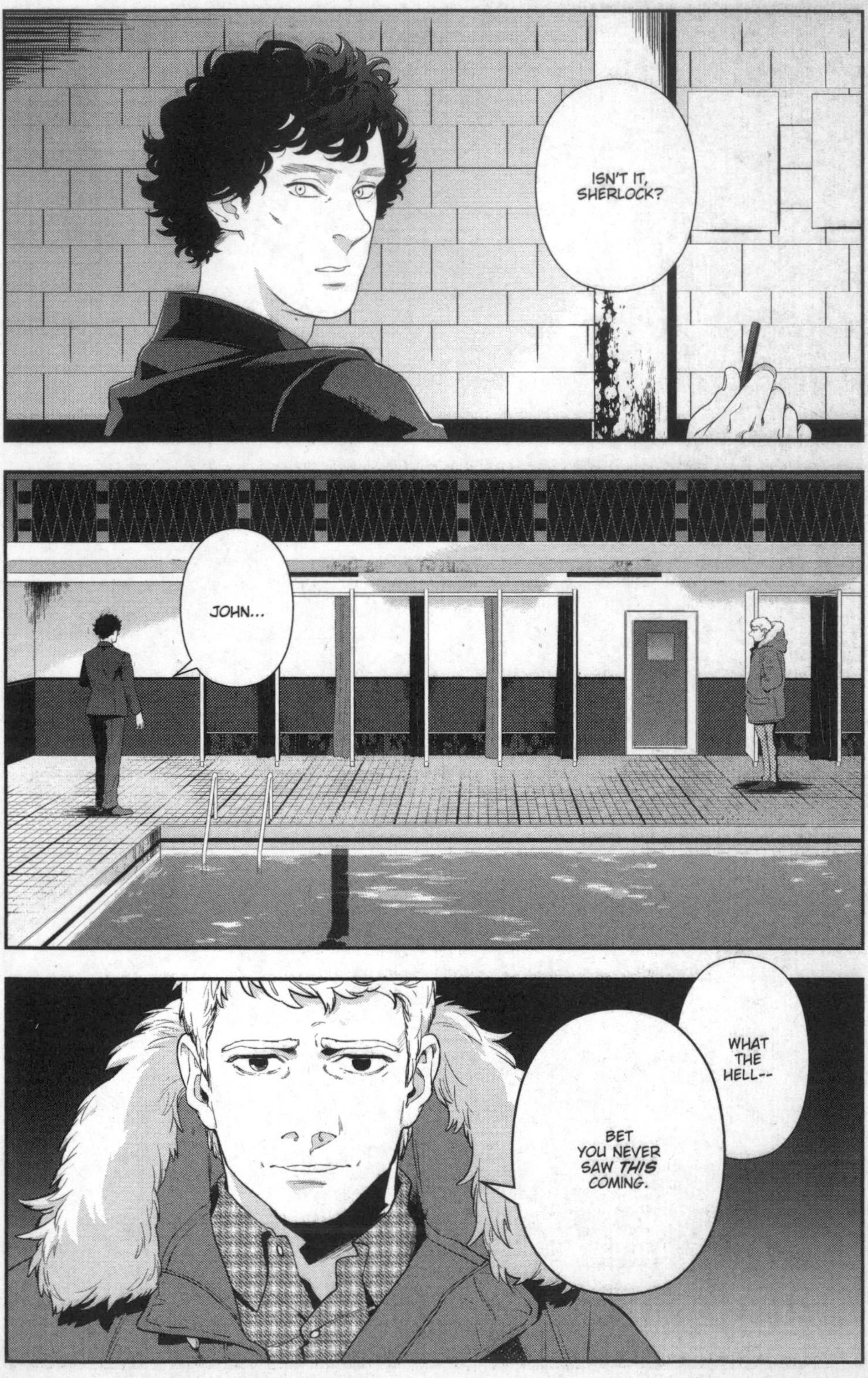
ISN'T IT, SHERLOCK?
JOHN...
WHAT THE HELL--
BET YOU NEVER SAW *THIS* COMING.

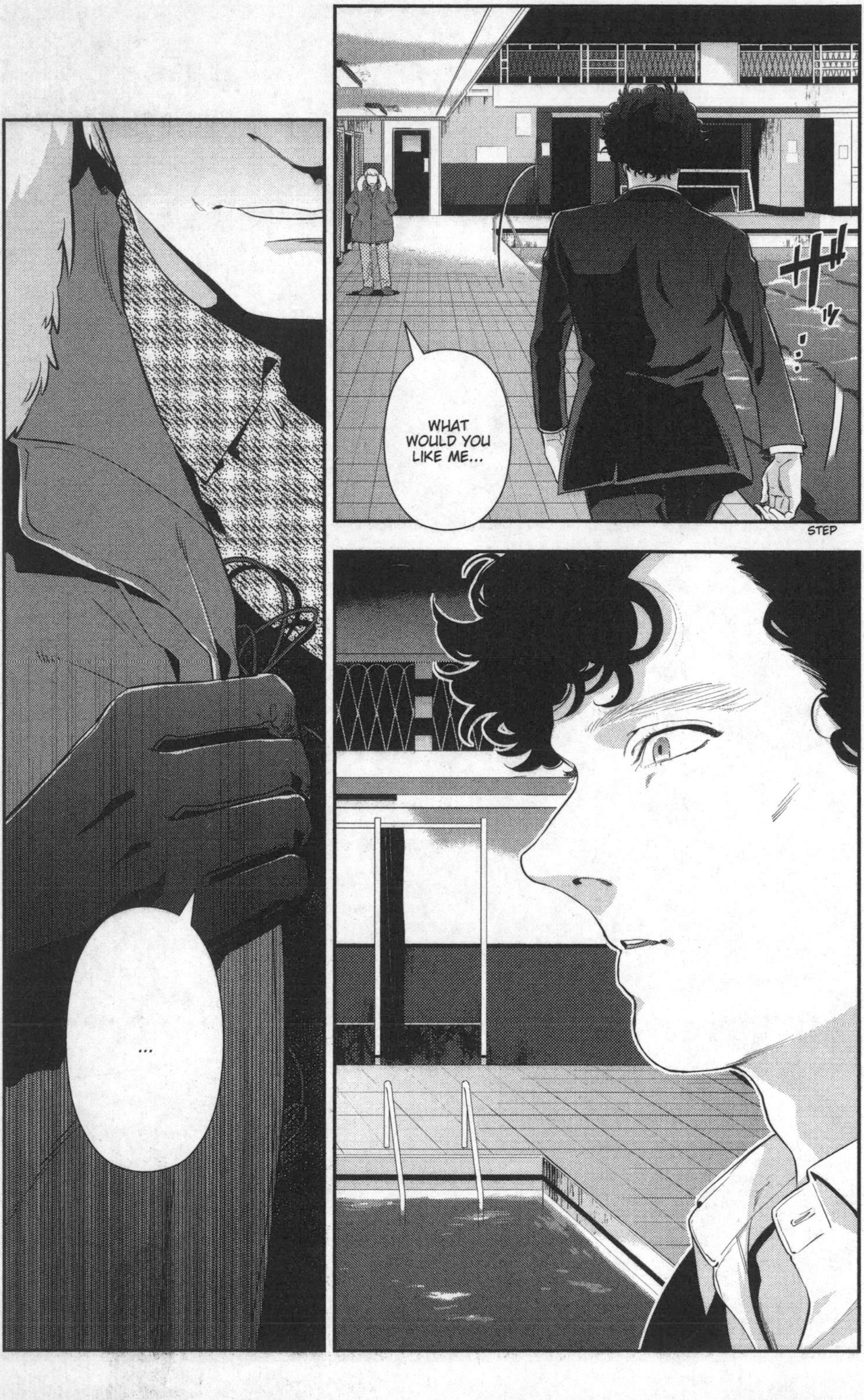
WHAT WOULD YOU LIKE ME...
STEP
...

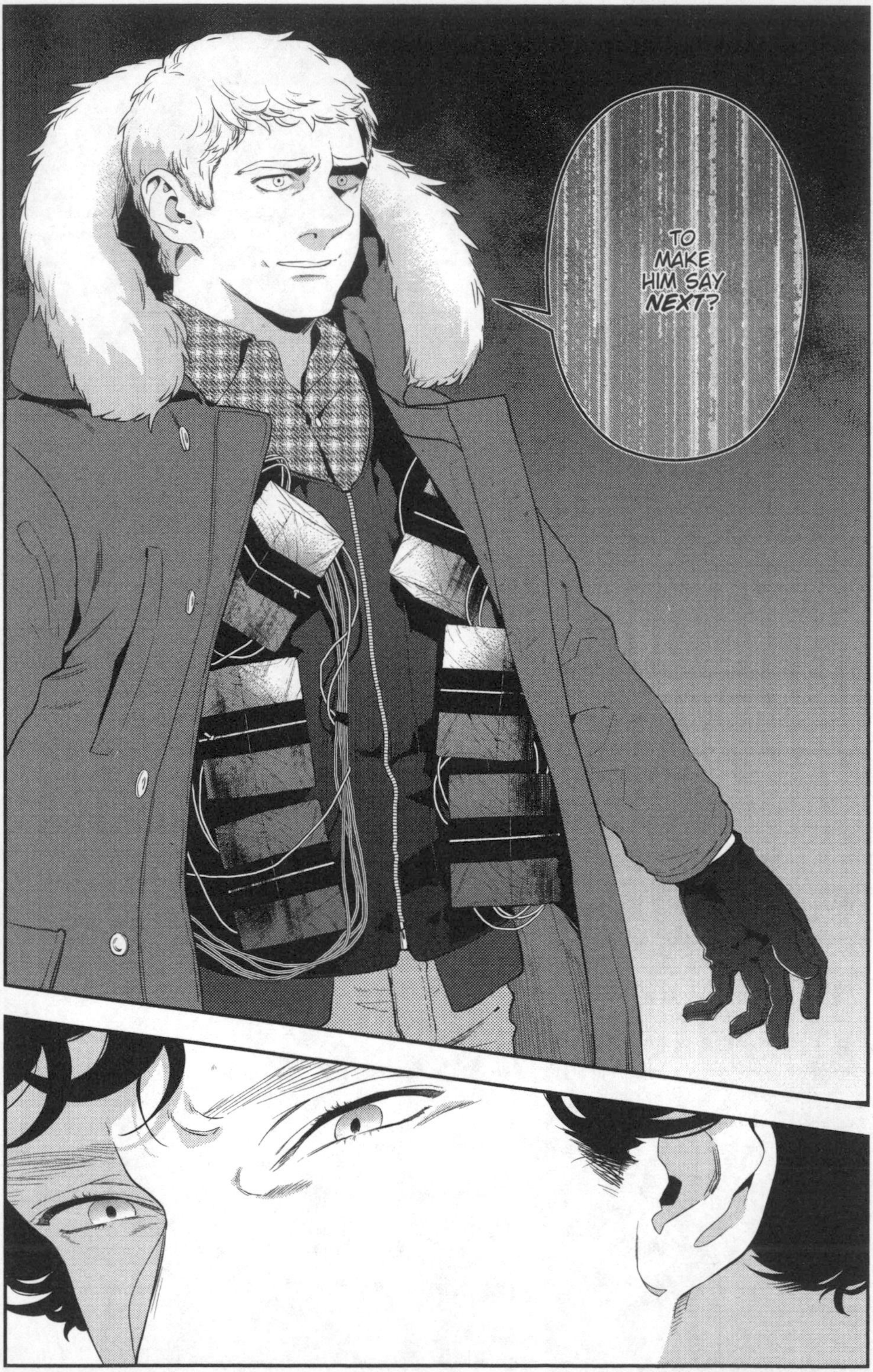
TO MAKE HIM SAY *NEXT*?

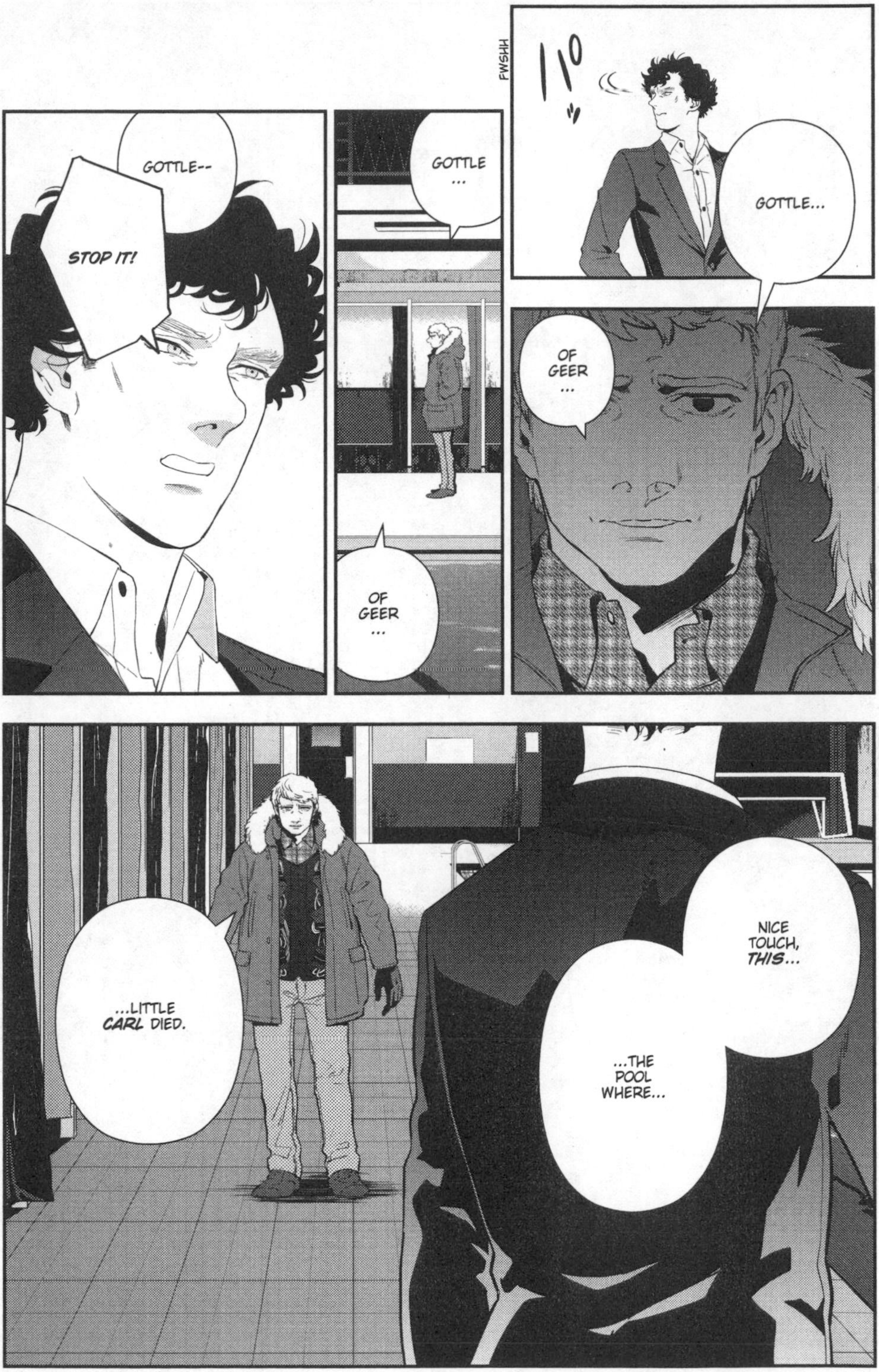
FWSHH
GOTTLE...
OF GEER ...
GOTTLE ...
OF GEER ...
GOTTLE--
STOP IT!
NICE TOUCH, *THIS*...
...THE POOL WHERE...
...LITTLE *CARL* DIED.

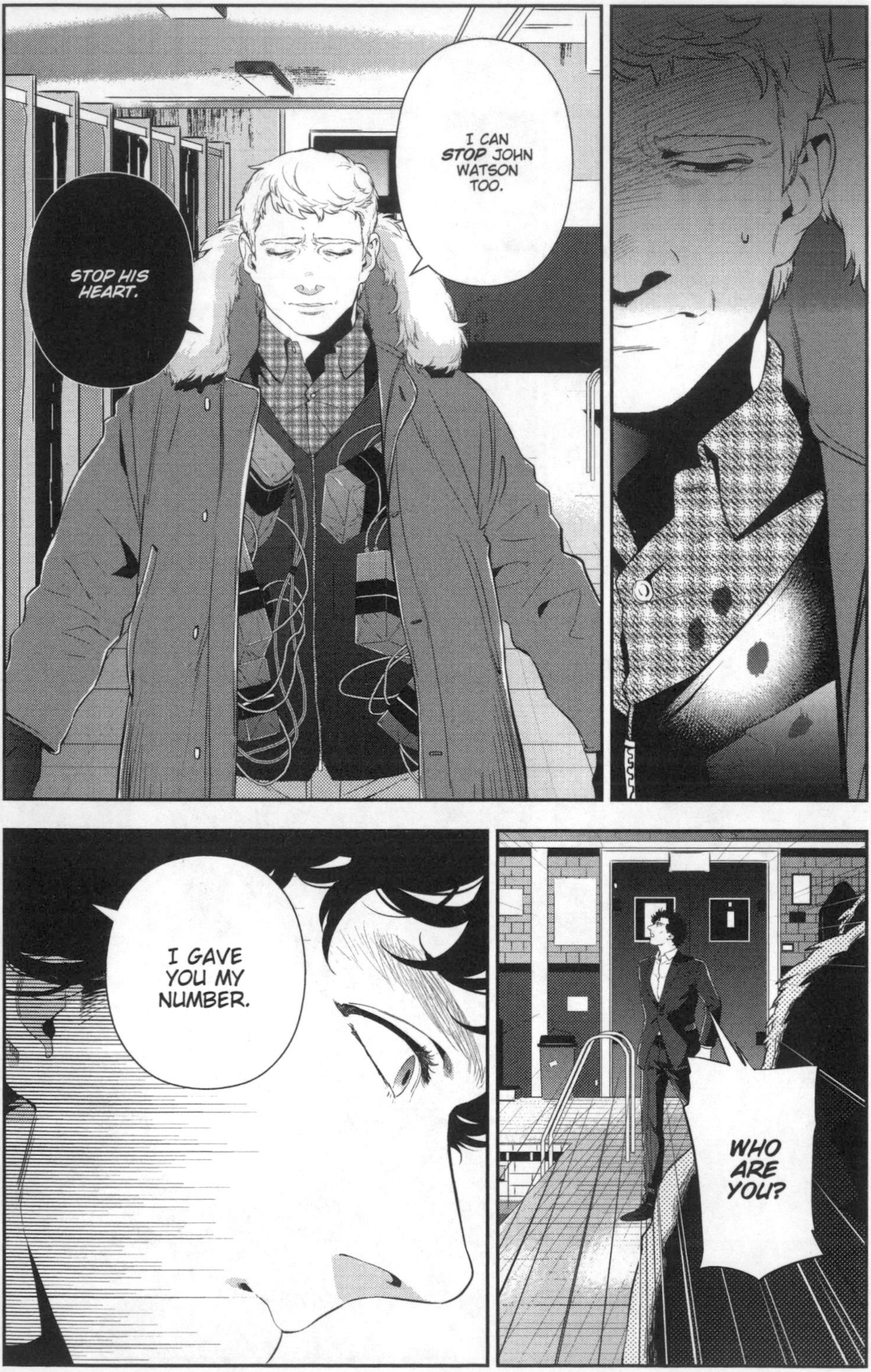
I CAN STOP JOHN WATSON TOO.
STOP HIS HEART.
WHO ARE YOU?
I GAVE YOU MY NUMBER.

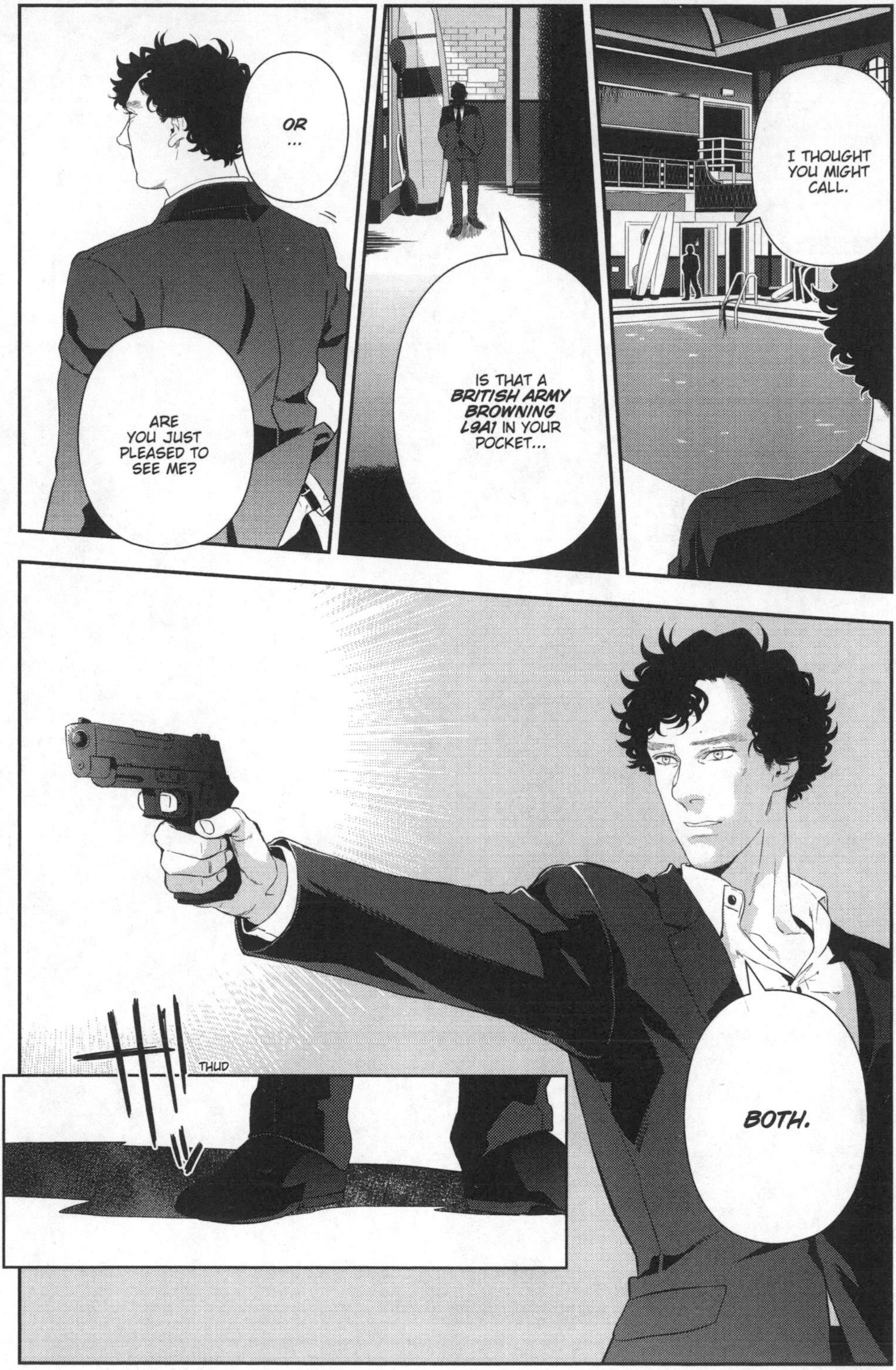
I THOUGHT YOU MIGHT CALL.
IS THAT A *BRITISH ARMY BROWNING L9A1* IN YOUR POCKET...
OR ...
ARE YOU JUST PLEASED TO SEE ME?
BOTH.
THUD

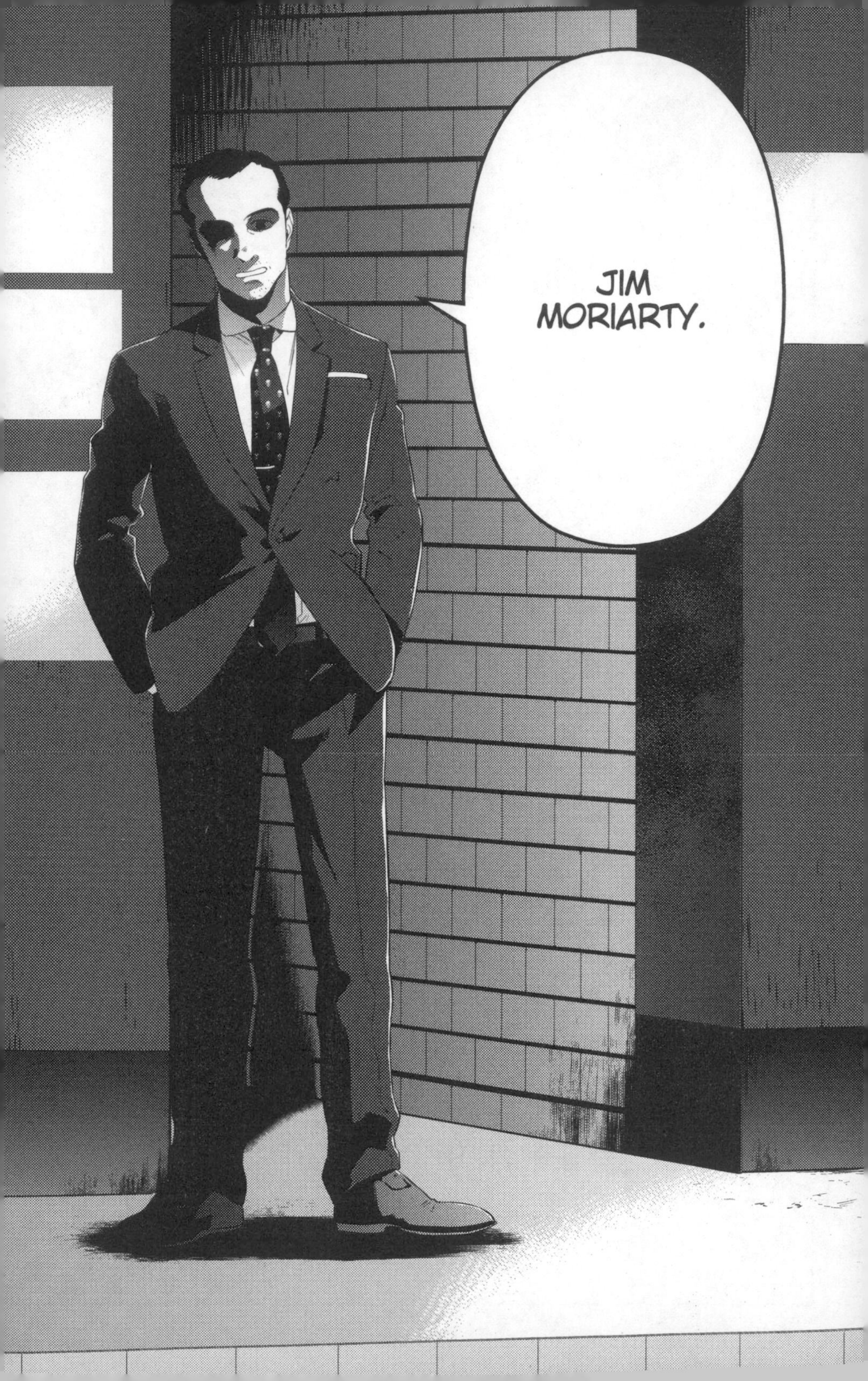
JIM MORIARTY.

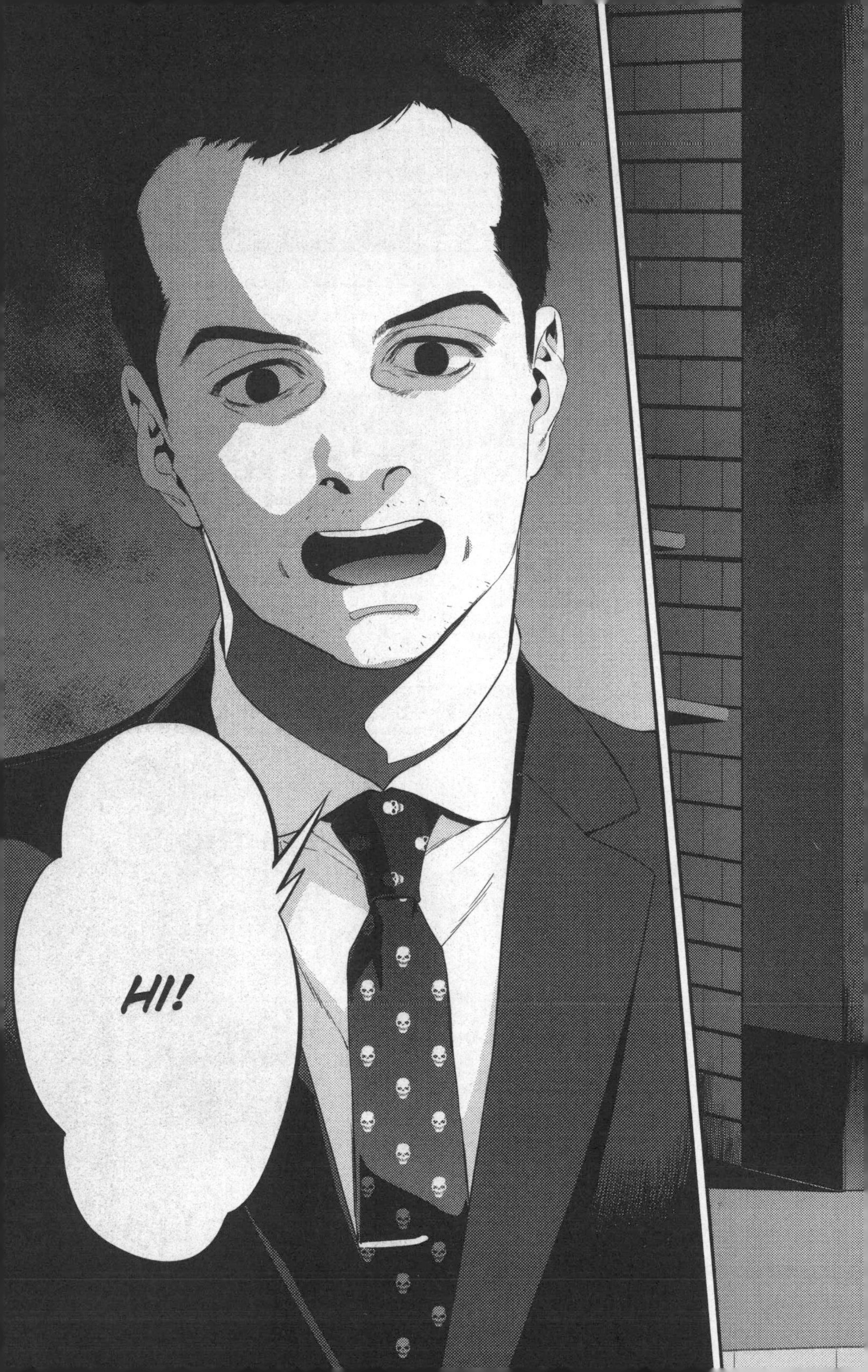
HI!

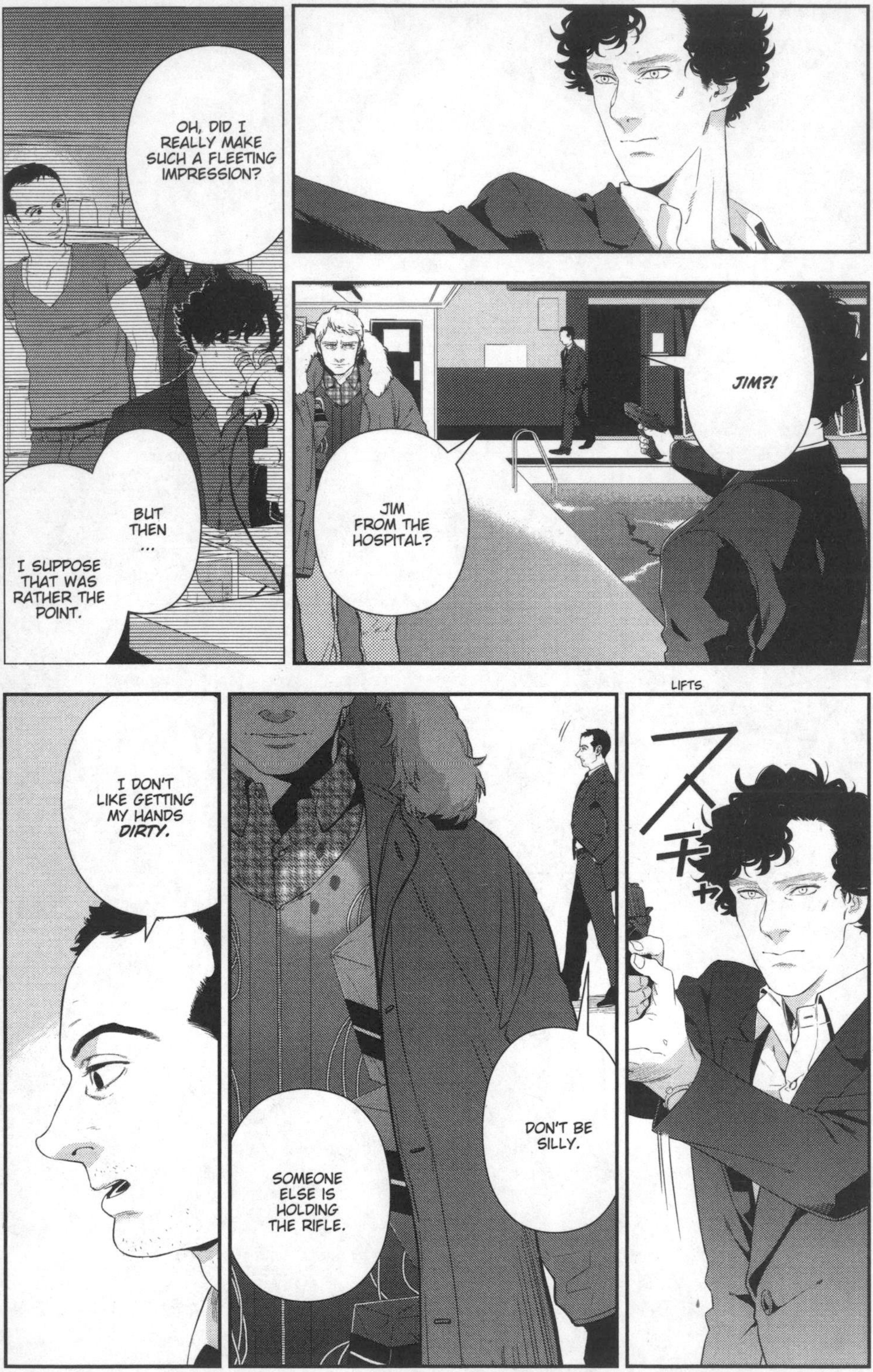
JIM?!
JIM FROM THE HOSPITAL?
OH, DID I REALLY MAKE SUCH A FLEETING IMPRESSION?
BUT THEN ...
I SUPPOSE THAT WAS RATHER THE POINT.
LIFTS
スチャ
DON'T BE SILLY.
SOMEONE ELSE IS HOLDING THE RIFLE.
I DON'T LIKE GETTING MY HANDS *DIRTY*.

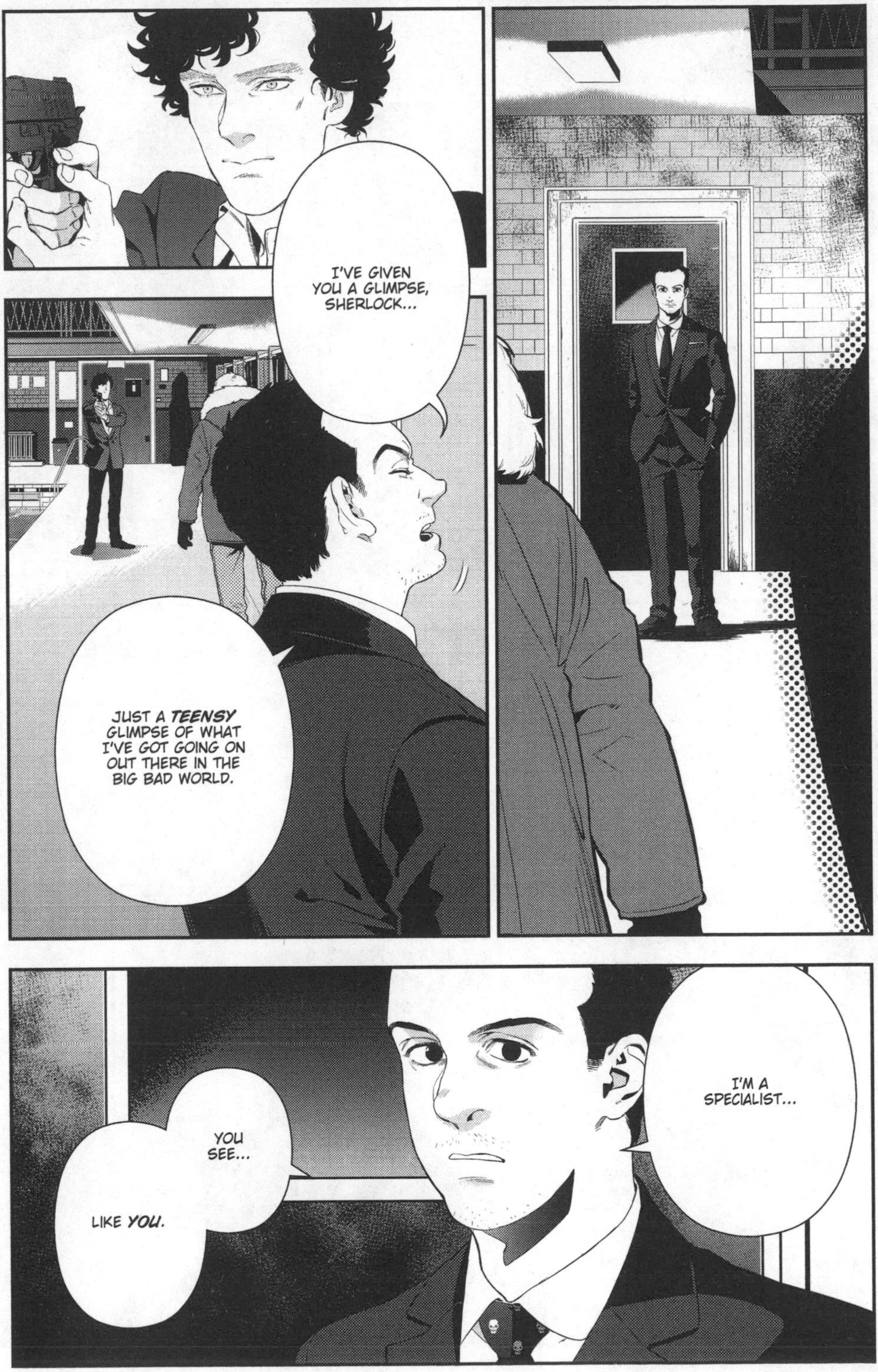
I'VE GIVEN YOU A GLIMPSE, SHERLOCK...
JUST A ***TEENSY*** GLIMPSE OF WHAT I'VE GOT GOING ON OUT THERE IN THE BIG BAD WORLD.
I'M A SPECIALIST...
YOU SEE...
LIKE ***YOU***.

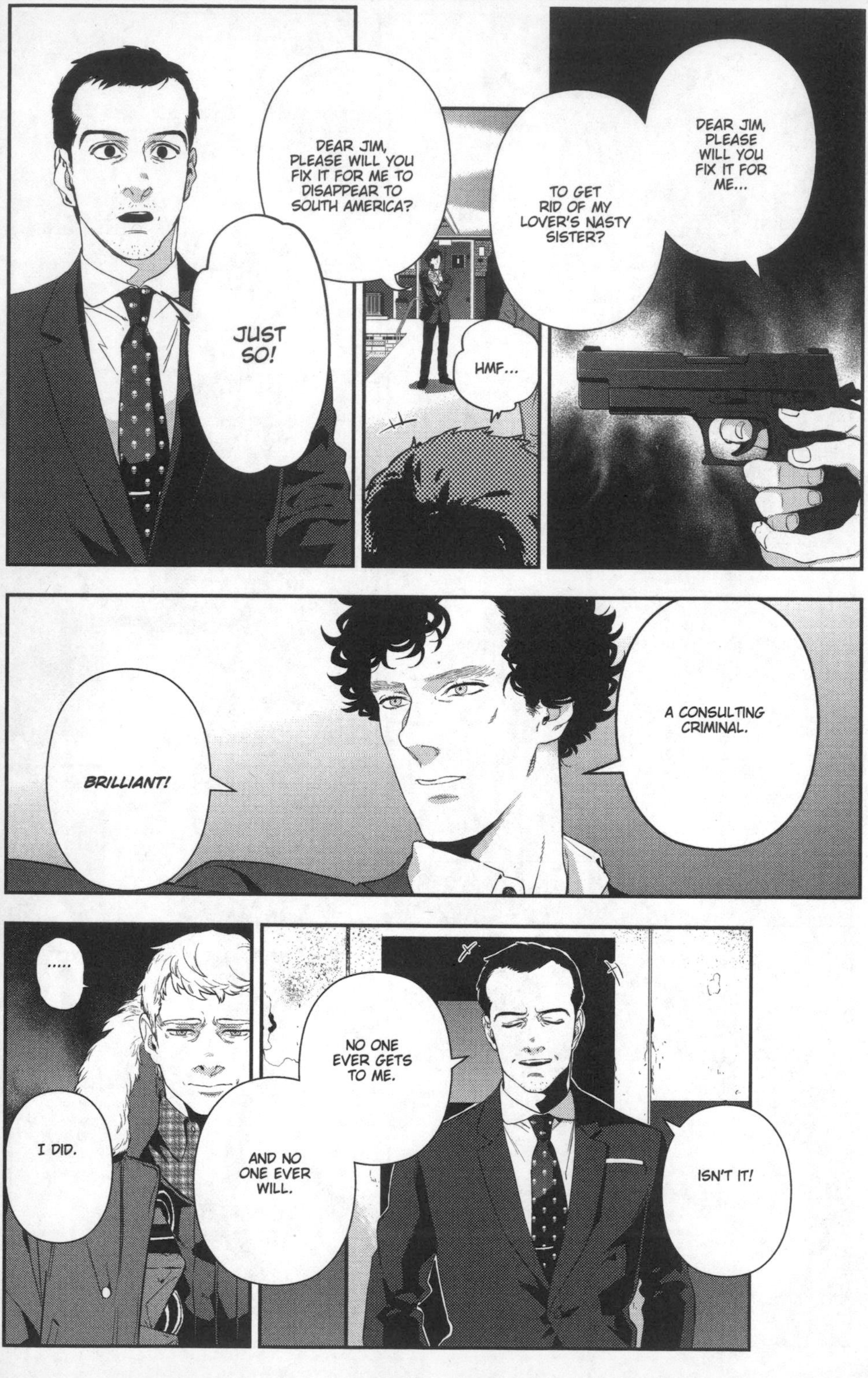
DEAR JIM, PLEASE WILL YOU FIX IT FOR ME...
TO GET RID OF MY LOVER'S NASTY SISTER?
DEAR JIM, PLEASE WILL YOU FIX IT FOR ME TO DISAPPEAR TO SOUTH AMERICA?
HMF...
JUST SO!
A CONSULTING CRIMINAL.
BRILLIANT!
ISN'T IT!
NO ONE EVER GETS TO ME.
AND NO ONE EVER WILL.
.....
I DID.

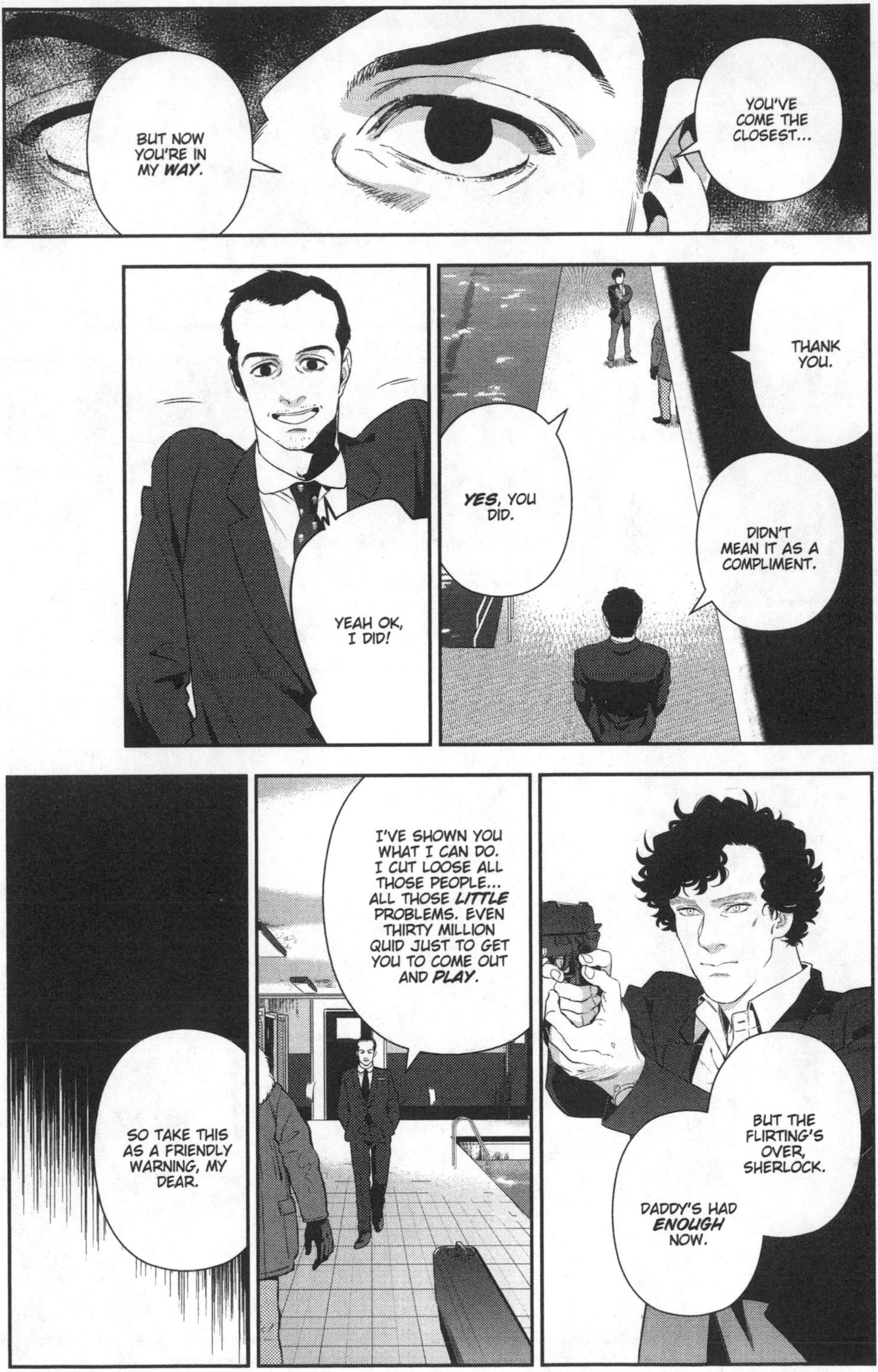
YOU'VE COME THE CLOSEST...
BUT NOW YOU'RE IN MY ***WAY***.
THANK YOU.
DIDN'T MEAN IT AS A COMPLIMENT.
YES, YOU DID.
YEAH OK, I DID!
BUT THE FLIRTING'S OVER, SHERLOCK.
DADDY'S HAD ***ENOUGH*** NOW.
I'VE SHOWN YOU WHAT I CAN DO. I CUT LOOSE ALL THOSE PEOPLE... ALL THOSE ***LITTLE*** PROBLEMS. EVEN THIRTY MILLION QUID JUST TO GET YOU TO COME OUT AND ***PLAY***.
SO TAKE THIS AS A FRIENDLY WARNING, MY DEAR.

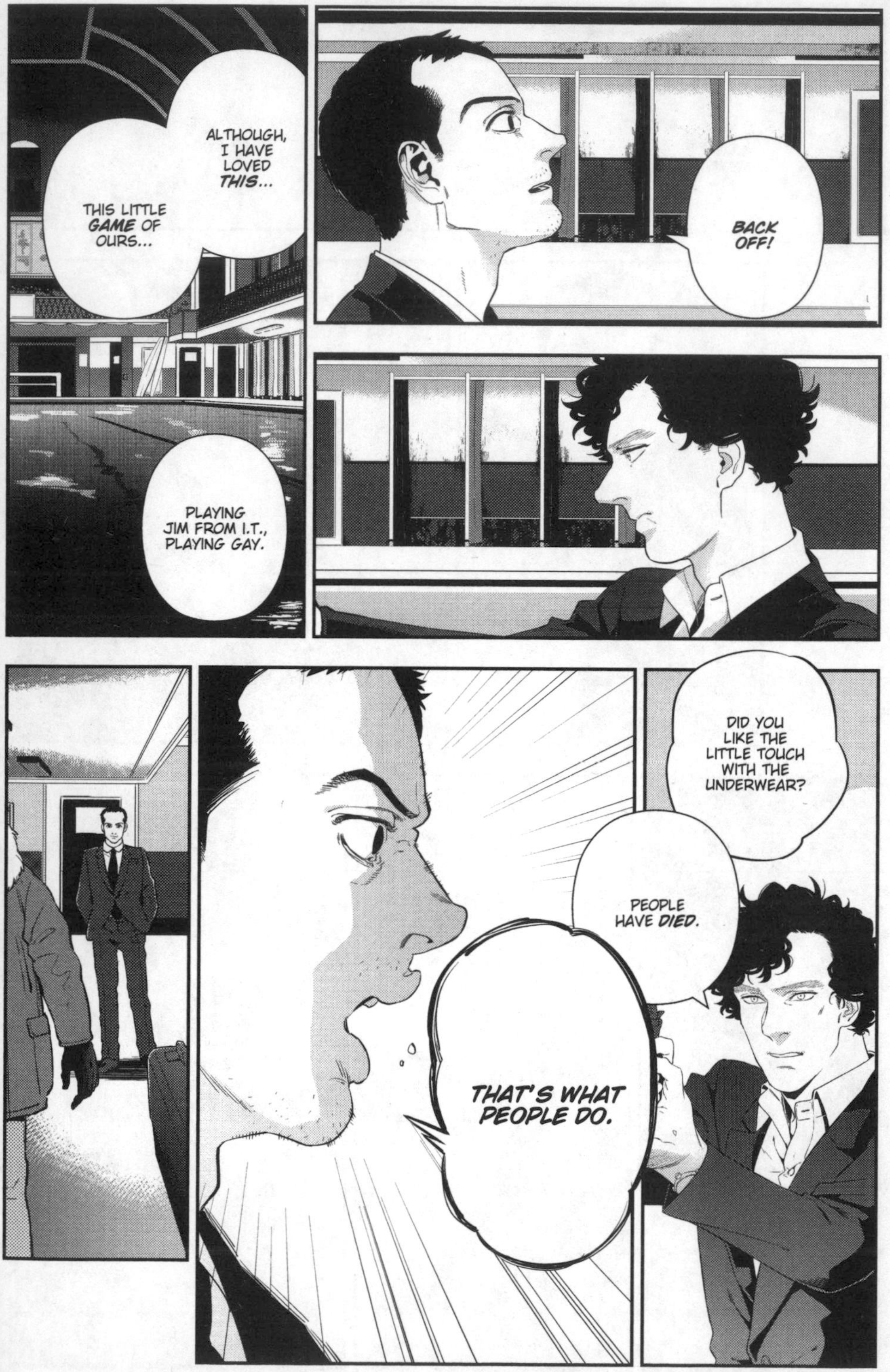
BACK OFF!
ALTHOUGH, I HAVE LOVED THIS...
THIS LITTLE GAME OF OURS...
PLAYING JIM FROM I.T., PLAYING GAY.
DID YOU LIKE THE LITTLE TOUCH WITH THE UNDERWEAR?
PEOPLE HAVE DIED.
THAT'S WHAT PEOPLE DO.

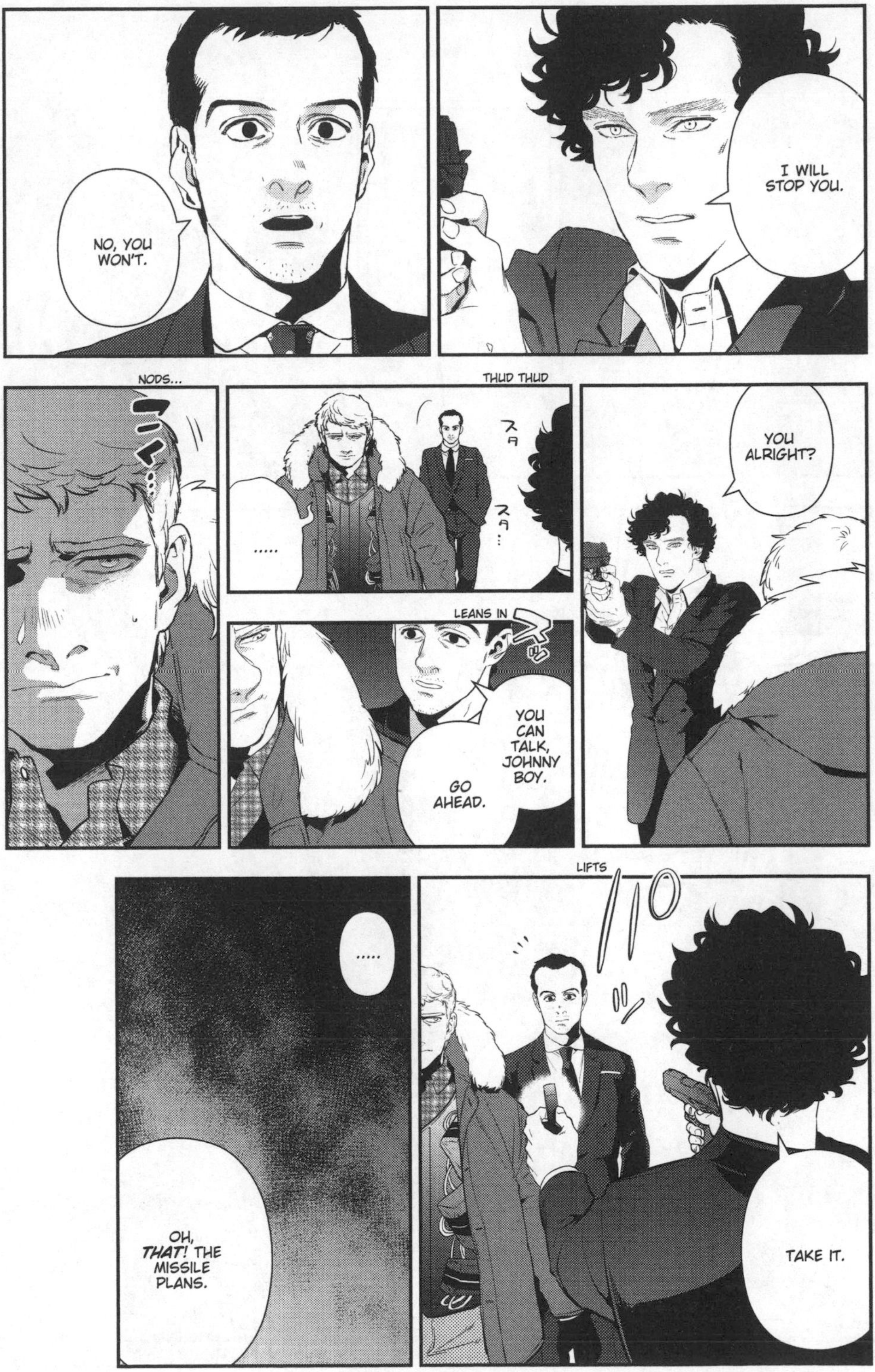
I WILL STOP YOU.
NO, YOU WON'T.
YOU ALRIGHT?
THUD THUD
スタ
スタ…
.....
LEANS IN
スッ
YOU CAN TALK, JOHNNY BOY.
GO AHEAD.
NODS...
LIFTS
TAKE IT.
.....
OH, *THAT!* THE MISSILE PLANS.

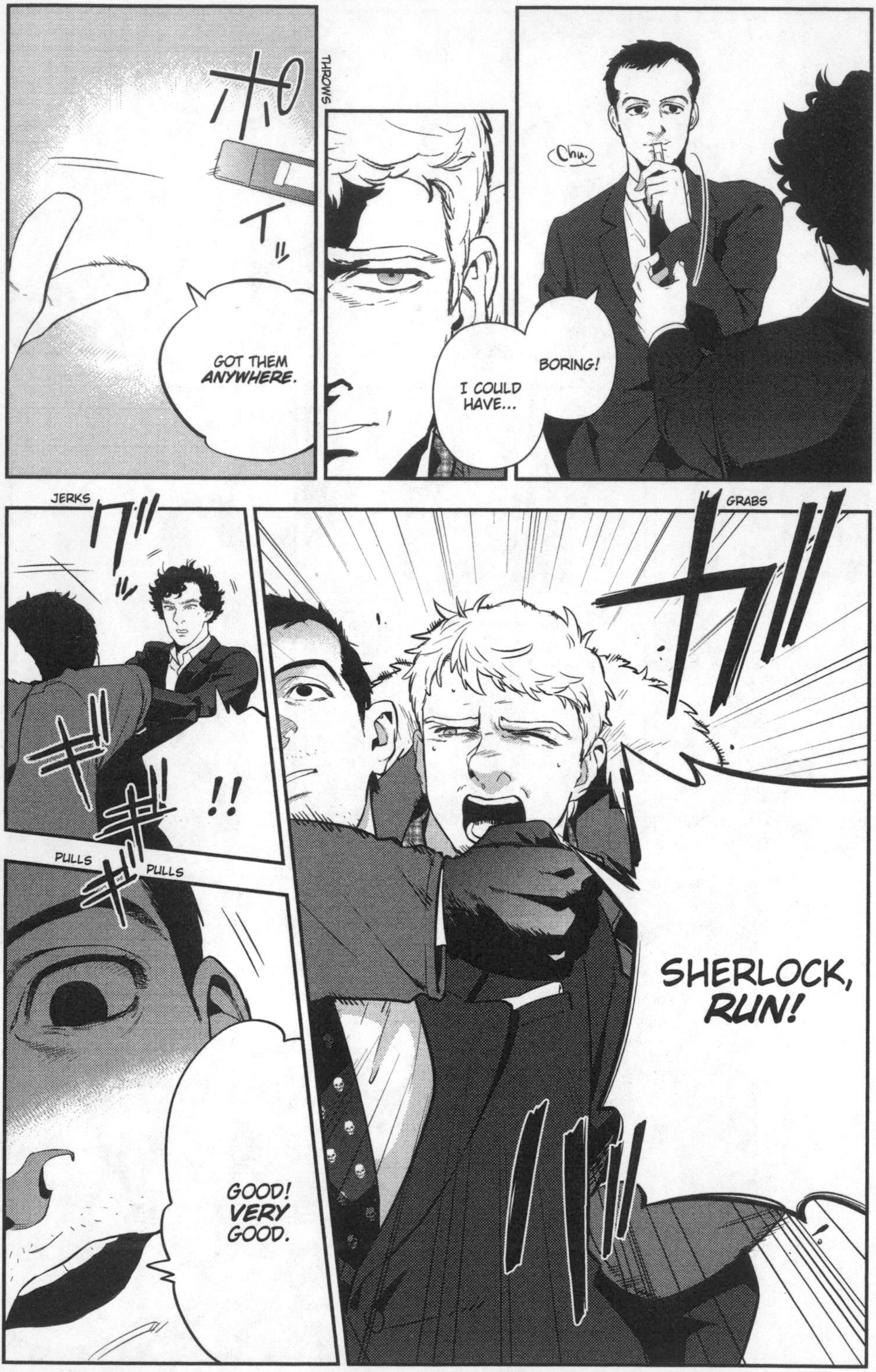
Chu.
BORING!
I COULD HAVE...
THROWS
GOT THEM ANYWHERE.
GRABS
SHERLOCK, RUN!
JERKS
!!
PULLS
PULLS
GOOD! VERY GOOD.

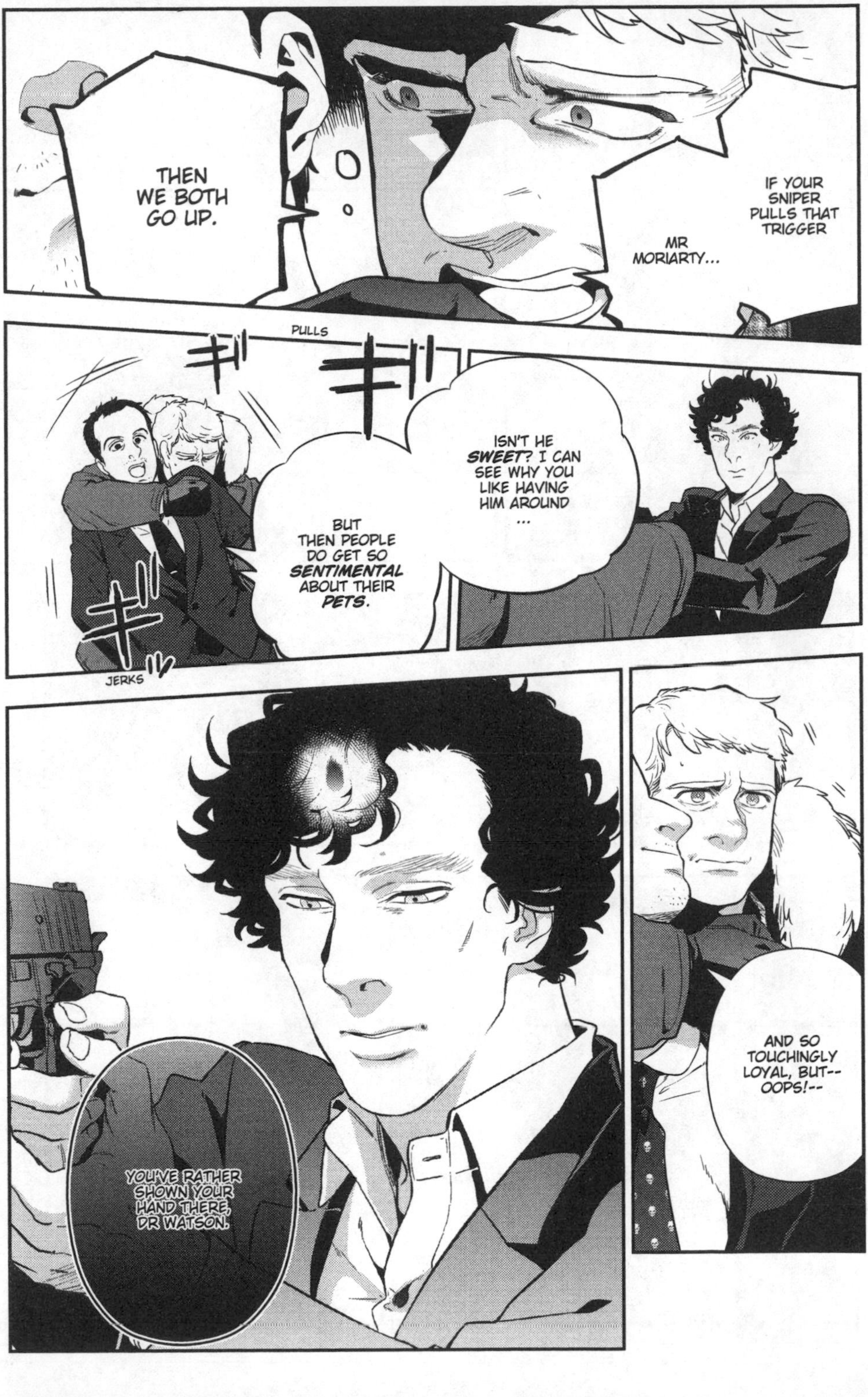
IF YOUR SNIPER PULLS THAT TRIGGER
MR MORIARTY...
THEN WE BOTH GO UP.
ISN'T HE **SWEET**? I CAN SEE WHY YOU LIKE HAVING HIM AROUND ...
BUT THEN PEOPLE DO GET SO **SENTIMENTAL** ABOUT THEIR **PETS**.
PULLS
JERKS
AND SO TOUCHINGLY LOYAL, BUT-- OOPS!--
YOU'VE RATHER SHOWN YOUR HAND THERE, DR WATSON.

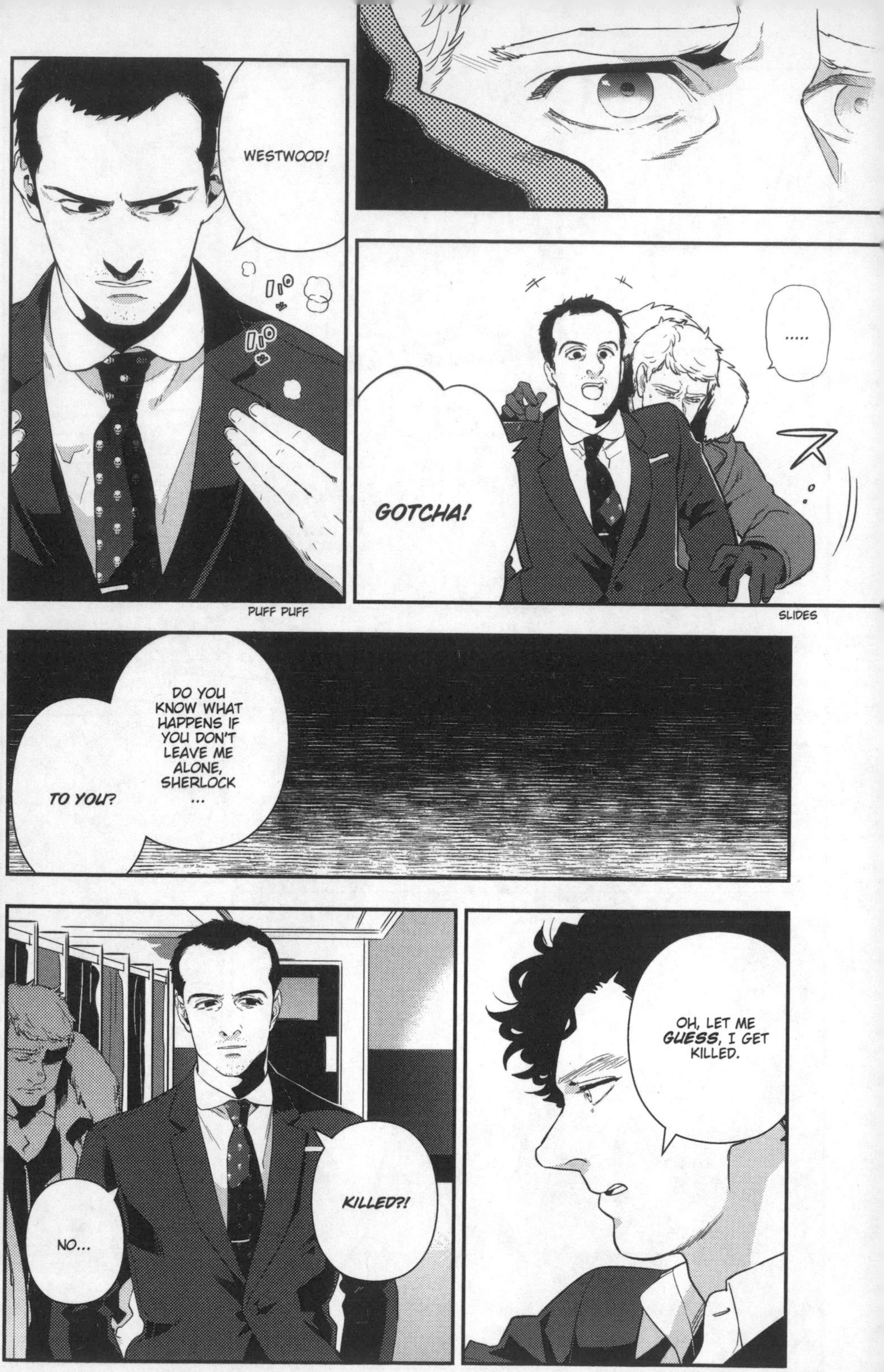
.....
GOTCHA!
SLIDES
WESTWOOD!
PUFF PUFF
DO YOU KNOW WHAT HAPPENS IF YOU DON'T LEAVE ME ALONE, SHERLOCK ...
TO YOU?
OH, LET ME GUESS, I GET KILLED.
KILLED?!
NO...

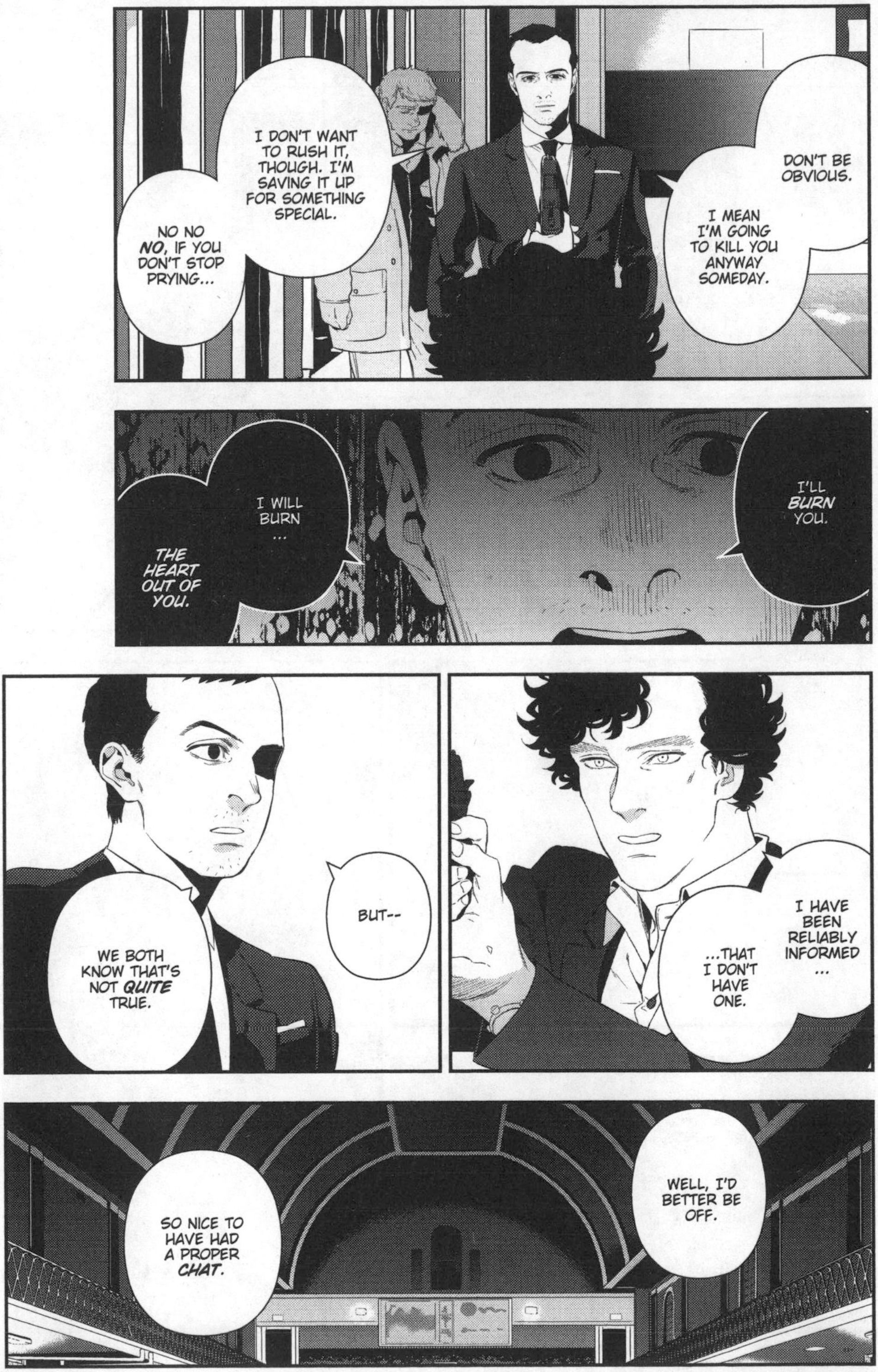
DON'T BE OBVIOUS.
I MEAN I'M GOING TO KILL YOU ANYWAY SOMEDAY.
I DON'T WANT TO RUSH IT, THOUGH. I'M SAVING IT UP FOR SOMETHING SPECIAL.
NO NO ***NO***, IF YOU DON'T STOP PRYING...
I'LL ***BURN*** YOU.
I WILL BURN ...
THE HEART OUT OF YOU.
I HAVE BEEN RELIABLY INFORMED ...
...THAT I DON'T HAVE ONE.
BUT--
WE BOTH KNOW THAT'S NOT ***QUITE*** TRUE.
WELL, I'D BETTER BE OFF.
SO NICE TO HAVE HAD A PROPER ***CHAT***.

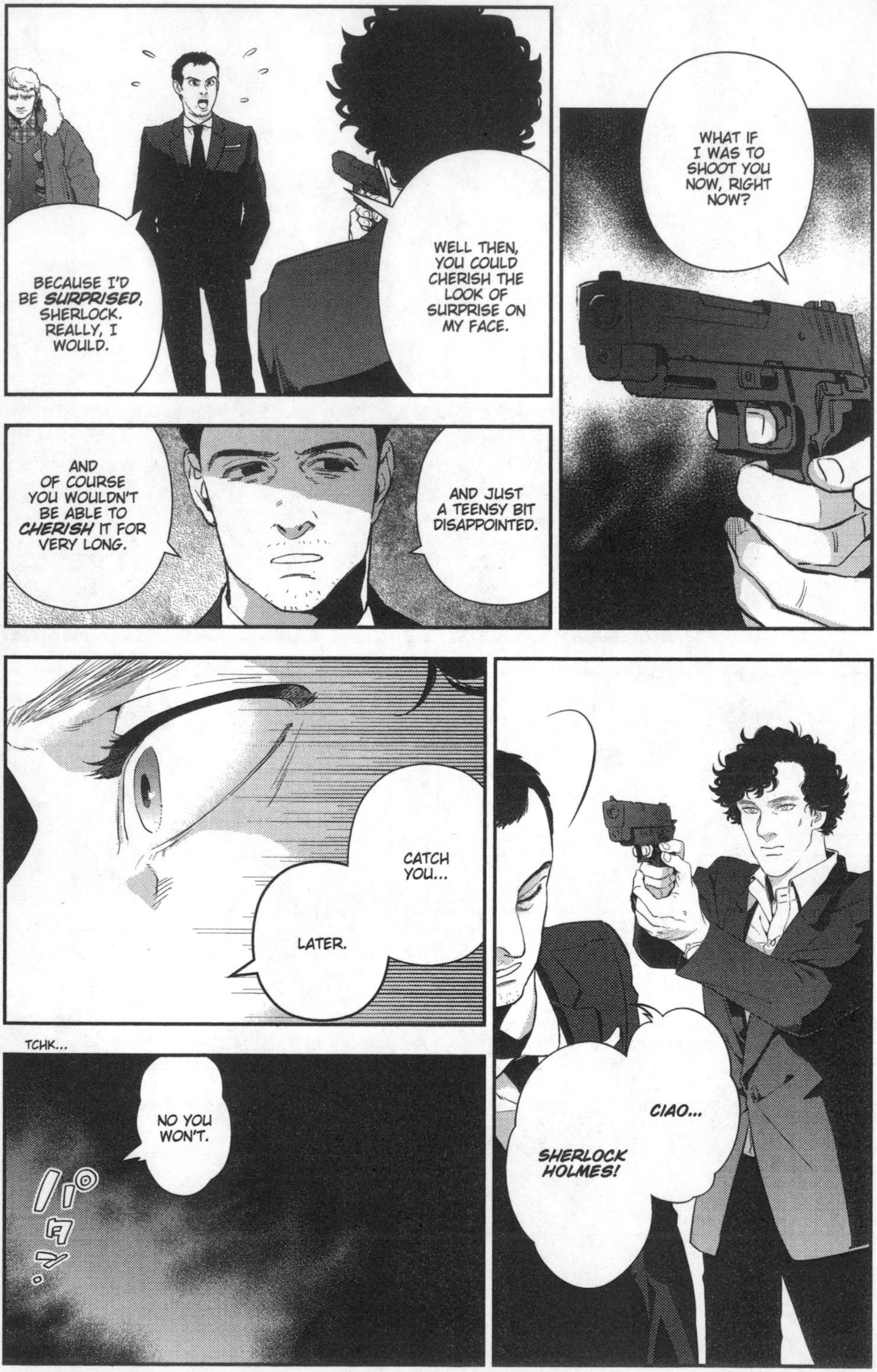
WHAT IF I WAS TO SHOOT YOU NOW, RIGHT NOW?
WELL THEN, YOU COULD CHERISH THE LOOK OF SURPRISE ON MY FACE.
BECAUSE I'D BE *SURPRISED*, SHERLOCK. REALLY, I WOULD.
AND JUST A TEENSY BIT DISAPPOINTED.
AND OF COURSE YOU WOULDN'T BE ABLE TO *CHERISH* IT FOR VERY LONG.
CIAO...
SHERLOCK HOLMES!
CATCH YOU...
LATER.
TCHK...
NO YOU WON'T.

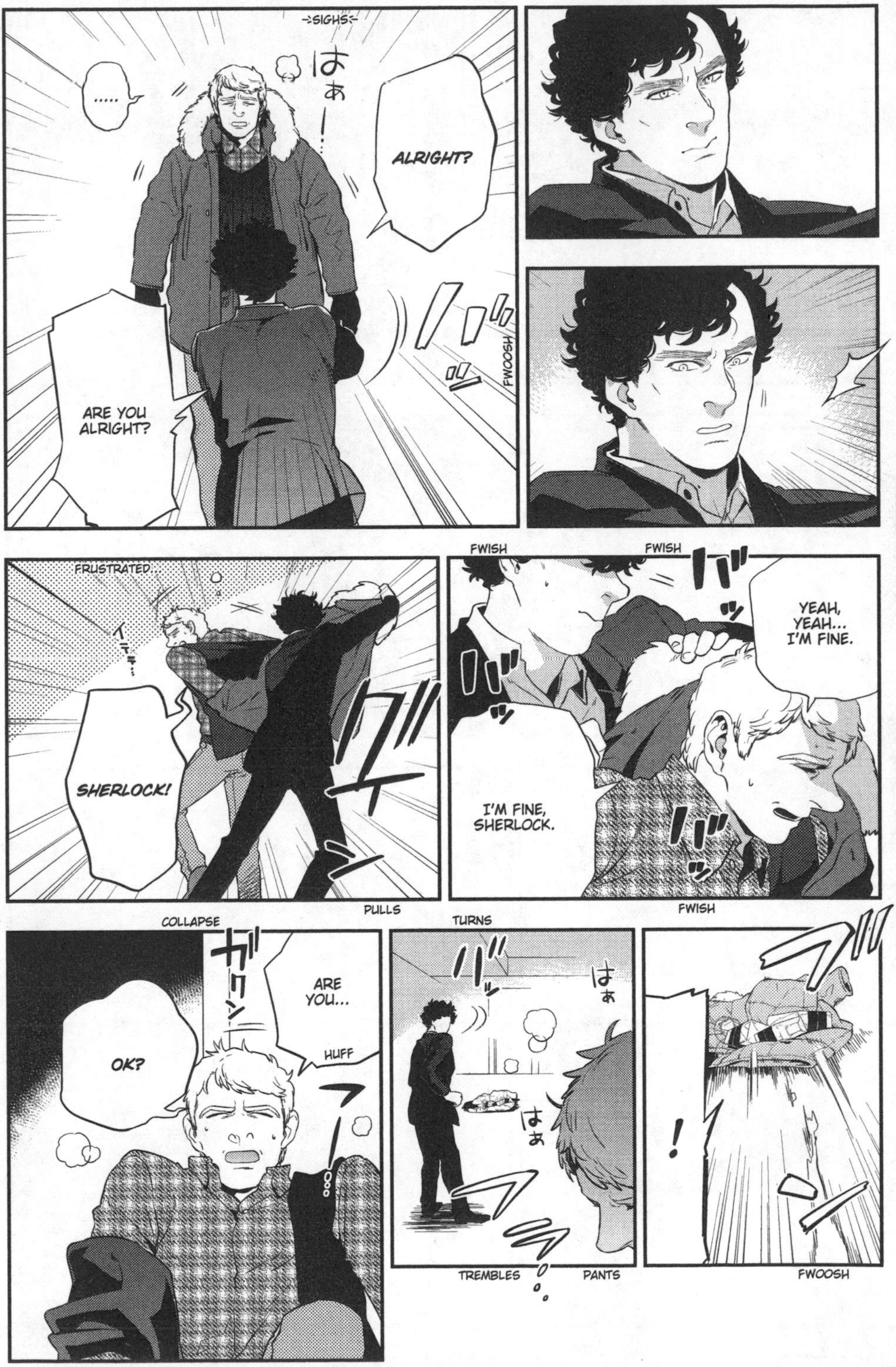

SIGHS
はぁー…
ALRIGHT?
......
FWOOSH
ARE YOU ALRIGHT?
FWISH
FWISH
YEAH, YEAH... I'M FINE.
I'M FINE, SHERLOCK.
FWISH
FRUSTRATED...
SHERLOCK!
PULLS
FWOOSH
!
TURNS
はぁ
はぁ
TREMBLES
PANTS
COLLAPSE
ARE YOU...
OK?
HUFF

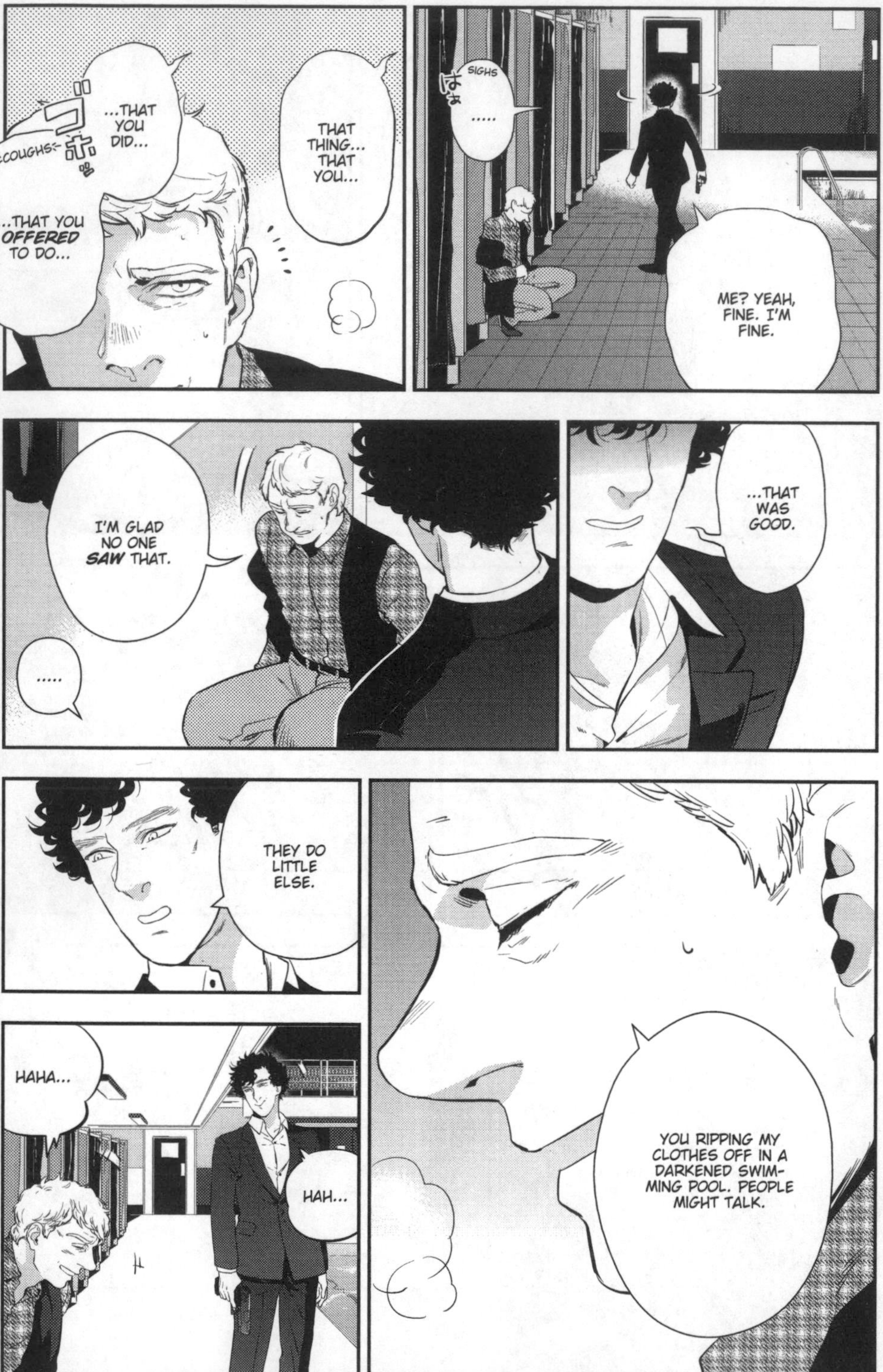
SIGHS
はぁ
.....
ME? YEAH, FINE. I'M FINE.
THAT THING... THAT YOU...
ゴホッ
COUGHS
...THAT YOU DID...
...THAT YOU OFFERED TO DO...
...THAT WAS GOOD.
I'M GLAD NO ONE SAW THAT.
.....
YOU RIPPING MY CLOTHES OFF IN A DARKENED SWIMMING POOL. PEOPLE MIGHT TALK.
THEY DO LITTLE ELSE.
HAHA...
HAH...

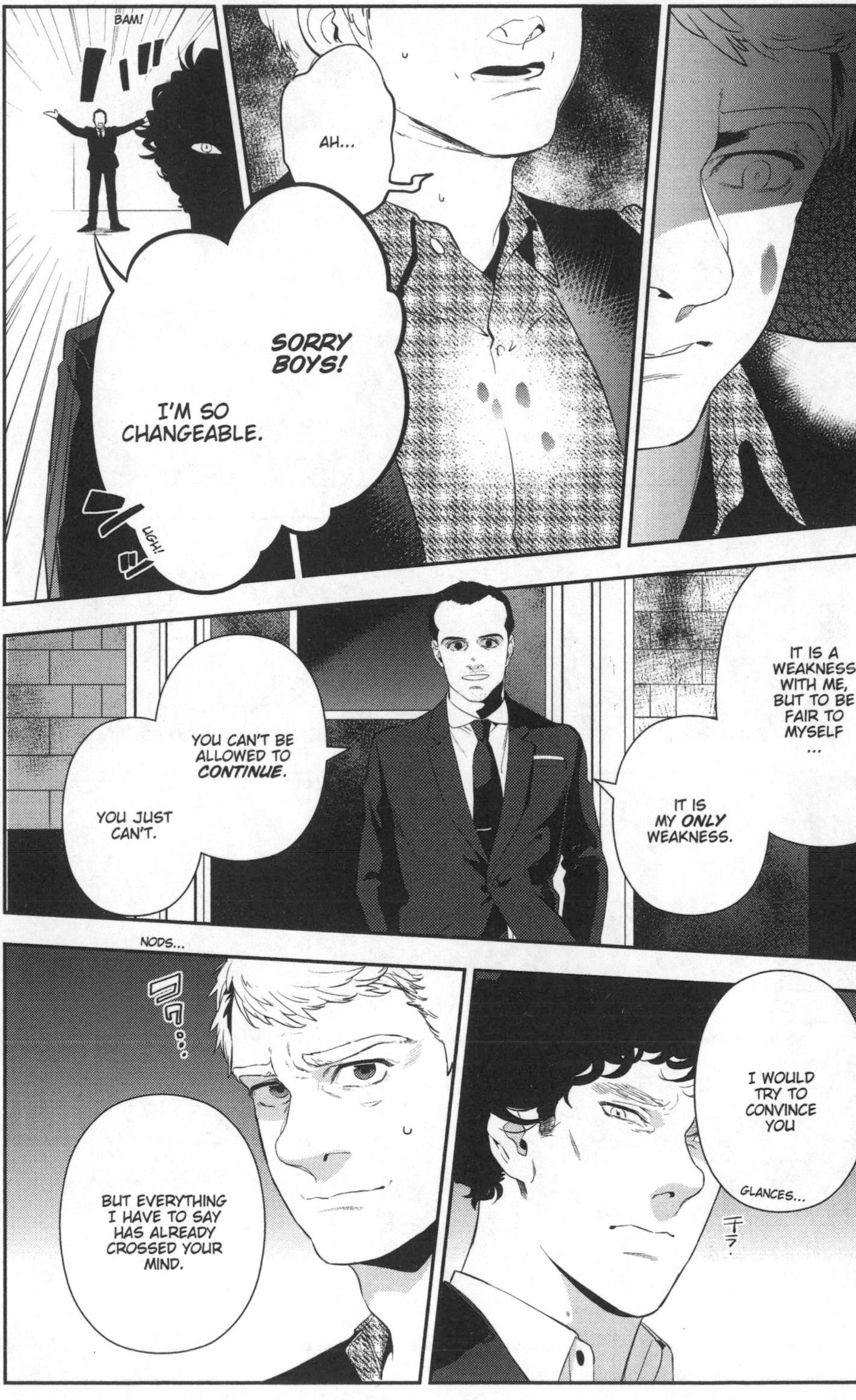
AH...
BAM!
SORRY BOYS!
I'M SO CHANGEABLE.
UGH!
IT IS A WEAKNESS WITH ME, BUT TO BE FAIR TO MYSELF ...
IT IS MY ONLY WEAKNESS.
YOU CAN'T BE ALLOWED TO CONTINUE.
YOU JUST CAN'T.
I WOULD TRY TO CONVINCE YOU
GLANCES...
NODS...
BUT EVERYTHING I HAVE TO SAY HAS ALREADY CROSSED YOUR MIND.

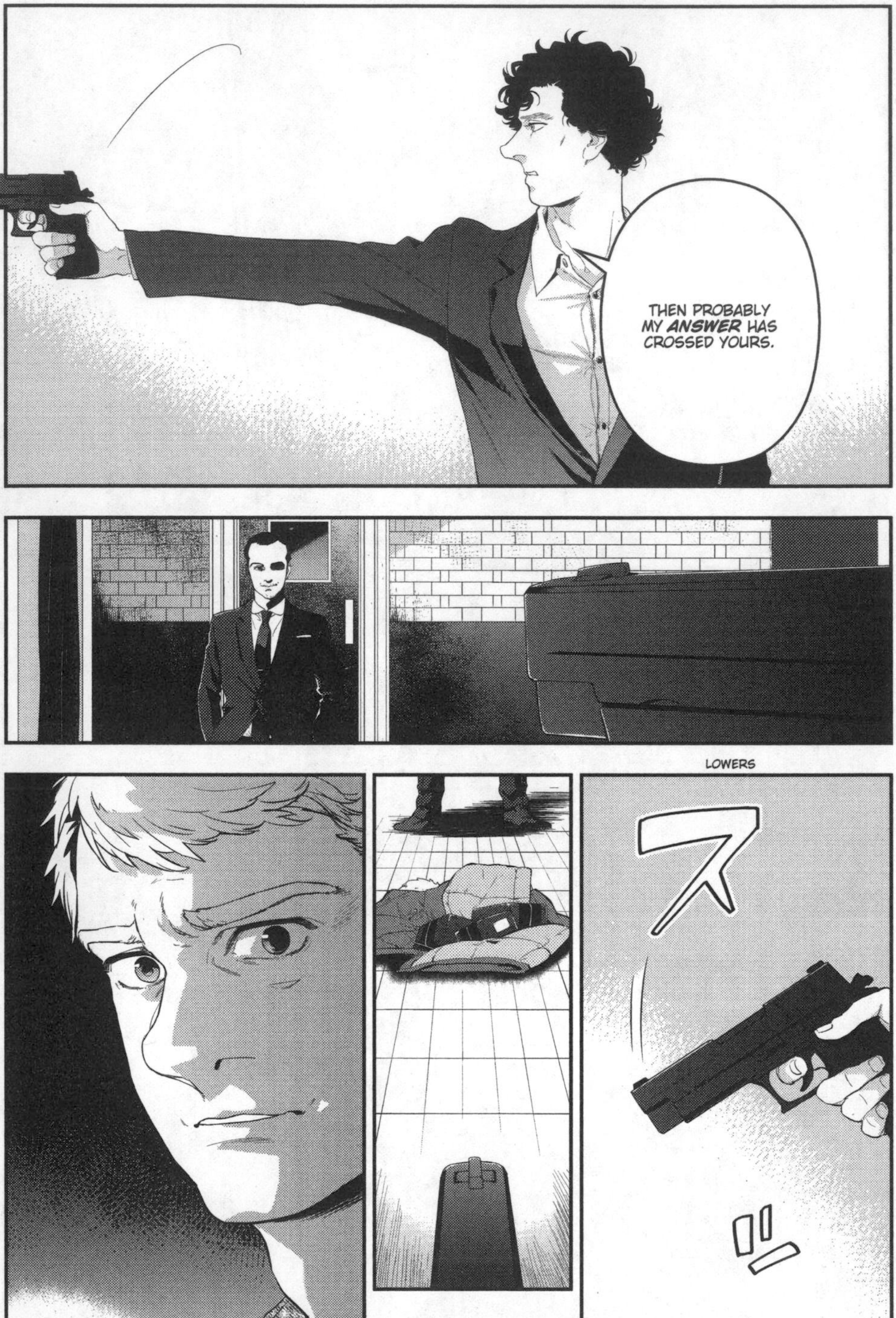
THEN PROBABLY MY **ANSWER** HAS CROSSED YOURS.
LOWERS

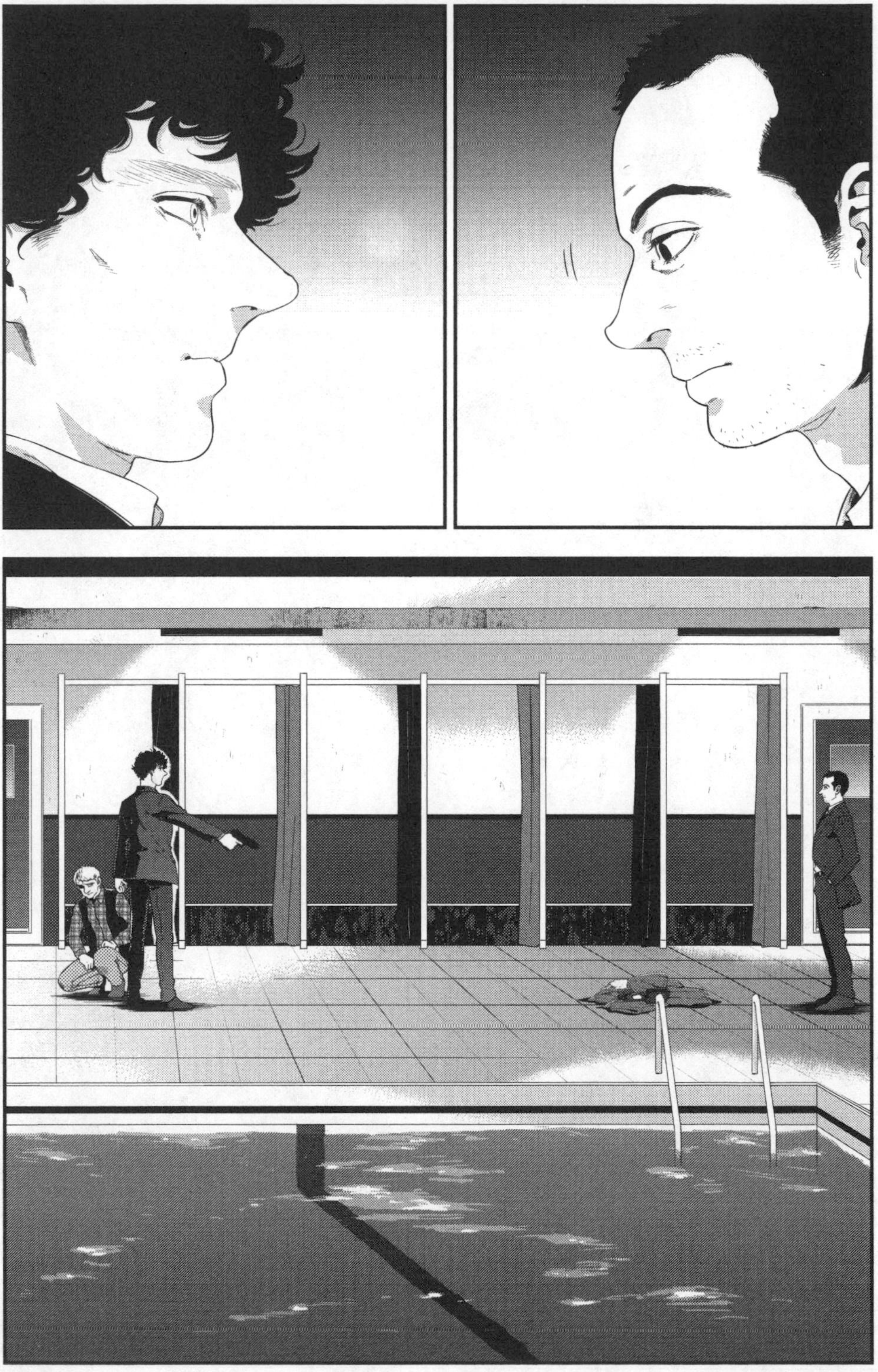

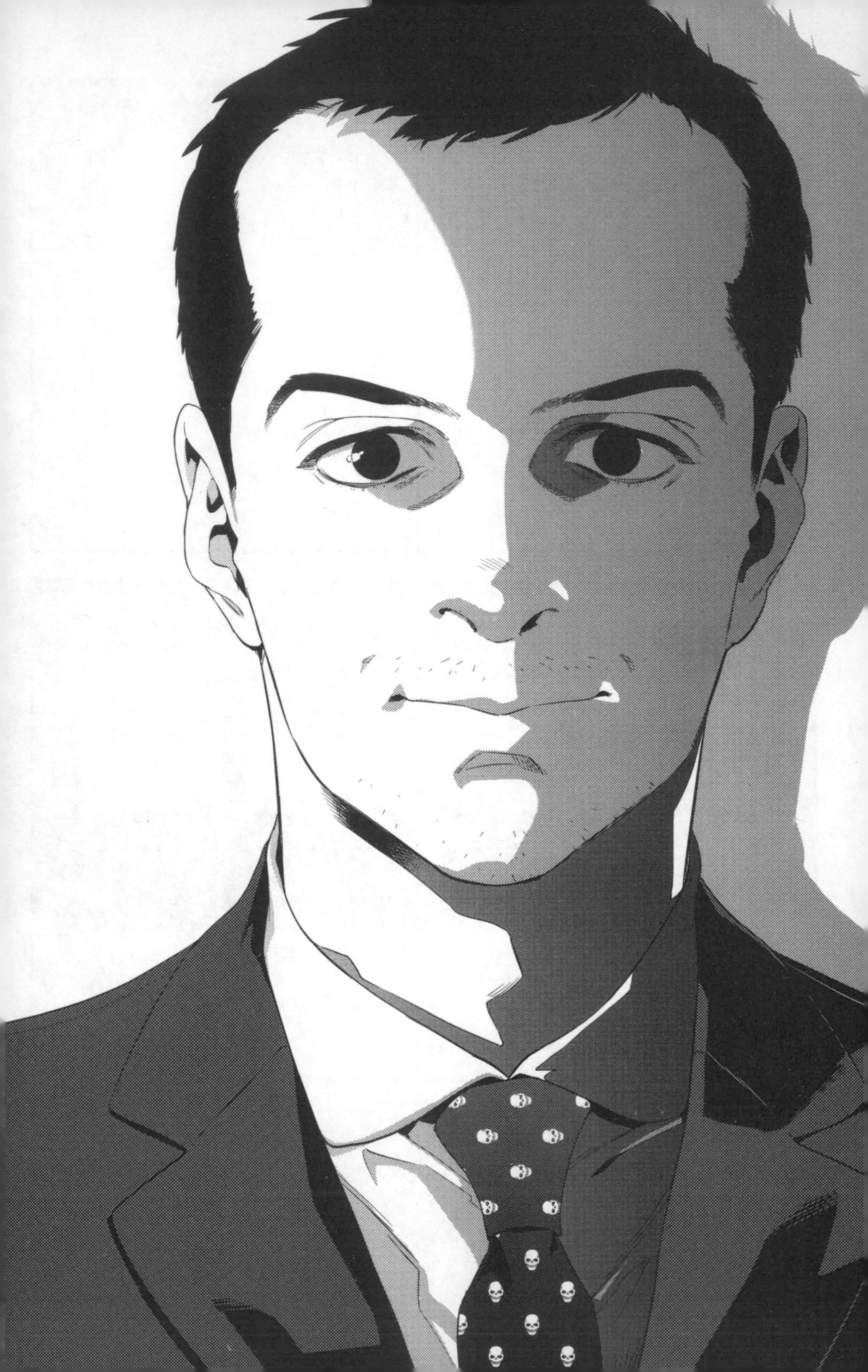

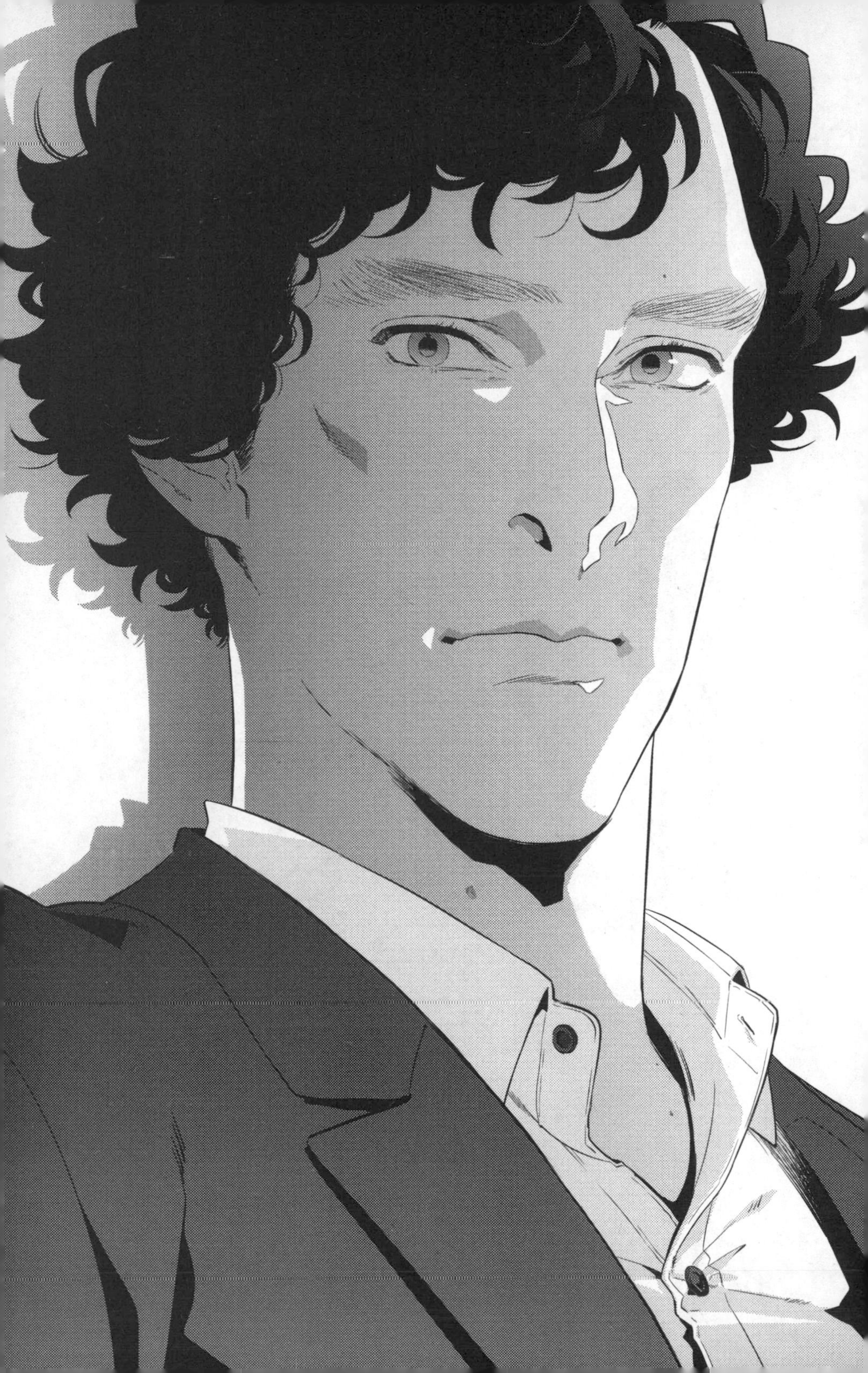

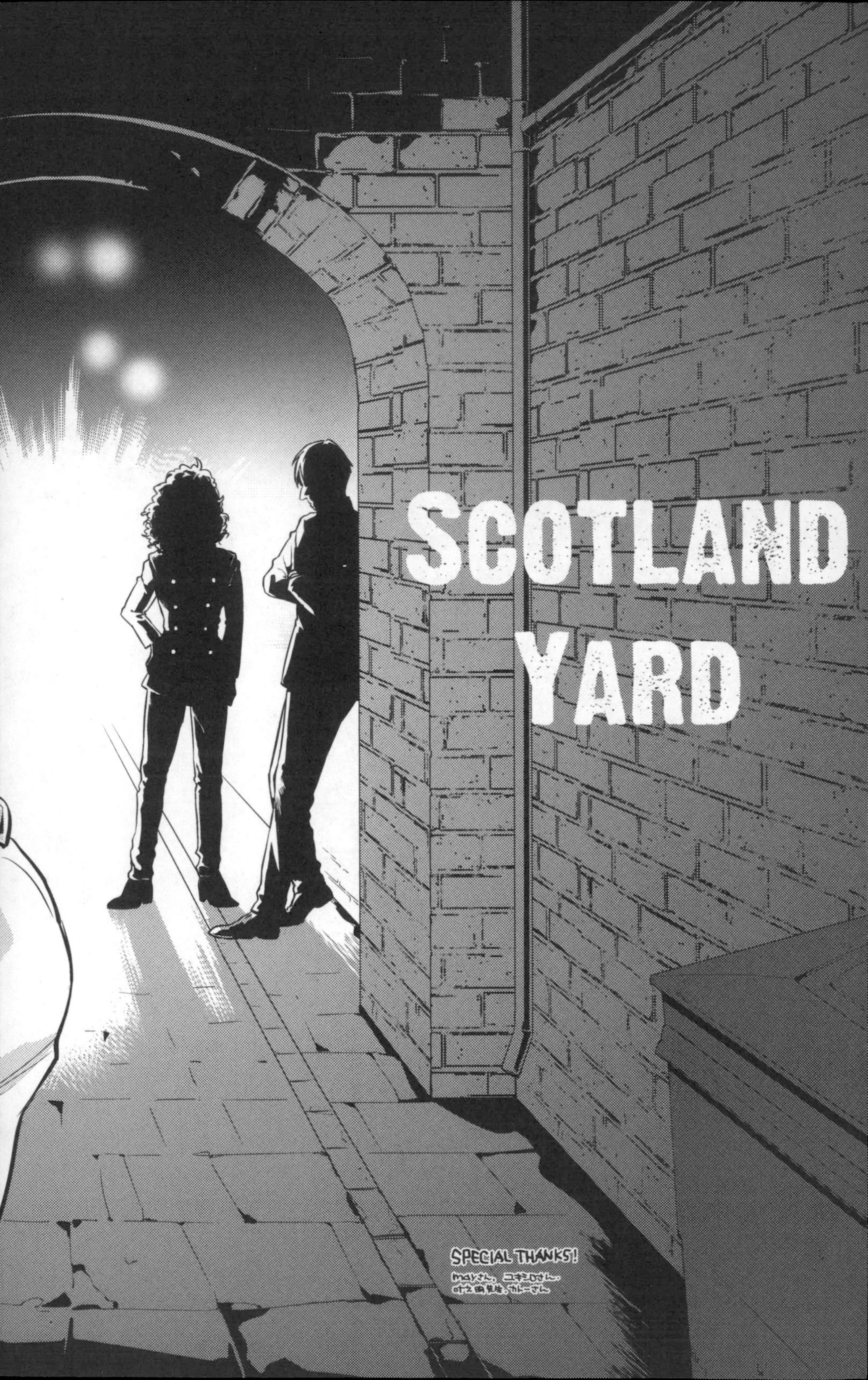
SCOTLAND YARD
SPECIAL THANKS!
mayさん、ユキシロさん、

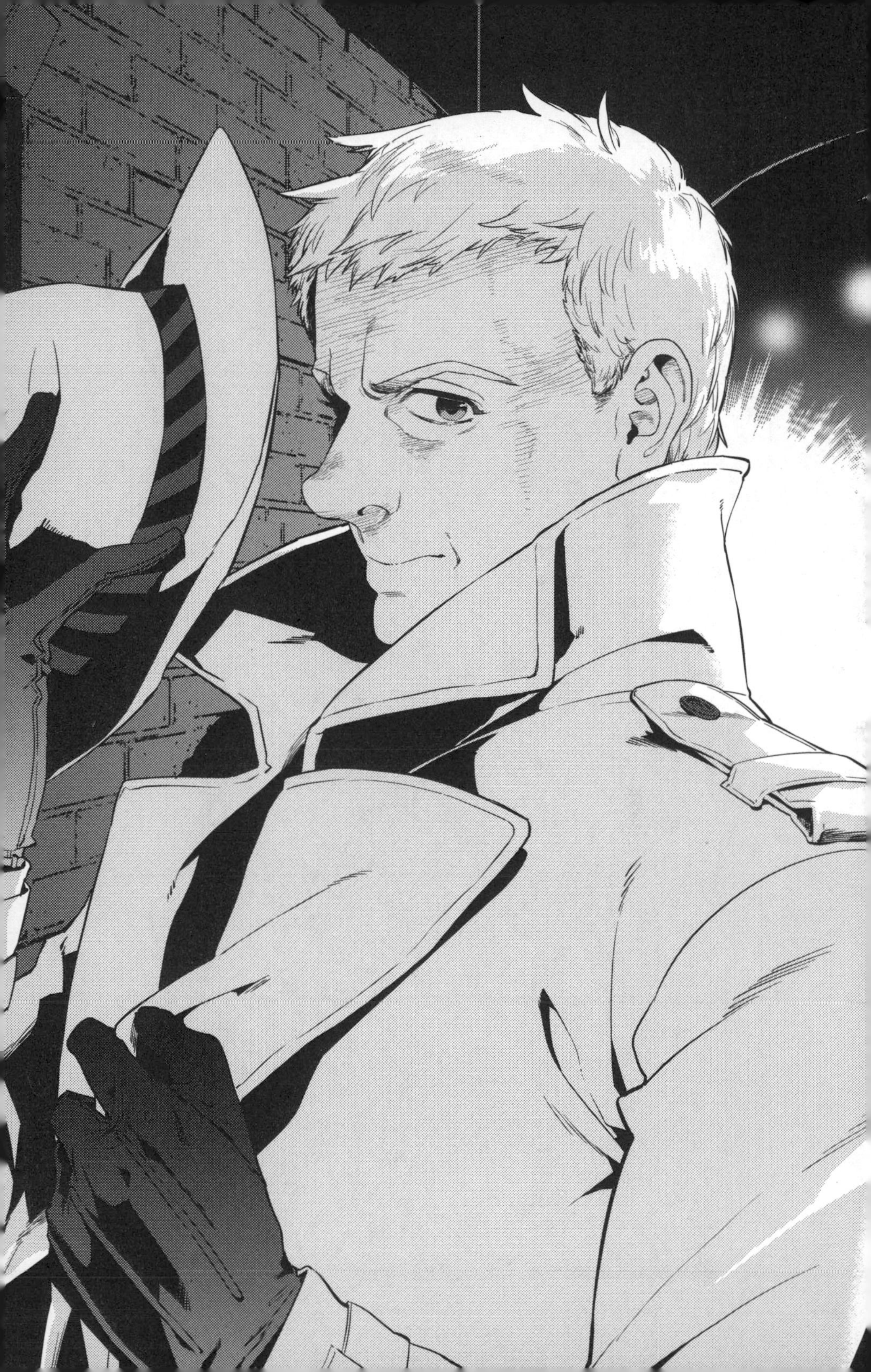

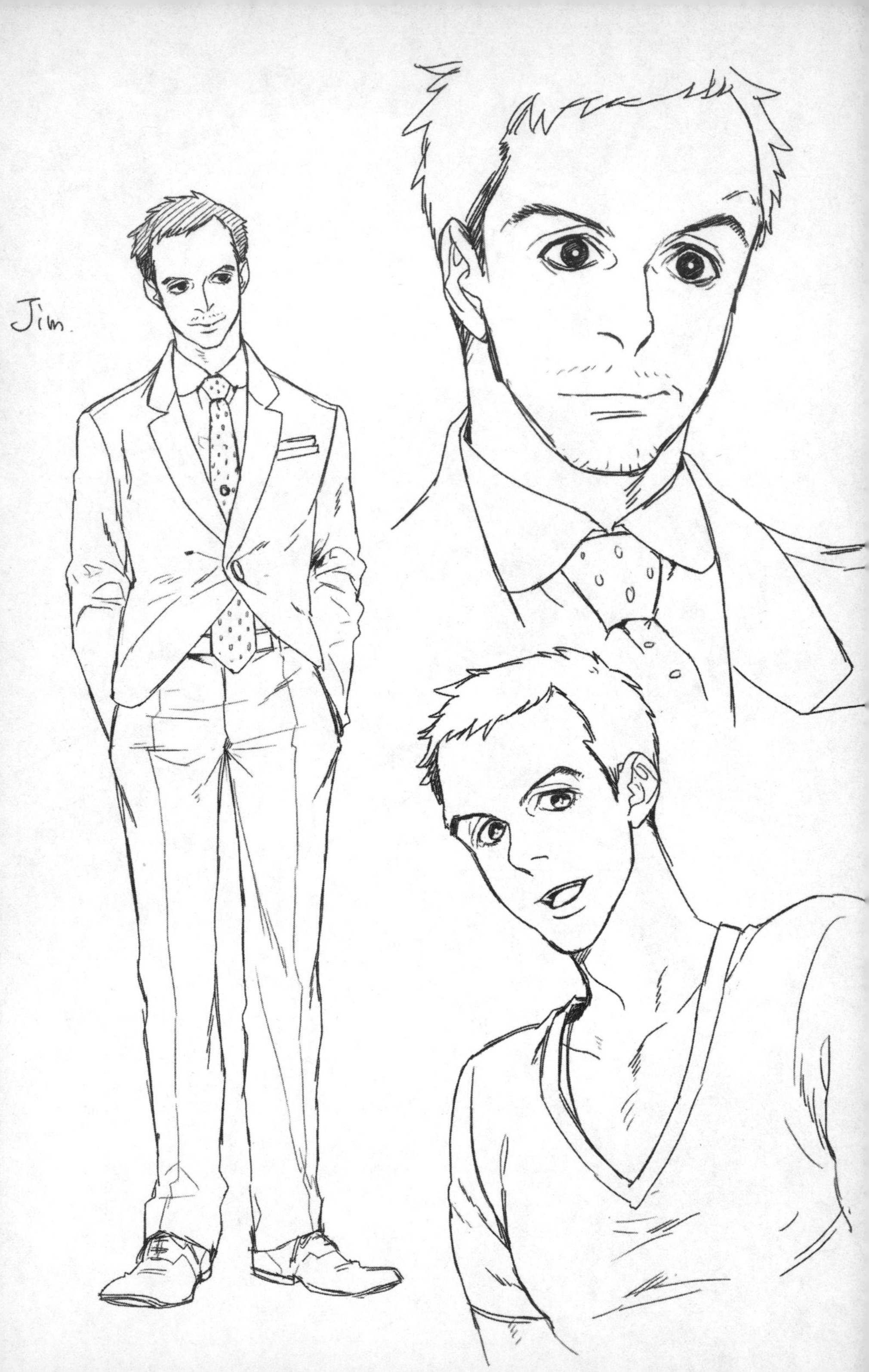
Jim.

COVER GALLERY

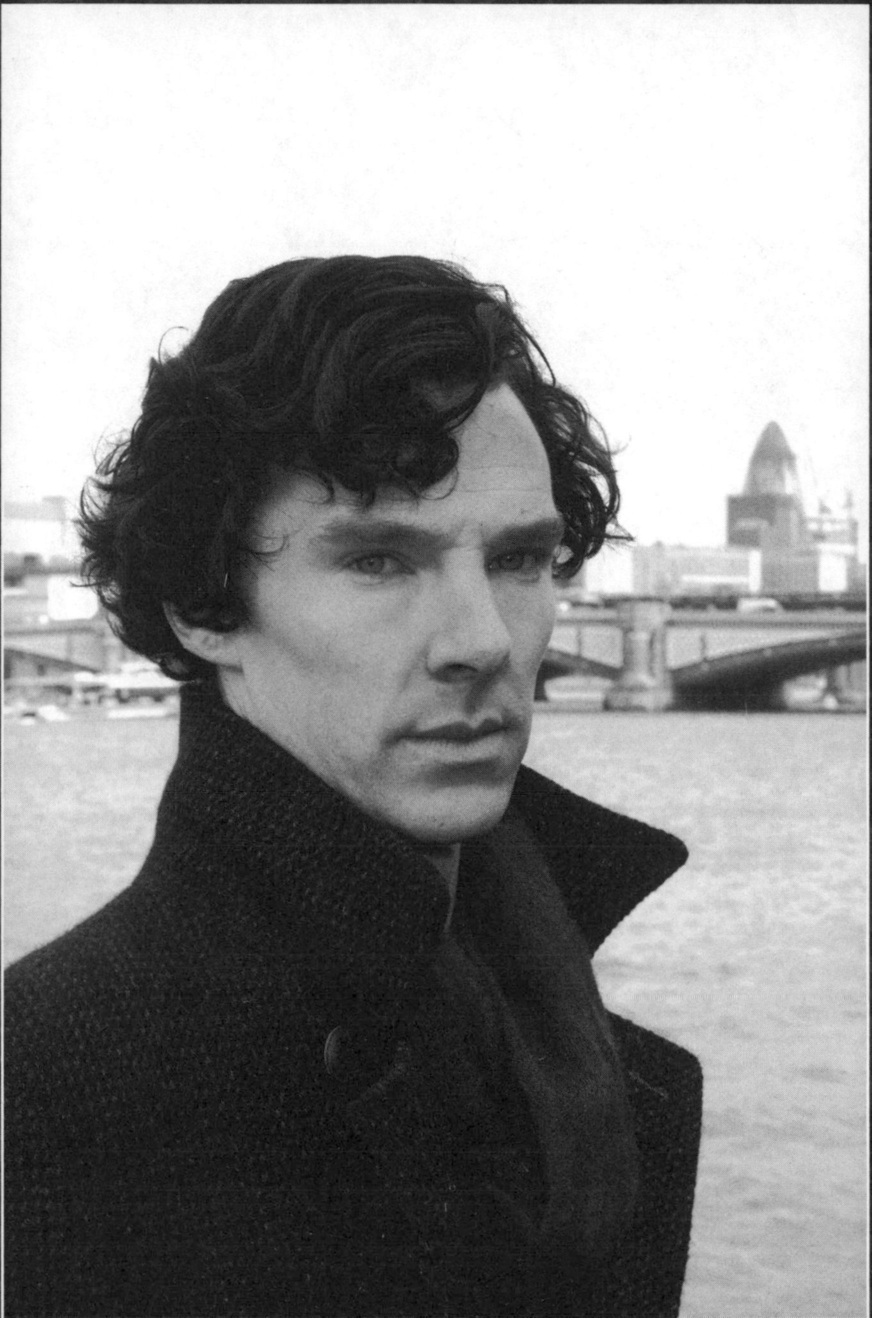

#1 COVER B
PHOTO

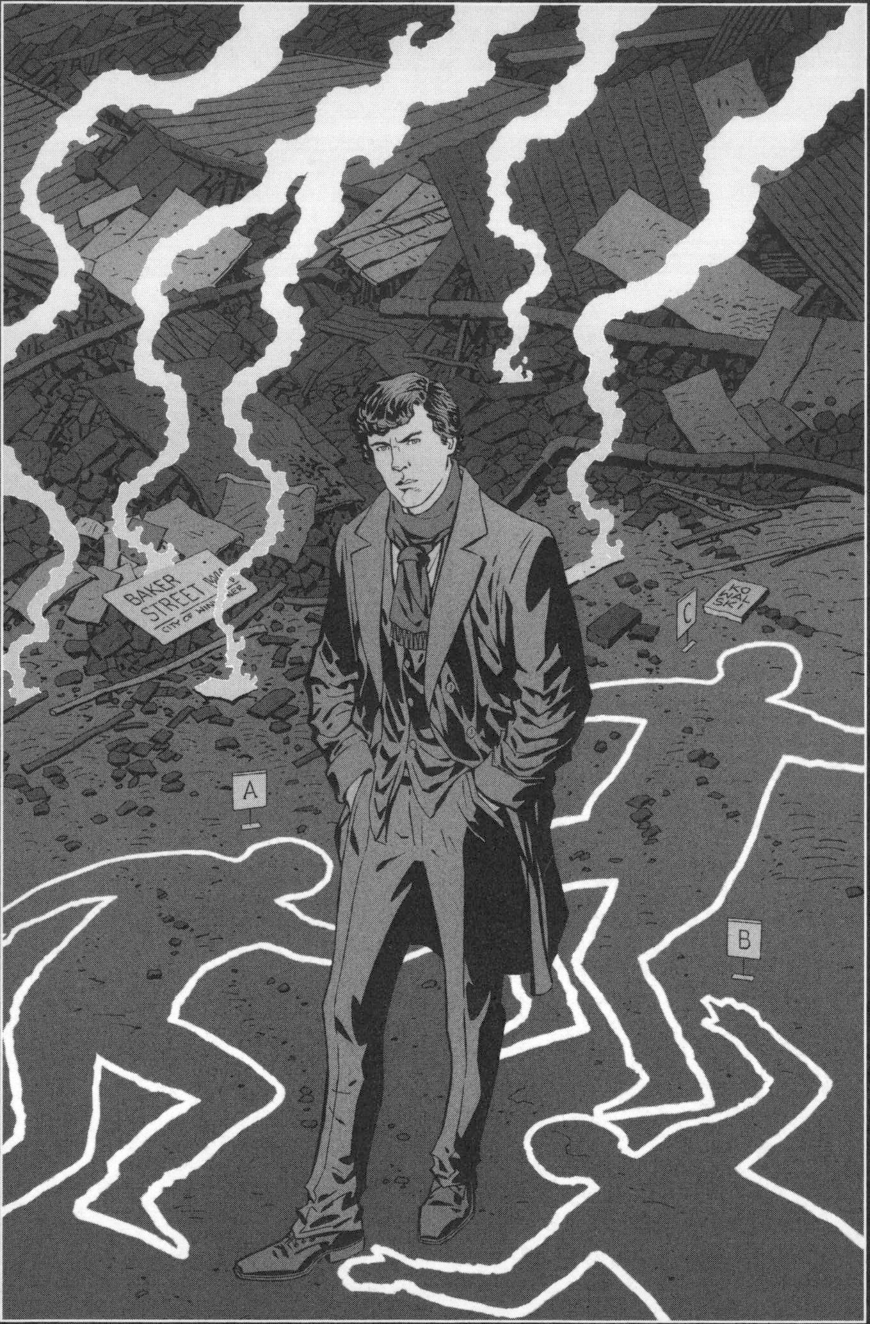
BAKER
STREET
KO
WAL
SKI
C
A
B

#1 COVER C
PIOTR KOWALSKI

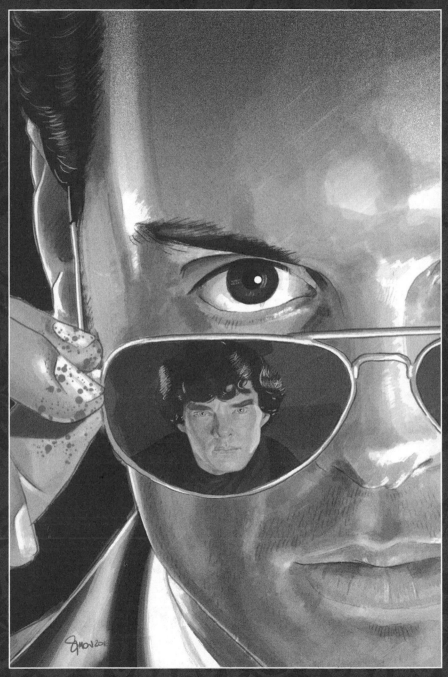

#1 COVER D
SIMON MYERS

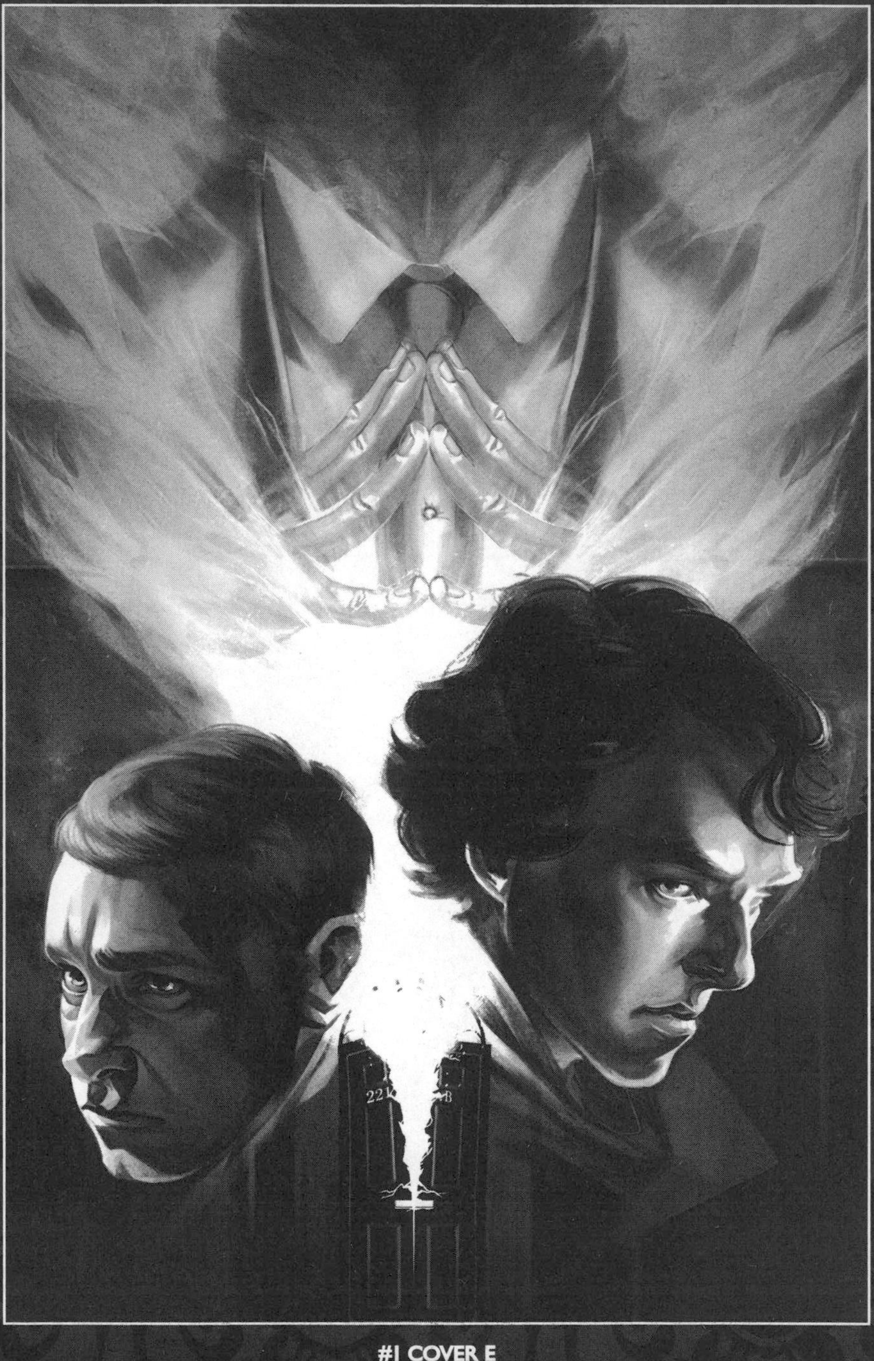

#1 COVER E
V.V. GLASS

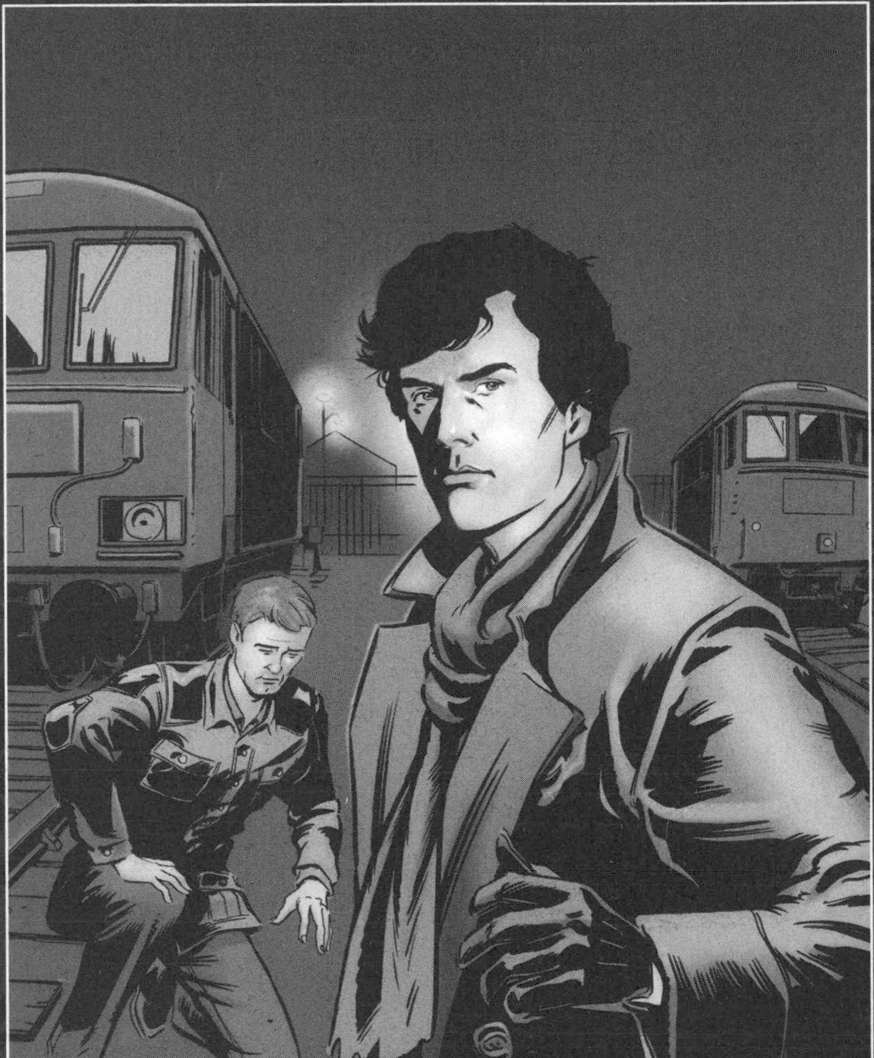

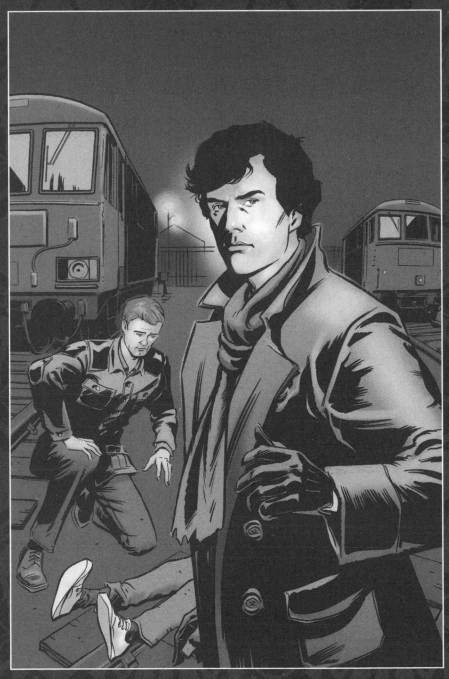

#2 COVER C
STEVE YEOWELL

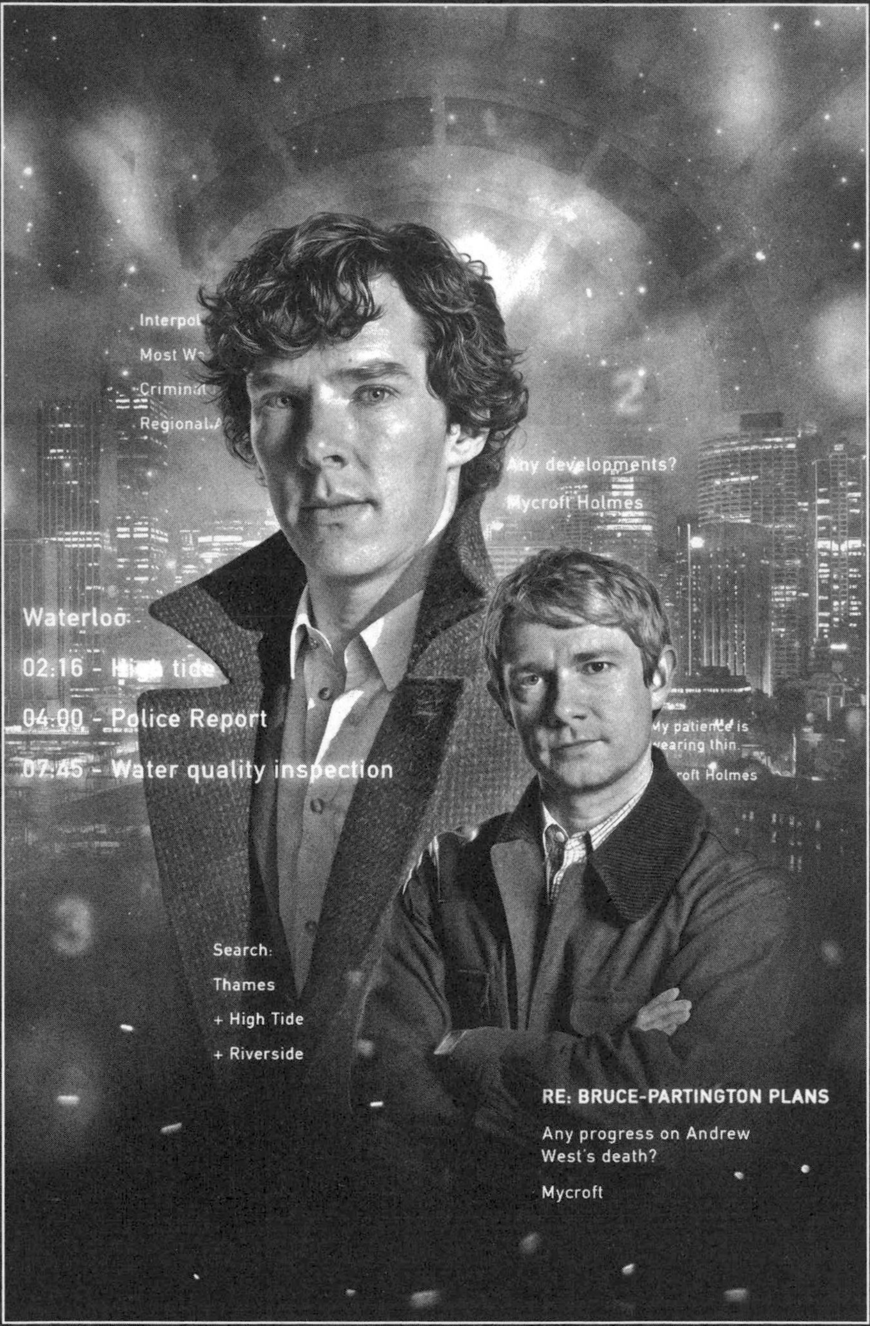

#3 COVER B
WILL BROOKS

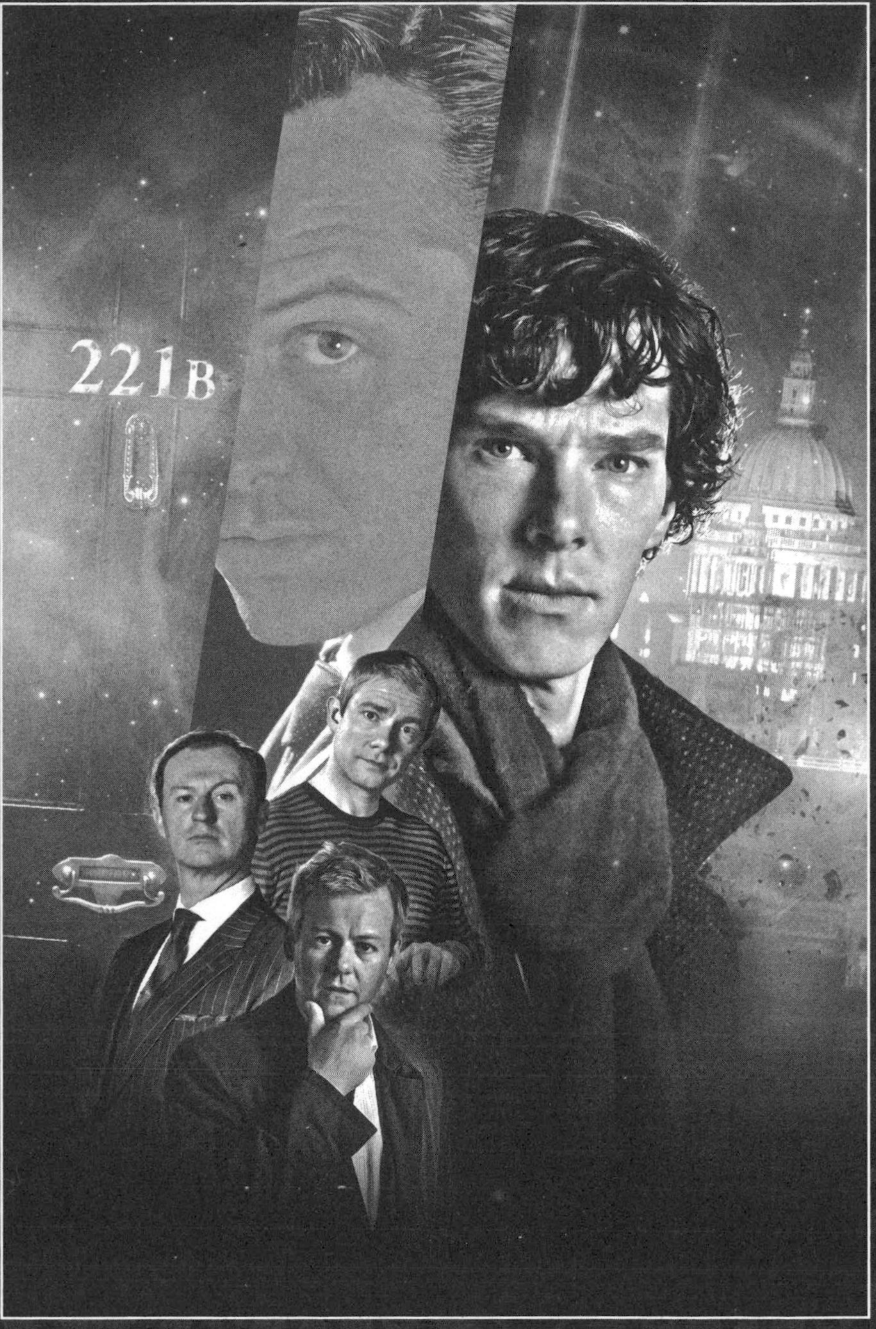
221B

#4 COVER B
WILL BROOKS

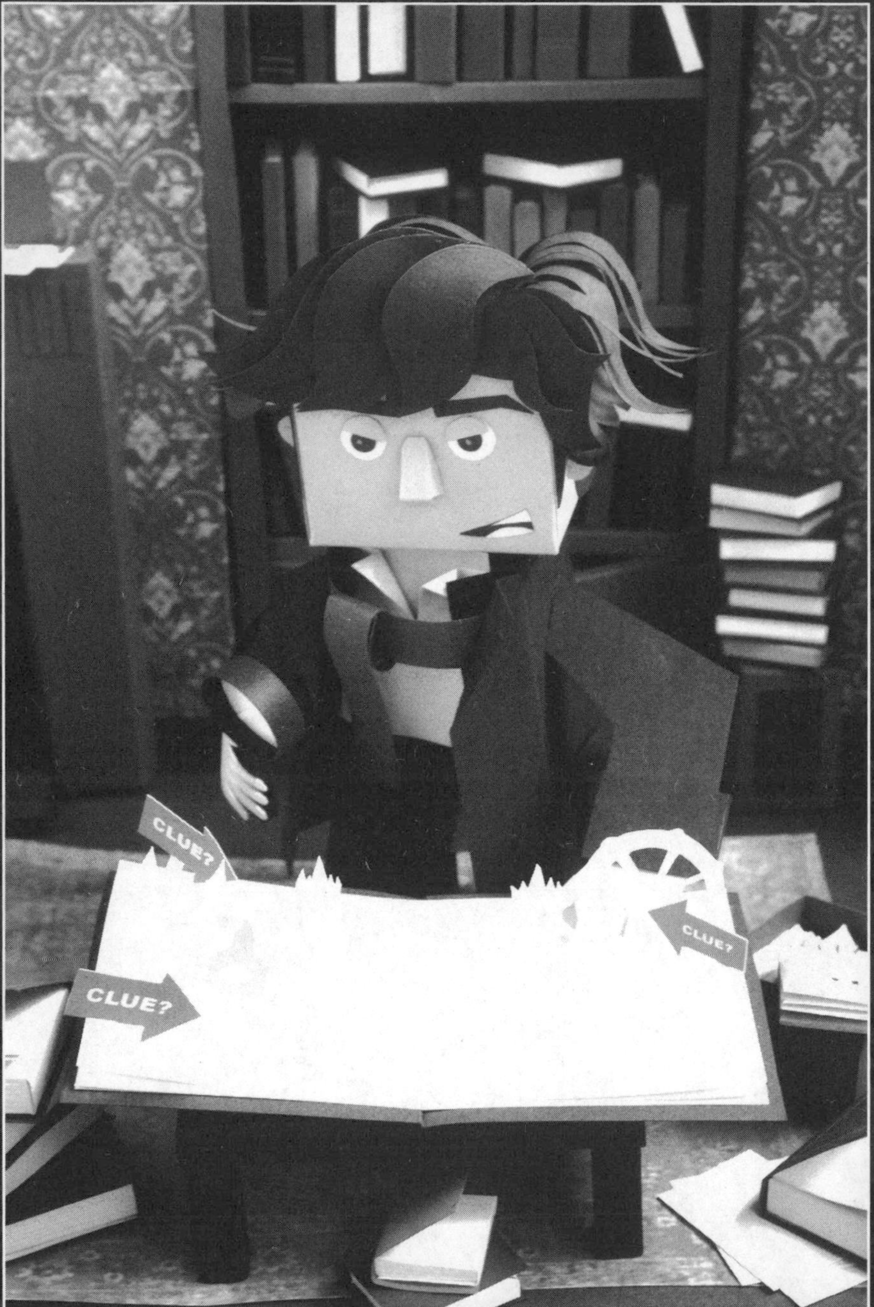
CLUE?
CLUE?
CLUE?

#5 COVER B
RYAN HALL

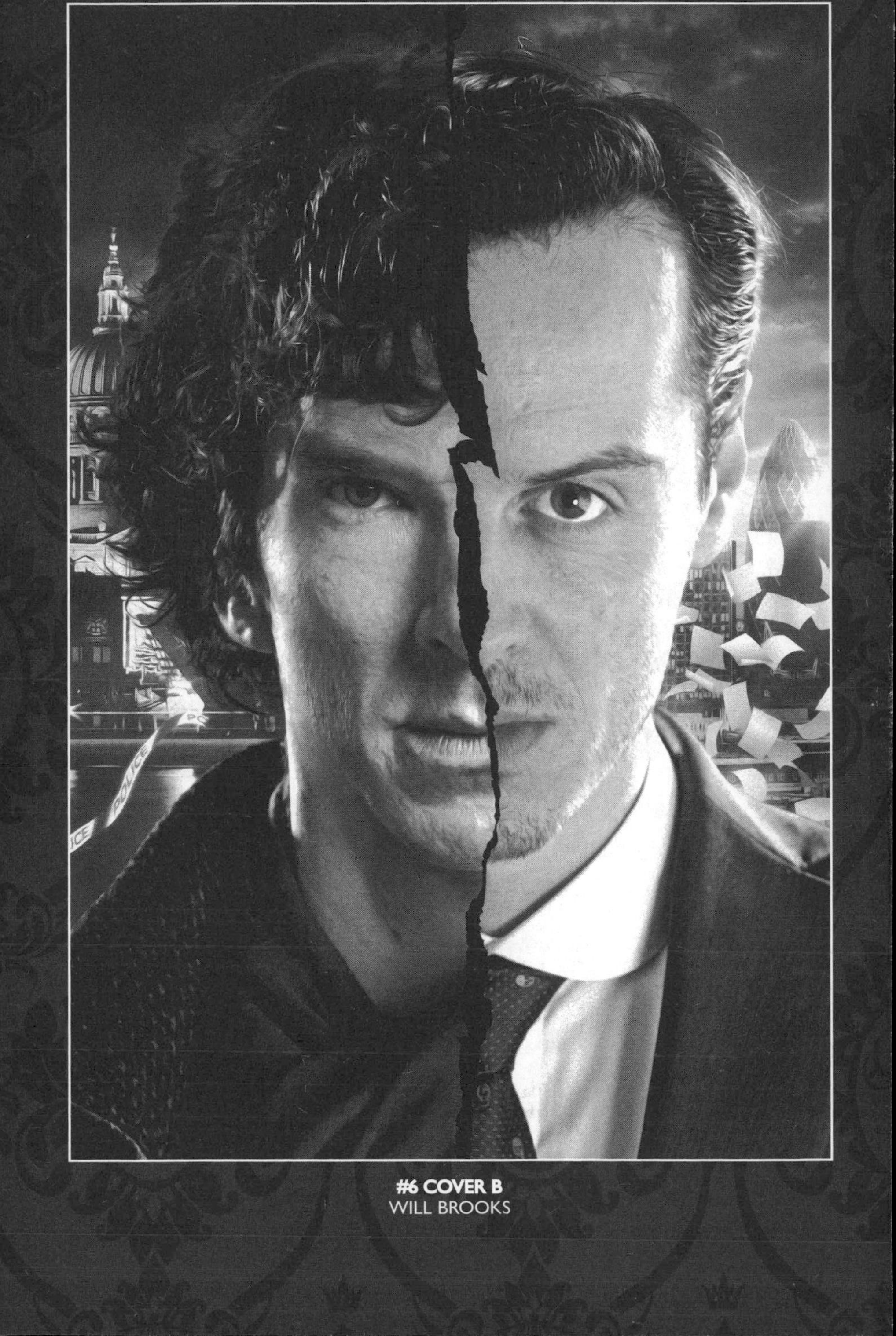
POLICE

#6 COVER B
WILL BROOKS

COMPLETE YOUR COLLECTION!

SHERLOCK

A STUDY IN PINK

"INJECTS NEW, WHOLLY UNEXPECTED LIFE INTO ONE OF POP CULTURE'S MOST WIDELY KNOWN PROPERTIES."

- NEWSARAMA

CO-CREATORS
Steven Moffat and Mark Gatiss

WRITER
Steven Moffat

ARTIST
Jay.

OUT NOW!

ISBN: 9781785856150

SHERLOCK
Steven Moffat
Mark Gatiss
Jay.
A STUDY IN PINK

SHERLOCK
THE BLIND BANKER

SHERLOCK

THE BLIND BANKER

"WELL DONE TO THE CREATIVE TEAM FOR DOING THE BELOVED SHERLOCK JUSTICE!"

- ALL-COMIC

CO-CREATORS
Steven Moffat and Mark Gatiss

WRITER
Steve Thompson

ARTIST
Jay.

OUT NOW!

ISBN: 9781785856167

HARTSWOOD FILMS

ON SALE NOW IN PRINT AND DIGITALLY
WWW.TITAN-COMICS.COM

TITAN COMICS

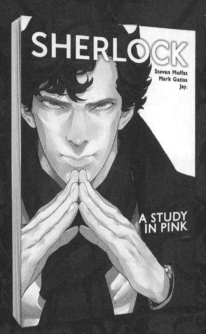

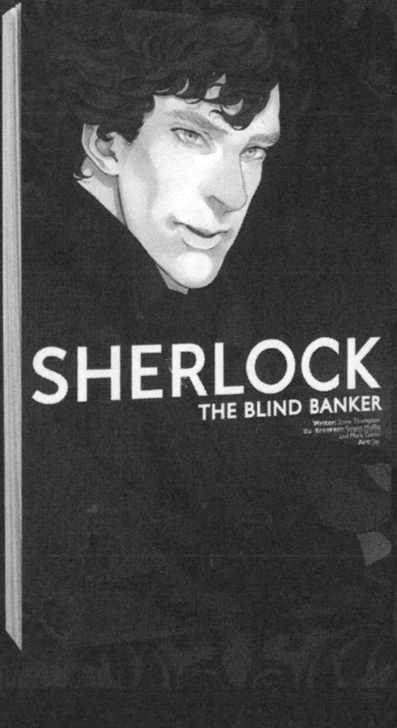

STOP!

This manga is presented in its original right-to-left reading format. This is the back of the issue!

Pages, panels, and speech balloons read from top right to bottom left, as shown above.
Sound effects are translated in the gutters between the panels.